Europe after Empire

Europe after Empire is a pioneering comparative history of European decolonization from the formal ending of empires to the postcolonial European present. Elizabeth Buettner charts the long-term development of post-war decolonization processes as well as the histories of inward and return migration from former empires which followed. She shows that not only were former colonies remade as a result of the path to decolonization: so too was Western Europe, with imperial traces scattered throughout popular and elite cultures, consumer goods, religious life, political formations, and ideological terrains. People were also inwardly mobile, including not simply Europeans returning 'home' but Asians, Africans, West Indians, and others who made their way to Europe to forge new lives. The result is a Europe fundamentally transformed by multicultural diversity and cultural hybridity and by the destabilization of assumptions about race, culture, and the meanings of place, and where imperial legacies and memories live on.

ELIZABETH BUETTNER is Professor of Modern History at the University of Amsterdam. Her publications include *Empire Families: Britons and Late Imperial India* (2004).

New Approaches to European History

Series editors
T. C. W. Blanning, *Sidney Sussex College, Cambridge*
Brendan Simms, *Peterhouse, Cambridge*

New Approaches to European History is an important textbook series, which provides concise but authoritative surveys of major themes and problems in European history since the Renaissance. Written at a level and length accessible to advanced school students and undergraduates, each book in the series addresses topics or themes that students of European history encounter daily: the series embraces both some of the more 'traditional' subjects of study and those cultural and social issues to which increasing numbers of school and college courses are devoted. A particular effort is made to consider the wider international implications of the subject under scrutiny.

To aid the student reader, scholarly apparatus and annotation is light, but each work has full supplementary bibliographies and notes for further reading: where appropriate, chronologies, maps, diagrams, and other illustrative material are also provided.

For a complete list of titles published in the series, please see:
www.cambridge.org/newapproaches

Europe after Empire

Decolonization, Society, and Culture

Elizabeth Buettner

University of Amsterdam

CAMBRIDGE
UNIVERSITY PRESS

University Printing House, Cambridge CB2 8BS, United Kingdom

One Liberty Plaza, 20th Floor, New York, NY 10006, USA

477 Williamstown Road, Port Melbourne, VIC 3207, Australia

314-321, 3rd Floor, Plot 3, Splendor Forum, Jasola District Centre, New Delhi-110025, India

79 Anson Road, #06-04/06, Singapore 079906

Cambridge University Press is part of the University of Cambridge.

It furthers the University's mission by disseminating knowledge in the pursuit of education, learning and research at the highest international levels of excellence.

www.cambridge.org
Information on this title: www.cambridge.org/9780521131889

First published 2016

A catalogue record for this publication is available from the British Library

Library of Congress Cataloging in Publication data
Buettner, Elizabeth, author.
Europe after empire : decolonization, society, and culture / Elizabeth Buettner.
Cambridge, United Kingdom : Cambridge University Press, 2016. | Series: New approaches to European history
LCCN 2015042963 | ISBN 9780521113861 (hardback : alkaline paper) | ISBN 9780521131889 (paperback : alkaline paper)
LCSH: Europe – Colonies – History. | Decolonization – Europe – History. | Postcolonialism – Europe – History. | Imperialism – History. | Multiculturalism – Europe. | Immigrants – Europe. | Europe – Ethnic relations. | Europe – Emigration and immigration. | BISAC: HISTORY / Europe / General.
LCC JV151 .B76 2016 | DDC 325/.34–dc23
LC record available at http://lccn.loc.gov/2015042963

ISBN 978-0-521-11386-1 Hardback
ISBN 978-0-521-13188-9 Paperback

Contents

Figures

Acknowledgements

This project would never have taken its current form without the tremendous support I have enjoyed from an ever-widening range of people and organizations. Special thanks go to John Breuilly, whose initial encouragement led me to embark on writing comparatively about issues that had started out as teaching interests and gradually turned into something much more. Similarly, I am grateful for the opportunities I've had to teach comparative courses on European imperialism and decolonization, migration and multiculturalism, and postcolonial cultures, both at the University of York, where I worked between 2000 and 2013, and now at the University of Amsterdam since 2014. The chance to discuss and debate these subjects with undergraduates and postgraduates did a great deal to influence my approach, so thanks very much to the students who signed on to courses like 'Border Crossings' and helped bring these topics to life – as did York conversations about mutual interests with Simon Ditchfield, David Clayton, Miles Taylor, Anna Bocking-Welch, Laura Price, and Magnus Niklasson.

This book started moving from initial conception to reality when I was chosen to take part in the International Research Seminar on Decolonization sponsored by the National History Center, Mellon Foundation, and Library of Congress. Its conveners (Roger Louis, Dane Kennedy, Marilyn Young, and Julia Clancy-Smith) in combination with my fellow 'seminarians' all offered an invaluable combination of friendly advice and constructive criticism over the course of four very hot weeks in Washington, DC in July 2006. If Washington shaped *Europe after Empire*'s beginnings, since 2012 Freiburg and then Amsterdam have provided ideal settings for completing it. I can't thank Ulrich Herbert, Wolfgang Eßbach, and Jörn Leonhard enough for welcoming me to the Freiburg Institute for Advanced Studies (FRIAS) as a senior research fellow in 2012–2013. While in Freiburg, conservations with John Horne, Joanna Wawrzyniak, Inka Racz, Edoardo Tortarolo, Lisa Heineman, and Mark Greengrass offered good guidance and sources of sanity, as did Jonas Lindner, whose help in navigating Freiburg's library facilities and tracking down copyright information was greatly appreciated. Alongside FRIAS, a British Academy Mid-Career Fellowship from January to December 2013 gave me both essential time to think and write and the chance to host three research workshops in York and London – for which thanks also go to Philip Murphy and Olga Jimenez at the Institute of Commonwealth Studies for their impeccable hospitality, and of course to the many people who shared their work at these events.

Generous invitations to speak at workshops, conferences, and seminars have been wonderful opportunities to exchange ideas and gain feedback along the way. Thanks very much to Ulrike Lindner, Mark Stein, Maren Möhring, and Eva Bischoff for including me in the 'Hybrid Cultures, Nervous States: Britain and Germany in a (Post)Colonial World' conference at the Westfälische Wilhelms-Universität Münster; Eva Bischoff and Ulrike Lindner for their kind follow-up invitations to Cologne; Mark Frey and Jost Dülffer, who organized the 'Trajectories of Decolonization: Elites and the Transformation from the Colonial to the Postcolonial' conference in Cologne; Sarah Stockwell and Larry Butler, who coordinated the 'Wind of Change' Fiftieth Anniversary Conference at the University of East Anglia; Angelika Epple, Ralf Schneider, and Sebastian Berg, for their invitations to speak at the University of Bielefeld; Moritz Föllmer (who I am now delighted to have as a colleague in Amsterdam) and Mark Smith, who sponsored an inspired series of workshops on 'New Approaches to European Urban History Since 1945' at the University of Leeds; Sonya Rose, Margot Finn, and Catherine Hall for providing me with such an excellent audience at the 'Reconfiguring the British: Nation, Empire, World' seminar, Institute of Historical Research, London; Emily Manktelow for inviting me to the University of Kent, and Paul Ward to Huddersfield; Britta Schilling for proposing a comparative discussion panel at the Modern European History Research Seminar at Cambridge; Rainer Emig for asking me to be a keynote speaker at the German Association for the Study of British Cultures annual conference in Hannover; Martin Thomas and Richard Toye, for coordinating the 'Rhetoric of Empire: Imperial Discourse and the Language of Colonial Conflict' conference at the University of Exeter; and Stuart Ward and Astrid Rasch for including me in workshops connected with the 'Embers of Empire' project at Copenhagen University. The German Historical Institute in London has extended its hospitality several times, most recently in hosting the workshop that Eva Bischoff and I co-organized on 'Remembering (Post) Colonial Violence: Silence, Suffering and Reconciliation'. Since I arrived at the University of Amsterdam, both the History Research Seminar and the NIOD Institute for War, Holocaust and Genocide Studies (alongside the Cultuurhistorisch Seminar at the University of Utrecht) have offered me supportive audiences and fresh Dutch insights into my research interests, engagements that I am excited about continuing in the years to come. Without these many chances to share my ideas and hear suggestions, this book would have been much the poorer intellectually, and certainly far less fun to think about.

A long list of friends – and friendly historians – has been more than generous in offering me countless suggestions about good readings and perceptive feedback on earlier drafts of many of *Europe after Empire*'s chapters. Martin Thomas and Jimmi Østergaard Nielsen both read far too much of this manuscript, so much that I'll never be able to thank them enough for their time (and endurance!), while Robert Bickers, Dane Kennedy, Roger Louis, Martin Shipway, Sonya Rose, Philip Murphy, Peter Romijn, Susan Legêne, Peter Marshall, Stuart Ward, and James Mark all passed along helpful suggestions at different junctures. Needless to say, I'm incredibly grateful to Michael Watson at Cambridge University Press for taking an interest in this project in the first place, for his receptivity to the ways it has evolved, and for waiting longer than he (and I) would have liked for its delivery. A number of people also helped with reproductions and images at critical moments, not least Paul Shields at the University of York and Koos Postma at the University of Amsterdam. Without them and the many artists and copyright holders who have kindly allowed me to include their material, *Europe after Empire* would have been a visually bereft book indeed.

Many of the people named above have lent not just academic insight but also a massive degree of moral support, as has my father, Don Buettner, ever a patient listener (a quality surely not unrelated to his hearing problems!). Fun evenings and long lunches with friends like John Williford, Justin Laur, Steve Clark, Kathy Castle, Sonya and Guenther Rose, Jonathan Williams and Konstanze Scharring Williams, Clive Cheesman and Roberta Suzzi Valli Cheesman, Eric Rath, Lora Sariaslan, Thomas and Elke Schauer, and Geert Janssen and Arnoud Visser made all the difference, lifting my mood and providing inspirations (and welcome distractions) of many kinds. Bernhard Rieger, however, remains in a class by himself as my husband and best friend, who not only listens (a lot), reads (too many drafts), and advises (whether asked to or not), but also always makes life fun and exciting. This book is dedicated to him, with profuse thanks and much love.

Introduction

Every year in mid-November, the Netherlands begins its extended round of Christmas season festivities which, unlike in many countries, peak not on 25 December but on 5 December, or *Sinterklaas* – Saint Nicholas' Eve. In cities and towns across the country and via broadcasts on national television, the Dutch equivalent of Santa Claus makes his arrival (*intocht*), coming not from the North Pole by sleigh but from Spain by boat. He is publicly welcomed by millions of spectators who typically brave inclement weather to watch him disembark from his steamboat, mount his white horse, and begin his procession through the streets. This national ritual captivates not only children and their parents but seemingly much of Dutch society, whose citizens treasure fond memories of the seasonal fun bookended by the local arrival ceremonies and the evening of the fifth, a family occasion when children receive presents from Sinterklaas. Even more beloved than Sinterklaas himself, an austere, almost larger-than-life elderly man dressed more like the Pope than the jolly Santa familiar in English-speaking countries, are the many helpers that make up his entourage: the clownishly boisterous group of men who collectively go by the name of 'Zwarte Piet', Black Piet. And every year, Zwarte Piet grows more controversial than before for the racist and colonial connotations he holds for a substantial minority of people in the Netherlands, once the heart of an overseas empire and now a postcolonial, multicultural society transformed by migration, much of it from former colonies.

Although commonly described as if its contours were age-old, like many European traditions Sinterklaas as celebrated today has only acquired its most recognizable aspects since the mid-nineteenth century, a time when the Netherlands had yet to abolish slavery in its colonies.[1] While Zwarte Piet is officially proclaimed to be a Moor dressed in Renaissance attire, his role and

---

[1] John Helsloot, 'De strijd om Zwarte Piet', in Isabel Hoving, Hester Dibbets, and Marlou Schrover (eds.), *Cultuur en migratie in Nederland: Veranderingen van het alledaagse 1950–2000* (The Hague, 2005), 249–71; John Helsloot, 'Zwarte Piet and Cultural Aphasia in the Netherlands', *Quotidian: Journal for the Study of Everyday Life*, 3 (2012), 1–20; Joy L. Smith, 'The Dutch Carnivalesque: Blackface, Play and Zwarte Piet', *Thamyris/Intersecting*, 27 (2014), 219–38.

Figure I.1 Sinterklaas *intocht* featuring 'Black Piets' (*Zwarte Pieten*),
Amsterdam, November 2014.
Photograph by Bernhard Rieger.

appearance bring forth connotations of slavery and the blackface traditions once
widely found in many Western societies scarred by racial inequality. Black Piet's
die-hard defenders – of which there are millions – deny that he is black because
he is or once was a slave from the West Indies, where the Netherlands ruled
plantation colonies such as Dutch Guiana (now Suriname) and islands in the
Antilles (West Indies) for centuries. Arguments that Piet's blackness comes from
having entered Dutch homes through the chimney to deliver children's presents
are dismissed by critics, many but not all of whom are of Afro-Surinamese or
Antillean origin. For them, the fact that Piet's clothing always remained improb-
ably spotless after the chimneys turned his face and hands black, together with
physical features such as coarse curly hair and exaggeratedly large red lips
(donned by an almost exclusively white band of performers for the occasion) are
clear evidence that the character is a holdover from a racist colonial order.

In a nation where many still suffer the consequences of discrimination and
cultural misunderstanding today, members of minority groups often feel that
Black Piet's status as Sinterklaas' menial servant and his characteristically

Figure I.2 Protest logo against *Zwarte Piet* posted on YouTube, November 2014. Its wording approximately translates as 'Black Piet doesn't belong, Black Piet shouldn't be, Black Piet is wrong, Black Piet symbol of colonialism'.

childish behaviour render him part of a contemptible heritage of racial stereotypes that should be abandoned. Other Dutch, mainly white, refuse to recognize Zwarte Piet's racist aspects and remain in thrall to a popular holiday icon, ardently rejecting requests even for slight adaptations to his persona let alone the demand that he be cut out of the festivities. While Zwarte Piet generated a low-level degree of controversy off and on for decades, debates and demonstrations surrounding the November *intocht* processions have grown far more vocal and organized since 2011, when several black performance artists were arrested for wearing T-shirts that read 'Zwarte Piet is racisme'. By 2014, there had been inconclusive judicial inquiries, numerous demonstrations and counter-demonstrations, polarized Facebook campaigns, more arrests, and Sunny Bergman's critical documentary entitled *Zwart als Roet* (*Black as Soot*, also released as *Our Colonial Hangover*).[2] Like much else, these attacks on the tradition and retaliations by its adherents demonstrate that cultures of empire not only remain alive in Europe; the fight over their meanings and survival also suggests that there is no end in sight to the halting process of coming to terms with them.

Heated discussions among the Dutch about what their nation's most prominent holiday festivities mean and whether they should be changed in a multicultural society have become as ritualized as the tradition now under severe attack. Through Zwarte Piet, festival organizers, the media, activists, and the general public perform yet another scene from the postcolonial drama of Europe after Empire, a story that has long outlasted formal decolonization. Having conceded the most treasured parts of its empire in the East Indies when Indonesia's independence was finally recognized in 1949 and agreed to Suriname's in 1975, decades later the Kingdom of the Netherlands still includes six small Antillean islands as part of its overall territory. Angry challenges to and strident defences of Zwarte Piet make the Netherlands one of a number of Western European nations that have experienced mass migration from their overseas dependencies and ex-colonies but have yet to work through their colonial histories, either with respect to their past empires' effects on far-away lands or their consequences at home in the early twenty-first century. Their extended domestic decolonization processes remain as incomplete as their grappling with postcolonialism's consequences in the form of multicultural societies and conflicted imperial memories.

Decolonization was never merely a chronologically and politically contained 'transfer of power' from rule by Europeans to independence as new Asian, African, and Caribbean nations after 1945. It had a pre-history stretching back though decades of rising contestation and lacked tidy closure when some flags were lowered and others raised at staged independence ceremonies. Just as important, it involved (ex-) colonizers and the (ex-) colonized alike at

---

[2] 'Betrogers tegen racisme opgepakt', *Het Parool* (Amsterdam), 14 November 2011; 'Een T-shirt is niet bedreigend', *AD/De Dordtenaar* (Dordrecht), 19 November 2011; Patrick Meershoek, 'Zwarte Piet verpest voor velen het feest', *Het Parool*, 15 November 2011; Hassan Bahara, 'Kijk maar naar zijn dommige gedrag; is Zwarte Piet racisme?', *De Groene Amsterdammer*, 28 November 2012; Eberhard van der Laan, 'Zwarte Piet maakt problemen en lost ze op', *nrc.next* (Amsterdam), 1 November 2013; 'Koloniale kater doet imago van Nederland weinig goed', *Het Parool*, 15 November 2014; 'Dit is het resultaat van effectief beleid', *nrc.next*, 17 November 2014; 'Een gezellige dag met een zwart rondje', *De Volkskrant* (Amsterdam), 17 November 2014; Patrick Meershoek, 'Amsterdam liet zien hoe het wel moet', *Het Parool*, 17 November 2014; www.facebook.com/Zwartepietniet, accessed 17 November 2014. Sunny Bergman's *Zwart als Roet* (alternatively, *Our Colonial Hangover*) can be viewed on www.youtube.com/watch?v=IVahza47h7c, accessed 15 January 2015.

every turn, whether the actors in question were situated in the empire, in Europe, or having undertaken journeys bridging metropolitan and colonial worlds. Not only were former colonies remade as a result of the path to decolonization: so too was Western Europe, both nationally as well as on local and international levels, which needed to decolonize itself.[3]

New times invited not only new politics but also new ways of thinking about identities – national, group, and individual – and their place in the world. While the Kenyan writer Ngũgĩ wa Thiong'o called on Africans to embark upon 'decolonising the mind' and their literary genres, Congolese nationalist Thomas Kanza described the 'mental decolonization' that gradually took root among the Congolese in the last years before they achieved formal independence from Belgium. The same could not be said for Belgians wedded to the colonial power structure that had transformed their nation from one of the smallest in Europe, geographically surrounded by far more powerful German and French states, into *la plus grande Belgique*, 'Greater Belgium'. Among Belgian policymakers together with army officers and colonial officials long based in Central Africa, Kanza observed the 'total absence of any mental decolonization' whatsoever even after Congo's independence at the end of June 1960.[4] As will be examined further in this book, prominent Belgians' failure to adapt their thinking and behaviour to a new order did much to sow the seeds of the neocolonial tragedies that afflicted the Congolese, some immediately following their nominal decolonization, others long afterwards.

Decolonization involved not just relinquishing formal control over territory but also coming to terms with the loss of the colonial order that had benefitted many Europeans and grappling with colonialism's far-reaching implications. 'For the former colony, decolonization is a dialogue with the colonial past, and not a simple dismantling of colonial habits and modes of life', Arjun Appadurai has argued. This was equally true for former colonizing countries, where no aspect of the process proved at all simple.[5] As the Zwarte Piet saga still being played out in the Netherlands shows, to this day discussions about the colonial and racial underpinnings of European culture are often entered into reluctantly, if at all, and could take more than a generation to develop significant momentum. Europe's transition from the colonial to the postcolonial era has involved considerable time lags between formal endings of empires and the process of reckoning with their implications and legacies. A Europe that is postcolonial in

---

[3] Robert J.C. Young, 'The Postcolonial Condition', in Dan Stone (ed.), *The Oxford Handbook of Postwar European History* (Oxford, 2012), 605.

[4] Ngũgĩ wa Thiong'o, *Decolonising the Mind: The Politics of Language in African Literature* (Nairobi, 1986); Thomas Kanza, *Conflict in the Congo: The Rise and Fall of Lumumba* (Harmondsworth, 1972), 41, 220.

[5] Arjun Appadurai, *Modernity at Large: Cultural Dimensions of Globalization* (Minneapolis, 1996), 89.

a literal, temporal sense needs to be distinguished from a Europe that has examined this past in depth and 'undo[ne] the ideological heritage of colonialism', as postcolonial theory insists it must.[6] This tortuous aftermath of empire is far from over, with celebrations of empire still competing with denunciations and wilful oblivion.[7] On countless occasions, returns to the past bear stronger resemblance to dialogues of the deaf than to meaningful efforts to arrive at informed understandings either of history or of different groups' relationships to it. And for much of the time, silence prevails over dialogue in any form.

* * *

Europe after Empire explores central aspects of the extended histories and present-day ramifications of decolonization with an emphasis on its metropolitan dimensions, taking on board the two largest European imperial powers, Britain and France, together with three smaller counterparts, the Netherlands, Belgium, and Portugal. Its scope spans the larger decolonization processes examined in Part I that lay the ground for Part II, which explores the histories of inward and return migration from former empires that have been responsible to a considerable degree for these nations' current ethnic and cultural diversity. Just as 'English society understood race through colonialism and its effects', as Sandhya Shukla notes, the same was true elsewhere in Europe where minority groups of colonial origins settled.[8] More than any other factor, their presence gave colonial history and its lasting impact new forms of visibility in postcolonial times, as metropolitan societies grappled with the implications of diversity and minorities demanded recognition for an overseas past that belonged not simply to them but to the nation at large.[9] 'Politically, socially and intellectually, the anti-colonial fight against inequality, against racism, against cultural hierarchy, has been fought within Europe in the postcolonial era by the subaltern subjects of the developing world who had migrated there', Robert Young summarizes.[10] Taken together, changes spanning the political to the demographic and cultural since 1945 have influenced how former empires have been remembered and forgotten in Europe, a topic that Part III examines.

As such, this project takes its place within an interdisciplinary scholarship that has emerged since the early 1990s and is commonly termed the 'new

---

[6] Robert J.C. Young, *Postcolonialism: An Historical Introduction* (Malden, MA, 2001), 65; Young, 'Postcolonial Condition'.

[7] Bill Schwarz, 'Actually Existing Postcolonialism', *Radical Philosophy*, 104 (2000), 17.

[8] Sandhya Shukla, *India Abroad: Diasporic Cultures of Postwar America and England* (Princeton, 2003), 62.

[9] Gert Oostindie, *Postcolonial Netherlands: Sixty-Five Years of Forgetting, Commemorating, Silencing* (Amsterdam, 2011), 160.

[10] Young, 'Postcolonial Condition', 607.

imperial history'.[11] Historians and academics in related disciplines, particularly literary studies and anthropology, rejected conventional approaches to the study of European countries that largely ignored their imperial histories. By and large, empire had long been abandoned to methodologically traditional academics interested mainly in political, military, and economic questions and whose geographies of analysis were centred on overseas arenas in combination with the decision-making corridors of power in London, Paris, The Hague, Brussels, and Lisbon. Researchers engaged in the 'new imperial history' or 'imperial turn', by contrast, have united 'home' and 'away' into a single conceptual category and insisted upon moving beyond a restricted, nation-bound approach to modern Western Europe.[12] Imperialism and the cultures and visions that grew from it did not solely pertain to the realm of high politics, nor were they contained on far-off continents or limited to the minority of Europeans who lived and worked in the colonies. Empires had deeply influenced everyday society and culture across Britain (the example that has received by far the most scholarly attention), the French 'hexagon' (as France has often been called on account of its approximate shape when seen on maps of Europe), and their neighbours with colonies of their own. European nations and their overseas possessions were indivisible, with cultures, practices, material objects, and ideas travelling in multiple directions, their traces scattered throughout European popular and elite cultures, consumer goods, literature, religious life, political formations, and ideological terrains. People were equally mobile, including not simply Europeans who travelled outwards but the small numbers of Asians, Africans, West Indians, and others who made

---

[11] Of especial importance in galvanizing subsequent work was Ann Laura Stoler and Frederick Cooper, 'Between Metropole and Colony: Rethinking a Research Agenda', in Ann Laura Stoler and Frederick Cooper (eds.), *Tensions of Empire: Colonial Cultures in a Bourgeois World* (Berkeley, 1997), 1–56. Scholars concerned with Britain and its empire have been the most prolific to date. Within this profusion of work, see Stephen Howe (ed.), *The New Imperial Histories Reader* (London, 2010); Kathleen Wilson (ed.), *A New Imperial History: Culture, Identity, and Modernity in Britain and the Empire, 1660–1840* (Cambridge, 2004); Catherine Hall (ed.), *Cultures of Empire: A Reader: Colonizers in Britain and the Empire in the Nineteenth and Twentieth Centuries* (Manchester, 2000); Catherine Hall and Sonya O. Rose (eds.), *At Home with the Empire: Metropolitan Culture and the Imperial World* (Cambridge, 2006); Andrew Thompson (ed.), *Britain's Experience of Empire in the Twentieth Century, Oxford History of the British Empire Companion Series* (Oxford, 2012). John M. MacKenzie has played a particularly important role in generating new approaches to British imperial culture by launching and overseeing the 'Studies in Imperialism' series of monographs and edited collections published by Manchester University Press (a series now edited by Andrew Thompson). Two of its many titles include John M. MacKenzie (ed.), *Imperialism and Popular Culture* (Manchester, 1986), and John M. MacKenzie (ed.), *European Empires and the People: Popular Responses to Imperialism in France, Britain, the Netherlands, Belgium, Germany and Italy* (Manchester, 2011), the latter being a promising example of Britain now being placed in comparative perspective.

[12] Antoinette Burton (ed.), *After the Imperial Turn: Thinking with and through the Nation* (Durham, 2003).

their way to Europe's capital cities, port communities, universities, and other sites of early colonial settlement. Empire's everyday, mundane presence at home was the most prominent sign of Europe's deep global entanglements, some imperial, others not. Metropolitan/colonial divides were thereby dissolved in a growing body of academic work, despite the ongoing doubts of some historians about empires' place at the heart of European life and European identities, both personal and national.

Many authors working within this field looked towards postcolonial, feminist, and literary theory and critical approaches to race, power relations, and cultural hybridity, drawing inspiration from scholars like Edward Said and Robert Young along with interpretations penned during the decolonization era by Frantz Fanon, Albert Memmi, and other authors whose arguments have since become canonical.[13] Other scholars situated within established lines of research and interpretation remained sceptical, however, and at times were openly resistant (if not outright hostile) to innovative studies and modes of analysis that they condemned as empirically deficient, underhistoricized, obtuse, and laden with academic jargon, or simply ignored these new approaches altogether.[14]

Despite the inevitable presence of detractors, since its inception the 'imperial turn' has inspired a growing number of scholars, myself included. Many of its pioneering figures now play leading academic roles in universities in the United States, Britain, and in other scholarly communities in the English-speaking world and (albeit to a much lesser extent) on continental Europe. Since the 1990s, the field has acquired favoured themes and habits of interpretation of its own. If its proponents have indeed succeeded (and some would deny that they have) in gaining a high level of recognition for their struggle to rethink European national histories and present-day circumstances with reference to imperial 'exteriors', the chronological and geographical scope of their work nevertheless remains decidedly uneven.

---

[13] Edward W. Said, *Orientalism* (New York, 1978); Edward W. Said, *Culture and Imperialism* (New York, 1993); Young, *Postcolonialism*; Barbara Bush, *Imperialism and Postcolonialism* (London, 2014); Dane Kennedy, 'Imperial History and Post-Colonial Theory', *Journal of Imperial and Commonwealth History*, 24:3 (1996), 345–63; Frantz Fanon, *Black Skin, White Masks*, translated by Charles Lam Markmann (New York, 1967; original French edition published Paris, 1952); Frantz Fanon, *The Wretched of the Earth*, translated by Constance Farrington (London, 1990; original French edition published Paris, 1961); Albert Memmi, *The Colonizer and the Colonized*, translated by Howard Greenfeld (Boston, 1991; original French edition published Paris, 1957); Albert Memmi, *Decolonization and the Decolonized*, translated by Robert Bononno (Minneapolis, 2006; original French edition published Paris, 2004).

[14] See Bernard Porter, *The Absent-Minded Imperialists: Empire, Society, and Culture in Britain* (Oxford, 2004); Bernard Porter, 'Further Thoughts on Imperial Absent-Mindedness', *Journal of Imperial and Commonwealth History*, 36:1 (2008), 101–17; John M. MacKenzie, '"Comfort" and Conviction: A Response to Bernard Porter', *Journal of Imperial and Commonwealth History*, 36:4 (2008), 659–68.

Historical research informed by these approaches on Britain and its former empire, for example, most commonly concentrates on the rise, consolidation, and heyday of imperial power between the eighteenth and early twentieth centuries. Far less work has been done to explore imperial declines and falls since the 1930s and particularly after 1945, and while the decolonization era and its aftermath now receive more attention than in the mid-2000s an imbalance nonetheless continues.[15] If Europe was 'literally the creation of the Third World' via the colonialism that long defined it, as the French Martinican-born revolutionary thinker Frantz Fanon memorably phrased it in *The Wretched of the Earth* (1961), much remains to be done to arrive at a full understanding of how Europe was *re-created* once its territorial expanse receded.[16] This re-creation was the product of innumerable changes occurring in the colonies, back in Europe, and via accelerating flows of peoples, practices, and ideas between them, processes not confined to (ex-) metropolitan and (ex-) colonial interactions but deeply shaped by wider global transformations. Not least were the effects of the Second World War and later the Cold War as Western Europe confronted a changed world order dominated by the United States and the Soviet Union that saw colonies come under new forms of governance and influence. More recently, the 'war on terror' since 2001 and its role in enhancing the Western demonization of Islam and Muslims have influenced both how late European imperialism and decolonization have been remembered internationally together with European reactions to the millions of Muslims now living in their midst, most of whom are descended from formerly colonized peoples.[17]

Among most scholars and much of the general public, post-1945 European history remains far more likely to be viewed through the lens of the post-war rather than as involving a series of radical transitions from the colonial to the postcolonial, even though it was both – and much more – at the same time.[18] Most national histories have operated along similar lines. As Benjamin Stora has written, France possessed a 'historical consciousness saturated by the weight of the Second World War, and soon dissolved by the cult of the new

---

[15] Signs of change began with Stuart Ward (ed.), *British Culture and the End of Empire* (Manchester, 2001), and have continued with Wendy Webster, *Englishness and Empire 1939–1965* (Oxford, 2005), Bill Schwarz, *Memories of Empire, Vol. 1: The White Man's World* (Oxford, 2011), Jordanna Bailkin, *The Afterlife of Empire* (Berkeley, 2012).

[16] Fanon, *Wretched*, 81.

[17] Derek Gregory, *The Colonial Present* (Oxford, 2004), 13; Marina Lazreg, *Torture and the Twilight of Empire: From Algiers to Baghdad* (Princeton, 2008), especially ch. 11.

[18] Tony Judt's *Postwar: A History of Europe since 1945* (London, 2005) counts as one valuable and influential study that pays passing attention to decolonization overseas and its European effects, yet these topics nonetheless remain marginal by comparison with other themes. More representative are Mark Mazower, *Dark Continent: Europe's Twentieth Century* (London, 1998); Dan Stone, *Goodbye to All That?: The Story of Europe since 1945* (Oxford, 2014).

and of the "modernity'" that ensued.[19] The same was true of Belgium and the Netherlands, which together with France shared the burden of having been 'the losers of 1940', as Pieter Lagrou notes, undergoing traumatic years of Nazi occupation followed by painful roads to recovery.[20] Coping with the problematic legacies of wartime resistance and collaboration came together with economic, political, and social reconstruction as societies struggled towards new democratic futures as part of the emergent Western bloc. While Britain never suffered German occupation and emerged on the winning side along with the United States, it too lived in the war's shadow, and all four of these nations' late imperial and decolonization histories were at least to some extent shaped by wartime experiences and their later repercussions. Portugal offers a distinct history as an imperial nation not comparably marked by the Second World War, having remained officially neutral throughout, and serves as an important reminder of the diversity of national experiences within the broader European (and even Western European) framework. In Portugal, it was 1974 rather than 1945 that became the defining watershed when the *Estado Novo* dictatorship in power since the 1920s finally was toppled in revolution – a revolution that was a direct consequence of over a decade of wars fought to hold on to its colonies in Africa.

Portugal's ultimately unsuccessful attempt to swim against the tide of Western European democracy and decolonization provides one of the clearest instances of mutually-influencing interconnectedness of a metropole and its colonies up to and beyond the dissolution of former empires. Others include the fall of France's Fourth Republic in 1958, a crisis provoked by the turmoil of the Algerian War being waged across the Mediterranean but whose effects reverberated throughout the hexagon itself. Countless examples abound across Western Europe, not simply encompassing political structures but regularly extending throughout domestic life. European-American relations; the role of European monarchies in national cultures; economic and societal modernization dependent on ethnic minority migrant workers, many of colonial and postcolonial origins; consumerism, affluence, and poverty; welfare state ideologies and structures; European youth cultures and emergent multicultures; new visions of national identity: all, and much else besides, were densely entangled with the histories of overseas colonies and ultimately ex-colonies and peoples, not evolving in isolation from them.

Europe after Empire benefits from the profusion of excellent analyses of these and other topics that have emerged to date, including studies penned by historians as well as scholars working within literary, cultural, and film studies

---

[19] Benjamin Stora, *La gangrène et l'oubli: La mémoire de la guerre d'Algérie* (Paris, 1991), 255.
[20] Pieter Lagrou, *The Legacy of Nazi Occupation: Patriotic Memory and National Recovery in Western Europe, 1945–1965* (Cambridge, 2000), 26.

along with geography, politics, anthropology, and sociology, to name several increasingly porous disciplinary configurations. In attempting to synthesize an ever-growing range of scholarship into an accessible and wider whole, it endeavours to address some of the innumerable gaps that remain, in part via a selective analysis of primary source materials, and to suggest new directions for further research. Samplings of texts by well-known Europeans, Indians, Africans, and others from the former colonial world take their place alongside subaltern and unfamiliar voices, providing glimpses of a spectrum of experiences and interpretations spanning from those of the powerful and exceptional to the disempowered and everyday. Sources drawn on range from autobiographical writings, political speeches, government publications and press reports to literature, songs, films, paintings, and material artefacts inhabiting European homes, museums, public spaces, and mental horizons. Writing with both experts in their respective fields as well as advanced students in mind, I aim to encourage fresh insights into topics with which some readers may already be familiar and introduce others to themes that remain either wholly new or relatively understudied. While more than twenty years of cumulative case studies and thematic innovations have generated a level of academic excitement that shows no sign of abating, they have also given rise to pleas for alternative approaches that go beyond the now-familiar call, now resoundingly answered, to rethink Western European national pasts and presents along imperial and post-imperial lines.

Taking their place alongside treatments focused on one European metropole and one (or occasionally several) colonies, a growing number of studies have productively situated this largely binary set of interactions within a wider geographical scope. Some scholars have explored networks and transfers that linked different parts of overseas empires together with one another in ways that did not necessarily or consistently run through Europe.[21] Others have sought to illuminate connections between intra-imperial and other transnational forms of interaction, a prominent example being Paul Gilroy's analysis of a 'Black Atlantic' world in which African diasporic peoples, cultural practices, and ideas routinely circulated between Britain, Europe, the United States, the Caribbean, and Africa.[22] Having recognized that European nations' imperial pasts could never be cordoned off from other global processes, historians have compared different empires (some continental and contiguous

---

[21] David Lambert and Alan Lester (eds.), *Colonial Lives Across the British Empire: Imperial Careering in the Long Nineteenth Century* (Cambridge, 2006); James Belich, *Replenishing the Earth: The Settler Revolution and the Rise of the Anglophone World, 1783–1939* (Oxford, 2009); Ulrike Lindner, *Koloniale Begegnungen: Deutschland und Großbritannien als Imperialmächte in Afrika 1880–1914* (Frankfurt am Main, 2011).

[22] Paul Gilroy, *The Black Atlantic: Modernity and Double Consciousness* (Cambridge, MA, 1993).

land empires, others maritime with a transoceanic reach), often covering a longer time period, or examined Europe's overseas empires as part of a broader set of global dynamics.[23] Many heeded Dipesh Chakrabarty's call to move beyond interpretive rubrics that had traditionally focussed on Europe and read other world histories primarily through a European prism. '"Europe" remains the sovereign, theoretical subject of all histories, including the ones we call "Indian," "Chinese," "Kenyan," and so on', he claimed in 2000. 'Provincializing Europe' would remove it from the centre of attention and destabilize it as a distorting point of reference that had produced the concepts, categories, and questions historians had conventionally used to study not just Europe itself but much of the rest of the world typically left to languish on its sidelines.[24]

With a wealth of studies having recast Europe as imperial at home as well as in its effects on the wider world, transcending the European metropole/overseas colonial 'dyad' (to borrow Durba Ghosh's term) is now an increasingly fruitful field of globalized inquiry.[25] Yet Chakrabarty's plea to move beyond Eurocentric areas of study and tools of analysis is both to be applauded and queried in equal measure. Europe-focused historiography and history teaching have finally made way for much greater attention to other parts of the world, shifts in emphasis and methods of interpretation that have changed how Europe *per se* has been conceived once the veil separating metropoles from empires was lowered. But having taken the 'imperial turn' and then partly transcended it en route to the global, most scholars have bypassed 'Europe' altogether.

While stressing Europe's geographic flexibility with the loss of empires and its permeability to outside influences and inward movements of peoples and cultures, many with colonial and postcolonial pedigrees, *Europe after Empire* nonetheless insists on the importance of Europe itself as an object of historical scholarship. It emphasizes that the ways and extent to which specific European nations experienced *decolonization themselves* come into much sharper focus

---

[23] C.A. Bayly, *The Birth of the Modern World, 1780–1914: Global Connections and Comparisons* (Malden, MA, 2004); Frederick Cooper, *Colonialism in Question: Theory, Knowledge, History* (Berkeley, 2005); John Darwin, *After Tamerlane: The Rise and Fall of Global Empires, 1400–2000* (New York, 2008); Jane Burbank and Frederick Cooper, *Empires in World History: Power and the Politics of Difference* (Princeton, 2010); Jörn Leonhard and Ulrike von Hirschhausen (eds.), *Comparing Empires: Encounters and Transfers in the Long Nineteenth Century* (Göttingen, 2011). Particularly relevant here is Durba Ghosh's insightful assessment of the scholarly state of play with respect to research on the British empire as of 2012. Durba Ghosh, 'Another Set of Imperial Turns?', *American Historical Review*, 117:3 (2012), 772–93. See also Simon J. Potter and Jonathan Saha, 'Global History, Imperial History and Connected Histories of Empire', *Journal of Colonialism and Colonial History*, 16:1 (2015), together with the other contributions to this special issue on 'Imperial History and Connected Histories of Empire'.

[24] Dipesh Chakrabarty, *Provincializing Europe: Postcolonial Thought and Historical Difference* (Princeton, 2000), 27.

[25] Ghosh, 'Another Set', 780, note 40.

when studied comparatively. In assessing five metropoles' transitions from the colonial to the postcolonial overseas and particularly at home, it brings together national-imperial trajectories that have largely been examined with respect to individual European cases alone, and rarely with an eye towards similar developments occurring in neighbouring countries. Important new comparative treatments of European decolonization published in recent years have not emanated from within the 'new imperial history' focused on domestic, social, and cultural themes, largely remaining focused on political dimensions and overseas locations.[26] Despite the profusion of insightful academic work about how distinct ex-metropoles experienced losing their empires and felt their legacy, scholarship concerning similar topics in different countries usually exists within a bubble, making few connections with parallel processes occurring elsewhere within decolonizing and postcolonial Europe. Ironically, however eagerly scholars have acknowledged the entangled histories of European nations and their former empires, taking the 'imperial turn' has not generated any comparable enthusiasm for a possible 'continental turn'. In fact, it may well help to account for the latter course remaining the road seldom taken.

Europe after Empire thus rejects both the older academic tendency to keep Western European nations separate from their empires but also the persisting one of keeping them separate from each other. As Konrad Jarausch, Thomas Lindenberger, and others have argued, the historiography of contemporary Europe remains dominated by national perspectives, with cross-national dimensions tending to receive short shrift.[27] The scholarly project of 'Europeanizing contemporary histories', as they call for, is an urgent one, and one in which historians of empire have played little part. Paradoxically, during the very decades when Europe became increasingly integrated and characterized by intra-continental transformations as the European Economic Community took root, expanded, and ultimately emerged as the European Union, academics directly concerned with comparative or transnational European processes remain small in number next to the majority whose interests fall within national boundaries.

---

[26] Martin Shipway, *Decolonization and Its Impact: A Comparative Approach to the End of Colonial Empires* (Malden, MA, 2008); Martin Thomas, Bob Moore, and L.J. Butler, *Crises of Empire: Decolonization and Europe's Imperial States, 1918–1975* (London, 2008); Martin Thomas, *Fight or Flight: Britain, France, and Their Roads from Empire* (Oxford, 2014). Miguel Bandeira Jerónimo and António Costa Pinto (eds.), *The Ends of European Colonial Empires: Cases and Comparisons* (Basingstoke, 2015) appeared too late to be consulted here.

[27] Konrad H. Jarausch and Thomas Lindenberger, 'Contours of a Critical History of Contemporary Europe: A Transnational Agenda', in Konrad H. Jarausch and Thomas Lindenberger (eds.), *Conflicted Memories: Europeanizing Contemporary Histories* (New York, 2007), 1–20; see also Martin Conway and Kiran Klaus Patel (eds.), *Europeanization in the Twentieth Century: Historical Approaches* (London, 2010).

Despite the undeniable importance of identifying nationally-specific contours, European imperialism was a shared phenomenon to such an extent that it often makes it 'better to speak of an internationalised discourse than of specific national cultures of empire', as Remco Raben suggests.[28] So too were the decolonizations, Europe-bound postcolonial migrations, and the divided memories of empire that followed.[29] Fighting against the fragmentation of post-1945 Western Europe into national histories (with or without their imperial dimensions) helps combat misleading notions of national and imperial exceptionalism regularly put forth by contemporaries, often in the course of defending their own nations' imperial records as uniquely benign and praiseworthy, as well as by historians keen to highlight the distinctiveness of their chosen nations or empires of study.[30] Upon closer comparative inspection, exceptionalist claims quickly reveal themselves as anything but, recurring across decolonizing and postcolonial Europe but perhaps nowhere more strikingly than in Britain.

Collectively, historians of Britain and its former empire count among the worst offenders of the wider tendency to examine national histories in a state of false isolation from their nearest – if not always dearest – neighbours.[31] Euroscepticism as recurrently manifest in the post-1945 political arena readily finds its equivalent among historians, both those whose approaches to Britain were literally insular and contained and those who cast their nets across the empire, Commonwealth, and globe, but typically neglected to cross the English Channel in their quest to re-write British history in terms of its connectedness with other places. Compelling analyses like Linda Colley's examinations of *both* French and imperial 'others' in 'forging the nation' in the eighteenth and early nineteenth centuries have yet to see their equivalent for the decades when

---

[28] Remco Raben, 'A New Dutch Imperial History?: Perambulations in a Prospective Field', *BMGN – Low Countries Historical Review*, 128:1 (2013), 23.

[29] Susan Legêne and Martijn Eickhoff, 'Postwar Europe and the Colonial Past in Photographs', in Chiara De Cesari and Ann Rigney (eds.), *Transnational Memory: Circulation, Articulation, Scales* (Berlin, 2014), 287–311.

[30] Dane Kennedy, 'Decolonization and Disorder', *East Asian Journal of British History*, 3 (2013), 95–111; Dina Khoury and Dane Kennedy (eds.), 'Comparing Empires', special issue of *Comparative Studies of South Asia, Africa and the Middle East*, 27:2 (2007). As Nora Fisher Onar and Kalypso Nicolaïdis note in 'The Decentring Agenda: Europe as a Post-Colonial Power', *Cooperation and Conflict*, 48:2 (2013), 289, 'exceptionalism, paradoxically, is one of the most common features of actors across the international system'.

[31] In including chapters about the 'imperial turn' as it pertained to French, Spanish, German, American, and Australian as well as British contexts, Antoinette Burton hoped that her *After the Imperial Turn* collection might help to 'interrogate the Anglocentric presumptions of new imperial histories and to open postcolonialism itself to critique as a carrier of unseen and subtle traces of British imperial hegemony' and 'encourag[e] students of Britain and its empire to come to terms with the ways in which historians of other national cultures are addressing the imperial turn, or not'. Unfortunately, these have largely failed to happen since its publication in 2003. Antoinette Burton, 'Introduction: On the Inadequacy and the Indispensability of the Nation', in Burton (ed.), *After the Imperial Turn*, 9–10.

Britain was simultaneously transformed from the hub of an empire and Commonwealth to a member of the EEC and EU.[32]

Although they are by no means alone in ignoring the vast majority of academic work on other nations' empires, scholars of Britain's interlinked domestic and imperial cultures dominated the 'new imperial history' in its early phases and correspondingly did much to influence researchers of France, Portugal, the Netherlands, and Belgium who embarked on imperial turns of their own. The preeminence of Anglophone scholarship continues today, whether it be research concerning Britain and its empire or produced by academics based in the United States, Britain, or other English-speaking countries about continental European empires. Interdisciplinary work on France and its colonies comes a distant second to that concerning Britain, with much of its initial inspiration coming from US-based historians of France.[33] Britain and France thus not only had the two largest modern empires but have also attracted the highest level of academic attention to the virtual exclusion of other former European colonizers. While fully appreciating the pioneering contributions made by those who have focused on these examples,

[32] Linda Colley, *Britons: Forging the Nation, 1707–1837* (New Haven, 1992); Linda Colley, 'Britishness and Otherness: An Argument', *Journal of British Studies*, 31:4 (1992), 309–29. This has also been pointed out by Wendy Webster, 'Home, Colonial and Foreign: Europe, Empire and the History of Migration in 20th-Century Britain', *History Compass*, 8:1 (2010), 32; Tony Kushner, *We Europeans?: Mass-Observation, 'Race' and British Identity in the Twentieth Century* (Aldershot, 2004), 32.

[33] Benjamin Stora, *La guerre des mémoires: La France face à son passé colonial* (Paris, 2007), 29; Florence Bernault, 'Colonial Syndrome: French Modern and the Deceptions of History', in Charles Tshimanga, Didier Gondola, and Peter J. Bloom (eds.), *Frenchness and the African Diaspora: Identity and Uprising in Contemporary France* (Indianapolis, 2009), 121. Leading American contributors to innovative approaches to French and French imperial history include Alice Conklin, Herman Lebovics, Kristin Ross, and Gary Wilder. Among their many publications, see Alice L. Conklin, 'Boundaries Unbound: Teaching French History as Colonial History and Colonial History as French History', *French Historical Studies*, 23:2 (2000), 215–38; Alice L. Conklin, Sarah Fishman, and Robert Zaretsky, *France and Its Empire since 1870: The Republican Tradition* (New York, 2011); Herman Lebovics, *Bringing the Empire Back Home: France in the Global Age* (Durham, 2004); Kristin Ross, *Fast Cars, Clean Bodies: Decolonization and the Reordering of French Culture* (Cambridge, MA, 1995); Gary Wilder, 'Unthinking French History: Colonial Studies Beyond National Identity', in Burton (ed.) *After the Imperial Turn*, 125–43. French contributions include Stora's many analyses of France and the Algerian War together with Pascal Blanchard, Sandrine Lemaire, and Nicolas Bancel (eds.), *Culture coloniale en France: De la Révolution à nos jours* (Paris, 2008), among a number of their edited collections. Tentative French explorations of Anglophone traditions of postcolonial studies include Marie-Claude Smouts (ed.), *La situation postcoloniale* (Paris, 2007); Catherine Coquery-Vidrovitch, *Enjeux politiques de l'histoire coloniale* (Marseille, 2009), especially ch. 3; Berny Sèbe, 'Itinéraires intellectuels et méthodologiques en Grande-Bretagne: De *l'imperial history* aux *postcolonial studies* en passant par les *French studies*', in Le Collectif Write Back (ed.), *Postcolonial Studies: Modes d'emploi* (Lyon, 2013), 89–104. See also the diverse perspectives and debates included in 'Racial France', special issue, *Public Culture*, 23:1 (2011), particularly essays by Jean-François Bayart, 'Postcolonial Studies: A Political Invention of Tradition', 55–84; Achille Mbembe, 'Provincializing France?', 85–119; Ann Laura Stoler, 'Colonial Aphasia: Race and Disabled Histories in France', 121–56.

this book strives to go beyond these usual suspects of colonial and postcolonial studies, situating them alongside three counterparts whose smaller geographical scale and lesser power on a European stage rendered the overseas colonies that expanded their dimensions of tremendous importance to their national identities. Just as ruling the Congo transformed Belgium into *la plus grande Belgique*, not least in its own national imaginary, the Netherlands counted as another 'small nation with a big empire', or 'a colonial giant but a political dwarf', as Vincent Kuitenbrouwer and H.L. Wesseling have respectively termed it.[34] This was equally if not more true for Portugal, whose spatial parameters were as modest as the political and economic weight it was capable of pulling if confined to its European dimensions alone.

This book, then, makes a strong plea for scholars and students of European metropoles and their (former) empires to grapple more deeply with the contributions and subject matter of those whose research targets different national-imperial cases. To date, scholars of France and even more markedly Belgium, the Netherlands, and Portugal have paid immeasurably more attention to research devoted to Britain than vice versa. Works concerning non-British colonial and postcolonial histories that have been taken up by English-language scholars remain exceptions that prove the rule, whether or not they appear in English.[35] The vast majority of research concerning the latter three cases remains largely neglected by non-specialists, despite the concerted effort made by a growing number of authors (particularly experts on the Low Countries and Portugal) to publish in English and thus render their writing accessible to a much larger international readership.[36] Ignoring it makes us not

---

[34] Vincent Kuitenbrouwer, '"A Newspaper War"?: Dutch Information Networks during the South African War (1899–1902)', *BMGN – Low Countries Historical Review*, 128:1 (2013), 150; H.L. Wesseling, 'The Giant that was a Dwarf, or the Strange History of Dutch Imperialism', *Journal of Imperial and Commonwealth History*, 16:3 (1988), 69.

[35] For every publication by Ann Laura Stoler, Frederick Cooper, or Todd Shepard (to name several leading figures who explore French and Dutch contexts in particular) to have influenced an international scholarly community, hundreds of books and articles by other contributors working on related questions remain relatively untapped. Revealing points about this issue are made by Frances Gouda, Remco Raben, and Henk Schulte Nordholt in their discussion of Stoler's book *Along the Archival Grain: Epistemic Anxieties and Colonial Common Sense* (Princeton, 2009), in 'Debate', *Bijdragen tot de Taal-, Land- en Volkenkunde*, 165:4 (2009), 551–67 (see especially 552, 555).

[36] Elleke Boehmer and Sarah De Mul (eds.), *The Postcolonial Low Countries: Literature, Colonialism, and Multiculturalism* (Lanham, MD, 2012); Vincent Viaene, David Van Reybrouck, and Bambi Ceuppens (eds.), *Congo in België: Koloniale cultuur in de metropool* (Leuven, 2009); Matthew G. Stanard, *Selling the Congo: A History of European Pro-Empire Propaganda and the Making of Belgian Imperialism* (Lincoln, NE, 2011); Guy Vanthemsche, *La Belgique et le Congo: L'impact de la colonie sur la métropole*, new and rev. edn. (Brussels, 2010), as well as its English translation entitled *Belgium and the Congo, 1885–1960*, translated by Alice Cameron and Stephen Windross, revised by Kate Connelly (Cambridge, 2012); Susan Legêne, *Spiegelreflex: Culturele sporen van de koloniale ervaring* (Amsterdam, 2010); Marieke Bloembergen and Vincent Kuitenbrouwer (eds.), 'A New Dutch Imperial History', special

only less informed about specific colonial and postcolonial histories but intellectually poorer in terms of broader conceptual tools of analysis. Greater familiarity with Portugal's understudied, 'subaltern' empire and its ideological underpinnings, for instance, provides an invaluable point of comparison and contrast with other European variants.[37] Yet as Nancy Naro, Roger Sansi-Roca, and David Treece put it, Lusophone (Portuguese-language) subject matter remains studiously neglected in an English-dominated field:

There is a certain irony in that, just as the Anglophone academic world was won over by a postcolonial theory critical of ethnocentrism, much of the academic production of this postcolonial turn adopted an Anglophone perspective. The 'Anglocentric' hegemony of intellectual production became consolidated in recent studies even when it was led by 'subaltern' studies.

Work on Lusophone equivalents to the 'Black Atlantic' world that Gilroy examined in English-language arenas also 'questioned the now fashionable terms "hybridity" and "syncretism" well before they were rediscovered by their Anglophone counterparts', they continue, but these intellectuals

are not considered 'cosmopolitan' scholars, because their publications in foreign languages have been relatively unknown or neglected in the English-speaking centers of cosmopolitan production. They have become 'local' or provincial scholars of 'exotic' cultures whose research, as cutting-edge as it is, is largely acknowledged only by a small body of specialists in their particular area.[38]

Encouraging readers to take a wider set of examples and approaches on board and view their own specific foci in fresh ways counts as a central aim of this book.

* * *

issue, *BMGN – Low Countries Historical Review*, 128:1 (2013); Oostindie, *Postcolonial Netherlands*.

[37] James D. Sidaway and Marcus Power, '"The Tears of Portugal": Empire, Identity, "Race", and Destiny in Portuguese Geopolitical Narratives', *Environment and Planning D: Society and Space*, 23:4 (2005), 529; Boaventura de Sousa Santos, 'Between Prospero and Caliban: Colonialism, Postcolonialism, and Inter-identity', *Luso-Brazilian Review*, 39:2 (2002), 9–43; Bela Feldman-Bianco, 'Colonialism as a Continuing Project: The Portuguese Experience', *Identities*, 8:4 (2001), 477–81; Miguel Vale de Almeida, *An Earth-Colored Sea: 'Race', Culture, and the Politics of Identity in the Postcolonial Portuguese-Speaking World* (New York, 2004); Paulo de Medeiros, 'Postcolonial Memories and Lusophone Literatures', *European Review*, 13:1 (2005), 151–61; Miguel Bandeira Jerónimo and António Costa Pinto (eds.), special issue on 'International Dimensions of Portuguese Late Colonialism and Decolonization', *Portuguese Studies*, 29:2 (2013).

[38] Nancy Priscilla Naro, Roger Sansi-Roca, and David H. Treece, 'Introduction', in Nancy Priscilla Naro, Roger Sansi-Roca, and David H. Treece (eds.), *Cultures of the Lusophone Black Atlantic* (New York, 2007), 11–12. Simon Potter and Jonathan Saha make similar valuable points about 'the Anglophone bias that continues to mark much supposedly "Global" history – often, in fact, a dialogue among English-speaking historians, built on English-language primary and secondary sources and centrally concerned with English-speaking parts of the world'. See Potter and Saha, 'Global History, Imperial History', 1–2.

That said, like any other, this book necessarily favours some locations over others. Its chapters on decolonization in Part I pay more attention to the loss of British India, French Algeria, the Dutch East Indies, the Belgian Congo, and Portuguese Africa, to name several, on account of their disproportionate importance for European policymakers and publics alike. Although many other examples also receive attention, for obvious reasons comprehensive and even coverage in a book of this length proved impossible. Similarly, Part II's discussions of European repatriation, ethnic minority immigration, and multicultural societies focus primarily on larger groups of migrants and more prominent instances of cultural diversity in postcolonial Europe, while Part III's examinations of European memories of empire reveal these to be equally selective in terms of their preferred events and places.

Moreover, although aiming towards a far broader Western European scope than the studies that evaluate one or perhaps two nations and their empires, *Europe after Empire* commits its own sins of omission by excluding Germany, Italy, and Spain from analysis. As Germany lost its own overseas colonies after the First World War, its role in post-1945 decolonization histories of other European countries is limited here to the ways in which the Nazi wartime enemy and occupier alongside the Jewish Holocaust influenced other nations' approaches and attitudes to empire and race, and later shaped memories of decolonization.[39] Nor are Italy's far shorter period of modern colonial rule in North Africa that came to an end with fascism or Spain's lingering colonial presence and ideologies after losing most of its empire in the early nineteenth century discussed. Available sources, space, and language limitations – that is, the languages with which this author has adequate reading abilities! – meant that neither could have received anywhere near the level of attention accorded to the five nations examined here.[40] Lastly, the roles played by Eastern European nations in Western European

---

[39] Recent works on German colonialism and postcolonial memories include Bradley Naranch and Geoff Eley (eds.), *German Colonialism in a Global Age* (Durham, 2014); Sebastian Conrad, *German Colonialism: A Short History* (Cambridge, 2012); Ulrike Lindner, Maren Möhring, Mark Stein, and Silke Stroh (eds.), *Hybrid Cultures – Nervous States: Britain and Germany in a (Post)Colonial World* (Amsterdam, 2010); Volker Langbehn and Mohammad Salama (eds.), *German Colonialism: Race, the Holocaust, and Postwar Germany* (New York, 2011); Jürgen Zimmerer (ed.), *Kein Platz an der Sonne: Erinnerungsorte der deutschen Kolonialgeschichte* (Frankfurt am Main, 2013); Britta Schilling, *Postcolonial Germany: Memories of Empire in a Decolonized Nation* (Oxford, 2014).

[40] Readers seeking introductions to these cases should consult Prem Poddar, Rajeev S. Patke, and Lars Jensen (eds.), *A Historical Companion to Postcolonial Literatures – Continental Europe and Its Empires* (Edinburgh, 2008); Christopher Schmidt-Nowara, 'A History of Disasters: Spanish Colonialism in the Age of Empire', *History Compass*, 5:3 (2007), 943–54; Zira Box, 'Spanish Imperial Destiny: The Concept of Empire During Early Francoism', *Contributions to the History of Concepts*, 8:1 (2013), 89–106; Juan B. Vilar, 'Franquismo y Descolonización: Española en África', *Historia Contemporánea*, 30 (2005), 129–58; Andreas Stucki, 'Imperium in iberischer Perspektive: Historiografie, Diskurse, Kultur', *Mittelweg*, 36 (2013–2014), 3–17;

decolonization histories pose different sets of questions, some of which are now being probed in an emergent scholarship. East-West European dynamics in a Cold War climate are just some of the many new directions that a transnational, intra-European, and globalized approach to decolonization and migration look set to take in future, a theme broached briefly in this book's main chapters as well as in its epilogue.

Scholarly orientations and traditions thus reveal themselves as much in flux as European ex-colonizing nations have been for decades. With their home-lands fundamentally transformed by the loss of empires, by multicultural diversity and cultural hybridity, and by the destabilization of older ideological assumptions about race, culture, and the meanings of place, some Europeans have responded enthusiastically and driven these changes forward. Others, by contrast, fight against what are perceived to be challenges to national cultures and identities. Zwarte Piet's uneasy position as a tradition in limbo exemplifies these tensions. Some Dutch want him eliminated from Sinterklaas rituals altogether as a racist caricature and colonial throwback, while others envision gradualist moves to make Piet less black but still recognizable – for instance, by proposing that performers and Piet-associated imagery engage in a phased shift from full blackface to merely dark smudges that would signify soot from the chimney, or by including pink, green, and blue Piets, dressed in familiar attire, alongside or in place of those who are black. Others still, meanwhile, protest that nay-sayers should stop trying to ruin a nice children's party that is best left just as it is, simultaneously exuberant and *gezellig* (a word ubiquitously used in Dutch to describe cosily pleasant social situations), unwilling to countenance the fact that many find it anything but in its current form.[41] With Zwarte Piet's longer-term fate and hue still hanging in the balance, his contentious status is symptomatic of the ever-changing approaches to and thoughts about racial legacies of empire specific to postcolonial places and moments within Europe after decolonization. The chapters that follow chart the process from the ending of empires to a postcolonial European present imbued with colonial traces and memories, conscious and unconscious, beginning with Britain and moving on to the Netherlands and their former colonizing European counterparts.

Ruth Ben-Ghiat and Mia Fuller (eds.), *Italian Colonialism* (New York, 2005); Jacqueline Andall and Derek Duncan (eds.), *Italian Colonialism: Legacy and Memory* (Bern, 2005); Patrizia Palumbo (ed.), *A Place in the Sun: Africa in Italian Colonial Culture from Post-Unification to the Present* (Berkeley, 2003); 'Colonial and Postcolonial Italy', special issue of *Interventions: International Journal of Postcolonial Studies*, 8:3 (2006).

[41] Patrick Meershoek, 'Zwarte Piet nieuwe stijl test de schoorsteen vast', *Het Parool*, 15 November 2014; Bas Blokker, 'Het duurde even, maar nu hebben we een Piet van roet', *nrc.next*, 17 November 2014; 'Hoe houden we het gezellig?', *Algemeen Dagblad* (Rotterdam), 17 November 2014.

Part I

Decolonization for colonizers

Europe's transition to the postcolonial era

1 Myths of continuity and European exceptionalism

Britain, decolonization, and the Commonwealth
family ideal

Britain, dominion 'daughters', and India's road to independence

At midnight on 31 December 1929, the Indian National Congress (INC) greeted the prospect of a new year and a new decade with a new set of political demands: *purna swaraj*. Urged on by incoming President Jawaharlal Nehru, the INC passed the Purna Swaraj Resolution and soon settled on 26 January as Independence Day. At meetings throughout the country, a pledge would be read out proclaiming that '[t]he British Government in India has not only deprived the Indian people of their freedom but has based itself on the exploitation of the masses, and has ruined India economically, politically, culturally and spiritually. We believe, therefore, that India must sever the British connection and attain Purna Swaraj or complete independence.'[1]

Purna swaraj marked a watershed within a nationalist struggle against Britain that originated in the late nineteenth century but whose momentum and mass participation had increased exponentially since the First World War. The 1930 pledge emerged as a product of British imperial policymaking since 1917, the Indian political demands it failed to fulfil, and the mounting non-cooperation campaigns they provoked. For the first time, India demanded not simply *swaraj* (home rule or self-rule) *within* the British empire but rather the right to break away *from* it. In so doing, India committed itself to a path that diverged sharply from precedents offered by Britain's dominions, which in 1930 included Canada, Newfoundland, Australia, New Zealand, South Africa, and the Irish Free State.[2]

---

[1] 'The Independence Pledge', issued at Allahabad, 17 January 1930 and jointly drafted by Mahatma Gandhi and Jawaharlal Nehru, reprinted in *Selected Works of Jawaharlal Nehru* (hereafter *SWJN*), Vol. 4 (New Delhi, 1973), 216.

[2] John Darwin, 'Britain's Empires', in Sarah Stockwell (ed.), *The British Empire: Themes and Perspectives* (Oxford, 2008), 2. The Irish Free State became a dominion in 1922; Newfoundland ceased to be one in 1933 when it forfeited responsible government during the depression, and ultimately become a province of Canada in 1949.

It would take another seventeen years for Britain to grant India its independence. During the interim, the rulers of empire proved reluctant to abandon their stated assumption that any future political advance in the Indian subcontinent would take place according to patterns established in white settler–dominated territories in the nineteenth century. In fact, the British proved as stubbornly resistant to shedding this notion as they once had been to accepting that India might one day follow in dominion footsteps in the first place. From the late 1830s and 1840s on, the so-called 'white' settler colonies enjoyed increasing autonomy over their internal affairs. Over time, they achieved 'responsible government' – effectively equivalent to full self-government – although Britain maintained control over their external relations. Starting in 1907, colonies with responsible government became known as 'dominions', a term distinguishing them from the Indian empire and other colonies directly ruled by Britain. 'Dominion status', as W. David McIntyre summarizes, was tantamount to 'a half-way house between colonial and independent status'.[3] Dominions' military, financial, and material contributions to Britain's 1914–1918 war effort allowed their leaders to demand an even fuller recognition of their sovereignty over matters foreign and internal alike. The Balfour Report of 1926 defined both Great Britain and the dominions as 'autonomous Communities within the British Empire, equal in status, in no way subordinate one to another in any aspect of their domestic or external affairs, though united by common allegiance to the Crown, and freely associated as members of the British Commonwealth of Nations'.[4] The 1931 Statute of Westminster legally formalized this devolution of authority, with the British Parliament relinquishing the power to legislate on dominions' behalf.

Indian nationalists had long observed these developments with keen interest. Just two years after dominions were given their name, Mohandas Gandhi stressed in *Hind Swaraj* that the INC 'has always desired self-government after the Canadian model'.[5] At the time, British authorities could not envisage a comparable road map for the subcontinent either then or at any point in the future. But the First World War wrought changed policies towards India which, like the dominions, made extreme sacrifices on the empire's behalf without consent. The INC's growing strength made Britain contemplate political concessions in the effort to conciliate Indian opinion and ensure wartime loyalty. The year 1917 brought the Montagu Declaration stating that Britain's goal for India was the 'gradual realization of responsible government' within the British

---

[3] W. David McIntyre, 'The Strange Death of Dominion Status', *Journal of Imperial and Commonwealth History*, 27:2 (1999), 194.

[4] Darwin, 'Britain's Empires', 16.

[5] *Hind Swaraj* (1909), in *The Collected Works of Mahatma Gandhi* (Electronic Book, accessible via www.gandhiserve.org/e/cwmg/cwmg.htm) (New Delhi, Publications Division of the Government of India, 1999, 98 volumes) (hereafter *CWMG*), Vol. 10, 251.

empire. This was followed by the 1919 Government of India Act granting Indians a power-sharing role in provincial affairs but maintaining full British control over the central administration, India's defence and internal security, foreign relations, and finance.[6]

The limited level of authority Indians actually acquired rendered it obvious that the promised progress towards 'responsible government' was by no means equivalent to gaining a significant degree of *self*-government. Moreover, reforms were immediately compromised by British crackdowns on civil and political dissent as wartime special powers were extended indefinitely, leading to protests and martial law. Free speech was suppressed; Indian activists could be held indefinitely without trial for alleged political crimes; trials could be held without jury; and police surveillance and army brutality increased – most notoriously during the massacre of civilians at a peaceful demonstration in Amritsar in the Punjab in 1919.[7] Repression made Britain new enemies, while the Government of India Act, intended to appease 'moderate' Indians, offered too little in the way of reform as compensation to win Britain many friends. The year 1920 saw nationalists led by Gandhi – widely revered as the 'Mahatma', or 'great soul' – embark upon a succession of transformative campaigns of non-cooperation and non-violent passive resistance to British rule.

By the time the 1919 Act underwent an official review and the viceroy, Lord Irwin, formally declared in 1929 that Britain intended dominion status for India in the future, it was too late. To ascendant INC leaders like Nehru, it was not simply that Irwin had specified nothing whatsoever about when India might expect to achieve this. It soon became clear that any short- and medium-term constitutional changes would involve 'safeguards' whereby Britain remained in control of India's defence, foreign relations, and currency, and the viceroy still enjoyed extensive powers.[8] 'Dominion Status was for some distant here-after', Nehru concluded; it was nothing more than 'political trickery, barely veiling the fixed intention to hold on to India as an imperial domain and possession for as long as this was possible. The claws of imperialism would continue deep in the living body of India.'[9] If Britain meant the 'Dominion Idea' to work towards 'the containment of colonial nationalism', as John

---

[6] Maria Misra, *Vishnu's Crowded Temple: India since the Great Rebellion* (London, 2007), 110, 126.

[7] Derek Sayer, 'British Reaction to the Amritsar Massacre 1919–1920', *Past & Present*, 131 (1991), 130–64.

[8] John Darwin, 'The Dominion Idea in Imperial Politics', in Judith M. Brown and Wm. Roger Louis (eds.), *The Oxford History of the British Empire, Vol. IV: The Twentieth Century* (Oxford, 1999), 79–81.

[9] Jawaharlal Nehru, *The Discovery of India* (New Delhi, 2000, first published 1946), 440. See also 'Presidential Address', Lahore, 29 December 1929, in *SWJN*, Vol. 4, 191. Nehru's many arguments contrasting dominion status with actual independence include 'Speech at the All Parties Conference', Lucknow, 29 August 1929, in *SWJN*, Vol. 3 (New Delhi, 1972), 57–61; Jawaharlal Nehru, *An Autobiography* (New Delhi, 2001, originally published 1936), 416–25.

Darwin has argued, by 1930 it had backfired spectacularly in India.[10] To INC leaders like Nehru who found themselves repeatedly jailed for their political activities, the dominion 'half-way house' seemed no different than an India that remained locked into the British empire.

Gandhi himself addressed the issue while visiting Britain in 1931. His twelve-week stay to attend the Round Table Conference on Indian constitutional reform took place during a lull in a four-year civil disobedience movement launched the previous year, when he captured world attention via campaigns like the salt march protesting British monopolies and taxation policies. He aspired to a future when Britain and India could be free to be partners on equal terms if they chose, not India's '"subjection" in glorified language'. Reflecting on his shift away from earlier aims, he commented to British audiences that 'I found that dominion status is a status common to members of the same family – Australia, Canada, South Africa, New Zealand etc.' Britain treated existing dominions as 'daughter nations' both because most of their populations were English-speaking and on account of 'natural links' that had 'grown out of the mother country'. But whereas biological, familial metaphors tied Britain and the dominions together, in India '[a]lien rule is like foreign matter in an organic body. Remove the poison and the body will at once start recuperating.'[11]

Although Gandhi did not explicitly mention race, his statements about dominions' 'natural' connection to Britain, common English mother tongue, and the mother/daughters familial analogy perceptively alluded to the power of 'race sentiment' within British thinking and imperial policymaking. Steady emigration from Britain to the white settler–dominated dominions created a strong sense of demographic and cultural community spanning these parts of the 'British world' – even in Canada and South Africa whose European populations were ethnically diverse and often divided, and which respectively included many French-speakers and Afrikaners alongside Britons and the British-descended.[12] '[A]n aggressive sense of cultural superiority as the representatives of a global civilization then at the height of its prestige' was common amongst Britons at home and dominion-based whites alike[13] – a superiority bestowed by whiteness and distributed among kith and kin of the same 'stock'. Indians, meanwhile, like other colonized peoples in Asia and

---

[10] Darwin, 'Dominion Idea', 64.

[11] C. Rajagopalachar and J.C. Kumarappa (eds.), *The Nation's Voice: Being a Collection of Gandhiji's Speeches in England and Sjt. Mahadev Desai's Account of the Sojourn [September to December, 1931]* (Ahmedabad, 1958; first published 1932), quotes taken from 192, 126, 195–6, 222; see also 79–80.

[12] James Belich, *Replenishing the Earth: The Settler Revolution and the Rise of the Anglo-World, 1783–1939* (Oxford, 2009).

[13] Darwin, 'Dominion Idea', 72.

Africa, fell outside Britain's racial family and were widely deemed insufficiently prepared to share its political privileges.

* * *

If the vague prospect of dominion status was no longer enough for the INC by 1930, it was still too much for Britons loathe to concede anything at all and for whom India was condemned to eternal political childhood. None voiced the latter position more often or with greater determination than the prominent Conservative Member of Parliament (MP) and former Colonial Secretary Winston Churchill.[14] In a series of speeches given in 1930 and 1931, he denounced as 'preposterous' the idea that India ever 'would be likely to live in peace, happiness and decency' with 'the same forms of government which prevail among the British, Canadian or Australian democracies'.[15] The 'lessons of history which we have learnt in our experience with the great self-governing dominions' did not remotely apply to India, he insisted:

Here you have nearly three hundred and fifty millions of people, lifted to a civilisation and to a level of peace, order, sanitation, and progress far above anything they could possibly have achieved themselves or could maintain. This wonderful fact is due to the guidance and authority of a few thousands of British officials responsible to Parliament who have for generations presided over the development of India. But if that authority is injured or destroyed, the whole efficiency of the services, defensive, administrative, medical, hygienic, judicial; railway, irrigation, public works and famine prevention, upon which the Indian masses depend for their culture and progress, will perish with it. India will fall back quite rapidly through the centuries into the barbarism and privations of the Middle Ages.

Britain should refuse to pander to 'the political aspirations towards self-government of a small number of intellectuals' who were categorically unrepresentative of the Indian population; such people had 'no real contact with the masses' and were 'incapable of giving them the guidance they require', Churchill intoned.[16] Unlike the disinterested Indian Civil Service presided over by benevolent British officials, '[n]epotism, back-scratching, graft and corruption in every form will be the handmaiden of a Brahmin domination.' So divided was the subcontinent along caste, class, and especially religious lines that any claim by the Indian National Congress to speak on behalf of 'the

[14] Sarvepalli Gopal, 'Churchill and India', in Robert Blake and Wm. Roger Louis (eds.), *Churchill* (Oxford, 1993), 457–71; Richard Toye, *Churchill's Empire: The World that Made Him and the World He Made* (London, 2010), ch. 6.
[15] 'India (Government Policy)', 3 December 1931, House of Commons, in Robert Rhodes James (ed.), *Winston S. Churchill: His Complete Speeches 1897–1963*, Vol. V, 1928–1935 (London, 1974), 5110.
[16] 'Our Duty in India', 18 March 1931, Albert Hall, London, in Rhodes James (ed.), *Churchill, Complete Speeches*, V, 5006–7, 5004; 'The March of Events', 26 March 1931, Constitutional Club, London, in Rhodes James (ed.), *Churchill, Complete Speeches*, V, 5011.

nation' could only be risibly self-serving. 'India' was merely 'an abstraction' and 'a geographical term', Churchill told his British listeners. 'It is no more a united nation than the Equator.'[17]

Britain not only had the 'duty' to act 'in the interests of India' and protect 'the masses', untouchables, Muslims, princes, Europeans, and others from the threat of 'Hindu despotism'.[18] With these duties came legitimate 'rights and interests' of its own, including 'the interest of Lancashire' that Churchill repeatedly invoked in the early 1930s.[19] India's effect on this northwest English county became a prime example of India's impact on the British nation. Nor was he alone in his assessment given the historic importance of the region's cotton industry within the British economy – a sector highly dependent upon global, and especially Indian, trade. Textiles (especially cotton cloth from Lancashire) remained Britain's largest export and India its largest overall market during the 1930s, but both had declined precipitously since the First World War. While 1,248 million yards of British cloth were sold in India in 1929, within just two years this had plummeted to 376 million – by which time approximately one-third of Lancashire's cotton workers were unemployed.[20] Although the causes of its economic crisis were in fact manifold (the global depression as well as stiff competition from Japanese manufacturers and other international producers also took their toll), within Britain a popular diagnosis of the stricken region's ills laid the blame squarely on the Indian National Congress' doorstep. More than any other factor, it was the Gandhi-led boycott of foreign textiles that 'spells the doom of Lancashire', as Churchill put it.[21] If the empire was striking back, it was commonly perceived as having scored its most destructive hit in Lancashire.

---

[17] 'March of Events', 5011.
[18] 'Our Duty in India', 5008–9. Churchill's wording stretched back to deeply-established British claims that 'oriental despotism' prevailed in pre-colonial India and to a longer history of British dismissals of elite Indian (especially Hindu) political aspirations; see especially Thomas R. Metcalf, *Ideologies of the Raj: The New Cambridge History of India*, III:4 (Cambridge, 1994), 37–8, 66; Mrinalini Sinha, *Colonial Masculinity: The 'Manly Englishman' and the 'Effeminate Bengali' in the Late Nineteenth Century* (Manchester, 1995). Similarly, Churchill's homage to the Indian Civil Service's virtues was (and remains) a familiar and resilient trope within hagiographical accounts of British rule; amongst other writings in this vein, see David Gilmour, *The Ruling Caste: Imperial Lives in the Victorian Raj* (London, 2005).
[19] 'India: "A Frightful Prospect"', 26 January 1931, House of Commons, in Rhodes James (ed.), *Churchill, Complete Speeches*, V, 4956; Andrew Muldoon, '"An Unholy Row in Lancashire": The Textile Lobby, Conservative Politics, and Indian Policy, 1931–1935', *Twentieth Century British History*, 14:2 (2003), 96.
[20] B.R. Tomlinson, 'India and the British Empire, 1880–1935', *Indian Economic and Social History Review*, 12:4 (1975), 339–40, 364; B.R. Tomlinson, *The Political Economy of the Raj 1914–1947: The Economics of Decolonization in India* (London, 1979), 2, 122; B. Chatterji, 'Business and Politics in the 1930s: Lancashire and the Making of the Indo-British Trade Agreement, 1939', *Modern Asian Studies*, 15:3 (1981), 528, 530.
[21] 'March of Events', 5012.

Cotton cloth had long played a central role within Indian anti-colonialism and ranked high among the INC's signature campaigns and symbols. By the 1930s, Gandhi's internationally famous persona owed much to his ascetic spiritualism, vegetarianism, fasts, and not least his clothing that rendered him an unconventional curiosity in Western eyes.[22] When Churchill notoriously dismissed him as 'a seditious Middle Temple lawyer, now posing as a fakir of a type well-known in the East, striding half-naked up the steps of the Vice-regal palace', he mocked Gandhi's habitual attire consisting of little more than a hand-spun cotton loincloth (*dhoti*), shawl, and sandals.[23] In tandem with his politics, the Mahatma's apparel had come a long way since his days as a young law student in the 1880s, freshly arrived in London and eager to dress like an English gentleman in tailor-made suits.[24] No longer content to play a part within the British imperial system, his instantly recognisable attire was emblematic of the INC's championing of import substitution and Indian-made products (*swadeshi* goods, or those 'of one's own land') that culminated in the civil disobedience campaign against textiles from abroad in the early 1930s.

For decades Gandhi had rallied against the combined havoc that Western civilization, its industrial machinery, and Manchester (the nucleus of Lancashire's cotton industry) had wreaked upon India. Building upon nineteenth- and early twentieth-century nationalist critiques of imperialism's economic drain of India, he and his Congress allies decried Britain's historic decapitation of indigenous Indian cloth manufacture for its own profit. Britain, nationalists claimed, had ruthlessly demoted the subcontinent to a mere producer of raw cotton for shipment to British mills, where it was woven into cheap fabric and re-exported to India.[25] Rural peasants paid the highest price, losing an invaluable source of extra income from making their own cloth that once supplemented the pittance they earned from agriculture, which provided employment for only half the year. 'Lancashire rose on the ruins of the Indian Village industry', Gandhi contended, turning the revival of cottage production of home-spun coarse cotton cloth (*khadi*) into a winning formula combining economic, cultural, and political nationalism and

---

[22] Sean Scalmer, *Gandhi in the West: The Mahatma and the Rise of Radical Protest* (Cambridge, 2011), Introduction and ch. 1; David Hardiman, *Gandhi in His Time and Ours: The Global Legacy of His Ideas* (London, 2003), ch. 9.

[23] 'A Seditious Middle Temple Lawyer', 23 February 1931, Winchester House, Epping, in Rhodes James (ed.), *Churchill, Complete Speeches*, V, 4985.

[24] Among countless studies of Gandhi, see standard works by Judith M. Brown, including *Gandhi: Prisoner of Hope* (New Haven, 1989); Judith M. Brown and Anthony Parel (eds.), *The Cambridge Companion to Gandhi* (Cambridge, 2011). His own assessment of his student years in London can be found in Mohandas K. Gandhi, *Autobiography: The Story of My Experiments with Truth*, translated by Mahadev Desai (New York, 1983; reprint of 1948 edn.), 38–72.

[25] Aside from his 1931 statements discussed later in this chapter, see also *Hind Swaraj*, 303–7; 'Presidential Address at Belgaum Congress', 26 December 1924, in *CWMG*, Vol. 29, 490–4.

regeneration.[26] As an explicit denunciation of imperialism and the harm it had done to India, his celebrated wardrobe provided a tangible illustration of anti-colonial alternatives. Spinning, weaving, and wearing *khadi* became iconic nationalist practices – the 'livery of freedom', in Nehru's estimation.[27] *Khadi* symbolized both the INC's fight against British exploitation and the nationalist elite's empathy and common cause with India's impoverished masses, acting as a direct refutation of the recurrent British charge that the INC was an unrepresentative organization with unrepresentative goals. 'In India several millions wear only a loin-cloth', Gandhi explained to a British reporter. 'That is why I wear a loin-cloth myself. They call me half-naked. I do it deliberately in order to identify myself with the poorest of the poor in India.'[28]

He also stressed his affinity to Britain's poor during his visit in the autumn of 1931. During the Round Table Conference he eschewed exclusive accommodations in favour of spartan lodgings in London's East End; every morning he started his day with a walk through its working-class districts, engaging in friendly exchanges with those he encountered along the way.[29] Amidst the suffering of the Great Depression, Gandhi had gained an international reputation as a symbolic hero to the poor and downtrodden that extended to Britain as well as the United States and other countries via intense media coverage of the 1930 salt march and other campaigns.[30] Regardless of his wider appeal and expressions of sympathy, however, he insisted that his primary concern was India's poor whose plight was exponentially worse than that of Britain's own. He repeatedly confronted this analogy during his 1931 stay, never more categorically refuting it than during his two-day excursion to Lancashire where many identified him and the INC's textile boycott as the main source of their troubles.[31] 'I am pained at the unemployment here', he said, and regretted whatever small part he personally might have played in it. 'But there is no starvation or semi-starvation. In India we have both', with 'half-starved skeletons, living corpses' in every village.[32] His duty was 'to the

---

[26] 'Speech at Meeting of Labour M.P.s', London, 16 September 1931, in *CWMG*, Vol. 53, 369.

[27] Susan S. Bean, 'Gandhi and *Khadi*, the Fabric of Indian Independence', in Annette B. Weiner and Jane Schneider (eds.), *Cloth and Human Experience* (Washington, DC, 1989), 355–76 (see 373 for Nehru's quote); Emma Tarlo, *Clothing Matters: Dress and Identity in India* (London, 1996), chs. 3 and 4; Lisa Trivedi, *Clothing Gandhi's Nation: Homespun and Modern India* (Bloomington, 2007); C.A. Bayly, 'The Origins of Swadeshi (Home Industry): Cloth and Indian Society, 1700–1930', in Arjun Appadurai (ed.), *The Social Life of Things: Commodities in Cultural Perspective* (Cambridge, 1986), 285–321.

[28] 'Interview to "The News Chronicle"', London, 17 September 1931, in *CWMG*, Vol. 53, 371; see also 'The Loin-Cloth', *Young India*, 30 April 1931, in *CWMG*, Vol. 52, 8–9.

[29] James D. Hunt, *Gandhi in London* (New Delhi, 1978), 205–7.

[30] Scalmer, *Gandhi in the West*, 33.

[31] Nicholas Owen, *The British Left and India: Metropolitan Anti-Imperialism, 1885–1947* (Oxford, 2007), 185–7.

[32] 'Speech in Lancashire', 26/27 September 1931, *Young India*, 15 October 1931, in *CWMG*, Vol. 53, 415.

starving millions of India, compared with whose poverty and pauperism the poverty of Lancashire dwindles into insignificance'.[33]

Gandhi hoped that face-to-face meetings with British cotton manufacturers and workers would give him the chance to explain Lancashire's deleterious effect on India and correct misunderstandings spread by his detractors about the rationale behind the INC's boycott. As a local newspaper reported,

Mr. Gandhi then went on to state his view that Indian poverty is the result of British policy through the overthrowing of India's old cotton industry by the machines of Lancashire more than a hundred years ago. He argued that the descendants of those who destroyed the supplementary means of livelihood ... could not now complain if the descendants of the dispossessed tried to rehabilitate themselves.[34]

For their part, Lancashire mill owners, trades unionists, workers, and the unemployed all hoped that seeing the grievous state of regional affairs first hand would lead him to call off the boycott. In this they were to be sorely disappointed. Noting that Britain's jobless received benefits nearly ten times higher than average Indian incomes, he told an unemployed workers' deputation that '[e]ven in your misery you are comparatively happy ... I wish well to you, but do not think of prospering on the tombs of the poor millions of India.'[35]

The *Manchester Guardian*'s account of Gandhi's meeting with cotton representatives suggests he succeeded in driving home the fact that local industry could expect no return to the past, when the colonizing nation had thrived at the expense of the colonized. One man left fearing a future in which 'fully 40 per cent of the spindles and looms in Lancashire will never run again'. But if many grudgingly faced up to economic reality, they struggled to accept Gandhi's deeper moral arguments about the comforts of even the least privileged social sectors within Britain when juxtaposed to the condition of India's peasantry struggling for sheer survival. 'It all depends on what one was accustomed to', one attendee reflected, while another reported that 'We put it to him that in the East a lower standard of life is the normal thing, and he agreed, but said that there were many millions in India who were below the lowest standard possible even in the Orient.'[36] British common-sense understandings of its cotton sector's predicament during the Great Depression thus reflected an ingrained sense of imperial entitlement vis-à-vis India, one laden with assumptions of poverty relativism that balked at acknowledging British culpability for colonial conditions. Whereas Gandhi insisted on

---

[33] 'Statement to the Press', Springvale Garden Village, 26 September 1931, from *The Sunday Observer*, 27 September 1931, in *CWMG*, Vol. 53, 412.

[34] 'Speech at Adult School', West Bradford, 27 September 1931, from *The Clitheroe Advertiser and Times*, 2 October 1931, in *CWMG*, Vol. 53, 418.

[35] 'Interview to Unemployed Workers' Deputation', West Bradford, 27 September 1931, in *CWMG*, Vol. 53, 419–20.

[36] 'Account of Meeting with Representatives of Cotton Trade', Edgeworth, 27 September 1931, from *The Manchester Guardian*, 28 September 1931, in *CWMG*, Vol. 53, 516, 514–15, 517.

Figure 1.1 Mohandas Gandhi and cheering mill workers while leaving one of
the textile mills at Spring Vale, Darwen, Lancashire, UK, 26 September 1931.
Credit: GandhiServe.

comparison, in Britain inequality between colonizers and colonized was taken as
the inevitable norm, part of a status quo in which Lancashire's right to India's
textile market and the local benefits it once bestowed were taken for granted.

Many Britons whom Gandhi met were as concerned about defending Britain's
'rights and interests' in India as Churchill was; unlike Churchill, however, who
refused even to meet Gandhi face to face, others had mastered the art of basic
courtesy and approached him without personal animosity or blatant disrespect.
Whether walking through working-class London or travelling on his many
excursions outside the capital, Gandhi repeatedly encountered public enthusiasm
and affection. 'People come out of their houses and shake hands with me and
wish me well', he reported of the East End. Even in Lancashire, where passions
often ran deepest and where he fully expected to be met with resentment, crowds
rushed to meet his train and lined the streets when he arrived.[37] 'Women mill

---

[37] 'Interview to Evelyn Wrench', London, on or after 17 October 1931, in *CWMG*, Vol. 54, 34;
'Statement to the Press', West Bradford, 27 September 1931, from *The Clitheroe Advertiser and
Times*, 2 October 1931, in *CWMG*, Vol. 53, 421–2; 'Speech at Plenary Session of Round Table
Conference', London, 1 December 1931, in *CWMG*, Vol. 54, 231.

workers shouted "Three cheers for Mr. Gandeye, hip hip – Hurrah'", one of his travelling companions recalled. Outside the factories, 'a number of women brought their babies and pushed them into [his] arms'.[38] Despite grave concerns about their own livelihoods, representatives of the cotton industry described him as 'one of the most remarkable men I have ever met' or went so far as to admit that 'If I were an Indian, I should be a disciple of Gandhi.'[39]

Gandhi and his cause, as these reports suggest, could claim friends as well as Churchillian-style foes at the heart of the empire. Alongside those who were casually sympathetic, open-minded, or simply curious to catch a glimpse of an exotic celebrity were others – Quakers, pacifists, communists, and some Independent Labour Party MPs like A. Fenner Brockway among them – broadly supportive of the INC's goals or at least willing to listen to nationalist arguments.[40] Churchill's views were by no means shared by all: his was an extreme voice even within his own Conservative Party strongly committed to empire, and his unbending stance on India denied him prominent Tory leadership positions even if it won him popularity among a considerable part of its electorate. Nonetheless, subsequent policy towards India in the wake of Gandhi's visit and the Round Table Conference underscored the extent to which the political climate reigning within 1930s Britain remained staunchly pro-imperialist.

* * *

The years ahead brought another cycle of Congress-led civil disobedience, stepped-up colonial repression, and the jailing of INC leaders (significantly, Gandhi was again in custody only a week after he returned from Britain).[41] Further political reforms also followed: with the 1935 Government of India Act, Britain resumed its process of bringing Indians into the administration. Whereas in 1919 the provinces of British India came partly under Indian control, 1935 brought full Indian provincial self-government as well as power-sharing at the centre. Like before, however, in 1935 the British were careful to keep a firm hold over imperial priorities – including defence, finance, and foreign relations – and the viceroy retained extensive discretionary powers. Furthermore, provincial ministries handed over to elected Indians could revert

---

[38] Mirabehn [Madeleine Slade], *The Spirit's Pilgrimage* (Arlington, VA, 1960), 141; on the 1931 visit, see 133–45.

[39] 'Account of Meeting with Representatives of Cotton Trade', 517, 515.

[40] Rajagopalachar and Kumarappa (eds.), *The Nation's Voice*, 113–17, 122–5, 129–31, 197; Hunt, *Gandhi in London*, 197–9, 205–11; more broadly, see Owen, *British Left*, ch. 7; Stephen Howe, *Anticolonialism in British Politics: The Left and the End of Empire, 1918–1964* (Oxford, 1993), ch. 2.

[41] Overviews providing further in-depth treatment of 1930s and 1940s India include Judith M. Brown, *Modern India: Origins of an Asian Democracy* (Oxford, 1994); Sumit Sarkar, *Modern India: 1885–1947* (Delhi, 1983); Misra, *Vishnu's Crowded Temple*; D.A. Low, *Britain and Indian Nationalism, 1929–1942* (Cambridge, 1997).

to direct British control if it was deemed necessary to maintain order. To many nationalists, it was obvious that the British did not consider the 1935 Act as a prelude to *purna swaraj* but rather intended to remain in India indefinitely. British policies also enhanced India's politicization along religious lines, which exacerbated communal divisions between Hindus and Muslims. The year 1935 entailed a continuation of 'divide and rule' approaches to India's diversity, with Britain rejecting INC claims to be a secular organization representing all of India whose reach extended beyond the Hindu majority and into mass society across the subcontinent. By the 1940s, this approach had provided far more political space for the Muslim League to emerge as a counterweight to the INC – a trajectory that took shape in the cauldron of the Second World War and reached its fullest extent once the war ended.

When the British viceroy, Lord Linlithgow, declared India to be at war against Nazi Germany along with Britain and the rest of the empire in 1939, he did so unilaterally without any consultation with the INC or any of the provincial ministries presided over by Indians – a clear demonstration of the limited autonomy over their own affairs Indians enjoyed in practice. The INC's elected leaders resigned from office in protest, civil disobedience resumed, and India's manpower and economic resources were again corralled to service the needs of the British empire at war in 1939–1945, just as they had been in 1914–1918. Renewed non-cooperation between 1939 and 1942 brought mass arrests, disruption, and a draconian British clampdown on dissent accompanied by a refusal to implement further political change demanded by the INC. Imperial intransigence was unsurprising, for not only was Britain hugely dependent on India's contributions to the war. Starting in May 1940, it was led by a prime minister whose categorical opposition to Indian nationalism had long rendered him a diehard imperialist since 1931: Winston Churchill.[42]

Wartime conditions gave rise to stepped-up anticolonial pressures to which Britain needed to formulate a credible response, and Churchill's was grudging at best. When he and United States President Roosevelt jointly issued the Atlantic Charter in August 1941 outlining common national priorities, their claim to 'respect the right of all peoples to choose the form of government under which they will live' and their 'wish to see sovereign rights and self-government restored to those who have been forcibly deprived of them' came high on the list. Yet not long after Churchill stressed that the declaration was not meant to apply to India or other British imperial territories; it concerned European nations that had fallen under Nazi occupation.[43] As he famously

---

[42] Yasmin Khan's *The Raj at War: A People's History of India's Second World War* (London, 2015) appeared too late to be drawn upon here.

[43] 'The Atlantic Charter, 14 Aug. 1941', and 'The Atlantic Charter: Extract from a Speech by the Prime Minister in the House of Commons', 9 September 1941, *Hansard Parliamentary Debates*, vol. 372, cols. 67–9, reprinted in A.N. Porter and A.J. Stockwell (eds.), *British*

declared a year later, 'We mean to hold our own. I have not become the King's First Minister in order to preside over the liquidation of the British Empire.'[44]

Over the coming months and years, Britain's empire in Asia was shaken to its core by another Axis occupier, Japan, and also challenged by the United States itself – an essential British ally which entered the war after Japan's bombing of Pearl Harbor, but equally a nagging thorn in Britain's side given its ideological opposition to European imperialism. Between late 1941 and spring 1942, Japan scored a rapid series of victories throughout Southeast Asia that rewrote the region's subsequent history. The next chapters discuss Japan's wartime impact on the Dutch East Indies and French Indochina, which resulted in a permanent weakening of European control and strengthened colonial nationalist movements, and the onslaught on Britain's territories was no less severe. Thought to be impregnable, Britain's naval base at Singapore fell to Japan, over 130,000 British imperial troops were taken prisoner, and the inability to defend a two-hemisphere empire was exposed for all to see. Japan occupied British Malaya at the cost of more military and civilian internments, redirected its rich sources of rubber, tin, and other commodities towards its own war machine, and advanced through Burma and thus to neighbouring India's gates.[45]

Britain's need for India's troops, money, and supplies had never been more desperate given the danger of Japanese invasion, yet never more at risk given the spread of nationalist non-cooperation with the 'Raj', as the British imperial Indian state was widely known. INC non-cooperation, American anti-colonialism, and pressure from Britain's own Labour Party (now part of the wartime coalition government) strengthened the conviction that concessions needed to be offered in order to guarantee India's wartime support. This forced Churchill, much against his will, to send a delegation headed by Sir Stafford Cripps, Labour MP and member of the War Cabinet, to India to negotiate in March 1942. The Cripps mission extended an unprecedented offer to Indian nationalists: the promise of dominion status tantamount to full independence after the war in exchange for cooperation vital to securing the victory. Yet it came with the crucial proviso that no individual province or princely state of the Indian subcontinent would be forced to become part of a unified, independent nation.

Depending on one's perspective, the Cripps mission could be chalked up either as a success or a fiasco. Crafted as a propaganda tool designed to appease American critics of empire and Labour Party supporters of Indian self-

Imperial Policy and Decolonization, 1938–64: Vol. 1, 1938–51 (Basingstoke, 1987), 101, 104–5; Wm. Roger Louis, *Imperialism at Bay 1941–1945: The United States and the Decolonization of the British Empire* (Oxford, 1977), 128–31.

[44] 'A New Experience – Victory', 10 November 1942, The Lord Mayor's Luncheon, Mansion House, London, in Robert Rhodes James (ed.), *Winston S. Churchill: His Complete Speeches 1897–1963, Vol. VI, 1935–1942* (London, 1974), 6695.

[45] Christopher Bayly and Tim Harper, *Forgotten Armies: Britain's Asian Empire and the War with Japan* (London, 2004), chs. 2–4.

government within Britain, it achieved its intentions. However, its refusal of the INC's demand for immediate participation in India's central government and its provincial opt-out clause when independence finally came led Congress to reject the offer as yet another sign of bad faith – further evidence that the British intended to remain indefinitely as well as strengthen their position by continuing to foster division and separatism among princes and provinces with a Muslim-majority population. Such suspicions were well-founded: Cripps' negotiations with nationalist leaders were impeded at every step by Churchill's obstructionism. For Churchill, limiting Cripps to making an unsatisfactory offer destined to fail in fact qualified as a success. The prime minister had not budged an inch from his position of 1931, and 'never doubted that the imperial interest would be best served by yielding nothing at all', as R.J. Moore surmised. Together with the viceroy, Lord Linlithgow, he 'espoused a do-nothing policy for the present and looked forward to a post-war British presence. Churchill favoured the eventual solution of the Indian problem whereby "we might sit on top of a tripos – Pakistan, Princely India and the Hindus"'. Linlithgow, for his part, believed Britain would remain in charge of India for another thirty years.[46]

Gandhi responded by calling on Britain to 'Quit India' at once and launched a mass movement under this banner in August 1942. He, Nehru, and other INC leaders great and small were rounded up and jailed, in many cases for the duration of the war; mass action took the form of urban strikes, peasant revolts, widespread sabotaging of India's communications infrastructure, and violent clashes with the police and army.[47] Imperial forces of law and order engaged in a ruthless backlash, with savage reprisals ranging from mass whippings of convicted rioters and the torturing of protestors to burning villages believed to harbour alleged 'terrorists'.[48] Approximately 2,500 people were shot and killed and up to 60,000 imprisoned, and the INC was outlawed and officially depicted as a revolutionary, underground organization. The Raj became increasingly ungovernable and its moral legitimacy was in tatters; communal tensions between Hindus and Muslims simultaneously grew in both violence and vehemence. The British authorities' need for amenable collaborators given the void left by the INC, meanwhile, enhanced the power of the Muslim League led by Mohammed Ali Jinnah, and with it the League's demand for a separate nation for India's Muslims: Pakistan.

By war's end in 1945, British rule in India was in its death throes. Cripps' promise of post-war independence had never been retracted, and the British could entertain no hope of re-establishing authority, order, and credibility, all

---

[46] R.J. Moore, *Churchill, Cripps, and India, 1939–1945* (Oxford, 1979), 43, 138; see also Wm. Roger Louis, *In the Name of God, Go!: Leo Amery and the British Empire in the Age of Churchill* (New York, 1992), 152–61; Toye, *Churchill's Empire*, 223–9.

[47] Moore, *Churchill, Cripps, and India*, 136.   [48] Bayly and Harper, *Forgotten Armies*, 244–53.

casualties of war and repression. It was no longer a question of postponing independence but of cutting British losses, attempting an exit from the sub-continent with as much dignity as possible under adverse circumstances in the face of escalating communal violence that the crippled imperial state could neither control nor contain. The British sought to secure a decolonization that would ideally salvage some shred of honour and influence and not be con-demned as an ignominious 'scuttle'. Policymakers invariably claimed they had hoped – one day – to hand over power to a united independent India. In the event, a long history of divide and rule tactics and wartime courting of the Muslim League to offset the power of a Hindu-dominated Congress created the conditions for the British Raj to be succeeded not by one independent state but rather two, India and Pakistan, headed respectively by Nehru and Jinnah. *Purna swaraj*, first demanded at midnight on the eve of 1930, finally came at midnight on 15 August 1947.

* * *

Post-war transitions and a new Commonwealth

In the coming decades, India's political evolution would become just one of many transformations to rock the British empire's foundations, ultimately resulting in widescale decolonization and a decline in Britain's world power status.[49] Britain's history of decolonization began in 1947–1948 under a Labour government headed by Clement Attlee, elected in July 1945 and remaining in office until 1951. Burma and Ceylon (later Sri Lanka) followed India and Pakistan on the road to independence, and Britain withdrew from the mandated territory of Palestine. But did the end of the Raj and the loss of its Indian 'Jewel in the Crown' in fact signal the end of the British empire? 'The British Empire is an Empire only because of India', Gandhi had stated in 1931, while Churchill predicted that '[t]he loss of India will be the death blow of the British Empire' and 'would be final and fatal to us. It could not fail to be part of

---

[49] What follows is an inevitably selective overview of Britain's decolonization history after 1945. Some of the many impressive wider treatments include Wm. Roger Louis, *Ends of British Imperialism: The Scramble for Empire, Suez and Decolonization: Collected Essays* (London, 2006); Brown and Louis (eds.), *Oxford History of the British Empire, IV*; John Darwin, *Britain and Decolonisation: The Retreat from Empire in the Post-War World* (Basingstoke, 1988); John Darwin, *The Empire Project: The Rise and Fall of the British World-System 1830–1970* (Cambridge, 2009), chs. 11–14; Martin Thomas, Bob Moore, and L.J. Butler, *Crises of Empire: Decolonization and Europe's Imperial States, 1918–1975* (London, 2008), Part I by L.J. Butler; Sarah Stockwell, 'Ends of Empire', in Stockwell (ed.), *The British Empire*, 269–93. Martin Shipway places the end of Britain's empire in comparative perspective in *Decolonization and Its Impact: A Comparative Approach to the End of Colonial Empires* (Malden, MA, 2008), as does Martin Thomas in *Fight or Flight: Britain, France, and Their Roads from Empire* (Oxford, 2014).

a process which would reduce us to the scale of a minor Power' – a rare instance of the two sharing common ground.[50] Come 1947, however, reigning British politicians and policymakers did not publicly view the independence of India and Pakistan as the beginning of an inevitable imperial decline and fall – nor had either Labour or the Conservatives resigned themselves to this prospect years later.

The history of South Asian nationalist struggles and British defences of their vested interests in the subcontinent in the face of the mounting challenges outlined earlier are crucial to recall when analyzing developments across the empire that followed. Just as importantly, they underpinned the consolidation of a powerful British narrative of what the Raj (and its end) meant, which became characteristic of common understandings of empire and decolonization that went on to enjoy a long metropolitan afterlife. The story that went to press in 1947 was one of continuity rather than rupture, one of a gradual, consensual devolution of power, and one in which laudable British intentions and not the untoward force of circumstances carried the day. It owed its basic plot to a pre-existing model that prescribed a preordained path from colonial to dominion status; in the post-war era, this was updated to emphasize a gradual, largely seamless, metamorphosis from British empire into a multiracial Commonwealth of nations. For when India and Pakistan became independent they officially did so *as dominions*, a transitional arrangement secured in exchange for an earlier British handover date despite the longstanding INC demand that India become an 'independent sovereign Republic'. To the delight of the last viceroy, Lord Mountbatten, the guise of dominionhood helped make Indian independence 'the greatest opportunity ever offered to the Empire', not a sign of its terminal condition.[51] Above all, the arrangement ideally distracted from the demeaning reality that Britain was being driven out of the subcontinent and hoped to withdraw as quickly as possible to avoid becoming embroiled in a communal civil war.[52]

Instead, in 1947 British commentators ranging from Mountbatten to Prime Minister Attlee to journalists from across the political spectrum packaged India's and Pakistan's independence as a success story for domestic consumption. Independence was a voluntary 'transfer of power', not a radical break; it was a credit to liberal British ideals and the intended, inevitable result of

---

[50] 'Answers to Questions', Oxford, 24 October 1931, in *CWMG*, Vol. 54, 89; 'India', 22 April 1931, Junior Imperial League Rally, Chingford, in Rhodes James (ed.), *Churchill, Complete Speeches*, V, 5015; 'India', 30 January 1931, in Rhodes James (ed.), *Churchill, Complete Speeches*, V, 4971; see also David Cannadine, *In Churchill's Shadow: Confronting the Past in Modern Britain* (London, 2002), 34.

[51] Wm. Roger Louis, 'The Dissolution of the British Empire', in Brown and Louis (eds.), *Oxford History of the British Empire*, IV, 335–6.

[52] John Darwin, 'British Decolonization since 1945: A Pattern or a Puzzle?', *Journal of Imperial and Commonwealth History*, 12:2 (1984), 193–4.

benevolent rule and careful planning that made colonial subjects 'ready' for self-rule. Indeed, it spelled no less than the fulfilment of British hopes dating back to the nineteenth century, a process ushered through critical stages of evolution in 1919, 1935, and ultimately in 1942, when the Cripps mission extended the generous offer of post-war independence.[53] Absent from official and media self-congratulation was any allusion to the decades-long history of British delaying tactics, national self-interest in the Raj, and ferocious repression of nationalists struggling for freedom; so, too, was any suggestion that Britain no longer had the power to govern or that communal divisions and violence owed anything to British policies that fomented Hindu–Muslim tensions and led to the tragic bloodbath following partition. As Chandrika Kaul outlines, two British narratives of independence came together in 1947 – 'a pro-empire version apparently co-existing with a celebration of decolonization'.[54]

After independence, this worked to absolve Britain from responsibility for the bloodshed that immediately followed, when up to one million died during the mass migration of as many as twelve million uprooted people between the new states of India and Pakistan. Communal massacres, in this reading, were but the unfortunate result of India's inherent, age-old divisions and evidence that anarchy ensued once Britain ceased to be in charge – just as Churchill and other imperial diehards had insistently prophesied.[55] Communalism even claimed Gandhi as a victim, murdered on 20 January 1948 in New Delhi by an anti-Muslim Hindu nationalist who disagreed with the Mahatma's commitment to a free India that welcomed all religious communities. Despite everything, however, after 1947 'India came to be seen as a paradigm of successful decolonization' within Britain, Nicholas Owen argues, 'deliberately portrayed as the tidy winding-up of a job well done' even though it marked 'the most violent of its retreats from empire, surpassing even the Mau Mau period in Kenya and the Malayan Emergency' still to come.[56] Far from being a source of shame on account of its human consequences, broken promises (for example, to the princely states forced to become part of India or Pakistan regardless of princes' wishes or previous British commitments), or for revealing Britain as unable to maintain its empire, 'transferring power' signified the opposite. As a Colonial Office report asserted in 1950, 'the transfer of power is not a sign of

---

[53] Nicholas Owen, '"More Than a Transfer of Power": Independence Day Ceremonies in India, 15 August 1947', *Contemporary Record*, 6:3 (1992), 415–51.

[54] Chandrika Kaul, '"At the Stroke of the Midnight Hour": Lord Mountbatten and the British Media at Indian Independence', *Round Table*, 97:398 (2008), 691. Excellent accounts of partition include Yasmin Khan, *The Great Partition: The Making of India and Pakistan* (New Haven, 2007); Ian Talbot and Gurharpal Singh, *The Partition of India* (Cambridge, 2009).

[55] Kaul, '"At the Stroke"', 690.

[56] Owen, '"More Than a Transfer"', 443, 416, 442; see also Wendy Webster, *Englishness and Empire 1939–1965* (Oxford, 2005), 58–68.

weakness or of liquidation of the Empire, but is, in fact, a sign and source of strength.'[57]

Given the long shadow cast by 1939–1945, pronouncements insisting on strength were as unsurprising as they were imbued by a combination of denial and wishful thinking. For Britain, the battle against the Axis powers had involved neither neutrality, as it had for Portugal, nor years of brutal Nazi occupation endured by the Netherlands, France, and Belgium. Undefeated at home, Britain emerged victorious in the fight against fascism, weathering the trials and tribulations and ultimately able to look back on the war as the nation's 'finest hour', as Churchill so memorably intoned. War had fortified existing national myths about Britain's imperial virtues and forged others anew, not least through flattering self-comparisons with enemies as well as allies. '[O]ur Empire, so magnificently united in this period of grave emergency, was not founded on conquest and oppression, like some Empires of the past, which the Germans are seeking to copy, but upon bold adventure, love of liberty and justice, and spiritual ideals', declared the President of the Empire Day Movement in the annual BBC radio broadcast to mark the occasion in 1943.[58] The Third Reich was defined by racism, aggression, invasions, and predatory foreign occupations; British imperial rule, by contrast, was benign, characterized by decency, moderation, lofty liberal ideals, racial tolerance, and noble plans for a future in which partnership, welfare and development initiatives, and a roadmap for planned self-government were all in the cards.

Conveniently ignoring conditions which prevailed within the South African dominion and across many of its colonies (not least in white settler territories like Northern and Southern Rhodesia as well as Kenya), Britain and its empire also claimed the moral racial high ground over the United States in which racial inequalities, segregation, and colour bars prevailed.[59] 'Being British meant being white', Sonya Rose summarizes, but also 'being tolerant, at least more tolerant than white Americans; it meant a paternalist stance that helped people of colour to "develop" and eventually "earn" their independence.'[60] These core ideals both bolstered national pride and helped defend the empire against American anti-colonial pressures that Britain could not afford to ignore, either before or after 1945.

[57] 'The colonial empire today: summary of our main problems and policies: CO International Relations Dept. paper. Annex: some facts illustrating progress to date' [May 1950], CO 537/ 5698, no. 69, reprinted in Ronald Hyam (ed.), *The Labour Government and the End of Empire 1945–1951, Part I* (*British Documents on the End of Empire*, Series A, Vol. 2) (London, 1992), 358.

[58] 'Empire Day Message', from Viscount Bledisloe, Empire Day, 1943 (PRO/CO 875/19/17), quoted in Sonya O. Rose, *Which People's War?: National Identity and Citizenship in Britain 1939–1945* (Oxford, 2003), 243.

[59] Webster, *Englishness and Empire*, 25–9, 42, 51–3.

[60] Rose, *Which People's War?*, 262; see also 258.

For if victory – militarily over its enemies, and morally over enemy and ally alike – was sweet, its costs were enormous. The Second World War left Britain politically hamstrung and economically destitute.[61] Despite the empire's massive contributions that included conscription and forced labour to enhance production for a wartime economy, Britain lost a quarter of its national wealth and went from being the world's largest creditor to the world's largest debtor nation. Not only did Britain incur close to £5 billion in war debts; over £1 billion in pre-war overseas assets had also been shed. American creditors imposed the most demanding terms and conditions, coupling loan agreements that fell far short of Britain's needs with intense political pressure to press forward with reform in the empire already seen in the Indian subcontinent. Britain continued to attempt American appeasement along similar lines as during the war itself, publicly committing to a process of political reform but stressing that social and economic development was the pre-requisite if the road to self-government – always at some unspecified time, and always within the framework of the empire and Commonwealth – was to advance on stable foundations. Meanwhile, initiatives like the Colonial Development and Welfare Act of 1945 legitimized a progressive new imperialism laden with good intentions to help colonial peoples that simultaneously provided desperately-needed aid to the metropole itself. Of the two goals, the latter took precedence: as Larry Butler rightly concludes, 'the aim of all this activity was less to benefit colonial populations than to restore Britain's economic independence.'[62]

Just as Gandhi and the INC had stressed the advantages Britain enjoyed at India's expense, policymakers in the second half of the 1940s looked to the empire to underwrite Britain's domestic recovery and reconstruction. George Orwell's pre-war prediction that without the empire England would be reduced 'to a cold and unimportant little island where we should all have to work very hard and live mainly on herrings and potatoes' would have resonated deeply in the immediate aftermath of war within a Britain suffering harsh winters alongside acute fuel and food shortages. Even basic staples such as bread – and the humble potato itself – became newly rationed.[63] Empire and imperial protectionism shone like a beacon of economic salvation for a metropole in crisis. Raw materials including tropical foodstuffs, metals, and other goods became targeted for increased production for export both to Britain and internationally.

---

[61] Philip Murphy, 'Britain as a Global Power in the Twentieth Century', in Andrew Thompson (ed.), *Britain's Experience of Empire in the Twentieth Century, Oxford History of the British Empire Companion Series* (Oxford, 2012), 48–61.

[62] L.J. Butler, in Thomas, Moore, and Butler, *Crises of Empire*, 58.

[63] George Orwell, *The Road to Wigan Pier* (New York, 1958; originally published 1937), 159–60; cited in Nicholas Owen, 'Critics of Empire in Britain', in Brown and Louis (eds.), *Oxford History of the British Empire*, IV, 208.

Produce from colonies that formed part of the Sterling Area could either be bought for the home market on favourable terms or sold outside the empire for the dollars Britain needed to restore its balance of payments deficit and gradually chisel away at its American loans. Britain increasingly relied upon oil supplies from its 'informal empire' in the Middle East, while the Gold Coast produced cocoa, Northern Rhodesia provided copper, and Malaya yielded lucrative quantities of rubber and tin.

Britain's need for Malayan exports underlay its crackdown on an insurgency in the colony that marked the start of the 'Emergency' declared in 1948. Like other revolts the Dutch and French confronted in Southeast Asia considered in Chapters 2 and 3, Malaya's was closely connected to the upheavals of Japanese occupation and the spread of communism across much of the region which gathered new momentum as China came under communist rule in 1949 and the Cold War increasingly dominated relations between East and West. Although its causes were manifold, the insurgency in Malaya can partly be seen as a popular backlash against intrusive economically inspired colonialism given the adverse impact of development policies Nicholas White aptly describes as 'hopelessly optimistic, ignorant of local conditions, and downright exploitative'.[64] In sub-Saharan Africa, Malaya, and elsewhere, the late 1940s and early 1950s brought what historians have termed a 'second colonial occupation' and an intensification of metropolitan investments which, in turn, had to be defended.[65] So too did white settlers in colonies like Kenya, Northern Rhodesia, and Southern Rhodesia, who played important roles in the agricultural and mining sectors geared towards international markets. Counterinsurgency campaigns pitting imperial troops (including many young British conscripts doing their obligatory National Service) against opponents variously dismissed as 'bandits', 'communist terrorists', or simply 'savages' were undertaken not just to preserve the empire from communist incursion but also to protect profitable economic interests deemed critical to the metropole's reconstruction.

* * *

Ultimately, the disruptive, self-serving imperialism of the second colonial occupation and the wartime upheavals that gave rise to it became signposts marking the road to decolonization.[66] But at the time, British officials remained

---

[64] Nicholas J. White, 'Reconstructing Europe through Rejuvenating Empire: The British, French, and Dutch Experiences Compared', *Past and Present*, 210: Supplement 6 (2011), 228. On the Malayan emergency, see Susan L. Carruthers, *Winning Hearts and Minds: British Governments, the Media and Colonial Counter-Insurgency 1944–1960* (London, 1995), ch. 2; T.N. Harper, *The End of Empire and the Making of Malaya* (Cambridge, 1999), ch. 4; Christopher Bayly and Tim Harper, *Forgotten Wars: The End of Britain's Asian Empire* (London, 2007), ch. 10.

[65] D.A. Low and J.M. Lonsdale, 'Introduction: Towards the New Order, 1945–63', in D.A. Low and Alison Smith (eds.), *History of East Africa*, Vol. 3 (Oxford, 1976), 13.

[66] White, 'Reconstructing Europe', 236.

convinced that colonial self-government could be safely postponed for the foreseeable future, in many cases for at least a generation. In the interim, imperial revival and the containment of radical change seemed possible. Insurgencies in Malaya, Kenya, and Cyprus during the 1950s could be broken, it was argued, and the 'hearts and minds' of colonized peoples won over. In many territories, organized nationalist demands for independence were all but invisible to colonial authorities. Some movements were still in their formative stages when the war ended; others simply had yet to take recognizable nationalist forms, or were denied recognition as nationalist. The Mau Mau revolt (predominantly among the Kikuyu) in Kenya, for example, was habitually depoliticized and psychologically pathologized, described as evidence of Africans' innate primitivism and savagery – not, as David Anderson summarizes, 'the product of frustrated legitimate nationalist aspiration against colonial oppression' that stemmed from land hunger and a thirst for freedom within a colony geared towards white settler interests.[67] Elsewhere, other movements were believed to appeal mainly to small elite minorities, as had long been the case in India. This was partly due to the fact that political pressures from colonial peoples resident in Britain were more perceptible than demands emanating directly from the colonies themselves. The 1945 Pan-African Congress seemed a case in point: organized in Manchester and taking a firm stand against imperial oppression, racism, and inadequate 'pretentious constitutional reforms', it was attended by West African and West Indian students, professionals, and activists along with African American supporters.[68]

Nationalism in Africa seemed an easy candidate for colonial containment or indeed pre-emption, posing nowhere near the threat it had in India in the immediate post-war period. Limited local concessions and the cultivation of amenable working relationships with 'moderate' (pro-Western) Africans, British authorities felt, would ensure measured political development along British-approved lines, while potential 'extremists' could be marginalized or suppressed. Not only was nationalism claimed to be in its infancy; so too were Africans, who were commonly seen by leading Labour and Conservative figures alike as far too politically immature to govern themselves. In 1943, Labour MP and Home Secretary Herbert Morrison had contrasted self-governing dominions that formed 'a family of adult nations' and India, which only had to wait until the

---

[67] David M. Anderson, 'Mau Mau at the Movies: Contemporary Representations of an Anti-Colonial War', *South African Historical Journal*, 48 (2003), 73. See also Dane Kennedy, 'Constructing the Colonial Myth of Mau Mau', *International Journal of African Historical Studies*, 25:2 (1992), 242–60; John Lonsdale, 'Mau Maus of the Mind: Making Mau Mau and Remaking Kenya', *Journal of African History*, 31 (1990), 393–421; Carruthers, *Winning Hearts and Minds*, 267.

[68] Frederick Cooper, *Africa Since 1940: The Past of the Present* (Cambridge, 2002), 58–9; Hakim Adi and Marika Sherwood, *The 1945 Manchester Pan-African Congress Revisited* (London, 1995).

war ended for self-government, with other colonies. 'It would be sheer non-sense – ignorant, dangerous nonsense – to talk about grants of full self-govern-ment to many of the dependent territories for some time to come', he argued. Acting with undue haste 'would be like giving a child of ten a latch-key, a bank account, and a shotgun'.[69] By 1950, the Colonial Office simultaneously pro-moted progressive objectives while still insisting on delaying political advance until colonial peoples were sufficiently 'adult', maintaining that '[o]ur aim is to create independence – independence within the Commonwealth – not to suppress it ... A vigorous, adult, and willing partner is clearly more to be desired than one dependent, adolescent, and unwilling' – hastening to add that 'there is no intention to abandon responsibilities prematurely.'[70] For all their expressed intentions, London-based officials and colonial administrators shared many out-looks with white settler advocates like Kenya-raised Elspeth Huxley, who habitually criticized whatever political concessions were contemplated as com-ing too fast and too soon. Africans suffered from superstition and 'tropical inertia' that made them averse to hard work, and depended upon colonial benevolence for their civilizational advance, she insisted in 1949: 'to give political freedom to countries at present too immature, backward and unstable to use it wisely' would potentially 'lead to chaos and perhaps Communist influence, and thence to the wiping out of economic gains ... and possibly even to the strategic encirclement of the west'.[71]

In this reasoning, Britain not only could but most decidedly *should* control the process of political change in order to ensure a moderate tempo and thereby a moderate, pro-Western tone. This would shore up what remained of the empire for the foreseeable future, and ideally with the United States' backing. For as the Cold War intensified in the late 1940s and early 1950s, playing the card of the communist threat, real or imagined, proved a highly effective means of strengthening Britain's hand in Anglo-American diplomatic stakes. The American political establishment retreated from the demand that Western European imperial powers advance steadily towards decolonization, opting instead to subsidize imperial rule as the best means of fighting the global advance of communism in Asia and Africa. 'For all the "holier than thou" attitudes of the Americans, the British and French Empires were propped up in the democratic cause of saving the global free market from communist annexa-tion', Wm. Roger Louis and Ronald Robinson emphasize.[72]

---

[69] 'Mr. Herbert Morrison Replies to Critics of Empire', *Manchester Guardian*, 11 January 1943.
[70] 'The Colonial Empire Today', CO 537/5698, no. 69, in Hyam (ed.), *Labour Government and the End of Empire 1945–1951, Part I*, 334–5; see also Ronald Hyam, 'Africa and the Labour Government, 1945–1951', *Journal of Imperial and Commonwealth History*, 16:3 (1988), 153.
[71] Elspeth Huxley, 'British Aims in Africa', *Foreign Affairs*, 28:1 (1949), 49, 54.
[72] Wm. Roger Louis and Ronald Robinson, 'The Imperialism of Decolonization', *Journal of Imperial and Commonwealth History*, 22:3 (1994), 493.

American support for the British empire was crucial, but Britain was equally determined to use the empire to maintain its position vis-à-vis America itself. However much the strains of war had weakened it, after 1945 Britain nonetheless remained the third-ranking world power after the United States and Soviet Union. For over a decade, British statesmen from across the political spectrum were determined to keep it that way. Britain's unpalatable dependence on American material aid and diplomatic acquiescence to its overseas ambitions could be tempered and complete subservience as the admittedly junior partner in the Anglo-American 'special relationship' avoided, it was believed, by retaining empire and remaining at the head of the 'Commonwealth of Nations' that expanded where empire had contracted.[73] Coupled with the assumption that Britain's rightful place was among the three great powers, the Commonwealth ideal as it coalesced under the Labour government after 1945 remained powerful well after the Conservatives returned to office in 1951, first under Churchill and then Anthony Eden. Its star only gradually faded during and after Harold Macmillan's period as prime minister from 1957 until 1963.

It was via the Commonwealth that the dominion idea emerged, alive, well, and reinvented, from the tunnel of the Second World War and the independence of India and Pakistan. Lord Mountbatten's satisfaction that both new states could initially be claimed as dominions despite the INC's obdurate opposition to all that this status had implied soon paved the way for a determined campaign to keep both under the Commonwealth umbrella. In the late 1940s, Britain's prior focus on the ultimate achievement of dominion status as the purported objective of imperial rule shifted to a rhetoric revolving around inclusion within the Commonwealth. '"Commonwealth", which began as a synonym for Empire, came to signify its antithesis', McIntyre notes; in place of 'Dominion Status' came 'fully independent Member of the Commonwealth', while 'British' no longer officially came before 'Commonwealth of Nations' after 1948.[74]

Above all, leading Labour politicians insisted that the Commonwealth was no longer limited to the exclusive 'club' consisting of the British 'mother country' plus its 'daughter nations', which Gandhi had distinguished from British–Indian relations in 1931. As Prime Minister Attlee explained to 'My dear Nehru' in a letter pleading him to support Indian membership, 'We have now reached another stage in the development of the Commonwealth. Hitherto

---

[73] Darwin, *Empire Project*, 561, 571; David Reynolds, *Britannia Overruled: British Policy and World Power in the Twentieth Century*, 2nd edn. (Harlow, 2000), ch. 7; Ronald Hyam, 'Introduction', in Hyam (ed.), *Labour Government and the End of Empire 1945–1951, Part I*, xlix, lxxi; David Goldsworthy, 'Introduction', in David Goldsworthy (ed.), *The Conservative Government and the End of Empire 1951–1957, Part I (British Documents on the End of Empire*, Series A, Vol. 3) (London, 1994), xxv–xxxiii, xlv.

[74] W. David McIntyre, 'Commonwealth Legacy', in Brown and Louis (eds.), *Oxford History of the British Empire*, IV, 693, 696.

the Dominions, although in South Africa the majority of the population are Dutch and in Canada a large percentage French, have been countries whose population has had a large element of United Kingdom stock' – a comment that revealingly ignored South Africa's African majority and Asian minorities, not to mention Canada's native American population. 'It has been a matter of pride to me that during my Premiership in Great Britain the family circle should have been enlarged by the coming of age, so to speak, of the nations in Asia. The British Commonwealth of Nations is now in effect the Commonwealth of British and Asiatic Nations', bound together by 'close association' but with 'complete freedom' for all its members – fully harmonious, in other words, with *purna swaraj*.[75] Nehru soon persuaded India's Constituent Assembly to concede to Commonwealth status by securing a formula whereby India was not required to recognize the British monarch as its formal head of state. As Nehru well knew, agreeing to Commonwealth membership could not stand in the way of India playing an independent role in world affairs that sharply deviated from Anglo-American priorities, as the coming era of non-alignment and public attacks on surviving forms of colonial domination would powerfully demonstrate.

Celebrated as a British triumph, the agreement with India made republicanism compatible with the Commonwealth and gave the organization the newly multiracial profile it needed if it hoped to win credibility as an entity fit for postwar modernity. This was bolstered when Pakistan and Ceylon joined soon after (although Burma stood aside, and Ireland withdrew). The evolving Commonwealth appeared to bode well for a future in which links between members could be maintained to mutual strategic and economic benefit on an increasingly bipolar world stage. Via the Commonwealth, Britain hoped to retain global power status and prestige as a 'third force' along with the American and Soviet superpowers. Instead of the loss of empire spelling Britain's decline, the growth and metamorphosis of the Commonwealth would attest to Britain's resilience, adaptability, and ability to dictate the course and pace of change, as well as indicate dedication to racial inclusivity and equality.[76]

Commitment to the Commonwealth was Labour Party orthodoxy between the late 1940s and early 1960s, but many of its attitudes were widely shared among Conservatives. Publicizing its newly multiracial character extended beyond the realm of party politics to become central to the British monarchy's self-fashioning as it entered a 'new Elizabethan era' with Queen Elizabeth II's ascent to the throne at the age of twenty-five in 1952. Significantly, she

[75] '[Relationship between India and the British Commonwealth]': Personal Letter from Mr. Attlee to Pandit Nehru, 11 March 1948, PREM 8/820, 29–37, reprinted in Hyam (ed.), *Labour Government and the End of Empire 1945–1951, Part IV*, 153–5.
[76] Patrick Gordon Walker, *The Commonwealth* (London, 1965; first published 1962), 307.

learned of her father's death while on holiday at a game reserve in Kenya – just one of many trips she and other members of the royal family made to Africa and other parts of the Commonwealth throughout her adult life. Another extended tour took place just months after her coronation in June 1953, when London had hosted a spectacular pageant of colonial and Commonwealth troops and leaders who came to take part in the parades and festivities. In her 1953 Christmas message broadcast from New Zealand, the Queen committed herself 'heart and soul' to upholding the Commonwealth as 'an equal partnership of nations and races' within which 'the United Kingdom is an equal partner with many other proud and independent nations, and . . . is leading forward yet other still backward nations to the same goal'.[77]

Queen and Commonwealth alike acted as powerful symbols of continuity and renewal in the 1950s, rooted in tradition but meant to signify the antithesis of aging relics belonging solely to the past. As the first British monarch to assume the title 'Head of the Commonwealth', Elizabeth II played an integral part in making monarchy a cord that tied Britain and the far-flung empire/ Commonwealth together as a unified, harmonious, and progressive 'family of nations'.[78] Within this Commonwealth family, still-'backward' members were being dutifully chaperoned and groomed to assume responsibility over themselves. Like the Queen herself, this was a family portrayed as youthful, attractive, fertile, and modern, its organizing values being equality and partnership – not one characterized by hierarchical power relations in which parental authority dominated.

Like the colonial and Commonwealth visitors who travelled to Britain to mark her coronation, moreover, the peripatetic Queen enacted her own high-level version of a key practice that had forged many of the links knitting Britain together with its colonies and Commonwealth and which was meant to sustain these ties after the Second World War: migration. 'A Commonwealth of scattered nations could only have been brought into being by the movement, mingling and interrelationship of its peoples across the seas' argued Patrick Gordon Walker, one of the Labour Party's most ardent Commonwealth

---

[77] Tom Fleming (ed.), *Voices Out of the Air: The Royal Christmas Broadcasts 1932–1981* (London, 1981), 74, quoted in Webster, *Englishness and Empire*, 93.

[78] Philip Murphy, *Monarchy and the End of Empire: The House of Windsor, the British Government and the Postwar Commonwealth* (Oxford, 2013), chs. 3–5 (especially ch. 4 on the coronation); Webster, *Englishness and Empire*, 93–5, 104, 118; Ben Pimlott, *The Queen: Elizabeth II and the Monarchy* (London, 2012; first published 1996), especially 182, 203–4, 217, 309–13; Peter H. Hansen, 'Coronation Everest: The Empire and Commonwealth in the "Second Elizabethan Age"', in Stuart Ward (ed.), *British Culture and the End of Empire* (Manchester, 2001), 57–72; Sonya O. Rose, 'From the "New Jerusalem" to the "Decline" of the "New Elizabethan Age": National Identity and Citizenship in Britain, 1945–56', in Frank Biess and Robert G. Moeller (eds.), *Histories of the Aftermath: The Legacies of the Second World War in Europe* (New York, 2010), 240–3.

devotees, in 1962.[79] The Commonwealth formed 'a true cultural community because its members could move freely amongst one another', its demographic fluidity rendering it 'a natural unit'.[80] 'Natural' did not mean biological, he insisted, denouncing assumptions that its 'cohesion rested in the last resort upon a community of kith and kin: that its political unity arose out of a biological unity' in which Britain as the 'mother country' presided over 'a Commonwealth of daughter states that had sprung from British loins'.[81] Nothing supported his argument more than Britain's dual commitment to unrestricted intra-Commonwealth migration and common citizenship.[82] This had been reaffirmed with the 1948 British Nationality Act, whereby all colonial and Commonwealth subjects – regardless of race – counted as British subjects sharing common citizenship and rights, including the right to settle in Britain itself.[83]

In making 'British subject' and 'Commonwealth citizen' formally synonymous, the 1948 legislation projected an overarching vision of nationality that encompassed domestic Britain, the former dominions of the 'Old Commonwealth', and Britain's Asian, African, and Caribbean colonies and ex-colonies in the process of building a 'New Commonwealth'.[84] As Chapter 7 will show, shared citizenship alongside unrestricted migration both to and from Britain created the conditions for unprecedented numbers of West Indians, Indians, Pakistanis, and others to settle in Britain between 1948 and 1962, when the first in a series of immigration restriction acts was passed with the implicit if not explicit aim of curbing the 'coloured' influx from the 'New Commonwealth'. Indeed, Gordon Walker's emphasis on the fundamental importance of free movement of peoples to the Commonwealth's cohesion and survival owed much of its urgency to the fierce public and parliamentary debates about whether to depart from this principle at the start of the 1960s. Legislation he passionately (if unsuccessfully) opposed that retreated from the 1948 Act was testament to the Commonwealth ideal's declining political purchase by the early 1960s, a theme explored further later in this chapter. However, tensions between Britain's stated commitment to a progressive, multiracial Commonwealth and the countless occasions when the interests of white British subjects, the erstwhile 'white dominions' of the 'Old Commonwealth', and white minorities in British colonial Africa received

[79] Gordon Walker, *Commonwealth*, 142. Gordon Walker had served as Undersecretary and then Secretary of State for Commonwealth Relations between 1947 and 1951. His positions receive fuller treatment in Elizabeth Buettner, '"This is Staffordshire not Alabama": Racial Geographies of Commonwealth Immigration in Early 1960s Britain', *Journal of Imperial and Commonwealth History*, 42:4 (2014), 712–15.

[80] Gordon Walker, *Commonwealth*, 231.   [81] Ibid., 232, 88.   [82] Ibid., 232.

[83] Ibid., 142, 193.

[84] Kathleen Paul, *Whitewashing Britain: Race and Citizenship in the Postwar Era* (Ithaca, 1997), ch. 1.

priority had been present from the outset. Formal citizenship was less important than a conception of national identity shared among a 'racial community of Britons' distributed across the metropole, Canada, Australia, New Zealand, East Africa, Central Africa, and most problematically of all, South Africa.[85]

In imperial and Commonwealth reality if not rhetoric, 'British stock' and white 'kith and kin' took precedence, denials notwithstanding. Britain's history of post-war migration was as much a story of white emigration as colonial immigration, for despite labour shortages at home the British government actively encouraged outward movement to arenas with established traditions of white settlement. Between 1945 and 1960, over 566,000 British-born nationals moved to Australia, 150,000 to New Zealand, 582,000 to Canada, 125,000 to South Africa, and 82,000 to Southern Rhodesia. British policy-makers believed that replenishing these parts of the empire/Commonwealth with 'British stock' would, as Kathleen Paul asserts, 'ensure that even as the dominions asserted their political autonomy, their cultural and economic links would still tie them to Britain'.[86] The family metaphor appeared repeatedly in political discourse about citizenship and was largely applied to whites. Persons of 'British stock' in settler colonies and dominions were likened to 'brothers and sisters', 'first cousins', or the 'true children' of Britons at home whether figuratively or literally, given the high volume of recent departures.[87] Africans, Asians, and West Indians, by contrast, were widely imagined as childlike in political and civilizational terms, but lacked the ancestry and cultural attributes that rendered overseas kith and kin part of the inner family circle, regardless of geographical distance.

* * *

From 1950s imperial crises to the 'wind of change'

For indigenous populations in Britain's white settler colonies, the multiracial family of empire in the 1950s spelled subordination with seemingly no end in sight. When the Conservative Party returned to power late in 1951 with Churchill resuming the role of prime minister until 1955, the new government did not adopt a fundamentally different approach to the empire and Commonwealth than had been devised under Labour. Colonial policy was neither a prominent nor a divisive electoral issue, and Britain's stated aim remained that of guiding its colonies towards responsible self-government within the Commonwealth – but without undue haste. Overall, however, Conservatives (including Churchill himself) showed as little enthusiasm

---

[85] Ibid., xv; Webster, *Englishness and Empire*, 11, 149, 175.
[86] Paul, *Whitewashing Britain*, 29 (see 25–34 for emigration data).   [87] Ibid., 20–3.

about many of the remaining colonial territories as they did for decolonization. As Philip Murphy argues, because for many Conservatives imperial priorities had long centred on the dominions and India, the empire that survived 'lost much of its emotional appeal after 1947 and became, for the most part, a series of intellectually demanding puzzles which they were no longer interested in solving'.[88]

Containing change remained a key objective, but non-settler colonies never had a strong hold on the British imagination; there, gradual progress towards independence within the Commonwealth continued apace and elicited little fervent Conservative reaction.[89] In West Africa, for example, the British political establishment persisted in the conceit that London remained fully in control, although nationalists had propelled political advance further and faster than had been hoped for or anticipated. Alongside Malaya, the Gold Coast achieved independence as Ghana in 1957, while Nigeria followed in 1960 and Sierra Leone in 1961.[90] West Africa's resident British population was small and limited largely to expatriate officials, development workers, and members of the business community, few of whom tried to stand in the way of independence under African majority rule. By contrast, the course of decolonization history proved far rockier, violent, divisive, and protracted where vocal minority communities of kith and kin had set down roots, as was the case in East Africa (especially Kenya) and Central Africa.[91]

White settlers in post-war British Africa succeeded in winning considerable support for their privileged status among colonial officials as well as a significant proportion of Conservative politicians at home, who redirected their imperial energies towards a commitment to settler interests.[92] Kenya as well as Northern Rhodesia, Southern Rhodesia, and Nyasaland (the three colonies brought together in 1953 within the framework of the Central African

---

[88] Philip Murphy, *Party Politics and Decolonization: The Conservative Party and British Colonial Policy in Tropical Africa, 1951–1964* (Oxford, 1995), 30–1. See also Toye, *Churchill's Empire*, 271, ch. 9. On the continuities and shifts across the period of Labour followed by Conservative rule, see David Goldsworthy, *Colonial Issues in British Politics, 1945–1961: From 'Colonial Development' to 'Wind of Change'* (Oxford, 1971).

[89] David Goldsworthy, 'Keeping Change Within Bounds: Aspects of Colonial Policy during the Churchill and Eden Governments, 1951–57', *Journal of Imperial and Commonwealth History*, 18:1 (1990), 81–108.

[90] In 1956 Sudan had preceded Ghana and Malaya to independence; Cyprus also became independent in 1960.

[91] Independence also proceeded more smoothly in East African colonies without significant white settler interests (as was the case with the decolonization of Tanganyika, later Tanzania, in 1961 and Uganda in 1962).

[92] Murphy, *Party Politics*, 58. On the history of the CAF, see especially Murphy's many treatments, including 'Introduction', in Philip Murphy (ed.), *Central Africa, Part I: Closer Association 1945–1958* (*British Documents on the End of Empire*, Series A Volume 5) (London, 2005), xxvii–cxvi, alongside Bill Schwarz, *Memories of Empire, Vol. 1: The White Man's World* (Oxford, 2011), ch. 6.

Federation) were arenas where Britain committed itself to 'multiracial partnership', but this stopped far short of racial equality. With the ratio of Europeans to non-Europeans being 1:93 in Kenya, 1:26 within the overall Federation (CAF), and 1:13 in Southern Rhodesia alone, white populations could never have held on to the disproportionate political, economic, and social status they enjoyed if political advance worked in the direction of majority rule.[93]

Settlers and their advocates in Africa as well as London thwarted meaningful political reform and successfully defended their position for much of the 1950s, which effectively meant consolidating white supremacy. It was only later in the decade that white minority privileges under alleged 'partnership' schemes appeared increasingly untenable – at least within the metropole and among the wider international community, if not to the settlers themselves or their diehard champions. The 1950s began with attempts to curb 'extremism' and minimize change in the name of gradual, reformist, and purportedly progressive multiracialism and power-sharing. As the decade drew to a close, however, Britain's reputation as an enlightened overseer with an unfailing ability to steer overseas events in desired directions – a reputation assiduously cultivated and eagerly asserted, regardless of its dubious veracity – had suffered severe blows.[94] For some (if certainly not all) Britons, the Kenya Emergency, the Suez Crisis, and the rising tensions within and surrounding the Central African Federation irrevocably damaged the British empire's legitimacy and called its future into question, even if they did not cause longstanding colonial mentalities to evaporate overnight.

* * *

Officially declared in October 1952 in response to the Mau Mau insurgency, the brutalities of the Kenya Emergency lasted until 1960. Violence perpetrated by Mau Mau insurgents driven by land shortages and opposition to white minority power gripped the settler community, domestic British opinion, and international observers alike. Mau Mau activists killed far more Africans than Europeans, but British reporting of the Emergency focused on white victims (both actual and potential), especially in its early stages.[95] Metropolitan media coverage portrayed 'a racial community of Britons ... under siege' by Mau Mau's regressive reign of terror, emphasizing threats to British kith and kin – not European violence or African deaths, internal divisions, political

---

[93] Murphy, *Party Politics*, 58.

[94] Martin Lynn (ed.), *The British Empire in the 1950s: Retreat or Revival?* (Basingstoke, 2006).

[95] Over the course of the Emergency, Mau Mau killed 32 Europeans and wounded 26 others, while over 2,600 African civilians were killed or wounded for opposing the rebellion. As David Anderson notes, 'More European civilians would die in road traffic accidents between 1952 and 1960 than were killed by Mau Mau.' David Anderson, *Histories of the Hanged: Britain's Dirty War in Kenya and the End of Empire* (London, 2005), 84.

grievances, and points of view. 'Imagery of violence in colonial wars often converged on a common theme', Wendy Webster notes: 'the threat to an Englishness symbolized by the idea of home.'[96] Never more sensationally did Mau Mau attacks on isolated rural settlers dominate British headlines than in reportage of the murders of the Ruck family at home on their farm in early 1953.

The Ruck incident possessed all the ingredients to guarantee its resonance among Kenya's European community and in the metropole. Peter and Esmée Ruck and their son Michael represented the Kenyan settler ideal and its imagined future, and thus became the ideal victims to galvanize white colonial society clamouring for the restoration of law and order by any means necessary.[97] The parents were the picture of an attractive couple with socially impeccable credentials living modestly on their African farm, he the son of an English clergyman who went to Kenya after the Second World War, she the African-born niece of a British Lord who trained as a physician and provided medical treatment to local Africans.[98] Attacked while taking an evening stroll in their garden, their assailants proceeded into the house itself and murdered six-year-old Michael in his bed. Mau Mau's invasion into the inner sanctum of white settler domesticity and the 'butchering' of the child rendered the tragic death of innocence in the hands of 'savages' complete. 'Into your midst there has come a vile, brutal wickedness of satanic power which has been unleashed in this land and is still at large', proclaimed the reverend leading the memorial service in Nairobi. And if words failed to capture the full horror of the killings, pictures came to their aid. The *Illustrated London News* accorded the Ruck murders a two-page spread, with several photographs featuring the blond child, his parents, and the bed where he died, now empty and bloodstained but still surrounded by teddy bears, a globe, and a toy 'model railway left ready for another day of play which never came'.[99]

The apparent involvement of one of the family's African servants in the killings made the Rucks' story even more horrifying. If the 'racial community of Britons' in Africa could not trust their 'houseboys' – as adult African men employed as domestics by Europeans continued to be called, their rhetorical

[96] Webster, *Englishness and Empire*, 124, 129 (on filmic portrayals of 1950s Kenya, see 122–34, alongside Anderson, 'Mau Mau at the Movies').
[97] Scholarly assessments of the Ruck murders include Lonsdale, 'Mau Maus of the Mind', 407; Carruthers, *Winning Hearts and Minds*, 136–7; Anderson, *Histories of the Hanged*, 93–8; Caroline Elkins, *Britain's Gulag: The Brutal End of Empire in Kenya* (London, 2005), 42–3.
[98] Some reports stated that Esmée Ruck was born in Kenya, others in South Africa; her maiden name was De Smidt, suggesting partial Afrikaner descent. 'Family of Three Found Slashed to Death', *Daily Mirror* (London), 26 January 1953; 'Murder Raid in Kenya', *The Times*, 26 January 1953.
[99] '"A Vile, Brutal Wickedness": The Murder of the Ruck Family by Mau Mau Terrorists in Kenya, A Shocking Crime Redeemed Only by the Heroism of an African Houseboy', *Illustrated London News*, 7 February 1953, 190–1.

equivalence to immature children continuing well into an era characterized by proclamations of multiracial equality within Britain's empire and Commonwealth 'family' – whom could they trust?[100] Many settlers believed their Kikuyu employees to have taken Mau Mau oaths, seeing it as 'a revolt of the domestic staff . . . as though Jeeves had taken to the jungle', in the words of Graham Greene.[101] The fact that some Africans remained loyal to their masters counted among Mau Mau's many uncertainties and complexities. Killed along-side the Rucks was another African 'houseboy' who died trying to help them during the attack; some commentators in the British press played up such evidence of Kikuyu loyalty, but most considered it an exception that proved the satanic rule. As the *Illustrated London News* concluded, '[a]n unusual aspect of the crime was the heroism of the African houseboy.'[102] Epitomizing the contradictions of Britain's multiracial empire in microcosm, the Ruck home was not the tranquil idyll inhabited by a symbolic multiracial family of equals so proudly celebrated within British post-war rhetoric. Instead, it was one in which vulnerable white kith and kin could never be sure which of their 'childlike' African subordinates might faithfully protect them, and which were 'savages' bent on murder who needed to be identified and crushed.

Settler demands that the Rucks' killers be brought to justice were swiftly met, and within months seven Kikuyu had been convicted and hanged.[103] Death sentences for the Kikuyu found guilty of the Ruck murders formed part of an intense British counterinsurgency campaign in which colonial authorities often turned to execution as a first resort rather than a last, regardless of the strength of evidence against the accused. Moreover, tens of thousands suspected or convicted of Mau Mau-related activity were subjected to attempted 'rehabilitation' in detention camps, where they suffered long-term internment (often without trial), hard labour, habitual beatings, torture and sexual violence, and collective punishments that achieved international notoriety among critics of colonialism.[104]

---

[100] Peter Evans, *Law and Disorder, or Scenes of Life in Kenya* (London, 1956), 83–4.

[101] Graham Greene, *Ways of Escape* (London, 1980), 188, cited in Lonsdale, 'Mau Maus of the Mind', 407.

[102] Peter G. Bostock, letter to the editor, 'Loyal Kikuyu', *The Times*, 30 January 1953; 'Murder Raid in Kenya'; '"A Vile, Brutal Wickedness"'. On the broader theme of Mau Mau as a civil war among the Kikuyu, with as many remaining loyal to the colonial government as rebelling, see Daniel Branch, *Defeating Mau Mau, Creating Kenya: Counterinsurgency, Civil War, and Decolonization* (Cambridge, 2009).

[103] '70 Mau Mau Killed in Week', *The Times*, 17 July 1953.

[104] Hangings and detention camps are the respective foci of studies by Anderson, *Histories of the Hanged*, and Elkins, *Britain's Gulag*, both of which appeared in 2005 and generated considerable public controversy, a theme Chapter 9 treats further. On British counterinsurgency campaigns in Kenya and elsewhere, see also Huw Bennett, *Fighting the Mau Mau: The British Army and Counter-Insurgency in the Kenya Emergency* (Cambridge, 2012); David French, *The British Way in Counter-Insurgency, 1945–1967* (Oxford, 2011).

Over time, the often indiscriminate brutality of Britain's methods to defeat the Mau Mau movement – officially labelled an 'Emergency', not a 'colonial war' – came under fire within Britain. Metropolitan opposition had initially been limited to a small segment of the political left spearheaded by, among others, the MP Fenner Brockway (introduced earlier as one of Gandhi's metropolitan supporters in the 1930s). Reports of abuses perpetrated by British troops, colonial administrators, and settlers (along with attempted cover-ups) gradually grew familiar to readers of many British newspapers, however, and were increasingly aired within the House of Commons by the mid-1950s. Mau Mau became one of the main issues that caused anti-colonial activists linked to a number of pre-existing organizations to form the Brockway-led Movement for Colonial Freedom (MCF) in 1954. The MCF quickly became the most influential metropolitan pressure group challenging the colonial status quo with a formal membership exceeding three million.[105]

It may have taken little to convince British audiences of Mau Mau's barbaric inhumanity given the stereotypes about African primitivism long prevalent within Western cultures, but stories of *British* atrocities publicized by Labour politicians affiliated with the MCF and reported in the press caused increasing unease about counterinsurgency tactics. The idea of Britain restoring the peace in Kenya was acceptable; draconian repression by security forces, however, compromised Britain's good name and moral reputation as a benevolent colonial ruler.[106] Particularly damning indictments of British methods compared counterinsurgency techniques to 'Gestapo tactics' and the collective persecution of the Jews by the Nazis – an analogy that also arose to question Dutch and French campaigns in the East Indies and Algeria, as will be discussed in the following chapters.[107] Likening British actions in Africa to the Nazism against which Britain had recently fought a war and celebrated its own racial tolerance revealed dangerous cracks weakening the foundations of multiracial colonial and Commonwealth proclamations.

* * *

The mid-1950s not only subjected Britain's conduct in Kenya to critical scrutiny. Like nothing else, the Suez Crisis of November 1956 revealed that 'Britain could not act independently of the United States, nor did the British state possess the economic or military strength to be ranked as a great power',

---

[105] Howe, *Anticolonialism*, ch. 6; Elkins, *Britain's Gulag*, 97–9, ch. 9; Owen, 'Critics of Empire', 205–6.

[106] Joanna Lewis, '"Daddy Wouldn't Buy Me a Mau Mau": The British Popular Press and the Demoralization of Empire', in E.S. Atieno Odhiambo and John Lonsdale (eds.), *Mau Mau and Nationhood: Arms, Authority and Narration* (Oxford, 2003), 227–50; Elkins, *Britain's Gulag*, 286; Howe, *Anticolonialism*, 318; Carruthers, *Winning Hearts and Minds*, 176–81, 267.

[107] Howe, *Anticolonialism*, 206; Elkins, *Britain's Gulag*, 117.

Roger Louis summarizes.[108] Maintaining Britain's international prestige and world power standing depended on the ability to assert authority in the strategically vital Middle East, considerable swathes of which counted as part of Britain's 'informal empire'. Assured use of the Suez Canal Zone was essential if Britain's military presence in the Middle East and Asia and access to oil supplies were to remain secure. Gamal Abdel Nasser's rise to power in Egypt during a 1952 coup and his nationalization of the Canal (formerly under British and French control) in July 1956 placed these interests in jeopardy. Prime Minister Anthony Eden (who had succeeded Churchill the previous year) became hell-bent on toppling him. Britain secretly forged an agreement with France and Israel whereby Israel would invade Egypt and pave the way for an Anglo-French intervention that would remove Nasser and reoccupy the Canal. But the Anglo-French assault on Egypt ground to a screeching halt thanks to the United States' furious opposition to the invasion that provoked a ceasefire followed by military withdrawal. Eden's covert machinations leading up to the invasion incurred the wrath of the Eisenhower administration with devastating and immediate consequences: Washington threatened to withhold support for a loan Britain sought from the International Monetary Fund, placing the value of the pound sterling at risk and leaving Britain no alternative but to toe the American line.

The Suez Crisis has rightly merited the inglorious distinction of a fiasco ever since. It forced Britain to learn a humiliating lesson like no other event in post-war history: that it could hold no hope of acting unilaterally without American acquiescence to its global aims. In Egypt in 1956, Washington's view that the Suez invasion ran counter to the struggle against communism decisively nipped Britain's attempt to reassert its interests by force in the bud. Britain's display of a style of colonialism the United States wanted consigned to history risked driving African, Middle Eastern, and Asian peoples into the arms of the Soviet Union. (Tellingly, the Eisenhower administration compared Britain's actions in Egypt with the Soviet invasion of Hungary that same year.) Like never before, Britain's status as a global power was exposed as a relic and its position as the manifestly junior partner in the Anglo-American special relationship visibly confirmed. As Nicholas Owen fittingly concludes, '[a]s a display of obsolete and ineffective imperialism, the Suez crisis could hardly be bettered'.[109]

---

[108] Wm. Roger Louis, 'Public Enemy Number One: Britain and the United States in the Aftermath of Suez', in *Ends of British Imperialism*, 696. Further analysis of the Suez Crisis can be found in William Roger Louis, 'American Anti-Colonialism and the Dissolution of the British Empire', *International Affairs*, 61:3 (1985), 409–16; Wm. Roger Louis and Roger Owen (eds.), *Suez 1956: The Crisis and Its Consequences* (Oxford, 1989); Darwin, *Empire Project*, 590–609.

[109] Owen, 'Critics of Empire', 206.

Suez inflicted both immediate and long-term damage. It ruined Eden's reputation and his already precarious physical health, forcing his resignation in a matter of weeks; Harold Macmillan succeeded him as prime minister early in 1957 and set about the task of repairing the ruptured special relationship.[110] Moreover, the crisis divided the Commonwealth, with Nehru openly supporting Nasser during the confrontation, and left Britain open to fierce opposition at the United Nations.[111] At home, Suez also divided British politicians and the wider public, with opponents of the invasion staging a large-scale demonstration in London's Trafalgar Square.[112] In retrospect, many have considered it as the most decisive development responsible for accelerating the pace of Britain's decolonization. Almost immediately afterwards, Ghana and Malaya became independent, and Macmillan requested an internal audit, which suggested that Nigeria, much of the West Indies, and a number of other territories would soon follow them.

Yet these had been agreed political objectives *before* the Suez Crisis erupted. Suez's impact, in short, came in combination with other events and emergent outlooks that changed the game. British decision-makers increasingly felt that the key to friendly postcolonial relations and to maintaining former colonies within the Commonwealth meant transferring power sooner rather than later to 'moderate', pro-Western politicians groomed as appropriate successors. Ideally, this would work not simply to marginalize 'extremists' but also curb the threat of new armed insurgencies. In any case, decisions taken in London soon after Suez meant that Britain would soon lack the ability to fight protracted revolts of the duration and scale of those it was still battling in Malaya, Cyprus, and Kenya. A 1957 Defence White Paper inaugurated a shift in Britain's overall military capacity from one dominated by conventional forces to one devoting increasing emphasis and expenditure to nuclear deterrence. With conscription (National Service) set to end starting in 1960 and thereby shrinking the available manpower, it was only a matter of time before Britain's capacity to fight lengthy colonial counterinsurgencies would become as militarily unsustainable as it was politically contentious.

* * *

British domestic misgivings about colonial brutality during Mau Mau did not yield the official inquiry many Labour MPs demanded, nor did it provoke mass protests against colonial policy. But by the late 1950s counterinsurgency rationales had become widely discredited – as had unquestioning support for

---

[110] Ritchie Ovendale, 'Macmillan and the Wind of Change in Africa, 1957–1960', *Historical Journal*, 38:2 (1995), 455–77.

[111] Louis, 'Public Enemy Number One'.

[112] Richard Whiting, 'The Empire and British Politics', in Thompson (ed.), *Britain's Experience of Empire*, 181–4.

white settler privileges in Kenya as well as the Central African Federation, where African mobilization resisting white dominance had become impossible to ignore. Revelations of the brutal deaths of eleven Kikuyu interned at the Hola detention camp in 1959 generated intense debates in the House of Commons spearheaded by Labour, with anticolonialism having moved from the party's margins to its mainstream.[113] News of Hola came alongside controversies surrounding emergencies declared in Nyasaland and Northern Rhodesia to crack down on African dissidents, who colonial authorities claimed were planning a massacre of Europeans, Asian communities, and African 'moderates'. Over fifty Africans were killed by security forces and over 1,000 detained without trial. The emergencies served as a convenient pretext for the Central African Federation's white rulers to stage a showdown with African opponents. Suppression 'had been carefully coordinated and it is clear that the Federal government was seeking a confrontation with the nationalists all of whom, by virtue of their very nationalism, were deemed to be extremists', Bill Schwarz notes. Yet far from killing off African nationalism, 'more than any other single act the imposition of the emergencies hastened the destruction of the Federation'.[114] A British investigation into events in Nyasaland generated the unwelcome verdict that the territory had effectively become a 'police state' within a Federation blatantly skewed in favour of white settler interests, not the multiracial power-sharing arrangement that protected the rights of its African population as trumpeted by its defenders. Together, Hola and the Central African emergencies put defenders of counterinsurgency tactics and white minority rule on the defensive themselves, and within British politics even the Conservatives grew increasingly divided about settler colonialism in Africa.

The years 1959 and 1960 found the British government under Macmillan contemplating a different future for multiracial colonial societies that diverged from the status quo that strongly favoured white interests. Independence under majority rule now became recognized as part of the immediate future in Britain's African colonies, with or without white settler populations. Nothing signalled this more famously than Macmillan's pronouncements during and after his six-week African tour early in 1960, when his travels took him first to independent Ghana, then to Nigeria and through the Central African Federation before concluding in South Africa. Macmillan's rhetoric contained a revealing

---

[113] Elkins, *Britain's Gulag*, ch. 10; Howe, *Anticolonialism*, 318–20; Lewis, "'Daddy Wouldn't Buy Me a Mau Mau'", 243–7; Anderson, *Histories of the Hanged*, 326–7; Richard Toye, 'Arguing About Hola Camp: The Rhetorical Consequences of a Colonial Massacre', in Martin Thomas and Richard Toye (eds.), *The Rhetoric of Empire: Arguing Colonialism in the Public Sphere* (Manchester, in press).

[114] Schwarz, *White Man's World*, 351. See also John Darwin, 'The Central African Emergency, 1959', *Journal of Imperial and Commonwealth History*, 21:3 (1993), 217–34.

combination of tried and tested ideologies alongside signs of new British approaches now in competition with them. He celebrated the transition of the Commonwealth from an organization of countries of 'predominantly British stock' to one encompassing India, Pakistan, Ceylon, Malaya, and Ghana within its 'brotherhood'.[115] 'The wind of change' was blowing through Africa 'whether we like it or not', he told both houses of South Africa's parliament in Cape Town – the 'wind' in question being that of 'African national consciousness' that could no longer be ignored, while the 'we' implicitly encompassed the British, white South Africans, and whites in East and especially Central Africa alike. Still publicly proclaiming an adherence to multiracialism, Macmillan also used his African tour to distance Britain from South African–style beliefs in white racial supremacy that found expression in apartheid, stressing that 'our policy is non-racial'.[116]

South Africa's commitment to apartheid that placed it at odds with most other member states soon led to its exclusion from the Commonwealth in 1961. Between 1960 and 1964, the 'wind of change' brought decolonization to much of British Africa along with many colonies in the Caribbean and further afield. In contrast to previous multiracial schemes which in reality had worked to strengthen the hand of white minorities, 'non-racial' approaches allowed Kenya to become independent under African majority rule in 1963 and Nyasaland and Northern Rhodesia to do likewise at the beginning of 1964 (when they respectively became Malawi and Zambia). By 1964, little was left of the empire aside from a range of small scattered islands, Hong Kong, and Southern Rhodesia, which subsequently became simply 'Rhodesia' – the rump of the discredited Central African Federation disbanded at the end of 1963. While much of the British empire that remained after the late 1940s was wound up between Suez and 1964, the resilience of white minority rule made Rhodesia an unresolved problem that remained contentious and divisive within Britain, the Commonwealth, and beyond until 1980.

* * *

Britain's high noon of decolonization between the late 1950s and mid-1960s thus brought a radical contraction of the nation's territorial reach and power, coupled with indisputable signs that Britain was the subordinate partner

---

[115] The Rt Hon. Harold Macmillan, MP, 'Africa', *African Affairs*, 59:236 (1960), 191, 194.

[116] 'Address by Mr Macmillan to Both Houses of the Parliament of the Union of South Africa, Cape Town', 3 February 1960, reprinted in Ronald Hyam and Wm. Roger Louis (eds.), *The Conservative Government and the End of Empire 1957–1964, Part I (British Documents on the End of Empire*, Series A Volume 4) (London, 2000), 167–74. The passages quoted here appear on 170–1. New assessments of the implications of Macmillan's African tour and speech in Cape Town can be found in Larry Butler and Sarah Stockwell (eds.), *The Wind of Change: Harold Macmillan and British Decolonization* (London, 2013).

within the Anglo-American special relationship that had fundamentally underpinned its international position since the Second World War. Regardless of how much had changed in reality, however, British political proclamations remained remarkably similar to those characteristic of the late 1940s and early 1950s: decolonization British-style was presented as voluntarily undertaken, long in the planning, and the fulfilment of imperial objectives. Upon returning from Africa in 1960, Macmillan contrasted the 'collapse and break-up' of the Austro-Hungarian and Ottoman empires after the First World War with Britain's recent imperial trajectory happening 'in the flood of its greatness, undefeated in war'. Great changes had come, but 'it has been an evolution, not a revolution – a process, I firmly believe, not of decline but of growth'.[117] His narrative crossed party lines to take similar form in contemporary Labour discourse. As Patrick Gordon Walker described it not long after, 'the evolution of the Commonwealth came about because British imperial rule increasingly assumed such a nature that it could fulfil itself only by annulling itself. Otherwise the normal process of imperial disintegration would have taken place.' Britain's course was an exceptional and elevated one, 'distinguishing it from other forms of European Imperialism'.[118]

Thus viewed through rose-coloured glasses, decolonization gave Britain much to be proud of. Although political differences of opinion and desired policy did emerge between (as well as among) the Conservatives and Labour, unseemly squabbles, schisms, and radical ruptures had largely been avoided. Nor had Britain's military forces or diehard colonial settlers directly intervened in ways that changed the face of Britain's decolonization process or dramatically reconfigured the metropolitan political order, as will be explored in later chapters with reference to France between 1958 and 1962 and Portugal in 1974.[119] Britain had no single decolonization episode that came even remotely close to French Algerian proportions, and staged its succession of colonial exits without becoming tainted by violent aftermaths comparable to those afflicting the Belgian Congo. Indeed, Belgian, and especially French, histories of decolonization had done much to influence British policymakers' own thoughts and actions. France's imminent departure from much of Africa in 1960 played a role in Britain's decision to move down the same road, while steering clear of crises like those raging in Algeria and the Congo had been high on Macmillan's and Colonial Secretary Iain Macleod's list of imperial priorities

---

[117] Macmillan, 'Africa', 199. His memoirs told a similar story in 1972; see Darwin, 'British Decolonization', 188–9.

[118] Gordon Walker, *Commonwealth*, 15.

[119] Miles Kahler, *Decolonization in Britain and France: The Domestic Consequences of International Relations* (Princeton, 1984); Hendrik Spruyt, *Ending Empire: Contested Sovereignty and Territorial Partition* (Ithaca, 2005), ch. 4.

in 1960 and 1961.[120] Britain needed to be on guard against becoming dragged down by France's struggle in Algeria, which placed it at risk of being 'tarred with a French colonial brush' among influential colonial critics at the United Nations and in the United States and Soviet Union. Above all, France's Algerian crisis demonstrated to British policymakers that settler extremism needed to be curbed so that 'nothing comparable should be allowed to develop in anglophone Southern Africa', as Martin Thomas has written.[121]

British commentators used other European colonial powers' hamstrung political orders, illiberal imperial policies, and ensuing colonial crises to show themselves to the best advantage, celebrating Britain's own colonial record as one of enlightenment, achievement, and continuity as empire morphed seamlessly – and seemingly painlessly – into Commonwealth with dignity.[122] Britain had valiantly coped with colonial 'emergencies' to restore peace, not fought bitter 'wars' against nationalists, the story went. To be sure, critical contemporaries (and most historians) have provided other accounts of British decolonization as rooted in messy, lethal realities as opposed to myths. Their work serves as an important reminder of Britain's own violent and deadly decolonizations, particularly those occurring soon after the Second World War in South Asia as well as the Middle East. Despite the million who died and the millions more displaced during the course of India and Pakistan's partition, for example, 'British government servants submerged these chaotic withdrawals within a broader narrative of managed decolonization that made little conces-sion to past British failures', Thomas emphasizes. '[T]he devastation left behind ... had limited material consequences for Britain, helping the idea of low-cost "escape" from empire take root in the public imagination and the British official mind.'[123] The fanciful tales tirelessly reiterated by powerful figures did much to shape wider metropolitan responses to the end of empire. Alongside many other voices, politicians made important contributions to the multifaceted narratives available to the British public about the empire and Commonwealth as they underwent decisive transitions, disseminating a story of continuity as opposed to radical rupture.

* * *

[120] Whiting, 'Empire and British Politics', 184–6; Darwin, 'British Decolonization', 203; 'Colonial Policy: Speech by the Rt Hon. Iain Macleod, Secretary of State for the Colonies, to the Conservative Party Conference, 11 Oct. 1961', reprinted in A.N. Porter and A.J. Stockwell (eds.), *British Imperial Policy and Decolonization, 1938–64, Vol. 2: 1951–64* (Basingstoke, 1989), 559.
[121] Martin Thomas, 'A Path Not Taken? British Perspectives on French Colonial Violence after 1945', in Butler and Stockwell (eds.), *Wind of Change*, 168, 172; see also Thomas, *Fight or Flight*, 329, 338, 345.
[122] Goldsworthy, 'Introduction', xli.
[123] Thomas, 'Path Not Taken?', 172; Thomas, *Fight or Flight*, 118.

The British public encounters decolonization

In the growing number of assessments of British domestic experiences of decolonization that now range from superficial asides to in-depth studies, scholars have found evidence of every conceivable attitude and level of engagement across society. Some point to visible expressions of anti-colonialism within the metropole such as the public outcry over the Suez invasion, unease that could extend to strident critiques of counterinsurgency tactics in 1950s Kenya, and the Movement for Colonial Freedom's three million-strong membership. As Stephen Howe qualifies, however, many Britons formally counted as MCF affiliates by virtue of being part of a trade union that had declared its collective support; those who were members on paper far exceeded the number of informed and dedicated anti-colonial activists. For most, 'imperialism as an issue was far too diffuse, distant, and apparently abstract to arouse widespread commitment outside the ranks of the already politicized'.[124] Staunch anti-colonialism was a 'minority pursuit' and British public opinion 'overwhelmingly apathetic'. But by the 1950s, 'the more informed it was the more critical it was likely to be', and 'such real faith as there had ever been in an imperial mission had been almost wholly lost'.[125]

Together with scholars working in related disciplines, historians have engaged in heated debates about the extent to which Britons at home were influenced by, interested in, or even conscious of the overseas empire. Howe himself counts among those taking a more sceptical view, rightly arguing that only focused empirical studies can convincingly substantiate general claims about empire's impact (or lack thereof) on various aspects of British life and thought.[126] Characteristic arguments that imperialism had little effect on metropolitan society and culture have been advanced by Bernard Porter.[127] Few Britons were passionately engaged with the empire during its heyday, he insists, let alone at the time of its decline and fall. Historians like Porter advocating the 'minimal impact' thesis point to public surveys conducted during and after the 1940s suggesting that many Britons had vague and highly inaccurate understandings of empire; some even seemed unable to name any British colonies. Aside from niche minorities who included imperialist zealots

---

[124] Howe, *Anticolonialism*, 237, 240.

[125] Ibid., 322, 326; see also Lewis, '"Daddy Wouldn't Buy Me a Mau Mau"'.

[126] Stephen Howe, 'Internal Decolonization? British Politics since Thatcher as Post-Colonial Trauma', *Twentieth Century British History*, 14:3 (2003), 286–304; Stephen Howe, 'When (if ever) Did Empire End? "Internal Decolonisation" in British Culture since the 1950s', in Lynn (ed.), *British Empire in the 1950s*, 214–37.

[127] Bernard Porter, *The Absent-Minded Imperialists: Empire, Society, and Culture in Britain* (Oxford, 2004); Bernard Porter, 'Further Thoughts on Imperial Absent-Mindedness', *Journal of Imperial and Commonwealth History*, 36:1 (2008), 101–17. Unsurprisingly, Porter's assertions provoked a hostile backlash; for a measured critique, see Stuart Ward, 'Echoes of Empire', *History Workshop Journal*, 62 (2006), 264–78.

and professionals earning their livelihoods from overseas careers, this argument ran, most Britons knew little and cared less about empire.

Polemics of this nature published in the 2000s, however, were made possible by the proliferation of interdisciplinary studies over more than twenty years that documented the opposite: namely, that imperialism had long been an important (albeit largely neglected) dimension of British popular culture, society, and material life. Starting in the mid-1980s, John MacKenzie's monographs, edited collections, and the 'Studies in Imperialism' series he launched with Manchester University Press provided space for an expanding group of authors to assess imperialism's far-from-minimal impact on Britain.[128] Imperial culture in Britain was never experienced uniformly and was not always consciously contemplated, let alone openly celebrated or condemned. It was often a 'banal imperialism' that permeated everyday metropolitan life in ordinary, mundane, and subtle ways to form part of schooling, religious and civic associational life, and a rich commodity and leisure culture across the social spectrum.[129] Empire and the Commonwealth remained widely present and highly influential during the decolonization era, as a growing body of scholarship convincingly demonstrates.[130] Even once empire seemed increasingly anachronistic and became subjected to critique and satirical portrayals in the 1950s and 1960s, it closely informed common understandings of national identity, patriotism, and race consciousness, structuring attitudes about racial 'others' and white Britishness alike.

Decolonization-era British engagements with empire and Commonwealth ranged from the participatory to the imaginative. As noted earlier, the high rate of post-war emigration to the old dominions and settler colonies in Africa gave many Britons first-hand encounters with these destinations. Even greater numbers gained second-hand exposure through ongoing links with relatives and friends who had recently relocated overseas. Stories relayed back home by and

---

[128] Among his many contributions, see John M. MacKenzie (ed.), *Imperialism and Popular Culture* (Manchester, 1986); John M. MacKenzie, 'Comfort and Conviction: A Response to Bernard Porter', *Journal of Imperial and Commonwealth History*, 36:4 (2008), 659–68; John M. MacKenzie, 'Passion or Indifference: Popular Imperialism in Britain, Continuities and Discontinuities over Two Centuries', in John M. MacKenzie (ed.), *European Empires and the People: Popular Responses to Imperialism in France, Britain, the Netherlands, Belgium, Germany, and Italy* (Manchester, 2011), 57–89.

[129] Krishan Kumar, 'Empire, Nation, and National Identities', in Thompson (ed.), *Britain's Experience of Empire*, 301. Excellent overviews include Catherine Hall and Sonya O. Rose (eds.), *At Home with the Empire: Metropolitan Culture and the Imperial World* (Cambridge, 2006), especially the editors' 'Introduction: Being at Home with the Empire', 1–31; Andrew Thompson's balanced, well-researched treatments, including *The Empire Strikes Back?: The Impact of Imperialism on Britain from the Mid-Nineteenth Century* (Harlow, 2005), esp. ch. 9; Andrew Thompson with Meaghan Kowalsky, 'Social Life and Cultural Representation: Empire in the Public Imagination', in Thompson (ed.), *Britain's Experience of Empire*, 251–97, along with other essays in this volume.

[130] Schwarz, *White Man's World*, esp. 1–32; Ward (ed.), *British Culture*.

about mobile 'kith and kin' made Australia, Canada, Rhodesia, and other places come alive as viable life choices for many, even if most never personally took them up (opinion polls conducted in Britain between 1948 and 1975 revealed that 30–40 per cent of those surveyed claimed they desired to resettle overseas).[131] Conscription, moreover, took many of the generation of young men coming of age after 1945 overseas for the first time via National Service performed in Malaya, Singapore, Kenya, and elsewhere.[132] For every colonial administrator, development worker, student volunteer, and affluent pleasure traveller who made their way to the colonies and former colonies for short trips or long periods of work were many more Britons who connected with the surviving empire and Commonwealth without ever leaving home via engagements fostered by Women's Institutes, Christian Aid, and other associational channels (some of which had explicitly-declared imperial and Commonwealth interests, others not). Other Britons extended hospitality to or studied alongside the growing numbers of colonial and Commonwealth students enrolled at British universities.[133] Perhaps most powerfully of all, encounters with recently-arrived migrants from the West Indies, South Asia, and elsewhere served as reminders of Britain's ties with empire in the age of decolonization, a theme that lies at the heart of Chapter 7.

Millions more were on the receiving end of media portrayals disseminated through British cinemas and theatres, on television, and through bookshops and libraries in the 1950s and 1960s.[134] Whether experienced up close and personally or from the proverbial armchair, each of these countless opportunities for direct and indirect engagement with the end of empire told its own story that was available to be received and interpreted in individualized ways. Like the allegedly factual versions propagated by political leaders, imaginative fictional portrayals also revealed both consciousness of imperial decline and denials that Britain's international position had fundamentally changed, sometimes simultaneously. Such was the case with Ian Fleming's James Bond novels published between 1953 and 1966 (when the last instalment penned by

---

[131] Thompson with Kowalsky, 'Social Life', 260–8; Schwarz, *White Man's World*, 57; A. James Hammerton and Alistair Thomson, *Ten Pound Poms: Australia's Invisible Migrants* (Manchester, 2005).

[132] Richard Vinen, *National Service: Conscription in Britain, 1945–1963* (London, 2014), ch. 13.

[133] Jordanna Bailkin, *The Afterlife of Empire* (Berkeley, 2012); Anna Bocking-Welch, 'The British Public in a Shrinking World: Civic Engagement with the Declining Empire, 1960–1970', PhD dissertation, University of York (2012); Ruth Craggs, 'Cultural Geographies of the Modern Commonwealth from 1947 to 1973', PhD dissertation, University of Nottingham (2009).

[134] Among many studies, see especially Webster, *Englishness and Empire*; Kathryn Castle, *Britannia's Children: Reading Colonialism Through Children's Books and Magazines* (Manchester, 1996); Rachel Gilmour and Bill Schwarz (eds.), *End of Empire and the English Novel since 1945* (Manchester, 2011).

Fleming himself appeared a year after his death), and never more clearly than in *Doctor No* (1958).

* * *

Along with the other books featuring British Secret Service agent 007, *Doctor No* gave its readers an elite Englishman's view of a world in transition at a time when the Cold War coincided with imperial retreat but when conventional racial and imperial assumptions nonetheless remained strong.[135] Written largely at 'Goldeneye', Fleming's home in Jamaica, the book emerged from a setting where imminent change was clearly on the horizon. The severe limitations on Britain's power on the international stage and subservience to the United States exposed by the Suez Crisis had become undeniable even in the rarefied and luxurious world of Goldeneye, where in 1957 Anthony Eden joined the ranks of the many famous personalities to visit Fleming while recovering from physical ailments after resigning as prime minister. Published the following year, *Doctor No* was one of several James Bond adventures set in Jamaica itself, where Bond battles a standard-issue foreign villain whose half German, half Chinese ancestry and financial backing by the Russians epitomized a composite merger of the Nazi adversary of yesteryear and the contemporary communist Cold War threat. As in the series' other novels, the Anglo-American alliance makes its appearance through Bond's relationship with CIA agent Felix Leiter. Unlike the actual special relationship in which the United States called the shots, however, Leiter never rises above his role as Bond's affable but largely inconsequential subordinate. In Fleming's imaginary world, it could easily seem as though Britain's post-war decline as a great power, Suez, and Eden's convalescent visit to Goldeneye immediately afterwards had never happened.

James Bond's Jamaican interlude finds him ably assisted by Quarrel, a black Cayman Islander with whom he had worked and forged a friendship on a past assignment. 'You haven't changed, Quarrel', Bond greets him, and neither had the tenor of their relationship: that between a privileged Briton indisputably in charge and a poor, perennially faithful colonial appendage – a man fondly described as having 'the simple lusts and desires, the reverence for superstitions and instincts, the childish faults, the loyalty and even love' for Bond.[136] Unlike the Chinese and 'Chigro' ('Chinese Negro') minions in the pay of the nefarious

---

[135] Valuable analyses of *Doctor No* (the novel as well as the 1962 film it inspired) along with other James Bond stories and their author include Cannadine, *In Churchill's Shadow*, ch. 12; James Chapman, *Licence to Thrill: A Cultural History of the James Bond Films* (New York, 2000), chs. 1 and 2; Cynthia Baron, 'Doctor No: Bonding Britishness to Racial Sovereignty', *Spectator: The University of Southern California Journal of Film and Television Criticism*, 14:2 (1994), 68–81.
[136] Ian Fleming, *Doctor No* (New York, 1971; originally published 1958), 31–2, 209.

Doctor No, black Jamaicans make few appearances in the novel. Readers encounter Jamaica and Jamaicans through the eyes of the colonial administrators Bond meets at King's House, the seat of British government in Kingston. 'All they think of nowadays . . . is their bloody self-importance', the colonial secretary complains. 'Self-determination indeed! They can't even run a bus service. And the colour problem! My dear chap, there's far more colour problem between the straight-haired and the crinkly-haired Jamaicans than there is between me and my black cook.' In response, 'Bond grinned at him . . . He had found an ally, and an intelligent one at that.'[137]

Their common outlook thus established, the pair proceed to lunch at Queen's Club where the clientele is seemingly limited to affluent whites served by black waiters and bartenders. 'It's like this', the colonial secretary tells Bond over his pipe. 'The Jamaican is a kindly lazy man with the virtues and vices of a child. He lives on a very rich island but he doesn't get rich from it. He doesn't know how to and he's too lazy. The British come and go and take the easy pickings, but for about two hundred years no Englishman has made a fortune out here' – an assessment imbued with implicit references to the era before the abolition of slavery when British planters grew rich from the proceeds of sugar plantations, anti-abolition tracts which insisted on blacks' incapacity for freedom and inability to maximize the island's abundant resources, and the long-term economic decline of Britain's Caribbean colonies in the wake of emancipation.[138] From the standpoint of 1958, further decline was soon to come:

Such stubborn retreats will not long survive in modern Jamaica. One day Queen's Club will have its windows smashed and perhaps be burned to the ground, but for the time being it is a useful place to find in a sub-tropical island – well run, well staffed and with the finest cuisine and cellar in the Caribbean.[139]

Après British rule, *le déluge* clearly lay eagerly in wait.

In *Doctor No*, long-standing racial stereotypes entangled with the fantasy of ongoing British world power coexist uneasily with explicit admissions that the old order verged on the brink of dissolution. Despite Fleming's portrayal of power relations in which Bond reigns supreme over both his white American CIA counterpart and black colonial assistant, by the novel's end the loyal Quarrel is dead, killed by Doctor No's henchmen. Colonial rule was on its

---

[137] Ibid., 48–9.

[138] Ibid., 54. The colonial secretary conjured up by Fleming provides a racialized assessment of Jamaicans and the island that shares common ground with Thomas Carlyle's dismissive portrayal first published in 1849. See Thomas Carlyle, 'Occasional Discourse on the Negro Question' (later retitled 'Occasional Discourse on the Nigger Question'), in Eugene R. August (ed.), *Thomas Carlyle, The Nigger Question, John Stuart Mill, The Negro Question* (New York, 1971), 1–37, alongside Catherine Hall's analysis in *White, Male and Middle Class: Explorations in Feminism and History* (New York, 1992), ch. 10.

[139] Fleming, *Doctor No*, 2.

way out, Jamaica becoming self-governing in 1959 and independent by 1962, when the film version of *Doctor No* was released. Through the character of Honeychile ('Honey') Rider, the beautiful blonde woman born and raised in Jamaica who becomes Bond's love interest, the vanished but lingering world of white-owned sugar plantations and palatial homes once serviced by slaves is presented in all its alluring decrepitude. (When Honey demands sexual favours from Bond, she revealingly insists that 'You owe me slave-time.') After Bond conquers his enemies and secures Honey's affections, the story ends with his visit to her ancestral plantation home, the 'Great House' suggestively named 'Beau Desert'. Burnt to the ground long ago, Beau Desert survives as a romantic ruin overrun by sugar cane, its basement somehow kept habitable – barely – by Honey with the help of the few surviving relics of better days gone by: a chandelier together with nineteenth-century furniture, silver, and glassware.[140] Otherwise penniless, orphaned, and left to fend for herself, Honeychile's combination of tropical sexiness, assertiveness, and vulnerability makes her irresistible to Bond. Symbolic of a precariously positioned white colonial society in need of British support, the Jamaica depicted in *Doctor No* is nonetheless one in which British power has been compromised and its remaining authority lives on borrowed time.

As with any popular cultural artefact, it is impossible to know how Fleming's large readership responded to the ideologies and images of white Britishness and colonialism in decline made available in *Doctor No*, either in 1958 or over the ensuing decades when it remained widely sold in print and regularly recirculated on film. Many British readers and viewers may well have considered *Doctor No*'s Caribbean settings replete with beaches, palm trees, cocktails, and attractive women first and foremost as a touristic dreamscape rather than as a colony in its last stages before independence. But Fleming's text nonetheless offers a potent example of what Bill Schwarz describes as 'internal mental structures of colonial power [that] outlive their epoch', whereby 'putatively racial truths … hold their ground in the metropolitan civilizations, apparently immune to the fact that the historical conditions which originally gave them life have come to their end'.[141] The colonial mentalities expressed in *Doctor No* showed no sign of faltering even as incipient decolonization is openly admitted.

Caribbean decolonization, including the independence of Jamaica alongside Trinidad and Tobago in 1962, was not overtly controversial in the metropole. The region had long ceased to be viewed as economically or strategically significant to Britain, and nationalist movements on the islands had not

---

[140] Ibid., 213–16.
[141] Bill Schwarz, 'Actually Existing Postcolonialism', *Radical Philosophy*, 104 (2000), 16; see also Howe, 'When (if ever) Did Empire End', 228, 233–4.

provoked the backlash in support of the status quo seen elsewhere. In *Doctor No*, Britain's white colonial kith and kin represented by Honeychile Rider are an important presence (Honey being a far more fully formed character than any non-white person in the novel barring Doctor No himself), but Jamaica's white community never assumed either the political or the cultural prominence of settlers in British Africa in mid-twentieth-century Britain. As a small minority of the resident population on an island neither envisioned nor promoted as a settler colony, white politics and society did not impede Jamaica's decolonization under majority rule or achieve notoriety, allowing Honey to emerge as a politically neutral figure with all her exoticized appeal intact.

* * *

Imperial endgames, Commonwealth doubts, European discomforts

Honey Rider's real-life counterparts in Central Africa, by contrast, grew ever more controversial from the late 1950s onwards. Once the Central African Federation broke up and Northern Rhodesia (Zambia) and Nyasaland (Malawi) became independent in 1964, Britain was left with only one remaining colony in the region, Rhodesia, where the most challenging nationalist threat it faced was white rather than black. Rhodesia's white minority not only clung to its privileges over blacks but sought to enhance them beyond what London would willingly countenance.[142] On 11 November 1965, its white government under Ian Smith proclaimed a Unilateral Declaration of Independence (UDI) that Britain refused to recognize, ushering in a stalemate that would take nearly fifteen years to resolve.

To its champions, Rhodesia became a key 'ideological space' – a last redoubt of imperial values where a white 'racial utopia' survived long after it had succumbed in other former colonies and within Britain itself.[143] 'The idea of Rhodesia evoked all that was most captivating in the imperial past', Schwarz proposes, offering 'living proof of the past in the present, and providing a necessary corrective for an England beset by disorder and subversion' – a significant cause of which was attributed to increased black immigration. 'To imagine the nation in this way – Rhodesia as England was – necessarily

---

[142] Europeans comprised less than 5 per cent of the territory's population, numbering roughly 228,000 in 1969 and increasing to 277,000 by 1977. Donal Lowry, 'Rhodesia 1890–1980: "The Lost Dominion"', in Robert Bickers (ed.), *Settlers and Expatriates: Britons over the Seas, Oxford History of the British Empire Companion Series* (Oxford, 2010), 122.

[143] Anthony Chennells, 'Rhodesian Discourse, Rhodesian Novels and the Zimbabwe Liberation War', in Ngwabi Bhebe and Terence Ranger (eds.), *Society in Zimbabwe's Liberation War* (Oxford, 1996), 102; Schwarz, *White Man's World*, 399.

entailed disavowing, in the imagination, the presence of the black Africans', whether they be those who had recently settled in the metropole or those fighting for their rights as Rhodesia's (Zimbabwe's) oppressed majority.[144] Exemplified by the Monday Club established in 1961 by old-school Conservative imperialists, segments of the political right and far right in Britain supported both the Rhodesia settler cause alongside measures to curb non-white Commonwealth immigration to Britain.[145]

Labour's response to UDI, meanwhile, proved indecisive and inadequate. In the 1950s, Britain had proved itself willing to undertake protracted military interventions in colonies where rebels were African, Malayan, or Cypriot, but not in the mid-1960s when they were white beneficiaries of racial inequality. Britain's Harold Wilson-led Labour government elected in 1964 ruled out sending British troops either to avert or crush UDI, in large part due to long-standing fears of the domestic political implications of pitting British soldiers against 'kith and kin' whom they might refuse to see as the enemy.[146] Instead, starting with Wilson a succession of British governments opted for ineffectual economic sanctions that Rhodesia readily circumvented with the help of supportive neighbours, particularly Portuguese-controlled Mozambique and South Africa. Although Wilson proclaimed Britain would only agree to Rhodesia's independence under majority rule, by stepping back from taking effective measures against Smith's illegal regime Britain repeatedly failed in its stated objectives of taking responsibility to resolve the imbroglio within its own colony and to protect Africans' rights.[147] Britain's economic sanctions would never achieve anything, the Zimbabwe African Peoples' Union (ZAPU) explained in 1969, because they were merely 'intended to serve as an umbrella to cover and facilitate ... a racialist-fascist settler minority rule' among 'kith and kinnery'. Powerful economic and business interests in Rhodesia rendered it impossible that Britain would 'enforce sanctions against herself'. Instead, she sought both to protect her investments and steer the international community 'into gradually rehabilitating her illegitimate child'.[148]

---

[144] Schwarz, *White Man's World*, 399, 406.
[145] Murphy, *Party Politics*, 203–7, 224–8; Daniel McNeil, '"The Rivers of Zimbabwe Will Run Red with Blood": Enoch Powell and the Post-Imperial Nostalgia of the Monday Club', *Journal of Southern African Studies*, 37:4 (2011), 731–45.
[146] Philip Murphy, '"An Intricate and Distasteful Subject": British Planning for the Use of Force Against the European Settlers of Central Africa, 1952–65', *English Historical Review*, CXXI:492 (2006), 746–77; Carl Watts, 'Killing Kith and Kin: The Viability of British Military Intervention in Rhodesia, 1964–5', *Twentieth Century British History*, 16:4 (2005), 382–415.
[147] Whiting, 'Empire and British Politics', 194–205.
[148] ZAPU, 'The Sanctions That Will Never Work', *Zimbabwe Review* (ZAPU, Lusaka), 1:2 (June 1969), reprinted in Aquino de Bragança and Immanuel Wallerstein (eds.), *The African Liberation Reader, Vol. 3: The Strategy of Liberation* (London, 1982), 74–8.

Scathing criticism did not emanate solely from African nationalist organizations like ZAPU or ZANU (the Zimbabwe African National Union). Opposition to Rhodesia under UDI and support for the colony's independence as Zimbabwe under majority rule rose among newly independent African and Asian nations of the Commonwealth and within Britain, where public opinion became increasingly sceptical.[149] White supremacist politics and policies in pre- and especially post-UDI Rhodesia were to all intents and purposes indistinguishable from apartheid South Africa, its critics insisted. As Donal Lowry summarizes, a sense of shared Englishness (or Britishness) with white Rhodesians increasingly fractured after UDI. '[E]mbarrassing relatives that the metropolitan British would rather forget': such did kith and kin in Rhodesia become to many within Britain, for whom they most decidedly did not symbolize 'Britain at its best'.[150] By the late 1960s, the Rhodesian cause, along with apartheid and the American war in Vietnam, became the focus of protests in London and the West Midlands staged by British students, leftists, liberals, and members of an increasingly politicized black and South Asian community. Public marches, demonstrations, and occupations were further evidence that awareness of empire was both considerable and often impassioned at home. White activists together with the Black People's Alliance (a Birmingham-based umbrella organization representing many immigrant groups) pitted themselves against a pro-Rhodesia, pro-apartheid, and anti-immigration right-wing minority most visibly represented by the National Front.[151] Diametrically opposed positions on white Rhodesia and South Africa came together with divergent verdicts on a multi-ethnic post-war Britain, a theme to which Chapter 8 will return.

Rhodesia only achieved independence as Zimbabwe under African majority rule in 1980 following seven years of guerrilla warfare waged by ZANU and ZAPU in a struggle to reverse UDI. White dominance long sustained by British impotence alongside South African and Portuguese support became ever more tenuous after Portugal's abrupt decolonization in 1974–1975, when independent Mozambique became a haven (and opened up a new war front) for guerrillas fighting for a free Zimbabwe. Even South Africa's support for

[149] Schwarz, *White Man's World*, 427.   [150] Lowry, 'Rhodesia 1890–1980', 116–17.

[151] 'LSE Student Threat to Bar Governors', *The Times*, 11 January 1969; 'Battle of the Strand in South Africa and Rhodesia Protest' and 'Battle Outside Rhodesia House', *The Times*, 13 January 1969; 'Five Arrested after Apartheid Rally', *The Times*, 27 May 1969; '43 Charged After Rhodesia Protest March in London', *The Times*, 14 February 1972; Dewitt John, Jr., *Indian Workers' Associations in Britain* (London, 1969), 161. Some aspects of these protests are explored in Josiah Brownell, '"A Sordid Tussle on the Strand": Rhodesia House during the UDI Rebellion (1965–80)', *Journal of Imperial and Commonwealth History*, 38:3 (2010), 471–99.

Rhodesia gradually faltered.[152] By independence, an estimated 27,500 Africans had been killed, 275,000 injured, and close to a million had become refugees and displaced persons; countless others suffered displacement, malnutrition, starvation, and harsh conditions imposed by martial law.[153]

'Apart from the odd historical anomaly, Britain is no longer a colonial power', *The Guardian* reflected upon Zimbabwe's independence in April 1980. *The Observer* offered a damning verdict, arguing that the 'fourteen years of UDI will surely figure as one of the more shameful periods in Britain's colonial history' on account of the failings of both Labour and Conservative governments to act decisively against a white supremacist settler order. For its part, *The Times* expressed relief that Britain was finally free of the embarrassing 'albatross' that had plagued British diplomacy and severely compromised Commonwealth relations (both Ghana and Tanzania, for example, had broken off diplomatic relations with Britain over the Rhodesia crisis). 'This is not only Zimbabwe's liberation day. It is also Britain's. Foreign policy in the Third World, and the cohesion of the Commonwealth, have been dogged for 15 years', concluded *The Guardian*.[154] This was an understatement. Not only had the long-standing Rhodesian 'problem' wreaked havoc on Commonwealth unity; it was a key reason why the Commonwealth ideal, once so politically powerful, underwent precipitous decline in 1960s Britain.

Perhaps the most resonant public denunciation of the Commonwealth came from Conservative MP Enoch Powell. In an anonymous contribution to *The Times* in 1964, Powell described how Britain's decline as a world power since 1939 had 'imposed a colossal revision of ideas' in which 'self-deception has been employed on the grand scale and has served a purpose. Now the wounds have almost healed and the skin formed again beneath the plaster and bandages, and they can come off'. Britain's attachment to the Commonwealth project constituted not just 'self-deception' but a 'farce', 'charade', and a 'pretence' – and most importantly, one whose time had come and gone. Rather than 'worshipping "the ghost of the British Empire"', Britain needed to rethink its place in the world and recognize itself as 'a power, but a European power', and 'base its patriotism on Britain's reality, not her dreams'.[155]

---

[152] Elaine Windrich, *The Rhodesian Problem: A Documentary Record 1923–1973* (London, 1975); Terence Ranger, 'Zimbabwe and the Long Search for Independence', in David Birmingham and Phyllis Martin (eds.), *History of Central Africa: The Contemporary Years since 1960* (London, 1998), 203–29.

[153] Dan van der Vat, 'The Country in Chaos Mr Mugabe is About to Inherit', *The Times*, 31 March 1980.

[154] 'Born in Unwonted Tranquillity', *Guardian*, 18 April 1980; 'Zimbabwe Ends an Era', *Observer*, 13 April 1980; 'A New and Free Zimbabwe', *The Times*, 18 April 1980.

[155] 'A Conservative', 'Patriotism Based on Reality Not on Dreams', *The Times*, 2 April 1964. On Powell and the Commonwealth, see especially Camilla Schofield, *Enoch Powell and the Making of Postcolonial Britain* (Cambridge, 2013), ch. 3.

That the much-lauded Commonwealth as an ideal and as a key plank in Britain's global policy might be nothing more than a 'farce' touched a nerve within official thinking, not least because Powell's intervention crystallized many reservations that had gradually taken root among many other politicians, officials, and the wider public. In 1967, the Secretary of State for Commonwealth Affairs circulated a report to Wilson's cabinet that took stock of the Commonwealth's value to Britain. Detractors not only labelled it a 'farce' but a 'wasting asset' with which British trade was in decline. Worse still, it was an organization over which Britain had lost leadership and authority. Among its twenty-six member states, the majority were developing countries in Africa and Asia that were 'emotionally involved in racial issues' and teamed together to subject Britain to 'pressure-group methods' over Rhodesia, South Africa, and development aid. Many considered Britain to be 'clutching vipers to her bosom', the report concluded:

Public opinion in this country is naturally affronted at the violent and blackguardly attacks made on Britain by some Commonwealth leaders in Africa or of African origin, and asks whether we are paying too high a price to maintain a Commonwealth association which includes such obnoxious critics.

What was more, Britain's Commonwealth connection was inseparable from the contentious issue of black and Asian immigration. Even though controls had already been implemented, the report stressed, the Commonwealth remained unpopular through its close association with an unwanted 'coloured' population.

All told, however, Britain had nonetheless reaped considerable advantages from the Commonwealth that could not be gainsaid. After all, the report concluded, 'the modern Commonwealth was a triumphant technique to cover the process of decolonialisation [sic], turning "Empire" into "Commonwealth". This both enabled us to extricate ourselves from colonial responsibilities with honour and psychologically cushioned the shock for the people of Britain in adjusting to a new era.' The Commonwealth remained a 'special asset which could give Britain a position ... out of proportion to her comparative economic and military strength' – a matter of no small importance given that '[w]e no longer command the resources of a major world power'.[156] Contradictory assessments such as these were characteristic of an

---

[156] 'The Value of the Commonwealth to Britain': Cabinet Memorandum by Mr Bowden. Annex, 24 April 1967, NA, CAB 129/129, C(67)59, reprinted in S.R. Ashton and Wm. Roger Louis (eds.), *East of Suez and the Commonwealth 1964–1971, Part II: Europe, Rhodesia, Commonwealth (British Documents on the End of Empire,* Series A Volume 4) (London, 2004), 418–29 (quoted passages taken from 420, 422, 429, 423, 421). On broader issues, see especially S.R. Ashton, 'British Government Perspectives on the Commonwealth, 1964–71: An Asset or a Liability?', *Journal of Imperial and Commonwealth History,* 35:1 (2007), especially 85–8.

era of transition during the later Macmillan and then Wilson governments, when political enthusiasm for the Commonwealth waned (but did not disappear) and Britain gradually curtailed its military presence East of Suez by the early 1970s. But in openly alluding to the dawn of 'a new era', this evaluation revealed a changing set of strategic geopolitical orientations in which Britain increasingly looked away from its Commonwealth 'family' and focused new attention on its next-door neighbours: the six nations that had come together to forge the European Economic Community (EEC) formally inaugurated by the Treaty of Rome in 1957.

* * *

Britain's growing interest in the EEC in the 1960s was not a clear-cut case of jettisoning old priorities for a wholly new foreign policy.[157] While acting as leader of the opposition during the Labour governments of the late 1940s and early 1950s, Churchill regularly spoke of Britain's unique international role as part of 'three circles': the British empire and Commonwealth, the 'English-speaking world' (within which the United States was paramount but which also included Canada and other dominions), and a 'united Europe' encompassing Western European nations outside the communist bloc. Great power status could be upheld via linking the spheres together in a way no other country could. Yet while he viewed engagements with all three as fully compatible rather than mutually exclusive, Churchill was nonetheless clear where Britain's priorities lay. Britain could 'draw far closer to Europe', he stressed, 'without abandoning the ties with our Dominions which to us are paramount and sacred, and comprise the ideal of the British Empire and Commonwealth of Nations'.[158] After returning to office in 1951, he clarified in a note to his cabinet that although Britain should encourage European unity 'I never thought that Britain ... should ... become an integral part of a European Federation':

We help, we dedicate, we play a part, but we are not merged and do not forfeit our insular or Commonwealth-wide character. I should resist any American pressure to treat Britain as on the same footing as the European States, none of whom have the advantages of the Channel and who were consequently conquered. Our first object is the unity and the

---

[157] Alex May (ed.), *Britain, the Commonwealth and Europe: The Commonwealth and Britain's Applications to Join the European Communities* (Basingstoke, 2001).

[158] '"The Three Circles" (Foreign Policy)', 20 April 1949, Economic Conference of the European Movement, in Robert Rhodes James (ed.), *Winston S. Churchill: His Complete Speeches 1897–1963, Vol. VII, 1943–1949* (London, 1974), 7810–11; see also 'European Unity', *The Times*, 9 October 1948. On the 'three circles', see Reynolds, *Britannia Overruled*, ch. 8; Anne Deighton, 'The Past in the Present: British Imperial Memories and the European Question', in Jan-Werner Müller (ed.), *Memory and Power in Post-War Europe: Studies in the Presence of the Past* (Cambridge, 2002), 104–5; Wolfram Kaiser, '"What Alternative Is Open to Us?": Britain', in Wolfram Kaiser and Jürgen Elvert (eds.), *European Union Enlargement: A Comparative History* (London, 2004), 9–10.

consolidation of the British Commonwealths [sic] and what is left of the former British Empire. Our second, the 'fraternal association' of the [English]-speaking world; and third, United Europe, to which we are a separate closely- and specially-related ally and friend.[159]

Churchill's interventions count among the many occasions when geographical and historical distinctions from other Western European nations came to the fore in political rhetoric. Not only did the English Channel separate the British Isles from the continent; Britain had avoided wartime invasion and occupation to emerge victorious alongside its American allies in 1945. Despite its weakened, impoverished, and subservient position vis-à-vis the United States outlined earlier, the war enhanced a sense of British difference and superiority over continental Europe that lasted long after 1945 and sowed a deep reluctance to partake in European integration.[160] Geopolitical priorities favouring empire and Commonwealth over European ties were broadly bipartisan in the early 1950s. As the Labour Party asserted in its *European Unity* manifesto in 1950, 'Britain is not just a small crowded island off the Western coast of Continental Europe. She is the nerve centre of a world-wide Commonwealth which extends into every continent. In every respect except distance we in Britain are closer to our kinsmen in Australia and New Zealand on the far side of the world, than we are to Europe.' Not only was Britain 'banker of the sterling area': 'We are closer in language and in origins, in social habits and institutions, in political outlook and economic interest.'[161]

Labour's resistance to Europe ultimately proved more resilient than was the case among most Conservatives. Little more than a decade later, Labour held fast to the Commonwealth ideal at a time when the Macmillan government launched Britain's first application to join the EEC in 1961. Propelled by shifts in British trade towards advanced industrial European markets and away from primary commodity-producing economies of the Commonwealth as well as by the very American pressure to which Churchill had alluded, the Conservative leadership feared that the only way to maintain Britain's influential standing with the United States was by assuming a position within Europe rather than remaining outside.[162] But as Labour leader Hugh Gaitskell countered in 1962, not only was the Commonwealth still a more important market than the EEC for British goods; it had provided essential aid to Britain in two world wars. Britain's entry into a European federation, he feared, would spell nothing less

---

[159] 'United Europe': Cabinet note by Mr Churchill, 29 November 1951, NA, CAB 129/48, C (51) 32, reprinted in Goldsworthy (ed.), *Conservative Government and the End of Empire 1951–1957*, Part I, 3–4.

[160] Antonio Varsori, 'Is Britain Part of Europe?: The Myth of British "Difference"', in Cyril Buffet and Beatrice Heuser (eds.), *Haunted by History: Myths in International Relations* (Providence, RI, 1998), 135–56; Kaiser, '"What Alternative"'.

[161] Labour Party, *European Unity: A Statement by the National Executive Committee of the British Labour Party* (London, 1950), 3, accessed via www.cvce.eu, 11 July 2013.

[162] Deighton, 'Past in the Present', 114; Kaiser, '"What Alternative"', 18.

than 'the end of Britain as an independent European state' (and thus 'the end of a thousand years of history'). This in turn would signal 'the end of the Commonwealth', for '[h]ow can one really seriously suppose that if the mother country, the centre of the Commonwealth, is a province of Europe ... it could continue to exist as the mother country of a series of independent nations?'[163]

Gaitskell and other Labour politicians were not alone in valuing the Commonwealth above Europe. In a 1961 Gallup poll asking which was most important to Britain, 48 per cent of the respondents chose 'the Commonwealth', 19 per cent 'America', and 18 per cent 'Europe' (with the remainder courageously opting for 'don't know'). But Britain's EEC membership application gave rise to intense discussions that framed Britain's Commonwealth and European commitments as necessitating a choice between the two.[164] If anything, Britain's overture to the EEC was not simply 'a tacit acknowledgement of the declining economic and political utility of the Commonwealth as a vehicle for British interests', as Stuart Ward has written, but became yet another factor among the many centrifugal forces already undermining Commonwealth cohesion.[165] By the late 1960s, concerns that the Commonwealth connection impeded Britain's superior prospects in Europe had joined the Rhodesian and immigration 'problems' as reasons for its waning political appeal, even among stalwart Labour supporters. Just six years after Harold Wilson argued that 'we are not entitled to sell our friends and kinsmen down the river for a problematical and marginal advantage in selling washing machines in Dusseldorf', his own government embarked on a second attempt to gain Britain entry into the EEC in 1967 after he became prime minister.[166]

Britain's second membership application met the same fate as the first in 1963: rejection on account of France's veto. The low priority accorded to the 'third circle' that was 'United Europe' since the late 1940s came back to haunt Britain and caused its exclusion from the EEC throughout the 1960s, with President de Gaulle invoking Britain's much-vaunted insularity and ties with distant Commonwealth countries as reasons why it was insufficiently

[163] 'Speech by Hugh Gaitskell (3 October 1962)', 7, reproduced from *Britain and the Common Market, Texts of Speeches Made at the 1962 Labour Party Conference by the Rt. Hon. Hugh Gaitskell MP and the Rt. Hon. George Brown MP together with the policy statement accepted by Conference* (London, 1962), accessed via www.cvce.eu, 11 July 2013.

[164] Alex May, '"Commonwealth or Europe?": Macmillan's Dilemma, 1961–63', in May (ed.), *Britain, the Commonwealth and Europe*, 98, 103–4; Richard Toye, 'Words of Change: The Rhetoric of Commonwealth, Common Market and Cold War, 1961–3', in Butler and Stockwell (eds.), *Wind of Change*, 140–58.

[165] Stuart Ward, 'A Matter of Preference: The EEC and the Erosion of the Old Commonwealth Relationship', in May (ed.), *Britain, the Commonwealth and Europe*, 162; see also Wolfram Kaiser, *Using Europe, Abusing the Europeans: Britain and European Integration, 1945–63* (Basingstoke, 1996), 120–2.

[166] Helen Parr, *Britain's Policy Towards the European Community: Harold Wilson and Britain's World Role, 1964–1967* (Abingdon, 2006), 18.

'European' to deserve membership. In reality, however, de Gaulle was far more concerned with Britain's second circle: the Anglo-American 'special relationship' in which the United States was the overwhelmingly dominant partner. Western European nations had become 'no more than satellites of the United States' after the war, he explained in 1962, and none more so than Britain. Europe's urgent need to achieve independence from the United States, he insisted, was incompatible with the unwelcome prospect of Britain being the thin end of an American wedge inside the EEC.[167] If Hugh Gaitskell had considered membership to portend 'the end of Britain as an independent European state', in de Gaulle's eyes this was a *fait accompli* – an established fact that had nothing whatsoever to do with the prospect of being 'a province of Europe' as opposed to the Commonwealth's 'mother country', but rather submission to the United States.

Britain only succeeded in entering the EEC in 1973 upon its third attempt after de Gaulle left office. Over the course of the three applications spanning 1961 and 1973, the Commonwealth continually receded as a factor within domestic British EEC debates.[168] Although the Conservative Party under Edward Heath demonstrated strong pro-European tendencies in the 1970s, Euroscepticism remained well-represented on its back benches and ultimately became more pervasive after Margaret Thatcher assumed leadership. Concerns about defending Britain's sovereignty against European encroachment were commonly aired in the 1980s, with reservations about national subordination within Europe rising in tandem with the inauguration of a new chapter in the Anglo-American special relationship.[169] Under Thatcher's governments, Britain distanced itself from Europe and prioritized Atlanticism – not only through a pro-American foreign policy, but also in mounting an ardent defence of one of the 'odd historical anomalies' remaining of colonial power to which *The Guardian* had referred when Zimbabwe became independent in 1980: the Falkland Islands.

Situated in the South Atlantic off the coast of Argentina, the remote, sparsely populated Falklands had been a British possession since 1833, largely as a sleepy backwater attracting little attention until Argentina lodged new claims to the islands (the 'Malvinas') starting in the 1960s. Britain appeared willing to negotiate a transfer, or 'leaseback', but encountered staunch opposition from the Islanders who ardently wished to remain

---

[167] Charles de Gaulle, quoted in Jussi Hanhimäki and Odd Arne Westad, *The Cold War: A History in Documents and Eyewitness Accounts* (Oxford, 2003), 332 (see also 331–6); Varsori, 'Myth of British "Difference"', 151; Julian Jackson, *Charles de Gaulle* (London, 2003), 100.

[168] Alex May, 'The Commonwealth and Britain's Turn to Europe, 1945–73', *Round Table*, 102:1 (2013), 29–39.

[169] Andrew Gamble, 'Europe and America', in Ben Jackson and Robert Saunders (eds.), *Making Thatcher's Britain* (Cambridge, 2012), 218–33.

British. Argentina's dictatorship finally forced the matter by initiating a military invasion in April 1982 – a move which provoked an eruption of jingoistic patriotic fervour within Britain in support of the Islanders' right to self-determination. Together with the mainstream media, much of Britain's political class supported recapturing the Falklands by force to protect their population of c. 1,400 who were 'British in stock and tradition', as Thatcher phrased it. Once again, Britain rallied around distant kith and kin – on this occasion those residing in a British colony (or 'dependent territory') rather than those within the 'Old Commonwealth'.[170]

Britain launched a naval task force that liberated the Falklands by mid-June, killing 255 British soldiers, 746 Argentine soldiers, and wounding over 2,000 in an operation costing over £3 billion. Back home, Thatcher and the Conservatives reaped the rewards of military success in a war fought on behalf of one of Britain's few remaining colonial possessions, which played a role in the party winning re-election with a substantially increased majority the following year. '[W]e fought for our own people and for our own sovereign territory', Thatcher proclaimed in a speech at a Conservative rally in July 1982. To all who had 'secret fears . . . that Britain was no longer the nation that had built an Empire and ruled a quarter of the world', she replied:

Well, they were wrong. The lesson of the Falklands is that Britain has not changed and that this nation still has those sterling qualities which shine through our history . . . now, once again, Britain is not prepared to be pushed around. We have ceased to be a nation in retreat. We have instead a new-found confidence – born in the economic battles at home and tested and found true 8,000 miles away. This confidence comes from the rediscovery of ourselves, and grows with the recovery of our self-respect.[171]

Historians provide differing assessments of the Falklands War of 1982, some calling it 'obviously imperial' while others rank it as a post-imperial conflict that, if anything, harkened back to Second World War Churchillism more than empire *per se*.[172] Ashley Jackson persuasively argues that the imperial past is closely linked to an ongoing imperial present, with the Falklands conflict signalling 'the resurgence of an interventionist Britain' that illustrates a high degree of continuity in 'Britain's deep involvement with the world beyond

---

[170] Paul, *Whitewashing Britain*, 185. The Falklands/Malvinas War also provoked critical opposition from the Left. See essays by Eric Hobsbawm, Robert Gray, and Tom Nairn in Stuart Hall and Martin Jacques (eds.), *The Politics of Thatcherism* (London, 1983); Anthony Barnett, 'Iron Britannia', *New Left Review*, 134 (1982), 1–96; James Aulich (ed.), *Framing the Falklands War: Nationhood, Culture, and Identity* (Milton Keynes, 1992).

[171] Margaret Thatcher, 'To Conservative Rally, Cheltenham, 3 July 1982', in *The Revival of Britain: Speeches on Home and European Affairs 1975–1988* (London, 1989), 160–4.

[172] Compare, for example, Stephen Howe, 'Decolonisation and Imperial Aftershocks: The Thatcher Years', in Jackson and Saunders (eds.), *Making Thatcher's Britain*, 242–3; Whiting, 'Empire and British Politics', 205–6.

Europe'.[173] The handover of Hong Kong to China in 1997 is often invoked as marking the end of an extended decolonization era that India and Pakistan's independence heralded fifty years earlier, but Britain today nonetheless retains a handful of small islands alongside a number of military bases scattered across the world. Not only had Britain never completely lost its empire; despite its relative decline in global power and reach 'it certainly never lost the appetite and capacity to perform a world role, despite the turn towards Europe', Jackson notes – a point borne out by early twenty-first-century British military interventions in Afghanistan and Iraq undertaken alongside the United States.[174]

Britain's 'turn towards Europe', moreover, remains a partial and often reluctant one punctuated by recurrent eruptions of hostility directed at the European Union. In 2013, the political successes of the Europhobic UK Independence Party (UKIP) spurred on Conservative Party demands for a referendum to determine whether Britain should even remain part of the EU, thereby adding yet another chapter to the long history of grumblings and doubts about the merits and meanings of the European connection. Long after the Commonwealth ceased to compete as an alternative source of British loyalties and attachments after the era of widescale decolonization, '[r]esistance to "Europe", an unhappy alternative to great powerdom, remained a powerful force in British politics', Anne Deighton aptly concludes.[175] While British Euroscepticism has many roots, its trajectory demands to be firmly embedded within domestic responses to decolonization and perceptions of the nation's postcolonial condition.

As the following chapters demonstrate, decolonization produced very different domestic responses among newly ex-colonial powers to the long-term process of European integration, along with much else besides. Not only were British and French experiences of the decolonization process and the evolving European project distinct; so too were those of smaller European colonizing nations long reliant on overseas territories to augment their status on the world stage and whose national identities owed an immeasurable debt to their imperial dimensions. It is the first of the latter, the Netherlands, that we will now consider.

---

[173] Ashley Jackson, 'Empire and Beyond: The Pursuit of Overseas National Interests in the Late Twentieth Century', *English Historical Review*, 122:499 (2007), 1352, 1365.

[174] Ibid., 1366.

[175] Deighton, 'Past in the Present', 109. See also Menno Spiering, *A Cultural History of British Euroscepticism* (Basingstoke, 2014).

2   Occupation, resistance, and liberation
The road to Dutch decolonization

Throughout the Second World War, the Dutch Cabinet remained closely attuned to the fate of the Netherlands within Europe and as an imperial power alike. Two of its most prominent members, Prime Minister Pieter Gerbrandy and Foreign Minister Eelco van Kleffens, wrote passionately both during and after the war about one part of the empire in particular: the East Indies. Territorially, the Kingdom of the Netherlands encompassed a small European nation in conjunction with the East Indies as well as the West Indies (which included Suriname on the mainland of South America along with Curaçao and other smaller islands of the Antilles in the Caribbean). But like most leading policymakers and commentators, Gerbrandy and Van Kleffens virtually ignored the western hemisphere and focused on the extensive Southeast Asian archipelago, whose collective population approximated 70 million and where Dutch control had originated over 300 years before. Although the Netherlands had also been present in the West Indies for centuries, the similarities ended there: by the mid-twentieth century, Dutch reflections on their nation's imperial past, present, and future had long looked east and rarely west, and the 1940s proved no different. Late in 1942 Van Kleffens discussed 'The Democratic Future of the Netherlands Indies' – apparently considering it so obvious that he meant the 'East Indies' he did not even bother with exact specification – as part of Queen Wilhelmina's government-in-exile based in London, where the monarch and her ministers had retreated in May 1940 when the Nazis invaded and occupied their homeland; Gerbrandy's book *Indonesia* appeared in 1950. Between them fell a series of watershed events, the end of the war, the end of the Netherlands East Indies, and the emergence of the Republic of Indonesia foremost among them.

Though penned under radically different circumstances and looking towards vastly different imagined futures, Van Kleffens' and Gerbrandy's accounts exhibited a high degree of consensus about the East Indies up until 1942. Van Kleffens was the more critical, contrasting Dutch rule after 1900 favourably with the preceding period. Previous eras may have seen 'colonial domination and economic exploitation for the benefit, first of the Dutch East India Company, then of the Dutch exchequer, and finally, under the liberal system of *laissez-faire*, of Dutch and foreign capitalism' – which, he hastened to add, was nonetheless of considerable advantage to indigenous peoples.[1] Yet once Queen Wilhelmina proclaimed the Netherlands' 'moral vocation' (often called the 'ethical policy' whose mission involved 'uplifting the natives') in 1901, Indonesians' welfare became the top priority. The 'beneficient effect of Dutch rule' across the next four decades included the inauguration in 1918 of a representative 'proto-parliament' (the *Volksraad*, or People's Council), the spread of education, and economic development prioritizing the production of commodities, including rubber, tin, oil, sugar, tea, coffee, and quinine.[2]

For his part, Gerbrandy dismissed portrayals of the much-maligned colonial order predating 1900. Whatever its flaws, by the turn of the century the Netherlands already had laid solid foundations to make 'a model colony' even better still. But like Van Kleffens he highlighted that by the 1940s 'we' had introduced modern agriculture, communications, and healthcare and established 'a free society, based on economic prosperity and an incorruptible administration'.[3] 'There was absolute freedom of speech, unless seditious', he insisted; 'There was a People's Council, a Parliament, which … could criticize Government actions and possessed considerable legislative power, and there were representative councils throughout the territories.'[4] Far from being 'usurpers who have exploited the Indies', Gerbrandy proclaimed that 'we made the Indies' and 'led the world' in creating 'colonial rule and development at its very best'.[5] 'Great tranquillity' and a 'unique excellence in the sphere of colonial relationships' prevailed, the people overwhelmingly assenting to Dutch rule.[6] Described as simple, traditional, and loyal, the archipelago's population was also a resoundingly apolitical one, both men emphasized.

Van Kleffens did his best to ignore the existence of nationalist activities when writing in 1942, while Gerbrandy's retrospective analysis of the years leading up to that point remained stubbornly dismissive of nationalism as a negligible phenomenon. And no wonder: much like Churchill had considered 'India' as only 'an abstraction', 'a geographical term', and 'no more a united nation than the Equator' in 1931, as Chapter 1 discussed, both Van Kleffens and Gerbrandy questioned the very status and concept of 'Indonesia' as a nation at

---

[1] Eelco N. van Kleffens, 'The Democratic Future of the Netherlands Indies', *Foreign Affairs*, 21:1 (1942), 92. Later historical treatments of Dutch policies in the East Indies provide more detailed, substantiated, and circumspect assessments, both of the 'ethical policy' as well as the heavily criticized 'culture system' predating it. See overviews provided by Bob Moore in Martin Thomas, Bob Moore, and L.J. Butler, *Crises of Empire: Decolonization and Europe's Imperial States, 1918–1975* (London, 2008), ch. 11; M.C. Ricklefs, *A History of Modern Indonesia since c.1200*, 4th edn. (Basingstoke, 2008), 183–94; Elsbeth Locher-Scholten, *Ethiek in fragmenten: Vijf studies over koloniaal denken en doen van Nederlanders in de Indonesische archipel 1877–1942* (Utrecht, 1981), 176–208.

[2] Van Kleffens, 'Democratic Future', 92–5.

[3] P.S. Gerbrandy, *Indonesia* (London, 1950), 21, 11.   [4] Ibid., 46.   [5] Ibid., 28, 48.

[6] Ibid., 40, 42.

all given the barriers posed by the islands' diversity across a vast geographical expanse.[7] The five largest and most important islands – Java, Sumatra, Borneo, Celebes (also known as Sulawesi), and the western part of New Guinea – formed only the tip of the Netherlands' East Indies iceberg, which extended to approximately 3,000 smaller, widely-dispersed islands. Van Kleffens claimed that any 'unity of the Netherlands Indies which now exists depends on the presence of Dutch rule ... Take the Dutch element of cohesion away, and the whole edifice would crumble into fragments.'[8] In the 1920s and 1930s, Gerbrandy argued, 'Nationalism was only preached by a relatively small minority of intellectuals, who played upon the word "Indonesia" and dreamed of a Union in one State of all the peoples of the archipelago. The vast majority of the people were either sceptical of this grandiose project or rejected it outright. By and large, the population were loyal to the Netherlands adminis-tration.' Of those few who actually 'saw Indonesia as a single unit ... it is needful to stress that this single unit was created by the Netherlands'.[9] Not only had 'we made the Indies'; the Dutch had seemingly made 'Indonesia' as well, insofar as it was acknowledged at all.

Gerbrandy and Van Kleffens' renditions were representative of a long-dominant attitude towards the East Indies among Dutch policymakers and elites, but owed their shape and tenor to the successive cataclysms wrought by war.[10] Starting in early 1942, the Netherlands suffered not just one foreign occupation but two as Nazi Germany's control over its European territory was joined by Japan's takeover of the East Indies. From London, the government-in-exile contemplated a nation and empire completely wrenched from Dutch control, with the only territories not overrun by Axis powers, Suriname and the West Indian islands, being protected by British and American Allies. Under these extraordinary circumstances, ministers like Van Kleffens and Queen Wilhelmina herself narrated versions of the recent imperial past fully in tune with present-day crisis conditions and wishes for a brighter future that involved, they dared hope, a return to the status quo *ante bellum* after an Allied victory. Fully dependent upon Allied support and above all on American

---

[7] Van Kleffens, 'Democratic Future', 90–2.   [8] Ibid., 97, 99.

[9] Gerbrandy, *Indonesia*, 24, 45. Benedict Anderson notes that 'although the very concept of "Indonesia" is a twentieth-century invention, and most of today's Indonesia was only conquered by the Dutch between 1850 and 1910', unlike Gerbrandy and Van Kleffens he explores Indonesia's modern origins under colonial domination in order to understand how a nationalist movement emerged to fight for a unified 'imagined community', not merely to delegitimize them both. See Benedict Anderson, *Imagined Communities: Reflections on the Origin and Spread of Nationalism*, revised edition (London, 2006), 11, 120.

[10] H. Colijn, *Koloniale vraagstukken van heden en morgen* (Amsterdam, 1928), 59, as discussed in Jacques van Doorn, *The Soldier and Social Change: Comparative Studies in the History and Sociology of the Military* (London, 1975), 114.

acquiescence to their projected future Indies policy, theirs was a finely-calibrated tale of a harmonious Indies idyll shattered only by the Japanese enemy.[11]

Dutch leaders in exile scripted their public statements with a watchful eye on American anti-colonial sentiments and expectations that a post-war world would also rapidly become a postcolonial one. If Van Kleffens' account published in English in the journal *Foreign Affairs* provided one instance (in which he took the opportunity to explain that the Indies had not even been a colony since 1922 but rather 'one of four component parts, equal in constitutional rank, of the Kingdom of the Netherlands'), Queen Wilhelmina's wartime speeches exemplified United States-oriented Dutch propaganda *par excellence*.[12] Speaking before Congress in August 1942, she described how previous steps 'toward full partnership in government on the basis of equality' and 'increasing self-government' had arrived at an impasse solely because 'the Japanese invasion temporarily interrupted their promising course'.[13] Her most noteworthy Indies-related pronouncement came via radio broadcast on 6 December 1942 when she envisioned (but significantly did not promise) a further devolution of power after the war. The Netherlands' relationship with Suriname, Curaçao, and 'Indonesia' – her use of the term a calculated concession to assuage anti-colonial feelings – would increasingly resemble that of Britain and its dominions within a Commonwealth model, with each territory having 'complete self-reliance and freedom of conduct ... regarding its internal affairs'. Such a development was simply part of 'a natural evolution' already well underway: 'After an age-old historical solidarity, in which had long since passed the era of colonial relationship, we stood on the eve of a collaboration on a basis of equality when suddenly we were both confronted by the present ordeal.'[14]

While these pronouncements by the monarch and her ministers succeeded in favourably impressing President Roosevelt and the American policymaking establishment, they went unheard in a Japanese-occupied Indonesia cut off from outside communication. Had they circulated within the archipelago, however, they would have been greeted with the same derision and disbelief

---

[11] Gerbrandy, *Indonesia*, 47, 73; Van Kleffens, 'Democratic Future', 100, 102.

[12] Van Kleffens, 'Democratic Future', 93.

[13] 'Address by Queen Wilhelmina, Delivered on the Occasion of Her Visit to the Congress of the United States, Thursday, August 6, 1942', in Netherlands Information Bureau, *The Netherlands Commonwealth and the Future* (New York, 1945), 13.

[14] 'Towards a Netherlands Commonwealth: Text of H.M. Queen Wilhelmina's Radio Address of December 6, 1942', in *Netherlands Commonwealth and the Future*, 20–2; see also analyses by C. Fasseur, 'A Cheque Drawn on a Failing Bank: The Address Delivered by Queen Wilhelmina on 6th/7th December 1942', *Low Countries History Yearbook*, 15 (1982), 102–16; Frances Gouda with Thijs Brocades Zaalberg, *American Visions of the Netherlands East Indies/ Indonesia: US Foreign Policy and Indonesian Nationalism, 1920–1949* (Amsterdam, 2002), 115; Jennifer L. Foray, *Visions of Empire in the Nazi-Occupied Netherlands* (Cambridge, 2012), 152–68.

as countless earlier colonialist portrayals of the Netherlands' Indies policy as enlightened and progressive among the very circles the Dutch were so eager to ignore or minimize in front of powerful outsiders: Indonesian nationalists. Prominent among early manifestations of political consciousness were small groups like Budi Utomo, established in 1908 and attracting elites and intellectuals, and especially Sarekat Islam, which grew into a mass movement revolving around a common religious identity with well over half a million followers within several years of its founding in 1912. A communist party calling for independence from the Netherlands was also in evidence by 1920. Other movements arose soon afterwards, coalescing under the leadership of western-educated Indonesians based at higher educational institutions in both the Netherlands and the Indies.[15] Mohammad Hatta was the key figure within Perhimpunan Indonesia, a group that emerged among colonial students attending Dutch universities in the early 1920s and the first organization to use 'Indonesia' in its name.[16] Through its title and content, its journal announced the group's aspirations and political demands: *Indonesia Merdeka*, a 'Free Indonesia' comprising 'the unity of an entire Indonesia independent of local differences'.[17]

Hatta's writings in *Indonesia Merdeka* and elsewhere laid bare the chasm between Dutch propaganda celebrating enlightened colonial policies and the brutal realities of foreign rule for the indigenous population. His eloquent accusations penned in the 1920s remained no less valid nearly twenty years later, with the conditions he and his sympathizers decried remaining virtually unchanged when the Japanese seized control. '[I]s it not said that Indonesia "is the cork on which Netherlands prosperity floats"?', he asked in 1928. '[T]he purpose of the colonisation is purely to quench material hunger with the rich colonial treasure. It is not, as is so often falsely suggested, to bring Western culture to the colonised people. Because never has colonisation been started in the service of philanthropy, to satisfy the wish for education of "less civilized" people.'[18] For Indonesians, the so-called '"blessings" of the Dutch rule' typically spelled impoverishment, taxes in excess of 40 per cent, press censorship, draconian forms of repression including arbitrary 'police terrorism', a harsh

---

[15] George McTurnan Kahin, *Nationalism and Revolution in Indonesia* (Ithaca, 1952), ch. 3; Jean Gelman Taylor, *Indonesia: Peoples and Histories* (New Haven, 2004), 293–5; Klaas Stutje, 'Indonesian Identities Abroad: International Engagement of Colonial Students in the Netherlands, 1908–1931', *BMGN – Low Countries History Review*, 128:1 (2013), 151–72.

[16] John Ingleson, *Perhimpunan Indonesia and the Indonesian Nationalist Movement 1923–1928* (Melbourne, 1975), 9–11; C.L.M. Penders (ed.), *Mohammad Hatta, Indonesian Patriot: Memoirs* (Singapore, 1981), chs. 4–9.

[17] Mohammad Hatta, 'National Claims', first published in *Indonesia Merdeka*, 1924–1925, reprinted in *Portrait of a Patriot: Selected Writings of Mohammad Hatta* (The Hague, 1972), 314.

[18] Mohammad Hatta, 'Indonesia Free': plea before the Court of Justice in The Hague, 9 March 1928, reprinted in *Portrait of a Patriot*, 210, 213.

penal code, and the banning of trades unions and political meetings.[19] As for the People's Council or *Volksraad*, repeatedly invoked by Dutch imperialists as testament to their progressive agenda, Hatta was just one of many contemporary critics (followed later by historians) to identify its limitations. Far from qualifying as a legitimate forum for political expression or enabling increased Indonesian autonomy, the *Volksraad* possessed no real power, and most nationalist groups refused to take part in it. The governor-general's unrestricted right to veto any of its decisions rendered it a 'mere advisory council' which had never been representative of the Indonesian majority in the first place, its membership voted in by a minuscule electorate and correspondingly dominated by a combination of Europeans and Indonesians broadly supportive of the Dutch-dominated colonial order.

Nor had the Netherlands ever intended the *Volksraad* to devolve greater autonomy onto the colonized or act as the 'proto-parliament' Van Kleffens later repackaged for American consumption. Never a selfless gesture of colonial goodwill, it came about as a reaction to increased Indonesian politicization exemplified by Budi Utomo, Sarekat Islam, and other organizations – an ill-disguised façade that amounted to mere '*sham* self-government'.[20] '[T]he mother country is not interested in *real* self-government for the colony', Hatta argued.[21] Instead, it habitually fell back on the conventional rationale that the Indies required a slow, 'gradual development' towards greater autonomy because its population was allegedly 'too immature for self-government'. This, he countered, was merely a 'fiction ... to cover self-interest'. It was not that Indonesia was unprepared to govern itself but rather that the Dutch were patently unwilling to allow it to do so, because conceding power meant relinquishing the long-proverbial 'cork on which Netherlands prosperity floats'.[22] In short, 'the Dutch colonial ideal' was anything but lofty, insisting only 'that Indonesia must eternally remain "a great coffee and sugar plantation for the State"!'[23]

Perhimpunan Indonesia's rise among Indonesian students living far from home was joined in 1927 by the Partai Nasional Indonesia (PNI)'s emergence in Java under Achmed Sukarno, an engineering student at the Technical College of Bandung whose charismatic leadership generated a mass following.[24] Other political organizations developed during these years,

[19] Ibid., 238, 224–43.
[20] Ibid., 250; for comparable verdicts, see 'Report of the First Public Meeting of Partindo Held in Batavia, 12 July 1931', in Chr. L.M. Penders (ed.), *Indonesia: Selected Documents on Colonialism and Nationalism, 1830–1942* (Queensland, 1977), 319–20; Ricklefs, *History of Modern Indonesia*, 194; Kahin, *Nationalism and Revolution*, 39–40; Robert J. McMahon, *Colonialism and Cold War: The United States and the Struggle for Indonesian Independence, 1945–49* (Ithaca, 1981), 30–1.
[21] Hatta, 'Indonesia Free', 251.   [22] Ibid., 254–5.   [23] Ibid., 256.
[24] J.D. Legge, *Sukarno: A Political Biography* (North Sydney, 1972), 86–8.

including communist groups, but all suffered similar fates: colonial suppression. If nationalism truly was a marginal phenomenon when the Second World War began, as Van Kleffens, Gerbrandy, and other Dutch statesmen continually claimed, this was not because it had never existed or had withered of its own accord through a lack of popular support. On the contrary, its presence and potential had been sufficiently worrying in the 1920s and 1930s for the colonial authorities to deploy the full extent of their powers in the attempt to quash it, and on a superficial level they succeeded. Political organizations calling for independence were outlawed, their membership subjected to intense police surveillance and harassment, and their leaders arrested, jailed, and exiled.[25] Tellingly, some of the most eloquent nationalist writings took the form of defence statements prepared for their trials, Hatta's 'Indonesia Free' (discussed earlier) and Sukarno's *Indonesia Accuses!* being paramount among them.[26] Detention and exile often occurred without even the semblance of a trial, however, and became the means through which the Dutch removed Hatta, Sukarno, and other major figures from the political scene by 1934. Their release only came after Japan's arrival in 1942.

Nationalism's revival and expansion took place under Japanese occupation that provided the air it needed to breathe. 'Given the success that the Dutch had in suppressing the small nationalist movement in Indonesia, the country would not have come into being without Japan's intervention', Adrian Vickers summarizes.[27] The Royal Dutch Indies Army (KNIL) could offer only weak resistance in the face of Japan's invasion of the archipelago and was rapidly overrun, its forces interned as prisoners of war. The colonial authorities surrendered and Dutch men, women, and children collectively were thrown into civilian internment camps. Over 42,000 European soldiers and approximately 100,000 civilians suffered horrific conditions in captivity that resulted in mortality rates of 1 in 5 and 1 in 6 respectively. With its representatives so rapidly and humiliatingly removed from public life, Dutch power and prestige were dealt a fatal blow as colonial society collapsed under what became a three-and-a-half-year occupation.[28]

---

[25] John Ingleson, *Road to Exile: The Indonesian Nationalist Movement 1927–1934* (Singapore, 1979); Kahin, *Nationalism and Revolution*, 90–4; McMahon, *Colonialism and Cold War*, 31–4.

[26] Soekarno, *Indonesia Accuses!: Soekarno's Defence Oration in the Political Trial of 1930*, edited, translated, and introduced by Roger K. Paget (Kuala Lumpur, 1975); Hatta, 'Indonesia Free'. Other contemporary Indonesian writings concerning the 'Call for Freedom' are gathered in Harry Poeze and Henk Schulte Nordholt (eds.), *De roep om Merdeka: Indonesische vrijheidslievende teksten uit de twintigste eeuw* (Amsterdam, 1996).

[27] Adrian Vickers, *A History of Modern Indonesia* (Cambridge, 2005), 85.

[28] L. de Jong, *The Collapse of a Colonial Society: The Dutch in Indonesia during the Second World War* (Leiden, 2002), 283, 421–2. This volume contains translations of selected chapters of L. de Jong, *Het Koninkrijk der Nederlanden in de Tweede Wereldoorlog, Deel 11b: Nederlands-Indië II*, 2 vols. (Leiden, 1985). The other Indies-focused volumes of this comprehensive overview of

At the outset, the Japanese received an enthusiastic reception from many Indonesians eager to welcome them as liberators from the Dutch. By 1942, few actively supported the colonial order aside from minority groups, particularly the Indisch Dutch (Eurasians) but also indigenous Christian communities such as the Ambonese, who provided much of the KNIL's manpower. But it was not long before initial support for the occupying forces haemorrhaged as Japan's economic exploitation of the islands' raw materials, forced labour and forced cultivation policies, military conscription, and endemic arbitrary brutality took their toll. Whatever admiration Indonesians may have felt towards the Japanese when they overthrew the Dutch turned to widespread hatred of a new set of ruthless foreign overlords.

To secure compliance with their war effort against the Allies, the Japanese looked to Indonesian nationalist leaders to secure mass support. Sukarno, Hatta, and others were allowed back from exile or out of prison as the Japanese promised eventual Indonesian self-government in return for wartime cooperation. Many agreed, not thanks to pro-Japanese sentiments but because temporary cooperation seemed the most effective tactic for securing their greater political goals: the permanent removal of the Dutch and full independence.[29]

Occupation created decisive new opportunities for nationalism to flourish and spread across social divides as Indonesians became politically mobilized on an unprecedented scale. Through conscription, developing paramilitary youth organizations, and provoking underground resistance against their occupation, the Japanese militarized Indonesian society in a way that proved critical after their capitulation in August 1945. When Allied forces arrived to assume control, they found a political, military, and mental Indonesian landscape changed out of all recognition in the absence of Dutch authority. Sukarno had taken advantage of the political vacuum opened up by Japan's surrender to declare an independent Republic of Indonesia on 17 August. For the Netherlands, the Second World War might have ended, but its catalytic effects meant there remained a colonial war still to be fought.

* * *

the Netherlands during the Second World War are *Deel 11a: Nederlands-Indië I*, 2 vols. (Leiden, 1984); *Deel 11c: Nederlands-Indië III* (Leiden, 1986). See also *Deel 12: Epiloog*, vol. 2 (Leiden, 1988), 710–1106, on the 1945–1949 conflict and its outcome, and *Deel 14: Reacties*, vol. 2 ('s-Gravenhage, 1991), 723–1031, assessing contemporary public responses *to Deel 11a-c* and *Deel 12*.

[29] Kahin, *Nationalism and Revolution*, ch. 4; H.W. van den Doel, *Afscheid van Indië: De val van het Nederlandse imperium in Azië* (Amsterdam, 2000), ch. 2; 'The Japanese Occupation in Southeast Asia': special issue of the *Journal of Southeast Asian Studies*, 27:1 (1996); Ricklefs, *History of Modern Indonesia*, ch. 17; William H. Frederick, *Visions and Heat: The Making of the Indonesian Revolution* (Athens, OH, 1989), ch. 3; Legge, *Sukarno*, 156–60.

Dutch approaches to the East Indies during and after 1945 were coloured by their own wartime experiences in both metropole and colony. Those in the Indies endured Japanese captivity, while those back home weathered Nazi rule as best they could. Some Dutch joined anti-German resistance movements, but for most the occupation years meant a gradual shift from reluctant adaptation to passive resistance, and in many cases civil disobedience, as Nazi occupation wore on. Alongside persecuting the Netherlands' Jewish population, German occupying forces demanded compulsory labour and material contributions to support their war effort; moreover, they cracked down on political resistance and strikes with deportations to concentration camps and public executions. The last year of the war saw German tyranny reach new heights. Once Allied forces had liberated the southern part of the country in September 1944, the suffering in the north became even more severe. A railway workers' strike aiming to block the arrival of German military reinforcements led the Nazis to prevent food and fuel from reaching western regions, resulting in the 'hunger winter' of famine that killed at least 15,000 people.[30]

Reprisals against Dutch anti-Nazi protests targeted not just captured resistance fighters but increasingly civilians, whether or not they appeared to be directly involved in resistance activities. The most infamous incident occurred in the village of Putten in October 1944 in the wake of a resistance attack nearby on a Wehrmacht car that killed a German officer. The German response was immediate and severe: the next day Putten was sealed off and its entire population rounded up. The Wehrmacht executed eight people on the spot and shipped virtually all men aged between 18 and 50 to a German concentration camp; after evacuating women and children they burnt the village. Of the 660 men deported fewer than one in ten survived until the end of the war, leaving over 750 fatherless children and 300 widows.[31]

Putten became a symbol of the collective punishment of the innocent by the fascist occupiers after the remainder of the Netherlands was liberated in May 1945. Whether or not they were part of the minority to have risked their lives through joining an underground resistance movement, most Dutch had remained loyal to their leaders in exile and rejected nazification efforts while suffering extreme deprivation and often far worse. Although in reality the dividing line between 'accommodation' and 'collaboration' with the German enemy was often a blurry and indeterminate one, a mythologized 'nation of

---

[30] Dick van Galen Last, 'The Netherlands', in Bob Moore (ed.), *Resistance in Western Europe* (Oxford, 2000), 189–221; Gerhard Hirschfeld, *Nazi Rule and Dutch Collaboration: The Netherlands under German Occupation 1940–1945*, translated by Louise Willmott (Oxford, 1988), 53–4; Jennifer L. Foray, 'The "Clean Wehrmacht" in the German-Occupied Netherlands, 1940–5', *Journal of Contemporary History*, 45:4 (2010), 768–87.

[31] Madelon de Keizer, 'The Skeleton in the Closet: The Memory of Putten, 1/2 October 1944', *History and Memory*, 7:2 (1995), 70–3, and her extended treatment, *Putten: De razzia en de herinnering* (Amsterdam, 2001).

heroes' coalesced during and after 1945 in opposition to the disreputable few branded as having actively collaborated and who faced arrest and purges after Germany's defeat.[32]

Writing in 1928, Mohammad Hatta had mused that '[t]he Dutch people of the 20th century have always been free. Therefore, it is very difficult for them to imagine in what conditions their own ancestors in the 15th and 16th centuries or in the days of Napoleon lived when they groaned under foreign rule. If they could imagine this situation, they would understand the feelings of the Indonesian students.'[33] The trauma of 1940 to 1945 rendered his statement obsolete, and by the time of their liberation the Dutch indeed had developed a new perspective on what occupation by a foreign power entailed. Jennifer Foray's research has uncovered a vibrant wartime conversation about the East Indies provoked by their loss of sovereignty to the Nazis, one conducted not just among the London-based government-in-exile but encompassing many resistance groups at home from across the political spectrum. 'In the Indies, as in the Netherlands, there now rules an oppressor', Queen Wilhelmina stated in her 6 December 1942 radio address, just one of many occasions when the Dutch equated their own condition to that of the Indies under Japanese domination. The leftist underground newspaper *Vrij Nederland* went further, claiming that 'the period of occupation through which we ourselves are passing has given us a greater appreciation of the Indonesians' urge for freedom'.[34]

Proclamations of solidarity had distinct limits, however. 'If the resisters of the political left and center had imagined a gradual, controlled process of reform, undertaken with an eye toward autonomy and eventual independence, their colleagues on the right believed that the restoration of the Kingdom of the Netherlands was not only possible but preordained', Foray demonstrates.[35] To varying degrees, conservative resisters dismissed the idea of colonial reform altogether and sought a return to the pre-war colonial order. For them, liberating the East Indies meant reconquering the archipelago. Many envisioned colonial liberation as a strictly *military* one whereby the colonized were freed from Japanese domination, and most decidedly not a *political* liberation from the Netherlands.[36]

Most Dutch thus sought a double liberation from fascist German rule at home and fascist Japanese rule over the Indies; very few (mainly communists) alluded to a possible triple liberation whereby Indonesia was fully freed from the Netherlands as opposed to simply granted greater autonomy that fell far

---

[32] Pieter Lagrou, *The Legacy of Nazi Occupation: Patriotic Memory and National Recovery in Western Europe, 1945–1965* (Cambridge, 2000), ch. 3; Louis de Jong, *The Netherlands and Nazi Germany* (Cambridge, MA, 1990), 27–50; Hirschfeld, *Nazi Rule*, 312, 321.

[33] Hatta, 'Indonesia Free', 244.

[34] 'Towards a Netherlands Commonwealth', and '"The Future of Holland: Indonesia and Holland", from the Dutch Underground Paper *Vrij Nederland*, July 30, 1943', in *Netherlands Commonwealth and the Future*, 22, 27.

[35] Foray, *Visions of Empire*, 306.   [36] Ibid., 172, 189, 214, 239, 263, 276.

short of independence.[37] Once the first liberation from the Germans had been achieved by the Allies in May 1945, the Dutch hoped to play an active role in accomplishing the second in the Indies rather than the passive one they had been forced to play in Europe. Assuming the mantle of *liberators* of their colonial subjects rather than merely *liberated* by the Allies bestowed a highly appealing form of agency they had long been denied under Axis occupation, not to mention a chance to restore national pride after humiliating losses of metropolitan and colonial sovereignty. This sentiment did much to inspire over 20,000 Dutch men, many of whom had been involved in wartime resistance groups, to answer the call for volunteers for a Dutch army that would valiantly embark to free the Indies from Japanese clutches.[38]

Yet high hopes that the 'nation of heroes' victimized by the Germans could not just take the wheel in freeing the Indies but also be welcomed back as liberators by Indonesians were doomed to disappointment. When the Dutch tried to regain control over the Indies they could only do so with Allied support once Japan had surrendered. In the short term, this took the form of a British and Australian military occupation between 1945 and 1946; in the longer term, it required American consent and economic aid, a theme discussed further later in this chapter.[39] Moreover, upon their return they confronted a bold new political order in the form of Sukarno's Republic of Indonesia that had declared its independence from colonial rule and an armed insurgency committed to the revolution's success.[40] Self-styled liberators in their own eyes, the Dutch were rejected as occupiers by the Republic whose legitimacy they denied. Despite being confronted by plentiful evidence that few welcomed their return, many only acknowledged this fact reluctantly or belatedly – and sometimes not at all.

* * *

[37] Ibid., 175.

[38] Ibid., 223, 260; see also Van Galen Last, 'Netherlands', 210; Van Doorn, *Soldier and Social Change*, 174–5; Tessel Pollmann, 'The Unreal War: The Indonesian Revolution Through the Eyes of Dutch Novelists and Reporters', *Indonesia*, 69 (2000), 94–5; Stef Scagliola, 'The Silences and Myths of a "Dirty War": Coming to Terms with the Dutch-Indonesian Decolonisation War (1945–1949)', *European Review of History – Revue européenne d'Histoire*, 14:2 (2007), 239; Peter Romijn, 'Learning on "the Job": Dutch War Volunteers Entering the Indonesian War of Independence, 1945–46', *Journal of Genocide Research*, 14:3 (2012), 317–36.

[39] Christopher Bayly and Tim Harper, *Forgotten Wars: The End of Britain's Asian Empire* (London, 2007), 158–89; Bob Moore, in Thomas, Moore, and Butler, *Crises of Empire*, 302–11; Van den Doel, *Afscheid van Indië*, ch. 3; Richard McMillan, *The British Occupation of Indonesia 1945–1946: Britain, the Netherlands and the Indonesian Revolution* (London, 2005).

[40] Invaluable studies of the Indonesian revolution include Kahin, *Nationalism and Revolution*; Benedict R. O'G. Anderson, *Java in a Time of Revolution: Occupation and Resistance, 1944–1946* (Ithaca, 1972); Anthony Reid, *The Indonesian National Revolution 1945–1950* (Hawthorn, Victoria, 1974); Frederick, *Visions and Heat*.

If resisters and collaborators were imagined as irrevocably opposed groups in the Netherlands, in the Indies they merged into one. During and indeed well after 1945, the pro-colonial Dutch political establishment steadfastly refused to recognize the Republic and its declaration of independence as legal on the grounds that its leaders and supporters allegedly had been Japanese collaborators.[41] 'This Indonesian republic from the first was indubitably a Japanese creation', Gerbrandy thundered, its leaders and backers merely a 'small body of intellectuals, collaborationists, self-seekers, who would sell their souls to the devil'.[42] Men like Sukarno and Hatta were mere 'quislings', 'lickspittles', and 'demagogues', their government an inept puppet one installed by the Japanese and lacking genuine popular support.[43] In a Europe then in the midst of war crimes trials, the ignoble day of the collaborator was said to have come and gone in the empire as well as at home. Such was the dominant line, relentlessly toed by the Dutch in the Indies and on the international stage. Now was the time to reclaim the Indies and with them an integral aspect of the nation's pride, prestige, power, and economic potential.

Recapturing control over the archipelago was a widely-shared national imperative deemed critical for reconstruction and the search for power and influence in the post-war global order. Such was the Indies' pre-war economic importance to the Netherlands that the well-known saying '*Indië verloren, rampspoed geboren*' – translated as 'Indies lost, misfortune born' or 'Indies lost, disastrous cost' – remained as fundamental to Dutch thinking in the mid-late 1940s as when used as the title of a pamphlet in 1914.[44] Responsible for approximately one-sixth of the Netherlands' national income during late 1930s, the Indies grew even more important to those contemplating a war-ravaged economy. Recovery at home and the desperate need for foreign exchange earnings tied hopes for future Dutch prosperity to Southeast Asia and its wealth of natural resources as never before, and political investments were higher still. Possessing the East Indies made the Netherlands a great power on the world stage; without them, proponents of empire continually maintained, it was merely a small, second-tier European nation whose international status was akin to Denmark's.[45] If imperial enthusiasts never tired of claiming that the

---

[41] Ironically, as Foray notes, Dutch collaborators with the Nazis had been 'especially quick to proclaim the enduring nature of these imperial ties'; *Visions of Empire*, 90.

[42] Gerbrandy, *Indonesia*, 68, 55.

[43] Ibid., 53, 79, 136; McMahon, *Colonialism and Cold War*, 37, 91; Van Doorn, *Soldier and Social Change*, 115–16, 121; Legge, *Sukarno*, ch. 7.

[44] C.G.S. Sandberg, *Indië verloren, rampspoed geboren* ('s Gravenhage, 1914), as discussed by Foray, *Visions of Empire*, 34–5, who also notes that Sandberg later belonged to the Dutch Nazi Party, 104–6.

[45] Pierre van der Eng, 'Marshall Aid as a Catalyst in the Decolonization of Indonesia, 1947–49', *Journal of Southeast Asian Studies*, 19:2 (1988), 336; McMahon, *Colonialism and Cold War*, 39–40; Hendrik Spruyt, *Ending Empire: Contested Sovereignty and Territorial Partition* (Ithaca, 2005), ch. 5; Marc Frey, 'Dutch Elites and Decolonization', in Jost Dülffer and Marc Frey (eds.), *Elites and Decolonization in the Twentieth Century* (Basingstoke, 2011), 57–8.

Netherlands had 'made the Indies', they also never forgot that the Indies made the Netherlands.

This belief accounted for the high level of Dutch support for retaining the Indies throughout the late 1940s among the political classes as well as the wider population, despite the lack of consensus and evidence of widespread general ignorance about the Dutch empire apparent in wartime discussions. The return of peace in Europe brought with it a Dutch political system that produced a recalcitrant state policy pitted against decolonization or even compromise. The predominant Catholic People's Party (KVP) worked alongside other centre-right, liberal, and Protestant parties in spearheading a hard-line approach to the new, allegedly illegitimate Republic that rejected negotiations, favouring the use of force against the nationalist insurgency and Indonesian revolution. In the immediate post-war years, no single Dutch political party was strong enough to win a national election with a clear majority, with the result being a series of coalition governments in which pro-Indies contingents pulled considerable weight. Consensus was the order of the day as leaders tried to prevent fragile multi-party coalitions from capsizing over disagreements about the Indies, pushing dissenting voices advocating negotiation and compromise to the margins and consolidating an inflexible stance determined by colonial diehards. Dutch public opinion, although not unanimous, by and large endorsed the stance of political elites who prioritized maintaining the Indies and fighting the Republic. Over the course of the Netherlands' ultimately futile attempt to quell the anti-colonial insurgency, most of the public (as well as the media) backed the deployment of Dutch troops in the archipelago to combat the violence that escalated upon Japan's surrender and the arrival of Allied forces.[46]

Between 1945 and 1949, over 150,000 soldiers fought on the Netherlands' behalf in Southeast Asia.[47] The colonial army (KNIL) contributed over 30,000 men to the forces pitted against the Indonesian republican army, while more than 120,000 embarked from the Netherlands. The latter included professional soldiers and volunteers, but the overwhelming majority – at least 95,000 – were conscripts.[48] Officially, they did not travel to the Indies to take part in 'war', for Dutch authorities refused to label it as such. Instead, they came head to head with the Republic's forces in campaigns to 'pacify' the Indies and protect the

---

[46] Spruyt, *Ending Empire*, ch. 5; Frey, 'Dutch Elites', 58–61; Van Doorn, *Soldier and Social Change*, 123; Pollmann, 'Unreal War', 102; J.J.P. de Jong, *Diplomatie of strijd: Een analyse van het Nederlands beleid tegenover de Indonesische Revolutie 1945–1947* (Amsterdam, 1988).

[47] See Bart Luttikhuis and A. Dirk Moses (eds.), *Colonial Counterinsurgency and Mass Violence: The Dutch Empire in Indonesia* (London, 2014), alongside the special issue of *Journal of Genocide Research*, 14:3–4 (2012), which contains overlapping content.

[48] Scagliola, 'Silences and Myths', 239, 259.

innocent local population from terrorist onslaught as part of 'a mission of mercy'.[49] Among the Dutch, the Indonesian revolution became subject to similar portrayals as nationalism – namely, as 'an affair of an extremist elite that was manipulating the masses through terrorism and propaganda' in which 'Dutch troops were not suppressing a freedom struggle but eliminating outlaws', as Petra Groen and Stef Scagliola phrased it.[50] In writing what became definitive studies of the conflict, Jacques van Doorn and Willem Hendrix recalled their own experiences as conscripts in Java when assessing official justifications that formed part of their indoctrination:

The Japanese occupation and its consequences – lawlessness, terror, poverty, hunger – destroyed the foundations and disintegrated the social order. This situation did not end with the Japanese surrender. Too many irresponsible elements . . . took advantage of the disorder and the lasting defencelessness of their own people . . . Remember that you are bearers of justice and security to a population that has long been subjected to terror and oppression.[51]

Dutch forces responded to the 'terror and oppression' they found after 1945 by unleashing their own – all in the name of the suffering 'poor peasant' supposedly against to the revolution. One of the earliest and most notorious 'pacification' exercises took place in South Sulawesi (formerly known as the Celebes) between late 1946 and early 1947. To break intense republican resistance in the region, Captain Raymond 'Turk' Westerling led special KNIL forces in a counterinsurgency campaign to quash the guerrilla movement. The search for 'terrorists' took him and his soldiers into a succession of villages suspected of harbouring the enemy, where they demanded that offenders be handed over. When the inhabitants refused to comply and denied knowledge of involvement, they responded by rounding up the villagers, separating the men, and shooting those whom intelligence activities purportedly 'proved' were active in the insurgency. Westerling's brutal methods resulted in a highly disputed death toll: by his own reckoning under 600 'terrorists' were killed, with the total casualties over three months ranging between 3,000 and 4,000; the Republic of Indonesia later claimed over 40,000 had perished, the majority being innocent civilians.[52]

---

[49] Romijn, 'Learning on "the Job"'; Pollmann, 'Unreal War', 95.
[50] Petra M.H. Groen, 'Militant Response: The Dutch Use of Military Force and the Decolonization of the Dutch East Indies, 1945–50', *Journal of Imperial and Commonwealth History*, 21:3 (1993), 36; Scagliola, 'Silences and Myths', 242.
[51] Van Doorn, *Soldier and Social Change*, 118. See J.A.A. van Doorn and W.J. Hendrix, *Ontsporing van geweld: Over het Nederlands/Indisch/Indonesisch conflict* (Rotterdam, 1970), especially chs. 3 and 4, for their fullest treatment.
[52] Raymond ('Turk') Westerling, *Challenge to Terror* (London, 1952), 115–17; 'Indonesian Ministry of Information', in *Illustrations of the Revolution 1945–1950: From a Unitary State to a Unitary State* (Djakarta, 1954), n.p.

Counterinsurgency in South Sulawesi set the tone for Dutch military tactics and their rationalization for the rest of the war, however the Netherlands chose to call it. Two military offensives undertaken in July–August 1947 and December 1948 were misleadingly labelled the first and second 'police actions', although Van Doorn and Hendrix rightly suggest that Westerling's previous campaign readily merits the inglorious distinction of counting as the first of many more than three.[53] Routine Dutch military behaviour relied upon brutal interrogation methods via torturing insurgents taken prisoner as well as civilians whose involvement was suspected but never proven; raiding villages at dawn in search of 'terrorists' and those accused of assisting them, then conducting random executions in the effort to intimidate locals into cooperating; and pillaging and burning entire 'suspect' villages in reprisal for attacks on Dutch forces.[54] Abu Hanifah, a medical doctor who became a leader of republican forces in Java, reflected that 'Westerling succeeded by using the most inhuman and brutal means. He burned down villages, he let whole districts be mowed down by his gunners. Killing, raping, and burning with a brutality only surpassed by the Japanese and the Germans was very common.'[55]

Ruthless violence first associated with Westerling was soon matched by other Dutch forces, and a host of later local atrocities – euphemistically referred to as 'excesses' – perpetrated in Java and elsewhere came to stand alongside South Sulawesi in the deadly history of Indonesia's decolonization struggle.[56] The massacre of 430 villagers in Rawagede in West Java on 9 December 1947 became the most notorious to the extent that it was later termed the 'Dutch My Lai', read through the prism of America's war in Vietnam starting in the late 1960s.[57] As Chapter 9 revisits, this counted among the numerous episodes that later resurfaced at moments when the Dutch, reluctantly for the most part, confronted unresolved aspects of their decolonization history.

If it was contentious to liken Rawagede to My Lai in the Netherlands even after decades had elapsed, the notion that it might qualify as an 'Indonesian

---

[53] Van Doorn and Hendrix, *Ontsporing van geweld*, 63–4; Van den Doel, *Afscheid van Indië*, 162–3.

[54] Van Doorn and Hendrix, *Ontsporing van geweld*, chs. 3 and 4; Van Doorn, *Soldier and Social Change*, 123, 137, 139, 156–7, 161–9; Jacques van Doorn and Willem J. Hendrix, *The Process of Decolonisation 1945–1975: The Military Experience in Comparative Perspective* (Rotterdam, 1987), 18, 23, 33–4.

[55] Abu Hanifah, *Tales of a Revolution* (Sydney, 1972), 153–4.

[56] *Nota: Betreffende het archievonderzoek naar gegevens omtrent excessen in Indonesië begaan door nederlandse militairen in de periode 1945–1950: Aan de Heer Voorzitter van de Tweede Kamer der Staten-Generaal, Zitting 1968–1969-10 008 3 (2)* ('s-Gravenhage, 1969) especially Bijlage 2, 7–19, Bijlage 5, 1–58; De Jong, *Koninkrijk, Deel 12: Epiloog*, vol. 2, 1011–60.

[57] Rawagedeh is an alternative spelling found in some sources. The precise death toll at Rawagehe was long disputed, with the Netherlands officially estimating it to be 150 while victims' advocates placed it at 430. Anne Barrowclough, 'Dutch Offer Formal Apology to the Widows of Rawagede', *The Times* (London), 10 December 2011.

Putten' comes uncomfortably much closer to home. To suggest that for every Putten to suffer at the hands of the Nazis in the occupied Netherlands there were many Rawagedes as the Dutch tried to regain military control over the Indies invites controversy, despite how often similar broader comparisons have been made by those who witnessed the Indonesian revolution firsthand. Indonesians like Abu Hanifah invoked them on more than one occasion. 'I thought you had learned a little from the hard times suffered during the Nazi regime and that you could understand that we also want to be free and independent', he recalled telling the Dutch officer who interrogated him while in detention in 1948.[58] Sukarno felt similarly, unequivocally stating late in 1945 that 'Indonesians will never understand why it is, for instance, wrong for the Germans to rule Holland if it is right for the Dutch to rule Indonesia. In either case the right to rule rests on pure force and not on the sanction of the populations.'[59]

For their part, most Dutch military personnel unsurprisingly distanced themselves from such analogies. '[T]he deployment of guerrilla tactics by the Indonesians has allowed the Dutch to focus on the use of "foul methods" by their enemies and deny full public acknowledgement of themselves as perpetrators of violence', Scagliola concludes.[60] Captain Westerling certainly did in his account of his activities in South Sulawesi, unapologetically describing summary executions of alleged 'terrorists' without trial amidst a host of other standard procedures. Dismissing widespread allegations concerning his conduct, he remained proud of acting on behalf of 'the little people'; winning so much 'affection of the simple Indonesians' was 'testimony to the popularity of my methods'. When his mission had been accomplished, 'thousands of the local inhabitants' came

to say goodbye and to thank me for what I had done for them – I had put an end to bloodshed by punishing the culprits without at the same time sacrificing the innocent. I had never bombed a village nor had I ever set fire to the huts of peaceful people. I had had criminals executed, but I had no undeserved or unnecessary deaths on my conscience.[61]

That said, some Dutch forces not only condemned counterinsurgency measures in Southeast Asia but also considered them on par with Nazi atrocities so recently perpetrated in the Netherlands. Among themselves, they spoke of 'nazi-methods' of interrogating prisoners and suspects; Van Doorn and Hendrix stressed how 'on the troop-transport ships going home' the systematic forms of abuse and torture inflicted 'were the subject of conversation and argument often ending in the unanimous comment that there was no need to

---

[58] Hanifah, *Tales*, 266. See also Gouda and Zaalberg, *American Visions*, 154, 231.
[59] McMahon, *Colonialism and Cold War*, 95.
[60] Scagliola, 'Silences and Myths', 241; Pollmann, 'Unreal War', 98–100.
[61] Westerling, *Challenge to Terror*, 71–2, 115.

reproach the Jerries'. A Dutch officer subsequently reflected that it was 'ironical that those who, like myself, had had personal experience of German interrogation methods and were determined that such a thing should never occur again ... were later, in Indonesia, to apply the same methods'.[62]

Not all would-be liberators of the Indies became perpetrators, no matter how self-critical or reluctant. But those who refused could pay a high price, as three Dutch marines who declined to take part in burning the village of Pakisadji in August 1947 learned. Considering this an unwarranted form of reprisal, they received lengthy prison sentences for not following orders.[63] Another case that generated protracted notoriety was that of Johan Cornelis (better known as 'Poncke') Princen, imprisoned by the Nazis during the war and later conscripted for service in the Indies against his will. He deserted the Dutch army in 1948 and joined the republican guerrilla forces, remaining in Indonesia after independence; back in the Netherlands, many continued to brand him a traitor long after the war's end.[64] It took until 1994 for him to be granted official permission to revisit the land of his birth, a stay that took place in the face of ongoing protests by veterans groups.

By 1949, an estimated 5,000 Dutch troops and well over 100,000 Indonesians had died.[65] The Dutch could claim considerable military success against their opponents, but their position had continually eroded in diplomatic terms. From 1946 on, they combined counterinsurgency campaigns against the Republic of Indonesia's army with a concerted effort to cripple it politically by pushing for the creation of a Netherlands-Indonesian Union symbolically presided over by the Dutch crown. Within this proposed Union, the Republic led by Sukarno and Hatta would be just one of many 'United States of Indonesia' (USI).[66] Conceiving of a future in which 'Indonesia' did not constitute a unitary state but rather a fragmented multitude of separate political entities that would remain soldered to the Netherlands formed a logical extension of conventional Dutch denials that a singular 'Indonesia' could ever grow

---

[62] Van Doorn, *Soldier and Social Change*, 157, 163, 162. As Maarten Kuitenbrouwer notes in 'The Never-Ending Debt of Honour: The Dutch in the Post-Colonial World', *Itinerario*, 20:2 (1996), 22, 'in private, the Roman Catholic Colonial Secretary E.M.J.A. Sassen admitted the use of "*Gestapo* methods"'. This is discussed in De Jong, *Koninkrijk, Deel 12*, 1009.

[63] Van Doorn, *Soldier and Social Change*, 137; Van Doorn and Hendrix, *Ontsporing van geweld*, 176; *Nota: Betreffende het archievonderzoek naar gegevens omtrent excessen in Indonesië*, Bijlage 5, 15, and Bijlage 12, 3–5.

[64] Poncke Princen, *Een kwestie van kiezen: Zijn levensverhaal opgetekend door Joyce van Fenema* ('s-Gravenhage, 1995); Kuitenbrouwer, 'Never-Ending Debt', 34.

[65] Kuitenbrouwer, 'Never-Ending Debt', 22.

[66] Marc Frey, 'The Indonesian Revolution and the Fall of the Dutch Empire: Actors, Factors, and Strategies', in Marc Frey, Ronald Pruessen, and Tan Tai Yong (eds.), *The Transformation of Southeast Asia: International Perspectives on Decolonization* (New York, 2003), 90–1, 95–6; Gouda and Zaalberg, *American Visions*, 231–2; Ricklefs, *History of Modern Indonesia*, 260–70; Reid, *Indonesian National Revolution*, 161–5; Moore, in Thomas, Moore, and Butler, *Crises of Empire*, 320, 326–34.

out of a plural 'Indies' as dictated by colonialism. Unable to countenance the legitimacy of an independent Republic of Indonesia on its own, the Netherlands struggled to curb its influence by binding it together with other federal states that emerged outside republican strongholds in Java and Sumatra – states that owed their very existence to Dutch sponsorship and military backing. Within this projected federal framework, the Republic thus would be severely circumscribed through forced association with Dutch-created puppet states governed by cooperative aristocrats who could be relied upon to safeguard the Netherlands' political and economic interests.

Such a policy aspiration amounted to a blatant effort to 'divide and rule' in reality while outwardly claiming sympathy with Indonesian aspirations for autonomy. The Netherlands' proposals predictably generated little enthusiasm among republican leaders, and several agreements rapidly fell apart in an atmosphere pervaded by increasing mistrust. The tide finally turned sharply in the Republic's favour in 1948, largely due to America's change of heart in line with the escalation of the global Cold War. The United States' position ultimately proved decisive as policymakers who previously had considered Dutch sovereignty as the best defence against the spread of communism thought differently of the Republic once its forces crushed a communist uprising at Madiun, thereby winning invaluable ideological credibility with the Truman administration. The Netherlands had already sacrificed much of their international reputation at the United Nations thanks to a transparently self-interested and obstructionist stance in Indonesia, but with the loss of US support its approach became completely untenable. While still valuing the Netherlands as a Western European ally and crucial to the post-war European Recovery Program, the United States concluded that the attempt to perpetuate colonial rule in Indonesia would do far more harm than good. In embarking on the second 'police action' in December 1948 the Netherlands went a step too far, forfeiting any remaining American goodwill and finding Marshall Plan aid earmarked for Indonesia (which had been necessary to sustain the counter-insurgency campaign) cut off.[67]

Fearing that desperately-needed Marshall aid for the Netherlands at home alongside inclusion in NATO might also be at risk and knowing full well that continuing a military campaign in Southeast Asia would be impossible without US financial and diplomatic backing, the Dutch finally consented to the Round Table conference that brought about a transfer of power on 27 December 1949. But the form of 'independence' this granted still fell considerably short of republican aspirations, for the Republic declared in August 1945 was enveloped within a new 'Republic of the United States of Indonesia' (RUSI) – a

---

[67] Van der Eng, 'Marshall Aid'; Gouda and Zaalberg, *American Visions*, 195–6, 300–2; Hong Lee Oey, *War and Diplomacy in Indonesia, 1945–50* (North Queensland, 1981), chs. 10–12.

construct that also encompassed the artificially-created Dutch-sponsored states. What prevailed at the end of 1949 was decolonization along Dutch lines, with RUSI forming a union with the Netherlands. Significantly, moreover, the Dutch did not consent to including West New Guinea (Irian Jaya) in the settlement in the face of republican insistence that the territory was rightfully part of Indonesia.

* * *

Like the federalism that underpinned it, RUSI stood on shaky ground from the outset and its life span proved extremely short. It was effectively stillborn from the start, a patently artificial entity designed to favour ongoing Dutch interests and scarred by Dutch actions both in the run-up to independence and in its immediate aftermath. In January 1950, Captain Westerling led 800 recently-demobilized KNIL troops in a coup attempting to overthrow Sukarno's new government, acting independently but with much high-level Dutch support suspected behind the scenes. Westerling failed, but the deplorable episode served as further evidence of a lack of good faith on the part of the Netherlands. The Westerling debacle acted as an additional spur to the unionist movement within most of the federal states, where the Republic enjoyed much mass enthusiasm that increasingly infiltrated the elites whose allegiance the Dutch had so carefully cultivated. The majority dissolved themselves and merged with the Republic, forming a new political entity that officially came into being on 17 August 1950. In the astute assessment of George McTurnan Kahin:

The very name of the new state – Republic of Indonesia – symbolized a return to the Unitarian pattern of the old Republic of Indonesia and a triumph of the nationalism which it represented. More than anything else the change from the federal R.U.S.I. to the new unitarian Republic represented the desire of the population to shake off the legacy of Dutch colonial rule. For despite the full sovereignty enjoyed by the R.U.S.I., the preponderant majority of the Indonesian population saw its federal structure as Dutch-imposed and a relic of colonialism. For them the liquidation of federalism meant the final triumph of the Republic of Indonesia proclaimed in August, 1945.[68]

Such that it was, opposition to becoming part of a unitary state came primarily from East Indonesia. A secessionist movement spearheaded by KNIL troops still loyal to the Netherlands and centred on the island of Ambon, whose substantial Christian population had long provided many recruits for the colonial army, declared independence as the Republic of the South Moluccas (*Republik Maluku Selatan*, or RMS) in April 1950. Republican forces defeated the rebellion by November, although a guerrilla struggle continued to fester in the coming years. The RMS's aspirations and failure

[68] Kahin, *Nationalism and Revolution*, 465–6.

led over 12,000 KNIL troops and their families to be resettled in the Netherlands, a theme Chapter 7 considers further. The Moluccan (mainly Ambonese) presence counted among the many ways Indonesia remained unfinished business within the metropole well beyond the incomplete decolonization of 1949.

If the RMS's fate and the plight of its adherents aroused considerable sympathy in the Netherlands, West New Guinea – called West Irian or Irian Jaya by Indonesians – remained another unresolved issue that attracted even more support. Its importance for the Dutch grew out of all proportion to its tangible worth. Within a Netherlands where only one-fifth of the population fully supported the 1949 settlement (and where an opinion poll taken in May 1950 ranked Westerling as the seventh most admired man in the nation), holding on to West New Guinea became a symbolic means of maintaining at least some degree of national grandeur – a sign that the Netherlands had *not* in fact sunk to the rank of Denmark with the loss of everywhere else in the Indonesian archipelago.[69] 'For many Dutch people, who had grown grey in the colonial service, it was very hard to accept the loss of Indonesia', Mohammad Hatta reflected in 1961:

Involved was a loss both of prestige and of what had long been called 'the cork supporting the welfare of the Netherlands.' The financial loss could be offset by an economic agreement favoring Dutch interests in Indonesia. But the loss of prestige? Memories of former 'colonial glory' could be kept alive only by retaining some part of the former Netherlands Indies under Dutch control. Hence the notion of excluding West Irian from the transfer of sovereignty.[70]

The zeal for retaining West New Guinea was never restricted solely to Dutch who had lived *in* Indonesia to whom Hatta alluded; it also abounded among colonial traditionalists who continued to live *by* the idea of the Dutch Indies, Pieter Gerbrandy prominent among them. After the Netherlands' liberation from German occupation, Gerbrandy never again enjoyed a level of public prominence comparable to his years as prime minister in the wartime government-in-exile. Yet he remained politically influential throughout the late 1940s as chairman of the pro-colonialist group *Handhaving Rijkseenheid*, a committee dedicated to the 'Preservation of the Unity of the Realm' – a group that dissolved early in 1950 upon its failure to achieve its objective of holding on to the East Indies. The *Stichting Rijksbehoud* (Foundation for the Preservation of the Realm) sprang up in its place shortly afterwards and also counted Gerbrandy on its executive council, along with 'almost all the prominent diehard conservatives in Holland', in the words of Arend Lijphart. Its stated

---

[69] Hans Meijer, 'Images of Indonesia in the Dutch Press 1950–1962', *Itinerario*, 17:2 (1993), 55, 60; Kuitenbrouwer, 'Never-Ending Debt', 22.

[70] Mohammad Hatta, 'Colonialism and the Danger of War', *Asian Survey*, 1:9 (1961), 12–13.

priorities focused on '[m]aintaining and defending that which is still left of the damaged Kingdom' along with '[p]romoting with vigor the prosperity of New Guinea and promoting the settlement there by Dutchmen from the Netherlands and Indonesia, and securing the safety of this territory against the clutches of Communism which are also extended toward it'.[71] The publication of *Indonesia* in 1950 was thus not Gerbrandy's last word on the subject, and until his death in 1961 he divided his time between lending support to the campaign for the breakaway Republic of the South Moluccas and what soon proved to be an equally lost cause: insisting on keeping West New Guinea Dutch.[72]

For Gerbrandy and other like-minded Dutch, it remained a matter of supreme importance that 'we have not been driven entirely from Far Eastern waters'.[73] To those contemplating West New Guinea through dispassionate eyes, the sparsely-populated, underdeveloped, and isolated territory's economic and strategic attractions were dubious at best and negligible at worst. In the event, promises of valuable raw materials as well as trade and investment opportunities remained castles in the air in the realm of Dutch fantasy. Arend Lijphart's analysis published in 1966 has stood the test of time in its resounding dismissal of West New Guinea's objective value in favour of its immense subjective and 'psychological' importance in the 1950s, not just for its most vocal right-wing champions but most politicians, much of the press aside from papers of the far left, and large and diverse segments of the Dutch public. Veterans who so recently had fought in Indonesia, for whom the trauma of a lost war was somewhat tempered by salvaging something of the Dutch East Indies from the wreckage of 1949; Dutch churches which saw West New Guinea as a promising field for new overseas mission work; other groups excited by its potential as a land ripe for colonization by white settlers as well as by Indisch Dutch citizens wanting to leave the newly-independent Republic: all believed the territory still offered vast scope for Dutch energies, abilities, and paternalistic good intentions.[74] The Dutch could still fulfil a moral, 'national duty' and bring Christianity and civilization to 'benefit the backward peoples' in a 'primitive' land where 'cannibalism is still practiced in parts' and 'disease is

---

[71] Arend Lijphart, *The Trauma of Decolonization: The Dutch and West New Guinea* (New Haven, 1966), 100, 118, 137.

[72] P.S. Gerbrandy, *Ambon en de A.R. Partij: De vrijheidsstrijd van de Republiek der Zuid-Molukken* (Kampen, 1956). For further context, see Cees Fasseur, *Eigen Meester, Niemands Knecht: Het leven van Pieter Sjoerds Gerbrandy, Minister-president van Nederland in de Tweede Wereldoorlog* (Amsterdam, 2014), ch. 27; see also chs. 14 and 25 on Indonesia.

[73] Gerbrandy, *Indonesia*, 184.

[74] For Lijphart's conclusions, see *Trauma of Decolonization*, 285–91; see also Meijer, 'Images of Indonesia'; Anderson, *Imagined Communities*, 176–8. Vincent Kuitenbrouwer offers new perspectives in 'Beyond the "Trauma of Decolonization": Dutch Cultural Diplomacy during the West New Guinea Question (1950–62)', *Journal of Imperial and Commonwealth History* (in press).

epidemic', Gerbrandy reminded his readers. 'The leadership of a white people is essential' in West New Guinea, where 'the Netherlands can still show something of the old spirit of enterprise which its people revealed in the past'.[75] Nor was he alone in his assessment. As a long-standing Dutch foreign secretary commented in hindsight, 'New Guinea was marginal to our interests, but central to our principles.'[76]

The high price the Netherlands paid for insisting on staying became increasingly clear in the late 1950s. Since Indonesia's independence, West New Guinea remained the biggest thorn in the side of postcolonial relations that poisoned virtually all spheres of interaction between former colonizers and the formerly colonized. The years 1956 and 1957 marked new lows with the Republic of Indonesia unilaterally abrogating the Union with the Netherlands agreed in 1949, expelling remaining Dutch nationals (a move that brought many more Indisch Dutch 'repatriates' to resettle in the Netherlands, as Chapter 6 explores), confiscating Dutch property, and nationalizing Dutch firms. In 1960, Indonesia severed diplomatic relations altogether. With intransigence over West New Guinea proving politically and economically counterproductive, domestic attitudes began to shift away from the previous commitment to standing firm long manifest among much of the Dutch press and public. The shift to a military confrontation in 1960 proved decisive, with the deployment of Dutch troops back in the region raising the question of whether conscripts would again be called upon to risk their lives as had been the case until 1949. While many in the Netherlands remained resentful over the loss of Indonesia and were unwavering in their hatred of figures like Sukarno, relatively few believed that keeping West New Guinea was worth another war. American pressure to end the confrontation achieved the rest, and an agreement was finally reached in September 1962 to pass the contested territory first to the United Nations and ultimately to Indonesian control in 1963.[77] Although bad blood remained, trade and diplomacy were free to attempt a hard road to renewal.

* * *

As the Netherlands bid a long and reluctant goodbye to its empire in Southeast Asia between 1949 and 1962, the nation contracted until its geographical reach was exclusively transatlantic. Post-war developments in the Dutch West Indies differed radically from those which led to a bitter decolonization history in Indonesia. The colonial Caribbean territories consisting of Suriname on the

---

[75] Gerbrandy, *Indonesia*, 184–8.
[76] J.M.A.H. Luns, cited in Kuitenbrouwer, 'Never-Ending Debt', 23.
[77] Hatta, 'Colonialism and the Danger of War', 13; Lijphart, *Trauma of Decolonization*, 287–8; Moore, in Thomas, Moore, and Butler, *Crises of Empire*, 353–8; Meijer, 'Images of Indonesia', 67–8.

South American mainland plus the six Antillean islands of Curaçao, Aruba, Bonaire, St Eustasius, St Maarten, and Saba had a combined total population of just under 250,000 in 1940. Compared to Indonesia's 70 million, the West Indies were a demographically insignificant part of the Dutch empire that lacked compensating economic or geopolitical advantages. Suriname's heyday as a plantation economy producing mainly sugar and coffee was a distant memory by the 1940s, but its ethnically diverse population still bore the imprint of a colonial order that had long depended upon African slaves and later upon importing Indian and Javanese indentured workers once slavery was abolished in the 1860s. Suriname and the Antilles remained underdeveloped economic backwaters centred on small-scale farming, the bauxite industry, and oil refineries but suffering from high unemployment and a chronic lack of social and economic opportunity. Until the 1940s there were few signs of nationalism like that which had already proliferated in Indonesia for well over a generation, but the Second World War did much to raise political awareness. Queen Wilhelmina's 6 December 1942 radio address gesturing towards a future with 'full partnership in government on the basis of equality' and greater local autonomy received an enthusiastic reception in the West Indies, spurring political mobilization and the formation of new political parties. In Suriname, parties developed along ethnic and class lines, with some representing the interests of Afro-Surinamese (Creole) communities and others catering to Indo-Surinamese of Javanese or Indian descent.[78]

While many throughout the West Indies looked forward to a greater degree of self-rule (epitomized by the appeal of being *baas in eigen huis*, or 'boss in your own home'), they stopped well short of demanding full political independence.[79] The year 1954 saw the passing of a new constitutional framework, the *Statuut* or Charter of the Kingdom of the Netherlands, which made the Netherlands, Suriname, and the Netherlands Antilles equal partners with full internal self-government and a common nationality (one similar to that granted to Britain's colonial and Commonwealth subjects in the 1948 British Nationality Act). Given that the European part enjoyed disproportionate wealth, power, and influence within the tripartite Kingdom and maintained control over foreign relations, defence, and the judiciary, true 'equality' was based more on illusion than fact. Nonetheless, the 1954 Charter generated a favourable international response that the Netherlands sorely needed in the wake of the intense global criticism over the recent (and still ongoing) Indonesian crisis, and it correspondingly became promoted as a sign that the traditional colonial relationship had been superseded by a mutually-approved

---

[78] Edward Dew, *The Difficult Flowering of Surinam: Ethnicity and Politics in a Plural Society* (The Hague, 1978); Moore, in Thomas, Moore, and Butler, *Crises of Empire*, ch. 15.

[79] Moore, in Thomas, Moore, and Butler, *Crises of Empire*, 366.

modern arrangement. Moreover, it also found widespread acceptance within Suriname and the Antilles.[80]

Dutch, still nursing the nation's wounds after Indonesian independence and keen on 'maintaining and defending that which is still left of the damaged Kingdom', to reiterate the Foundation for the Preservation of the Realm's stated aspiration, would have found as much acceptance of their aims as they could possibly have wished for in the West Indies – had only they cared to look. Even from within the redoubt of staunchly patriotic colonial organizations, however, few Dutch bothered to redirect their attention from West New Guinea or the South Moluccas to find solace across the Atlantic.[81] The new political framework inaugurated in 1954 failed to make up for losing the sparkling East Indies 'belt of emeralds', as the saying went, and the Caribbean territories became no more alluring than before. Neither Dutch elites nor the press nor the public ever managed to muster significant interest in Suriname or the Antilles, and for the better part of the next twenty years the Charter remained a largely unchallenged status quo at home and in the Caribbean alike.

The political relationship between the Dutch and the West Indies only entered a new phase between the late 1960s and the mid-1970s. The year 1969 saw civil disturbances and strikes in Suriname and Curaçao, with Dutch military forces called in to restore calm in the latter. Coming at the end of a decade that marked the high point of European decolonization, the unrest of 1969 also coincided with intense debates in the Netherlands over the question of so-called military 'excesses' in Indonesia in the late 1940s, making the deployment of Dutch marines to Curaçao a highly sensitive issue that gave rise to unwelcome historical analogies.[82] Thereafter, more and more Dutch came to view residual bonds rooted in colonialism, even once they had taken a progressive turn with the 1954 Charter, as both outmoded and placing the Netherlands at risk of provoking international condemnation for engaging in colonialist behaviour reminiscent of an earlier and still-contentious era. The tripartite Kingdom of the Netherlands instituted by the Charter, it was widely felt, should be considered a transitional phase between colonialism and full independence, not a permanent arrangement.

In 1973 a newly-elected, left-leaning Dutch coalition government presided over by Prime Minister Joop den Uyl was eager to encourage independence in the West Indies. Research by Gert Oostindie, Inge Klinkers, and others persuasively argues that a main reason why increasing numbers of Dutch favoured

---

[80] Gert Oostindie and Inge Klinkers, *Decolonising the Caribbean: Dutch Policies in a Comparative Perspective* (Amsterdam, 2003), ch. 5. This book is an abridged translation of the authors' three-volume *Knellende Koninkrijksbanden: Het Nederlandse dekolonisatiebeleid in de Caraïben, 1940–2000* (Amsterdam, 2001), which provides an invaluable in-depth treatment; see volume 1 (*Deel 1*) on the years between 1940 and 1954.

[81] Oostindie and Klinkers, *Decolonising the Caribbean*, 64.   [82] Ibid., 96–9.

Caribbean independence rather than a continuation of the terms agreed in 1954 was the mounting anxiety about West Indian (particularly Afro-Surinamese) settlement in Dutch cities and towns in the 1960s and early 1970s.[83] Like their counterparts from other colonies and ex-colonies entering Britain and other European nations thanks to citizenship rights, growing numbers of Surinamese took advantage of their Dutch nationality to live and work in the European Netherlands, a topic to which Chapter 7 returns. Dutch who were concerned about the ramifications of a 'mass exodus' towards metropolitan shores increasingly looked to complete decolonization as a means of stemming an unwanted flow. Severing ties with Suriname and the Antilles seemed to offer a ready solution to what many denigrated as the 'problem of immigration' but which more accurately could be described as racially-motivated concerns about the rights of fellow citizens to free internal migration within the kingdom.

Yet in the West Indies the response to Dutch initiatives intended to end in decolonization was tepid and divided. When Suriname's leader Henck Arron suddenly called for independence by the end of 1975 the Dutch government hastened to move the process forward despite a resounding lack of consensus within Suriname itself. No referendum on independence was ever conducted, but Creole opinion was said to be evenly divided on the possible benefits of sovereignty while the vast majority of the Javanese and Hindustani communities were firmly against change, fearing Creole domination if the Dutch ceased to safeguard their rights.[84] Vocal though it was, opposition was of no avail, with Suriname gaining independence at the end of November 1975. To secure what had become a cross-party Dutch policy aim in the face of widespread reluctance across the Atlantic, the Netherlands agreed to support Suriname in the form of substantial development aid as well as by permitting unrestricted immigration to continue over a five-year transition period. In light of Dutch insistence, however, Hans Ramsoedh's description of Suriname's decolonization as 'forced independence' is apt.[85]

In stark contrast to Indonesia's protracted fight for sovereignty in the face of long-term Dutch resistance to leaving the East Indies, then, the later experience of the Dutch Caribbean qualifies as an 'upside-down decolonisation with the metropolis, not the former colonies, pressing for independence', as Rosemarijn Hoefte and Gert Oostindie phrased it.[86] But while Dutch pressure produced results in Suriname, the Netherlands Antilles refused to be swayed. In the bleak

---

[83] Ibid., 103; Kuitenbrouwer, 'Never-Ending Debt', 30.
[84] Rosemarijn Hoefte and Gert Oostindie, 'The Netherlands and the Dutch Caribbean: Dilemmas of Decolonisation', in Paul Sutton (ed.), *Europe and the Caribbean* (London, 1991), 74–5; Oostindie and Klinkers, *Decolonising the Caribbean*, ch. 6.
[85] Hans Ramsoedh, 'De geforceerde onafhankelijkheid', *Tijdschrift voor Surinaamse Taalkunde, Letterkunde, Cultuur en Geschiedenis*, 7 (1993), 43–62.
[86] Hoefte and Oostindie, 'The Netherlands and the Dutch Caribbean', 94; see also Oostindie and Klinkers, *Decolonising the Caribbean*, 119.

aftermath of its independence, Suriname plunged into growing ethnic conflict, underwent political crises including a 1980 coup that resulted in a dictatorship, and faced a dire economic future – hardly an inspiration for the Antilles to follow in its footsteps. Few Antilleans believed any of the six small islands to be viable as either one or many independent nations. However ardently the Netherlands desired to be rid of the kingdom's remaining Caribbean territories, it lacked the power to terminate the 1954 Charter unilaterally without consent of all parties – consent which to this day has never been forthcoming. Decolonization remains incomplete to intense Dutch regret. Although divisions within the Netherlands Antilles widened to such an extent that it ceased to exist as a collective entity in 2010, none of the six islands that formerly comprised it opted to go it alone when offered the chance in referendums in the early 2000s. Instead, Aruba, Curaçao, and St Maarten now qualify as autonomous countries but still remain within the Kingdom of the Netherlands, while Bonaire, St Eustasius, and Saba have become 'public bodies' that share a similar status as Dutch municipalities.

Dutch attitudes to the West Indies since the 1954 Charter have remained remarkably consistent over time, characterized first and foremost by a resounding lack of public and political enthusiasm about the region. As Hoefte notes, whenever the West Indies managed to make the headlines in the early twenty-first century, it was usually for negative reasons. They were resented as an economic drain on the metropole and a source of unwanted Surinamese and Antillean immigration (which continued to grow after 1975 despite Dutch hopes that the former's independence would substantially restrict it), and seen as places where corruption and drug-related problems are rife.[87] Long considered far more of a liability than an asset, it is fair to say that if 'The Hague's priorities were anywhere but in the Caribbean' by the 1970s, this remains equally true today.[88]

After intensely-felt disappointments in the East Indies, the Netherlands refocused attention not on the West Indies but rather looked inwards as well as towards the United States and Europe when reimagining a national future upon a reconfigured international stage. Economic recovery after the devastation wrought by the Second World War proved remarkably successful thanks to programmes like the Marshall Plan that aided domestic reconstruction, while in geopolitical terms the Netherlands acquired an important status within NATO and as a loyal American ally. Europe assumed growing importance in the 1950s, when the Netherlands became one of the six original members of what began as the European Coal and Steel Community and gradually evolved

---

[87] Rosemarijn Hoefte, 'The Difficulty of Getting it Right: Dutch Policy in the Caribbean', *Itinerario*, 25:2 (2001), 70.

[88] Oostindie and Klinkers, *Decolonising the Caribbean*, 145.

into the fledgling European Economic Community (and ultimately the European Union) over the coming decades.[89]

Swimming with the tide of European integration dominated the agenda for most Dutch politicians, albeit not all. One holdout was none other than P.S. Gerbrandy, who wholeheartedly refused to endorse the Treaty of Rome in 1957 that established the EEC. Supporting it would be tantamount to the '*inlijving van Nederland bij Frankrijk-Duitsland*', he argued – nothing short of 'the annexation of the Netherlands by France and Germany'.[90] As he had previously insisted in the grim and embittered ruminations on the closing pages of his book *Indonesia*, minus the East Indies not only was the dreaded '*Indië verloren, rampspoed geboren*' prophecy destined to become a reality to the Netherlands' severe economic detriment. The small nation's entire identity and sovereignty was at stake, under threat from being engulfed within a 'united Europe' dominated in large part by its recent wartime enemy and hated occupier:

> In future the Netherlands will be no more than a part of Western Europe, a country of limited possibilities such as Denmark or Switzerland, but one with a dislocated economy lacking spiritual and political balance ... Is then Bismarck's prophecy that the Netherlands of her own volition will incorporate herself with Germany likely to be realized? ... The Netherlands are fast moving towards the political-economic melting-pot, together with possibly the whole of Western Europe. Whether, in these circumstances, the Netherlands will retain its identity will depend on the spirit of the coming generation.[91]

Unlike Gerbrandy, by then an elderly and marginal figure determined not to adapt his views to new times, most Dutch came to recognize Europe as far more a promise than a threat to their future. Being part of Western Europe's post-war economic resurgence and embarking on the path towards integration did much to make up for Indonesian decolonization in economic and political terms, even if many Dutch continued to regret the forfeiture of the East Indies and doubt the value of the remaining West Indian territories.[92] As will be seen in the coming chapters, other neighbouring nations underwent a similar reorientation towards Europe during the era of widescale decolonization. If they did experience new forms of identity (or indeed identity crises) as Gerbrandy suggested they might,

---

[89] Duco Hellema, *Buitenlandse Politiek van Nederland: De Nederlandse rol in de wereldpolitiek* (Utrecht, 2006), chs. 5–7; William Mallison, *From Neutrality to Commitment: Dutch Foreign Policy, NATO and European Integration* (London, 2010); Mathieu Segers, *Reis naar het continent: Nederland en de Europese integratie, 1950 tot heden* (Amsterdam, 2013).

[90] 'Parlement & Politiek', entry for Mr P.S. Gerbrandy, www.parlement.com/9291000/biof/00446, accessed 13 August 2012.

[91] Gerbrandy, *Indonesia*, 179; see also 26–7, 29, 177–8.

[92] Henri Baudet, 'The Netherlands after the Loss of Empire', *Journal of Contemporary History*, 4:1 (1969), 127–39; H.L. Wesseling, 'Post-Imperial Holland', *Journal of Contemporary History*, 15:1 (1980), 125–42 (especially 131–3); Moore, in Thomas, Moore, and Butler, *Crises of Empire*, 353, 375.

these were just as likely if not more so to stem from the social and cultural effects of late-colonial and postcolonial migrations, noted earlier in passing and addressed in depth in Part II, that irrevocably changed the Netherlands and other countries into the multicultural nations they have become since 1945. Decolonization, postcolonial migrations, and new intra-European relationships in the wake of the Second World War did not occur in isolation; rather, they were interconnected, walking hand in hand and able to exert considerable influence upon one another at critical historical moments.

Some contemporaries contemplated Western Europe with an eye towards their nations' postcolonial futures; others did so to compare distinct histories of colonialism and the prospects for decolonizations that were sometimes yet to come. In the 1950s and 1960s, Dr Abu Hanifah, introduced earlier in connection with his role in coordinating insurgent activities during the Indonesian revolution, served as a cabinet minister and became a leading international representative of Indonesia. Making his first visit to Europe in 1950 as the Minister for Education and Culture, his journey took him to the Netherlands and other countries, including France. By the end, he recalled,

I left Paris and France with an impression I couldn't get rid of. The country and the people who really invented the revolution, and had as a slogan, freedom, equality and fraternity, was still the most colonial country in the world, with the possible exception of Belgium and Portugal. They exported the idea of revolution but now they had to import back into France some of the old ideas of freedom and equality before France could again be considered the centre of the enlightened world.[93]

It is to these nations that we now turn, beginning with France.

---

[93] Hanifah, *Tales*, 356.

3   Soldiering on in the shadow of war
Decolonizing *la plus grande France*

'All men are created equal; they are endowed by their Creator with certain
inalienable Rights; among these are Life, Liberty, and the pursuit of
Happiness.' Standing before his supporters in Hanoi on 2 September 1945,
Ho Chi Minh delivered a Declaration of Independence of the Democratic
Republic of Vietnam whose opening words invoked the United States'
Declaration of Independence from Britain of 1776. But his focus immediately
shifted to the revolutionary ideology of France, which had gradually assumed
control over Vietnam's three component territories of Tonkin, Annam, and
Cochin China starting in the 1850s. 'The Declaration of the French Revolution
made in 1791 on the Rights of Man and Citizen also states: "All men are born
free and with equal rights, and must always remain free and have equal rights"',
he continued. But the French systematically denied to their colonial subjects
what they had claimed for themselves starting in 1789. For the better part of a
century, 'the French imperialists, abusing the standard of Liberty, Equality, and
Fraternity, have violated our Fatherland and oppressed our fellow citizens.
They have acted contrary to the ideals of humanity and justice', Ho insisted.
As colonizers, the French had long withheld democratic political liberties from
the Vietnamese, blocked their national unity, and 'built more prisons than
schools'. Economically, they 'robbed us of our rice fields, our mines, our
forests, and our raw materials', dominated the financial and export sectors,
extracted extortionate taxes that impoverished the Vietnamese peasantry, and
exploited workers. Dismissing France's claims to and policies in Vietnam as a
hypocritical affront to its own revolutionary national pedigree all along, Ho
simultaneously declared independence and insisted that as far as France was
concerned Vietnam was already free. Japan's occupation of much of Southeast
Asia during the Second World War had effectively dissolved French authority;
Japan's surrender opened up a power vacuum comparable to that Sukarno
stepped into in Indonesia that allowed the Viet Minh – the nationalist front
Ho spearheaded – to seize the reins. If the Japanese had begun the process of
removing the French, the Viet Minh completed it during the August Revolution
of 1945. 'The truth is', Ho emphasized, 'we have wrested our independence

from the Japanese and not from the French'; by 2 September, French rule was already history.[1]

Second World War experiences in Southeast Asia as well as Europe and across France's overseas territories were central to the French empire's decline and ultimate fall. But although transformations between 1939 and 1945 decisively shaped post-war developments and colonial contests, this discussion begins by examining their roots in colonial policies and anti-colonial critiques sown in the preceding World War of 1914–1918 and the interwar years. The year 1945 saw the end of one war that soon led to another in Vietnam, for the French refused to recognize what Ho Chi Minh said was blindingly obvious: that their days as a colonial power in Vietnam (and indeed throughout French Indochina, which encompassed Cambodia and Laos alongside Vietnam's three constituent parts) were over. Like the Netherlands and Britain, in the mid-late 1940s France looked to empire in a quest to reassert its standing in a post-war world. Vietnam's long struggle for freedom was inseparable from France's response to its domestic history of wartime defeat in Europe that brought brutal and divisive years of Nazi occupation, Vichyite collaboration, and resistance movements situated both within and outside metropolitan France. Free French resistance forces led by General Charles de Gaulle staged their assault on the Axis powers thanks to crucial support not simply from the Allies but also from the French empire.

From the European battlefields of the First World War to the succession of French defeats and imperial withdrawals between 1940 and the end of the Algerian War in 1962 (with the ultimately unsuccessful attempt to regain decisive authority in Vietnam between 1945 and 1954 being only the most important event to fall in between), France's army played a leading role in France's long road to decolonization. Soldiers fighting *for* France, however, occasionally fought *against* France. They became central actors within a series of Franco-French disputes that were simultaneously civil, domestic, and imperial in scope, raging across both the metropole (often called the hexagon) and *la France d'outre-mer* – overseas France. These spanned the end of the Third Republic in 1940 and ensuing years of German occupation, the Fourth Republic which emerged from the embers of war in 1946 but fell as a result of the fight over Algeria in 1958, and culminated in the Fifth Republic that emerged under de Gaulle's leadership and finally signalled the end of French

[1] 'Declaration of Independence of the Democratic Republic of Vietnam (September 2, 1945)', in Ho Chi Minh, *On Revolution: Selected Writings, 1920–66*, edited by Bernard B. Fall (New York, 1967), 143–5. This address has been discussed by (among others) Mark Philip Bradley, *Imagining Vietnam and America: The Making of Postcolonial Vietnam, 1919–1950* (Chapel Hill, 2000), 4, 107; Mark Atwood Lawrence, 'Explaining the Early Decisions: The United States and the French War, 1945–1954', in Mark Philip Bradley and Marilyn B. Young (eds.), *Making Sense of the Vietnam Wars: Local, National, and Transnational Perspectives* (Oxford, 2008), 23; Fredrik Logevall, *Embers of War: The Fall of an Empire and the Making of America's Vietnam* (New York, 2012), 97–8.

Algeria – the settler-dominated territory that proved the most difficult to relinquish, not least because it was long deemed more than a colony but rather an integral part of France.[2] Debates about the future, meanings, and geographical limits of the French nation, its empire, and its place on the post-1945 world stage were as 'one and indivisible' as the republic itself was widely proclaimed. These divided the French among themselves just as they pitted French colonizers against the colonized who, like Ho Chi Minh, knew their national liberty was well worth the fight.

* * *

The French empire from the First World War to the 1930s

The First World War brought France's empire into the French hexagon in unprecedented ways. As was seen in the British case, *la France d'outre-mer* contributed immeasurably to the metropolitan war effort in the form of financing, food, materiel, and especially manpower. Divided from its North African territories only by the Mediterranean, France drew essential grain supplies and other staples from Algeria, Morocco, and Tunisia. Given the mass diversion of its workers to the war front, France also depended upon recruits from overseas to fill industrial and agricultural labour needs. Approximately 220,000 men from Algeria, Indochina, and other colonies along with China worked in French ports and munitions factories, in mines, and on farms.[3] If a global labour force maintained the home front, it was a multi-ethnic army that manned the war front. Alongside over 90,000 European settlers from Algeria, over half a million more troops were mobilized from colonized populations across France's empire, including approximately 270,000 Algerian, Tunisian, and Moroccan Muslims, 181,000 West Africans, 49,000 Indochinese, and 41,000 from Madagascar.[4] Best known of those stationed on French soil and along the

[2] Important overviews include Martin Thomas, *Fight or Flight: Britain, France, and Their Roads from Empire* (Oxford, 2014); Robert Aldrich, *Greater France: A History of French Overseas Expansion* (Basingstoke, 1996), ch. 8; Raymond F. Betts, *France and Decolonisation, 1900–1960* (Basingstoke, 1991); Martin Thomas, Bob Moore, and L.J. Butler, *Crises of Empire: Decolonization and Europe's Imperial States, 1918–1975* (London, 2008), Part II by Martin Thomas. For France's decolonization in comparative perspective, see Bernard Droz, *Histoire de la decolonisation au xxe siècle* (Paris, 2006); Martin Shipway, *Decolonization and Its Impact: A Comparative Approach to the End of the Colonial Empires* (Malden, MA, 2008).
[3] Tyler Stovall, 'Colour-Blind France?: Colonial Workers during the First World War', *Race & Class*, 35:2 (1993), 35–55; Tyler Stovall, 'The Color Line Behind the Lines: Racial Violence in France During the First World War', *American Historical Review*, 103:3 (1998), 737–69; John Horne, 'Immigrant Workers in France During World War I', *French Historical Studies*, 14:1 (1985), 57–88.
[4] Robert Aldrich and Christopher Hilliard, 'The French and British Empires', in John Horne (ed.), *A Companion to World War I* (Oxford, 2012), 524–39 (for data, see 526).

western front were the *tirailleurs sénégalais*, the light infantry recruited from Senegal alongside neighbouring colonies of French-ruled West Africa.

Exposed to colonized peoples up close like never before, French reactions derived partly from pre-existing colonial ideologies and racial stereotypes and partly from new wartime circumstances. Colonial soldiers often experienced racist treatment, and wartime portrayals readily revealed condescending and paternalistic attitudes. African troops stationed in their midst typically were imagined as primitive, simple, and childlike in French eyes, and often as a sexual threat to white women.[5] Nonetheless, their services, loyalty, and bravery became widely recognized as invaluable to a nation in grave need of defenders. Even before the war, West African soldiers were promoted as an essential source of military manpower that would help compensate for France's low birth rate compared to Germany, and their sacrifices for France were celebrated as easily worthy of public gratitude in official statements and popular culture as death tolls escalated.[6] In 1915, the smiling, brave, docile, and obedient *tirailleur sénégalais* (who 'gave his blood for France', as his champions continually reiterated) first became the trademark image for Banania, a French breakfast drink made from cocoa and banana flour – quintessential colonial commodities. Despite successive visual adaptations and lapses in his usage, the *tirailleur* remains the visible face of Banania in the present day, much modernized but still recognizable by his dark skin and red hat with the blue tassel. Until the 1970s, his image appeared accompanied by the slogan '*Y'a bon*' – 'this be good'. Epitomizing the simple, ungrammatical French supposedly spoken by the charming but culturally inferior unschooled 'native', the language accorded to the childlike *tirailleur* was long considered apt for a product widely consumed by French children.[7]

---

[5] Annabelle Melzer, 'Spectacles and Sexualities: The "Mise-en-Scène" of the "Tirailleur Sénégalais" on the Western Front, 1914–1920', in Billie Melman (ed.), *Borderlines: Genders and Identities in War and Peace, 1870–1930* (New York, 1998), 213–44; Richard S. Fogarty, *Race and War in France: Colonial Subjects in the French Army, 1914–1918* (Baltimore, 2008), ch. 6; Alison S. Fell, 'Nursing the Other: The Representation of Colonial Troops in French and British First World War Nursing Memoirs', in Santanu Das (ed.), *Race, Empire, and First World War Writing* (Cambridge, 2011), 158–74.

[6] Marc Michel, *Les Africains et la Grande Guerre: l'appel à l'Afrique (1914–1918)* (Paris, 2003); Antoine Champeaux and Éric Deroo, *La Force noire: gloire et infortunes d'une légende coloniale* (Paris, 2006), 49–125; Éric Deroo, 'Mourir, d'Appel à l'empire (1913–1918)', in Pascal Blanchard, Sandrine Lemaire, and Nicolas Bancel (eds.), *Culture coloniale en France: De la Révolution à nos jours* (Paris, 2008), 163–72. Important studies in English include Gregory Mann, *Native Sons: West African Veterans and France in the Twentieth Century* (Durham, 2006), ch. 4; Joe Lunn, *Memoirs of the Maelstrom: A Senegalese Oral History of the First World War* (Portsmouth, NH, 1999); Myron Echenberg, *Colonial Conscripts: The Tirailleurs Sénégalais in French West Africa, 1857–1960* (Portsmouth, NH, 1991), ch. 3.

[7] Champeaux and Deroo, *La Force noire*, 104–5; Dana S. Hale, *Races on Display: French Representations of Colonized Peoples, 1886–1940* (Bloomington, 2008), 95–6; Anne Donadey, '"Y'a bon Banania": Ethics and Cultural Criticism in the Colonial Context', *French Cultural Studies*, 11:31 (2000), 9–29; Sylvie Durmelat, 'Introduction: Colonial Culinary Encounters and Imperial Leftovers', *French Cultural Studies*, 26:2 (2015), 116–18.

Figure 3.1 Advertisement for Banania breakfast drink, France, used starting in 1936.
Credit: The Advertising Archives, London.

The years 1914–1918 rightly qualified as a 'world war' while the fighting raged, and its aftermath had equally global implications as territories once controlled by the collapsed German, Austro-Hungarian, Russian, and Ottoman empires came under new governance with the 1919 Treaty of Versailles. Like Britain, France too reaped imperial rewards, gaining control over substantial parts of German Togoland and Cameroon in West Africa in addition to the ex-Ottoman territories of Syria and Lebanon in the Middle East, all of which counted as 'League of Nations mandates' as opposed to colonies *per se*. Second in geographical reach only to Britain's, France's empire reached its widest territorial extent in the interwar years, becoming *la plus grande France* (Greater France) literally as well as imaginatively.[8] Together with three North African territories that were not formally colonies (these being the protectorates of Tunisia and Morocco, and most importantly Algeria, which consisted of three *départements* claimed as part of France itself), the empire spread from French Indochina to the Antillean (Caribbean) islands of Martinique and Guadeloupe and French Guiana on the coast of South America. Among other territories scattered across the globe, Greater France also encompassed the small Indian Ocean island of Réunion, the much larger island of Madagascar off the coast of Southeast Africa, and the large territorial groupings comprising French West Africa and French Equatorial Africa.

France's newly-enlarged empire reached its apogee as a reservoir of national pride in the 1920s and 1930s, when political and cultural investments in imperial ambitions scaled new heights. French colonial ideology had long been geared towards the goal of assimilation, whereby colonized peoples were believed capable of becoming culturally recast in the French image and thus elevated both morally and intellectually (indicatively, such people were considered *évolués* – those who had 'evolved' to reach a higher stage of civilization). Universalist, centralized, and ostensibly colour-blind, French proponents of assimilation imagined a single, unified imperial community of 'one hundred million Frenchmen'. Albeit still powerful in the interwar years, assimilationism was joined by claims to favour 'association', which left space for accommodating cultural differences and accelerated the co-option of selected local elites into colonial governance. Whatever their distinctions, both approaches legitimated French imperialism, allowing its attendant civilizing mission to reign supreme. France's stated imperial aim involved reforming societies it condemned as culturally backward or barbaric as it bestowed the civilizational benefits of France's language, culture, and political and economic oversight.[9]

---

[8] Martin Thomas, *The French Empire Between the Wars: Imperialism, Politics and Society* (Manchester, 2005).

[9] Raymond F. Betts, *Assimilation and Association in French Colonial Theory* (New York, 1961); Gary Wilder, *The French Imperial Nation-State: Negritude and Colonial Humanism Between the Two World Wars* (Chicago, 2005), Part I; Alice L. Conklin, *A Mission to Civilize: The Republican*

Assimilation and association's dual but overlapping imperial ideologies featured a combination of republicanism and racist exclusivity, extolling France as superior and generously prepared to share its gifts with inferior 'others' deemed nowhere near ready to look after themselves. These values received a full airing in the early 1930s French children's books by Jean de Brunhoff featuring Babar, an orphaned young elephant. Babar leaves his forest home (seemingly in Africa) for a city bearing a marked resemblance to Paris, where he is introduced to 'civilization' by the wealthy and kindly 'Old Lady' (personifying France) who happily gives him clothing and education and exposes him to unfamiliar foods and customs, such as eating with silverware. She continues to lend a helping hand after he returns to the forest to become the king who sets about remaking his homeland in the urban (French) image. Introducing schools, orderly urban planning, and culture to an emergent city that acquires all the trappings of a colonial capital, Babar serves as the évolué conduit through which a higher (French) civilization is altruistically bestowed upon a hitherto primitive society to its immeasurable benefit.[10] Like Banania's retention of the *tirailleur sénégalais* in its advertising, Babar remains a well-known character in children's literature today long after the French imperial world that gave birth to him was torn apart.

Published in 1931, the first Babar book *Histoire de Babar* (*The Story of Babar*) coincided with the colossal fair held between May and November in the Vincennes park in Paris that showcased imperial ideals like no other event or cultural artefact. This *Exposition Coloniale* was the latest and largest in a long line of overseas-related international exhibitions, many having taken place between the 1870s and 1920s in the Mediterranean port city of Marseille, one of France's main 'gateways to empire' through which a high volume of trade and many inward- and outward-bound travellers passed.[11] Part of the Vincennes exhibition revolved around displays of exotic animals from Asia and Africa, including elephants that may have provided some of the inspiration for Babar; this became the basis for the permanent zoo still open on the site today. The exposition also featured colonial peoples, cultures, and buildings, most famously the massive reconstruction of the Angkor Wat temple (which

---

Idea of Empire in France and West Africa, 1895–1930 (Stanford, 1997); Alice L. Conklin, 'The Civilizing Mission', in Edward Berenson, Vincent Declert, and Christophe Prochasson (eds.), *The French Republic: History, Values, Culture* (Ithaca, 2011), 173–81.

[10] Claire-Lise Malarte-Feldman and Jack Yeager, 'Babar and the French Connection: Teaching the Politics of Superiority and Exclusion', in Meena Khorana (ed.), *Critical Perspectives on Postcolonial African Children's and Young Adult Literature* (Westport, CT, 1998), 69–77; Stephen O'Harrow, 'Babar and the *Mission Civilisatrice*: Colonialism and the Biography of a Mythical Elephant', *Biography*, 22:1 (1999), 86–103; Ariel Dorfman, 'Of Elephants and Ducks', in *The Empire's Old Clothes: What the Lone Ranger, Babar, and Other Innocent Heroes Do To Our Minds* (New York, 1983), 17–64.

[11] Pascal Blanchard and Gilles Boëtsch (eds.), *Marseille Porte Sud, 1905–2005* (Paris, 2005).

the French had painstakingly restored in Cambodia) along with a series of pavilions dedicated to each colony. Together with zoos containing animals were human zoos – displays of colonial subjects brought to Paris to populate the 'native villages' and thus add to their alleged authenticity for curious French visitors. African and Asian craftsmen, performers, colonial troops, and others proved as big a draw as the animals, architectural replicas, and exhibits designed to show off France's colonial achievements in agriculture, forestry, missionary work, education, and just administration praised for setting the colonies on the road to peace and prosperity.[12]

The exposition amounted to a sprawling propaganda piece designed to convince the over eight million people attending it of the value of France's colonial enterprise and the civilizing mission's achievements. Significantly, however, the images of cultural difference, exoticism, and primitivism on display underscored the yawning gap that still divided the vast majority of the 'non-evolved' colonial 'natives' and the civilized French. Whatever colonial achievements France could celebrate, the colonized remained far too backward to merit equal rights or be seen as candidates for political freedoms. Rather than merely applauding a civilizing mission accomplished, then, the 1931 exposition represented French rule and benevolent tutelage as a noble work still well in progress.

With over thirty million tickets sold and attracting many repeat visitors, the exposition indisputably qualified as a commercial and popular success. But whether the enjoyment of exotic, stereotypical spectacles translated into the wider enthusiasm for empire its organizers hoped would result remains open to question.[13] Much of the French public remained seemingly indifferent both to the civilizing mission's allure as well as to its counter-narrative: allegations of colonial abuses, injustice, greed, and misrule, accompanied by growing demands that France recognize colonial aspirations to rights and liberty. In 1931 Paris, protests against colonial conditions in reality as opposed to the fantasy-laden portrayals of French altruism pervading the Vincennes park took the form of a small *Exposition anti-impérialiste*. Organized by African and Vietnamese students along with French artists connected to the surrealist movement, communists, and socialists, it highlighted not laudable colonial

[12] Charles-Robert Ageron, 'L'Exposition coloniale de 1931: Mythe républicain ou mythe impérial?', in Pierre Nora (ed.), *Les Lieux de mémoire, vol. 1: La République* (Paris, 1984), 561–91; Herman Lebovics, *True France: The Wars over Cultural Identity, 1900–1945* (Ithaca, 1992), 51–104; Panivong Norindr, *Phantasmatic Indochina: French Colonial Ideology in Architecture, Film, and Literature* (Durham, 1996), 14–51; Patricia A. Morton, *Hybrid Modernities: Architecture and Representation at the 1931 Colonial Exposition, Paris* (Cambridge, MA, 2000); Nicola Cooper, *France in Indochina: Colonial Encounters* (Oxford, 2001), ch. 4; Hale, *Races on Display*; Steve Ungar, 'L'Exposition coloniale (1931)', in Blanchard, Lemaire, and Bancel (eds.), *Culture coloniale*, 259–67.

[13] Thomas, *French Empire Between the Wars*, 199–202, 349.

achievements bestowed upon grateful, primitive natives, but forced labour, economic exploitation, and political oppression.[14] Dwarfed in size, funding, and publicity by the officially-endorsed monumentalism at Vincennes (which it futilely asked the public to boycott), the modest anti-colonial alternative none-theless attested to the coexistence of imperial triumphalism and condemnation across *la plus grande France* that was audible at the heart of the empire to those caring to listen.

Protests by colonized peoples against the newly-aggrandized and embol-dened imperial status quo spread and diversified after the First World War. Paris-based students and intellectuals from the French Antilles and West Africa became active in the *négritude* movement, part of the literary and cultural efflorescence propelled by writers like Aimé Césaire from Martinique (who first advanced the term in the 1930s), the Senegalese poet Léopold Sédar Senghor, and other black expatriates. Influenced by transnational black cultural conversations of the interwar era (not least the Harlem Renaissance in African-American culture), *négritude* championed a black identity that had cultural importance, validity, and dignity. In so doing, it assertively countered the racist and disparaging imagery peddled by proponents of the Western civilizing mission and assimilation.[15]

Alongside politicized cultural initiatives were new and overtly nationalist political organizations, some of the most important of which were established by colonial activists who, like Césaire and Senghor, had formative experiences in the metropole. As the first party to demand Algerian independence, the *Étoile Nord-Africaine* (North African Star) was founded in 1926 in Paris by Ahmed Messali Hadj, who had first crossed the Mediterranean as a conscripted soldier in 1918 and later returned as one of the growing numbers of Algerian men to work in France in the interwar period. Messali Hadj's movement not only won a following among Algerian workers but enjoyed the support of the French Communist Party (the PCF, *Parti Communiste Français*), itself a fledgling organization that had come into being just six years before.[16] Other nationalist groups developed in the colonies themselves, among them the Viet Nam Quoc Dan Dang (the VNQDD, or National Party of Vietnam) in Hanoi in 1927. A revolutionary party that looked partly to the Kuomintang in China for its inspiration, the VNQDD demanded independence and committed itself to a nationalist, democratic, and socialist agenda, capitalizing on the spread of mass

---

[14] Alongside the aforementioned studies on the *Exposition Coloniale*, see also Lynn E. Palermo, 'L'Exposition Anticoloniale: Political or Aesthetic Protest?', *French Cultural Studies*, 20:1 (2009), 27–46; for a broader discussion of interwar anticolonialism, see Claude Liauzu, *Histoire de l'anticolonialisme en France: Du XVIe siècle à nos jours* (Paris, 2007), ch. 4.

[15] Wilder, *French Imperial Nation-State*, especially Part III.

[16] Benjamin Stora, *Messali Hadj: Pionnier du nationalisme algérien (1898–1974)* (Paris, 1986); Neil MacMaster, *Colonial Migrants and Racism: Algerians in France, 1900–62* (Basingstoke, 1997), 99, 153.

discontent at French economic incursions and political repression. But while conditions within the colonies caused much local political ferment, the importance of the migration experience to the interwar flowering of nationalist thought cannot be denied. Prominent among the rising generation of future leaders was Nguyen Tat Thanh (*né* Nguyen Sinh Cung), born in Annam in c.1890 and better known by the names he subsequently assumed to reflect his anti-colonial politics: first Nguyen Ai Quoc ('Nguyen the Patriot'), and most famously Ho Chi Minh – 'He who enlightens'.[17] Having left Vietnam in 1911 as a cook on a French steamship, sailed the world, and worked in London as a busboy, Ho had resided in Paris since 1917, doing a range of odd jobs while honing his political outlooks in conversation with other Vietnamese expatriates.

Ho Chi Minh was one of many colonial nationalists for whom the First World War and the Paris peace process that followed provoked increasing condemnation of predatory imperialism and raised political expectations. US President Woodrow Wilson's Fourteen Points stressing the principles of democracy and self-determination galvanized their hopes, only to dash them. Uninvited, Ho came to the peace conference in 1919 in the attempt to deliver one of his first political manifestoes: a petition redolent with Wilsonian-style rhetoric he sought to bring to the President's attention. It demanded the Vietnamese right to choose their own government, launched a plea for the amnesty of political prisoners and judicial reform, and sought freedom of speech, the press, association, migration, and education; it concluded by asking for indigenous representation in the French parliament.[18] Although he proclaimed Vietnamese confidence that the French would uphold their ideals of liberty, justice, and fraternity, his petition was ignored. For Wilson as for other Western leaders responsible for crafting the peace, self-determination in practice applied to the European territories of the defeated Central Powers – *not* to extra-European territories which remained colonies, or had become transferred mandates that counted among the victors' spoils.

Realizing that Wilsonian self-determination left no space for Vietnamese aspirations, Ho Chi Minh soon turned to an alternative political model in his quest for freedom from European colonialism: communism inspired by Lenin and the Bolshevik Revolution.[19] A year later Ho became one of the founding members of the French Communist Party and grew increasingly active as a critic of French colonialism, leaving France in 1923 for stays in Russia and

---

[17] Pierre Brocheux, *Ho Chi Minh: A Biography*, translated by Claire Duiker (Cambridge, 2007), ch. 1; William J. Duiker, *Ho Chi Minh: A Life* (New York, 2000), ch. 2.

[18] Ho Chi Minh (Nguyen Ai Quoc), 'Revendications du peuple annamite', Paris, 1919, in Alain Ruscio (ed.), *Ho Chi Minh: Textes 1914–1969* (Paris, 1990), 22–3.

[19] Erez Manela, *The Wilsonian Moment: Self-Determination and the International Origins of Anticolonial Nationalism* (Oxford, 2007), 3–4.

China. His tract *French Colonization on Trial* emerged in the mid-1920s and cynically highlighted the wartime abuse of colonial troops, many of them brutally impressed into military service, to demonstrate the extortionate 'blood tax' France demanded of Africans and Asians – not to mention the lack of gratitude they received in return:

> Before 1914, they were only dirty Negroes and dirty Annamese, at the best only good for pulling rickshaws and receiving blows from our administrators. With the declaration of the joyful new war, they became the 'dear children' and 'brave friends' of our paternal and tender administrators ... They (the natives) were all at once promoted to the supreme rank of 'defenders of law and liberty'.

Sent to 'rot on the battlefields of Europe', '[a]s soon as the guns had had their fill of black or yellow cannon fodder, the loving declarations of our leaders were magically silenced'. The 'Negroes and Annamese', 'dirty' once again 'after valiantly defending right and justice, returned empty-handed to their indigenous state where right and justice are unknown'.[20]

Unfortunately for the Vietnamese, Ho's statements rang true. In a colonial society where 90 per cent of the indigenous population was poor and rural, French interwar economic policies considerably worsened the plight of the peasant majority, while the small working class employed in mines or in cities fared little better. Regressive taxes and rising indebtedness resulted in the transfer of vast swathes of peasant land into the hands of better-off Vietnamese landlords or French-run plantations.[21] Indochina's colonial economy was geared towards increasing the output of rice, coal, rubber, and other raw materials for export and required a large, cheap, and submissive labour force – one which landlessness, debt, and abject poverty drove peasants to join. The colonial state aided French capitalist enterprises through condoning forced labour along with coercive recruitment methods to secure an indentured workforce that became subject to gross maltreatment.

Conditions on the rubber plantations to which Michelin gained concessions in the late 1920s serve as a case in point. Recruited with false promises and often under complete duress, peasants taken far from home effectively became imprisoned on remote plantations, suffering habitual beatings, malnutrition, accidents, malaria, dysentery, and other ills as they cleared the land and then grew and harvested rubber for pitifully low wages.[22] Looking back on his years as one of the nearly 18,000 workers on Michelin's Phu Rieng plantation, Tran Tu Binh remembered a 'hell on earth' where '[o]ne's strength today was never

---

[20] 'French Colonization on Trial', in Ho Chi Minh, *On Revolution*, 68, 72–3.

[21] Samuel L. Popkin, *The Rational Peasant: The Political Economy of Rural Society in Vietnam* (Berkeley, 1979), ch. 4.

[22] Pierre Brocheux and Daniel Hémery, *Indochina: An Ambiguous Colonization, 1858–1954*, translated by Ly Lan Dill-Klein *et al.* (Berkeley, 2009), 168, 208.

what it had been the day before. Every day one was worn down a bit more, cheeks sunken, teeth gone crooked, eyes hollow with dark circles around them, clothes hanging from collarbones. Everyone appeared almost dead, and in fact in the end about all did die.'[23] A far cry from the cheerful demeanour of the 'Michelin Man' who served as the company's popular logo then and now, his rotund body composed of a stack of tires, the skeletal and subjugated Michelin men (and women) peopling Tran's account present a more accurate if unsavoury corporate image that most French preferred to overlook, if not condone.[24]

Colonial abuses during a time when Vietnam was savaged by the effects of the Great Depression sparked growing rural unrest, dissent, and strikes among plantation, mining, and factory labourers that the colonial army and police attempted to stamp out in campaigns of violent retribution.[25] Worker and peasant agitation became linked to political dissidence, especially once communists made contact with plantation coolies and other desperate communities. Tran Tu Binh's account of Phu Rieng described how representatives of the Vietnamese Revolutionary Youth League established by Ho Chi Minh from his base in China in 1925 politicized the rubber workers and took up their grievances.[26] By the time Ho founded the Indochinese Communist Party (ICP) in 1930, his stance and aims had radicalized considerably from the petition he prepared for Versailles in 1919. In his inaugural statement, Ho condemned French colonialism as working hand in hand with deepening capitalist exploitation after the 1914–1918 war depleted the national economy, oppressing the colonized poor to aid France's own recovery. He called on 'workers, peasants, soldiers, youth, and pupils' to join the struggle not just 'to make Indochina completely independent' from France – a demand coming at the same time as the Indian National Congress resolved to fight for *purna swaraj* and not settle for increased self-government within the British empire – but to rid it of the capitalism that crippled the majority. Establishing a government controlled by workers, peasants, and soldiers, taking over banks, redistributing land to peasants, abolishing unfair taxes, initiating an eight-hour workday, bringing back 'all freedoms to the masses' who would enjoy universal education, and equality between the sexes all constituted central planks of the ICP's platform.[27]

[23] Tran Tu Binh, *The Red Earth: A Vietnamese Memoir of Life on a Colonial Rubber Plantation*, translated by John Spragens, Jr., edited by David G. Marr (Athens, OH, 1985), 23, 26.

[24] Stephen L. Harp, *Marketing Michelin: Advertising and Cultural Identity in Twentieth-Century France* (Baltimore, 2001).

[25] Martin Thomas, *Violence and Colonial Order: Police, Workers and Protest in the European Colonial Empires, 1918–1940* (Cambridge, 2012), ch. 6.

[26] Tran Tu Binh, *Red Earth*, 47–53.

[27] 'Appeal Made on the Occasion of the Founding of the Communist Party of Indochina (February 18, 1930)', in Ho Chi Minh, *On Revolution*, 127–9.

In the years to come, the ICP's emphasis on the plight and revolutionary potential of workers and especially peasants set it apart from other nationalist organizations that focused their energies on the cities and more educated social sectors as vehicles for change. Its strong appeal among the peasant and worker majority was one of the most important reasons why the ICP ultimately won the battle for popular support over rival nationalist groups such as the VNQDD, which had been left in tatters following French crackdowns on their leadership and activities in the early 1930s.[28] The VNQDD's involvement in triggering a military mutiny among *tirailleurs tonkinois* at the Yen Bay garrison in 1930 in the attempt to galvanize a widespread uprising was promptly quelled by the French, who proceeded to unleash a campaign of terror in the surrounding region.[29] VNQDD activists faced *en masse* arrests, imprisonment, and in many cases execution, leaving the party decimated; French repression also wiped out many ICP-affiliated militants, and it took until the Second World War for communism to emerge as a leading political force.

Across the French empire of the 1930s, recurrent moves to contain and punish political and socio-economic dissent prevailed over modest efforts to undertake colonial reform or accord any legitimacy to nationalist grievances. The decade witnessed a spiralling cycle of unrest, uprising, and state violence, with the economic hardships of the Great Depression and the growing demand for political rights both playing their part in colonial ferment and radicalization. In 1936, the election of France's Popular Front government opened up limited prospects for reform, but these bore little fruit. In Algeria, the Blum-Viollette Bill's proposal to extend the suffrage enjoyed almost exclusively by the approximately one million-strong white settler population but withheld from all but a handful of the c. eight million Muslims raised the expectations of Algerian nationalist groups based in Algeria and among migrant workers across the Mediterranean. Blum-Viollette would have granted political equality (and thus equality with French citizens) and the vote to approximately 25,000 Muslims without demanding that they first abandon their Muslim legal status – had it passed. As it was, the powerful, pro-settler colonial lobby derailed Blum-Viollette, and like other proposed reforms it came to nought. Algerian nationalists felt betrayed and disenchanted, losing whatever confidence they once had in the prospect of political advance or the amelioration of conditions privileging settlers and discriminating against indigenous populations. The Popular Front soon dissolved

---

[28] William J. Duiker, *The Communist Road to Power in Vietnam* (Boulder, 1981), ch. 2; William J. Duiker, *Sacred War: Nationalism and Revolution in a Divided Vietnam* (New York, 1995); Brocheux and Hémery, *Indochina*, ch. 7.

[29] Thomas, *French Empire Between the Wars*, ch. 7; Martin Thomas, 'Fighting "Communist Banditry" in French Vietnam: The Rhetoric of Repression after the Yen Bay Uprising, 1930–1932', *French Historical Studies*, 34:3 (2011), 611–48.

organizations like the *Étoile Nord-Africaine*, arrested Messali Hadj and other leading activists, and banned successor parties like the *Parti du Peuple Algérien* (Algerian People's Party).[30] When the Second World War erupted in 1939, many nationalist organs had been outlawed, their adherents detained or driven underground. With the advent of war, however, neither the French metropole nor *la France d'outre-mer* would ever be the same again.

* * *

Vichy, war, and the French Union

France's failure to fend off Nazi Germany's invasion in May 1940 set in train a cascade of national humiliations with long-term consequences for metropole and empire alike. Upon France's surrender in June, the remnants of its government under Marshal Pétain relocated to the southern spa town of Vichy, whereupon France became split between German-occupied regions in the north and territory controlled by the ultraconservative Vichy regime that owed its survival to collaboration. In 1940, the Third Republic born in 1870 came to an end, and collaboration with and resistance to the Nazis and Vichy began. Never homogeneous, France's wartime resistance movement operated both within and outside the hexagon. General Charles de Gaulle fled to London, and with Churchill's backing this largely unknown figure assumed the mantle of self-designated leader of the emergent 'Free French' forces, at first minuscule in number. De Gaulle's 'Appel' broadcast from London on 18 June refused to recognize France either as defeated or alone, because the wider battle was not confined to Europe. This was a world war, de Gaulle proclaimed, and France still 'has a vast empire behind her.'[31]

At first, however, most of the empire stood behind Pétain rather than de Gaulle. With few exceptions (most importantly French Equatorial Africa), French colonial governors and their administrations from North and West Africa to Syria and Lebanon to Indochina were ardent Vichyites. So too were most white settlers in Algeria and elsewhere, who fully supported administrations which seized the opportunity to roll back the paltry reforms enacted in the 1930s and further disenfranchise colonized populations.[32] If metropolitan France was divided between the German-occupied territory, the Vichy-controlled zone, and a disparate resistance struggle, in the empire the Franco-French split took the form of Vichy loyalism and Free French republicanism, with the balance gradually shifting from the former to the latter. One by one, between 1940 and 1944

---

[30] Martin Evans, *Algeria: France's Undeclared War* (Oxford, 2012), 64–75.

[31] Martin Shipway, *The Road to War: France and Vietnam, 1944–1947* (Oxford, 1996), 13–14.

[32] Eric T. Jennings, *Vichy in the Tropics: Pétain's National Revolution in Madagascar, Guadeloupe, and Indochina, 1940–1944* (Stanford, 2001).

every French colonial administration apart from Indochina's transferred allegiance to the Free French, often following invasions in which Free French units operated together with other Allied military forces.

Radically different though they were in goals and ideology, Vichy and the Free French nonetheless concurred on the empire's fundamental importance to France. As Martin Thomas has summarized, 'Vichy was a quisling state which found in empire a refuge from which it could govern relatively unfettered', whereas in the hexagon it remained under Germany's watchful eye. 'By contrast, Free France was a metropolitan government-in-waiting temporarily confined to colonial territory' as well as London exile.[33] Free France's active role in helping to topple Vichyite colonial regimes and thereby expand control over the empire provided de Gaulle with sorely-needed legitimacy vis-à-vis the British and American Allies upon whose support he relied, together with access to colonial troops, supplies, and income. After the American and British 'Operation Torch' landings in Algeria and Morocco in November 1942, Vichy forces succumbed to Free French control and de Gaulle shifted his base of operations from London to Algiers. French Algeria's capital city thus turned from the symbolic hub of overseas France under Vichy into the seat of his provisional government until mainland France itself was liberated – with considerable assistance from Free French troops from the colonies. In short, the empire (especially French Africa) had enabled de Gaulle's movement both to form its army and reassert French sovereignty.

In Indochina, meanwhile, Vichy-affiliated colonial authorities were toppled not by the Free French or the Allies but the Japanese. Although Japan had allowed the French to remain in place (under sufferance) after gaining effective control of the region and subsuming the colonial economy within its own war effort, in March 1945 Japan moved to a direct occupation and imprisoned French administrators. By the time Japan surrendered in August, French authority in Indochina had disintegrated and colonial unrest and political demands escalated, providing crucial space for the Viet Minh to consolidate its own standing as a nationalist liberation front and for Ho Chi Minh to declare Vietnam's independence.

Wartime conditions and depredations sparked dissent in other imperial arenas as well, whether they fell under Japanese, Vichy, or Free French control. A key event occurred late in 1944 at the Thiaroye military compound outside Dakar in Senegal, when *tirailleurs sénégalais* recently released from German prisoner-of-war camps and repatriated to West Africa mutinied to demand equivalent pay, pension rights, and compensations as their French infantry counterparts. French troops mercilessly crushed the revolt of their fellow French imperial men-in-

---

[33] Martin Thomas, *The French Empire at War, 1940–45* (Manchester, 1998), 227.

arms, killing 35 and sowing the seeds of future anti-colonial misgivings.[34]
Algeria also witnessed growing Muslim nationalist politicization propelled by
leaders like Ferhat Abbas after de Gaulle's provisional government established
itself in Algiers. In 1943, Abbas led other nationalists in drawing up a 'Manifesto
of the Algerian People' demanding meaningful political rights and representation
for Algerian Muslims and calling on France to honour its own principles of 1789.
Like Ho Chi Minh, Abbas and his co-signatories looked back both to the First
World War as well as to the Second World War in formulating their platform.
'The French colony only admits equality with Muslim Algeria on one level:
sacrifices on the battlefield', and the 1943 manifesto called for full liberty and
equality without distinction of race or religion, highlighting the desperation of
Muslims denied adequate land, living wages, work opportunities, medical provi-
sions, and schooling.[35] 'Conscious of their recruitment into the Free French
Army, they [Algerians] wanted to know that their fight to liberate Nazi Europe
would lead to their own liberation through self-government', Martin Evans
notes, together with the amelioration of dire socio-economic conditions suffered
by the overwhelming majority.[36] Asserting their rights vis-à-vis Algeria's
European population, Abbas tactically contrasted the Muslims fighting on Free
France's behalf with the majority of the European settler community, which had
'interpreted the Vichy regime and new order instituted by Marshal Pétain as the
intimate expression of its ideal and the possibility of satisfying its thirst for
domination'. Settlers had 'received German officers at their table' and 'set
[themselves] up against the Muslims whom they portrayed as communists and
dangerous revolutionaries'.[37]

De Gaulle responded in March 1944 with an offer to bestow citizenship on
65,000 Algerian Muslims – a gesture as hated by resident Europeans as its
actual scope was minimal, applying as it did to less than 1 per cent of Algeria's
non-European population. Intended in part to appease Algerians at a time when
many were fighting in Italy together with Allies, his greater purpose was to
enhance Free France's authority in a North Africa dominated by British and
American forces and assuage American anti-colonial pressures. Algerians like
Abbas dismissed such proposals, their insufficiency acting as a spur to further
political activism. For his part, when he left Algiers in August 1944 upon the
liberation of Paris after the fall of Vichy, de Gaulle ordered the colonial army
and police forces to keep a close watch on nationalist activity and quell
opposition by force if necessary.[38]

---

[34] Armelle Mabon, 'La tragédie de Thiaroye, symbole du déni d'égalité', *Hommes et migrations*,
1235 (2002), 86–95; Mann, *Native Sons*, 116–19.
[35] Alistair Horne, *A Savage War of Peace: Algeria 1954–1962* (New York, 1979), 42; 'Manifeste
du Peuple Algérien', in Claude Collot and Jean-Robert Henry (eds.), *Le Mouvement national
algérien : Textes 1912–1954* (Paris, 1978), 155–65, especially 161.
[36] Evans, *Algeria*, 78.   [37] 'Manifeste du Peuple Algérien', 162.   [38] Evans, *Algeria*, 78–9.

De Gaulle's approach to Algeria was entirely consistent with the outcomes of the conference convened to discuss plans for the post-war, post-metropolitan liberation empire held in Brazzaville, the capital of French Equatorial Africa, in January and February. While reforms were promised, many were vaguely defined at best; other proposals merely replaced one form of subordination of the colonized (such as forced labour, which was to be phased out over a five-year period) with another (a '*service obligatoire du travail*', or mandatory labour service). Wider French citizenship for colonial subjects was also promised, as was colonial representation in France's Constituent Assembly – although in only a handful of seats. The Brazzaville meetings of 1944 were in large part a Free French propaganda exercise that took little account of colonial demands, evidenced by the fact that few Africans were even present, let alone had their concerns taken seriously, at an event dominated by French officials. Like Dutch and British wartime discursive initiatives, Brazzaville aimed to deflect American anti-colonial pressures and map out a future for a restored French empire, not prepare to wind it down.[39]

At Brazzaville, the Free French intended to appear liberal and generous while conceding little in the way of imperial devolution. Indeed, attendees envisaged what emerged in 1946 as a federal French Union soldering metropole and overseas territories together, befitting what would become a 'one and indivisible' Fourth Republic soon to rise from the ashes of Nazi occupation and Vichy. War had not blunted France's espousal of older imperial values but rather reinforced them. 'The ends of the civilising mission accomplished in the colonies exclude any idea of autonomy, all possibility of evolution outside the French bloc; also excluded is the eventual establishment of self-government in the colonies, even in a distant future', its proceedings stressed. Indicatively, so foreign was the notion of '*le self government*' to the French colonial mindset prevailing at Brazzaville that the English term was used instead.[40]

To colonial subjects, the response to the Thiaroye mutiny of the *tirailleurs sénégalais* and pronouncements at Brazzaville signalled all too clearly that metropolitan liberation did not portend colonial liberation in the view of the Free French. Events in Algeria on 8 May 1945 revealed this disjuncture most starkly. Celebrations across Algeria of 'Victory in Europe' Day – a victory that colonial troops, including over 136,000 Algerian Muslims, had helped make possible – erupted into a widespread revolt in Sétif and other towns, where disputes over land ownership and severe food shortages brought long-simmering tensions between Algerians and European settlers and colonial authorities to a boil. One hundred and two Europeans were killed and over a hundred others injured, often mutilated, in Sétif; French reprisals were savage and unyielding. Ten thousand soldiers (French as well as Moroccans, West Africans, and others)

---

[39] Shipway, *Road to War*, 20, 28–38.   [40] Ibid., 35–6.

combed the countryside to hunt down insurgents, burning houses and villages and conducting arbitrary executions and mass arrests. These measures were coupled with naval and aerial bombardments.[41]

If the number of Algerians killed was a subject of contention – French estimates tended to be a fraction of the 45,000 claimed by Algerians – Sétif's larger impact was indisputable. The chasm dividing Muslims and Europeans widened and hatreds deepened, and wider swathes of Algerian society were drawn to nationalism. For ever-greater numbers of Algerians, not least Muslim troops returning home from Europe after demobilization, the 'disjunction between the ideal of anti-Nazi liberation and the reality of French Algeria could not have been more startling', as Martin Evans has written.[42] In the coming years, many veterans ultimately assumed the role of anti-colonial liberation fighters who looked to violence as the only means to rid Algeria of French rule and settler domination. The Second World War may have ended in Europe in May 1945, but the simultaneous tragedy at Sétif marked what Alistair Horne has called 'the first volley of the Algerian War' that was to tear apart the hexagon and Algeria alike from 1954 until 1962.[43] In between, the French had another war to wage in Indochina, where Japan's surrender ushered in a new phase of the Vietnamese independence struggle against a liberated France determined to fight decolonization as part of its post-war road to reconstruction.

* * *

By mid-1945, France could celebrate the completion of the liberation process begun the previous summer in some parts of the hexagon in which multi-ethnic Free French forces had played an active role alongside the Allies. But liberation euphoria could not dispel a history of humbling defeat in 1940, the cruelties and civil divisions wrought by Vichyite collaboration and German occupation, and the Free French dependence on Allied wartime assistance that seemed set to continue well after 1945. The Second World War had dealt a severe blow to France's standing as a global power, and politicians after 1945 made the recovery of French grandeur a top priority. 'France cannot be France without greatness', de Gaulle famously stated in his *War Memoirs*, and he was far from alone in construing that greatness as closely tied to empire.[44] As Gaston Monnerville put it as Chair of France's Consultative Assembly in May 1945, 'let us never forget: without the Empire, France would be merely a liberated

---

[41] Jean-Louis Planche, *Sétif 1945: Histoire d'un massacre annoncé* (Paris, 2006); Martin Thomas, 'Colonial Violence in Algeria and the Distorted Logic of State Retribution: The Sétif Uprising of 1945', *Journal of Military History*, 75:1 (2011), 523–56; Evans, *Algeria*, 78–95.

[42] Evans, *Algeria*, 95.   [43] Horne, *Savage War*, 28 (see 23–8 for a longer discussion).

[44] Tony Smith, 'The French Colonial Consensus and People's War, 1946–58', *Journal of Contemporary History*, 9:4 (1974), 243.

country. Thanks to her Empire, France counts amongst the victors'. A public opinion poll conducted that same month found that 90 per cent of those responding believed that France counted as a great power once again, concluding that 'If France was still great, it was because of the Empire and its resources.'[45] Not only was empire deemed imperative to France's post-war economic reconstruction as a source of raw materials and foreign exchange earnings; it would give France international standing in a political arena in which the United States and the Soviet Union would clearly be dominant players, with Britain and its empire/Commonwealth trailing in third place.[46]

Yet preserving the French empire meant rhetorically killing it off as part of a wider effort to relegitimate it in tune with a reconfigured global political landscape. 'The colonial empire is dead', proclaimed the reporter general of the Constituent Assembly in 1946. 'In its place we are setting up the French Union. France, enriched, ennobled, and expanded, will tomorrow possess a hundred million citizens and free men.'[47] From 1946, the Constitution formally turned France and its empire into a single and comprehensive entity, with 'colony' now assiduously avoided in political discourse in favour of new nomenclature. Martinique, Guadeloupe, and Guiana in the French Antilles became '*départements d'outre-mer*' ('overseas departments'), as did Réunion. Colonies in sub-Saharan Africa and the Pacific along with Madagascar became '*territoires d'outre-mer*' ('overseas territories'), the mandated territories of Cameroon and Togo became 'associated territories', and the protectorates of Tunisia and Morocco alongside the five territories comprising the Indochinese Federation were recast as 'associated states'.[48] French Algeria maintained its pre-war status as three French *départements*, thus perpetuating the Third-Republic fiction that it remained integral to the nation into the Fourth Republic.

But to what extent did new names reflect new French policies and outlooks? As befitted a Union that encompassed metropolitan and overseas France, the new Constituent Assembly consisted of elected deputies hailing from both, albeit in vastly disproportionate numbers. Among 586 delegates in total, only 64 had been returned by overseas-based populations of the Union whose inhabitants exceeded 70 million, the remainder representing the 40 million

---

[45] Shipway, *Road to War*, 88. Gaston Monnerville was a lawyer born in French Guiana; descended from slaves, he had been active in metropolitan political life and in the resistance since the 1930s. See Jean-Paul Brunet, *Gaston Monnerville (1897–1991): Un destin d'exception* (Paris, 2013); on Monnerville's political career as long-time president of the Senate and ultimate political marginalization directly after Algerian independence, see Todd Shepard, *The Invention of Decolonization: The Algerian War and the Remaking of France* (Ithaca, 2006), 251–61.

[46] Nicholas J. White, 'Reconstructing Europe Through Rejuvenating Empire: The British, French, and Dutch Experiences Compared', *Past & Present*, 210, Supplement 6 (2011), 214.

[47] Martin Thomas, in Thomas, Moore, and Butler, *Crises of Empire*, 141.   [48] Ibid., 141–3.

residing within the hexagon. Moreover, only about half the overseas delegates had been elected by indigenous populations while the rest represented the French settler and expatriate minority whose numbers were minuscule by comparison.[49] Even so, delegates returned by Africans, Antilleans, and Algerians made a marked difference in shaping the 1946 Constitution and the French Union's framework and provisions. They included key figures such as Léopold Sédar Senghor, Ferhat Abbas, and Aimé Césaire; indeed, it was thanks to Césaire, now a communist deputy for Martinique, that the Antilles and Réunion were accorded the status of *départements d'outre-mer*. African delegates were responsible for securing the abolition of forced labour and the hated *indigénat*, which had long entailed a distinct and prejudicial system of justice for indigenous subjects. Most importantly, however, in 1946 these erstwhile subjects became citizens of the French Union via a law named after Lamine Guène, a Senegalese deputy.[50]

Generalized French Union citizenship was not won easily: overseas delegates had to fight hard against conservative forces determined to contain its implications. What ultimately emerged as article 80 of the Constitution proclaimed that 'All *ressortissants* [inhabitants] of overseas territories have the quality of citizen, on the same basis as French nationals of the metropole or of the overseas territories. Specific laws will establish the conditions under which they will exercise their rights as citizens.'[51] This vague and guarded formulation worked to dilute the rights of citizenship (and underpinned unequal suffrage provisions) even as it proclaimed equivalence regardless of racial and religious distinctions. Despite its egalitarian features, the Constitution thus marked a prime example of 'the schizophrenic character of post-war French colonialism', as Frederick Cooper notes: 'Africans could sit in the French legislature, and African labour unions could organize, strike, and claim equal pay and benefits for equal work. At the same time, anything that fell into the category of "insurrection" received the full colonial treatment', as subsequent French brutality in confronting uprisings in 1947 Madagascar and the 1954–1962 Algerian War of independence proved.[52] As many of the French Union's proverbial 'hundred million citizens' came to recognize, they were not free to envision an alternative national future fully independent of the federalized Union structure. If the Union put an end to the colonial order in name, it

---

[49] Jacques Frémeaux, 'L'Union française: le rêve d'une France unie (1946–1960)', in Pascal Blanchard, Sandrine Lemaire, and Nicolas Bancel (eds.), *Culture coloniale en France: De la Révolution à nos jours* (Paris, 2008), 406–7.

[50] The best in-depth analysis of these topics is Frederick Cooper, *Citizenship between Empire and Nation: Remaking France and French Africa, 1945–1960* (Princeton, 2014), chs. 2 and 3.

[51] Ibid., 121.

[52] Frederick Cooper, 'Reconstructing Empire in British and French Africa', *Past & Present*, 210, Supplement 6 (2011), 201.

was also intended to perpetuate many features of French domination in substance.

* * *

Indochina's fight for independence

Within the 'associated states' of the Indochinese Federation, Vietnamese committed to the Viet Minh soon put France to the test. In Vietnam, the coming years saw French nationalism seeking to restore world grandeur come head to head with Vietnamese nationalism and ultimately lose. Even before France's liberation when Indochina remained under Japanese domination, de Gaulle made it clear that France intended to re-establish sovereignty over Indochina and ensure its place within the French Union. But in August 1945 the Free French were far too weak to achieve this on their own. Since the Allies agreed that the French should ultimately return (American anti-colonialism had already started to wither with the growing fear of the spread of communism), Chinese troops were deployed to reoccupy territory north of the sixteenth parallel while British imperial forces undertook the same task to the south. This project paid no heed to Ho Chi Minh's Declaration of Independence of the Democratic Republic of Vietnam on 2 September. The British aimed to restore order and hand southern Vietnam (Cochin China and part of the central state of Annam) back to the French, who tried to clear Viet Minh forces from the region but lacked both the manpower and money to achieve an effective reoccupation.[53]

Weakness brought the French reluctantly to the negotiating table, and on 6 March 1946 an accord was signed with Ho Chi Minh that recognized the Republic of Vietnam as a free state with its own government, parliament, army, and finances. Crucially, however, this 'free state' would form part of the Indochinese Federation and the French Union – thereby compromising the very nature and extent of its freedom. In return, the Viet Minh permitted France to maintain its economic interests in the region as well as a limited number of troops to protect them, but insisted on a future plebiscite in Vietnam's three states of Tonkin, Annam, and Cochin China to determine whether each would join the Republic or arrive at an alternative arrangement with France. Ho looked to the agreement to secure two key objectives: the departure of Chinese occupiers and the emergence of a unified and independent Vietnam comprising all three regions following the plebiscites. While the former was successful, the latter failed because France failed to uphold its part of the

---

[53] David G. Marr, *Vietnam 1945: The Quest for Power* (Berkeley, 1997); Stein Tønnesson, *Vietnam 1946: How the War Began* (Berkeley, 2010); Shipway, *Road to War*, Part II; Brocheux and Hémery, *Indochina*, ch. 8.

bargain. The French also welcomed Chinese withdrawal as the chance to re-establish their troops north of the sixteenth parallel (the agreement stipulating their own withdrawal within five years), but were unwilling to allow the plebiscites to go forward. Instead, the French representative backed a separatist and ultimately short-lived republic in Cochin China as a counterweight to the Republic of Vietnam. This was of many manoeuvres undertaken in the next years intended to undercut the Viet Minh by sponsoring alternative Vietnamese players (such as the emperor Bao Dai) on the political stage whose lack of popular local support and utter reliance on French endorsement effectively rendered them puppets. As the Viet Minh's leading military strategist General Vo Nguyen Giap reflected, the French merely used the 6 March accord 'as a provisional expedient ... a delaying stratagem for preparing for the war they intended to continue'.[54] Relations between the French and the Viet Minh degenerated over the coming months and military skirmishes became more frequent. Eight years of Franco-Vietnamese war started late in 1946 after the French bombing of the port of Haiphong and the Viet Minh's retaliatory attack on French military installations in Tonkin.

France's determination to reassert control over Vietnam after the wartime abyss received cross-party support in the metropole. After de Gaulle resigned in early 1946, a series of unstable multi-party coalition governments held office that were characterized by an uneasy political cohabitation between the recently-formed *Mouvement républicain populaire* (MRP), socialists, and communists in the PCF, whose star had never been higher following their contributions to the wartime resistance struggle. The MRP's conservative leadership strongly favoured maintaining empire under the cloak of the French Union and consistently took a hard line on Indochina, but it was the socialist Prime Minister Léon Blum who reluctantly approved military repression in December 1946 and his socialist successor Paul Ramadier who reinforced this commitment soon after. Ramadier's rationale was telling. He declared in a speech before the National Assembly 'that France must stay in Indochina, that her succession there is not in question and that she must carry out there her civilizing work'. France stood neither for domination nor subjugation but association, he continued, adding that 'we respect the independence of peoples' – but on decidedly French terms. 'In Vietnam we will see new republics built with new liberties knowing, after all, that if the word liberty can be spoken in the Far East it is because France spoke it there first ... But this cannot be realized except within the framework of the French Union.'[55]

[54] General Vo Nguyen Giap, 'The War of Liberation, 1945–1954', in Russell Stetler (ed.), *The Military Art of People's War: Selected Writings of General Vo Nguyen Giap* (New York, 1970), 84.
[55] Prime Minister Ramadier, 'The French Stand in Indochina, March 18, 1947', reprinted from the *Journal Officiel de la République française*, Débats Parlementaires, 18 March 1947, pp. 904–5,

Liberty in Vietnam thus owed its conceptual origins to French influences and could only evolve though French-approved political frameworks: such was the view of many socialists, the MRP, and other parties on the centre and right of the French political spectrum in the late 1940s. The stance of French communists was more complex. France's refusal to countenance the kind of liberty Ho Chi Minh and the Viet Minh sought – Vietnam's independence as a unified state not hemmed in by either the Indochinese Federation or the French Union, which they rightly suspected would simply mean the continuation of colonial domination – was closely connected to dismissals of Ho and his party as agents of international communism. This occurred at precisely the moment when the Cold War doctrine consolidated under the Truman administration and shaped both American and European responses to anti-colonial nationalist movements.

As long as the *Parti Communiste Français* formed part of governing coalitions its ability to proclaim unqualified support for the Viet Minh was compromised, and the turning point came in May 1947 when the tense tripartite arrangement finally came to an acrimonious end and Ramadier rid his cabinet of communist ministers. The PCF then became free to declare open opposition to the French war, while their political opponents inside and outside government forfeited the opportunity to negotiate with the Viet Minh, since dialogue with Vietnamese communists meant strengthening the hand of French communists.[56] Over the coming years, this fractious French domestic political landscape impeded political solutions to the Indochina war and the conflict became submerged within the wider Cold War that divided Southeast Asia, Europe, and the French hexagon itself.[57] A Franco-French split had pitted Vichyites against the Free French and other resistance fighters not long before; it now characterized the chasm between French communists and other political parties.

The French and the Viet Minh contemplated one another through the lenses of both the war that had just ended and the Cold War that followed. 'The last avatar of the Second World War': such was the subsequent verdict of General René du Biré on France's war in Indochina.[58] If many French authorities considered Vietnam part of a wider effort at France's global reassertion after the nation's humbling loss of power after June 1940, Ho Chi Minh continued to

translated by Tony Smith, in Tony Smith (ed.), *The End of the European Empire: Decolonization after World War II* (Lexington, MA, 1975), 124, 126, 127; see also Smith, 'French Colonial Consensus', 226–7.

[56] Alain Ruscio, *Les communistes français et la guerre d'Indochine, 1944–1954* (Paris, 1985); Martin Thomas, 'French Imperial Reconstruction and the Development of the Indochina War, 1945–1950', in Mark Atwood Lawrence and Fredrik Logevall (eds.), *The First Vietnam War: Colonial Conflict and Cold War Crisis* (Cambridge, MA, 2007), 130–51.

[57] Shipway, *Road to War*, 107–9.

[58] 'Témoignage: Général (CR) René du Biré', in Pierre Journaud and Hugues Tertrais (eds.), *1954–2004: La bataille du Dien Bien Phu entre histoire et mémoire* (Paris, 2004), 201.

evoke the Atlantic Charter and other Allied wartime proclamations and condemn French colonialists who 'sabotaged their fathers' principles of liberty and equality'. Moreover, like the Japanese occupiers, they had sent Vietnamese militants to prisons and 'concentration camps, which are more horrible than the ones set up by the German fascists to torture their victims'. Ho insisted that the Viet Minh's struggle was not against the French people but rather against French colonialism that operated only in the interests of 'a handful of administrators and militarists or capitalists':

We know that having struggled against the Germans, and maintained a firm spirit during the darkest days of their history, the French people will feel our pains and sacrifices more than any other people. They will intervene with their Government to stop the bloodshed, and save honest people's lives.[59]

This confident claim made in November 1945 was about to be put to the test by Henri Martin, an eighteen-year-old marine then on board a ship bound for Vietnam.

Henri Martin's decision to enlist in the French Navy extended from his wartime resistance activity as a young communist in the last months of German occupation. Having participated in the liberation of French towns from Nazi control near where he grew up, he volunteered for five years' naval service to help expel the Japanese from Indochina. Yet he quickly grew disillusioned with what he witnessed of French colonialism and military behaviour once the focus shifted to snuffing out Viet Minh opposition after Japan's surrender. 'In Indochina, the French army conducts itself like *les Boches* [Germans] acted at home', he told his parents in a letter in May 1946 – an analogy enhanced by his focus on French Foreign Legion forces, which he estimated to consist of 40 per cent German nationals. 'To kill one guy, they burn eight villages', he reported, asking: 'Why do our soldiers pillage, burn, and kill? To civilize?' In firing upon defenceless fishermen and villagers and abusing wounded prisoners, 'the army forfeits all France's prestige in the Far East'; in failing to uphold 'our ideal of liberty', they were sacrificing France's good name. What Martin found were not the rebels commonly disparaged by the French but men fighting for their own liberty from the French, who in response were unwilling to tolerate any Vietnamese who proved insufficiently grateful for the golden opportunity to become 'civilized', at gunpoint if necessary.[60]

[59] 'Speech Delivered in the First Days of the Resistance War in South Vietnam (November, 1945)', in Ho Chi Minh, *On Revolution*, 158–9; 'Appeal to Vietnamese Residents in France (November 5, 1945)', in ibid., 156–7.

[60] Henri Martin, letters of 18 May 1946 and 3 June 1946, in Jean-Paul Sartre *et al.*, *L'Affaire Henri Martin* (Paris, 1953), 40–1, 44.

Thoroughly disgusted by what he saw, Martin finally received permission to return to the metropole after two years in Indochina. Stationed at the Toulon dockyard, he attempted to politicize new army recruits about to be sent overseas by distributing leaflets calling on them to oppose the war, and in 1950 he was arrested on charges of demoralizing the army and given a five-year prison sentence.[61] His case generated sufficient public notoriety and controversy to merit the sublimely French distinction of an *affaire* after communists and prominent intellectuals embarked on a battle to defend his actions and secure his release and pardon by the summer of 1953. In a collection of testimonials edited by the leading existentialist philosopher Jean-Paul Sartre, Martin's supporters commended him for struggling to uphold the principles of the French Revolution and the anti-Nazi resistance alike in contesting French injustices in Indochina deemed comparable to those France itself had recently suffered. One champion, Marc Beigbeder, alluded to 'barbaric behaviour' meted out in Indochina 'which, in the manner of Hitler, was unleashed on civilian populations by bombing villages with napalm and by collective massacres comparable to those at Oradour, and by arbitrary executions'.[62] In this, he referred to the events of 10 June 1944, when Oradour-sur-Glane became France's equivalent to the Dutch village of Putten when Waffen-SS troops rounded up and killed 642 French women, children, and men and burnt the village to the ground.

By the time of '*L'Affaire Henri Martin*' in the early 1950s, Oradour was so deeply entrenched in the French national consciousness as the archetypal 'martyred village' where innocent French civilians had been slaughtered by Nazis trying to crack down on resistance activity that drawing a parallel between its fate and that of the Vietnamese at the hands of the French made for a uniquely powerful indictment of French conduct in Indochina.[63] Invoking Oradour-sur-Glane, as a number of French detractors did, worked to condemn French actions and, relatedly, 'inscribe the Viet Minh into French national history and into the resistance mythology', Sylvain Pons has written. At a stroke, this turned the Viet Minh into 'brothers in arms' of the anti-Nazi French and the French expeditionary forces who had so recently liberated France into forces of occupation akin to Nazis. Viet Minh leaders freely deployed similar rhetoric. 'We're resisters too', Ho Chi Minh proclaimed, making reference to the Viet Minh's recent struggle against the Japanese; or, as Tran Van Giau,

[61] Alain Ruscio, '*L'Affaire Henri Martin*: Genèse et grandes étapes', in Alain Ruscio (ed.), *L'Affaire Henri Martin et la lutte contre la guerre d'Indochine* (Pantin, 2005), 43–107; Ruscio, *Les communistes français*, 266–87; Paul Clay Sorum, *Intellectuals and Decolonization in France* (Chapel Hill, 1977), 55–6, 151–5; Liauzu, *Histoire de l'anticolonialisme*, 418–20.

[62] Marc Beigbeder, 'Un héros de la raison commune', in Sartre *et al.*, *L'Affaire Henri Martin*, 251.

[63] Sarah Farmer, *Martyred Village: Commemorating the 1944 Massacre at Oradour-sur-Glane* (Berkeley, 1999).

another senior Viet Minh figure, put it in an interview with a French journalist, '*C'est vous les Allemands*' ('It's you who are the Germans').[64]

Beigbeder was one of a number of early post-war writers to invoke Nazi European atrocities in connection with European colonialism. Better known was Aimé Césaire's *Discours sur le colonialisme* (*Discourse on Colonialism*), published first in 1950 and in revised form in 1955, which provided a searing assessment of how

colonization works to *decivilize* the colonizer, to *brutalize* him . . . to awaken him to . . . violence, race hatred, and moral relativism . . . each time a head is cut off or an eye put out in Vietnam and in France they accept the fact . . . a universal regression takes place, a gangrene sets in, a center of infection begins to spread.

With Nazism, Europe experienced what Césaire called a 'boomerang effect': before Europeans were victims of Nazism, 'they were its accomplices; that they tolerated that Nazism before it was inflicted on them, that they absolved it, shut their eyes to it, legitimized it, [was] because, until then, it had been applied only to non-European peoples'. The reason why 'the very distinguished, very humanistic, very Christian bourgeois of the twentieth century' could not forgive Hitler, Césaire argued,

is not *the crime* in itself, *the crime against man*, it is not *the humiliation of man as such*, it is the crime against the white man, the humiliation of the white man, and the fact that he applied to Europe colonialist procedures which until then had been reserved exclusively for the Arabs of Algeria, the 'coolies' of India, and the 'niggers' of Africa.[65]

With Nazism and genocide in Europe still but a recent memory, anti-colonial deployments of Nazi analogies to condemn European attempts to reassert the upper hand overseas exemplify how, as Michael Rothberg concludes, '[n]ot only has imperialist violence produced a "decivilization" of Europe; European fascism inflects and infects colonial discourse in the age of decolonization'.[66]

To what extent did metropolitan society share the verdicts of Henri Martin and his supporters on France's Indochina policy? Sartre's review *Les Temps modernes* had come out against the war from the start, publishing editorials as early as December 1946 that caused outrage by comparing it with the Nazi occupation of the hexagon, a charge it reiterated in later years.[67] Politicians and press organs at the centre and on the right supported France's effort to restore its authority and combat the Viet Minh; liberals and leftists increasingly moved

[64] Sylvain Pons, 'Les visages d'un ennemi: la fabrication du Viêt-Minh, 1945–1946', *Relations Internationales*, 130 (2007, no. 2), 39–40.

[65] Aimé Césaire, *Discourse on Colonialism*, translated by Joan Pinkham (New York, 2000), 35–6.

[66] Michael Rothberg, *Multidirectional Memory: Remembering the Holocaust in the Age of Decolonization* (Stanford, 2009), 77, and his extended analysis of Césaire throughout ch. 3.

[67] David Drake, '*Les Temps modernes* and the French War in Indochina', *Journal of European Studies*, 28:1–2 (1998), 29–30, 36.

towards calls for French representatives to negotiate with the Viet Minh, concede independence, and withdraw French forces. Calls for peace came alongside criticisms of the mounting cost of the military operations and rising death tolls, particularly from French communists and the *Confédération Générale du Travail* (the federation of trades unions). The war provoked significant protests among dock workers in Marseille and other port cities who staged strikes in 1949 and 1950, refusing to load ships carrying munitions and troops destined for Vietnam – an example of those uniquely situated at the metropolitan/overseas geographical interface adopting perspectives based on personal experiences, in this instance the unloading of coffins and wounded soldiers from inbound ships that provided a potent indication of the brutality and sacrifices of a faraway war.[68] For reasons examined further later, however, between the two extremes of pro-war and anti-war politics and militancy lay what Alain Ruscio describes as a 'swampland' of public indifference about a conflict that seemed remote from everyday concerns.[69]

The prevalence of French communists among Indochina war dissenters was testament to the Cold War underpinnings of the conflict whose front ran through France itself as well as through Vietnam and led to its internationalization. The global Cold War heating up in the late 1940s changed the scale, nature, and rationales of the independence struggle between the Viet Minh and France, allowing France to justify retaining its foothold under the guise of fighting a war against communism. France denied that its ambitions were colonial in nature. The stated intention became that of supporting a non-communist Vietnamese nationalist alternative to the Democratic Republic of Vietnam in the form of a unified and independent 'Associated State' (within the French Union) headed by Bao Dai, the former emperor – a figure who never succeeded in attracting significant Vietnamese backing. Ho Chi Minh's calls for the French to honour the Vietnamese demand for national freedom were thus pitted against French self-justifications that they sought to defend the free world from insidious communist encroachment.

The Viet Minh's communist credentials made anti-colonialism in Vietnam vastly different from the leading nationalist organization the Dutch battled in the East Indies. Because Sukarno and his allies had proven their anti-communism to American satisfaction, the United States backing for the Dutch position eroded in 1948, as explored in the last chapter. By

---

[68] Ruscio, *Les communistes français*, Part II, chs. 4 and 5; Rosemarie Scullion, 'On the Waterfront: Class Action and Anti-Colonial Engagements in Paul Carpita's *Le Rendez-vous des quais*', *South Central Review*, 17:3 (2000), 35–49.

[69] Alain Ruscio, 'L'opinion française et la guerre d'Indochine (1945–1954): Sondages et témoignages', *Vingtième Siècle*, 29:1 (1991), 37; Alain Ruscio, 'French Public Opinion and the War in Indochina: 1945–1954', in Michael Scriven and Peter Wagstaff (eds.), *War and Society in Twentieth-Century France* (New York, 1991), 117–20.

contrast, starting in 1950 the United States grew ever more involved in directly aiding France against her Vietnamese opponent. American financing and military advisors came in combination with the increased weaponry and funding the Viet Minh received from the new communist People's Republic of China after Mao Zedong's victory in 1949. Internationalizing and escalating the war rendered it infinitely more costly and changed the nature of battle, together with the Viet Minh's military fortunes. Since 1946, the Viet Minh had mainly waged a guerrilla war, managing to spread their influence across many regions of Vietnam's rural interior, both in the northern parts of the country where their main strongholds were located and increasingly across many parts of Cochin China. As General Giap recalled, '[t]he soil of the fatherland was being freed inch by inch right in the enemy's rear lines. There was no clearly defined front in this war. It was wherever the enemy was. The front was nowhere, it was everywhere.'[70] Guerrilla skirmishes never ceased, but after 1949 the Viet Minh's ability to stage large-scale conventional battles gradually grew stronger. Early 1950s Viet Minh victories at Cao Bang and Hoa Binh came at the price of heavy casualties, while other set-piece battles ended in catastrophic defeats.[71]

French war-weariness increased as the conflict morphed into a long war of attrition while the Viet Minh maintained and strengthened its appeal among the peasant majority, not least via land redistribution programmes in areas where they assumed control. For the Viet Minh, the war was decidedly a 'people's war' that derived its power from mass support and sacrifices, with the goals of independence, national reunification, and social revolution rallying huge swathes of an overwhelmingly impoverished agrarian society behind its cause.[72] In France, by contrast, politicians and the politically-engaged sectors of public opinion grew progressively more resentful at the loss of life and financial burdens. By 1952, the war with no end in sight devoured 40 per cent of France's defence budget despite spiralling contributions from the United States, which paid over three-quarters of France's war costs by 1953.

With more and more territory falling under effective enemy control and the Viet Minh's military capabilities growing, the French looked to a combination of military and political solutions to a conflict that had become increasingly

[70] Giap, 'War of Liberation', in Stetler (ed.), *Military Art of People's War*, 88.
[71] Among many excellent studies of the Franco-Viet Minh conflict too numerous to mention here, see discussions by Duiker, *Communist Road to Power*, ch. 7; Jacques Dalloz, *The War in Indo-China, 1945–54*, translated by Josephine Bacon (Dublin, 1990); Anthony Clayton, *The Wars of French Decolonization* (London, 1994), chs. 3 and 4; William J. Duiker, 'Ho Chi Minh and the Strategy of People's War', in Lawrence and Logevall (eds.), *First Vietnam War*, 152–74, along with other contributions to this collection; Logevall, *Embers of War*.
[72] Giap, 'War of Liberation', in Stetler (ed.), *Military Art of People's War*, 92–8.

unpopular at home and hindered the pace of the metropole's economic revival. Negotiations at Geneva were planned for mid-1954, and both adversaries aimed to arrive at the table holding the strongest hand possible. General Henri Navarre adopted a new strategy to turn French fortunes around, seeking to block the Viet Minh's supply of weaponry flowing in from China and stem its activities across the border in Laos by occupying Dien Bien Phu, an isolated basin in the mountainous region of northwest Tonkin. This area had long been a Viet Minh stronghold where it held an overwhelming geographical advantage, and Giap gambled that it could build up sufficient forces and artillery to defeat the heavily fortified French garrison defended by 16,000 troops. Tens of thousands of Viet Minh troops and peasant recruits contributed to a logistical triumph, carrying in munitions and supplies on foot and on bicycles. They painstakingly constructed an intricate system of tunnels, trenches, and offensive positions, encircling the supposedly impregnable French camp and launching their attack in mid-March 1954. Fifty-six days later the French surrendered on 7 May, having ignominiously forfeited their hilltop defensive positions one by one and lost the ability to resupply Dien Bien Phu by plane with food, weapons, and troop reinforcements once the Viet Minh destroyed the airstrip that had served as the garrison's main connection to the outside world. Losses were heavy on both sides, with Viet Minh casualties totalling more than 25,000 while the French expeditionary corps troops counted more than 1,500 killed and 4,000 wounded. Over 10,000 became prisoners of war, suffering horrific conditions in Viet Minh internment camps that killed many more. As General du Biré later recalled, a far higher percentage of men captured at Dien Bien Phu perished than those subjected to Nazi death camps.[73] As the worst military defeat suffered in the nation's colonial history, Dien Bien Phu heralded the end of France's involvement in the war in Indochina, but analogies drawn between the enemy and the Nazis (this time by French officers looking back fifty years later) long outlived it.

Dien Bien Phu was just the debacle needed to secure France's departure from Vietnam. Although the United States pressured the French to continue the fight, at Geneva they recognized Vietnam north of the seventeenth parallel as under the control of Ho Chi Minh's government, leaving the region south of the divide in the hands of the Bao Dai regime which soon gave way to another American-backed political order equally wanting in stability and legitimacy. France's retreat soon extended to conceding independence to Cambodia and Laos, bringing its era of colonial control in Southeast Asia to a close and leaving the Americans to carry on the struggle against communism in the region until 1975.

* * *

[73] 'Témoignage: Général (CR) René du Biré', 203.

Reckoning with Indochina and the struggle over
Algérie française, 1954–1958

Writing in 1956, General Navarre defended himself from accusations that he bore responsibility for this monumental defeat. He shifted the burden of Dien Bien Phu – and the loss of Indochina – onto the Fourth Republic, whose approach to the war he characterized as pervaded by vacillation, cowardice, and chronic indecision and miscalculations. French politicians had 'allowed the army to be stabbed in the back' and 'tolerated the continuous betrayal by the Communist Party and all its reserves', he wrote, a verdict shared by many other French officers whose experiences in Indochina sowed intense feelings of betrayal at the hands of an uninterested French public, French communists and other anti-war voices, and most of all the men who held office in weak, unstable, and ephemeral governments.[74] Of more than 500,000 troops to have fought on France's behalf, over 100,000 had been killed (as against more than 400,000 Viet Minh dead). Nonetheless, the Indochina war was quickly forgotten within France after May 1954, the widespread amnesia undoubtedly contributing to the resentment that took root among surviving soldiers and officers. France's fight to maintain its hold over Vietnam was promptly overshadowed by the struggle in Algeria that broke out only months after the surrender at Dien Bien Phu. The contrasts between the Indochina conflict and that which raged in Algeria between 1954 and 1962 do much to explain why the former so readily became marginalized within French public memory.

First, the French did not battle the Viet Minh alone: indeed, two-thirds of those who fought on France's behalf were not French nationals. France drew heavily on the French Union, the French Foreign Legion, and indigenous recruits from Vietnam, Cambodia, and Laos, increasingly so the longer the war dragged on. Soldiers from North Africa and West Africa (largely Moroccans, Algerians, and Senegalese) made up 43.5 per cent of the French Expeditionary Corps in 1954. Of the 488,560 men to embark for the Far East, 233,467 were French, 72,833 were legionnaires, 122,932 came from North Africa, and 60,340 from sub-Saharan Africa.[75] In his famous analysis of a saluting African boy whose photograph donned the cover of the popular French weekly magazine Paris-Match in 1953, Roland Barthes claimed that the image was meant to demonstrate 'that France is a great Empire, that all her sons, without any colour discrimination, faithfully serve under her flag, and that there is no better answer to the detractors of an alleged colonialism than the zeal

---

[74] Henri Navarre, Agonie de l'Indochine, 1953–1954 (Paris, 1956), cited in Dalloz, War in Indo-China, 183.

[75] Michel Bodin, Les africains dans la guerre d'Indochine, 1947–1954 (Paris, 2000), 5; Michel Bodin, La France et ses soldats: Indochine, 1945–1954 (Paris, 1996), 7. Clayton, Wars of French Decolonization, 74, notes that in the summer of 1953 there were 151,000 Vietnamese and 26,000 forces from Cambodia and Laos fighting the Viet Minh.

shown by this Negro in serving his so-called oppressors'. If an African soldier (or potential future soldier, given the young age of the boy in the image) could act as the mythical 'signifier' of the French empire, this was due as much to his engagements in Indochina as to his previous involvement in two world wars.[76]

French troops formed a minority of the total fighting force and of the total numbers killed (the war claimed 20,000 French lives, including nearly 2,000 officers along with 11,000 legionnaires, 15,000 North and West Africans, and 46,000 Indochinese).[77] Crucially, French nationals fighting in the Indochina war were professional soldiers and volunteers, never conscripts. This rendered the French experience of the 1946–1954 war in Southeast Asia vastly different from the Algerian War that followed it, when over two and a half million French men were drafted to serve across the Mediterranean. This was just one of many ways that the war was brought home to every French community in the metropole, turning the fight in Algeria into a personal and family experience for millions more French men and women in the hexagon than were directly affected by the Indochinese conflict preceding it.[78] 'There is not a single Frenchman who does not have a cousin in Algeria', anti-colonial critic Frantz Fanon noted in 1957, which meant that 'the whole French nation finds itself involved in the crime against a people and is today an accomplice in the murders and tortures that characterize the Algerian war'.[79]

Second, just as Indochina was never a destination for French conscripts, it was never inhabited by a substantial French expatriate or settler population. Approximately 30,000–35,000 French nationals lived in Vietnam between 1940 and 1954, forming a drop in the bucket within Vietnam's population that exceeded 20 million. By contrast, the French 'cousins' in Algeria to whom Fanon alluded included even more settlers than soldiers. Amidst a Muslim population of nine million lived one million European settlers, most of them born in Algeria; although not all were originally of French descent (a substantial number had family origins in Spain, Malta, and Italy), they had long enjoyed French nationality, as had Algeria's Jewish population.

---

[76] Roland Barthes, 'Myth Today', in *Mythologies*, translated by Annette Lavers (London, 1993), especially 116, 129, 143. First published in French in 1957, the essays compiled in *Mythologies* were written between 1954 and 1956; Barthes analysed the cover of the 25 June–3 July 1953 issue of *Paris-Match*.

[77] Dalloz, *War in Indo-China*, 185.

[78] On the intersections of France's history of decolonization, especially in Algeria, with French society and especially the experience of modernization and proliferating consumer culture in the metropole, see the landmark study by Kristin Ross, *Fast Cars, Clean Bodies: Decolonization and the Reordering of French Culture* (Cambridge, MA, 1995), together with many later studies including Raphaëlle Branche and Sylvie Thénault (eds.), *La France en guerre 1954–1962: Expériences métropolitaines de la guerre d'indépendance algérienne* (Paris, 2008).

[79] Frantz Fanon, 'French Intellectuals and Democrats and the Algerian Revolution (1957)', in *Toward the African Revolution*, translated by Haakon Chevalier (Harmondsworth, 1970; original French text published in 1964), 93.

Third, whereas French Indochina was 12,000 kilometres distant and was historically composed of a colony and protectorates, Algeria lay directly across the Mediterranean and was reachable from mainland France by ship in under two days. Algeria had long been far more than a colony, or a protectorate like its Tunisian and Moroccan neighbours: since 1848, it had been constitutionally part of France itself and divided into three *départements*, falling under the jurisdiction of France's Ministry of the Interior as opposed to the Ministry of Colonies. France had insistently tried to corral Indochina, like other overseas territories, into the French Union; Algeria, however, *was* France. '*Algérie, c'est la France*', its defenders continually insisted; or, as General Raoul Salan proclaimed in 1958 while acting as the French army's commander-in-chief in Algeria, '[t]he Mediterranean runs through France as the Seine runs through Paris'.[80] So conceptually integral was Algeria to France, so large (and politicized) was its white settler population, and so geographically proximate was it to the hexagon that the war of decolonization which erupted on 1 November 1954 readily spilled across the Mediterranean. Over the next eight years, it was to engulf French politics and society in ways Indochina never did. Nonetheless, the devastating *dénouement* of France's attempt to remain in Vietnam survived in the imaginations of those who became embroiled in the violence pervading Algeria and shaped their goals and tactics. So too did the legacy of fascism, which continued to affect French responses to the Algerian conflict just as it had structured perceptions of the last years of French Indochina.

* * *

The Algerian insurrection that broke out late in 1954 did not emanate from an established political party led by familiar leaders like Messali Hadj or Ferhat Abbas.[81] The *Front de Libération Nationale* (FLN) was a new and hitherto unknown grouping initially led by nine men and their supporters, many of whom already claimed prior involvement in nationalist organizations suppressed by the French. Its inner circle gradually built up a committed group of armed insurgent cells that announced their arrival onto the anti-colonial scene in a series of seventy coordinated attacks across Algeria on 1 November. The FLN's emergence and support network extended from long-brewing tensions and Muslim anger that became radicalized and

---

[80] Pierre Vidal-Naquet, *Torture: Cancer of Democracy: France and Algeria 1954–62*, translated by Barry Richard (Harmondsworth, 1963), 107.

[81] Overviews of the 1954–1962 Algerian War include Horne, *Savage War*; Benjamin Stora, *Histoire de la guerre d'Algérie (1954–1962)*, 4th ed. (Paris, 2004), published in English translation as Part I of Benjamin Stora, *Algeria 1830–2000: A Short History*, translated by Jane Marie Todd (Ithaca, 2001); Jean-Charles Jauffret (ed.), *Des hommes et des femmes en guerre d'Algérie* (Paris, 2003); Mohammed Harbi and Benjamin Stora (eds.), *La guerre d'Algérie* (Paris, 2004); Sylvie Thénault, *Histoire de la guerre d'indépendance algérienne* (Paris, 2005); Evans, *Algeria*.

militarized on the back of decades of political disappointments and ongoing mass poverty and dispossession. Just as the modest Blum-Viollette reform proposals had been scuppered by settler activists in the late 1930s, the 1947 Statute of Algeria further affirmed the political, social, and economic pre-eminence of the European minority in an Algerian Assembly divided into two separate electoral colleges. Each college contained sixty elected repre-sentatives, but one side was voted in by 460,000 Europeans and 58,000 'assimilated' Muslims, while the other was returned by 1,400,000 'unassi-milated' Muslims. With a two-thirds vote required to pass legislation, the settlers never failed to achieve the political result they sought and to stymie proposals they feared would dilute their power by redistributing it to the Muslim majority. Within a system that was blatantly unequal as it was, French authorities further bolstered the status quo by rigging elections.

France's repeated capitulations to the settler minority left moderate Algerian nationalists who looked to achieve change via legal channels hamstrung, ultimately rendering the middle ground of Muslim Algerian politics a scorched earth where little survived to harvest. By blocking the efforts of Muslim moderates to secure concessions and sowing deep-seated distrust in the pro-spects for reform, the French were left to do battle with an ascendant nationalist enemy that demanded not reform – or an independent Algeria connected to France as part of a federation, as Abbas' *Union Démocratique du Manifeste Algérien* (UDMA) party called for – but a full-scale revolution. Under the FLN banner, this enemy matched French and settler intransigence and reciprocated a long colonial history of ruthless repression not by pleas for fair access to the ballot box but by insisting that violence was the only way to secure Algeria's complete independence. Frantz Fanon, the psychiatrist and political theorist from Martinique who gained first-hand exposure to colonial racism at home, as a student in France, and as a doctor at a hospital in Algeria, joined the FLN in 1956 and quickly became one of its most renowned and eloquent political advocates. His succinct encapsulation of the colonial situation accurately summed up the FLN's core ethos, which dismissed non-violent tactics as ineffectual – 'an attempt to settle the colonial problem around a green baize table, before any regrettable act has been performed or irreparable gesture made, before any blood has been shed'. Faith in non-violence was inherently misguided, Fanon argued, as it went against the entire nature of the colonial system in which untold amounts of blood had always been shed: 'colonialism is not a thinking machine, nor a body endowed with reasoning faculties. It is violence in its natural state, and it will only yield when confronted with greater violence'.[82]

---

[82] Frantz Fanon, *The Wretched of the Earth*, translated by Constance Farrington (London, 1990; originally published as *Les damnées de la terre*, Paris, 1961), 48.

The 1 November proclamation issued by the FLN leadership accordingly declared that theirs was a revolutionary struggle to be carried forward 'by all means until our goal is achieved', demanding Algerian national independence predicated on 'the respect of all fundamental liberties without racial or confessional distinction' but within the 'framework of Islamic principles'. The campaign fought inside Algeria itself needed to involve an '*assainissement politique*' (politics of sanitation, or purification) by 'placing the national revolutionary movement on its true path and the annihilation of all traces of corruption and reformism'. Curing Algeria of the sickness which was colonialism required 'gathering and organizing all the healthy energies [*toutes les énergies saines*] of the Algerian people in order to liquidate the colonial system'.[83] This involved terrorist acts including bombings, assassinations, and brutal physical attacks on European settlers, soldiers, and police as well as Muslims perceived to support the colonial order – or simply Muslims who had not subscribed to the FLN's programme. Indeed, the Algerian War was more than a struggle against the French for national independence: it was a fratricidal civil war in which the FLN successfully deployed violence and intimidation on a massive scale to absorb, neutralize, or eliminate Algerians who supported rival nationalist movements (such as the latest incarnation of Messali Hadj's organization). To take a prominent example, Ferhat Abbas switched allegiance to the FLN and became the head of its provisional government after having lost faith in the ability of political moderation to achieve change (going so far as to assert that 'there is no other solution but the machine-gun') *and* because the FLN executed his nephew, another moderate, as one of the many condemned as traitors whose fate was meant to serve as a lesson to others not yet committed to their cause.[84]

From the start, the FLN correctly identified its liberation struggle within Algeria as inseparable from its external dimensions, beginning with its inspirations. The decisive defeat General Giap's army inflicted upon France's forces at Dien Bien Phu that hastened the end of French rule in Vietnam just six months before the FLN launched its insurgency made a strong mark on Algerian militant consciousness, in part because many North African soldiers who had served with the French expeditionary forces returned home and became incorporated into the FLN's campaign to cleanse Algeria of French toxins. Reflecting on its global import in 1961, Fanon perceived that '[t]he great victory of the Vietnamese people at Dien Bien Phu is no longer, strictly speaking, a Vietnamese victory. Since July 1954, the question which the

[83] 'Proclamation', in Jabhat al-Tahrir al-Qawmi (ed.), *Le Peuple Algérien et Sa Révolution* (Éditions Résistance Algérienne, n.d., 1956 or 1957), 24.
[84] Matthew Connelly, *A Diplomatic Revolution: Algeria's Fight for Independence and the Origins of the Post-Cold War Era* (Oxford, 2002), 25; Horne, *Savage War*, 140.

colonized peoples have asked themselves has been "What must be done to bring about another Dien Bien Phu? How can we manage it?"[85]

Alongside international encouragements and stimuli came direct support from outside Algerian territory. In its 1 November 1954 proclamation, the FLN stressed its aim to 'internationalize the Algerian problem' and involve the United Nations directly as part of its propaganda war to win support for its cause. This ultimately proved crucial to its victory in securing independence, but nurturing relationships spanning North Africa had always been the most important plank in its external agenda.[86] Although the FLN sought national independence for Algeria, it emphasized 'the realization of North African Unity within its natural Arab-Muslim framework'.[87] Throughout the course of the conflict, Algeria's closest neighbours proved integral to the FLN's fight. Once France granted independence to its protectorates of Morocco and Tunisia in 1956 (a process heavily influenced by its struggle to contain the Algerian revolt), the FLN insisted that their independence could be nothing other than a 'delusion' as long as Algeria remained 'under the colonial yoke'.[88] In fact, independent Morocco and Tunisia provided crucial bases for FLN leaders living in exile and gave the insurgency supplies and bases from which to stage attacks into Algeria. Nor can Cairo's importance be underestimated, with Egypt under the Nasser regime giving the movement essential political and military backing.

France responded to the internationalization of the Algerian War with a barrage of tactics they hoped would contain it. The French army fortified the borders with Tunisia and Morocco with hundreds of miles of electrified barbed wire, watchtowers, and landmines to stem cross-border penetrations and cut the internal insurgency off from inward flows of men and materiel. Political leaders, meanwhile, insisted that Nasser was the real guiding light behind the FLN and blamed its successes and survival largely on the moral and material sustenance it received from Egypt. Like British Prime Minister Anthony Eden, France's socialist premier Guy Mollet would not budge from his conviction that Nasser was both a representative of world communism and a new version of Hitler with whom the West must not repeat the mistake of 1930s appeasement. After Nasser nationalized the Anglo-French Suez Canal in July 1956, France's decision to join forces with the British and Israelis to invade in November was largely taken to stop the FLN from receiving the Egyptian backing that was essential for their insurrection. The Suez invasion failed once intense pressure from the United

[85] Fanon, *Wretched*, 55.
[86] On the international diplomatic dimensions of the Algerian War that worked decisively in the FLN's favour, see Connelly, *Diplomatic Revolution*.
[87] 'Proclamation', in al-Qawmi (ed.), *Le Peuple Algérien*, 24.
[88] 'Doctrine révolutionnaire et programme politique de la Résistence Algérienne', in al-Qawmi (ed.), *Le Peuple Algérien*, 29.

States rendered it impossible for the British to continue, as Chapter 1 discussed. Once Britain backed down, the French had no choice but to do likewise.[89]

Suez failed to stop Egypt from assisting the FLN, sabotaged France's standing with many Arab states, and worsened relations with both the United States and Britain as Cold War allies the French political establishment felt could not be fully trusted. Anger and doubts about the 'Anglo-Saxons' continued to simmer afterwards, contributing in the longer term to de Gaulle's refusals to allow a Britain that was far too likely to do America's bidding to become part of the European Economic Community and his decision to withdraw France from NATO's integrated military alliance in the 1960s (themes that receive further attention in this chapter's conclusion).[90] Tensions that dated back to difficult relations during the war years when de Gaulle had relied on Anglo-American support for the Free French had taken a new turn in the late 1940s, a time when concerns about the impact of American economic and political dominance and popular culture gave rise to the fear of France becoming '*coca-colonisé*' – colonized by invasive American influences like Coca-Cola.[91] In November 1953, Ho Chi Minh had insisted that America compromised not only Vietnam's independence but also that of France itself, with 'U.S. imperialists' pressuring France to continue the fight 'in hopes of replacing France in Indochina' as well as determining France's European defence policy.[92] His prognosis for the French had never seemed truer than at Suez three years later, nor for the Vietnamese over the course of the next twenty.

Spectacularly backfiring with far-reaching consequences, the Suez campaign exemplified how, as Matthew Connelly observes, 'nothing "internationalized" the [Algerian] war so much as France's increasingly desperate attempts to isolate it'.[93] France rejected recurrent United Nations criticisms of its Algerian policy as inappropriate meddling in an internal, metropolitan French affair that required 'pacification' and 'actions to maintain order'. The Algerian revolt was no more acknowledged as a 'war' than Algeria was recognized as a colony, the French claiming they were conducting 'police operations' and 'operations to restore civil peace' in response to 'events' within French *départements*.[94] But if the argument that 'Algeria is France'

---

[89] Connelly, *Diplomatic Revolution*, 108–9, 119–23; Irwin M. Wall, *France, the United States and the Algerian War* (Berkeley, 2001), 66, 263 (and ch. 2 more generally); Jean-Pierre Rioux, *The Fourth Republic, 1944–1958* (Cambridge, 1987), 272–5; Evans, *Algeria*, 159–61, 183–4.

[90] Horne, *Savage War*, 163; see also 157–64; Martin Thomas, *The French North African Crisis: Colonial Breakdown and Anglo-French Relations, 1945–62* (Basingstoke, 2000), especially 125–9.

[91] Richard F. Kuisel, *Seducing the French: The Dilemma of Americanization* (Berkeley, 1993), 55.

[92] 'Replies to a Foreign Correspondent (November 26, 1953)', in Ho Chi Minh, *On Revolution*, 257.

[93] Connelly, *Diplomatic Revolution*, 8.

[94] Benjamin Stora, 'Algeria: The War Without a Name', *Journal of Imperial and Commonwealth History*, 21:3 (1993), 208.

was a French article of faith, its feebleness was derided as 'damn nonsense' by US President Eisenhower and mocked by FLN supporters.[95] As André Mandouze (a French teacher at the University of Algiers who became committed to the fight against colonialism) pointed out in his journal *Consciences Maghribines*, 'one wouldn't so often and so violently repeat that Algeria is French if it really was. She simply would be – and that would suffice.'[96]

France's determination to restore 'law and order', crush the revolt, and keep Algeria French involved an internal counterinsurgency campaign to match the effort to insulate Algeria from external aid and reinforcements. The FLN's massacre staged in and around Philippeville in August 1955 exemplified the war's brutality and cycle of retributional violence. Targeting cafés with grenades and ambushing a nearby mining village, 123 were killed and/or mutilated, including 71 European men, women, and children, 31 soldiers, and 21 Algerians (Abbas' nephew counting among them). In response, French forces gunned down or summarily executed as many as 12,000 Algerians, most of whom were completely innocent of any involvement.[97] Philippeville typified the worsening pattern of attack followed by retaliation described by Fanon as a symbiotic process:

The violence of the colonial regime and the counter-violence of the native balance each other and respond to each other in an extraordinary reciprocal homogeneity. This reign of violence will be all the more terrible in proportion to the size of the implementation from the mother country. The development of violence among the colonized people will be proportionate to the violence exercised by the threatened colonial regime.[98]

Philippeville became a critical episode in the war's escalation, leading France to deploy vastly increased levels of manpower and institutionalize ferocious counterinsurgency techniques. These ranged from mass population resettlements to collective reprisals against villages and urban neighbourhoods believed to be harbouring FLN militants and, most notoriously, to torture as a means of extracting information and breaking the resistance movement. In the aftermath of Philippeville, France augmented its professional army and police forces already in Algeria. Alongside the 35,000 West African troops who served, France drew on hundreds of thousands of young conscripts from the metropole, first by recalling reservists who had already fulfilled their national service duties and then by sending those freshly drafted across the Mediterranean, where the required period of service gradually lengthened to twenty-seven months.[99] French troop levels in Algeria multiplied until they

[95] Connelly, *Diplomatic Revolution*, 120.
[96] André Mandouze, 'Le gouvernement français et son "complexe" à l'égard de l'opinion', *Consciences Maghribines*, no. 8–9 [n.d.], in al-Qawmi (ed.), *Le Peuple Algérien*, 80.
[97] Evans, *Algeria*, 119–22; Horne, *Savage War*, 140–1.   [98] Fanon, *Wretched*, 69.
[99] Cooper, *Citizenship*, 262–3.

amounted to 450,000 by the summer of 1957. By the spring of 1956, moreover, the state of emergency declared the year before had led the Mollet government to bestow special powers on the army, thereby consolidating the shift from civil to military rule over Algeria. This greatly enhanced the supremacy of French officers, paratrooper units, and the rank and file, whether career soldiers or draftees, who together with the police engaged in large-scale operations to hunt down militants or those who allegedly assisted them, conduct mass arrests and on-the-spot executions, or haul in supposed 'suspects' at will for 'questioning'. Victims were subjected to interrogations that involved physical and psychological torture that often ended in their execution or disappearance without trace.[100] One of the most intense, focused, and protracted bouts of counter-insurgency activity lasted from January to September 1957, when the army under the command of General Jacques Massu fought the Battle of Algiers that concentrated on killing off the FLN on the narrow, winding, densely-populated streets of the Casbah.

The Battle of Algiers qualified as a military success that achieved the objective of ridding the capital of an FLN presence but came with adverse political repercussions, the magnitude of which would only become clear during and after May 1958. In granting emergency powers and absolute authority to General Massu, the head of the Tenth Parachute Division, Paris effectively legalized the army's pre-eminence. 'Algeria had come to the parting of the ways, and the road taken led straight to the unconditional surrender of the civil power to the military, in other words of the French Republic to the "Generals"': such was the verdict of Pierre Vidal-Naquet, one of a growing number of prominent French intellectuals to speak out against the war and its recourse to systematized inhumane methods to fight the insurgency. The ramifications extended beyond Algeria and stabbed at the very heart of the French political order:

When the war in Algeria broke out, the French Authorities had a choice between two policies: either to admit that a fundamental political question was at the root of the Algerian problem, or to decide that this problem could be solved by military and police methods. The adoption of emergency legislation meant that the Government, and with it the National Assembly, had chosen the second alternative and had, in fact, surrendered to the torturers. Instead of increasing its authority the State had embarked upon a process of self-destruction.[101]

Transferring civil authority in Algeria to the higher echelons of the French army ensured that extreme tactics and ideologies would prevail, with equally profound reverberations. For many senior and non-commissioned officers as

---

[100] Raphaëlle Branche, *La Torture et l'armée pendant la guerre d'Algérie, 1954–1962* (Paris, 2001).
[101] Vidal-Naquet, *Torture*, 50, 66.

well as professional soldiers, Algeria became the (undeclared) 'war that could not be lost' and *Algérie française* a cause to which they became as devoted as the most intransigent, right-wing European settlers.[102] The diehard commitment to keeping Algeria French and the rejection of any suggestion of negotiation with the FLN that crystallized among significant numbers of French officers and career soldiers was closely linked to the humiliations incurred in Indochina with the surrender at Dien Bien Phu, the sufferings of French prisoners-of-war in Viet Minh camps, and France's withdrawal from Southeast Asia soon after.[103] Indochina had taught the French army far more than counterinsurgency tactics it later used against guerrillas in North Africa; it also rendered Algeria the site of its redemption and severely compromised its political neutrality.

General Raoul Salan, the commander-in-chief during the Battle of Algiers, spoke for many fellow officers when he rooted his stance in a longer trajectory that encompassed a history of French colonial military glory combined with devastating disappointments that were national as well as personal. In 1962, he looked back on over forty years of army command that stretched from French West Africa, where he headed contingents of Senegalese troops as part of the Free French forces helping to liberate the hexagon in 1944, to long periods of service in Indochina between the wars and again after 1945. Referring to the First and Second World Wars, he recalled that '[w]hen the hour of peril struck, twice, for the old metropole, I saw the peoples of the empire rush to her aid: Algerians, Moroccans, Tunisians, Vietnamese, and Senegalese fought with us and often under my orders. When one has known the France of courage, one can never accept the France that gives up [*la France de l'abandon*].' Yet in pulling out of Indochina in 1954, this was exactly what France did: abandoning Vietnamese soldier and civilian allies to the mercy (or lack thereof) of the Viet Minh. 'Had we not promised them that the French flag would never be lowered on the soil of Indochina? ... They had cause to believe us because they knew the efforts and the sacrifices of the French army', Salan insisted. This confidence was betrayed by Paris at the cost of many lives, and once French soldiers moved on to Algeria to confront the new rebellion their resolve was clear: 'Their role would be to protect these

---

[102] George Armstrong Kelly, *Lost Soldiers: The French Army and Empire in Crisis, 1947–1962* (Cambridge, MA, 1965), chs. 9 and 10.

[103] Stephen Tyre, 'The Memory of French Military Defeat at Dien Bien Phu and the Defence of French Algeria', in Jenny Macleod (ed.), *Defeat and Memory: Cultural Histories of Military Defeat in the Modern Era* (Basingstoke, 2008), 214–33; Martin S. Alexander, 'Seeking France's "Lost Soldiers": Reflections on the French Military Crisis in Algeria', in Kenneth Mouré and Martin S. Alexander (eds.), *Crisis and Renewal in France, 1918–1962* (Oxford, 2002), 242–66; Martin Evans, 'The French Army and the Algerian War: Crisis of Identity', in Scriven and Wagstaff (eds.), *War and Society*, 147–61.

French *départements* from Indochina's fate and maintain the integrity of national territory.'[104]

'Never again': such was the attitude of many influential French army officers in Algeria who became as vigilantly on their guard as the European settlers against the prospect that the government would renege on its commitments to keeping Algeria French. In May 1958, tensions that had fomented between *Algérie française* partisans (civilians and soldiers) and Paris reached the tipping point. Fed up with the chronic instability and indecisiveness of the Fourth Republic, which had seen a total of twenty-five different ministries and eighteen different prime ministers come and go since 1946, fears that an incoming government headed by Pierre Pflimlin, a self-declared liberal on Algerian policy who called for negotiations, intended to do a deal with the FLN provided the backdrop for the widespread disorder that erupted in Algiers on 13 May. A mass demonstration following the brutal FLN killings of four French soldiers degenerated into mob violence as settler militants descended upon public buildings and rioting broke out, while the elite paratroopers did nothing to stop them. In response, Generals Massu and Salan established a 'Committee of Public Safety', an act tantamount to a full seizure of power by senior officers allied with settler extremists. The generals at the helm in Algiers suggested that Paris was in dire need of the same medicine. A weak and indecisive political order rife with party factionalism had long proven itself incapable of ruling France and even less able to resolve the Algerian crisis; the solution for the quagmire within and outside the hexagon, many believed, would come in the form of a strong leader capable of reforming a crippled political apparatus.

'*Vive de Gaulle!*' Salan publicly announced in Algiers, a cry which echoed across the Mediterranean as observers watched the gathering military storm that appeared to be blowing northwards towards the hexagon itself. The sixty-seven-year-old Free French hero of the Second World War, although technically in retirement from political life, seemed the ideal solution to the nation's political turpitude and Algerian imbroglio. General de Gaulle had stood outside the political mainstream he condemned for the past twelve years and was thus unscathed by its recurrent impasses, and many critics looked to him as the saviour capable of reforming the political order through exerting decisive leadership. Ironically, the return of *the* general was seen as the only way to avoid the spread of a military takeover to the metropole by the senior generals who had already assumed control in Algiers, and who openly threatened to send paratroopers under Massu's command into Paris. With paras already having assembled on Corsica and in Toulouse, the seemingly imminent occupation of Paris led to Pflimlin's resignation. De Gaulle all too

---

[104] 'Déclaration de M. Raoul Salan', in *Le Procès de Raoul Salan: Compte rendu sténographique* (Paris, 1962), 76.

eagerly came out of political retirement and assumed leadership of what
became the Fifth Republic, one with a new constitution and far stronger
executive authority over the parliamentary system that had become dogged
by party squabbling. While he was welcomed back by popular mandate, his
return to power, like the fall of the Fourth Republic and birth of the Fifth, had
been precipitated by the coup emanating from Algiers.[105] The question that
remained, however, was whether de Gaulle would fulfil the great expectations
of the *Algérie française* champions who had been instrumental in securing his
return. What would change under de Gaulle, and what solutions to the Algerian
crisis would ultimately emerge under his presidency?

* * *

De Gaulle, the new Republic, and the ongoing crisis in North Africa and the hexagon, 1958–1962

Initially, de Gaulle's return brought continuity in France's approach to Algeria.
With Algeria only becoming independent in July 1962, France's undeclared
war in its North African *départements* lasted longer under the Fifth Republic
than it had under the Fourth. De Gaulle promptly travelled to Algeria, arriving
on 4 June 1958 to be greeted with a rapturous reception by settlers and soldiers
who felt their confidence in him to be vindicated when he proclaimed 'I have
understood you' and commended the army for its 'magnificent work of understanding and pacification'. Speaking in Mostaganem two days later, he went so
far as to proclaim '*Vive l'Algérie . . . française!*' – the only time he was to do so
either in the course of the visit or indeed over the next four years.[106] Once de
Gaulle took power, France continued to use the same weapon of torture as a
means of interrogation, stepped up other counterinsurgency techniques, and
initiated new military offensives in its battle against the FLN, with the result
that public outcry within France already apparent before May 1958 increased
thereafter. Debates about the institutionalized use of torture and what it meant
for France spanned Republics as well as the hexagonal/overseas divide, counting as just one of many ways that the Algerian conflict increasingly crossed the
Mediterranean and permeated metropolitan life that will be discussed in the
pages that follow.

Torture's pervasiveness during the Battle of Algiers of 1957 gave rise to
public exposés and controversy thanks to accounts disseminated by victims and

---

[105] Christophe Nick, *Résurrection: Naissance de la Vᵉ République, un coup d'État démocratique* (Paris, 1998); Rioux, *Fourth Republic*, 300–13; Nicholas Atkin, *The Fifth French Republic* (Basingstoke, 2005), chs. 1 and 2; Thénault, *Histoire de la guerre*, ch. 8.
[106] Evans, *Algeria*, 237; Guy Pervillé, 'Discours d'Alger (4 juin 1958)', in Claire Andrieu, Philippe Braud, and Guillaume Piketty (eds.), *Dictionnaire de Gaulle* (Paris, 2006), 363.

by leftist French intellectuals who took up their cause. In 1957 and 1958, two cases in particular dominated metropolitan discussions, both involving Frenchmen arrested in Algiers after being accused of supporting the FLN's campaign. In June 1957, Maurice Audin, a communist who taught physics at the University of Algiers, was accused of assisting the FLN and taken into custody, suffering extreme torture before being 'disappeared'; his friend Henri Alleg, a journalist affiliated with banned anti-colonial newspapers, was also arrested and tortured but lived to tell the tale in a manuscript smuggled out of prison one page at a time. Activists in France led by Pierre Vidal-Naquet formed a committee to investigate Audin's disappearance and publicized it extensively, while Alleg's *La Question* was widely printed and circulated despite becoming the first book since the eighteenth century to be banned in France.[107] Alleg's account detailed the brutalities of torture and interrogation in custody in Algiers, describing water torture, beatings, electrodes applied to his genitals, the infliction of burns, and psychological manipulation through threats to his family at the hands of his paratrooper captors who were determined (but ultimately failed) to make him divulge what he knew of enemy activities.

Alleg's metropolitan supporters extended as high into the intellectual pantheon as Jean-Paul Sartre, who had a long involvement in anti-colonial critique that included his support for Henri Martin in the early 1950s.[108] Contributing the preface to Alleg's story, Sartre began with recourse to a well-established set of analogies:

In 1943, in the Rue Lauriston (the Gestapo headquarters in Paris), Frenchmen were screaming in agony and pain: all France could hear them. In those days the outcome of the war was uncertain and the future unthinkable, but one thing seemed impossible in any circumstances: that one day men should be made to scream by those acting in our name.

There is no such word as impossible: in 1958, in Algiers, people are tortured regularly and systematically. Everyone, from M. Lacoste (Minister Resident for Algeria) to the farmers in Aveyron, knows this is so, but almost no one talks of it ... France is almost as mute as during the Occupation, but then she had the excuse of being gagged.

Invoking the Nazi massacre at Oradour, Sartre despaired that 'fifteen years are enough to transform victims into executioners'.[109] But if Sartre recoiled in

---

[107] James D. Le Sueur, *Uncivil War: Intellectuals and Identity Politics during the Decolonization of Algeria*, 2nd ed. (Lincoln, NE, 2005), especially 221–8; James D. Le Sueur, 'Introduction', in Henri Alleg, *The Question*, translated by John Calder (Lincoln, NE, 2006; first published Paris, 1958), xiii–xxv.

[108] See, alongside Jean-Paul Sartre, *Colonialism and Neocolonialism* (London, 2001), Le Sueur, *Uncivil War*; Sorum, *Intellectuals*, especially 119–44; David L. Schalk, *War and the Ivory Tower: Algeria and Vietnam* (New York, 1991), ch. 3; Liauzu, *Histoire de l'anticolonialisme*, ch. 6.

[109] Jean-Paul Sartre, 'A Victory', in Alleg, *Question*, xxvii–xxviii. See Michael Rothberg's excellent analysis of the resurfacing of Nazi occupation memories in France in the context of debates about torture in Algeria in *Multidirectional Memory*, especially 192–216.

horror, Alleg's description of his ordeal stressed that some of his tormentors 'flattered themselves that they were like the Gestapo', with one shouting:

'You're going to talk! Everybody talks here! We fought the war in Indo-China – that was enough to know your type. This is the Gestapo here! ... Now it's the tenth Paratroop Division who are doing it to you' ... Ir – hammered my face with blows and jabbed my stomach with his knee. 'What we are doing here, we will do in France ... And your whore of a Republic, we will blow it up into the air, too!'[110]

After the Fourth Republic's collapse triggered by the French army acting in concert with settlers in Algeria, French authorities heading the Fifth Republic proclaimed that torture had become a thing of the past – a creature of the discredited old regime. In its place, the story ran, came progressive initiatives in the field of socio-economic development and a willingness to contemplate new measures for political reform in Algeria. Regardless of state denials, however, army and police practices remained much the same as before; so too did the links critics made between the French in Algeria and the Germans in occupied France. Two further victims of torture became French *causes célèbres*, both of whom were young Algerian Muslim women: Djamila Bouhired, tortured during the Battle of Algiers after having been apprehended for acting as a messenger liaising between leading FLN militants and given a death sentence for planting a bomb, and Djamila Boupacha, captured in early 1960 for having thrown a bomb into a café, hidden FLN insurgents, and done other work to aid the revolt. Their cases illustrate both the significant roles played by Muslim women in Algeria's independence struggle and their importance in the publicity war waged by French intellectuals protesting against torture. Like the white French men subjected to torture or who were killed or disappeared while in custody (a mere handful of victims when compared with the thousands of Algerians who suffered the same fate), Algerian women became favoured subjects of metropolitan exposés which often focused in depth on the sexual violations meted out by their French captors.[111]

Djamila Boupacha's case achieved its notoriety largely through the efforts of two influential women who came out in her defence and galvanized other

---

[110] Alleg, *Question*, 47.

[111] Frantz Fanon, 'Algeria Unveiled', in *A Dying Colonialism*, translated by Haakon Chevalier (Harmondsworth, 1970; original French text published 1959), 21–52; Khaoula Taleb Ibrahimi, 'Les Algériennes et la guerre de libération nationale: L'émergence des femmes dans l'espace public et politique au cours de la guerre et l'après-guerre', in Harbi and Stora (eds.), *La Guerre d'Algérie*, 281–323; Raphaëlle Branche, 'Sexual Violence in the Algerian War', in Dagmar Herzog (ed.), *Brutality and Desire: War and Sexuality in Europe's Twentieth Century* (Basingstoke, 2009), 247–60; James D. Le Sueur, 'Torture and the Decolonization of French Algeria: Nationalism, "Race" and Violence during Colonial Incarceration', in Graeme Harper (ed.), *Colonial and Postcolonial Incarceration* (London, 2001), 168–72; Judith Surkis, 'Ethics and Violence: Simone de Beauvoir, Djamila Boupacha, and the Algerian War', *French Politics, Culture and Society*, 28:2 (2010), 38–55.

critics to follow suit: Tunisian lawyer Gisèle Halimi and Simone de Beauvoir, who published widely about the injustices Boupacha endured after her arrest. Her ordeals involving rape with a bottle, torture with electrodes, beatings, and the arrest and brutalization of family members illustrated that de Gaulle's return to political leadership had not ended abuses and in fact further safeguarded torturers' and assassins' legal immunity from prosecution for their actions. De Beauvoir appealed to readers of her articles on Boupacha in *Le Monde* and in the book she published with Halimi to take a stand against torture by arguing that 'the alternatives are simple and clear-cut':

Either – despite your willing and facile grief over such past horrors as the Warsaw ghetto or the death of Anne Frank – you align yourselves with our contemporary butchers rather than their victims, and give your unprotesting assent to the martyrdom which thousands of Djamilas and Ahmeds are enduring in your name, almost, indeed, before your very eyes; or else you reject, not merely certain specific practices, but the greater aim which sanctions them, and for which they are essential. In the latter case you will refuse to countenance a war that dares not speak its true name – not to mention an Army that feeds on war, heart and soul, and a Government that knuckles under to the Army's demands.[112]

De Beauvoir's activism on Boupacha's behalf was about more than combatting French public indifference to the conduct of war (which critics perceived to be socially widespread) by reactivating Nazi parallels guaranteed to touch nerves. It also linked the abusive treatment suffered by Boupacha and thousands of other Algerians to the power that France's military wielded over political authorities both in Algiers and Paris that extended beyond May 1958. Others agreed, including Sartre (de Beauvoir's partner). As James Le Sueur has written, 'Sartre and members of the new left detested de Gaulle's rise through "fascist" forces originating from the extreme right and the army. As Sartre stated: "The Algerian *colons* [settlers] want to colonize France"; they were holding de Gaulle as their "hostage."'[113] French anti-colonial critics may have protested against self-interested assumptions that 'Algeria was France', yet they readily agreed that the war's influence had increasingly seeped into the hexagon itself. '[W]as there not a danger that France would become another Algeria – a proving-ground for a police force, and later an army, both determined to use every means, even torture, to achieve their ends?', Pierre Vidal-Naquet asked. After May 1958, 'what was happening was that France was being "Algerianized" imperceptibly, day by day'.[114]

---

[112] Simone de Beauvoir, 'Introduction', in Simone de Beauvoir and Gisèle Halimi (eds.), *Djamila Boupacha: The Story of the Torture of a Young Algerian Girl Which Shocked Liberal French Opinion*, translated by Peter Green (New York, 1962; originally published Paris, 1962), 20–1; on the lack of change after de Gaulle's return, see 19, 207, 246.

[113] Le Sueur, *Uncivil War*, 228.   [114] Vidal-Naquet, *Torture*, 107.

Metropolitan France was much more than a source of manpower to fight the FLN, or an arena where vigorous debates about Algeria's status and the morality and ends of war did battle with public apathy and many people's unwillingness to think too much about torture and other counterinsurgency practices. The hexagon itself became another theatre of war. Some public figures on the left actively preached military insubordination, calling on conscripts to refuse to do their service in Algeria in the 'Manifesto of the 121' of 1960, a petition newspapers initially were banned from printing.[115] Moreover, several thousand French men and women became directly involved in illegal underground activities in aid of the FLN, with many explaining their anti-colonial motivations through recourse to the memory of wartime resistance to Nazi occupation.[116] Affiliates of Francis Jeanson's network, among other clandestine supporters, were able to aid the FLN by forging links with its representatives among the Algerian community then resident in the metropole – the growing population of labour migrants totalling c. 350,000 living in shantytowns and slums around Paris and other French cities. They helped to hide Algerian insurgents from the authorities and transport funds across the Mediterranean raised among Algerians working in the metropole.[117]

In autumn 1958, the FLN took their independence struggle directly into France in a way the Viet Minh never had, opening a 'second front' in the hexagon. Mainland France was declared the 'seventh *wilaya*', adding to the six *wilayas* (or insurgency zones) into which Algeria itself was divided.[118] French police and military personnel were targeted for assassination, as were other Algerians who tried to remain neutral or supported Messali Hadj. The violence of war spanned the metropolitan and overseas divide, as did the FLN insurgents and the forces that France pitted against them. Maurice Papon assumed the position of Paris Prefect of Police after earlier postings in occupied wartime France (where he had played an important role in the deportation of Jews to German concentration camps) and later in Morocco and Algeria, with the tools of repression moving across borders along with him and countless other police and army personnel. Under Papon, the Paris police engaged in intensive surveillance activities and crackdowns on Algerian shantytowns, using French personnel as well as Algerian *harki* military auxiliary forces to terrorize

---

[115] Ibid., 145–8; Schalk, *War and the Ivory Tower*, 105–8.

[116] Martin Evans, *The Memory of Resistance: French Opposition to the Algerian War (1954–1962)* (Oxford, 1997); see also testimonies of leading French anti-war activists including André Mandouze and Georges Mattéi in Martin S. Alexander, Martin Evans, and J.F.V. Keiger (eds.), *The Algerian War and the French Army, 1954–62: Experiences, Images, Testimonies* (Basingstoke, 2002), 243–53.

[117] See Fig. 7.1 (included in Chapter 7) showing Jean Pottier's photograph of the Algerian *bidonville* (shantytown) of Nanterre outside central Paris as it looked in the late 1950s and early 1960s.

[118] Ali Haroun, *La 7ᵉ Wilaya: La Guerre du FLN en France, 1954–1962* (Paris, 1986).

the migrant community through harassment, round-ups, and internments. These peaked in September and October 1961, when police murdered more than 120 Algerians in and around Paris. The climax came on and in the days after 17 October, when up to 30,000 Algerians staged a peaceful public demonstration in the centre of Paris to protest against endemic police violence and the recently-imposed night-time curfew affecting their community. Police arrested, detained, and interrogated over 14,000, with the exact numbers killed through street violence, drowning in the Seine, or in custody – together with those tortured – never clearly established.[119]

The 17 October massacre (along with Papon's inglorious career that ranged from Jewish persecution during the occupation to atrocities perpetrated during the decolonization era) became only the most notorious example of police and military brutality on metropolitan soil, one of many wartime episodes and controversies still intensely debated more than fifty years later, as Chapter 9 will take further. The repression of Algerians suspected of FLN activity was not new in 1961 Paris. Countless examples had already received immense publicity, including the testimonies of five men, most of whom were students arrested and tortured in 1959, that were collected and published under the title *La Gangrène*.[120]

Gangrene was one of a number of disease metaphors repeatedly used in connection with the Algerian War's effects by critics and apologists alike.[121] Edmond Michelet, France's minister of justice after de Gaulle's return, counted among the latter. Having been deported to Dachau and tortured for his own resistance activities during the Second World War, Michelet at once deplored instances of torture in Algeria yet was reluctant to recognize it as the generalized practice it was, regretfully chalking it up as a '*raison d'État*' (reason of state). Michelet preferred to understand torture as exceptional and unfortunate, and most importantly as a sickness introduced during the occupation that had yet to be fully eradicated from the French body politic. 'The consequences of the Nazi virus' and 'after-effects of the Nazi totalitarian pox [*de la vérole, du totalitarianisme nazi*]', he concluded, telling representatives of the committee formed to defend Djamila Boupacha that '[t]he Nazis are responsible for this

---

[119] Jim House and Neil MacMaster, *Paris 1961: Algerians, State Terror, and Memory* (Oxford, 2006), especially 100, 106, 129, 161–7 (and Part I, chs. 1 and 3 more generally); Linda Amiri, *La Bataille de France: La guerre d'Algérie en métropole* (Paris, 2004); Jean-Luc Einaudi, *La Bataille de Paris: 17 octobre 1961* (Paris, 1991); Benjamin Stora, *La gangrène et l'oubli: La mémoire de la guerre d'Algérie* (Paris, 1991), 92–100; Mathieu Rigouste, *L'Ennemi intérieur: La généalogie coloniale et militaire de l'ordre sécuritaire dans la France contemporaine* (Paris, 2009), 100–4.

[120] Béchir Boumaza *et al.*, *La Gangrène* (Paris, 1959; reprinted 2012).

[121] Elizabeth Buettner, 'Extended Families or Bodily Decomposition?: Biological Metaphors in the Age of European Decolonization', in Martin Thomas and Richard Toye (eds.), *The Rhetoric of Empire: Arguing Colonialism in the Public Sphere* (Manchester, in press).

canker in our midst. It spreads everywhere, and corrupts all it touches. You can't eradicate it'.[122]

Michelet was not alone in framing France's conduct in Algeria in this manner, but many who attacked French practices and assessed their ramifications considered other disease analogies such as gangrene (or cancer) as more apt.[123] Considering torture as akin to a pox or virus suggested it to be a contagious disease with which France (whether in French Algeria, or in the hexagon) had been infected from without, in this case by the Nazi German wartime enemy ever-present in French memory during Algeria's independence struggle. Comparing torture to gangrene, however, suggests a refusal to externalize responsibility by displacing it onto the Nazi past, a readiness to face up to its long-term colonial and metropolitan incubation, and an admission that France had only itself to blame for its self-inflicted festering wounds. With colonialism and all its adverse effects equated to a degenerative and insidious form of internal deterioration in which the rot persistently crept further throughout the French national body, the solution lay not in helpless fatalism ('you can't eradicate it') or resurrecting the Nazi past as a source of contagion. Rather, it required radical action in the form of surgery to amputate infected organs and thus stem the body's progressive contamination of itself.[124]

* * *

How were France and Algeria to be cured of festering colonial maladies? Much of the French public looked to de Gaulle in and after 1958 to act as the doctor who would find acceptable remedies, if necessary by taking up the scalpel and acting as the dismembering surgeon. Thus, alongside the continuities in France's approach to the Algerian insurrection and the sharp intensification of military operations against the FLN after de Gaulle took office, the next years saw gradual moves towards negotiations and announcements starting in September 1959 indicating that France was willing to consider Algerian self-determination. Signs of a shift in approach in Algeria came alongside initiatives that led to the decolonization of French-ruled sub-Saharan Africa in 1960, a theme returned to later in this chapter, but despite changes simultaneously occurring elsewhere in the French Union (renamed the French Community in

---

[122] Edmond Michelet, quoted in Vidal-Naquet, *Torture*, 92; 'Les Éditeurs', 'Dans la légalité', in Boumaza *et al.*, *La Gangrène*, 7; de Beauvoir, 'Introduction', 14. On his life and career, see Guillaume Mouralis, 'Edmond Michelet (1899–1970)', in Andrieu, Braud, and Piketty (eds.), *Dictionnaire de Gaulle*, 767–8.

[123] Compare views included in de Beauvoir and Halimi, *Djamila Boupacha*, 210, 243, to Vidal-Naquet's framing of torture as a 'cancer of democracy'.

[124] Rigouste, *L'Ennemi intérieur*, 54–5. See Stora, *La gangrène*, 8, who in 1991 condemned France's refusal to address the war or the issue of 'collective culpability' in the decades after 1962 as a 'denial [that] continues, like a cancer, like a gangrene, to gnaw at the very foundations of French society'.

1958) Algeria continued to take centre stage in France's national and overseas affairs. In de Gaulle's version of events as later recounted in his memoirs published in 1970, the French public had grown 'weary of the military and financial commitment and shocked by deplorable incidents during the repression'. Remaining wedded to the status quo of keeping Algeria French at any price meant that France would remain, he wrote,

politically, financially, and militarily bogged down in a bottomless quagmire when, in fact, she needed her hands free to bring about the domestic transformation necessitated by the twentieth century and to exercise her influence abroad unencumbered. At the same time, it would condemn our forces to a futile and interminable task of colonial repression, when the future of the country demanded an Army geared to the exigencies of modern power.

Self-determination was the only alternative, for 'the "French Algeria" for which I heard people clamoring in the early days of my administration was a ruinous Utopia'.[125]

Along with alluding to the decline in metropolitan public acceptance, the conflict's adverse effects on France's economy and world standing, and the need to modernize its military capacities, de Gaulle's description of the army's actions in Algeria as 'colonial repression' involved a radical change of terminology from what had long been characteristic. By the time of writing, de Gaulle claimed not just to have concluded that France could not hold onto Algeria but that it was a 'colonial' scenario, not a French internal matter. His framing was indicative of what Todd Shepard identifies as a rapid readjustment in French thinking between 1959 and 1962: 'the large-scale abandonment of arguments that "Algeria is France" and the acceptance that "Algeria is a colony that must be decolonized"'.[126] Once this shift was underway, the battle fought by France's mainstream political establishment became one pitted as much against FLN violence as it was against the social groups who remained staunch (and increasingly belligerent) defenders of conventional *Algérie française* positions. More than ever, the last years of French rule in Algeria were a time of escalating Franco-French conflicts that overlay Franco-Algerian divides.

Once de Gaulle publicly came out in support of a negotiated road towards an 'Algerian Algeria' as opposed to the French Algeria he came to consider an 'impossibility' (and where the costs far outweighed the benefits) in autumn 1959, he and other advocates for a change of course faced the growing wrath of settler hardliners ('ultras') and their sympathizers in the army.[127] De Gaulle was keenly aware of the threat the army posed to civil authority, having

---

[125] Charles de Gaulle, *Memoirs of Hope: Renewal 1958–62, Endeavour 1962–*, translated by Terence Kilmartin (London, 1971; first published in French in 1970 and 1971), 44, 45, 46.
[126] Shepard, *Invention of Decolonization*, 55.
[127] Alain Peyrefitte, *C'était de Gaulle* (Paris, 1994), 59.

previously courted veterans and been the biggest personal beneficiary of the military coup that toppled the Fourth Republic and rolled out the red carpet for his presidency in May 1958. Soon after Algiers-based generals catapulted him back to power he strove to rein in the military in order to consolidate the state's (and his own) authority, writing to General Salan in October of the necessity for the army to cease playing political roles in Algeria prior to recalling him to Paris before the year was out.[128] With clear evidence mounting that de Gaulle would refuse to be their 'hostage', as Sartre had accused, and was in fact acting in a way that went against their cause, *Algérie française* partisans denounced him as a traitor and grew increasingly militant in their fight against a sell-out of settler interests – interests they defined as identical to those of the French nation. A defining moment came with 'Barricades Week' in late January 1960, when extremist settler ringleaders staged an insurrection and took over university buildings in central Algiers they had stockpiled with weaponry and supplies. Street violence caused a number of deaths and received widespread settler backing. Rather than being crushed by the French army, which held back in a show of support, the revolt fizzled out as some instigators surrendered, others fled into Spanish exile, and a number joined the Foreign Legion as a means of avoiding jail sentences. Many would later redirect their energies into what emerged the following year as the illegal *Organisation de l'Armée Secrète* (OAS, or Secret Army Organization).

Looking back on the episode in his memoirs, de Gaulle stressed that since 'the immediate objective of the rioters was simply to force me to renege on self-determination, I was determined to lance the abscess, make no concessions whatever and obtain complete obedience from the Army'.[129] If the settlers seemed increasingly uncontrollable, he could at least act to curb army excesses by draining the wound of its most virulent toxins with the use of a blunt surgical instrument. Like General Salan before them, many officers (General Massu among them) whose loyalties to Paris and de Gaulle were deemed suspect were transferred out of Algeria and often pushed into retirement from active service. This did as much to increase civil-military tensions and fuel officers' plots against the government as it did to reduce the immediate threat of high-level insubordination. Bolstered by the results of a referendum in January 1961 that showed a metropolitan voter approval rate of Algerian self-determination that exceeded 75 per cent, de Gaulle announced at a press conference in April that 'decolonization is our interest, and is therefore our policy' in Algeria.[130] This proved the catalyst for a putsch clumsily attempted by four newly-retired generals, Raoul Salan, Maurice Challe, Henri Zeller, and Edmond Jouhaud, who had surreptitiously returned to Algiers in the interim.

---

[128] Stora, *La gangrène*, 83–4; Kelly, *Lost Soldiers*, 225, 318.
[129] De Gaulle, *Memoirs of Hope*, 79.   [130] Shipway, *Decolonization*, 199.

Army successes in changing the course of metropolitan politics in May 1958, however, were not destined to be repeated in April 1961: de Gaulle's radio broadcasts appealing to French conscripts to stand behind him as their president rather than obey the orders of the renegade generals achieved their aim and the poorly-organized revolt rapidly disintegrated. Rumours that paratroopers following the rebellious generals' orders would invade Paris never materialized, and de Gaulle used the occasion of the failed putsch to step up purges of senior army personnel. Two hundred officers were arrested for their involvement; Challe and Zeller, who gave themselves up, were sentenced to fifteen years in prison; and Jouhaud and Salan, who went on the run, handed death sentences *in absentia*.[131] As official negotiations with FLN leaders began in Évian in May, those who had supported the failed military coup banded together with settler 'ultras' to open what was to become one of the war's closing chapters. Assuming leadership of the recently-established underground *Organisation de l'Armée Secrète*, they were determined to unleash their own wave of terror in a last-ditch effort to keep Algeria French after Paris – and indeed the overwhelming majority of French in the hexagon – had abandoned the faith and embarked on the road towards an 'Algerian Algeria'.

Salan became one of the principal OAS figureheads. Having famously proclaimed 'Vive de Gaulle!' in May 1958, less than three years later he stood at the helm of a terrorist organization that made repeated attempts to assassinate him. Targeting de Gaulle – who always escaped without a scratch – was part of the OAS's campaign to take violence against the FLN, against 'Arabs' in general, against French authorities who favoured negotiations (including de Gaulle's political inner circle), and against European settlers who looked likely to give up on *Algérie française* to such apocalyptic heights that moves to withdraw or hand power to the FLN would have to be scrapped. Fuelled by fury and desperation, the OAS went on the rampage and was responsible for thousands of killings in 1961 and 1962. Its reign of terror encompassed Algeria as well as the hexagon, where victims included the mayor of Évian who was murdered to ensure their message was heard at the very spot where negotiations were set to begin.[132] The organization attracted considerable support from among the settler community who looked to it as their last hope for salvaging the Algeria they loved – one which was France, French-dominated, and in its death throes.

Rather than saving *Algérie française* from the brink, however, OAS violence scuppered whatever slim chances there still were for the settlers to remain in an independent 'Algerian Algeria', hastened the mass European exodus that peaked over the summer of 1962, and cemented de Gaulle's resolve and the

---

[131] Evans, *Algeria*, 294–9; Shipway, *Decolonization*, 212–14.
[132] Vincent Quivy, *Les Soldats perdus: Des anciens de l'OAS racontent* (Paris, 2003), 85.

French public's ardent desire to find a way out of the Algerian morass as soon as possible. In French cities north of the Mediterranean, communists and other leftists organized anti-OAS demonstrations, including one in Paris where eight protestors were killed at the Charonne metro station as police attempted to contain the violence through beating participants. By the time Algerian independence was agreed in July 1962, both the OAS and the majority within metropolitan French society who hated and feared them had resorted once again to tried-and-tested Second World War comparisons. Most French on the mainland equated the OAS (together with the settlers as a collective group) with 'fascists', while the OAS, for their part, styled themselves the new resistance and cast the back-stabbing de Gaulle, erstwhile leader of the Free French and their sworn public enemy number one, in the role of Pétain.[133]

For those who waged the losing battle to uphold *Algérie française* until the bitter end, the independent Algeria governed by the FLN that emerged in July 1962 meant betrayal and the loss of a fight against the death of empire and the dismemberment of France itself. Most were unrepentant, not least Salan, who was finally captured in Algiers and brought before a military tribunal in Paris in May 1962. Despite the likelihood of being sentenced to the firing squad, he defiantly began his declaration by acknowledging his role as the head of the OAS and claiming full responsibility. He defended his actions as a legitimate form of protest against France's repetition of its abandonment of Indochina in Algeria, where the land, the settlers, and loyal Muslims would be left at the hands of FLN 'murderers' and faced with the distinct possibility of a future either in exile or in the coffin. Claiming the army to be the guarantor of French Algeria, he argued his actions in pursuit of this goal to be logical as well as just, whatever means had proven necessary to deploy.[134]

De Gaulle begged to differ and made no secret of the fact. The previous November, he had summoned a large gathering of senior army officers to Strasbourg in the wake of the putsch and the ensuing purges of their ranks, lecturing them on the need to align their aims with those of the state and obey its authority, regardless of their personal feelings on the issues in question. '[O]nce the State and the nation have chosen their path, the soldier's duty is irrevocably laid down', he insisted. 'Outside that duty, soldiers are lost men.'[135] *Soldats perdus* (lost soldiers) thus described men like Salan, the hundreds of OAS affiliates still at large and determined to wreak havoc, and other resolutely

---

[133] Stora, *La gangrène*, 87–9, 109–12, 204–5; Shepard, *Invention of Decolonization*, chs. 3 and 7; Rémi Kauffer, *OAS: Histoire d'une guerre franco-française* (Paris, 2002); Olivier Dard, *Voyage au coeur de l'OAS* (Paris, 2005); Kelly, *Lost Soldiers*, ch. 16; Evans, *Algeria*, 304–17; Paul Henissart, *Wolves in the City: The Death of French Algeria* (London, 1971); Martin Thomas, 'Repression, Reprisals, and a French Rhetoric of Massacre at Empire's Close', in Thomas and Toye (eds.), *Rhetoric of Empire*.
[134] 'Déclaration de M. Raoul Salan', 75, 86, 82.
[135] De Gaulle, *Memoirs*, 124; Kelly, *Lost Soldiers*, 360–1.

militant *Algérie française* devotees whose conception of the state and the nation had diverged radically from those of de Gaulle and indeed the French metropolitan majority.

To the shock of almost everyone and to de Gaulle's intense fury, the judges spared Salan the death penalty and sentenced him to life imprisonment instead – a sentence, as it turned out, that would be cut short in 1968 under a general amnesty for officers still in custody for participating in the putsch. In between, Salan filled his hours by penning voluminous memoirs in which he ruminated on multiple losses that merged into one. 'To lose an empire is to lose yourself', he mused; 'It takes all meaning away from the life of a man, the life of a pioneer.'[136] Losing Algeria entailed more than 'inventing decolonization' and redrawing the boundaries of France to exclude its three North African *départements* so long claimed as integral national territory.[137] For millions who had become personally embroiled in its fate, it meant reinventing their lives anew in 1962 while rarely leaving Algeria behind in memory, even if they were destined never to set foot there again. As later chapters of this book explore, this was true not only for France's army but for former settlers, the *harkis* who made it out of Algeria alive when most of their fellow Muslim troops fighting on behalf of France were horrifically massacred by the FLN, and countless others in postcolonial France.[138]

* * *

French decolonization, *grandeur,* and Europe

De Gaulle, unsurprisingly, insisted on reading the end of *Algérie française* and the end of France's empire very differently than Salan. In his memoirs he took all the credit for making French decolonization a reality, claiming all the while that having to be the man to 'extricate [France] from the constraints imposed upon her by her empire and no longer offset by any compensating advantages' was 'bitterly cruel'. France, he proclaimed, rightly

took pride in the human achievement represented by the basis of modern development laid down in these rough lands as a result of the activities of countless soldiers, administrators, settlers, teachers, missionaries, and engineers. What an agonizing ordeal it was to be then for me to hand over our power, furl our flags and close a great chapter of History!

---

[136] Raoul Salan, *Mémoires: Fin d'un empire*, Vol. 2 (Paris, 1971), 442, cited in Tyre, 'Memory', 214.
[137] Shepard, *Invention of Decolonization*.
[138] Estimated numbers of *harkis* killed range from 10,000 to 150,000; Evans, *Algeria*, 337, suggests 30,000.

However distasteful the task, 'I was obliged, in order to achieve my aim, to coerce and sometimes punish other Frenchmen who opposed it but whose first impulse may have been well-intentioned. I was obliged to overcome the anguish which gripped me as I deliberately put an end to a colonial domination which was once glorious but would henceforth be ruinous'.[139] Just as French colonial achievements in the past could rightly be applauded, so too could the decision to draw the era to a close.

However improbable, de Gaulle's 'decolonization narrative ... reinvented historical perspectives and made the end of the Algerian War into a victory', as Martin Evans phrases it, despite the fact that any reading of the evidence should have given France nothing to celebrate.[140] Close to eight years of endemic conflict had taken a huge human toll. Algerians commonly invoked their 'one and a half million martyrs' who were killed or wounded during their independence struggle, while French sources put the figure at up to 300,000 Algerian dead in addition to approximately 25,000 French troops killed and 65,000 wounded.[141] Together with mortalities, the intense sufferings inflicted through forced population resettlements, torture, and other endemic human rights abuses became domestically divisive and internationally notorious, making the so-called 'pacification' of Algeria a French diplomatic disaster that more than offset any military successes against the FLN. The manner and spirit in which the settlers departed *en masse* in the summer of 1962, moreover, inflicted even more damage and bitterness. As de Gaulle wrote of the OAS, 'once the agreements had been signed, they switched to a "scorched earth" policy. Now the Europeans must get out of Algeria at all costs and leave nothing but ruins. "Let us leave it as we found it in 1830!" was the slogan', and they coordinated countless arson attacks on public buildings and infrastructure, offices, and homes. Many departing settlers preferred to destroy their farms and set their cars and any other property on fire which they could not carry with them as they crossed the Mediterranean heading northward.[142]

With neither the last blood-drenched years of French Algeria nor its ignominious end that rendered the entire struggle to maintain it futile likely to do France's reputation any favours, de Gaulle took comfort in having presciently diagnosed *Algérie française* as 'not the remedy but the sickness' and having finally 'turned the page' by wielding the scalpel – a painful act, yet one 'necessary for the health of the country'.[143] To tell more convincing French success stories of the decolonization era he needed to look elsewhere, starting with the end of empire in sub-Saharan ('Black') Africa that had culminated two years earlier in 1960.[144] Unlike Algeria and Vietnam, the spate of

---

[139] De Gaulle, *Memoirs*, 37, 82.   [140] Evans, *Algeria*, 349.   [141] Ibid., 335–6.
[142] De Gaulle, *Memoirs*, 127; Evans, *Algeria*, 319.   [143] Peyrefitte, *C'était de Gaulle*, 73, 257.
[144] In 1960, alongside Madagascar, Togo, and Cameroon, territories in French Equatorial Africa that became independent included Oubangui-Chari (later the Central African Republic), Chad,

decolonizations in French West and Equatorial Africa and Madagascar had not come at the end of drawn-out, divisive, and costly wars but rather were presented as having occurred in a planned and peaceful manner in an atmosphere of mutual consent. Such a reading leaves endless African stories untold, especially those of non-elites marginalized in high-level discussions about how the future of their newly-postcolonial nations would look and who would enjoy the greatest stake in them.[145] Yet it goes far in explaining the common neglect of French sub-Saharan Africa both in much of the historical scholarship on decolonization and in French public memories of empire and the manner of its ending.

French politicians largely concurred across party lines on the understanding that 'Black' Africa was a tale of 'successful decolonization' in which France could take unmitigated pride.[146] De Gaulle certainly did his best to promulgate this verdict and, as was his wont, place his own personal stamp on the entire course of events. 'France, through my voice, opened the road which has taken the African territories toward self-determination', he told an audience in Brazzaville in 1958, rewriting his own history as a born champion of decolonization by misleadingly claiming to have had precisely this end in mind as far back as the conference hosted by the same city in 1944.[147] Referendums held across French African territories in 1958 offered voters the options of 'sovereignty combined with continued association with metropolitan France', as de Gaulle phrased it, or outright independence outside the French Community.[148] Any territory choosing the second road was threatened with the severance of all ties and the consequent forfeiture of all forms of French economic, administrative, and military support – a threat on which France eagerly made good once Guinée's electorate had the audacity to nail its colours to the mast of independence. In response to Ahmed Sékou Touré's speech proclaiming that 'There is no dignity without freedom. We prefer poverty in freedom to wealth in slavery', France duly proceeded to punish Guinée's misbehaviour by making an ostentatious show of cutting off all forms of aid.[149] Still, Guinée was held up as the

---

Moyen-Congo (later Congo-Brazzaville), and Gabon; those in French West Africa included Dahomey (later Benin), Guinée, Haute-Volta (later Burkina Faso), Ivory Coast, French Sudan (later Mali), Mauretania, Niger, and Senegal.

[145] Frederick Cooper, *Decolonization and African Society: The Labor Question in French and British Africa* (Cambridge, 1996).

[146] For in-depth discussions of the decolonization of sub-Saharan French Africa, see especially Cooper, *Citizenship*; Tony Chafer, *The End of Empire in French West Africa: France's Successful Decolonization?* (Oxford, 2002); Charles-Robert Ageron and Marc Michel (eds.), *L'Afrique noire française: L'Heure des indépendances* (Paris, 1992); John D. Hargreaves, *Decolonization in Africa*, 2nd ed. (London, 1996). For succinct overviews, see Shipway, *Decolonization*, 185–91, 205–9; Thomas, in Thomas, Moore, and Butler, *Crises of Empire*, 171–7.

[147] Shipway, *Decolonization*, 206.   [148] De Gaulle, *Memoirs*, 53.

[149] Shipway, *Decolonization*, 206; Cooper, *Citizenship*, 314–17, 372.

exception that proved the rule when every other French African territory and Madagascar proved themselves 'determined to remain linked to France while at the same time becoming their own masters', de Gaulle wrote contentedly. Madagascar stood for the rest of France's former African territories when it was pronounced to be 'grateful ... to France for restoring her independence while at the same time helping her to make her way in the future'.[150]

The extent to which Africans really did become 'their own masters' in 1960 as de Gaulle claimed remains highly questionable. In many respects, their independence was nominal and incomplete, for the countries that opted to remain within the French Community and therefore in France's good graces did so at the price of France remaining in charge of their foreign affairs, defence, currency, media, and communications. Presided over by loyal Francophone African elites, sub-Saharan Africa's relationship with its former colonial ruler remained one strongly marked by political subservience and economic dependency – precisely the scenario Frantz Fanon had warned would be pervaded by 'the snares of neo-colonialism'.[151] Yet however the tenor of Franco-African relations after 1960 was described, sub-Saharan ex-colonies remained an important French sphere of global influence in the post-decolonization era.[152] Africa became one of the cornerstones of French foreign policy together with Europe and the United States, both of which had crucial parts to play as France looked for new ways to reassert itself globally upon making the transition from decolonization to the postcolonial era.

For de Gaulle, a France without a formal empire or its Algerian *départements* did not mean that France had sacrificed its quest for *grandeur*, the all-important determinant of its national identity. In a conversation with his spokesman, Alain Peyreffite, less than a month before Algerian independence, he insisted that if France was no longer a 'great power she is no longer anything', continuing: 'Look at Portugal, which was once great. This small people conquered Brazil and the coasts of Africa, India, and China. The Pope granted it half the world, and the other half to Spain. Today, it's just a poor small country. Will France decline too?' In de Gaulle's estimation, France faced two futures: '*Va-t-elle se portugaliser?*' – 'will she turn herself into Portugal?' – or would she 'climb back up the hill?'[153]

In invoking Portugal and apparently deeming Portugal's remaining overseas empire in Africa as too insignificant to bear mention, he raised the first question

---

[150] De Gaulle, *Memoirs*, 57, 64.

[151] Chafer, *End of Empire*, ch. 8; Frantz Fanon, 'Accra: Africa Affirms Its Unity and Defines Its Strategy', in *Toward the African Revolution*, 165; see also other essays in this volume, in particular Fanon's points on 127–59.

[152] Earlier French ambitions to consolidate a 'Eurafrique' that would coexist with its position in the emerging EEC are explored in Cooper, *Citizenship*, 202–10, 263–70; Peo Hansen and Stefan Jonsson, *Eurafrica: The Untold History of European Integration and Colonialism* (London, 2013), and mentioned briefly in this book's epilogue.

[153] Peyrefitte, *C'était de Gaulle*, 280.

only to reject it immediately. For de Gaulle believed that 'France cannot be France without greatness' as ardently in and after 1962 as he had before. France would never resign herself to Portuguese depths, even if, 'of course, we are no longer *le gros animal*, we no longer have the power we once did. There are rockets, but there are also ideas. France's majesty is moral. In Africa, in Asia, in South America, our country is the symbol of racial equality, the rights of man, and the dignity of nations', he asserted in February 1963. France stood for 'something essential' and was distinguished by her 'vocation that was more disinterested and more universal' than any other nation's; she could take credit for having once championed 'American independence, the abolition of slavery, and the right of peoples to self-determination. Because she is the champion of the independence of nations, against all forms of hegemony'.[154]

However much he expounded on the importance of 'ideas' and fantasized about the high esteem in which France allegedly was held by others – especially developing countries where France had just expended so much energy in the attempt to withhold the very rights he extolled – de Gaulle did not neglect the value of rockets as a means of re-establishing France's global standing on new footing. By the end of the Algerian War, France had shifted its defence policy towards building up a nuclear deterrent and scaling back the conventional standing army that had been both essential to fighting the FLN and other colonial wars as well as politically threatening as renegade senior officers repeatedly tried to steer French politics to their own ends. Through an independent modern nuclear strike force, France aimed to hold her own in a world presided over by two superpowers and avoid becoming subsumed into their orbit as yet another mere 'satellite', which was how de Gaulle dismissively viewed not just the Eastern European nations that had become part of the Soviet bloc but also Western European countries whose policies were now determined by the United States. Although France was part of the Atlantic alliance and remained steadfastly outside the Soviet bloc, in fundamental ways the United States had become de Gaulle's main source of anxiety.[155] By taking the lead among the six nations which were founding members of the European Economic Community, France could fight against the EEC's subordination to the United States and what he repeatedly referred to as '*la colonisation américaine*', in which 'America tries to control Europe as she looks to control Latin America and Southeast Asia' as a venture dedicated to 'global hegemony'.[156] Ho Chi Minh's warning about the threat 'U.S. imperialists' posed to France's independence as well as Vietnam's in 1953, in sum, was one de Gaulle would have readily agreed with ten years later.

[154] Ibid., 283.
[155] Frédéric Bozo, *Two Strategies for Europe: De Gaulle, the United States, and the Atlantic Alliance* (Lanham, MD, 2001); Thomas, *French North African Crisis*, 192–201, 207.
[156] Peyrefitte, *C'était de Gaulle*, 355, 367.

De Gaulle's aim in the early to mid-1960s was to use the EEC alongside a strengthened Franco-German alliance as a means of counteracting American domination. As such, it was imperative both to maintain control over French defence and to keep Britain from joining the EEC. Britain, having caved into American pressure at Suez in 1956, had gone on to surrender ultimate control over its nuclear capabilities to American oversight; France was determined not to do the same, a defining moment coming with de Gaulle's decision to take France out of NATO's integrated command structure in 1966. NATO was merely an American invention to camouflage its own dominance, he argued, and Britain would simply become America's 'trojan horse' if allowed into the EEC.[157] This conviction dictated his decision to veto two British applications for EEC membership in 1963 and again in 1967, insisting that it was up to France to refuse 'to allow ourselves to be absorbed by the Anglo-American giant. It is we who will not allow Europe to drown itself in an Atlanticism which is just a cover for American hegemony'.[158]

Far more important than Europe's independence vis-à-vis the United States was France's own. Having just undertaken the decolonization of the vast majority of its erstwhile empire (with exceptions including the small overseas *départements* of Martinique, Guadeloupe, French Guiana, and Réunion, which remained French), France needed be on guard against becoming colonized itself. As de Gaulle stipulated early in 1963, France was not prepared to become tantamount to a 'protectorate'; if it was not careful, 'France would be to the United States that which Morocco was to France'.[159] Having lost its sovereignty under Nazi occupation and been forced to play a manifestly junior role to its American and British allies in the Second World War and pay heed to American demands after 1945, de Gaulle declared that the era of 'subordination was over' in June 1962, both for France's colonies and for France itself. 'What is good for France will not be decided in Washington, but in Paris. What is good for the Senegalese will not be decided in Paris, but in Dakar. Each people must take its destiny in its own hands.'[160] With France entering the postcolonial era determined to defend her own independence and take the lead within a 'European Europe', her leader never forgot to remain as vigilant about the 'snares of neo-colonialism' as Fanon had insisted Africa needed to be.

---

[157] Ibid., 282; see also 299, 336, 371.   [158] Ibid., 355.   [159] Ibid., 374.   [160] Ibid., 293.

4   Long live the king?

Belgium, the monarchy, and the Congo between the
Second World War and the decolonization years

In mid-1955, Belgium's media was abuzz with the story of a young man's first
trip to Central Africa. Departures for the Congo were nothing new: ships sailed
regularly between the ports of Antwerp and Matadi, carrying colonial administrators, missionaries, officers, businessmen, settlers, and their families
between metropole and colony. Whether or not they themselves were part of
the colonial community or personally knew others who were, by the 1950s
many Belgians were familiar with the seaborne colonial rites of passage of
European departures and African arrivals, if only through the comic book hero
Tintin and his small white dog Milou (Snowy), whose global misadventures
had famously taken them to the colony in *Tintin au Congo* in 1930.
Subsequently reissued with some revision and new colour illustrations soon
after the Second World War, Tintin's journeys as a 16-year-old 'boy reporter'
grew even better known in the 1950s than when Georges Remi (known as
Hergé) first drew him, enhancing his status as a national icon and cult figure – a
position he maintains to this day despite recurrent controversies concerning the
strips' anti-Semitic and racist content. But in 1955, the traveller in question was
neither the standard-issue colonial representative nor a figure as beloved as
Tintin: he was none other than King Baudouin I, making his first royal tour of
the Congo and Rwanda-Burundi at the age of 25. And unlike most ordinary
Belgians setting off for Africa (and extraordinary ones like Tintin and Milou),
King Baudouin went not by ship but on a state-of-the-art aircraft via Sabena,
Belgium's national airline.[1]

   Baudouin's tour of his nation's Central African territories was intended to turn
the page on one of the most challenging and divisive periods in Belgian history.
Just as in 1914, Belgium suffered another wartime German invasion in 1940.

---

[1] Hergé, *Tintin au Congo* (Paris, 2006), 9. *Tintin au Congo* first was serialized in 1930 in *Le Petit
Vingtième*, the children's supplement of the Brussels newspaper *Le Vingtième Siècle*; in 1931 it
appeared in book form. For a reprint of this 1930/1931 black-and-white edition, see *Les
aventures de Tintin au Congo,* in *Archives Hergé,* 3rd edn. (Tournai, 1973), 181–293. In 1946
the revised, colour version was published by Casterman, the edition that remains in print today
and now exists in English as *Tintin in the Congo*, translated by Leslie Lonsdale-Cooper and
Michael Turner (London, 2005).

King Léopold III (Baudouin's father) capitulated after only eighteen days, surrendering the army without the elected government's consent. Unlike the British royal family who famously toughed out the war years in London and unlike Queen Wilhelmina of the Netherlands who went into London exile when her country was occupied and later returned home in triumph, the Second World War did not ultimately emerge as Léopold III's finest hour or enhance his reputation.[2] He chose to remain in Nazi-occupied Belgium when his government ministers fled into exile and had extensive dealings with the Nazi 'New Order' until the country was finally liberated by the Allies in September 1944. The king went into Swiss exile as Belgians began their protracted confrontation with the aftermath of occupation and collaboration with the Nazis. Between 1944 and 1949, over 340,000 people were accused of collaborationist activities, approximately 58,000 of whom were found guilty and 241 executed.[3] Hergé counted among the many arrested for their wartime behaviour, in this case his continued publication of the Tintin stories in *Le Soir*, a newspaper placed under the control of the Nazi occupiers. Despite his associations with *Le Soir* and right-wing collaborators, not to mention the derogatory, caricatured depictions of Jews at the height of Nazi repression in his cartoons, he was never put on trial, purportedly because his drawings were judged 'inoffensive' but quite possibly on account of Tintin's wide public appeal.[4]

Occupation followed by accusations, repression, trials, and purges wreaked havoc upon a nation whose inherent regional, ethnic, and linguistic divisions already had deepened during the interwar years which saw the ascent of Flemish nationalism and, to a lesser extent, Walloon nationalism. Although support for (and resistance to) the Nazis came from French-speaking Wallonia and Dutch-speaking Flanders alike, after the war politically conservative Flemish Catholic royalists became particularly identified with collaboration, while an anti-royalist coalition of liberals, socialists, and communists took up the legacy of resistance.[5] The issue of Léopold III's return from exile brought

[2] Peter Romijn and Ben Frommer, 'Legitimacy in Inter-War Europe', in Martin Conway and Peter Romijn (eds.), *The War on Legitimacy in Politics and Culture 1936–1946* (Oxford, 2008), 50–1; Louis de Jong, *The Netherlands and Nazi Germany* (Cambridge, MA, 1990), 51–75.

[3] John Fitzmaurice, *The Politics of Belgium: A Unique Federalism* (London, 1996), 43.

[4] Joël Kotek, 'Tintin: un mythe belge de remplacement', in Anne Morelli (ed.), *Les grands mythes de l'histoire de Belgique, de Flandre et de Wallonie* (Brussels, 1995), 281–9; Pierre Assouline, *Hergé: The Man Who Created Tintin*, translated by Charles Ruas (Oxford, 2009), 105–19; Benoît Peeters, 'A Never Ending Trial: Hergé and the Second World War', *Rethinking History*, 6:3 (2002), 261–71; Hugo Frey, 'Tintin: The Extreme Right-Wing and the 70th Anniversary Debates', *Modern & Contemporary France*, 7:3 (1999), 361–3; Hugo Frey, 'Contagious Colonial Diseases in Hergé's *The Adventures of Tintin*', *Modern & Contemporary France*, 12:2 (2004), 177–88.

[5] On Walloon and Flemish collaboration, see respectively Martin Conway, *Collaboration in Belgium: Léon Degrelle and the Rexist Movement, 1940–1944* (New Haven, 1993); Bruno De Wever, *Greep naar de macht: Vlaams-nationalisme en Nieuwe Orde: Het VNV 1933–1945* (Gent, 1994). On the aftermath of occupation, see Pieter Lagrou, *The Legacy of Nazi*

domestic divisions to a head. Over a six-year period, Belgians grappled with *la question royale*, the 'royal question': should the king, condemned by many as the greatest traitor and collaborator of them all, be allowed to reassume his role as sovereign?[6]

If Belgians hoped that the March 1950 national referendum on Léopold III's return would finally resolve *la question royale*, they were sadly mistaken. As over 57 per cent casting their ballot supported his return, the king and his family resumed residence in the palace of Laeken outside Brussels, but the controversy did not end there. The vote revealed the extent to which the political gulf separating the regions had widened. 72 per cent had favoured the king in Flanders but only 42 per cent did so in Wallonia and 48 per cent in Brussels, sparking off a series of violent mass demonstrations in Wallonia and a march on Laeken in protest. With Belgium seemingly on the verge of civil war, Léopold III was persuaded to abdicate in favour of his son, who assumed the throne the following year.[7]

Barely 21 years old, Baudouin was meant to mark a new beginning and finally enable the nation to leave the taints and discords of the Nazi era and its immediate aftermath behind. With *la question royale* having escalated divisions between Flemings and Walloons, the young king faced the daunting challenge of reconciling the two communities and restoring the monarchy's legitimacy and popularity.[8] In a small and divided nation, the monarchy needed to resume its status as a unifying symbol – one of the few in a country whose official motto ironically was 'Union creates strength'.[9] But Baudouin did not win immediate national acceptance, and in the early 1950s he was widely suspected of remaining under the influence of his discredited father.[10]

Baudouin finally succeeded in recasting his image as a callow dependent by turning to the colonial arena that had been an integral aspect of the Belgian dynasty ever since King Léopold II claimed the Congo Free State as his private domain in 1885. A constitutional monarch at home, in Africa Léopold II's rule was absolute, the territory having been recognized as his personal property at the Berlin Conference. Over the next twenty years, it

---

Occupation: Patriotic Memory and National Recovery in Western Europe, 1945–1965 (Cambridge, 2000).

[6] Lagrou, *Legacy*, 48; Martin Conway, *The Sorrows of Belgium: Liberation and Political Reconstruction, 1944–1947* (Oxford, 2012).

[7] Lagrou, *Legacy*, 33, 45; Mark Van Den Wijngaert, Lieve Beullens, and Dana Brants, *Pouvoir et monarchie: La Belgique et ses rois*, translated from the Dutch by Anne-Laure Vignaux (Brussels, 2002), 60–1, 391, 404.

[8] Conway, *Sorrows of Belgium*, 371–2.

[9] Antoon Van den Braembussche, 'The Silence of Belgium: Taboo and Trauma in Belgian Memory', *Yale French Studies*, 102 (2002), 37.

[10] Van Den Wijngaert *et al., Pouvoir et monarchie*, 222, 356.

became internationally notorious for the extent to which Africans were abused and exploited in ways that greatly exceeded practices typical in other European colonies. The state attempted to maximize profits through land expropriation alongside punitive methods of gathering ivory and especially rubber, with the practice of severing hands becoming the most abominable of many ways African populations were coerced into delivering rubber quotas. Ultimately, the state and its concessionary companies focused heavily on developing railways and mining as the vast extent of the region's mineral wealth became apparent. Although Léopold justified taking control on the grounds that this liberated the indigenous population from the horrors of the slave trade run by 'Arabs' from Africa's east coast, in his Congo Free State the Congolese were in fact anything but 'free'. They suffered forced labour, shocking levels of physical brutality and mutilation, and other forms of state-orchestrated terror and intimidation in the interest of extracting wealth for Léopold himself, Europeans employed by him as administrators and army officers, and others connected with the international mining industry and export companies. Millions died from disease, exhaustion, starvation, and outright murder. Following an international humanitarian campaign led by Britons and Americans, the Belgian government eventually pressured Léopold to transfer the Congo to direct rule by Belgium – for which he received immense financial compensation that added to the vast profits already earned from his territory. In 1908 it officially became a colony, the Belgian Congo.[11]

A year after the Belgian state took control of the Congo from the throne, Léopold II died, largely unloved and controversial among his subjects at home and widely criticized abroad for his regime's brutality in Africa. The year 1908 gave Belgium the opportunity to make a fresh start in its colony by instituting new systems of governance that fully rectified previous conditions and by distancing the royal family from association with Central Africa. Revealingly, both largely failed to happen. Although some of the worst abuses of the Congolese were gradually ameliorated, many previous

---

[11] For overviews of the Congo Free State and the international scandals surrounding its systematic human rights abuses, see Isidore Ndaywel è Nziem, *Histoire générale du Congo: De l'héritage ancien à la République Démocratique* (Paris and Brussels, 1998), 311–65; Guy Vanthemsche, *La Belgique et le Congo: L'impact de la colonie sur la métropole*, new and rev. edn. (Brussels, 2010), as well as its English translation entitled *Belgium and the Congo, 1885–1960*, translated by Alice Cameron and Stephen Windross, revised by Kate Connelly (Cambridge, 2012); Jules Marchal, *L'État Libre du Congo: Paradis perdu: l'histoire du Congo, 1876–1900*, 2 vols. (Borgloon, 1996); Jules Marchal, *E.D. Morel contre Léopold II: l'histoire du Congo, 1900–1910*, 2 vols. (Paris, 1996); Daniel Vangroenweghe, *Rood rubber: Léopold II en zijn Kongo* (Brussels, 1985); Adam Hochschild, *King Leopold's Ghost: A Story of Greed, Terror, and Heroism in Colonial Africa* (New York, 1998); Kevin C. Dunn, *Imagining the Congo: The International Relations of Identity* (New York, 2003), ch. 2; Kevin Grant, *A Civilised Savagery: Britain and the New Slaveries in Africa, 1884–1926* (New York, 2005), ch. 2.

practices long remained in place. These included forced labour, punishments with the whip (*chicotte*), and a lack of any political rights – a feature of Belgian colonialism which became more and more striking by the 1940s and 1950s as other European imperial powers slowly granted their own colonial populations varying degrees of self-government and rights that might extend to circumscribed forms of citizenship as opposed to subjecthood. The Belgian Congo's export-driven economy dominated by mining companies working hand in hand with the colonial administration grew ever more powerful.[12]

Although the Belgian monarchs who succeeded Léopold II lacked his direct authority over the colonial state, the royal family maintained an intimate association with (as well as a considerable financial stake in) the Congo. As Crawford Young describes, in comparison with other European empires 'there is no real parallel in colonial history for the vital role the royal family has played in the Congo'. Without Léopold II, the Congo Free State would never have come into existence in the first place, nor would it subsequently have been 'bequeathed' to the nation. Thereafter, 'the royal family always retained a special interest ... and a powerful conviction that tradition called for the King to take an active part in the formulation of Congo policy'.[13] Successor monarchs and their supporters worked harder with every passing generation to enhance the Congo's symbolic role as part of both royal and national identity, a process that reached its culmination under Baudouin.

Léopold II's posthumous reputation as a colonizer was thoroughly white-washed, quickly becoming legendary in a positive sense rather than in an infamously negative one, at least among Belgians. In the metropole, what Guy Vanthemsche and Adam Hochschild respectively have called 'collective amnesia' or the 'Great Forgetting' about the horrors of the Congo Free State and the man largely responsible for them took hold through intense colonial propaganda, in which state education, museums like the Royal Museum for Central Africa in the Brussels suburb of Tervuren, monuments, periodic fairs and exhibitions, and eventually filmmaking all played their role.[14] Members of

---

[12] Georges Nzongola-Ntalaja, *The Congo from Leopold to Kabila: A People's History* (London, 2002), 26–41; Jean-Luc Vellut, 'Mining in the Belgian Congo', in David Birmingham and Phyllis M. Martin (eds.), *History of Central Africa*, Vol. 2 (London, 1983), 126–62.

[13] Crawford Young, *Politics in the Congo: Decolonization and Independence* (Princeton, 1965), 47–8; see also Vanthemsche, *La Belgique et le Congo*, 44–5, 54–9, 80–3.

[14] Vanthemsche, *La Belgique et le Congo*, 44–5; Hochschild, *King Leopold's Ghost*, ch. 19; Matthew G. Stanard, *Selling the Congo: A History of European Pro-Empire Propaganda and the Making of Belgian Imperialism* (Lincoln, NE, 2012); Mathew G. Stanard, 'Learning to Love Leopold: Belgian Popular Imperialism, 1830-1960', in John M. MacKenzie (ed.), *European Empires and the People: Popular Responses to Imperialism in France, Britain, the Netherlands, Belgium, Germany and Italy* (Manchester, 2011), 124–57; Vincent Viaene, David Van Reybrouck, and Bambi Ceuppens (eds.), *Congo in België: Koloniale cultuur in de metropool* (Leuven, 2009); Jan Vandersmissen, 'Cent ans d'instrumentalisation de Léopold II, symbole

white colonial society, for their part, not only readily acquiesced to the Léopoldian cult but did much to consolidate it, both while residing in the Congo and through pro-colonial activities once they returned home. Léopold II's glorification became central to reinforcing the link binding the reputation of the royal family to the nation's cumulative 'achievement' in the Congo both before and after 1908, while the Congo habitually became portrayed as integral to Belgium's self-identity and international standing alike up until the end of the 1950s.

In contrast to European empires that ruled over diverse portfolios of overseas dependencies, in Belgium the Congo reigned supreme within its imperial identity. Indeed, until the end of the First World War the Congo was virtually its *only* overseas territory, and the small adjoining territories of Rwanda and Burundi transferred from German to Belgian administrative oversight by a League of Nations mandate after Germany's defeat never came close in terms of their political, economic, or symbolic importance.[15] Domestically, monarchy and colony were used symbiotically in the effort to create a sense of national unity across the festering Walloon–Fleming divide. Internationally, the Congo – over seventy-five times the size of Belgium – gave a small nation surrounded by more powerful neighbours immeasurably more status on the world stage as *'une plus grande Belgique'*, or 'Greater Belgium'.[16]

Already a source of Belgian pride well before the Second World War, the Congo grew even more important to a nation and its dynasty trying to recover from the political humiliations and domestic upheaval lingering in the wake of Nazi occupation. Like the other imperial powers discussed in previous chapters, after the war Belgium envisioned the Congo not as a candidate for decolonization but as a going concern, a region that would remain under its indefinite control. Social welfare and development initiatives were stepped up after 1945, but commonly-held Belgian views of the Congo and its peoples were characterized much more by continuity than change between the 1930s and the 1950s. This becomes readily apparent when Hergé's *Tintin au Congo* (especially the 1946 re-issued edition which, despite slight textual revisions and new colour drawings, was broadly similar to the original 1930 version) is juxtaposed to state-sanctioned depictions of King Baudouin's 1955 royal tour.

controversé de la présence belge en Afrique centrale', in Sébastien Jahan and Alain Ruscio (eds.), *Histoire de la colonisation: Réhabilitations, Falsifications et Instrumentalisations* (Paris, 2007), 223–40.

[15] Mahmood Mamdani, *When Victims Become Killers: Colonialism, Nativism, and the Genocide in Rwanda* (Princeton, 2001); Gérard Prunier, *The Rwanda Crisis: History of a Genocide* (London, 1995), 23–54; Peter Uvin, *Life after Violence: A People's Story of Burundi* (London, 2009), ch. 1. Belgium also established a small concession in the north China city of Tianjin in 1902. I thank Robert Bickers for bringing this to my attention.

[16] Vanthemsche, *La Belgique et le Congo*, 80–9; Dunn, *Imagining the Congo*, 28–9; Stanard, *Selling the Congo*, 92, 198, 248–50.

Figure 4.1 Hergé, *Tintin au Congo* (Paris: Casterman, 2006), 9.
Credit: ©Hergé/Moulsinart 2013.

Long-prevalent ideas revolved around Belgium and its representatives as benevolent colonizers successfully implementing their 'civilizing mission' among primitive Africans who, almost without exception, stood in awe and appeared grateful for their good works.

Images of Tintin and Baudouin in Central Africa performed much the same function for Belgian audiences, being emblematic of the affirmative story of colonialism they told to themselves. Upon disembarking from their steamship on arrival, the adolescent Tintin and his fox terrier sidekick Milou are greeted by a cheering crowd of adoring Africans, some wearing loincloths and carrying spears, others in Western attire. Regardless of dress, all were drawn in a similarly condescending and stereotypical fashion with exaggerated simian facial features, and all were clearly in agreement about their visitors' deservedly elevated status (throughout their adventure, the heroic pair are repeatedly seen carried on the shoulders of ecstatic Congolese or on palanquins by obedient porters). Quickly donning the khaki clothing and sun helmet favoured by white colonials, Tintin set out into the bush accompanied by Milou and Coco, the African 'boy' who faithfully served them. Throughout their misadventures Tintin proved himself a colonial jack of all trades, performing by turns the roles of administrator, doctor, and teacher at a Catholic mission school, not to mention indiscriminate hunter of big game whenever the opportunity to kill a herd of antelope, a monkey, an elephant, or a rhinoceros arose. With Milou, he ordered Africans whose train became derailed to place it back on the tracks as opposed to standing by lazily, defended them from leopards they seemed too cowardly to confront themselves, prescribed quinine to heal a sick man whose wife believed him to be possessed by evil spirits, and dealt with superstitious rural peoples baffled by modern technology. He unmasked a sorcerer as a fraud who not only had exploited gullible tribespeople but had teamed up with one of the story's white villains (none other than American gangsters sent to Africa by Al Capone in a plot to win control of the African diamond trade), and succeeded by the end in handing the criminals over to the colonial authorities. While doing battle with their enemies, Tintin and Milou were rescued by a kindly missionary and taken back to a mission boasting a hospital, chapel, and school – an encapsulation of many core features of Belgium's purportedly selfless aim of introducing forms of 'progress' that Africans desperately needed. 'When we arrived here a year ago this was all bush', the missionary proudly informs them, illustrating how much had been achieved in a miraculously short space of time thanks to hard work and dedication.[17]

During his visit to the mission in the 1930 version, Tintin gave the African children a geography lesson ('My dear friends, today I'm going to tell you about your fatherland: Belgium!').[18] In the post-war re-issue this was changed to instruction in simple arithmetic, but the story's underlying message remained constant. As Pierre Halen has observed, the small and young coloniz-ing nation of Belgium, represented by Tintin and Milou, was not a vicious racist brandishing a whip but idealistic, peace-loving, and 'paternalist yet also very attentive to the "protection of the natives"'. Still awaiting 'civilization', colo-nized Africans were 'good savages, naïve, whom one should and must educate, care for, instruct, pacify, reassure'.[19] Or, as Georges Van Den Abbeele pro-poses, Tintin personified 'a child-nation attempting to lord it over another people through an infantilizing ideology issued in the overt paternalism of Belgian colonial rule'.[20] Together with their African 'boy' Coco, a scene in which Tintin mistakes an elderly Pygmy for a child on account of his short stature, calling him '*fiston*' ('lad', or 'sonny'), marks another example of how Tintin/Belgium could shed a diminutive status while retaining an image as innocent, unthreatening, and well-meaning vis-à-vis the African 'other' who still needed – indeed *wanted* – supervision by a capable, rational 'adult', even if the adult in question was a still an adolescent.[21] Portrayed as undereducated, invariably speaking broken French, prone to irrational ideas and susceptible to malevolent influences, living amongst wild animals, and usually as half-naked,

[17] Hergé, *Tintin au Congo*, 36.

[18] Hergé, *Les aventures de Tintin au Congo*, in *Archives Hergé* (1973), 247.

[19] Pierre Halen, *'La petit Belge avait vu grand': Une littérature coloniale* (Brussels, 1993), 160, 165. See also Nancy Rose Hunt, 'Tintin and the Interruptions of Congolese Comics', in Paul S. Laudau and Deborah D. Kaspin (eds.), *Images and Empires: Visuality in Colonial and Postcolonial Africa* (Berkeley, 2002), 90–123. On Belgian colonial paternalism, see also Young, *Politics in the Congo*, ch. 4; on colonial maternalism, see Nancy Rose Hunt, *A Colonial Lexicon: Of Birth Ritual, Medicalization, and Mobility in the Congo* (Durham, 1999), ch. 6.

[20] Georges Van Den Abbeele, 'The Children of Belgium', in Tyler Stovall and Georges Van Den Abbeele (eds.), *French Civilization and Its Discontents: Nationalism, Colonialism, Race* (Lanham, MD, 2003), 332.

[21] Hergé, *Tintin au Congo*, 49.

the Congolese were nowhere near sufficiently 'mature' to govern themselves. The thriving Catholic mission may have shown how much had already been accomplished, but much remained to be done – a Belgian belief that remained unshaken in the 1950s.

Tintin au Congo continually portrayed the Congolese as living under Belgian rule not by coercion but through their own desire. Offered warm receptions when they first land in the colony and again as they arrive amongst the Babaorum people ('Welcome, noble stranger! You are good white man'), Tintin and Milou are repeatedly elevated to the status of royalty, with Tintin declared 'chief of Babaorum' and 'king of the M'Hatuvu' and Milou given a crown and a throne, all offers Tintin politely declined. The pair leave the Congo at the end of the story to embark upon further adventures around the world, but their memory remains alive. The book closes with an image of Africans congregating outside their huts and discussing their departed guests with wonder and admiration, worshipping them as effigies on pedestals.[22]

King Baudouin was nowhere as reluctant as Tintin to accept the status as sovereign in the Congo. On the contrary: affirming and consolidating his authority and legitimacy as the latest head of the royal house was one of the main purposes of his visit. Accompanied by a hundred journalists and the documentary filmmaker André Cauvin, Baudouin's tour and the renditions of it produced for metropolitan, colonial, and international audiences were stage-managed to showcase the deep reservoir of devotion and loyalty to the monarchy as an institution and to the king as an individual amongst everyone in the Congo, whether white colonials or indigenous Congolese.[23] Displaying the monarchy to good effect went hand in hand with flagging colonialism's diverse achievements. As Baudouin stressed in his first public speech upon arrival, he was proud to be the fourth generation of his family to pay 'much sollicitous [sic] attention to the lot of the native' ever since the Congo came under Belgian sovereignty by 'the genius of Léopold II'. Belgium's royal family, along with the 'pioneers' and successive generations of colonials who went to Africa, had worked together to ensure that 'the civilizing rôle of Belgium' bore fruit.[24]

Cauvin's film *Bwana Kitoko* (1955) and the illustrated book published to accompany it continually depicted how 'tradition and modernism rub shoulders

---

[22] Ibid., 21, 27, 30, 50, 62.

[23] For a detailed discussion of the tour's press coverage, see Bernard Piniau, *Congo-Zaïre 1874–1981: La perception du lointain* (Paris, 1992), 79–87, 93–116; on the royal tour more generally, see Zana Aziza Etambala, *Congo '55–'65: Van koning Boudewijn tot president Mobutu* (Tielt, 1999), 17–39; Erik Raspoet, *Bwana Kitoko en de koning van de Bakuba: Een vorstelijke ontmoeting op de evanaar* (Antwerp, 2005).

[24] André Cauvin, *Bwana Kitoko: A Book Written on the Occasion of the Visit of the King of the Belgians to the Congo and Ruanda-Urundi* (Brussels, 1956), ix–x.

at every turn'.[25] Airplanes and airports; ships and harbours; the contemporary architecture of the colony's capital city (then still known, indicatively, as Léopoldville); hydroelectric dams and copper mines in the Katanga province; army bases and the disciplined African soldiers of the *Force publique*: from start to finish, *Bwana Kitoko* presented modernity as having strictly Belgian or wider Western origins. Tradition, by contrast, applied both to Belgians' devotion to their African territories and the ways of African peoples. Baudouin and his entourage were treated to a continual display of folkloric spectacles during which 'the collective soul of the black men finds its most eloquent expression'; African chiefs wore elaborate ceremonial garb, animal skins, and headdresses to pay homage to their Belgian ruler.[26]

In its depiction of Africans as primitive and enthralled by chiefs and kings, Cauvin picked up where Hergé's Tintin and countless other renditions of Central Africa available within Belgian popular culture left off. In 1930 and 1946, Tintin and Milou arrived by ship to great acclaim and left the Congo not long after revered as royalty; in 1955, a new 'young King' descended from his Sabena aircraft 'to greet his subjects and to receive their homage'. Not just King of the Belgians, 'the King is also the Great Chief of the Black Peoples, and the visit of their King is a great event in their lives'.[27] Cauvin's film and book repeatedly foregrounded demonstrations of 'deference and affection' by Africans who came *en masse* to see Baudouin from the moment he was driven from the airport into Léopoldville:

All along the route ... gaiety and joy burst forth in shouts and cheers and dances, – all the hullabaloo of a simple and childlike people out to celebrate a great occasion. No sooner had the King set foot on land than he was given a new name. The people of the Congo have christened Baudouin I, King of the Belgians, 'Bwana Kitoko' or 'Noble Lord'.[28]

As if to underscore this 'childlike' status of his African subjects, Baudouin was often photographed with black children who welcomed him with flowers, reportedly 'paying special attention to the welfare work for children' at every stop on his journey.[29]

[25] Ibid., 9. The book's text and film's voiceovers are often identical, and when they differ the tone and message are broadly the same. First released in 1955, *Bwana Kitoko* was reissued in 2010 following restoration as part of the DVD *Belgisch Congo Belge* (www.cinematek.be). For analyses of *Bwana Kitoko* and other colonial propaganda films, see Florence Gillet, *André Cauvin: Portrait d'un cinéaste* (Brussels, 2006); Francis Ramirez and Christian Rolot, *Histoire du cinéma colonial au Zaïre, au Rwanda et au Burundi* (Tervuren, 1985), 27, 55, 101, 167, 196–7, 200, 209, 247; Stanard, *Selling the Congo*, ch. 6, especially 224–5, 230–3. Cauvin also made another film, *Le Voyage royal* (1955), documenting the same tour but more oriented towards Baudouin's encounters with white colonial society.
[26] Cauvin, *Bwana Kitoko*, 51.   [27] Ibid., 5–6, 9.   [28] Ibid., 42, 13.
[29] Ibid., x, 12, 21, 28; see also Nathalie Tousignant's excellent points in 'Imaginaires coloniaux dans la Belgique "nouvelle" (1999–2004): Enjeux mémoriels', paper presented at the 'Colloque

Figure 4.2 King Baudouin in the Congo, 1955.
Photograph by André Cauvin.
Credit: Collections CEGESOMA – Brussels.

Thanks to its extensive multimedia coverage, Baudouin's African tour had significant repercussions in both metropole and colony. When he left Belgium he was largely an unknown quantity, a hesitant and youthful figure yet to emerge from his father's contentious shadow and find widespread acceptance amongst a Belgian public for whom *la question royale* was unfinished business. A few short weeks later he flew back to Brussels in triumph, basking in the glow of colonial adulation. Congolese, Rwandans, and Burundians alongside

"Expériences et mémoire: partager en français la diversité du monde"', Bucarest, septembre 2006', 16, available at www.celat.ulaval.ca/histoire.memoire/b2006/Tousignant.pdf., accessed 24 August 2011.

white colonials had faithfully performed the roles of loyal subjects with a seemingly boundless enthusiasm for their monarch that had hitherto proved fitful at best within Belgium itself. This gave him a newfound status and relaxed self-assurance that survived his inbound flight and did much to alter public opinion at home. Upon return Baudouin was hailed as 'Bwana Kitoko' yet again, his reputation as 'noble lord' consolidated and the prestige of the compromised royal house revitalized via African sustenance that marked his personal and regal coming of age.[30] In the decades that followed this colonial rite of passage, he retained the respect and affection of most Belgians, whether Fleming or Walloon, becoming a rare popular figure of consensus within a nation growing ever more fractured along ethnic, linguistic, and regional lines.

* * *

Baudouin's visit also continued to resonate among the Congolese after his departure. To a considerable extent, Belgians found in the Congo (and eagerly publicized) exactly what they had come looking for: a 'happy', 'model colony' whose peoples venerated Belgian authority and seemed overwhelmingly content with the status quo. Fomented and orchestrated by the colonial authorities though it was, the highly visible, public relations-friendly 'gaiety and joy' directed towards Baudouin appeared genuine for the most part, yet attitudes among the colonized were far more complex. Congolese responses to the king revealed resistant understandings of a racialized 'natural' colonial hierarchy that destabilized the image of the white colonizer as a paternal authority figure and the black colonized as a child too immature to rule itself without parental guidance. Significantly, although the Belgians involved in publicizing the king's tour eagerly circulated the story that the Congolese had greeted Baudouin as 'Bwana Kitoko', they had initially called him 'Mwana Kitoko' ('beautiful child', or 'handsome boy'). As 'Mwana Kitoko' highlighted the king's youth and inexperience in Congolese eyes, it compromised his grandeur; affectionate though it was, its seeming lack of deference led to its suppression in official accounts of the visit.[31]

Many Congolese thought highly of the new king not simply as the pinnacle of traditional Belgian authority but more importantly because he was seen as heralding a new era of race relations. Baudouin's enjoyment in meeting the Congolese and the positive rapport between them appeared heart-felt rather than scripted and dictated by protocol; his proclamations, respectful demeanour, and informality made him seem different from many if not most whites

---

[30] Piniau, *Congo-Zaïre*, 85–6; Van Den Wijngaert *et al., Pouvoir et monarchie*, 356–7; Tousignant, 'Imaginaires coloniaux', 16–17.

[31] Etambala, *Congo '55–'65*, 27; Thomas Kanza, *Conflict in the Congo: The Rise and Fall of Lumumba* (Harmondsworth, 1972), 78.

living in Central Africa. The Belgian Congo still denied Africans political rights and access to higher-level jobs, subjecting all but the most privileged few to a colour bar that excluded them from restaurants, hotels, shops, and other public places to which whites wanted sole access. As such, Baudouin stood out simply for saying that blacks and whites should be allowed to eat and drink together.[32] In speeches given in the Congo and later back in Brussels, he made a deep impression by describing Belgium and the Congo as 'form[ing] but one nation' comprising a 'Belgo-Congolese community' (modelled on the French Union) that would 'guarantee to everyone, white and black, a share in the government of the country according to his merits and capabilities'. Improving standards of living was not enough, he insisted: what was needed was for 'whites and natives to show greater mutual understanding in their daily inter-actions' and behave with 'respect for the human individual'.[33]

Although Baudouin never went beyond vague statements about the form a Belgo-Congolese community might take, what new roles blacks might play, and what rights they might enjoy within it, to an increasingly vocal contingent of African intellectuals his words boiled down to one core message: change. Patrice Lumumba, a leading spokesman among Congolese évolués ('the evolved' who valued their exposure to European culture through the colonial education system), invoked Baudouin's proclamations and the concept of a Belgo-Congolese community with approval on many occasions in his writings dating from 1956 and 1957.[34] Lumumba viewed this initiative as offering the prospect for a racialized colonial system to be reformed and the Congo 'administered and directed *jointly* by the Belgians and the Congolese ... working side by side'. 'Administrative paternalism and all official measures which unintentionally or incidentally favour the superiority of the White over the Black, in the social, economic or political sphere, should be ... replaced by rather more liberal measures, more democratic and more in keeping with the basic principles of the Belgo-Congolese community', Lumumba continued. The *évolués* 'consider themselves to be true citizens, the equals of the Belgians, both in dignity and in civic rights', an equality demanding none other than

---

[32] François Ryckmans, *Mémoires noires: Les Congolais racontent le Congo belge, 1940–1960* (Brussels, 2010), 83–6; Etambala, *Congo '55–'65*, 34–5, 37; Piniau, *Congo-Zaïre*, 105.

[33] King Baudouin, 'Ayez confiance en la Belgique', allocution prononcée au Stade Baudouin à Léopoldville, le 17 mai 1955; 'La communauté belgo-congolaise', allocution prononcée au Cercle Royal Africain, le 1er juilliet 1955', in M. John Bartier (ed.), *Messages Royaux: Un choix de messages de S.M. le Roi Baudouin* (Brussels, 1973), 98–103. On the concept of a 'Belgo-Congolese community' inspired by the French Union, see Young, *Politics in the Congo*, 48–56; Ndaywel è Nziem, *Histoire générale du Congo*, 464; Vanthemsche, *Le Belgique et le Congo*, 67, 120–1.

[34] Patrice Lumumba, *Congo, My Country*, translated by Graham Heath (London, 1962), 32, 154, 157, 188.

'brotherly collaboration' and 'friendship' in place of a condescending and exclusionary paternalism.[35]

If Baudouin's visit and suggestions that the colonial authorities would implement reforms that gave Africans a stake in the colonial hierarchy raised hopes, these were soon to be disappointed. White colonials resisted any suggestion that their privileges vis-à-vis blacks might be reduced, and the colonial state never implemented even the most cautious forms of power-sharing with an African elite that constituted only a small sliver of the indigenous population. In retrospect, Baudouin's 1955 tour served as a point of departure for further politicization among évolués when it failed to yield any significant concessions.[36] Not long after, Congolese elites who had endorsed the Belgo-Congolese community idea came to dismiss it as merely an insincere 'manoeuvre to delay the advance of their emancipation', as Isidore Ndaywel è Nziem put it.[37] An indication of just how delayed this might be came in a pamphlet penned by A.A.J. Van Bilsen, a professor at the University Institute for Overseas Territories in Antwerp, which proposed a 'thirty-year plan for the political emancipation of Belgian Africa'.

Gradualist though it was, Van Bilsen's statement 'was a political bombshell in colonial and évolué circles', Georges Nzongola-Ntalaja notes. 'Van Bilsen was denounced by the defenders of the colonial order as a lunatic or subversive', while politically-minded African writers responded in two ways.[38] One group contributed the *Conscience africaine* (*African Consciousness*) manifesto in 1956 that supported the thirty-year plan, seeing it as a promising beginning that would lead to political change, the Africanization of administrative cadres, and an end to racial discrimination. Albeit a seminal document in the development of Congolese nationalist politics, its moderate stance generated a counter-manifesto issued by the *Alliance des Bakongo* (Abako) that demanded reforms at a greatly accelerated pace; Abako's leader Joseph Kasavubu, moreover, spoke of 'immediate independence' that surpassed loosely-conceived talk of 'emancipation'.[39]

[35] Ibid., 182, 188, 68.
[36] Ryckmans, *Mémoires noires*, 88–90; Nzongola-Ntalaja, *Congo from Leopold to Kabila*, 79–80.
[37] Ndaywel è Nziem, *Histoire générale du Congo*, 464.
[38] Nzongola-Ntalaja, *Congo from Leopold to Kabila*, 81; A.A.J. Van Bilsen, *Vers l'indépendance du Congo et du Ruanda-Urundi: Réflexions sur les devoirs et l'avenir de la Belgique en Afrique centrale* (Brussels, 1958). Van Bilsen's 'thirty-year plan' was first published in Dutch in 1955 and in French in 1956.
[39] Nathalie Tousignant (ed.), *Le manifeste Conscience africaine (1956): Élites congolaises et société coloniale: Regards croisés* (Brussels, 2009); Ndaywel è Nziem, *Histoire générale du Congo*, 511–20; Nzongola-Ntalaja, *Congo from Leopold to Kabila*, 82; Jean Stengers, 'Precipitous Decolonization: The Case of the Belgian Congo', in Prosser Gifford and Wm Roger Louis (eds.), *The Transfer of Power in Africa: Decolonization 1940–1960* (New Haven, 1982), 321–5; René Lemarchand, *Political Awakening in the Belgian Congo* (Berkeley, 1964), 153–8.

From the Belgian point of view, in 1956 there appeared to be no end to colonial rule in sight. Whether living in metropole or colony, the overwhelming majority of Belgians looked to the Congo with pride and a sense of national entitlement, seemingly envisioning no immediate or even medium-term substantive changes to the prevailing system. A survey taken within the metropole that year showed that over 80 per cent of the 3,000 polled believed Belgium's presence in the Congo to be legitimate and beneficial to the Congolese and to Belgium alike (with the remaining being largely of 'no opinion' as opposed to unsupportive of the colonial mission). Many justified their beliefs, and Belgium's ongoing presence in Central Africa, on the grounds of all Belgium had achieved to the good of the colony.[40] Deep-seated attitudes about Belgian colonialism and the Congolese people appeared unshaken two years later when Brussels hosted the 1958 World's Fair (Expo '58), which conveniently served as an occasion to celebrate the fiftieth anniversary of the 1908 takeover when Léopold II's territory became a Belgian colony. Belgium's own exhibitions included a number of pavilions applauding its colonial endeavours, honouring the role played by Léopold II, and portraying the Congolese as backward, primitive, and unchanging, fit for display in a 'native village' or as loyal soldiers of the *Force publique*, well trained and tightly controlled by an exclusively white officer corps.[41] Like the narratives circulated about King Baudouin's 1955 visit, Expo '58 became yet another platform for 'showing off the Congo with all its wealth and its happy colonized people', as Thomas Kanza sarcastically phrased it, to Belgians and millions of international visitors.[42]

Expo '58 also enabled more Congolese *évolués* to visit the metropole than ever before as participants or spectators. Unlike neighbouring colonial powers with well-established traditions of educating their colonized elites at British and French universities, Belgium had actively restricted the Congolese presence in the metropole, fearing that time in Europe would provide exposure to radical ideas that would destabilize the colonial order and its hierarchy – a theme to which Chapter 7 returns. Kanza himself was the first Congolese ever to graduate from university with a degree in anything other than theology following his studies at the Catholic University of Leuven (or Louvain) between 1952 and 1956, by which time his peer group enrolled in Belgian higher educational institutions amounted to just a few dozen. Attending Expo

---

[40] Vanthemsche, *La Belgique et le Congo*, 114–15.
[41] Stanard, *Selling the Congo*, especially 66–76, 236–44, 257–9; Matthew Stanard, '"Bilan du monde pour un monde plus déshumanisé": The 1958 Brussels World's Fair and Belgian Perceptions of the Congo', *European History Quarterly*, 35:2 (2005), 267–98; Sarah Van Beurden, '"Un panorama de nos valeurs africains": Belgisch Congo op Expo 58', in Viaene *et al.* (eds.), *Congo in België*, 299–311.
[42] Kanza, *Conflict in the Congo*, 39.

'58 was often part of a greater political awakening or the beginning of their 'mental decolonization', he argued:

For the first time they had spoken on an equal footing with Europeans, Americans, Russians, Chinese, Arabs, Japanese, Indians. For them, Belgium was to be from then on just one country like any other, with good and bad aspects . . . [they] achieved a mental decolonization during the Fair which would make it hard for them ever to accept the colonial yoke again.[43]

Congo's *évolués* expanded their political horizons in many ways in 1958. Nationalism galvanized wider swathes of the Congolese population as political parties emerged that year with specific political platforms now demanding far more than a stake for indigenous elites in the colonial system or slow and partial Belgian concessions. Most parties grew out of new or pre-existing ethnic associations and as such attracted adherents who shared a 'tribal', linguistic, or regional origin, such as Kasavubu's Abako or Moïse Tshombe's *Confédération des Associations Tribales du Katanga* (Conakat). By contrast, Patrice Lumumba was a leading founder of the *Mouvement National Congolais* (MNC), which rapidly won mass support with an explicitly multi-ethnic platform that emphasized the need for national unity and denounced ethnic and regional separatism. As nationalism gained further momentum between 1958 and 1960 and decolonization arrived at a speed unimaginable just two years before, these competing variants proved decisive in debates concerning the shape a postcolonial Congo would take – debates in which Belgium proved keenly self-interested.

Events occurring within as well as outside the Congo were responsible for what Jean Stengers termed its 'precipitous decolonization' and independence on 30 June 1960. Congolese nationalists like Lumumba drew inspiration from signs that colonial rule was drawing to a close elsewhere in Africa, with Ghana's independence from Britain in 1957 and de Gaulle's announcement in 1958 that France's sub-Saharan African territories could choose between outright independence or membership within the French Community being key turning points. In the Congo itself, mass mobilization and radicalization was on the rise. Socio-economic discontent mixed with rising nationalism, with the Congolese becoming increasingly impatient with Belgian dithering in implementing political change and setting an accelerated timetable for independence. Widespread rioting in Léopoldville in January 1959 involved violence against Europeans and their property and caused considerable alarm amongst Belgians, who feared the colonial state lacked sufficient military force to quell future uprisings, which looked likely to recur. In its hopes of containing the spread of unrest Belgium conceded independence, which arrived just eighteen months later.

[43] Ibid., 40–1; see also Ryckmans, *Mémoires noires*, 150–9.

Like the Congolese nationalists, Belgium also looked to recent events in other colonial arenas and within other European countries attempting to keep hold of them when contemplating how best to approach colonial discontent that could no longer be ignored. 'Elsewhere, emancipation movements had been engaged in battle, and in the end – in Indochina as in ... the Netherlands Indies – the result was defeat of the colonial power, a defeat leaving catastrophe and often ruins in its wake. Profiting by these lessons, Belgium must avoid such errors', Stengers summarized. Should the *Force publique* prove unable to quell insurgency on its own, Belgian 'public opinion would not tolerate the engagement of Belgian troops in operations to maintain or restore order in the Congo ... It wanted no resort to force. It wanted no Algerian policy; the French example served as a powerful deterrent.'[44] Yet agreeing to decolonization to steer clear of these pitfalls did not mean that Belgium had simply resigned itself to cutting all ties with its colony. Instead, Ludo De Witte asserted, the metropolitan 'government accelerated the pace of decolonisation precisely to cut short any process of radicalising the Congolese masses ... [and] curtail the period of politicisation ... Brussels thus hoped to put inexperienced and weak Congolese politicians in power and continue to pull the strings behind the scenes.'[45]

In aiming to usher in a nominally 'independent' Congolese government that would preserve its interests in full, Belgium did its utmost to promote a central government with limited powers that left room for significant regional self-determination. As King Baudouin insisted in a speech given in January 1960, conversations with countless Congolese convinced him of the 'general wish to organize the future state based on considerable provincial autonomy'.[46] A federalist outcome was favoured both by Belgium and by Congolese political parties like Abako and Conakat that campaigned on ethnic or regional platforms. Ironically, the increasingly tense nature of Belgium's own ethnic pluralism was taken up by Congolese wanting a federal state, seeing the metropolitan model as a strong argument for a federal alternative. In a 1959 essay asking 'What is a People and a Nation', Abako put it thus:

It suffices to observe the perpetual mistrust and misunderstandings between Flemings and Walloons to convince oneself of the danger there is to unite men of different origins ... we cannot help saying that if the union between Flemings and Walloons were conceived on a federal basis, the almost interminable quarrels which have often broken forth between these two tribes would have been avoided.[47]

---

[44] Stengers, 'Precipitous Decolonization', 328, 332; see also Vanthemsche, *La Belgique et le Congo*, 130–1.

[45] Ludo De Witte, *The Assassination of Lumumba*, translated by Ann Wright and Renée Fenby (London, 2001), 180.

[46] King Baudouin, 'L'Honneur de nos deux pays', allocution prononcée à la Radio le 9 janvier 1960, in Bartier (ed.), *Messages Royaux*, 107.

[47] *Notre Kongo*, 19 November 1959, cited in Young, *Politics in the Congo*, 267–8.

Pitted against this approach was Patrice Lumumba's wing of the MNC. 'What we wish to create in the Congo is a nation of brothers, a homogeneous society, and we will do everything in our power to combat, to destroy every vestige of colonialism and tribalism', Lumumba argued; 'there are those who are trying to set the various sectors of the Congolese population against each other, using the word "federalism" as a cover-up ... what they are really advocating is separatism'.[48] For Lumumba and his party, Belgium's stance favouring ethnic and regional autonomy was nothing more than a cynical ploy to maintain control after formally granting 'freedom' to its colony through a 'divide and conquer' decolonization policy. Colonialism and tribalism worked hand in hand, and fomenting the latter enabled a continuation of the former. 'The hopes and wishes of certain Belgians were set on the Congo's finally becoming some six different states, nominally independent, with the periodic bonus of major or minor tribal conflict ending in fratricide,' wrote Thomas Kanza, who had become one of Lumumba's close associates within the MNC. 'Belgium would still possess all the means of pressure and persuasion she needed to continue to act there, whether directly or indirectly, and to safeguard her financial, economic, missionary and humanitarian undertakings.'[49]

Belgian efforts to secure an independence settlement in 1960 that favoured federalist Congolese parties at the MNC's expense did not initially succeed. Elections held in the run-up to 30 June saw Lumumba's MNC emerge as the leading party, and although it failed to secure a majority of seats in assemblies at either the national or regional level it was able to form a coalition government together with allied parties. Lumumba was to become prime minister upon independence – precisely the scenario Belgium had hoped to avoid at all costs and one with which its resident minister tried to tamper by appointing Kasavubu, Abako's leader, as the head of state. 'Even though Belgium publicly came out in favor of the independence of the Congo, its intention nonetheless was to set up a government that would be under its thumb', Lumumba complained.[50] This lent direct support to his regionalist opponents who otherwise could not have survived on their own, and its consequences were felt immediately after the official transfer of power.

* * *

When the ceremonies marking Independence Day arrived on 30 June, genuine decolonization as demanded by Lumumba and his nationalist allies was nowhere

---

[48] Patrice Lumumba, speech given to the Amis de Présence Africaine in Brussels, 6 Feb. 1960, reprinted in Jean Van Lierde (ed.), *Lumumba Speaks: The Speeches and Writings of Patrice Lumumba, 1958–1961*, translated by Helen R. Lane (Boston, 1972), 166.

[49] Kanza, *Conflict in the Congo*, 37, 80.

[50] Patrice Lumumba, press conference published in *Indépendence*, 15 June 1960, reprinted in Van Lierde (ed.), *Lumumba Speaks*, 201.

in sight. Given the dearth of Congolese with the higher education or professional training qualifying them for senior administrative duties, Belgian colonial administrators remained in their posts. Moreover, no Africanization whatsoever had occurred within the officer corps of the *Force publique*, which remained exclusively white, the Congolese confined to its subaltern ranks with no indication of any change in the foreseeable future. As a series of eight postage stamps released to mark the occasion illustrated, Belgian official pride in the nation's colonial achievements remained unshakeable – a confidence that underpinned the assumption that its administrative, military, and economic presence in the region would remain extensive. Thanks to Belgium, the Congo and its peoples had received the gifts of Western modernity ranging from radio broadcasting technology, river navigation, and forestry to primary education and medicine – pictorial evidence of an ambitious and altruistic civilizing mission accomplished. But just because Belgium had chosen to 'give' the Congo its independence did not mean that the Congolese were seen to have reached adulthood and gained the full capacity to rule themselves. The stamp featuring a smiling small boy standing by a globe in a schoolroom testified to a resilient colonial mindset that cast the Congolese as grateful children with many lessons still to be learned from a well-intentioned and dedicated teacher.

'Mental decolonization' was practically non-existent among many Belgians involved in the colonial enterprise, not least King Baudouin. His speech at the independence festivities was redolent with the same paternalistic rhetoric, celebratory arrogance, and wilful amnesia as had pervaded his Congo-related proclamations since he ascended to the throne nine years before. Congo's independence, he began, 'is the conclusion of a work conceived by the genius of King Léopold II . . . For eighty years, Belgium has sent to your land the finest of her sons, first to free the Congo basin from the appalling slave traffic that was decimating her populations; then to unite ethnic groups which had been enemies'. Léopold II 'did not come in the guise of a conqueror, but of a civilizer', Baudouin stressed. In consequence, '[t]he Congo has been given railways, roads, waterways and air routes which, by bringing your people into contact with one another, have fostered their unity'; 'a medical service . . . which has delivered you from devastating illnesses'; modern agriculture, cities, improved housing and hygiene, and industrial development that has 'increased the well-being of your populations'; and primary education via mission and state schooling. 'We are happy to have thus, despite the gravest difficulties, given to the Congo the elements needed to prepare a country on its way to development . . . It is for you, gentlemen, to prove that we were right thus to place our confidence in you.'[51]

---

[51] King Baudouin, 'L'Indépendence du Congo', allocution prononcée à Léopoldville, le 30 juin 1960, in Bartier (ed.), *Messages Royaux*, 110–13. Portions of Baudouin's speech appear in translation in Kanza, *Conflict in the Congo*, 155–7.

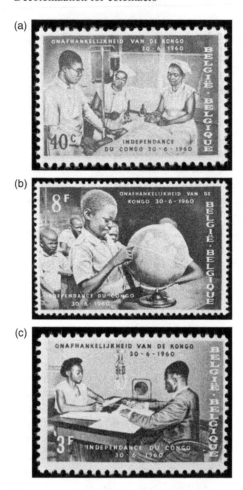

Figure 4.3a–c Belgian postage stamps dated 30 June 1960 and commemorating the independence of the Congo, illustrating medical staff with a patient, a boy with a globe, and a man and woman with radio transmission equipment.
Copyright: bpost.

In the official programme coordinated by the colonial authorities, the king's proclamation was meant only to be followed by a speech by Kasavubu; Lumumba, although the elected prime minister, was not scheduled to speak at all. But after Kasavubu delivered an inoffensive response scripted for him in advance, Lumumba seized the initiative and the microphone, issuing a blistering rebuttal to the standard Belgian colonial narrative revolving around benevolent 'gifts' for which Baudouin, once again, had served as mouthpiece. The Congolese, he countered, had 'fought to win' independence 'to put an end to the humiliating slavery that had been forced upon us' during 'eighty years under a colonialist regime'. Along with suffering loss of land, '[b]ack-breaking work ... in return for wages that did not allow us to satisfy our hunger', and legalized inequality between blacks and whites, he described how '[w]e have been the victims of ironic taunts, of blows that we were forced to endure morning, noon and night because we were blacks':

We have known that there were magnificent mansions for whites in the cities and ramshackle straw hovels for blacks, that a black was never allowed into the so-called European movie theaters or restaurants or stores; ...
  Who can forget, finally, the burst of rifle fire in which so many of our brothers perished, the cells into which the authorities threw those who no longer were willing to submit to a rule where justice meant oppression and exploitation? ...
  But we ... whose bodies and souls have suffered from colonialist oppression, loudly proclaim: all this is over and done with now.

Lumumba insisted upon 'our complete and sovereign independence', 'our economic independence', and described Belgium and the Congo as 'two equal and independent countries' – all of which generated immense applause, both from his audience in the room and among those listening to radios across the country.[52]

Lumumba's speech turning the conventional version of colonialism on its head caused grave insult to the king and to Belgium, leading to tremendous media outcry in Brussels. Belgian authorities involved in coordinating the transfer of power already considered Lumumba the worst possible leader of the Congo precisely because he demanded full independence, which placed Belgian and other Western economic interests in danger. His pronouncements on 30 June simply confirmed what many firmly believed before, namely that Lumumba would have to be removed from the scene for Belgium's ongoing stake in and control over an 'independent' Congo to be guaranteed. Demonizing Lumumba and destabilizing his fledgling national government became a top priority.[53] Belgium correspondingly took advantage of crises that erupted almost immediately, crises for which it had actively laid the foundations: the mutiny by soldiers in the *Force publique*, and the secession of the Katanga province.

As noted earlier, in June 1960 only whites held the posts of commissioned officers in the colonial army, and this remained so after Independence Day. General Émile Janssens continued as its commander-in-chief, and his response

[52] Patrice Lumumba, speech at proclamation of independence, reprinted in Van Lierde (ed.), *Lumumba Speaks*, 220–4.
[53] Pierre Halen and János Riesz (eds.), *Patrice Lumumba entre dieu et diable: Un héros africain dans ses images* (Paris, 1997); Dunn, *Imagining the Congo*, ch. 3.

to seething discontent among African troops and non-commissioned officers at the lack of promotions, poor pay, and retention of Belgian officers was conveyed in no uncertain terms, written on a blackboard before a large meeting convened on 4 July: '*avant l'indépendance* = *après l'indépendance*' – 'before independence = after independence'. Mutiny broke out the following day, spreading among various units throughout the country and resulting in physical attacks on European officers, their families, and their property and spreading panic among the white population. Thousands of Europeans fled the Congo on land into neighbouring territories and more spectacularly via a massive airlift back to Belgium on Sabena aircraft, themes that Chapter 6 on European repatriations treats in greater detail. As Lumumba's government tried to restore order and introduce Africanization, General Janssens was dismissed and sent back to Brussels, taking his dramatic flair with him. To publicly express his disapproval at the Belgian government's decision to grant independence to a 'still savage' people – a savagery to which the Congo's rapid descent into chaos during the mutiny supposedly attested – he promptly made a pilgrimage to the statue of Léopold II on Brussels' Place du Thrône, before which he proclaimed that the former monarch and his colonial legacy had been defiled. Lumumba's verbal assault on Belgium's colonial record in front of Baudouin opened the floodgates to physical attacks on whites, he argued in books written as part of his subsequent campaign to absolve himself of responsibility. Like others, Janssens eagerly attributed the soldiers' seditious violence to Lumumba's provocation rather than his own.[54]

The *Force publique* mutiny gave Belgium the pretext to launch a military intervention to ensure the safety of Belgian nationals. This effectively resulted in a neo-colonial reconquest less than two weeks after the official transfer of power. 'Within the Belgian government's narrative, the Congolese proved within the first few days of independence that they were not "developed" enough for the "gifts" of sovereignty and self-rule, so the gifts could and should be taken back', Kevin Dunn argues; independence was premature because the Congolese remained immature, with Lumumba's 'insolence' in front of King Baudouin being a prime example. 'The "inherent" savagery and barbarism of the Congolese had returned to the surface now that Belgium's civilizing hand had been removed.'[55] It was not only Belgian lives that were endangered but wider economic interests, especially the security of the mining concerns concentrated in Katanga. Belgian troops flown in from the metropole ostensibly to quell the munity and protect whites in affected areas were mainly sent to

[54] É. Janssens, *J'Étais le Général Janssens*, 2nd edn. (Brussels, 1961), 230; Général e. r. Émile Janssens, *Au fil d'une vie* (Brussels, 1972), 438–41.
[55] Dunn, *Imagining the Congo*, 79, 82, 84.

Katanga, where nearly one-third of the Congo's white residents were located, not to mention much of its vast mineral wealth.[56]

Belgium's military invasion immediately became crucial to propping up the province's secession orchestrated by Moïse Tshombe's party, Conakat, on 11 July. Although technically an African organization, in reality Conakat and its leader were puppets manipulated by Katanga's white settler population together with the *Union Minière de Haut Katanga* (UMHK, the region's most powerful mining company), and their Belgian political backers. Under cover of this breakaway government, Katanga became Belgium's 'bridgehead ... to fight Congolese nationalism' and 'the prime weapon in its fight against Lumumba's government', Ludo De Witte has written. Seeing it as the most promising way to realize its federalist agenda at the expense of an independent and unified nation state, 'Brussels had amputated Katanga from the body of the Congo in the hope that Léopoldville would not survive the operation.'[57] By casting Tshombe and Kasavubu as loyal moderates and Lumumba as 'irrational', 'extreme', and 'communist', Belgium thus brought its collective military, political, and economic weight to bear on the Congo's political landscape and thereby ensured Lumumba's elimination. It was aided by a United Nations intervention coupled with American involvement that extended to the White House and the CIA as Cold War anxieties about the possibility of Soviet influence over mineral-rich Central Africa came to the fore.[58] Using Kasavubu as the intermediary, Lumumba was removed from office within weeks and soon imprisoned; he was ultimately transferred to Katanga and into the hands of his political enemies headed by Tshombe and his white backers, where he was beaten, tortured, and murdered in early 1961.

Belgium assiduously sought to distance itself from Lumumba's death by attributing it to African political infighting, dismissing it as a 'Bantu affair' and further evidence that the Congolese were not able to govern themselves in a civilized manner. Long a source of controversy, conjecture, accusations, and denials, it took close to forty years for Lumumba's assassination to be subjected to an intensive Belgian parliamentary inquiry stemming from debates that resurfaced in response to the publicity surrounding Ludo De Witte's study, as Chapter 9 explores further. Although countless issues remain murky even after the

---

[56] On the mutiny and the secession of Katanga in July 1960, see (alongside Chapter 6's discussion) J. Gérard-Libois and Benoît Verhaegen, *Congo 1960: Les dossiers du CRISP*, 2 vols. (Brussels, 1961), especially vol. 1, 371–460, and vol. II, 469–517; W.J. Ganshof van der Meersch, *Fin de la souveraineté belge au Congo: Documents et Réflexions* (Brussels, 1963), 132–77, 399–462; Louis-François Vanderstraeten, *De la Force publique à l'Armée nationale congolaise: Histoire d'une mutinerie juillet 1960* (Brussels, 1985); Ndaywel è Nziem, *Histoire générale du Congo*, 568–80.

[57] De Witte, *Assassination*, 31.

[58] John Kent, *America, the UN and Decolonisation: Cold War Conflict in the Congo* (London, 2010).

commission of inquiry released its findings, nevertheless it clarified the extent to which Belgian complicity and direct involvement in Lumumba's murder encompassed officers in Africa, the highest echelons of its political establishment at home, and the innermost circles of its royal palace, including King Baudouin himself.[59]

Baudouin openly expressed his support for Tshombe's secessionist regime and spoke as though Katanga were a legitimate state, doing his utmost to influence public opinion. 'Entire ethnic groups, led by men of honesty and courage, have pledged their friendship and begged us to help them build their independence amid the chaos of what was once the Belgian Congo', he told his countrymen in late July 1960. 'It is our duty to respond to all those who loyally ask for our help.' An argument rather different from his proclamation that Belgium had long worked to 'unite ethnic groups' and 'fostered their unity' made on Independence Day less than a month before, it was nonetheless a more accurate portrayal of Belgium's policies, in the Congo as well as its mandated territories of Rwanda and Burundi, that actively fomented ethnic divisions and favoured tribalism and regionalism at the expense of national unity.[60] As the findings of the official inquiry confirmed in 2001, Baudouin had direct knowledge of plans to murder Lumumba in Katanga and did nothing to prevent it; his inner aristocratic circle of advisors had aided and abetted the unlawful assassination with royal encouragement. Alongside the strong symbolic link that had bound Belgium's monarchy and the Congo closely for eighty years, the vested interests of the royal house and nation's upper classes extended to their financial portfolios in which investments in mining and affiliated concerns in the Congo were of immeasurable importance. With the Congo's postcolonial political order being inseparable from Belgian (and wider Western) economic interests and access to mineral wealth, no punches were pulled in the urgent quest to ensure a favourable neo-colonial outcome in a global landscape shaped by Cold War rivalries.

By 1965 this seemed to have been achieved. Five years of successive insurrections, provincial secessionist movements, ongoing political upheaval, and several military coups resulted in a re-unified Congo (soon to be renamed Zaïre) under the control of General Mobutu, who proved happy to play the role of biddable Western stooge Lumumba had rejected and for which Tshombe and other 'moderates' were no longer needed. Mobutu remained in power until 1997 as a

---

[59] Georgi Verbeeck, 'Coming To Terms with the (Post-)Colonial Past in Belgium: The Inquiry into the Assassination of Patrice Lumumba', in Harriet Jones, Kjell Östberg, and Nico Randeraad (eds.), *Contemporary History on Trial: Europe Since 1989 and the Role of the Expert Historian* (Manchester, 2007), 56–7; Colette Braeckman, *Lumumba, un crime d'État: Une lecture critique de la Commission parlementaire belge* (Brussels, 2009), 45–50; Van Den Wijngaert *et al., Pouvoir et monarchie*, 358–61; Vanthemsche, *La Belgique et le Congo*, 135–8.

[60] De Witte, *Assassination*, 36–42; King Baudouin, 'L'Intérêt national et l'amour du pays', allocution prononcée au micro de l'I.N.R. à l'occasion du 21 juillet 1960, in Bartier (ed.), *Messages Royaux*, 115.

ruthless dictator presiding over a state kleptocracy, propped up for decades by foreign governments including the United States and France, which valued him as the safest means of protecting their economic investments and as a Cold War ally.[61] Belgium also preserved cordial relations with Mobutu for much of this period, with King Baudouin personally remaining a key figure within his nation's diplomatic initiatives with its erstwhile colony. Baudouin visited the Congo/Zaïre at Mobutu's personal invitation on several occasions, and was a guest of honour at celebrations in 1970 and 1985 marking the tenth and twenty-fifth anniversaries of independence. He extended hospitality to Mobutu in return, hosting gala dinners on his behalf at the royal palace in Brussels. Relations only soured in the late 1980s and early 1990s when Mobutu's government came into increasing international disrepute on account of its endemic human rights violations at a time when the end of the Cold War made him less politically useful to the West. Moreover, during his struggles with the International Monetary Fund over Zaïre's foreign debts, Mobutu pressured Belgium for aid in part by developing an argument alluding to the 'colonial debt' it still owed in Central Africa, a debt he implied was moral and material alike. Accusations hinting at exploitation and abuses during the colonial era, however, did nothing to mend relations – rather the opposite.[62] When his hold on power weakened in the mid-1990s and collapsed in 1997, Belgium had finally distanced itself from the regime – a sign that its financial interests in the region were no longer what they had been in 1960.

As for King Baudouin, if the 2001 findings of the parliamentary commission confirmed allegations implicating him in Patrice Lumumba's murder from afar, his fall from grace (when he became 'a saint with dirty hands', as Colette Braeckman termed it) was a posthumous one.[63] Baudouin died of cardiac arrest in 1993 aged only 63, having spent his last three decades on the throne presiding over Belgium's gradual fragmentation as regional political demands grew ever more vociferous. The suggestion that the independence of the Congo in 1960 followed by Rwanda and Burundi in 1962 helped further weaken an already-divided nation by removing colonialism as a common denominator of Belgian national identity remains hypothetical: far more research is needed to build a convincing case for a direct connection between decolonization

---

[61] Nzongola-Ntalaja, *Congo from Leopold to Kabila*, chs. 3 and 5; Odd Arne Westad, *The Global Cold War: Third World Interventions and the Making of Our Times* (Cambridge, 2005), 131–43.

[62] Mobutu [Sese Seko], *Dignité pour l'Afrique: Entretiens avec Jean-Louis Remilleux* (Paris, 1989), 177, 180, 187–98; Gauthier de Villers, *De Mobutu à Mobutu: Trente ans de relations Belgique-Zaïre* (Brussels, 1995), Part III (see especially 202); Claude Roosens, 'Belgique-Zaïre: la Grande crise', in Olivier Lanotte, Claude Roosens, and Caty Clement (eds.), *La Belgique et l'Afrique Centrale: De 1960 à nos jours* (Brussels, 2000), 135–48; Van Den Wijngaert *et al., Pouvoir et monarchie*, 361–4; Dunn, *Imagining the Congo*, 124–5, 130, 134, 163; De Witte, *Assassination*, 165–6; Vanthemsche, *La Belgique et le Congo*, 273–9; Ndaywel è Nziem, *Histoire générale du Congo*, 814.

[63] Braeckman, *Lumumba, un crime d'État*, 45.

overseas and creeping federalism at home.[64] In any case, because Francophone Belgians had presided over the top levels of the colonial administration and French was the main language of colonial public life, many Flemish nationalists at home had lacked an ardent commitment to the Congo, seeing it as an emblem of the unitary Belgian state in which Flemings suffered from their own form of 'internal colonization' at Francophone hands.[65]

Whether or not African decolonization and domestic federalism were causally linked, however, it remains deeply ironic that Belgium's own national integrity became progressively enfeebled by internal divisions between Flemings and Walloons that grew exponentially after the end of an empire in which Belgium cultivated and exploited regional and ethnic (or 'tribal') differences among Africans to its own advantage. Whether by fomenting distinctions and animosities between Hutus and Tutsis in the case of Rwanda or supporting federalism and regionalist movements like Tshombe's Conakat to undercut Lumumba's nationalist government in the case of the Congo, Belgian policies did much to sow the seeds of postcolonial tragedies. Lumumba's murder and the 1994 Rwandan genocide count as just two examples.[66]

* * *

If Belgium placed an order for a high level of regional autonomy in the Congo in 1960, it was delivered to its home address not long after, first in the form of a linguistic frontier implemented in 1963 and later via a series of constitutional changes beginning in 1970 and culminating in a federal state in 1993, immediately prior to Baudouin's death.[67] His reign began in an effort to reconcile the communal rifts between Flanders and Wallonia worsened by the Second World War and *la question royale*, and ended with a federal solution that optimists, Baudouin included, hoped would come to the nation's rescue by acting as a bulwark against separatism. Between the 1950s and 1993 the king worked hard to resuscitate the monarchy as an institution that bridged Belgium's internal divisions rather than enhanced them, and the intense national mourning upon his death attested to the extent of his popularity among both communities.[68] Flemings

---

[64] For a critical perspective on such a connection posited by Stanard, *Selling the Congo*, 250, see Vanthemsche, *La Belgique et le Congo*, 90.

[65] Vanthemsche, *La Belgique et le Congo*, 75, 78–9, 89–90. On this complex topic in longer-term perspective, see Bambi Ceuppens, *Congo Made in Flanders?: Koloniale vlaamse visies op 'blank' en 'zwart' in Belgisch Congo* (Gent, 2003).

[66] Mamdani, *When Victims Become Killers*, chs. 1–3.

[67] Xavier Mabille, *Histoire politique de la Belgique: Facteurs et acteurs de changement* (Brussels, 1997), 327–432.

[68] Van Den Wijngaert *et al.*, *Pouvoir et monarchie*, 392–8, 405. As Martin Conway stresses in *Sorrows of Belgium*, 371, under Baudouin 'the monarchy recovered much of its former centrality' after the cataclysms of the 1940s. 'Indeed, precisely because of the reduced power of many of the other institutions of the central state, its importance as the manufacturer of political compromises and coalitions, and as a focus of patriotic sentiments, emerged all the more prominently. The

and Walloons came together to lament the passing of a beloved and venerated monarch, not forgetting the Congo's decisive role in creating his public persona that in turn reinvigorated the royal house's reputation. Looking back on his life, the Flemish- and French-language press reactivated his status as 'the last king of the Congo', invoking his youthful incarnation as 'Bwana Kitoko' once again.[69]

Reflecting on Belgian identity in 2002, Nancy Rose Hunt underscored the importance of Tintin and his creator within a national culture whose unifying symbols were few and far between:

Hergé and Tintin are as basic and everyday to a common Belgian national imaginary as Magritte paintings or mussels with fries, no small feat in a country ever more fractured by linguistic boundaries, especially since the Belgian state was federalized. Indeed, the cuisine, the monarchy, and Tintin comics join Belgium's post-colonies, corruption scandals, wartime occupations and Sabena Airlines as some of the few widely resonant forms of imagining Belgium as a nation.[70]

Many of these have ebbed if not vanished altogether in the years since. Baudouin's death dealt a blow to the monarchy; as he and his wife had no children, his younger brother Prince Albert ascended the throne but never won a comparable degree of public affection. Sabena Airlines – one of many visible Belgian representatives in mid-twentieth-century Congo, as Chapter 6 takes further – also fell by the wayside, one of the many airlines to go bankrupt in the wake of 11 September 2001. Only two years before its demise, Sabena reinvoked its colonial heritage through an advertising campaign featuring a white child contemplating the cover of *Tintin au Congo*, with the accompanying caption reading 'Remember your first trip to Africa'.[71] As Chapter 9 considers in greater detail, in a Belgium plagued by recurrent political stalemates and appearing closer to national disintegration than ever before, Tintin's survival alongside narratives and memories of the nation's colonial record in Africa remain central (albeit hotly debated) facets of the national past that retain powerful purchase in the present.

enduring power of the monarchy as the vehicle for a certain sense of "Belgianness" could not, however, offset the broader problem of the decline of the prestige and effectiveness of the state', which led to 'negative mobilization against the state' starting in the 1960s.

[69] Hugues Le Paige (ed.), *Questions royales: Réflexions à propos de la mort d'un roi et sur la médiatisation de l'événement* (Brussels, 1994), 124, 130, 138.

[70] Hunt, 'Tintin', 92–3; see also Kotek, 'Tintin: un mythe belge'.

[71] Norimitsu Onishi, 'Tintin at 70: Colonialism's Comic-Book Puppet?', *New York Times*, 8 January 1999.

5   From rose-coloured map to Carnation Revolution

Portugal's overseas amputations

'Portugal não é um país pequeno' – 'Portugal is not a small country', read a poster advertising the 1934 Colonial Exhibition held in the city of Porto. This slogan accompanied a map of Europe upon which Angola, Mozambique, and other faraway Portuguese-ruled territories had been lifted out of Africa and Asia, placed side by side, and repositioned as a geographical extension of Portugal itself, superimposed so that they fanned out to cover much of Spain, France, Germany, and Eastern Europe, even extending into Russia. While literally distant and discontinuous, figuratively the colonies were amalgamated and moved towards home to transform Portugal – in reality dwarfed by larger, wealthier, and more politically powerful neighbours – into a European giant. Never mind that Portugal was just one of a number of European nations with an overseas empire: colonies were a source of national pride and aggrandisement, creating an impressive rose-coloured map and an affirmative story Portugal could tell itself, and others, as evidence of an importance that greatly exceeded limited European territorial confines and capabilities.[1]

Not coincidentally, Portugal's insistent colonial propaganda of the 1930s came at a critical historic juncture as the *Estado Novo*, or 'New State', consolidated itself after a military coup in 1926 had ended a republic and ushered in nearly fifty years of dictatorship, mainly under the rule of António de Oliveira Salazar. This half century started with European overseas empires at their peak but gradually witnessed the intensification of international pressures that led to a protracted decolonization process after 1945. During that period, Portugal's experience attested to imperialism's fundamental impact not only on colonized peoples but also *within* Europe's colonizing nations themselves. In Portugal's case, the importance of overseas engagement to national identity dated back nearly five hundred years to the time when Prince Henry the Navigator and explorers like Vasco da Gama launched the era of the 'Discoveries' that made Portugal the pioneering maritime power it became in the early modern era. Assertions of the longevity of its history outside Europe were far more than mere statements of

---

[1] Manuela Ribeiro Sanches (ed.), *'Portugal não é um país pequeno': Contar o 'império' na pós-colonialidade* (Lisbon, 2006), 22–3.

190

Figure 5.1 'Portugal não é um país pequeno' ('Portugal is not a small country'), poster designed by Henrique Galvão for the 1934 Colonial Exhibition, Porto, Portugal.
Credit: Arquivo Histórico Militar, Lisbon.

historical fact in the twentieth century: rather, they were politically-motivated pronouncements predicated upon at least as much myth as reality. Defending its global heritage and right to remain overseas was a crucial dimension of Portugal's national identity and culture, particularly in the face of growing challenges that both stemmed from and followed the Second World War.

Portugal was not only the first European imperial power; it also became the last, holding steadfastly to its far-flung territories and its rationale for maintaining them long after Britain, the Netherlands, France, and Belgium had embarked upon decolonization and gradually adopted new national priorities and ideologies. In 1973, Portugal's Ministry of Foreign Affairs issued *Portuguese Africa: An Introduction*, one of countless similar publications aimed at an English-language international readership. Within it, spokesmen on behalf of the *Estado Novo* dictatorship reiterated Portugal's grounds for remaining in Africa in terms that had become wearyingly familiar to critics across the globe. To those insisting on an end to Portuguese colonial rule that had sparked a series of violent nationalist liberation struggles in Guinea, Angola, and Mozambique, Portugal categorically refused to 'accept the charge of colonialism' in the first place. Its 'overseas provinces' were *not* colonies but rather 'an integral, inseparable part of Portugal', a model multiracial society 'based on the equal dignity of the human person within a single national family, regardless of ethnic or geographical origin'. Those living in European Portugal or Portuguese Africa all counted as Portuguese citizens who, 'whatever their colour or place of origin, enjoy the same juridical and political rights and opportunities'. In sum, 'the Portuguese provinces in Africa are not under Portuguese sovereignty: they are constituent parts of that sovereignty'. Defending Portuguese Africa meant nothing less than preserving Portugal's 'national unity' and respecting 'the fundamental values which constitute its moral and spiritual heritage'.[2]

Opponents of Portugal's continued overseas presence reading *Portuguese Africa: An Introduction* when it first appeared would have found little that was credible and even less that was new in its line of argument. Instead of enduring forced labour, rampant structural racial inequalities, and economic exploitation under colonialism as its detractors claimed, page after page declared that Africans in the 'overseas provinces' benefitted from marked advances in regional infrastructure, economic development, and widening healthcare and educational provisions. The book insisted that Portugal was the victim of false international allegations (the United Nations being the worst offender) and illegitimate attempts to interfere in its internal affairs; moreover, Portuguese, black and white alike, confronted not 'freedom fighters' making a stand against colonial injustice but rather suffered 'terrorist' attacks instigated and funded by communist outside forces. But if these diametrically opposed readings of Portugal's legitimacy (or lack thereof) in Africa seemed irreconcilable by the early 1970s, it soon became clear that the lengthy stalemate pitting the dictatorship and its supporters against anti-colonialists was entering its final days. In hindsight, *Portuguese Africa: A Conclusion* would have been a more fitting title for a book published just a year before the military coup of 25 April 1974 toppled the Lisbon regime and simultaneously spelled the end of the 'overseas provinces'. Emanating directly from strains built up over thirteen years of wars in Africa, the metropolitan revolution that brought decolonization in its wake ironically lent support to the long-standing assertion that metropolitan and overseas Portugal under the *Estado Novo* were inseparable parts of a whole. As Norrie MacQueen has observed, it 'confirmed the "indivisibility" of the empire – though in the context of dissolution rather than perpetuation'.[3]

* * *

---

[2] Portugal, Ministry of Foreign Affairs, *Portuguese Africa: An Introduction*, 2nd edn. (Lisbon, 1973), 20, 97, 22, 25, 48.

[3] Norrie MacQueen, *The Decolonization of Portuguese Africa: Metropolitan Revolution and the Dissolution of Empire* (London, 1997), 209.

This chapter revisits Portugal's tenacious hold on an empire whose very existence it denied between the 1950s and its eventual implosion in 1974, insisting until the end that Portugal formed a single pluricontinental and multiracial nation.[4] Beyond southwest Europe, Portugal also encompassed Guinea-Bissau in West Africa and the islands of Cape Verde and São Tomé and Príncipe off its coast, Angola and Mozambique on each side of southern Africa, and small enclave territories in Asia (Goa, Damão, and Diu flanked by India, the trading port of Macau engulfed by China, and Timor in the Indonesian archipelago). Geographically dispersed and 'deterritorialized', Portugal's constitutive parts scattered across the globe were nonetheless cohesive, unified, and sustained by the sea. One author evaluating Goa's place within the Portuguese universe in 1953 phrased it thus: 'the sea plays the role . . . of the blood vessels of the human body; it guarantees the circulation of the blood and the life of the whole organism'.[5]

Although this conceptualization of the nation had deep roots, it became further entrenched in the 1950s and 1960s in response to wider global trends pushing Western European empires to set their colonies on the road to independence. In line with the constitutional amendment recasting 'colonies' as 'overseas provinces' in 1951, the dictatorship that was controlled by Salazar until 1968 consolidated its defensive stance in the face of mounting international opposition (particularly from the United Nations) and anti-colonial nationalism.[6] Recurrent public proclamations reinforced the constitution's assertion that Portugal's destiny entailed a 'historic mission' to bring civilization to the lands its great seafaring explorers had 'discovered' starting in the fifteenth century, a mission for which Portugal was ideally suited.[7] Having spearheaded the 'Discoveries', Portugal proudly stressed how it continued to take precedence over other European powers following it into the 'tropics' by establishing uniquely harmonious relations with the peoples it encountered in America, Africa, and Asia. To lend intellectual credibility to this version of the

[4] Good overviews include António Costa Pinto, *O Fim do Império Porguguês* (Lisbon, 2001); Stewart Lloyd-Jones and António Costa Pinto (eds.), *The Last Empire: Thirty Years of Portuguese Decolonization* (Bristol, 2003).

[5] Armando Gonçalves Pereira, *My Personal Deposition in the Case of Goa, Pamphlet* (1953), 30, cited in Caroline B. Brettell, 'Portugal's First Post-Colonials: Citizenship, Identity, and the Repatriation of Goans', *Portuguese Studies Review*, 14:2 (2006–7), 142–3.

[6] A tract by Portugal's long-standing Foreign Minister provides one example of many; see Franco Nogueira, *The United Nations and Portugal: A Study in Anti-Colonialism* (London, 1963). Bruno Cardoso Reis, 'Portugal and the UN: A Rogue State Resisting the Norm of Decolonization (1956–1974)', *Portuguese Studies*, 29:2 (2013), 251–76, provides helpful context.

[7] Article 133, *Political Constitution of the Portuguese Republic* (Lisbon, 1957), 36, in Ronald H. Chilcote (ed.), *Emerging Nationalism in Portuguese Africa: Documents* (Stanford, 1972), 18; James D. Sidaway and Marcus Power, '"The Tears of Portugal": Empire, Identity, "Race", and Destiny in Portuguese Geopolitical Narratives', *Environment and Planning D: Society and Space*, 23:4 (2005), 527–54.

Portuguese national character, the *Estado Novo* found its guru not at home but in Brazil, which had been ruled by Portugal until its independence in 1822. In the scholarship of Gilberto Freyre, a sociologist who rose to fame following his publication of *The Masters and the Slaves* in 1933 and later extended his geographical remit beyond Brazil to encompass the wider Lusophone (Portuguese-speaking) world, the Portuguese dictatorship identified an appealing rationale for its overseas presence that seemed as fit for the present as it was for its illustrious past: lusotropicalism.[8]

Freyre's thinking served as a highly convenient ideological prop for the Salazar regime as it confronted escalating international criticism and anti-colonial nationalism in the 1950s and 1960s. The dictatorship selectively appropriated his ideas and sponsored him on tours across the 'overseas provinces' as well as to Portugal itself.[9] Wherever he looked across the Lusophone world, Freyre saw copious historical and contemporary testament to the Portuguese people's exceptional benevolence, empathy and respect for different customs and mores, willingness to mix across racial lines, and lack of racial prejudice, all of which added up to a laudable tropical vocation and national ethos.[10] He singled out sexual relationships between Portuguese men and 'tropical women' as evidence of Portuguese 'sensitivity' and commitment to the 'assimilation of tropical values' in daily life, such as their adoption of new eating habits and forms of dress. Mixed-race relationships and 'half-breed' populations were part of a wider 'new reality – new since the sixteenth century – that can be characterized as Lusotropical, diverse expressions of a single symbiotic culture that can be called Lusotropical culture', Freyre wrote in 1958. Within this 'single system', the 'surpassing of the ethnic condition by the cultural characterizes the Lusotropical civilization', to the extent that 'when I refer to a Portuguese, it is a social Portuguese or a cultural Portuguese that I mean; and who can be either yellow, dark, red, black or white'.[11]

What is more, Freyre argued that Portuguese arriving in the tropics stood apart from northern Europeans in that 'before trying to transform the tropics,

[8] Yves Léonard, 'Salazarisme et lusotropicalisme, histoire d'une appropriation', *Lusotopie 1997* (Paris, 1997), 211–26; Andreas Stucki, '"Beyond Civilization": Rhetoric of Empire in the Portuguese and Spanish "Overseas Provinces"', in Martin Thomas and Richard Toye (eds.), *The Rhetoric of Empire: Arguing Colonialism in the Public Sphere* (Manchester, in press). *Luso* derives from the Latin *Lusus*, Portugal's legendary founder; Portugal was thus called Lusitania by the Romans.

[9] Cláudia Castelo, *'O modo português de estar no mundo': O luso-tropicalismo e a ideologia colonial portuguesa (1933–1961)* (Porto, 1998), 87–107.

[10] Miguel Vale de Almeida, *An Earth-Colored Sea: 'Race', Culture, and the Politics of Identity in the Postcolonial Portuguese-Speaking World* (New York, 2004), 46–61, 74–7; Castelo, *'O modo português'*, 35–43; Gerald J. Bender, *Angola Under the Portuguese: The Myth and the Reality* (Trenton, NJ, 2004; originally published London, 1978), ch. 1.

[11] Gilberto Freyre, *Integração Portuguesa nos trópicos/Portuguese Integration in the Tropics* (Lisbon, 1958), 88, 103, 118.

they themselves have been changing into Lusotropicals in body and soul'.[12] Freyre's cultural and historical narrative of lusotropical exceptionalism was music to the regime's ears because it provided a welcome rationale for holding fast in the face of demands to pull out. Portugal's distinctive approach to the tropics, in short, explained why it insisted on staying at the very moment when other empires were winding down. 'Because such spirit was lacking in them, except for superficial assimilations and technical improvements,' Freyre concluded, 'other Europeans have lately been retiring from the warm areas, after centuries of political and economic domination over their populations, without having been able to develop there civilizations which can remotely be compared with the ... Lusotropical ones.'[13]

Salazar and his supporters continually returned to Freyre's arguments in public justifications for Portugal's stance on Asia and Africa. Portugal's 'national territory knows no form of discrimination and ... multi-racial societies have been formed, redolent of the spirit of friendly intercourse and co-operation', Salazar noted in a speech at the United Nations in 1961. Speaking of Angola and Mozambique, he insisted they were peopled by 'a community of races living together in perfect harmony and understanding'.[14] Similarly, in earlier declarations on Goa he stressed that 'Portuguese blood mingled liberally with that of the local peoples' and declared that integrating its population within the 'Portuguese community' had been the nation's aim ever since the sixteenth century. A Goan was 'as Portuguese as he who lives and is born in Lisbon', and in consequence 'Goans do not anywhere consider or call themselves Indians but Portuguese of Goa'. Integral to the Portuguese nation for centuries, Goa and its overseas counterparts must not be alienated from it. Doing so, Salazar concluded, would be 'no more than the political impossibility of a state voluntarily amputating itself as though it did not constitute a moral unity'.[15]

Like countless other commentators, Salazar explicitly invoked Portugal's centuries-old history overseas to explain why it deserved to feel at home there. Portuguese national culture as endorsed by the *Estado Novo* had long placed the 'Discoveries' at the core of the nation's identity, but never more than in the early 1960s. 1960 marked the five hundredth anniversary of Prince Henry's death, an occasion officially commemorated with great fanfare that took the

---

[12] Ibid., 118.   [13] Ibid., 88, 94.

[14] *The Portuguese Overseas Territories and the United Nations Organization: Speech delivered by H.E. the Chairman of the Council of Ministers, Prof. Dr. Oliveira Salazar, during the Extraordinary Session of the National Assembly, held on June 30th 1961* (Lisbon, 1961), 18. For further representative statements concerning Portugal and its overseas territories, see Oliveira Salazar, *Entrevistas 1960–1966* (Coimbra, 1967), 51, 80, 126, 184.

[15] *Goa and the Indian Union: Speech Delivered through the National Broadcast by the Prime Minister Prof. Oliveira Salazar on April 12th, 1954* (Lisbon, 1954), 17; Oliveira Salazar, 'Goa and the Indian Union: The Portuguese View', *Foreign Affairs*, 34:3 (1956), 421–2.

form of monuments, celebratory events, and publications. Freyre for his part contributed to 'the Navigator's' textual memorialization with his book *The Portuguese and the Tropics*, published in Lisbon under the auspices of the executive committee entrusted with coordinating the fifth centenary programme. He drew a direct line between past and present in chapters purportedly revealing 'Prince Henry as a pioneer of a social policy of integration of non-Europeans in the Luso-Christian system of human relations' and 'Portuguese civilization as a style of integrative civilization, marked by the influence of Prince Henry'. Another section considered 'Camões, lusist and tropicalist', positioning the author of the 1572 epic poem *Os Lusíadas* (*The Lusíads*) that exalted da Gama's voyage to India between 1497 and 1498 as another venerable precedent for a durable patriotic ethos.[16] The ubiquity of fifteenth- and sixteenth-century historical figures within the state-sanctioned Portuguese culture of the mid-twentieth century was as celebrated at home as it was remarkable to outside observers. Reckoning with Camões' centrality formed part of American diplomat George Ball's steep learning curve when he met with Salazar in the early 1960s as Under Secretary of State in the Kennedy administration. 'During our talks, history constantly intruded', he reflected. 'Salazar was absorbed by a time dimension quite different from ours; it seemed as though he and his whole country were living in more than one century, and the heroes of the past were still shaping Portuguese policy.' Portugal was not simply presided over by a dictator, Ball concluded: it was 'ruled by a triumvirate consisting of Vasco da Gama, Prince Henry the Navigator, and Salazar'.[17]

Yet beneath its elaborate lusotropical trappings, the foundations of Portugal's metropolitan and overseas standing relative to other European nations and empires were as materially impoverished as their justificatory ideology was rich. As the dictatorship's opponents readily asserted then and ever since, Portugal eagerly looked overseas to offset and counteract its low status as Western Europe's poorest and least developed country that was treated dismissively for much of the period following its early modern heyday. Widely scorned as degenerate, primitive, provincial, and backward, Portugal and its people had long been viewed with contempt by richer neighbours, analogous to colonized 'others' or as uneasily situated between the categories of European and non-European.[18] Lusotropicalism's celebration of racial mixing (long referred to as miscegenation), for instance, meant recasting sexual practices,

---

[16] Gilberto Freyre, *The Portuguese and the Tropics: Suggestions inspired by the Portuguese methods of integrating autochthonous peoples and cultures differing from the European in a new, or Lusotropical complex of civilization*, translated by Helen M. D'O. Matthew and F. de Mello Moser (Lisbon, 1961), chs. 6, 15, and 16; see also Freyre, *Integração Portuguesa*, 97, 123.

[17] George W. Ball, *The Past Has Another Pattern: Memoirs* (New York, 1982), 277.

[18] Boaventura de Sousa Santos, 'Between Prospero and Caliban: Colonialism, Postcolonialism, and Inter-identity', *Luso-Brazilian Review*, 39:2 (2002), 21–4.

Figure 5.2 Monument to the 'Discoveries', Belém, Lisbon, inaugurated in 1960 as part of the commemorations of Prince Henry the Navigator's death 500 years earlier.
Photograph by author, 2012.

cultural borrowings, and mixed populations which had been conventionally condemned among foreign observers and making them a source of pride and a sign of intercultural understanding. Sanjay Subrahmanyam proposes that:

the Portuguese claim to being non-racist colonisers (a view that is *not* limited, it should be stressed, to supporters of the *Estado Novo*) is in large measure a result of their having internalised but inverted the categories imposed on them by cultures on which they were, by the late nineteenth century, dependent... Rather than being a sign of weakness, miscegenation was portrayed as the great Portuguese strength, that which gave their tropical culture its resilience, and above all a sign of their humane attitude towards the colonised.[19]

Portuguese defenders of this supposedly egalitarian, hybrid, transcontinental national 'body' through whose veins the sea coursed as lifeblood relentlessly harkened back to the 'Discoveries', when Portugal could claim its place at the

[19] Sanjay Subrahmanyam, 'The "Kaffirs of Europe": A Comment on Portugal and the Historiography of European Expansion in Asia', *Studies in History*, 9:1, n.s. (1993), 141; see also 146.

vanguard and centre of Europe's new global encounters.[20] Lusotropical ideas constituted the antithesis of withering dismissals of Portugal as an inferior, 'semiperipheral' country on the world stage since the 1600s. Occupied by Spain for sixty years starting in 1580 and subsequently towered over by Britain and its empire, Portugal could plausibly be argued to rank as a client state or informal colony of Britain – 'an empire within an empire', as Norrie MacQueen summarizes.[21] A colonizer in denial, Portugal's was nonetheless a 'subaltern colonialism', according to Boaventura de Sousa Santos – a colonialism practiced by a nation weak within Europe and thus all the more reliant upon retaining colonies to enhance its economic and political stature.[22]

Celebratory claims about Portugal's overseas history and the conditions prevailing in its African and Asian territories indeed bore little if any relationship with reality. Critiques by historians and contemporary opponents of Portuguese colonialism have accumulated since the 1960s, decisively demolishing arguments that good race relations, equality, or intercultural empathy ever prevailed in its Asian and African possessions. As Charles Boxer and Gerald Bender asserted in their respective studies of the early period of exploration and colonization and the later occupation of Angola, the Portuguese behaved no better than other Europeans, believing that other races and cultures were inferior and treating them as such. Willingness to mate with 'tropical' women did not equate with a lack of racial prejudice among Portuguese men, for example; those who suggested as much 'misperceive lust for respect or confuse eroticism with egalitarianism', Bender insisted.[23] In fact as opposed to theory, interracial sexual liaisons were condemned much more often than not, while non-European peoples and cultures were firmly believed in dire need of exposure to Western civilization and Christianity. Indeed, Salazar himself openly admitted as much in his *Declaration on Overseas Policy* in 1963. 'We have before us a task of social uplift, of civilization, initiated, carried on and based on moral principles' for hundreds of years, he observed:

Is the language which we teach those peoples superior to their dialects or not? Does the religion preached constitute a nation of civilized expression and world projection by the missionaries surpass fetishism [*sic*] or not? ... If our reply to these questions is

---

[20] Brettell, 'Portugal's First Post-Colonials', 152; Luís Madureira, 'Tropical Sex Fantasies and the Ambassador's Other Death: The Difference in Portuguese Colonialism', *Cultural Critique*, 28 (1994), 158–9.

[21] MacQueen, *Decolonization of Portuguese Africa*, 7; Sandro Sideri, *Trade and Power: Informal Colonialism in Anglo-Portuguese Relations* (Rotterdam, 1970); Pedro Aires Oliveira, 'Live and Let Live: Britain and Portugal's Imperial Endgame (1945–1975)', *Portuguese Studies*, 29:2 (2013), 186–7.

[22] Santos, 'Between Prospero and Caliban', 9, 11–12, 37.

[23] Amongst Boxer's voluminous output, see C.R. Boxer, *Race Relations in the Portuguese Empire 1415–1825* (Oxford, 1963), 40; Bender, *Angola Under the Portuguese*, 35.

affirmative, we cannot but conclude that the state of national conscience created by the Portuguese among such divers peoples has been a benefit to all, a benefit which would be wholly lost if we agreed to retrogress.[24]

In accordance with this outlook, during the *Estado Novo* Portugal long retained the native statute (*indigenato*) instituted in 1917 in most of its overseas territories. This legal framework distinguished those deemed 'uncivilized', 'native', and 'unassimilated' (*indígena*) from those qualifying as 'civilized', 'non-native', and 'assimilated' (*não-indígena*), and hence as full Portuguese citizens. While Portugal's spokesmen never tired of stating that no official colour bars or laws prohibiting mixed marriages existed in its Asian and African lands, the *indigenato* code prevailing in most of Portuguese Africa effectively institutionalized racial inequality to all intents and purposes. Very few Africans ever achieved the privileged status of *não-indígena* and *assimilado*, nor did many mixed-race persons (*mestiços*); by contrast, all whites residing in the overseas provinces automatically fell into this category, even when they manifestly lacked the attributes Africans needed to prove in order to qualify. Counting as assimilated and non-native required social, economic, and cultural credentials that were well out of reach for most non-Europeans, such as a salaried occupation, the ability to read and speak Portuguese fluently, and a range of Portuguese cultural competencies. Acquiring these forms of 'civilization' proved impossible for the overwhelming majority: few schools imparting these credentials existed, and those that did were beyond the limited financial means of most Africans. Class, culture, and education thus barred most non-whites from counting as civilized citizens, yet the same limitations did not apply to the many poor, unskilled, and uneducated Portuguese emigrants arriving in Angola and Mozambique in growing numbers after 1945, a substantial proportion of whom were completely illiterate.[25]

For the African majority falling outside the minute portion of the territories' population declared to be *não-indígena*, the *indigenato* regime meant forced labour, forced cultivation of particular crops for export, land expropriation, heavy taxation, a complete lack of political and civil rights, and the risk of arbitrary imprisonment without trial and brutal corporal punishment.[26] The

[24] *Declaration on Overseas Policy, by H.E. Prof. Oliveira Salazar, Prime Minister of Portugal, Broadcast on 12 August 1963* (Lisbon, 1963), 6–7.
[25] Malyn Newitt, *Portugal in Africa: The Last Hundred Years* (London, 1981), 168.
[26] Peter Karibe Mendy, 'Portugal's Civilizing Mission in Colonial Guinea-Bissau: Rhetoric and Reality', *International Journal of African Historical Studies*, 36:1 (2003), 35–58; Bender, *Angola Under the Portuguese*, 149–59, 200–1, 212–13; Allen Isaacman and Barbara Isaacman, *Mozambique from Colonialism to Revolution, 1900–1982* (Boulder, 1983); Jeanne Marie Penvenne, *African Workers and Colonial Racism: Mozambican Strategies and Struggles in Lourenço Marques, 1877–1962* (Portsmouth, NH, 1995); Allen Isaacman, *'Cotton Is the Mother of Poverty': Peasants, Work, and Rural Struggle in Colonial Mozambique, 1938–1961* (Portsmouth, NH, 1996).

indigenato statute was not repealed until 1961, and only then did everyone in the overseas territories technically rank as equal Portuguese citizens regardless of race. In practice, however, for most Africans much stayed the same as before. Forced labour remained widespread years later, and many Africans still needed to grow cash crops in demand by the state and to provide manual labour for public works projects, plantations, and settler enterprises to pay their taxes. Social, educational, and occupational discrimination was no less pernicious for being implicitly, as opposed to explicitly, based upon race, and most Africans and many *mestiços* still faced insurmountable barriers to upward mobility.[27]

Both before and after 1961, Portugal's overseas provinces were exploited for the benefit of the metropolitan and white-dominated African economy alike, which in Angola and Mozambique revolved around state-sponsored white settlement schemes that reached their peak after 1950. (Guinea-Bissau and the Cape Verde Islands, by contrast, never became home to more than small numbers of whites, their economies continuing to rely on African peasant agriculture in the former and on migrant remittances in the latter.) The overseas territories, particularly those designated for settlers in southern Africa, played a vital role in the Portuguese economy, acting as a source of cheap raw materials such as cotton, sugar, coffee, rice, tea, vegetable oils, and sisal. In time, Angola contributed growing supplies of diamonds and oil. Some products were consumed within Portugal, while others were re-exported for foreign exchange earnings that helped offset its chronic balance of payments deficit. Uncompetitive Portuguese industries like textile manufacture relied upon African cotton supplies and preferential access to African markets for finished cloth, cheap wine, and other goods. Migration also provided crucial support for the underdeveloped economies of both metropolitan and overseas Portugal. White emigrant remittances sent home from Africa helped sustain the former, just as territories like Mozambique and Angola generated considerable revenues for the state through African migrant workers' wages earned in mining and agriculture in South Africa, Rhodesia, and elsewhere.[28]

Many white settlers found better opportunities and standards of living than in the metropole, but the main beneficiaries were Portugal's political elites and economic oligarchies who profited from overseas enterprises and investments.[29]

---

[27] Amílcar Cabral, 'At the United Nations: Extracts from a statement made in Conakry in June 1962 to the United Nations Special Committee on Territories under Portuguese Administration', in *Selected Texts by Amílcar Cabral: Revolution in Guinea, and African People's Struggle* (London, 1969), 20–3; Eduardo Mondlane, *The Struggle for Mozambique* (Harmondsworth, 1969), 35–57.

[28] Gervase Clarence-Smith, *The Third Portuguese Empire 1825–1975: A Study in Economic Imperialism* (Manchester, 1985), ch. 6.

[29] Kenneth Maxwell, *The Making of Portuguese Democracy* (Cambridge, 1995), ch. 1; Hendrik Spruyt, *Ending Empire: Contested Sovereignty and Territorial Partition* (Ithaca, 2005), 177, 181, 190; MacQueen, *Decolonization of Portuguese Africa*, 51–2.

Yet the African majority and growing numbers of *mestiços* (including those of both groups who had gained *assimilado* status under the *indigenato* statute) saw little reward from being 'Portuguese' and no realistic hope for improvement. With economic progress limited and uneven at best, political rights and self-government seemed altogether impossible prospects. The *Estado Novo* categorically refused to tolerate political and labour organization, deploying its secret police and other arms of the state in draconian crackdowns on nationalist groups and their leaderships. Devolved self-government and decentralization in any form was rejected, as was even a long-term transition to independence. As Salazar had said, alienating territories that counted as part of an integrated nation was not accepted as decolonization but as akin to amputations that would fundamentally compromise, if not kill, the national body.

* * *

Escalating tensions between Portuguese defenders of the pluricontinental and multiracial nation of the *Estado Novo*'s fertile imagination and African and Asian nationalist opponents finally came to a head in the early 1960s. Nationalist movements coalesced under educated, charismatic figures like Amílcar Cabral, the Cape Verdian who became the leader of the PAIGC (*Partido Africano para a Independência da Guiné e Cabo Verde*/African Party for the Independence of Guinea and Cape Verde), and Eduardo Mondlane, who headed Mozambique's FRELIMO (*Frente de Libertação de Moçambique*/Mozambique Liberation Front).[30] Such men had no qualms about denouncing Portuguese rhetoric and hollow reforms, like the repeal of the *indigenato* statute, as a self-interested sham, and categorically rejected Portuguese efforts to deny they were colonizers with colonies. Their speeches and writings closed the gap between misleading lusotropical assertions and the brutal realities of economic exploitation and political and military repression, raising the issue of Portugal's shortcomings and weaknesses in no uncertain terms. Mondlane argued that 'one can see why the colonies are important to Portugal: their resources can compensate for Portugal's own lack; they provide for a mass of poverty-stricken and frequently unemployed people an emigration outlet which, at the same time, keeps them within the jurisdiction of Portugal, contributing to the national income and liable for military service; since the colonies have a favourable trade balance with countries other than Portugal, they help her to retain reserves of foreign exchange.'[31] Similarly, in 1961 Cabral stressed that 'Portuguese colonialists try, in vain, to convince the world that they have no colonies and that our African countries are "provinces of Portugal"'. What they were in fact doing was 'pursuing, arresting, torturing,

---

[30] Patrick Chabal, *Amílcar Cabral: Revolutionary Leadership and People's War* (London, 1983).
[31] Mondlane, *Struggle for Mozambique*, 78; see also 216.

killing, massacring, launching a colonial war in Angola and feverishly preparing for a new war in Guinea and Cabo Verde'.[32] Africans suffering under Portuguese domination experienced not simply colonialism, Cabral continued, but a colonialism meted out by a nation that itself had been little more than a 'semi-colony of England' since the early eighteenth century. How else could such 'an underdeveloped and backward country' maintain its colonies unless the status quo suited the interests of stronger nations?[33]

The year 1961 marked a decisive turning point in Portugal's relations with its 'overseas provinces'. At a time when other European empires were largely being phased out, Portugal's refusal to contemplate meaningful change made many decide that violent resistance was the only way forward. Armed liberation struggles broke out first in Angola early in 1961, as Cabral noted, then in Guinea in 1963 and Mozambique in 1964. In contrast to these three guerrilla conflicts which stretched over more than a decade, it took only two days of military pressure to bring Portugal's presence in South Asia to an end. By 1961, Goa's status quo most certainly was *not* in the interest of a stronger nation, in this case an independent and assertive India under Prime Minister Jawaharlal Nehru. Since 1947 India had made repeated attempts to negotiate over the small enclaves comprising the so-called 'Portuguese State of India' upon which it bordered, but to no avail. Like African nationalists, Indians and Goan exiles in India wrote prolifically against Portugal's position, insisting that geographically and culturally Goa, Damão, and Diu were rightfully part of India and that Goans were Indian, not Portuguese. Refuting Salazarist arguments that it was Portugal's centuries-long historical presence that determined sovereignty and that Goans were fully equally to Portuguese, these critics underscored instead that segregation, discrimination, and exploitation prevailed in what was 'a blatant case of colonialism'.[34]

Goa acquired tremendous symbolic importance for both sides, and a long-festering diplomatic impasse resulted. Nehru finally lost patience and sent 30,000 Indian troops to annex Goa in December 1961, having observed the onset of Angola's wars of liberation several months before.[35] Portugal's poorly-equipped garrison numbering just 900 rapidly surrendered, and India and its supporters on the international stage celebrated its takeover as a liberation. The Portuguese state, however, refused to see it as anything other than an illegal invasion and occupation. Goa was 'transformed from a flourishing State

---

[32] Amílcar Cabral, 'Guinea and Cabo Verde against Portuguese Colonialism: Speech made at the 3rd Conference of the African Peoples held in Cairo, March 25–31, 1961', in *Selected Texts*, 10.

[33] Ibid., 12.

[34] Carmo Azevedo, *Salazar's Bluff Called (The Goa Question)* (Delhi, 1956), 45; Vijaya Lakshmi Pundit, 'India's Foreign Policy', *Foreign Affairs*, 34:3 (1956), 437.

[35] Philip Bravo, 'The Case of Goa: History, Rhetoric and Nationalism', *Past Imperfect*, 7 (1998), 125–54; M.N. Pearson, *The New Cambridge History of India, vol. 1, no. 1: The Portuguese in India* (Cambridge, 1987), 154–61.

into a colony of the Indian Union by force', Salazar proclaimed, and it was not until the fall of the dictatorship in 1974 that Portugal recognized India's claims.[36] Until then, the *Estado Novo* persisted in the view that the 'Portuguese State of India' was merely under temporary occupation, 'colonized' by India but rightfully continuing to belong within a pluricontinental Portugal. Its governor and military commanders who dared surrender in the face of insurmountable odds after having been ordered to fight to the death became scapegoats, facing court martial and exile from Portugal on the charge of high treason.

For Portuguese army officers, the fate of their counterparts following their capitulation of Goa cast a long and ominous shadow over the wars of liberation that engulfed Angola, Guinea-Bissau, and Mozambique over the coming years. Between the early 1960s and mid-1970s, anti-colonial guerrilla movements in all three territories became drawn into the global Cold War shaped by international intervention. Marxist-oriented groups such as the PAIGC, FRELIMO, and the MPLA (*Movimento Popular de Libertação de Angola*/Popular Movement for the Liberation of Angola) led by Agostinho Neto received funds, training, and equipment from the Soviet Union, Cuba, and other communist countries. In Angola, the MPLA competed with Holden Roberto's FNLA (*Frente Nacional para a Libertação de Angola*/Angolan National Liberation Front) and Jonas Savimbi's UNITA (*União Nacional para a Independência Total de Angola*/National Union for the Total Independence of Angola), which found assistance from neighbouring countries in southern Africa, China, and periodically from the United States. Portugal itself won diplomatic support from apartheid South Africa and Rhodesia, which considered it a critical bulwark against the further spread of black majority rule, and from its NATO allies thanks to its insistence that perpetuating Portuguese rule was critical to containing the spread of communism in Africa. United States aid for the dictatorship's counterinsurgency campaigns against African guerrillas grew considerably during Richard Nixon's presidency, its contributions becoming increasingly necessary the longer the fighting continued.[37]

Although Portugal faced a unified foe in Guinea-Bissau and Mozambique and divided rival movements in Angola where it engaged in separate battles with the MPLA, FNLA, and UNITA, militarily the situation soon settled into a lengthy stalemate in all three territories. For years, Portuguese forces limited

---

[36] Salazar, *Declaration on Overseas Policy*, 28.
[37] Odd Arne Westad, *The Global Cold War: Third World Interventions and the Making of Our Times* (Cambridge, 2007), ch. 6; Witney W. Schneidman, *Engaging Africa: Washington and the Fall of Portugal's Colonial Empire* (Lanham, MD, 2004); MacQueen, *Decolonization of Portuguese Africa*, 52–6; Miguel Bandeira Jerónimo and António Costa Pinto (eds.), special issue on 'International Dimensions of Portuguese Late Colonialism and Decolonization', *Portuguese Studies*, 29:2 (2013).

FRELIMO's successes in Mozambique and held their own in Angola, where fighting remained largely confined to frontier regions away from the major urban and white settler concentrations. Guinea, however, posed the greatest challenge, becoming akin to 'Portugal's Vietnam'. Conflict raged across the entire territory and the PAIGC gained control over huge swathes, despite Portugal's vast commitment of troops, weaponry, and merciless counterinsurgency tactics borrowed from prior and ongoing American and European campaigns against guerrilla opponents in Africa and Asia (Vietnam itself being one of the most important arenas).[38]

Back in Lisbon, Salazar remained Prime Minister until a severe stroke in 1968 prevented him from holding office. After the dictator's death in 1970, Amílcar Cabral reflected that he had been 'unable to survive the affirmation of Africa's existence: the victorious armed resistance of the African peoples to the Portuguese colonial war. Salazar was nothing more than a fanatical believer in the doctrine of European superiority and African inferiority.' While the stroke literally was brought on by his fall off a collapsed deck chair, Cabral preferred a figurative explanation: 'Africa was the sickness that killed Salazar.'[39] Under his successor Marcelo Caetano, Portugal's basic position on Africa did not substantially change despite talk of new policies, and the government remained steadfast in its refusal to withdraw from Africa or contemplate meaningful political reforms. In a fundamental sense, Africa ultimately proved to be the *Estado Novo*'s cause of death as well – a chain of events Cabral had presciently anticipated as early as 1961. '[W]e are certain that the elimination of Portuguese colonialism will bring about the elimination of Portuguese fascism', he proclaimed. 'Through our liberation struggle we are making an effective contribution towards [its] defeat.'[40]

But it took time before Portugal's dictatorship suffered the repercussions of anti-colonialism, and their assassinations in the interim meant that neither Cabral nor Mondlane lived to enjoy them. Initially, increased military expenditure helped the nation's economy, and India's takeover of Goa and the outbreak of wars in Africa generated a defensive patriotic response within the metropole that boosted Salazar's popularity.[41] To bolster its case for Portugal staying put, the dictatorship repeatedly invoked the crises that erupted in connection with Congolese and Algerian independence as lessons about the dire consequences of European departures from Africa.[42] All told, however,

[38] Norrie MacQueen, 'Portugal's First Domino: "Pluricontinentalism" and Colonial War in Guinea-Bissau, 1963–1974', *Contemporary European History*, 8:2 (1999), 209–30.

[39] Amílcar Cabral, 'Second Address Before the United Nations', October 16, 1972, in Africa Information Service (ed.), *Return to the Source: Selected Speeches by Amílcar Cabral* (New York, 1973), 26.

[40] Cabral, 'Guinea and Cabo Verde against Portuguese Colonialism', 16.

[41] Newitt, *Portugal in Africa*, 224; Clarence-Smith, *Third Portuguese Empire*, 193.

[42] For one example of many, see Portugal, Ministry of Foreign Affairs, *Portuguese Africa*, 99–100.

over the long term armed conflict in Angola, Mozambique, and Guinea in particular cost Portugal dearly. In Western Europe's poorest nation with a metropolitan population of less than nine million, fighting the wars eventually ate up nearly half the state budget and close to 8 per cent of its gross domestic product. Roughly one million men experienced military service in Africa between 1961 and 1974, mainly as conscripts. Nearly 9,000 troops died and approximately 30,000 others were wounded. Mandatory service took soldiers and officers to Africa for periods extending up to six years, and by 1974 over 25 per cent of men of military age were in the army. As Chapter 7 will revisit, many faced with this unappealing prospect voted with their feet, evading military service by emigrating to work in France and other Western European countries for a combination of economic and ideological reasons, or simply to escape the draft.[43] Morale plummeted as guerrilla fighting stretched on and casualties grew, with most in uniform against their will and having reached the conclusion that the wars were unwinnable. As officers knew well in the wake of Goa, however, surrender was not an option, yet the threat of their professional humiliation loomed increasingly large.

Portuguese responses to the African wars thus ranged from avoidance and hostility to indifference and bitter resignation. Given the lack of freedom of expression and pervasive censorship under an authoritarian government, it is difficult to gauge genuine popular reactions to the official ethos fixated on lusotropical ideals and a conception of the nation that extended beyond Europe and into other continents. Expressions of national pride in overseas Portugal and its illustrious centuries-long history so assiduously cultivated by the state were indeed evident, but in time the wars in Africa took a heavy toll. Such as they were, ideals foregrounding Portugal's destiny as a pluricontinental nation increasingly appeared ill-founded or unsustainable, particularly to those risking their lives to little avail in African conflicts with seemingly no end in sight.

By the beginning of 1974, signs of discontent among army officers had become impossible to ignore, emanating from among the most junior con-scripted officers in Africa (who often exhibited even less enthusiasm for war than the troops under their command) and from the highest cadres alike. General António de Spínola was the most prominent figure among the latter. Drawing on extensive wartime experience in Africa and especially his years in Guinea as its governor-general and army commander, Spínola concluded that the wars could never be won on the battlefield and instead demanded new political solutions. Early in 1974 he published a book entitled *Portugal and the Future* that outlined proposals for progressive steps towards self-government in

---

[43] João Medina, 'The Old Lie: Some Portuguese Contemporary Novels on the Colonial Wars in Africa (1961–74)', *Portuguese Studies*, 15 (1999), 149; Westad, *Global Cold War*, 218; Clarence-Smith, *Third Portuguese Empire*, 194; MacQueen, *Decolonization of Portuguese Africa*, 37, 49, 76.

Portuguese Africa. Significantly, this would lead not to a severing of ties but to a 'federation of Portuguese states' comparable to a Lusophone commonwealth.[44] Spínola advocated widening political participation and representation, increased provincial autonomy, and decentralization, while also stressing that foreign relations, defence, and financial matters would remain in the hands of the central government in Lisbon.[45] He thus fell considerably short of advocating complete independence and a full break with the past, repeatedly arguing that implementing these changes would provide 'the proper structure for our continued existence as a pluri-continental and multi-racial country'.[46]

Though pressing for new approaches, his book nonetheless continually returned to deeply established understandings of the nation and its place in the world. His federal vision reserved an important place for Brazil, Portugal's erstwhile but long-independent colony, and Freyrian lusotropical ideology along with it. Revealingly, he shared common ground with Salazarist rhetoric from the 1950s and 1960s that imagined Portugal as an integrated national body confronted with the threat of debilitating 'amputations' like that of Goa:

We celebrated the independence of Brazil as if it were the birth of a son ... we have in Brazil today a cultural extension on which can be based the most sanguine hopes. The Portuguese language is spoken there, and in certain circles, the links with Lusitanian culture and with our way of being, of life and of co-existence in a society with a genuine mingling of the races ... but in remembering this, we are reminded of Goa, which was the amputation of a limb.[47]

Federal reforms, he insisted, were imperative in order to 'save our country which otherwise is set on the road to disintegration, its African territories being amputated, one by one'. Indeed, for Spínola losing Africa altogether and contemplating an exclusively European future remained unthinkable:

The overseas provinces are essential to the survival of our nation as a free and independent nation. Without our African territories our country would be reduced to an insignificant corner of a gigantic Europe without any trump cards left to deal in our dealings with other nations – our existence a mere formality in a grouping of nations, in which we enjoy no real independence.[48]

In favouring gradual change and only partial autonomy, Spínola's programme promised far too little that would satisfy African nationalists. Nonetheless, it diverged from the regime's recalcitrant stance which had long refused to entertain the notion of even moderate changes to the overseas status quo, and Spínola was dismissed from his post as a result. *Portugal and the Future*

[44] MacQueen, *Decolonization of Portuguese Africa*, 72–5, 92–3.
[45] António de Spínola, *Portugal and the Future*, translated into English from *Portugal e o futuro* (Johannesburg, 1974), 100, 139.
[46] Ibid., 109.   [47] Ibid., 71–2.   [48] Ibid., 141–2.

quickly became one of the immediate catalysts that converted long-simmering resentment among officers into the April 1974 *coup d'état*. But if Spínola had advocated reform, others demanded a revolution. On 25 April, discontented officers who had formed the *Movimento das Forças Armadas* (the Armed Forces Movement, or MFA) descended upon Lisbon with tanks and rapidly overthrew the Caetano regime. Long the *Estado Novo's* mainstay, the armed forces ultimately proved its undoing. An ecstatic public reception greeted this virtually bloodless 'Carnation Revolution' (so-called on account of the flowers inserted into soldiers' guns) which signalled the transition from dictatorship to democracy.

Military anger that finally spilled over to form the MFA and led to the 25 April coup ranged from professional grievances over promotion and status that divided officers among themselves to a complete unwillingness for war to continue in Africa. The revolution took a moderate course at first, with Caetano relinquishing power to General Spínola, who was initially supported by the MFA. Yet differing agendas within the military proved fundamentally irreconcilable. Once in office, Spínola persisted with his dream for a Lusitanian federation and remained wedded to the ideas contained within *Portugal and the Future*, envisioning independence coming to Portuguese Africa only 'in a generation or so' – an unfeasible path that boded nothing but ongoing violent conflict with nationalist guerrilla forces.[49] Determined to avoid this prospect at all costs, in September 1974 MFA officers secured Spínola's resignation, after which Portugal's revolution moved leftwards under the influence of socialists and communists who favoured immediate decolonization.

Historians differ on the extent to which the Armed Forces Movement was politically inspired and radicalized by the struggles for national liberation raging in Guinea, Mozambique, and Angola. Nevertheless, many broadly concur with Agostinho Neto of Angola's MPLA, who declared that Portuguese officers constituted 'the fourth Liberation Movement'.[50] In this, the MFA liberated the metropole from dictatorship and helped finish the job of ridding Africa of Portuguese colonialism others had begun more than a decade before, just as Cabral had prophesied. If not fully influenced by African nationalists' fights against the *Estado Novo*, thirteen years of counterinsurgency certainly determined their actions in 1974 and 1975. 'Not one more soldier for the colonies and the return of those already there' was the demand underpinning MFA demonstrations during the summer following the coup;

---

[49] Kenneth Maxwell, 'Portugal and Africa: The Last Empire', in Prosser Gifford and Wm Roger Louis (eds.), *The Transfer of Power in Africa: Decolonization, 1940–1960* (New Haven, 1982), 357.

[50] Ibid., 367. Compare the interpretations by Douglas Porch, *The Portuguese Armed Forces and the Revolution* (London, 1977); Maxwell, *Making of Portuguese Democracy*, 60; MacQueen, *Decolonization of Portuguese Africa*, 75, 82–93.

leftist officers contended that the Portuguese people had been sent to fight and die in Africa to protect the profits of elites and companies with overseas interests that exploited the impoverished metropolitan majority and Africans alike.[51] Spínola's successors therefore abandoned his gradualist and moderate aims and hastened negotiations towards independence as soon as possible. Plans were hammered out for handing over power throughout Portuguese Africa (including in Cape Verde and São Tomé and Príncipe, which had not experienced armed insurrections), and by November 1975 all of the African 'overseas provinces' had become independent.

Tragically, Portugal's withdrawal did not spell an end to brutal civil strife and international intervention for those it once ruled. In Angola above all, violence continued as different political groupings continued to fight each other with considerable support from outside proxies, long remaining a Cold War battleground and the epicentre of southern African geopolitical conflicts dominated by the interests of apartheid South Africa. Nor was the future a happy one for the population of East Timor. Portugal readily agreed to its self-determination, but the region was invaded by neighbouring Indonesia in 1976. East Timor then suffered decades of occupation, political repression, and martial law that saw hundreds of thousands killed before independence came in 2002. Macau's future was altogether more peaceful if equally drawn out, its gradual transfer to Chinese sovereignty in 1999 proceeding on a consensual basis.[52]

* * *

With few exceptions, to all intents and purposes Portugal thus terminated five centuries as an overseas power in well under two years. What, then, was Portugal's fate once it had lost its 'overseas provinces', long imagined as so essential to national identity that contemplating their forfeiture had seemed inconceivable – even tantamount to 'an amputation of limbs'? Just as many poor Portuguese had looked to Western Europe as a more promising source of work and opportunity and chose to migrate northwards rather than head to settler societies in Angola or Mozambique, so too did the nation's economic oligarchies gradually turn their attention towards the continent in search of alternatives to conventional overseas arenas. Indeed, in economic terms Portugal's shift towards Western Europe had already begun during the 1960s and early 1970s as the continent rose in importance relative to Portuguese Africa.[53] Once freed from the dictatorship, between 1974 and 1976 the revolution evolved into a democratic republic under moderate socialist governments,

---

[51] MacQueen, *Decolonization of Portuguese Africa*, 179; Maxwell, 'Portugal and Africa', 359.

[52] Westad, *Global Cold War*, ch. 6; Arnaldo M.A. Gonçalves, 'Macau, Timor, and Portuguese India in the Context of Portugal's Recent Decolonization', in Lloyd-Jones and Pinto (eds.), *Last Empire*, 53–66.

[53] Clarence-Smith, *Third Portuguese Empire*, 13, 17–18, 193, 202, 217.

after which Portugal turned its full attention towards closer political as well as economic ties with its neighbours at the urging of Prime Minister Mário Soares and other leading figures. This culminated in Portugal's entry into the European Economic Community (later the European Union) in 1986.

For Portugal, democracy, decolonization, and the road to European integration went hand in hand, a process most Portuguese endorsed wholeheartedly – not least those like Soares who had long opposed the dictatorship as exiled dissidents. 'The empire is dead, long live the EU', wrote António de Figueiredo, a leading opponent of the *Estado Novo* and commentator on Portuguese colonialism long based in Britain.[54] Promising to be 'the best drug to overcome the postcolonial hangover', the EEC/EU provided substantial compensation for overseas losses, not least far superior prospects for higher domestic standards of living, economic development, and prosperity.[55] In the process, it offered Portugal the chance to develop a new national identity whose primary orientation was continental and European as opposed to pluricontinental and oceanic.

Unlike other postcolonial European nations that promptly entered into neocolonial relationships with former dependencies, Portugal may well have been too poor to 'neo-colonize' – which to a considerable extent explained why the dictatorship fought to the death to retain its African and Asian territories and the pluricontinental construct with which the Salazar and Caetano regimes became inseparable.[56] Yet this did not preclude future attempts to reinvigorate relations with the Portuguese-speaking international community from the late 1980s onwards at times when Europe's allure was placed in doubt.[57] Should concerns over Portugal's peripheral (and hugely indebted) position within an enlarged, early twenty-first-century EU become more deeply embedded, as seems likely to be the case, it remains to be seen whether looking further afield across the Lusophone world for economic, diplomatic, or cultural allegiances rooted in imperial history – albeit from a position of far less relative power than once was the case – may once again help offset a sense of marginality closer to home.[58]

---

[54] António de Figueiredo, 'The Empire Is Dead, Long Live the EU', in Lloyd-Jones and Pinto (eds.), *Last Empire*, 127–43.

[55] Michael Harsgor, 'Aftereffects of an "Exemplary Decolonization"', *Journal of Contemporary History*, 15:1 (1980), 159; António Costa Pinto and Nuno Severiano Teixeira, 'From Africa to Europe: Portugal and European Integration', in António Costa Pinto and Nuno Severiano Teixeira (eds.), *Southern Europe and the Making of the European Union, 1945–1980s* (New York, 2002), 3–40.

[56] MacQueen, *Decolonization of Portuguese Africa*, 52; Maxwell, *Making of Portuguese Democracy*, 19; Figueiredo, 'The Empire Is Dead', 133.

[57] See Chapter 8 for an account of the emergence of the Community of Portuguese Language Countries (CPLP) in 1996.

[58] António Goucha Soares, 'Portugal and the European Union: The Ups and Downs in 20 Years of Membership', *Perspectives on European Politics and Society*, 8:4 (2007), 460–75; Dietmar Rothermund, 'The Self-consciousness of Post-imperial Nations: A Cross-national Comparison', *India Quarterly: A Journal of International Affairs*, 67:1 (2011), 13.

Decades after the Carnation Revolution, moreover, Portugal's centuries-old history as a maritime nation whose caravels and navigators pioneered the 'Discoveries' and which long retained confidence in the imagined virtues of its lusotropical domain lingers on, continuing to play a pre-eminent role within national culture and heritage (themes returned to in Chapters 8 and 9). As Part II now explores, late-colonial and postcolonial migrations into Portugal as well as other former colonizing powers in Western Europe have been essential to keeping selective memories of empire alive. Long after its demise as a pluricontinental nation with the severing of the 'overseas provinces' from the national body, Portugal, like other postcolonial European nations, continues to experience what Salman Rushdie, writing of Britain, called the 'phantom twitchings of an amputated limb', or the 'recrudescence of imperialist ideology' in the aftermath of empire.[59] Such ongoing imperial reverberations and hauntings are inseparable from the many human links to empires lost that have survived into the late-twentieth and early twenty-first centuries.

---

[59] Salman Rushdie, 'Outside the Whale' (1984), in *Imaginary Homelands: Essays and Criticism 1981–1991* (London, 1991), 92.

Part II

Migrations and multiculturalisms in
postcolonial Europe

6   Ending empires, coming home
The ghost worlds of European colonial repatriates

Introduction

In the last pages of *Faded Portraits*, a novel first published in 1954 under his pseudonym E. Breton de Nijs, Rob Nieuwenhuys provided a fictional portrayal of a Dutch East Indies family who had resettled in the Netherlands after Indonesia became independent in 1949. Nieuwenhuys' account was decisively shaped by his Indies roots. Born in Java in 1908 and the son of a *totok* – or 'pure Dutch' – father and a mother of combined Dutch and Indonesian descent, his family had been linked to Southeast Asia for generations. Aside from his time in the Netherlands as a student, he had seldom lived anywhere else prior to his departure in the early 1950s. *Faded Portraits* fittingly concluded with a brief account of its transplanted characters' new lives in cities like The Hague and Arnhem, both of which had traditions of attracting Indies people, *totoks* and those of mixed ancestry alike:

Dubekart ... the *totok* of the Indies, now lives in The Hague as an old Indies hand. I imagine you see him walking regularly along Frederik Hendrik or Meerdervoort Avenue on his way to the Hotel De Kroon or L'Espérance. There he and several companions from the same generation preserve an old world, a ghost world set against a purely colonial decor ... They live somewhere near Beuk Square or Thomson Avenue, that typical Indies quarter where they have formed their own community and follow their own way of life with its endless visits and dinners ('*Ajo*, come again soon, Toet; I'll make you some delicious *gado-gado*') ... They left because that country no longer offered them anything, because it was not *their* country anymore ... It is beyond retrieval.

What awaited such Indies repatriates? At least at the outset, Nieuwenhuys suggested, they continued to rely on a network of fellow ex-colonials and subsisted largely on nostalgia and discontent:

In The Hague alone there are thousands like them: uprooted Indies emigrés. Some of them sit aimlessly in front of a window looking out at the wet streets and leafless branches and thinking of their *kebonan* with its fruit trees and *melatti* bushes, flower beds, and palm trees. They are homesick, and have an aching desire for *their* Indies and say to each other: 'Too bad it went the way it did, it used to be so good over there.' Others sit all day near a red hot stove in their pajamas and slippers ... [and] are bitter about the government. They feel betrayed and abandoned, and an old rancor grows. Yet they will still partially adjust – at least the younger ones will – and sooner or later they will find their place in Dutch society. From them will come the next generation, with a lighter complexion, until they will all be indistinguishable from the *totoks*, both in appearance and opinion.[1]

Nieuwenhuys' intimate acquaintance with the late colonial world and its collapse made him an apt and astute commentator on the repatriation experience that irrevocably changed the lives of over 300,000 Dutch nationals who left Indonesia between the late 1940s and early 1960s. These protracted waves of departure from Indonesia constituted an early example of decolonization and the ensuing dispersals of colonial communities. The end of European overseas empires elsewhere in subsequent decades created new episodes of migration as colonizers were faced with stark choices: after extended periods, entire lifetimes, or even generations of residence in the colonies, what came next?

European nationals who had lived and worked in the colonies were certainly not alone in feeling the effects of decolonization. As was outlined in the Introduction and Part I, Europeans were part of colonizing communities whether or not they themselves had ever left their homeland, making decolonization and its postcolonial aftermath part of broader European societal experiences for those 'at home' and 'away' alike. Yet those personally based in the empires indisputably counted among those whose lives were most indelibly marked by their passing. Colonizers' returns collectively constituted a migration phenomenon of considerable demographic significance in Western Europe. Over the forty-year period following the Second World War, between 5.4 and 6.8 million people arrived in Western Europe from former colonies, of whom between 3.3 and 4 million were Europeans and Eurasians.[2]

Supplementing existing research literature with new source material, this chapter compares distinct nations' repatriations, examining the lives of Dutch, British, Belgian, French, and ultimately Portuguese colonials who re-entered metropolitan societies between the late 1940s and the mid-1970s and beyond.[3] Who were they, and what had their colonial roles and experiences been before decolonization? Their national, geographical, occupational, cultural, and socio-

---

[1] E. Breton de Nijs, *Faded Portraits*, translated by Donald and Elsje Sturtevant (Amherst, MA, 1982 [1954]), 151–2.

[2] Bouda Etemad, 'Europe and Migration after Decolonization', *Journal of European Economic History*, 27:3 (1998), 457–70.

[3] Italians based in North Africa unfortunately cannot be included here. See, however, Romain Rainero, 'Rapatriés et réfugiés italiens: un grand problème historique méconnu', in Jean-Louis Miège and Colette Dubois (eds.), *L'Europe retrouvée: les migrations de la décolonisation* (Paris, 1994), 23–34; Charles Burdett, 'Memories of Italian East Africa', *Journal of Romance Studies*, 1:3 (2001), 69–85; Charles Burdett, 'Colonial Associations and the Memory of Italian East Africa', in Jacqueline Andall and Derek Duncan (eds.), *Italian Colonialism: Legacy and Memory* (Bern, 2005), 125–42; Pamela Ballinger, 'Borders of the Nation, Borders of Citizenship: Italian Repatriation and the Redefinition of National Identity after World War II', *Comparative Studies in Society and History*, 49:3 (2007), 713–41.

economic diversity defies any attempt at summary description. Colonial communities included settlers whose ancestors had emigrated several generations before, more recent arrivals whose intentions to stay permanently were destroyed with the end of empire, and temporary sojourners who included officials, businesspeople, and a wide range of other non-officials and their families. They encompassed those who were fully of European ancestry as well as those descended from colonizers and colonized alike – the Indisch Dutch, Anglo-Indians, and other *métis* and *mestiços* from French– and Portuguese-speaking imperial arenas. Crucial factors affecting their return included the conditions of their departure, the timing of their arrival in Europe, and the wider social, economic, and political circumstances prevailing in the countries whose populations they either joined or re-joined.

Although often generating much national concern at their moment of arrival and during their initial resettlement period, subsequent scholarly engagement with these decolonization migrants long proved limited and highly uneven. Recent academic interest in the wider themes of race, migration, and the effects of empire within Europe has begun to yield new work on neglected topics, yet much remains to be done.[4] Interdisciplinary explorations of 'whiteness' as a racial and cultural identity have done much to generate and intellectually inform new studies of decolonization repatriations.[5] Europeans returning from overseas empires long attracted little attention because, unlike those commonly understood as racial 'others', they did not physically stand out – particularly in nations that experienced unprecedented levels of Asian, Caribbean, and African immigration during roughly the same period. However distinct they may have become as a result of being part of colonial communities, they often continued to count as a part of the national community – in other words, as 'us' – in public understandings. Those with European nationality or claims to belonging who arrived from the colonies who *did* attract the most notice were, indicatively, those whose ability to count as 'white' and/or as 'European' appeared most tenuous or compromised: persons of mixed ancestry, and those who had never before spent time in the metropole. Geographical, cultural, and racial affiliations frequently worked in combination to shape perceptions about belonging and national concerns about arrivals' ability to integrate.

---

[4] Miège and Dubois (eds.), *L'Europe retrouvée*; Andrea L. Smith (ed.), *Europe's Invisible Migrants* (Amsterdam, 2003).

[5] Catherine Hall, *White, Male, and Middle Class: Explorations in Feminism and History* (New York, 1992); Ruth Frankenberg (ed.), *Displacing Whiteness: Essays in Social and Cultural Criticism* (Durham, 1997); Ann Laura Stoler, *Race and the Education of Desire: Foucault's History of Sexuality and the Colonial Order of Things* (Durham, 1995); Ann Laura Stoler, *Carnal Knowledge and Imperial Power: Race and the Intimate in Colonial Rule* (Berkeley, 2002); Richard Dyer, *White* (London, 1997).

European resettlement experiences were thus far from uniform, but taken together they constitute a key indicator of the ways in which individuals, groups, and newly postcolonial metropoles responded to the loss of overseas territories. As Frederick Cooper has argued, ex-colonizers coming 'home' could appear as 'the living embodiments of a history repudiated around the world'.[6] Repatriates personified the failures of colonial projects and ambitions, in some instances in the wake of long, costly, bloody, and embarrassing fights to preserve empires against anti-colonial nationalists and opponents of traditional imperial orders. How did postcolonial metropoles confront the need to rein-corporate such persons within national boundaries and cultures that were newly reconfigured upon decolonization? Moreover, how did repatriated individuals and groups respond and adapt?

In his analyses of settler colonialism in French North Africa, Frantz Fanon asserted that 'the settler, from the moment that the colonial context disappears, has no longer any interest in remaining or in coexisting'.[7] Even if settlers and other colonials often would not, or could not, remain or co-exist within the ex-colonies that had achieved political independence (although exceptions com-plicate Fanon's general rule, as will be discussed later), they nonetheless refused to disappear, needing instead to carve out new lives elsewhere follow-ing decolonization. For many, the mere thought of doing so was overwhelming, which at least partly explains why so many clung to and defended the colonial order so tenaciously. As one elderly settler woman who had lived in Mozambique for decades wrote in her diary in 1975, members of her commu-nity fleeing for Portugal faced an uncertain future which, in her eyes, seemed like no future at all: 'a cousin, to whom I was very close, left. Later, destitute in Lisbon, he killed his wife and then himself. They were good people. They were dead anyway, they only made it official'.[8] Metaphorically dead they may have been, yet in reality most repatriates, coupled with the ghosts of dead empires they represented, lived on to haunt European nations long past the demise of the colonial worlds that gave rise to them.

* * *

The Netherlands and repatriates from Indonesia

Given its long history of Dutch rule and substantial European-descended population, the Netherlands East Indies unsurprisingly dominates the story of

---

[6] Frederick Cooper, 'Postcolonial Peoples: A Commentary', in Smith (ed.), *Europe's Invisible Migrants*, 172.
[7] Frantz Fanon, *The Wretched of the Earth*, translated by Constance Farrington (London, 1990 [1961]), 35.
[8] Ester Lee, *I Was Born in Africa* (Atlanta, London, and Sydney, 1999), 75.

decolonization migrations to the metropole. Compared with the 300,000 Europeans and Eurasians who either returned to Holland or came for the first time after Indonesian independence in 1949, those from the Dutch West Indies fade into numerical and visible insignificance. Most East Indies arrivals came between the end of the Second World War (when most Dutch nationals had experienced years of internment during the Japanese occupation) and the 1960s, and qualified for entry into the Netherlands on the basis of nationality.[9] 80,000 were metropolitan Dutch – the temporarily resident *totoks* or their children, who were usually fully of European descent – and over 180,000 were Eurasians, or 'Indisch Dutch', of mixed ancestry.[10] Strictly speaking, 'repatriation' did not accurately describe the experience of most Indisch Dutch who had never before set foot in the Netherlands. What is more, their status as 'Dutch', legal though it may have been, proved contentious and jostled uneasily with cultural as well as racial conceptions of national belonging.

Within contemporary discussions of Indies repatriation, the metropolitan Dutch *totoks* were all but ignored.[11] Despite this group's considerable size, accounts of their returns at the end of empire mainly emerged in fictional works such as Nieuwenhuys' *Faded Portraits* or in autobiographies; references to *totoks* in wider public discourse tended to be incidental and impressionistic. These families, whether they belonged to the official or non-official sector, constituted the highest social class in colonial society, and most had sufficient financial and social resources so as not to require urgent material help or attention from the Dutch government. In 1958, one report following an official investigation correspondingly devoted little attention to them since they had not posed 'problems' meriting state concern: 'They were entitled to repatriation at the expense of their employers and for many it meant no more than a somewhat early end to their colonial careers', the author summarized. Most 'moved in with family or friends' and eventually found permanent housing on their own. Nonetheless, the report alluded to private dilemmas following the upheaval that brought an entire way of life to an end, one of which was the tendency to nurture resentment at the Dutch government for its failure to prevent decolonization through what they considered inept policies. Like the

[9] A small portion of these Indies arrivals – 7,000 Chinese, 1,000 Papuans, 8,000 Indonesians, and 12,500 Moluccans (also known as Ambonese) – were treated as separate from European and Eurasian citizens; Chapter 7 considers Moluccan migration to the Netherlands in greater detail.

[10] Herman Obdeijn, 'Vers les bords de la mer du Nord: Les retours aux Pays-Bas induits par la décolonisation', in Miège and Dubois (eds.), *L'Europe retrouvée*, 70.

[11] This was also true of much subsequent historiography, although the following studies have helped rectify this: Hans Meijer, *Indische rekening: Indië, Nederland en de backpay-kwestie 1945–2005* (Amsterdam, 2005); Lizzy van Leeuwen, *Ons Indisch erfgoed: Zestig jaar strijd om cultuur en identiteit* (Amsterdam, 2008); Ulbe Bosma, *Terug uit de koloniën: Zestig jaar postkoloniale migranten en hun organisaties* (Amsterdam, 2009); Gert Oostindie, *Postcolonial Netherlands: Sixty-Five Years of Forgetting, Commemorating, Silencing* (Amsterdam, 2011), 26–33, chs. 3 and 4.

totoks Nieuwenhuys described and like many home on leave or retired before colonialism ended, residing in The Hague, maintaining contact with other ex-colonials, and perpetuating colonial understandings and cultural practices adopted over the course of long periods spent overseas was common.[12] Yet their difficulties and choices remained at the personal level, whereas transitions among the Indisch Dutch generated immense social concern.

Indisch experiences after the transfer of power to Indonesian nationalists stemmed from their colonial status in the last decades of Dutch rule. Although they were a socially diverse group, most occupied an intermediary position between the influential, white, expatriate Dutch community and the indigenous population that approximated 70 million. Most were Dutch speaking with a European-style education, and although relatively few had travelled to the Netherlands, they derived their identity from their cultural and racial affiliations with the colonizers. Even so, most *totoks* looked down upon them as social and racial inferiors – mere '*Indos*' – despite their legal status as Dutch, and most earned their livelihoods from subordinate positions in state and commercial employment. Underprivileged within colonial society though the majority undoubtedly were, they nonetheless were set apart, and above, most of Indonesian society. Even poorer Indisch who bore more resemblance to the indigenous population derived benefits that extended from their European ancestry and loyalty to the colonial state, and saw themselves as distinct from, and often superior to, Indonesians.[13]

Between independence and the late 1950s, the Dutch government persisted in viewing the Indisch Dutch as a group which ideally should remain in Indonesia. Despite their legal right to resettle in the Netherlands, Dutch authorities actively tried to hinder this and minimize the number joining metropolitan society. This disinclination was especially marked with respect to those described as 'Oriental Dutch', or those of mixed ancestry seen as most strongly rooted in Indonesia by virtue of their colour, culture, and often limited economic means.[14] In this era, the Netherlands was envisioned as a nation of emigration, not immigration, with the government encouraging overseas migration to countries like Australia, Canada, and the United States in light of post-war housing and employment shortages. But during the 1950s, more and more Indisch felt their future in independent Indonesia to be increasingly insecure, not least due to the ongoing political tensions between the

---

[12] J.H. Kraak, 'The Repatriation of the Dutch from Indonesia', *R.E.M.P. Bulletin*, 6:2 (1958), 32–3, 37.

[13] Stoler, *Carnal Knowledge*.

[14] John Schuster, 'The State and Post-War Immigration into the Netherlands: The Racialization and Assimilation of Indonesian Dutch', *European Journal of Intercultural Studies*, 3:1 (1992), 47–58; Guno Jones, 'Dutch Politicians, the Dutch Nation and the Dynamics of Post-Colonial Citizenship', in Ulbe Bosma (ed.), *Post-Colonial Immigrants and Identity Formations in the Netherlands* (Amsterdam, 2012), 36–8.

Netherlands and the Sukarno governments, and ever larger numbers succeeded in leaving over the course of the decade. After the diplomatic rupture caused by the Netherlands' refusal to leave West New Guinea and hand control over to Indonesia, the Sukarno government expelled most remaining Dutch nationals and confiscated their property in 1957. Regardless of its reluctance to accept Indisch Dutch into the Netherlands, the Dutch government then became forced to recognize that they could not remain where they were and increased its involvement in the repatriation process.[15]

Dutch authorities then shifted towards public rhetoric that stressed the need to welcome and accommodate those who often arrived nearly penniless, and established agencies to aid their integration. Many arriving in the 1950s initially had nowhere to go since they lacked a family network in the Netherlands, and began by staying at state-run boarding houses run by staff who helped men find work and instructed families on how best to adapt to Dutch life. Official Dutch proclamations and resettlement policy involved a contradictory set of aims. On the one hand, authorities commonly extolled the nation's history as a society tolerant of outsiders with a long tradition of accommodating refugees; according to this narrative, racism had no place in the national culture. On the other hand, however, new Indisch arrivals, most of whom were visibly recognizable as ethnically and culturally distinct, faced immense pressure to assimilate. While phenotypes were unamenable to change, Dutch authorities strove to alter newcomers' cultural practices in ways that revealed an intolerance of difference that linked culture with race, regardless of the widespread official denials that racism existed.

Starting on ships bound for the Netherlands and continuing in boarding houses upon arrival, Indisch Dutch faced a barrage of lessons and strictures about how to behave in the society they were entering. Metropolitan Dutch responsible for assisting with resettlement exhibited clear biases against mores deemed inferior. One sociologist's study published in 1960 diverged from most accounts, strongly sympathizing with the adjustment difficulties of those who had left everything familiar behind – homes, jobs, possessions, friends, a warm climate, and indeed an entire way of life that prioritized hospitality over Dutch frugality. Metropolitan prejudices and preconceptions about mixed-race persons from the nation's former colony only compounded their difficulties. Negative '*Indo*' stereotypes they repeatedly encountered revolved around how they and their habits were seen as distinct from valued Dutch norms: 'the Indo is lazy, unreliable, supine, listless, lacking initiative and economical sense'; 'melancholic brown big eyed nowhere belongers . . . with a basketful of kroepoek, lombok and emping, [foods] which are protected as their most

---

[15] Wim Willems, 'No Sheltering Sky: Migrant Identities of Dutch Nationals from Indonesia', in Smith (ed.), *Europe's Invisible Migrants*, 33–59.

beloved possessions'; 'mysterious people too, full of strange Eastern tricks and magic forces', common wisdom suggested.[16] That these citizens were viewed as 'foreigners' and 'strangers' was evident even in academic studies sponsored by the state that publicly insisted that Indisch Dutch should be regarded as 'long lost children', not to mention in responses from the 'man on the street'.[17]

Social workers responsible for inculcating new practices and urging that Indies ways be stamped out continued their efforts to reshape Indisch domestic life if they received state assistance when resettling in homes of their own. Indisch Dutch were widely understood to be 'bad housekeepers, debt-makers, party loving irresponsible neglectors of the necessary floor- and staircase-scrubbing', not to mention inordinately generous to all visitors 'but having at the same time not even a carpet on the floor and no money for next week'.[18] Many metropolitan stereotypes and attempts at intervention revolved around reforming deviant household routines, and women repatriates bore the brunt of injunctions to change their habits. Not only did they face learning new house-keeping regimes without the servants that had been an accustomed part of Indies life to help with cleaning, cooking, or childcare; they were also expected to lead the way as the family abandoned old customs.[19]

Repatriates' food habits incurred much adverse attention, with reports lamenting that they persisted in eating '*sambal* [hot peppers]' and 'returned to using the staple food of their homeland, namely rice' once they moved out of state-run boarding houses that served only meat, potatoes, and tasteless vege-tables. Once settled in homes of their own, Dutch neighbours resented 'the strange and unpleasant odours caused by the preparation of Indonesian dishes'.[20] A colonial Indies culinary culture that revolved around welcoming guests with an elaborate array of spicy dishes was meant to be superseded by the austere, unseasoned foods that formed the basis of Dutch meals where visitors rarely, if ever, joined the family circle.[21] Repatriates' succinct under-standings of 'how to become a good Hollander' boiled down to the following domestic criteria: 'Stop eating rice, become a solid potato-eater'; 'Wash your laundry on the prescribed Monday morning'; 'Never tire of cleaning the

---

[16] Topaas de Boer-Lasschuyt, 'Eurasian Repatriants in Holland', *R.E.M.P. Bulletin*, 8:2 (1960), 41, 27.

[17] J. Ex, *Adjustment after Migration* (The Hague, 1966), 9, 20, 26, 76, 93; Andrew Goss, 'From *Tong-Tong* to Tempo Doeloe: Eurasian Memory Work and the Bracketing of Dutch Colonial History, 1957–1961', *Indonesia*, 70 (2000), 15–22.

[18] Boer-Lasschuyt, 'Eurasian Repatriants', 41.   [19] Ex, *Adjustment after Migration*, 30–1, 102.

[20] Ibid., 71; Kraak, 'Repatriation', 40.

[21] Anneke H. van Otterloo, 'Chinese and Indonesian Restaurants and the Taste for Exotic Food in the Netherlands: A Global-Local Trend', in Katarzyna Cwiertka with Boudewijn Walraven (eds.), *Asian Food: The Global and the Local* (Richmond, Surrey, 2002), 157–60. As Van Otterloo notes, 157, 'The Dutch have never had a "Rembrandt in the kitchen"'.

house'; 'be not too generous and not too hospitable'; 'Be business-like, pay respect to money'.[22]

Given the emphasis on changing private habits, it is unclear how much Indisch repatriates complied with social workers' instructions behind closed doors. Chapter 8 explores how many retained Indies culinary customs which ultimately spread outwards to reshape Dutch diets and certainly the nation's restaurant scene. Yet when critical outside observers initially paid a visit, the pressure to conform encouraged some to demonstrate 'feigned integration' and proclaim that they ate potatoes, offered guests commendably little in the way of refreshments, and had only limited contact with others who had come from Indonesia.[23] Indeed, Dutch authorities actively discouraged excessive social interactions with fellow Indisch Dutch. Housing policies aimed to disperse them throughout the country instead of concentrating them in one area where they might form a 'ghetto' that would stand in the way of integration.[24] Yet many evaded such efforts aimed at relinquishing Indies ties and habits: those who did not require state housing assistance often gravitated towards The Hague, like so many former East Indies residents had done before them.[25] Others continued to find solace and support through maintaining a largely Indies-linked social circle and privately persisting in familiar cultural practices.[26]

Although publicly they appeared to be integrating as men found employment (facilitated by a booming economy after the early 1950s) and families settled into local life, the rapid assimilation upon which the state insisted was compromised both by repatriates' own desires and the biases they habitually encountered. Indisch Dutch experiences belie public proclamations that the Netherlands was not a racist society: the Dutch, they reported,

feel superior, they look down on us. In their eyes we are a lesser sort of people, who possess few abilities and are lax. Many are badly informed about who we actually are or what we were out there. They think that we are Indonesian or else Ambonese, that we lived in straw huts, that we have never walked in shoes and that we used to sleep on the ground. Many are amazed we speak Dutch. We are not seldom looked upon as intruders, who make the labour market difficult for people here and for whom extra taxes have to be paid.

Repatriates confronted cultural stereotypes, wilful ignorance, and direct racist taunts from Dutch children who addressed them as 'black nigger' and 'chin-chin-chinaman'.[27] Within a society where many in the 1950s and 1960s were eager to forget the Indies once Indonesian nationalists had forced the Dutch out,

---

[22] Boer-Lasschuyt, 'Eurasian Repatriants', 42.   [23] Ibid., 37.   [24] Ibid., 37–8.
[25] Esther Captain et al. (eds.), De Indische zomer in Den Haag: Het cultureel erfgoed van de Indische hoofdstad (Leiden, 2005).
[26] Ex, Adjustment after Migration, 65; Goss, 'From Tong-Tong to Tempo Doeloe', 22.
[27] Ex, Adjustment after Migration, 42, 53.

they acted as a unwelcome reminder of a past now seen to reflect poorly on the Netherlands' national status.[28]

Given the reality of racism as well as most repatriates' refusal to abandon all aspects of their culture upon resettling, it became clear over the longer term that assimilation had been neither rapid nor complete. The importance of selected aspects of Indies culture and identity that persisted and spread within Dutch society will be addressed further in subsequent chapters. But outwardly, in the eyes of hopeful observers, their supposed assimilation became celebrated as a success. In an early academic study one prominent scholar asserted that by the mid-1970s, despite the racialization that greeted many upon arrival, 'after twenty years the group was so completely incorporated into [Dutch] society that a representative study of these people was made virtually impossible'.[29] A growing number of studies now contest a history of smooth and unproblematic integration, illuminating the difficulties most Indisch Dutch arrivals encountered, the manifold ways they responded to them over time, and how colour and class differences among repatriates created very different experiences of settlement in both the short term and the long term.[30]

Yet the fact remains that the *myth* of their assimilation was widely influential and distinguished them from non-European immigrant groups arriving in their wake, whether they hailed from overseas Dutch territories in the Antilles, the ex-colony of Suriname, or outside the former empire. As was seen in the earlier quote, Indisch Dutch repatriates themselves contributed to this early on by asserting their own distinctiveness from the Ambonese (also known as Moluccans), another group of arrivals from the former Dutch East Indies who lacked European descent. Moreover, as Lizzy van Leeuwen's research demonstrates, the arrival of many labour migrants from Turkey and Morocco in the 1960s and 1970s worked to enhance repatriates' Dutch patriotic sentiments as well as their assertions of difference vis-à-vis other minority groups. Many Indisch repatriates strongly resented any intimation of resemblance to Turkish and Moroccan 'guest workers' on account of skin colour. Additionally, since most were Protestant or Roman Catholic, they also distinguished themselves in religious terms from Turkish or Moroccan Muslims who shared the faith of the Indonesian majority against whom they had defined their identity both under

[28] Boer-Lasschuyt, 'Eurasian Repatriants', 30; Goss, 'From *Tong-Tong* to Tempo Doeloe', 11–12.

[29] Hans van Amersfoort, *Immigration and the Formation of Minority Groups: The Dutch Experience, 1945–1975*, translated by Robert Lyng (Cambridge, 1982), 81.

[30] Annemarie Cottaar and Wim Willems, *Indische Nederlanders. Een onderzoek naar beeldvorming* (The Hague, 1984); Annemarie Cottaar and Wim Willems, 'De Geassimileerde Indische Nederlander: Mythe of Werkelijkheid?', *De Gids*, 148, 3:4 (1985), 257–70; Wim Willems and Leo Lucassen (eds.), *Het onbekende vaderland: De repatriëring van Indische Nederlanders (1946–1964)* ('s-Gravenhage, 1994); Wim Willems, *De Uittocht uit Indië: 1945–1995* (Amsterdam, 2001); Meijer, *Indische rekening*; Van Leeuwen, *Ons Indisch erfgoed*; Bosma, *Terug uit de koloniën*.

colonialism and upon decolonization. Indeed, in the 1970s and 1980s (and continuing in the present day), some Indisch Dutch and their Netherlands-born children became supporters of, and occasionally politicians in, right-wing political parties with anti-immigrant, anti-Muslim platforms.[31]

Those of mixed ancestry who were once perceived as worryingly more Indonesian than European are now widely considered as the reverse. As John Schuster argued in the early 1990s, 'even the phenotypical and cultural characteristics which set them apart from the Dutch have become less significant. From highly visible people, the Indonesian Dutch have become socially invisible, and have been made very much part of the Dutch imagined community.'[32] By the time the Netherlands developed multicultural policies starting in the late 1970s they targeted later migrants from Suriname and the Antilles as well as Moroccans and Turks but not the Indisch, who do not officially count as a minority group.[33] In light of this, has Nieuwenhuys' suggestion in *Faded Portraits* that those of mixed descent might gradually 'find their place in Dutch society' and become 'indistinguishable from the *totoks*' come to pass? To answer in the affirmative would require forgetting their history of racialized treatment that involved patronizing demands for conformity to national 'norms', and equally ignoring a resilient sense of postcolonial group identity and ongoing identity politics. Nonetheless, the process through which Indisch Dutch repatriates' former visibility decreased and their Europeanness became accentuated depended upon comparisons made with other newcomers who lacked European ancestral and cultural capital upon which to build.

* * *

Resettling imperial Britons

In an article entitled 'Who Goes Home?' published shortly after Tanganyika achieved independence in 1961, a former British administrator described a European colonial community on the eve of its disintegration. Its overriding characteristic was its cultural distance from Britain as well as from the African majority surrounding it:

---

[31] Van Leeuwen, *Ons Indisch erfgoed*, 149–50; Lizzy van Leeuwen, 'Wreker van zijn Indische grootouders: De politieke roots van Geert Wilders', *De Groene Amsterdammer*, 36, 2 September 2009.

[32] Schuster, 'The State and Post-War Immigration', 56; see also Guno Jones, 'Biology, Culture, "Postcolonial Citizenship" and the Dutch Nation, 1945–2007', *Thamyris/Intersecting*, 27 (2014), 324–6.

[33] Ulbe Bosma and Marga Alferink, 'Multiculturalism and Settlement: The Case of Dutch Postcolonial Migrant Organisations', *Journal of International Migration and Integration*, 13:3 (2012), 277–8; Oostindie, *Postcolonial Netherlands*, 30–3.

As the expatriates' service lengthened, their contacts with Britain weakened; they shared no interests with friends at home ... They remained British but not part of Britain: at the same time, they failed to establish a correspondingly permanent position in the country where they were spending most of their lives. The only group with whom they identified was an essentially artificial and transient society.[34]

For imperial Britons who had long lived far from 'home', the end of colonialism typically spelled the end of accustomed lifestyles and occupations. Like their Dutch and other European counterparts, British expatriates (as well as many settlers) needed to start over, and their futures took many forms.

Starting with India and Pakistan's independence in 1947, thousands of Britons who had lived and worked in the colonies experienced displacement. The numbers returning to the metropole were immense, but repatriation received little public attention and subsequently attracted limited scholarly interest. Although 1991 census figures suggested that as many as 560,000 whites then residing in Britain had been born in former colonies – numbers in fact comparable to Britain's Afro-Caribbean- or Pakistan-born populations – they generated so little wider attention that one historian likened them to 'dogs that did not bark'.[35] Nor, as distinct from the Netherlands, did Eurasians become widely construed as a 'problem', perhaps because they arrived in smaller numbers (by one estimate, only about 25,000 Anglo-Indians had resettled in Britain by 1970).[36] And unlike the cases of Belgium, France, and Portugal discussed in the following sections, Britons returning from the colonies did not arrive *en masse*. Successive decolonization episodes occurred over the course of decades, and some ex-colonizers did not leave the moment the Union Jack was lowered. Moreover, knowledge of the personal upheaval experienced by many who did rejoin metropolitan society could serve as an incentive to others to remain overseas either temporarily or permanently after decolonization.

Detailed pictures of colonizers' return largely concern the middle classes, despite the colonies having white populations from every socio-economic level. Officials' experiences remain the best documented, with memoirs along with colonial service and pensioners' publications providing insight into the transition back to home life. Some of their problems were not new: Britons coming back at the end of empire responded in many of the same ways as their late nineteenth- and early twentieth-century predecessors.[37] Returnees

---

[34] Ralph Tanner, 'Who Goes Home?: An Analysis of Up-country European Communities in Tanganyika', *Transition*, 3:8 (1963), 31.

[35] Ceri Peach, 'Postwar Migration to Europe: Reflux, Influx, Refuge', *Social Science Quarterly*, 78:2 (1997), 271–3; Etemad, 'Europe and Migration', 465; Michael Twaddle, 'British Nationality Law, Commonwealth Immigration and the Ending of the British Empire', in Miège and Dubois (eds.), *L'Europe retrouvée*, 45–6.

[36] Alison Blunt, *Domicile and Diaspora: Anglo-Indian Women and the Spatial Politics of Home* (Malden, MA and Oxford, 2005), 105.

[37] Elizabeth Buettner, *Empire Families: Britons and Late Imperial India* (Oxford, 2004), ch. 6.

commonly felt estranged – or, as the writer quoted earlier put it, 'British but not part of Britain'. Many resented losing the status they enjoyed in the colonies, where being white, British, and middle class placed them near the top of the social ladder; back in Britain, by contrast, they retreated into relative obscurity on more modest incomes and pensions.

The radical differences between colonial lifestyles and their metropolitan aftermath took private and public forms, and were experienced in age- and gender-specific ways.[38] For women, the loss of colonial households where large numbers of servants had been the norm necessitated new domestic routines. Even middle-class families in post-war Britain often proved unable to find, or afford, domestic help, and women accustomed to having most of their cleaning, cooking, shopping, and childcare done by others had to undertake most domestic tasks on their own. One Anglo-Indian woman later recalled that 'when I came to England, I was an ayah [nursemaid], I was a bearer, I was a sweeper, I was everything!' – an experience shared by most white middle-class women as well.[39] Men retired from colonial professions were counselled on how to cope with the boredom of 'pensioned idleness', but this was a predicament to which few women could relate. 'Your wife *never* retires', an ex-army officer wrote in 1955. 'Bereft of her native cook, she'll find herself for the first time regarding the baleful glare of a very dead cod on a plate and wondering how on earth to turn it into lunch'.[40] After the privileges of imperial life, such women found themselves occupying social roles once marked as appropriate for 'natives'. Indeed, back in Britain, they were once again 'native' themselves – unless, if Anglo-Indian, they needed to struggle to become accepted as such in the first place.

For men who had served as colonial officials, the end of empire might have coincided roughly with retirement age; alternatively, it meant early retirement before they could draw full pensions. The younger generation needed to carve out new professional lives once decolonization rendered their original posts obsolete, a problem the British government addressed by setting up organizations like the Overseas Services Resettlement Bureau starting in the late 1940s. Business was a common destination, but metropolitan stereotypes about their former lives dogged some ex-colonials' efforts to find work. 'There is a general view current that anyone who has served overseas has lived a life of indolent luxury', the head of the OSRB summarized in 1959, complaining that British employers were often unaware just how demanding imperial work had been.[41]

---

[38] Elizabeth Buettner, '"We Don't Grow Coffee and Bananas in Clapham Junction You Know!": Imperial Britons Back Home', in Robert Bickers (ed.), *Settlers and Expatriates: Britons over the Seas*, *Oxford History of the British Empire Companion Series* (Oxford, 2010), 302–28.

[39] Blunt, *Domicile and Diaspora*, 126.

[40] W.P.A. Robinson, *How to Live Well on Your Pension* (London, 1955), 14–15, 72–3.

[41] R.L. Peel, 'O.S.R.B.', *Corona*, XI:4 (1959), 149.

'Music hall jokes about irascible gentlemen in topees [sun helmets], swigging gin under the waving palms and waited on by a host of servants, were accepted as not too wide of the mark', commented another. 'They might be good at dealing with a tribal riot but most unlikely to be of much use in modern industry'.[42] In this view, ex-colonials had little to offer to a changing, modernizing, post-war metropole in which the empire and those Britons once associated with it seemed equally anachronistic.

Many ex-colonial officers ultimately found new jobs in public administration in Britain, some in the Home Civil Service. Others continued to work overseas as diplomats or else circulated as colonial administrators in other territories still under British rule once the colony where they initially had been posted became independent. Still others returned overseas as development experts and as employees of multinational companies which, unlike some at home, valued their prior professional experiences as an asset.[43] Officials and non-officials alike commonly had careers that spanned the globe: many actively sought professional opportunities outside the United Kingdom, thus remaining part of expatriate communities in Asia, Africa, and the Middle East well past formal decolonization.[44]

For many such postcolonial Britons, remaining overseas offered valued types of work, community, and culture that the metropole could not. Many settlers and retirees also chose not to return to Britain when empire or their working years ended for the same reason. Pensioners from colonial occupations and their families had a long history of retiring to other parts of the colonial and Commonwealth world such as British Columbia, Nova Scotia, Cyprus, and Australia before the end of empire, and this tradition continued during and after decolonization.[45]

White communities in East, Central, and South Africa had particular appeal for many who had long grown accustomed to overseas life and wanted to 'stay on' – if not where they originally were based, then in other colonial or ex-colonial arenas promising similar amenities. Kenya attracted British retirees from other parts of Africa throughout the 1950s (despite the instability during the Mau Mau insurgency) and also maintained a significant white minority settler presence following independence in 1963. Both the British government and the Kenyan nationalists assuming power saw potential economic and

---

[42] Sir John Rankine, 'Selling the Service to Employers', *Corona*, XIV:4 (1962), 146.

[43] Joseph M. Hodge, 'British Colonial Expertise, Post-Colonial Careering and the Early History of International Development', *Journal of Modern European History*, 8:1 (2010), 24–46.

[44] Anthony Kirk-Greene, *Britain's Imperial Administrators, 1858–1966* (London, 2000), 260–73; Anthony Kirk-Greene, 'Decolonisation: The Ultimate Diaspora', *Journal of Contemporary History*, 36:1 (2001), 133–51.

[45] Buettner, *Empire Families*, ch. 6; Buettner, '"We Don't Grow Coffee"', 318–21. Many Anglo-Indians similarly opted for Australia rather than Britain after the end of the Raj; see Blunt, *Domicile and Diaspora*, ch. 6.

political benefits in reaching a settlement that enabled many white farmers to remain on their land.[46] Similarly, the colony once known as Southern Rhodesia and later simply as Rhodesia attracted considerable numbers of retirees both before and after a white minority government embarked upon its Unilateral Declaration of Independence from Britain in 1965. One former colonial official from Tanganyika spoke for many others when he explained why he and his family chose to relocate there instead of returning to Britain: colonials 'may have but a flimsy nostalgic interest in the land of [their] birth' and would rather spend their advancing years enjoying an accustomed sociability, familiar topics of conversation, 'warmth and servants', and 'a reasonably adjacent golf course'.[47] The colonial lifestyle many families had cherished during men's careers – plentiful domestic help, a warm climate, affordable opportunities for sports, and a full social calendar – depended upon being white, reasonably well-off expatriates with ready access to African domestic labourers. As such, Rhodesia and South Africa continued to attract Britons migrating from other colonial arenas until the former became independent as Zimbabwe under African majority rule in 1980; white privileges in the latter, meanwhile, only declined with the end of apartheid. As will be seen later in the chapter, colonizers from other nations also found South Africa more appealing than returning to Europe because they too could continue to enjoy the privileges of whiteness there more than at home.

Those opting for resettlement abroad did not limit themselves to British colonies, ex-colonies, or Commonwealth countries, however. Since the nineteenth century, Britons accustomed to overseas life sometimes chose to grow old in Europe, most commonly in expatriate communities on the French or Italian Rivieras. Continental retirement destinations continued to beckon many who hesitated to return to a Britain from which they felt estranged.[48] In the late 1960s, pensioners were informed that in places like Portugal they could 'retire to the sun and live the kind of life you used to live in the Colonies. Conditions are good and cost of living reasonable in the Algarve.'[49] One Briton long based in the Algarve remembered the 1960s as 'a bit like the days of the Raj down there then – servants were a-plenty, booze was cheap and the climate was good'.[50] The Algarve also became home to a number of white settlers departing from Kenya upon its independence under African majority rule. Such Britons appear not to have been deterred by the prospect of moving to a country under

[46] Gary Wasserman, *Politics of Decolonization: Kenya Europeans and the Land Issue, 1960–1965* (Cambridge, 1976).

[47] 'Why Not Rhodesia?', *Corona*, XII:7 (1960), 258–61.

[48] W.R. McGeagh, 'Retire to France', *Corona*, XI:5 (1959), 185–8; Buettner, *Empire Families*, 239–45.

[49] 'Members' Announcements: Portugal', *Overseas Pensioner*, 13 (1967), 22.

[50] Russell King, Tony Warnes, and Allan Williams, *Sunset Lives: British Retirement Migration to the Mediterranean* (Oxford, 2000), 63–5, 84–6.

dictatorship that clung on to its 'overseas provinces' in Africa and categorically refused to contemplate decolonization until it collapsed under the weight of anti-colonial wars in 1974. In fact, it is plausible to suggest that the *Estado Novo*'s stubborn hold on Africa may well have counted among Portugal's attractions. Such was the prominence of British ex-colonials among the Algarve's retirement population that a book written in 1974 claimed that 'Great Britain may have lost an empire but seems to be gaining a province' – an assessment that surely would have been relished by critics noted in the previous chapter who dismissed Portugal as a poor, underdeveloped 'semiperipheral' nation and empire that had long ranked as little more than a 'semi-colony of England'.[51]

For some, returns to Britain only took place after overseas life was prolonged through temporary residence in other British colonies, ex-colonies, or parts of Europe recommended for their affordability, weather, and congeniality. The majority who ultimately did resettle in Britain commonly felt misunderstood by society at large; like repatriates in the Netherlands, they too often continued to fraternize with others who shared colonial experiences and understandings. If most largely escaped the notice of mainstream British society and appeared to have readily become re-acclimated to domestic life, their colonial past nonetheless remained a potent source of identity and nostalgia. Once colonial life was over memories of it typically lived on, even if long dormant, remaining available to be reactivated both privately and publicly long after empire became history.

* * *

Belgians and the Congo

For Belgians living and working in the Congo, the transfer of power in 1960 led to a dramatic decolonization migration then unprecedented in scale and speed.[52] When the Congo became independent on 30 June, Belgium had hoped that most of its nationals (who numbered close to 89,000 out of a total non-African population of approximately 114,000) would remain in Africa to continue their work.[53] Commentators in the press persisted in extolling the nation's 'civilizing mission' as a worthy goal that had yet to reach completion and justified ongoing personal, and national, commitments. Yet as Chapter 4 introduced, the former colony plunged into political chaos and violence when Congolese soldiers in the

---

[51] Charles E. Wuerpel, *The Algarve* (Newton Abbot, 1974), 164.

[52] Pierre Salmon, 'Les retours en Belgique induits par la décolonisation', in Miège and Dubois (eds.), *L'Europe retrouvée*, 191–212.

[53] René Lemarchand, *Political Awakening in the Belgian Congo* (Berkeley, 1964), 75.

Force publique mutinied just days after independence. Belgians became caught in the fray, and some suffered physical assault.

Lurid reports poured back into Belgium concerning attacks at military bases in towns like Thysville. Emotive stories dominated the headlines of newspapers from across the political spectrum telling tales of Belgian martyrdom. The press paid particular attention to rapes of white women and young girls by frenzied African soldiers, but also reported the supposed decapitation of Belgian infants alongside a host of other atrocities.[54] With fear and rumours running rampant throughout the Congo in mid-late July, tens of thousands of Europeans desperately sought refuge either in neighbouring European colonies or through hasty departures for Belgium via an airlift run by the Sabena airline. Approximately 38,000 flew home from the Congo in under a month.[55] Stories and photographs inundated the media showing tearful, injured, and distraught Belgians landing at the Brussels airport with little but the clothes on their backs; the majority were women and children, the latter clinging to the one toy they had managed to carry with them.

Blame for these attacks was attributed not only to the African soldiers who had mutinied but also to the new Congolese administration headed by Patrice Lumumba and to Belgian politicians. Prime Minister Eyskens' government was derided for orchestrating a premature decolonization, providing expatriate nationals with false assurances of their safety, encouraging them to remain in the Congo after the transfer of power, and then dragging its feet over how best to coordinate a response once violence erupted. The ranks of former colonials whose returns to the metropole had taken place well before independence swelled with mounting numbers of the newly repatriated, and together with other interest groups they organized a series of demonstrations in Brussels attended by several thousand people.[56] Rallying around the statue of King Léopold II as was their custom during ceremonial gatherings with a Congo connection, the placards they carried spoke volumes about the rhetoric deemed most likely to sway wider metropolitan public opinion and shape political decisions. 'Our massacred and mutilated children, our raped women'; 'Belgian politics lost us an empire'; 'We're ruined!'; and, perhaps most evocatively, 'Send Mrs Eyskens and the parliamentarians' wives to Thysville' were just some of the sentiments and accusations vented by irate ex-colonials who felt betrayed by politicians who had agreed to a Congolese independence that

---

[54] 'L'arrivée des premiers réfugiés à l'aéroport de Bruxelles', *La Libre Belgique* (Brussels), 11 July 1960, 8; 'Ce que disent les réfugiés et les rapatriés', *Le Peuple* (Brussels), 11 July 1960, 1; 'Les heures pénibles d'un dramatique exode', *La Libre Belgique*, 27 July 1960, 1; 'Deux enfants ont été décapités par des mutins – leur mère est devenue folle', *La Libre Belgique*, 20 July 1960, 9.

[55] Guy Vanthemsche, *La Belgique et le Congo: L'impact de la colonie sur la métropole*, new and rev. edn. (Brussels, 2010), 318; 260–1.

[56] Peter Verlinden, *Weg uit Congo: Het drama van de Kolonialen* (Leuven, 2002), 177, 191, 201.

failed to provide desired guarantees.[57] Demanding that the 'black assassins', 'beasts', and 'savages' be held to account, repatriates played a critical role in pressuring the government to act.[58]

Renditions of Belgians' plight in a newly-independent Congo were far from politically and culturally neutral. Newspapers repeatedly compared the mass departures of terrified Belgian 'refugees' (a term indicatively preferred over the less provocative and loaded 'repatriates') from the Léopoldville airport to the exoduses from Belgium upon German invasions in 1914 and 1940.[59] On this occasion, however, flights occurred not away from the motherland but rather towards it. Yet again, Belgium – in the shape of a white colonial woman with a child – had been raped, this time by a Congolese enemy rather than a German one. As Pedro Monaville aptly observes, the raped Belgian women of July 1960 served as 'the natural incarnation of the nation'.[60] Colonizers turned ex-colonizers overnight immediately became cast as helpless and innocent victims of extreme or threatened brutality, rendered as feminine or childlike in their vulnerability.

Gendered representations of Belgian disempowerment in the face of Congolese 'savagery' unleashed the instant they were freed from colonial rule ran through what amounted to a flood of sensationalist journalism. The state promptly took up its dominant elements, enlisting media renditions of the July mutiny to rationalize its course of action: the deployment of metropolitan troops to the Congo less than two weeks after independence ceremonies had taken place.[61] To counter international criticism at the United Nations, officials appropriated individual Belgians' misfortunes, whether real, imagined, or potential, to vindicate military intervention. Personal testimonials were compiled and circulated at home and abroad to spell out the full horrors of a world turned upside down that desperately needed the restoration of civilization from without.

No detail of physical maltreatment or psychological injury allegedly meted out by Congolese soldiers on the rampage seemed too salacious or too delicate to be endlessly recycled within the Belgian press and in published official enquiries disseminated with the express intention to shock. Atrocity narratives

---

[57] 'Manifestation de coloniaux à Bruxelles', *La Libre Belgique*, 9/10 July 1960, 1; 'Une manifestation du "Rassemblement pour la défense des Belges au Congo"', *La Libre Belgique*, 18 July 1960, 8; 'Impressionnante manifestation des Blancs d'Afrique', *Le Soir* (Brussels), 12 July 1960, 7.

[58] 'Quelques centaines de manifestants crient "Eyskens au Poteau"', *Le Peuple*, 11 July 1960, 2.

[59] 'La situation au Congo', *Le Peuple*, 9/10 July 1960, 3; 'Ce que disent les réfugiés et les rapatriés', 1; 'Le problème des réfugiés', *Le Peuple*, 13 July 1960, 3.

[60] Pedro Monaville, 'La crise congolaise de juillet 1960 et le sexe de la décolonisation', *Sextant*, 25 (2008), 98.

[61] Bernard Piniau, *Congo-Zaïre 1874–1981: La perception du lointain* (Paris, 1992), ch. 7; Monaville, 'La crise congolaise'.

regaled readers with successive cases of ritualized humiliation. Mutinying *Force publique* troops separated Belgian officers from their wives and children and subjected them to highly symbolic forms of violence and insult that blatantly upended colonial racial hierarchies and flaunted deep taboos.[62] White men were captured, hit, spat upon, forced to undress in public and go barefoot, and undertake menial labour; the indignities officers suffered included being made to crawl on all fours with ropes around their necks.[63] The Congolese rank and file, it was implied, relished this inversion of conventional power relations, taking immense delight in reducing their commanders to a degraded and dehumanized status – one indeed bearing resemblance to their own circumstances over much of the colonial era. Revealingly, several Congolese commentators writing about the munity believed that it 'showed the Belgians that the Congolese were not "animals who could be kicked about and abused" but human beings who if not treated properly would react'. Just as importantly, it proved 'that the immediate, total and undiluted independence which had been so long demanded was a reality' – in stark contrast to Belgian assumptions that much would remain the same as before. After Europeans had fled the port city of Matadi, Congolese reportedly came together 'to drink a toast to the Belgians who had been humiliated for the very first time since their arrival in the Congo'.[64]

Stripping Belgians of their authority and subjecting them to demeaning forms of mistreatment that Africans had endured for generations extended to women. As Congolese Information Minister Anicet Kashamura insisted during a 19 July radio broadcast, 'Belgium exterminated 12.5 million blacks during the course of the colonial period; as for Belgian troops ... they raped black women and acted "like bandits"'.[65] With their husbands and fathers unable to protect them, white women and their children were abandoned to what was habitually described as their worst possible fate – the 'Black Peril' that imagined European women as permanently threatened with sexual assault by African men. Women gang-raped for hours at a time, some while pregnant; women raped in front of their children, sometimes while holding infants in their

---

[62] Catherine Hoskyns, *The Congo since Independence: January 1960-December 1961* (London, 1965), 89–104, 122–4; Crawford Young, *Politics in the Congo: Decolonization and Independence* (Princeton, 1965), 315–21; Monaville, 'La crise congolaise', 98–100.

[63] Among voluminous examples, see those related in W.J. Ganshof Van Der Meersch, *Fin de la souveraineté belge au Congo: Documents et Réflexions* (Brussels, 1963), 441–52; J. Gérard-Libois and Benoît Verhaegen, *Congo 1960: Les dossiers du CRISP*, 2 vols. (Brussels, 1961), vol. 1, 455–6, and vol. II, 472–8; Louis-François Vanderstraeten, *De la Force publique à l'Armée nationale congolaise: Histoire d'une mutinerie juillet 1960* (Brussels, 1985).

[64] Simon-José Diboka, *Matadi – sous l'aggression des Belges* (Léopoldville, 1961), 21, 39, quoted in Hoskyns, *Congo since Independence*, 102.

[65] A. Stenmans, *Les premiers mois de la République du Congo (Léopoldville) (1er juillet–22 novembre 1960): Relation coordonnée des événements et réflexions d'ordre general* (Brussels, 1961), 21.

arms; women who sacrificed themselves sexually hoping that their daughters would be spared, but to no avail: in vivid Belgian public renditions of the horrors that ensued the instant that merciless 'savages' gained the upper hand, deep-seated colonial racial nightmares became a reality that minutely-detailed reports were meant to substantiate.[66]

While some Belgians clearly did suffer terribly at the hands of Congolese soldiers and about a dozen were killed, scholars have suggested that actual instances of physical brutality were nowhere near as widespread as the media or official investigations implied. The numbers of sexually assaulted women were, and remain, impossible to verify (estimates varied considerably, with some sources suggesting up to one hundred, others far fewer). Nevertheless, even at the time proven eyewitnesses and victims of violence, male or female, could be as elusive as rumour and hearsay were ubiquitous.[67] Indisputably pervasive, however, was the potent combination of white panic and media spectacle together with Belgian officials who fanned their flames.

Belgian ministers and politicians lent their full support to the mass evacuation procedure and publicly sympathized with repatriates' woes, ostensibly because 'the security of Belgians living in the Congo, above all their children and their wives' needed to be ensured.[68] But the Sabena aircraft that had carried women and children to safety in Belgium returned to the Congo filled with Belgian soldiers. This was not merely a virile rush to the aid of the defenceless in the name of national honour, but a military intervention involving 10,000 troops. Significantly, Belgian forces were not invariably posted to the regions most deeply affected by the munity. Instead, many were sent to protect the mineral-rich Katanga province that boasted not just a substantial white population but also immense natural resources and a regional secessionist movement deemed infinitely more favourable to Western economic and political interests than the assertive central Congolese government presided over by Lumumba. If white women and children served as a convenient pretext for intervention, Belgium's real agenda was all too clear to Congolese nationalists. The Belgian and Congolese governments traded increasingly bitter recriminations that resulted in formal relations being broken off in mid-July, with both sides protesting that they had been 'violated'. Angry Belgians invoked '*les femmes et fillettes violées*' – raped women and girls; Lumumba stressed that the Belgian invasion lacking the Congolese government's approval constituted both 'a violation of our national sovereignty' and 'a violation of our treaty with Belgium'.[69]

---

[66] See Van Der Meersch, *Fin de la souveraineté belge*; Gérard-Libois and Verhaegen, *Congo 1960*; Vanderstraeten, *De la Force publique*.

[67] Piniau, *Congo-Zaïre*, 221; Vanderstraeten, *De la Force publique*, 447–9.

[68] Gérard-Libois and Verhaegen, *Congo 1960*, Vol. II, 508.

[69] 'Belgians Attacked', *The Times* (London), 15 July 1960, 12; 'Belgian Troops Fly to Aid Elisabethville Europeans', *The Times*, 11 July 1960, 10.

Belgian military forces soon were restricted to their bases and replaced by United Nations troops sent to maintain order, but at home raped white women, murdered and mutilated children, and men attacked while valiantly trying to defend them or restore order dominated public discussions throughout the weeks when Belgian departures peaked. Belgians in the metropole responded to the repatriates' plight by supporting a well-publicized campaign backed by the state and the royal family to assist those who had 'lost everything' with financial donations. A National Congo Committee rapidly took shape as a fundraising and solidarity association that utilized familiar imagery of suffering women and children (as well as Belgians more generally 'who dedicated their lives to the civilizing mission on African soil') and succeeded in raising over 16 million francs by early August.[70] One initiative involved the issue of three postage stamps available for purchase with a surcharge donated to the committee, one picturing a woman holding a child and all three featuring the aircraft – national heroes in their own right – that had been essential to the mass evacuation procedure.[71]

Such demonstrations of support suggest that Belgians fleeing the Congo enjoyed considerable sympathy among metropolitan society. Yet two years later officials remained undecided about the level, and form, of compensation that colonial repatriates should receive.[72] Once their situation no longer served the immediate purpose of justifying the military intervention that in turn had supported the Katanga secession, repatriates ceased to pay political dividends. What is more, many Belgians may well have restricted their support for Congo repatriates to a one-time small donation or to briefly lending an ear to emotive talk which, in the end, was even cheaper still. Since the government's decision to grant independence in the summer of 1960 was strongly influenced by the fear that Belgians at home would refuse to consent to sending large numbers of troops to maintain order in the Congo, it was likely that widespread sympathy for those directly affected by decolonization in Central Africa had decided limitations.

Some Belgians who had lived and worked in the Congo undoubtedly continued to nurse deep resentments against the government they believed had

---

[70] 'Le Prince Albert fait un appel en faveur des réfugiés du Congo', *Le Soir*, 21 July 1960, 7; 'Le "Comité national Congo" a déjà recueilli plus de 16 millions', *La Libre Belgique*, 2 August 1960, 6.
[71] Nancy Rose Hunt discusses the wider symbolic resonance of airplanes in the Congo in *A Colonial Lexicon: Of Birth Ritual, Medicalization, and Mobility in the Congo* (Durham, 1999); see especially ch. 2. Writing decades later just after the airline had gone bankrupt, Guy Vanthemsche described its mass evacuation of Belgians from the Congo in July 1960 as 'one of the greatest achievements in Sabena's history'. Guy Vanthemsche, *La Sabena 1923–2001: Des origines au crash* (Brussels, 2002), 162.
[72] 'L'indemnisation du préjudice professionel subi au Congo', *Le Soir*, 31 May 1962, 2.

Figure 6.1a–c 'Pont aérien'/'Luchtbrug' series of three Belgian postage stamps issued in support of the Comité National Congo/Nationaal Comité Congo, 3 August 1960.
Credit: bpost.

betrayed them.[73] Metropolitan commentators worried that without appropriate reintegration policies, repatriated colonials would risk becoming 'wrecks', 'desperados', and 'eternally unadapted' to life back home. But public discussions focused not on the difficulties of emotional readjustment for individuals, but rather on how men who had worked as colonial officers and officials could be saved from unemployment via new occupations.[74] Revealingly, the 'violated' women whose plight had served as the main catalyst for the exodus and military intervention retreated into public obscurity after their repatriation once they no longer served a sense of national purpose.

While most Belgian men ultimately did succeed in re-establishing themselves following the collapse of their previous way of life (thanks in large part to a low unemployment rate), many only did so after a period ridden with apprehension and uncertainty. One ex-colonial officer recalled the early 1960s as a precarious and anxious time of professional incoherence as he drifted from one short-term job to the next, ultimately becoming part of Belgium's diplomatic service. Although his new career involved returning to an independent Congo, he recounted his sense of relief upon finally making a definitive professional transition: 'it was not displeasing to be thus assured that I, too, was "decolonizable"', he put it.[75]

Other Belgians, particularly those supported by private-sector employment, also remained in the Congo well past 1960. Some who had initially fled during the mutiny subsequently returned when assured that their lives, work, and property would be protected. Forming part of the ongoing multinational Western presence in Central Africa following the formal transfer of power, many Belgians continued to seek livelihoods in the former colony well into (and in some cases beyond) the 1970s, when the Mobutu regime's Zaïrianization projects reduced their employment prospects in foreign companies.[76]

* * *

[73] In the early 1960s, some took part in extremist pro-colonial groups like the Comité d'Action et de Défense des Belges d'Afrique, which was soon renamed the Mouvement d'Action Civique. Although these organizations have been identified as precursors to later far-right political parties (some of their members later joined the Francophone Belgian National Front), at the time they were short-lived and marginal on the Belgian political landscape. Overall, the connection between Belgians who returned from the Congo in 1960 and the emergence of far-right postcolonial politics was far less pronounced than among France's *pieds-noirs* from Algeria (as discussed later in this chapter and in Chapter 8). See Vanthemsche, *La Belgique et le Congo*, 289, 391; David Art, *Inside the Radical Right: The Development of Anti-Immigrant Parties in Western Europe* (New York, 2011), 66–7; 'Mouvement d'Action Civique', www.ResistanceS.be/r0201.html#036, accessed 26 October 2012.

[74] 'Le problème des réfugiés', *Le Peuple*, 12 July 1960, 3; 'Le problème de la réintégration', *La Libre Belgique*, 23/24 July 1960, 1; Hoskyns, *Congo since Independence*, 469.

[75] Jan Hollants van Loocke, *De la colonie à la diplomatie: une carrière en toutes latitudes* (Paris, 1999), 57–8.

[76] Salmon, 'Les retours', 201; Lieve Joris, *Back to the Congo*, translated by Stacey Knecht (London, 1992), 1–14.

France: *pieds-noirs* and others

Like Belgians and Britons, not all French residing overseas returned to the metropole when colonial rule ended, since French decolonizations created a variety of possibilities. The French community in many newly independent West African nations like Senegal remained and indeed expanded in decades following independence.[77] Although ongoing or growing European communities largely were composed of those employed by the private sector, some former colonial administrators also 'stayed on', at least temporarily, as diplomats or as technical and development advisors of agencies sponsored by the French government. Most officials, however, were transferred back to the metropole, where France's Colonial Ministry was responsible for finding them new state jobs – a benefit Britain's colonial civil servants never enjoyed.[78] They became integrated into other official services, sometimes being reposted overseas but more often in provincial France. Since the Ministry of Culture's establishment in 1958 coincided with decolonization, ex-colonial personnel were prominent among its early staff. While unemployment or an even more radical career change was thus avoided, many failed to achieve comparable satisfaction in their new posts, finding that they enjoyed less power, responsibility, and independence than they had 'in the bush'. As one transferred administrator later recalled, 'imagine a man having ruled millions of people for ten years without any supervision suddenly finding himself piling up files in a tiny office'. On a personal level, many colonial officials turned metropolitan civil servants regretted the loss of their previous professional status.[79]

Yet French officials formed only a minute proportion of the total number of overseas French who entered the metropole when a succession of territories became independent. Between the early 1950s and the mid-1960s approximately 1.5 million people were 'repatriated', a term used to refer not only to French born in France, but also to those born overseas who only arrived in the metropole when empire ended. Repatriates thus constituted over 3 per cent of the 44 million French citizens within the 'hexagon', or metropolitan territory. As many ex-colonies had only a few thousand Europeans residing in them, most decolonization episodes resulted in a comparative trickle of returns home. North African territories with large white settler communities provide the exception: over 230,000 Europeans left Morocco, 170,000 left Tunisia, and close to a million left Algeria. Departures from Algeria were the most dramatic by far and have correspondingly been the subject of most historical studies due to the large size of

[77] Rita Cruise O'Brien, *White Society in Black Africa: The French of Senegal* (London, 1972).
[78] William B. Cohen, *Rulers of Empire: The French Colonial Service in Africa* (Stanford, 1971), 194–9.
[79] Véronique Dimier, 'For a New Start: Resettling French Colonial Administrators in the Prefectoral Corps', *Itinerario*, 28:1 (2004), 49–66; Herman Lebovics, *Bringing the Empire Back Home: France in the Global Age* (Durham, 2004), ch. 2.

the French community and the circumstances that led to its departure, *en masse*, mainly during the summer of 1962. In just a few months, about half a million fled across the Mediterranean to disembark in port cities of southern France.[80]

While Tunisia and Morocco had been French protectorates whose independence was not preceded by lengthy anti-colonial insurgencies, Algeria only freed itself of French control following nearly eight years of brutal violence waged between the *Front de Libération Nationale*, or FLN, and France. As summarized in Chapter 3, the war in Algeria divided the French at home like no other colonial struggle. Indeed, Algeria had not technically been construed as a colony at all, but rather as an integral part (or more precisely as three *départements*) of the French nation. Moreover, in its last years, the Algerian War not only became one that pitted Algerian independence fighters against the French, but also a Franco–French conflict. Increasing numbers of metropolitan French wanted their government to negotiate with the FLN and lost the will to remain in North Africa given the death toll of French soldiers, the moral dilemmas that ensued with mounting revelations of the widespread use of torture to curb the insurgency, and the financial costs of the conflict. But the large French settler community remained staunchly committed to the cause of *Algérie française*, or keeping Algeria French. The years 1961 and 1962 saw the emergence and growth of the *Organisation de l'Armée Secrète* (OAS), an underground group that drew upon settlers and segments of the French army who remained dedicated to the fight to continue French control. The OAS's efforts to force France to stay in Algeria through escalating the violence to ever-higher and more savage levels proved to be in vain, and by the time Algeria became independent in July 1962 the OAS's campaign had effectively rendered it impossible for the settlers to remain. Rather than achieving its aims, the OAS's desperate actions led to the mass exodus of all but a few thousand settlers, who felt that their choices were either 'the suitcase or the coffin': leaving Algeria, or facing the FLN's wrath.

The drama, and trauma, of the departure from Algeria stemmed in part from the conflicts that preceded and produced it, and in part from the nature of settler society. Unlike better-off colonial officials residing overseas on a temporary basis, close to 80 per cent of Algeria's Europeans had been born in North Africa, reflecting the history of settlement that dated back to France's conquest in 1830.[81] For over a century, French as well as Spanish, Italian, Maltese, and

---

[80] Colette Dubois, 'La nation et les français d'outre-mer: rapatriés ou sinistrés de la décolonisation?', in Miège and Dubois (eds.), *L'Europe retrouvée*, 92; William B. Cohen, 'Legacy of Empire: The Algerian Connection', *Journal of Contemporary History*, 15 (1980), 98.

[81] Benjamin Stora, 'The "Southern" World of the *Pieds Noirs*: References to and Representations of Europeans in Algeria', in Caroline Elkins and Susan Pedersen (eds.), *Settler Colonialism in the Twentieth Century* (New York, 2005), 226.

other Europeans who became included in the category of French nationals augmented the settler community, which for the most part consisted of people who were a far cry from the *grands colons* (wealthy colonists) of popular imagination back home. Most settlers were, at best, of modest social status, having worked for the government or in the private sector as office staff, shopkeepers, or artisans.[82] A large proportion were working class, making 'poor whites' – like the characters Albert Camus featured in his fictional and semi-autobiographical writings – a substantial portion of Algerian French society.[83] While their overall social status was lower than that of most French people in the metropole, their position was vastly superior to that of indigenous North African Arabs and Berbers and was predicated upon benefits derived from being part of a European minority.

The vast majority of Algeria's white settlers had never been to the metropole prior to the panicked departures of 1962, and unwillingly left North Africa knowing no other lifestyle.[84] Although Frenchness was the crux of their identity, they had long since diverged from most French north of the Mediterranean and became increasingly distinct throughout the 1954–1962 war. This difference extended to the name by which they popularly became known: *pieds-noirs*, or literally 'black feet'. The origins of this label remain unclear, with some commentators suggesting that it derived from the black boots worn by soldiers or the shoes worn by Europeans that served as one of the physical markers that distinguished them from members of indigenous society. *Pied-noir* only came into widespread usage in the late 1950s, and initially it had pejorative connotations when articulated by metropolitan commentators whose patience with the war, and with the settlers increasingly deemed responsible for France's problems in Algeria, was rapidly becoming exhausted. Yet settlers soon appropriated the *pied-noir* appellation for themselves, and after leaving Algeria for mainland France its proliferation amongst the erstwhile settler community symbolized the ways in which this identity was perpetuated, and indeed strengthened, within the postcolonial metropole. As Jean-Jacques Jordi asserts, a new group identity emerged in the postcolonial period, and 'it was not in Algeria but in France, and not until May 1962, that the "pied-noir" was born. The 1962 repatriation would become the foundational event for a community in exile, a community that had not existed as such in Algeria'.[85] Paradoxically, an identity that harkened back to colonial origins became fully contingent upon

[82] David Prochaska, *Making Algeria French: Colonialism in Bône* (London, 1990).
[83] Albert Camus, *The First Man*, translated by David Hapgood (London, 1995; first published 1994).
[84] Jeannine Verdès-Leroux, *Les Français d'Algérie de 1830 à aujourd'hui: Un page d'histoire déchirée* (Paris, 2001), ch. 5.
[85] Jean-Jacques Jordi, 'The Creation of the Pieds-Noirs: Arrival and Settlement in Marseilles, 1962', in Smith (ed.), *Europe's Invisible Migrants*, 73; Jean-Jacques Jordi, *De l'exode à l'exil: Rapatriés et pieds-noirs en France: L'exemple marseillais, 1954–1992* (Paris, 1993), 223, 240.

decolonization and postcolonial upheavals. Moreover, from the very moment *pieds-noirs* entered metropolitan society they asserted their specificity within and differences from it, forging an identity with cultural, social, geographical, and political manifestations that still endures among many today.

Pieds-noirs' distinction from mainstream French society was apparent to all observers from the first dramatic moments of their arrival, when thousands disembarked each day from ships at Marseille and other port cities in the south of France. Most entered with little more than a few suitcases and strong resentment towards French people – President Charles de Gaulle first and foremost – who had turned their backs on the *Algérie française* cause and to whom they attributed their current plight. Metropolitan onlookers in turn viewed *pieds-noirs* as the main cause of what had stretched into a long and unpopular war, and many showed little sympathy for their predicament and losses.[86] Had it not been for the intractability of racist, extremist settlers, common wisdom went, France could have avoided the divisive and deadly imbroglio that the Algerian conflict had become. Such reasoning amounted to wilful amnesia about the extent to which metropolitan France had created the conditions for the evolution of settler society and aided and abetted its ability to shape Algerian policy. Attempts to absolve the metropole of its own culpability for Algeria's descent into nationalist insurrection, spiralling violence, and ultimately the manner in which the French-Algerian connection was severed altogether cast the settlers as the root of the nation's Algerian 'problem' that was solved so unsatisfactorily.[87] Widely seen to have gotten what they deserved, once exiled in France *pieds-noirs* confronted considerable resentment for being a drain on national resources in light of their needs for housing, jobs, and social services. Furthermore, metropolitan opinion deemed them politically suspect, attributing far-right sympathies to the entire community. As one newspaper feared, *pieds-noirs'* arrival would bring 'the OAS, torturing policemen and fascists, paratroopers plotting putsches' into 'the heart of France'.[88]

The atmosphere of suspicion and hostility that greeted them provided solid foundations for an ongoing *pied-noir* identity. Many sought to preserve what aspects they could of their former way of life and social world, and chose to remain in the south of France after disembarking. France's Mediterranean provinces, known as the Midi, offered a warmer climate and a culture that bore a stronger resemblance to that of North Africa than elsewhere in the hexagon, helping explain why at least 60 per cent of *pieds-noirs* (along with

---

[86] Benjamin Stora, *La gangrène et l'oubli: La mémoire de la guerre d'Algérie* (Paris, 1991), 256–61.
[87] Todd Shepard, *The Invention of Decolonization: The Algerian War and the Remaking of France* (Ithaca, 2006), 192–204.
[88] Cohen, 'Legacy of Empire', 106.

repatriates from Tunisia and Morocco) opted to resettle there rather than spread throughout France. Although the government was anxious that a geographically concentrated *pied-noir* community could pose political dangers and actively tried to encourage them to go north, new arrivals overwhelmingly opted for southern cities despite the relative lack of employment opportunities in the region. In places like Marseille, Avignon, Toulon, Nîmes, Toulouse, Nice, and particularly in a new town they established on their own, Carnoux-en-Provence, French repatriates made a deep mark, comprising up to 10 per cent of the population (and close to 100 per cent in Carnoux).[89] Most of those who did move north headed for the Paris region, where they formed a less visible and concentrated presence.

Clustering together allowed *pieds-noirs* who felt isolated within the metropole to perpetuate familiar social circles and cultural practices. Living near family and friends had obvious attractions for those lacking any pre-existing network of acquaintances in France. Daily proximity was further enhanced by more occasional contacts maintained with those living further afield through numerous *pied-noir* associations, several hundred of which had been formed in France since 1962.[90] Members of such organizations periodically met to renew old ties forged across the Mediterranean as well as work together to achieve political, economic, and cultural goals. During the first twenty years after their mass repatriation, demands for indemnification for lost property in North Africa often dominated their agenda.

The government's delayed, and then grudgingly given, financial compensations worked to enhance the unity of a postcolonial community long after its transfer to France. After indemnification campaigns began to bear fruit, *pied-noir* associations increasingly took on a social character that encouraged the preservation of French Algerian culture and memory. The years after repatriation saw numerous publications on *pied-noir* history; on *pataouète*, the language spoken by working-class settlers of Algiers; and on *pied-noir* cuisine.[91] Books like Irène and Lucienne Karsenty's *Le livre de la cuisine pied-noir* (1973) promised much more than recipes for couscous, *merguez* (a spicy sausage), and *mouna* (a type of bread). 'We lost everything in leaving our country', its preface began. 'Only one thing remains ours, always alive at the bottom of our hearts: memory. And nothing keeps this memory alive more than our cooking, this warm and colourful tradition that ties us to all we loved.' Far

[89] Jordi, *De l'exode à l'exil*; Pierre Baillet, 'L'intégration des rapatriés d'Algérie en France', *Population*, 30:2 (1975), 303–14.

[90] Andrea L. Smith, *Colonial Memory and Postcolonial Europe: Maltese Settlers in Algeria and France* (Bloomington, 2006).

[91] Anne Roche, 'Pieds-noirs: le "retour"', *Modern & Contemporary France*, NS 2:2 (1994), 151–64; Roland Bacri, *le roro: Dictionnaire pataouète de langue pied-noir, étymologique, analogique, didactique, sémantique et tout* (Paris, 1969).

more than simply 'an ensemble of "specialities"', *pied-noir* cuisine acted as 'the indispensable fertilizer through which an entire people continues to nourish its roots'.[92] That which was preserved in daily speech and cuisine might thereby be passed on and become documented for posterity, both for subsequent generations of *pieds-noirs* further removed from direct experiences of *Algérie française* and for a wider public that remained largely ignorant of their history. Chapter 9 further examines *pieds-noirs*' '*nostalgérie*', or nostalgia for French Algeria, and efforts to ensure that their North African past is remembered – *in the ways they want to it be remembered* – and not forgotten.

Over the more than fifty years since their decolonization 'exodus' from North Africa, *pied-noir* unity has tapered off for some ex-settlers and the second generation. Having arrived during France's so-called 'thirty glorious years' of post-war prosperity, most succeeded in re-establishing themselves economically, and in many respects they gradually merged with other metropolitan social sectors. One group from North Africa never displayed an ex-settler identity to any degree comparable to most *pieds-noirs*: the 120,000 Jews who had French citizenship but whose ancestors' presence in Algeria, Morocco, and Tunisia preceded that of other European settlers by centuries. When they settled in France, they foregrounded an identity based upon Frenchness and Jewishness rather than playing up a colonial past.[93] Today, those who migrated from North Africa after 1945 form a large proportion of France's Jewish population in the wake of the pre-war Jewish community's devastation through emigration and deportation to Nazi death camps during the Vichy era.

Other non-Jewish *pieds-noirs* have also largely 'turned the page' and now identify little, if at all, with ex-settlers *per se*. But although it has become diluted and diminished over time, the degree to which a recognizable *pied-noir* community still survives in France remains striking. Political behaviour provides a final manifestation of a distinctiveness which nonetheless demonstrates crucial affinities with French lacking North African settler origins. While *pieds-noirs* never materialized as an extreme-right force capable of derailing mainstream politics, they have periodically supported far-right presidential and local candidates in considerable numbers. An implacable hatred for de Gaulle led many to vote for an adamantly pro-*Algérie française* presidential contender in 1965; since the 1970s and 1980s, many have sympathized with Jean-Marie Le Pen's *Front National*, which derives considerable support from the southern provinces where much of the ex-settler population lives.[94] Le Pen, a former paratrooper who had served in Algeria during the war, has actively courted the

---

[92] Irène Karsenty and Lucienne Karsenty, *Le livre de la cuisine pied-noir* (Paris, 1973), preface by Enrico Macias, n.p.; see also Joëlle Hureau, *La mémoire des pieds-noirs* (Paris, 2001), 281–9.
[93] Jordi, *De l'exode à l'exil*, 212–19.
[94] On the *Front National* and its *pied-noir* support base, see Chapter 8.

so-called 'couscous vote', yet it is important to stress that the *Front National's* appeal is not limited to *pieds-noirs*. The party's anti-immigration platform – one which targets France's Muslim population of North African origin as a major source of social and cultural ills – not only appeals to ex-settlers long accused of racism but to other metropolitan French opposed to non-white communities which form a substantial presence in southern cities like Marseille. *Pieds-noirs'* European ancestry thus enables them to occupy common ground with a portion of the white French majority at the same time that a cultural distinctiveness as former North African settlers ironically reveals similarities, such as eating couscous, with North African 'immigrants' they have long defined themselves against – both across the Mediterranean before 1962 and within the hexagon thereafter.

* * *

Portugal's *retornados*

While France's mass repatriation from Algeria in 1962 and its longer-term consequences has dominated accounts of colonial departures, Portugal's equivalent in the mid-1970s was more demographically significant by far. The vast majority of Portuguese returning to the metropole during and after the collapse of empire and the 'Carnation Revolution' of April 1974 came from just two territories: Angola, which had an estimated white population of 335,000, and Mozambique, where Europeans totalled approximately 200,000.[95] The remainder of Portugal's African territories had comparatively minute numbers of European Portuguese residents, and their repatriations went largely unnoticed at home. Estimated numbers of *retornados* ('returnees') from Angola, Mozambique, and elsewhere vary widely, but fall between 500,000 and 800,000. These included over 500,000 settlers in addition to over 200,000 troops returning home after the fight against African anti-colonial insurgents ended after over thirteen years of armed struggle.[96] At least 25,000–35,000 were either *mestiços* or Africans who arrived as Portuguese citizens, often as the spouses or children of persons born in Portugal.[97] Given that Portugal's population did not then exceed 9 million, *retornados* from Africa formed, relatively speaking, the most numerically significant influx of

[95] Jeanne Marie Penvenne, 'Settling Against the Tide: The Layered Contradictions of Twentieth-Century Portuguese Settlement in Mozambique', in Elkins and Pedersen (eds.), *Settler Colonialism*, 86.

[96] Colette Dubois, 'L'épineux dossier des retornados', in Miège and Dubois (eds.), *L'Europe retrouvée*, 230–1.

[97] Stephen C. Lubkemann, 'The Moral Economy of Portuguese Postcolonial Return', *Diaspora*, 11:2 (2002), 199.

all decolonization migrations into Europe, causing the resident population to grow by 5–10 per cent.

What is more, as with the Belgian and French examples, Portugal's decolonization influx occurred in a very short space of time, with much of it compressed into little over one year. Unlike Britain and the Netherlands where European-descended nationals arrived in smaller numbers and over a protracted period, Portugal's *retornados* were depicted as engaged in a panicked mass exodus from an Africa which, in many places, appeared on the brink of violence and chaos, if indeed it had not already fallen into the abyss thereof. When Portugal's African territories gained independence late in 1975, there were signs of white settler resistance to decolonization and a willingness by some to assume control themselves. Given settlers' political and military weakness, however, white minority governments stood no chance of success.[98]

Although some did initially hope to remain in Africa, in the end few did so: civil unrest and the nationalization of their property by newly independent African governments further speeded up the departure of nearly all Europeans and many *mestiços*. Ryszard Kapuściński, a journalist observing the last days of Portuguese rule in Angola, described a general mood and conditions in the second half of 1975 that recall those prevailing among Belgians in the Congo in July 1960 and European settlers' departures from Algeria soon afterwards. Scrambling for the Luanda airport and fighting for seats on the next flight out,

they took it apathetically, with dismal resignation . . . The revolution [in Portugal] was to blame for everything, they said, because before that it had been peaceful. Now the government had promised the blacks freedom and the blacks had come to blows among themselves, burning and murdering. They aren't capable of governing . . . I put forty years of work in here. The sweat of my damn brow. Who will give it back to me now? Do you think anybody can start life all over again?[99]

Departing Portuguese abandoned businesses, houses, cars, and often pets – in many cases nearly everything they owned aside from the bare minimum of luggage.[100]

That many landed in Lisbon with few belongings was a reflection not only of the circumstances of their departure: their impoverished status upon arrival in turn illustrated the poorer socio-economic backgrounds of many Portuguese both before and during their years in Africa. Middle- and upper-class Portuguese, although not completely absent from colonial society, were not the preponderant classes to make their way to Africa during the decades after

[98] Malyn Newitt, *Portugal in Africa: The Last Hundred Years* (London, 1981), 246; Norrie MacQueen, *The Decolonization of Portuguese Africa: Metropolitan Revolution and the Dissolution of Empire* (Harrow, 1997), chs. 5 and 6.
[99] Ryszard Kapuściński, *Another Day of Life* (New York, 2001 [1976]), 10–11.
[100] Ibid., 18, 25, 46; Lee, *I Was Born in Africa*, 77, 91.

the Second World War when the government stepped up its promotion of white settlement in the nation's 'overseas provinces'. Typically of impoverished rural peasant origins and often illiterate, Portuguese who had sought a new life in Mozambique or Angola did so because few opportunities for advancement were available locally. Just as many left rural areas of northern Portugal to seek work in northern Europe (France and West Germany being the most popular destinations), others opted for Africa, sometimes to work in agriculture but more often to live in cities and find employment as manual workers, staff the lower echelons of the service sector, or run small businesses. Like Europeans in French North Africa, many remained relatively poor overseas, others moved into the lower middle class, and few counted among the wealthy. Upon return-ing home with decolonization, most had scant economic resources on which to draw.

Just as significantly, *retornados* arrived back in a nation that had long counted among the poorest and least developed in Western Europe and that was in the midst of a definitive political transformation at a time of global economic downturn. In the mid-1970s, Portugal's unemployment rate already stood at close to 10 per cent, and this was further aggravated by demobilized soldiers and settlers seeking jobs upon return from Africa.[101] Work and housing were in perennially short supply, and the new government's programmes to assist repatriates in the resettlement process often proved unable to meet their needs. Many *retornados*, particularly the majority who had gone to Africa less than a generation before, turned to family members who had remained at home for help, returning to their places of origin (frequently to the rural northeast). Others whose ties with the metropole had become attenuated – perhaps because they had been born in Africa or simply had resided there for decades without paying a return visit, or because they were mixed race – lacked a family network to turn to for support. Without an ancestral or childhood home in which to take refuge when their colonial world collapsed, many stayed in Lisbon, Setúbal, Porto, or Faro, where finding housing and work seemed more likely.[102] The least fortunate ended up living in shantytown settlements outside Lisbon and other cities, a 'temporary' form of accommodation that sometimes lasted years.

Retornados of all descriptions experienced strong resentment from their fellow countrymen, family included. Interviews conducted by Stephen Lubkemann suggest some of the sentiments that Portuguese who had not been part of overseas communities in Africa felt not only about repatriates, but about the nation's failed African projects. Upon return, 'even our family

[101] William J. Carrington and Pedro J.F. de Lima, 'The Impact of 1970s Repatriates from Africa on the Portuguese Labor Market', *Industrial and Labor Relations Review*, 49:2 (1996), 330–47.
[102] R. Pena Pires *et al.*, *Os Retornados: Um Estudo Sociográfico* (Lisbon, 1984), 56–60.

members did not want to know us . . . They said that we had exploited the blacks to have an easy life and now we wanted to exploit our families too' after leaving Africa destitute.[103] 'Even though we had lost everything, people would say that we had not worked to get what we had in the first place', recalled another. Those who had profited at Africans' expense subsequently became viewed as parasites upon a Portuguese host: 'when I wanted to work I was called an "exploiter" . . . If I could not find work, then I was called a degenerate who wanted to "abuse the charity of the Portuguese".'[104]

Some commentators accused *retornados* of being anti-revolutionary reactionaries, dangerously out of step with the new political order after April 1974. Such views appeared prominently in the leftist press, which condemned them as 'minions of colonial repression' who now posed a threat to the post-dictatorship democracy at home.[105] Widely seen as the agents and beneficiaries of the nation's former colonial dreams that had proved costly failures, they became discredited in tandem with empire itself after Portugal failed to fulfil its overseas ambitions.[106] At times, insults levelled against *retornados* placed them outside the boundaries of legitimate Portugueseness on account of their African ties. One woman who had struggled to find work as a cleaner recalled how 'the crew boss was very abusive and always said that we *retornadas* stole work from the Portuguese and should go back to our own place in Africa'.[107] Whether *retornados* were white or of mixed Portuguese and African ancestry, many comments suggest that they became racialized following their return from settler communities: refusals to rent houses to *retornados* were attributed to the idea that 'we would not act civilized because we were used to the way things were in Africa'.[108]

In the face of widespread suspicion, hostility, and impoverishment, some *retornados* opted to re-emigrate. A significant minority resettled in the world's largest Portuguese-speaking nation that had achieved independence from the metropole in a decolonization episode more than a century before: Brazil. Others chose not to return in the first place, preferring to move to nearby South Africa or Rhodesia – in effect embarking upon a path similar to that chosen by Britons and other ex-colonizers who wanted to continue living outside Europe in areas where white minority rule remained firmly ensconced.[109] Yet most did resettle permanently in Portugal and embarked

---

[103] Stephen C. Lubkemann, 'Race, Class, and Kin in the Negotiation of "Internal Strangerhood" among Portuguese Retornados, 1975-2000', in Smith (ed.), *Europe's Invisible Migrants*, 83.

[104] Lubkemann, 'Moral Economy', 197–8.   [105] Ibid., 191.

[106] Ricardo E. Ovalle-Bahamón, 'The Wrinkles of Decolonization and Nationness: White Angolans as Retornados in Portugal', in Smith (ed.), *Europe's Invisible Migrants*, 162–5.

[107] Lubkemann, 'Moral Economy', 201.   [108] Ibid., 197.

[109] Dubois, 'L'épineux dossier', 228–31; Jim R. Lewis and Allan M. Williams, 'Portugal's Retornados: Reintegration or Rejection?', *Iberian Studies*, 14:1–2 (1985), 13; Marcos Toffoli da Silva, 'Entre vítimas e algozes: dilemas da "comunidade portuguesa" na África do

on the struggle to find work and accommodations. *Retornados'* attempts to win state compensation for having 'lost everything' in Africa never succeeded and anger at the government they held responsible for decolonization persisted, yet repatriated Portuguese never materialized as the right-wing political threat some in the metropole had initially feared.[110] Instead, the occupational and educational skills gained while living in Africa ultimately helped many situate themselves considerably higher on Portugal's socioeconomic ladder than would have been likely had they never lived overseas.[111] Having worked in service-sector occupations or lower-level government jobs in the colonies enabled many to gain a foothold in these niches back home, even if they had started out as impoverished peasants prior to living in Africa. Small businesses, groceries, and restaurants with names such as 'Café Luanda' or 'Lourenço Marques Market' served both as spatial memorials of Portugal's recent history in southern Africa and as evidence of the diverse ways *retornados* came to earn their livelihoods over the medium term.

Portugal's improved economic fortunes during the 1980s facilitated *retornados'* reintegration within mainstream society.[112] In time, they effectively disappeared as a topic of wider discussion and as a outwardly proclaimed identity.[113] Colonial names of businesses and ongoing private *retornado* friendship networks aside, many publicly downplayed their connection with Africa that had turned into a stigma in the mid-1970s. They preferred to stress what they had in common with other Portuguese rather than the ways that having once belonged to a colonial settler society set them apart. A key factor underlying the tendency for many to suppress an identity rooted in colonialism and decolonization was the racial connotation contained within the *retornado* label. As noted earlier, metropolitan hostility towards repatriates encompassed accusations that they were racist exploiters of Africans and also suggested that their status as Portuguese had become qualified by virtue of having been part of a multiracial African society. In contrast to the deeply rooted ideology of lusotropicalism that stressed racial equality as a central plank within official justifications of the nation's imperial projects during the dictatorship (as discussed in Chapter 5), biases against *retornados* partly hinged on the 'connotations of potential racialized difference' of the term within the popular

Sul pós-*apartheid*', in Daniel Melo and Eduardo Caetano da Silva (eds.), *Construção da Nação e Associativismo na Emigração Portuguesa* (Lisbon, 2009), 273–301.

[110] António Costa Pinto, 'Dealing with the Legacy of Authoritarianism: Political Purges and Radical Right Movements in Portugal's Transition to Democracy, 1974–1980s', in Stein Ugelvik Larsen (ed.), *Modern Europe after Fascism, 1943–1980s*, Vol. II (Boulder, 1998), 1707–8.

[111] Lewis and Williams, 'Portugal's Retornados', 17–19.

[112] Stephen C. Lubkemann, 'Unsettling the Metropole: Race and Settler Reincorporation in Postcolonial Portugal', in Elkins and Pedersen (eds.), *Settler Colonialism*, 265.

[113] Rui Pena Pires, *Migrações e Integração* (Oeiras, Portugal, 2003), ch. 4.

imagination.[114] Because of the noticeable minority who were *mestiço* or African, those who were white often sought to ease their own reintegration by distancing themselves from those whose skin colour rendered them visibly 'other'.[115]

While *'retornado'* was thus originally a multiracial category, this quality ultimately explained its near-disappearance as those who were white simultaneously dissociated themselves from the stigma of defunct colonialism and from those who remained socially excluded on account of their colour and ancestry. The former largely merged with the white Portuguese majority, while the latter suffered ongoing rejection as 'Africans' or 'blacks' like other postcolonial migrants considered in Chapter 7.[116] Yet for all that they largely failed to constitute a notable public presence in the decades immediately after migration, a substantial segment of Portugal's population continued to claim direct ties with the nation's imperial past that had only recently passed into history. As Chapter 9 will show, *retornados'* stories ultimately resurfaced and acquired new public resonance in the early twenty-first century. Like repatriates elsewhere in Europe, those in Portugal would also emerge to help shape how imperial pasts are remembered, reinvented, and forgotten at a later date.

* * *

Decolonizing the colonizer

Repatriates have recurrently acted as a barometer for wider European attitudes about lost empires at particular historical moments. Were they ideally to be reincorporated and assimilated into metropolitan societies and their imperial pasts obliterated? Rendering former colonials who came home socially invisible and ignoring their overseas histories arguably facilitates a similar erasure of the domestic dimensions and aftereffects of European empires. Failing to attend to what stories of their imperial lives and afterlives can tell about the decline, fall, and aftermath of colonialism constitutes a missed opportunity to gain a deeper understanding of how these processes affected Europe and Europeans, not just peoples and places formerly under European rule.

---

[114] Lubkemann, 'Moral Economy', 199.
[115] Ibid., 199, 203, 206; Lubkemann, 'Unsettling the Metropole', 258, 299; Lubkemann, 'Race, Class, and Kin', 88–9, 92. Luís Batalha discusses related themes in *The Cape Verdean Diaspora in Portugal: Colonial Subjects in a Postcolonial World* (Lanham, MD, 2004), ch. 4.
[116] Cecilie Øien, 'Of Homecomings and Homesickness: The Question of White Angolans in Post-Colonial Portugal', in Eve Rosenhaft and Robbie Aitken (eds.), *Africa in Europe: Studies in Transnational Practice in the Long Twentieth Century* (Liverpool, 2013), 183–200; see especially 189–94.

Important though it is to keep the history of ex-colonials alive, rationales for doing so can serve drastically different agendas. Ghost worlds of former empires and former colonizers periodically have gained a new lease on life in postcolonial Europe, often through the concerted efforts of repatriated individuals and groups eager for their own, and their nation's, overseas histories to be remembered after the fact. In critical respects former colonials share common ground with scholars who insist on the connected, entangled histories of European nations and their former empires and the need for them to be better known, not neglected or forgotten; moreover, they know firsthand that the experience of colonialism continued to resonate and shape both Europe and Europeans long after decolonization. The similarities end, however, when scholarly critiques of colonialism, decolonization, and those personally implicated clash with accounts which are nostalgic, revisionist, or largely celebratory – a topic that will be taken up again later in this book.

As this chapter has indicated, a variety of labels became applied to persons of European origin who re-established themselves in the Netherlands, Britain, Belgium, France, or Portugal when overseas empires came to an end. Taken literally, 'repatriate' did not accurately describe those embarking on their first trip to Europe, and its use suggested a willingness to accept people whose identities had taken shape far away as legitimate members of a reconfigured national community by emphasizing what they shared in common with the metropolitan majority. 'Refugees' or 'victims' were appellations intended to garner public sympathy for those who, as was repeatedly asserted, had 'lost everything' when they left former colonial arenas where their presence had become untenable through violent conflicts involving metropolitan policymakers and armies, anti-colonial nationalists, and settlers. Other designations such as 'Indisch Dutch' or '*pieds-noirs*' singled out some decolonization arrivals as distinct on the grounds of their ethnicity and/or their colonial heritage. The variety of terms used at different times and in different places serves as an important reminder that such people lacked uniform experiences of empire and decolonization alike. Equally important, they reveal the ambivalent, changing, and often controversial place of former colonials within nations engaged in the drawn-out process of decolonizing themselves.

Racial identity has proven one of the most crucial determinants shaping how ex-colonizers have become part of postcolonial Europe. Repatriates who were of mixed racial ancestry had to struggle far more to be accepted as Europeans, while white ex-colonials were often promptly forgotten after their return and subsequently neglected by historians because they appeared to blend in with the metropolitan majority. The mid- to late twentieth-century resettlement of colonial Europeans and Eurasians alike occurred alongside the arrival of substantial ethnic minority populations from colonies and former colonies, a

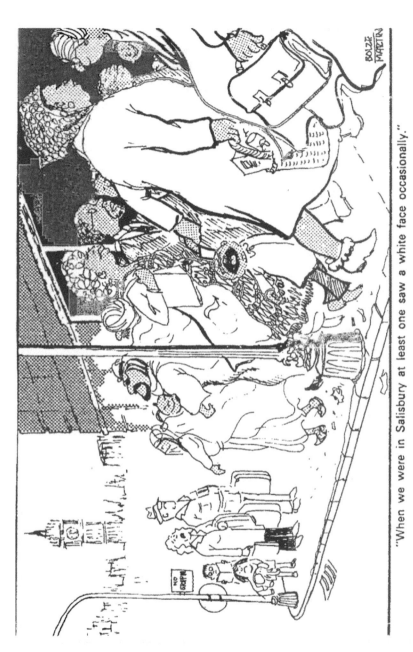

"When we were in Salisbury at least one saw a white face occasionally."

Figure 6.2 Louis Bolze and Rose Martin, *The Whenwes of Rhodesia* (Bulawayo: Books of Rhodesia Press, 1978), 23. Depiction of white Rhodesians newly returned to London, observing a multiethnic population that visually dominates the image.

topic to which Chapter 7 now turns. More than any other factor, the growing presence of formerly colonized racial 'others' in post-1945 Europe enabled ex-colonizers who had been overseas to converge with those who had never left their homeland – often on account not only of shared ethnicity, but also shared understandings of racial difference.

7   Ethnic minority immigration
from empires lost

Introduction

In 1965, *The Times* published a series of reports discussing Britain's 'Dark Million' – 'immigrants' from the nation's former colonies who had settled in large numbers, mainly after the Second World War. Rendering the link between Britain's imperial history and its current experiences of migration explicit, one segment launched with a stanza from Rudyard Kipling's 1899 poem 'The White Man's Burden', referring to the populations colonizers governed in the empire. The journalist reflected:

The heavy harness has been thrown off. The British Empire is gone. 'New caught sullen peoples' have been given independence and may live next door to old men who were alive when Kipling's verse was written. Well may they think that the British have been in retreat ever since they won the last war, and that the debris of a falling Empire has crashed into their own backyards.

    In a Bradford café . . . I overheard two old men talking . . . They were lamenting the change – the coming of the Pakistanis with their alien habits. 'Once we were great,' [one] said. 'We had the most powerful navy in the world. We used to export to India. Now their blokes come over here . . . Another old man, in Warwickshire, who had fought for his country and been badly wounded, also spoke of the days of glory when the Navy was strong. When coloured people came, he bought property to stop them coming next to his, to prevent the value falling.[1]

In this rendition, imperial decline followed former greatness as Britain proved unable to defend its shores against the arrival of Pakistanis and others, peoples now rhetorically reconfigured as 'debris' once they came too close to home and encroached upon neighbourhoods, streets, and private homes.

With the decline and loss of empire, postcolonial migration became imagined as the new 'white man's burden' and 'heavy harness' as venerable aging war veterans made valiant efforts to protect the value of their homes. Peoples long ruled by the British overseas arrived deeply imbued with the history of empire – a history white Britons remembered and misremembered in equal measure. While some commentators imagined empire as signifying both a burden and a source of greatness for Britain, others provided less affirmative

---

[1] 'British workers see ghosts of their past in immigrants' trials', *The Times* (London), 23 January 1965.

assessments. When asked whether he thought 'coloured colonials should be allowed to go on coming into this country' in a mid-1950s survey, a British machine operator in Coventry offered an alternative response. Nonetheless, his too was similarly steeped in allusions to a longer history, both of empire and immigration: 'We've been there long enough and exploited them, so now they come here – just like the Irish and others.'[2]

Had empire been a burden for the colonizers or exploitation for the colonized? Regardless of how the imperial past was judged in the decades when it drew to a close, commentators were in no doubt about the direct link between Britain's activities overseas and their demographic repercussions at home. Both the old men at the Bradford café and the worker in Coventry described the arrival and settlement of 'coloured' people as a recent phenomenon – a symptom of the post-war 'now'. Understandings of immigration from the colonies and former colonies as new and unprecedented after 1945 were equally apparent within other Western European nations during the decades of overseas decolonization. But as was also the case in France, the Netherlands, Portugal, and Belgium (if to varying degrees), in Britain centuries of overseas colonization had involved not only European comings and goings between metropole and colony but also a long-term presence of colonized peoples 'at home' as well as 'away'. Scholars have charted a history of blacks and Asians in Britain, for example, that predates the modern era but which expanded during the eighteenth, nineteenth, and early twentieth centuries.[3] Similarly, during as well as between the First and Second World Wars, Britain and France both experienced a substantial colonial influx as West Indians, Africans, and Asians travelled to Europe as workers, soldiers, artists, intellectuals, and in countless other capacities.[4] What changed after 1945 was not the mere

---

[2] Michael Banton, *White and Coloured: The Behaviour of British People Towards Coloured Immigrants* (London, 1959), 84–5.

[3] Peter Fryer, *Staying Power: The History of Black People in Britain* (London, 1984); Rozina Visram, *Asians in Britain: 400 Years of History* (London, 2002); Humayun Ansari, *'The Infidel Within': Muslims in Britain since 1800* (London, 2003); Antoinette Burton, *At the Heart of the Empire: Indians and the Colonial Encounter in Late-Victorian Britain* (Berkeley, 1998); Michael H. Fisher, *Counterflows to Colonialism: Indian Travellers and Settlers in Britain, 1600–1857* (New Delhi, 2004); Jonathan Schneer, *London 1900: Imperial Metropolis* (New Haven, 1999).

[4] Barbara Bush, *Imperialism, Race, and Resistance: Africa and Britain, 1919–1945* (London, 1999); Philippa Levine, 'Battle Colors: Race, Sex, and Colonial Soldiery in World War I', *Journal of Women's History*, 9:4 (1998), 104–30; David Omissi, 'Europe Through Indian Eyes: Indian Soldiers Encounter England and France, 1914–1918', *English Historical Review*, 122:496 (2007), 371–96; Paul Rich, *Race and Empire in British Politics* (Cambridge, 1986), 120–68; Sonya O. Rose, *Which People's War?: National Identity and Citizenship in Wartime Britain, 1939–1945* (Oxford, 2003); ch. 7; Bill Schwarz, 'Black Metropolis, White England', in Mica Nava and Alan O'Shea (eds.), *Modern Times: Reflections on a Century of English Modernity* (London, 1996), 176–207; Laura Tabili, *'We Ask for British Justice': Black Workers and the Construction of Racial Difference in Late Imperial Britain* (Ithaca, 1994); Hakim Adi, *West Africans in Britain: 1900–1960* (London, 1998). On France, see citations listed below.

existence of colonized and formerly colonized peoples within Western Europe, but the fact that their arrival and permanent settlement involved far greater numbers than before in response to political and social transformations.

While not identifying the so-called 'coloured' newcomers of his own times with more deeply entrenched patterns of travels and settlement by colonial peoples, the Coventry worker explicitly juxtaposed non-European and European minorities. As he noted, 'the Irish and others', including Jews, were equally central to Britain's history of immigration. Although white, Europeans of many national and religious backgrounds had also been singled out as racially or ethnically distinct in ways that evolved throughout the modern period, and which remained in evidence after the Second World War.[5] The late 1940s, for example, saw Britain recruit European Volunteer Workers, or EVWs, including many Eastern Europeans whom the war had turned into displaced persons or refugees.[6]

In consequence, it would be inaccurate to describe the immense variety of migrations that changed the face of Western Europe's decolonizing and former imperial powers as strictly colonial or postcolonial in nature.[7] Global migration created transnational diasporas that were not restricted to colonized and formerly colonized peoples settling in the particular metropole that governed, or once governed, their territories. Congolese travelled not only to Belgium but just as commonly relocated to France, while Moroccans migrated to Belgium and the Netherlands alongside France. What is more, many of Britain's, Belgium's, and France's immigrants came from Eastern and Southern Europe. Portugal, meanwhile, long sent many more migrants to France and other European countries than it received from its own erstwhile colonies in Africa, taking much longer than other postcolonial metropoles to become a nation of immigration as well as emigration. These population flows were part of a wider phenomenon whereby peoples from underdeveloped or politically oppressive or unstable regions sought greater opportunities in more economically advanced countries, not just in Western Europe but also in North America.

---

[5] David Cesarani (ed.), *The Making of Modern Anglo-Jewry* (Oxford, 1990); Enda Delaney, *The Irish in Post-war Britain* (Oxford, 2007); Todd M. Endelman, *The Jews of Britain, 1656 to 2000* (Berkeley, 2002); David Feldman, *Englishmen and Jews: Social Relations and Political Culture, 1840–1914* (New Haven, 1994); Mary J. Hickman, 'Reconstructing Deconstructing "Race": British Political Discourses about the Irish in Britain', *Ethnic and Racial Studies*, 21:2 (1998), 288–307; Roger Swift and Sheridan Gilley (eds.), *The Irish in Britain, 1815–1939* (London, 1989).

[6] Kathleen Paul, *Whitewashing Britain: Race and Citizenship in the Postwar Era* (Ithaca, NY, 1997), ch. 3; Diana Kay and Robert Miles, *Refugees or Migrant Workers?: European Volunteer Workers in Britain, 1946–1951* (London, 1992).

[7] For an exemplary discussion that juxtaposes Commonwealth and European migration to Britain, see Wendy Webster, 'The Empire Comes Home: Commonwealth Migration to Britain', in Andrew Thompson (ed.), *Britain's Experience of Empire in the Twentieth Century, Oxford History of the British Empire Companion Series* (Oxford, 2012), 122–60.

These caveats aside, the extent to which these Western European nations have been remade in social, cultural, and economic terms by the settlement of peoples from their own former empires remains decisive, even when other factors must necessarily render the story far more complex. With the exception of Belgium, ex-colonized peoples have dominated new arrivals to these countries both numerically and in the popular and official imagination. The following sections consider the social and ethnic diversity along with the timing of these migrations, examining both newcomers' experiences and common responses to different groups within the receiving countries. The racism that greeted ethnic minorities from declining empires and recently decolonized regions after the Second World War owed much to both the lasting impact of colonial institutions and outlooks along with the resilient mentalities they bred among Europeans accustomed to viewing the colonized as unequal inferiors. But despite its destructive prevalence, racism does not tell the whole story of encounters between white Europeans and non-European immigrants, and instances of tolerance, cultural exchange, and accommodation can be identified throughout the period. Nonetheless, anxieties about new forms of proximity were unquestionably widespread when the 'empire struck back', with many fearing that European nations and cultures were under threat and 'invaded' from without. This chapter explores the first phases of mass migration and settlement which occurred at different junctures after 1945, when those long viewed from a distance suddenly came close to home and possibly even moved in next door. Chapter 8 then takes up longer-term consequences as Western Europe became increasingly multicultural over the course of several generations.

* * *

Britain's late imperial and New Commonwealth settlers

The 1948 arrival of the *S.S. Empire Windrush* carrying 492 West Indians seeking new lives in the 'mother country' proved an emblematic event in the history of black Britain. Symbolically inaugurating the mass settlement of people from the Caribbean and coinciding with the British Nationality Act, it signalled not only a more numerous and permanent black presence, but also reflected their belief that they belonged. Their sense of entitlement was fully justified: as Chapter 1 noted, the 1948 Nationality Act aimed to strengthen Britain's relations with its colonies and former colonies within the Commonwealth by formalizing migration and settlement rights for all subjects of these territories, irrespective of colour. Colonial and Commonwealth subjects were British citizens by law. As such, although commonly referred to as 'immigrants' both then and now, other terminology such as 'migrants', 'settlers', or 'black Britons' is more apt, as Winston James has argued. The movement of people from the British West Indies, India and Pakistan, and British Africa was 'more akin to internal migration' as those travelling were legally British citizens circulating within the empire and Commonwealth.[8]

Passengers aboard the *Windrush* sailed from the West Indies with a spirit of optimism and confidence in their claims to a rightful place in Britain, an outlook crystallized in a calypso lyric composed en route by the Trinidadian Aldwyn Roberts. More famously known as Lord Kitchener, he sang 'London is the Place for Me' on camera for reporters upon arrival, celebrating 'this lovely city' where 'the English people are very much sociable':

> Well, believe me I am speaking broad-mindedly
> I am glad to know my mother country
> I've been travelling to countries years ago
> But this is the place I wanted to go
> London, that's the place for me.[9]

Lord Kitchener succinctly captured the high hopes of those embarking for Britain while also alluding to the well-established patterns of labour migration within the empire and the colonial culture underpinning their journeys and outlooks.[10] Britain was responsible for the black diaspora's very existence in its West Indian possessions, having participated in the African slave trade until its abolition in 1807. The Caribbean's plantation economy persisted beyond the abolition of slavery in 1833–1834, although the once-lucrative sector fell into steepening decline thereafter. Chronically high unemployment and economic underdevelopment in the West Indies meant that many residents had prior histories of 'travelling to countries years ago', like the United States and Panama, for work; Britain was only one destination within a constellation of others.[11] Indeed, migration to Britain reached much higher levels after 1952 when the United States' McCarran-Walter Immigration Act placed severe restrictions on the number of West Indians permitted to enter annually, thereby redirecting most prospective immigrants to other labour markets. Jamaica sent

---

[8] Winston James, 'The Black Experience in Twentieth-Century Britain', in Philip D. Morgan and Sean Hawkins (eds.), *The Black Experience and the Empire, Oxford History of the British Empire Companion Series* (Oxford, 2004), 349; Paul, *Whitewashing Britain*, chs. 5–7; Randall Hansen, *Citizenship and Immigration in Post-war Britain: The Institutional Origins of a Multicultural Nation* (Oxford, 2000), ch. 2.

[9] Lord Kitchener, 'London is the Place for Me', *London is the Place for Me: Trinidadian Calypso in London, 1950–1956*, Honest John Records (London, 2002).

[10] Hugh Hodges, 'Kitchener Invades England: The London Calypsos of Aldwyn Roberts', *Wasafiri* 45 (summer 2005), 24–30; Stuart Hall, 'Calypso Kings', *Guardian* (London), 28 June 2002.

[11] Harry Goulbourne and Mary Chamberlain (eds.), *Caribbean Families in Britain and the Trans-Atlantic World* (London, 2001); Mary Chamberlain, *Narratives of Exile and Return* (London, 1997).

the largest numbers of migrants to Britain, although Trinidad, Barbados, British Guiana, and other territories were also well represented.

In the late 1940s and early 1950s, Britain's post-war labour shortage and expanding economy meant that policymakers and employers actively recruited workers from the colonies, the Commonwealth, and Europe. Like West Indians, South Asians arriving in Britain often hailed from regions and social sectors long decisively shaped by mobility within an imperial political economy which became reworked upon decolonization. Britain's South Asian population largely claims its origins in Punjab, Azad Kashmir ('free Kashmir', controlled by Pakistan), Gujarat, Sylhet (in Bengal, now part of Bangladesh), and East Africa, the latter effectively having become 'twice migrants' after having first left India for Africa and then relocating to Britain.[12] Punjab and Kashmir suffered from rural underdevelopment alongside political and population upheaval with the partition of British India into independent India and Pakistan in 1947, with the former being divided and the latter becoming a disputed territory between the two states. Moreover, since the nineteenth century Punjabi Sikh and Muslim men along with Kashmiris had been prominent within the British armed forces. Military service both elsewhere in South Asia and further afield in the British empire made these communities ideally positioned to be aware of, and take advantage of, employment opportunities within an imperial or post-imperial rubric. Men from the Mirpur district of Azad Kashmir and from Sylhet were also well represented in the labour force of British steamships and thus familiar with overseas travel, work, and residence. Most South Asians who relocated to British East Africa in the nineteenth and twentieth centuries, meanwhile, hailed from Gujarat. Some went as indentured workers to build the railways, while others found opportunities in the commercial and service sectors. As British passport holders, East African Asians either were expelled from, or fled, Kenya, Uganda, or other neighbouring regions following their decolonization and the assumption of power by African nationalist governments in the late 1960s and early 1970s.[13]

Although significant numbers of South Asians, Africans, and others did migrate to Britain in the late 1940s and 1950s, until the early 1960s West Indians constituted the vast majority of Britain's new arrivals from the colonies and Commonwealth and thus dominated public discussions of 'immigration'. One study published in 1960 estimated that the non-white population then

[12] Roger Ballard (ed.), *Desh Pardesh: The South Asian Presence in Britain* (London, 1994); Avtar Brah, *Cartographies of Diaspora: Contesting Identities* (London, 1996); Judith M. Brown, *Global South Asians: Introducing the Diaspora* (Cambridge, 2006); Parminder Bhachu, *Twice Migrants: East African Sikh Settlers in Britain* (London, 1985).

[13] Nasreen Ali, 'Imperial Implosions: Postcoloniality and the Orbits of Migration', and Ceri Peach, 'Demographics of BrAsian Settlement, 1951–2001', in N. Ali, V.S. Kalra, and S. Sayyid (eds.), *A Postcolonial People: South Asians in Britain* (London, 2006), 158–67 and 168–81.

living in Britain totalled approximately 210,000, including 115,000 West Indians, 25,000 West Africans, 55,000 Indians and Pakistanis, and 15,000 from other territories.[14] Most had arrived during the mid-1950s on account of the British economy's labour needs. The 1960s saw South Asian new arrivals peak when the Indian and Pakistani governments stopped restricting emigration and raised the number of passports they issued to their nationals. Foreseeing moves by the British government to place limits first on numbers and then on primary migration altogether (which respectively came to pass with the 1962 and 1968 Commonwealth Immigration Acts and subsequent legislation), Indian and Pakistani efforts to 'beat the ban' characterized the 1960s. In combination with the East African Asian influx starting at the end of the decade, this caused Britain's population of South Asian origin to grow to 112,000 in 1961 and then increase to 516,000 by 1971.[15] As will be explored later in this chapter, 1971 marked the end of primary immigration from these regions.

Of highly diverse social and regional origins, most colonial and Commonwealth citizens arrived as blue-collar workers, but a minority were middle or upper class. During the post-war decades, colonial and Commonwealth students became a growing presence at British universities and other higher education institutions, and in the mid-1950s they already numbered about 11,000.[16] Most students intended to return home once they completed their studies, but some stayed to embark upon careers. Others arrived having completed degrees overseas and entered the professions, with Indian doctors staffing the National Health Service being a prime example of the cross-class nature of migration and settlement. West Indian intellectuals and writers like George Lamming, C.L.R. James, and Sam Selvon, alongside their Asian and African counterparts, often had formative experiences in Britain which decisively shaped their writing and thinking, whether or not they were to remain permanently or return home.[17]

---

[14] Donald Wood, 'A General Survey', in J.A.G. Griffith, Judith Henderson, Margaret Usbourne, and Donald Wood (eds.), *Coloured Immigrants in Britain* (London, 1960), 9.

[15] Peach, 'Demographics', 168–9.

[16] A.T. Carey, *Colonial Students: A Study of the Social Adaptation of Colonial Students in London* (London, 1956), 11; Political and Economic Planning, *Colonial Students in Britain* (London, 1956); J.M. Lee, 'Commonwealth Students in the United Kingdom, 1940–1960: Student Welfare and World Status', *Minerva* 44:1 (2006), 1–24; A.J. Stockwell, 'Leaders, Dissidents and the Disappointed: Colonial Students in Britain as Empire Ended', *Journal of Imperial and Commonwealth History*, 36:3 (2008), 487–501; Jordanna Bailkin, *The Afterlife of Empire* (Berkeley, 2012), ch. 3.

[17] Bill Schwarz (ed.), *West Indian Intellectuals in Britain* (Manchester, 2003); Shompa Lahiri, 'South Asians in Post-imperial Britain: Decolonisation and Imperial Legacy', in Stuart Ward (ed.), *British Culture and the End of Empire* (Manchester, 2001), 200–16; Bhikhu Parekh (ed.), *Colour, Culture and Consciousness: Immigrant Intellectuals in Britain* (London, 1974).

Equally important, while men initially dominated colonial and Commonwealth migration in numerical terms, women were present among the 'coloured' population throughout this period. Prior to family reunification when wives (and children) came in larger numbers to join men who had previously settled, women also came independently or with family members to study or to work in their own right. West Indian nurses and other hospital staff, for example, played central roles in running the National Health Service alongside Indian doctors.[18] Britain's post-war welfare state, not to mention many industries, relied heavily upon personnel from overseas from its very outset. Recognition of this fact generated some appreciation but also widespread concern about the social and cultural consequences.[19]

Despite the heterogeneity of Britain's growing black and Asian population along class, gender, and other lines, however, men – and young working-class men specifically – formed the bulk of these expanding communities. In the British popular imagination of the 1950s, the 'typical immigrant' was likely to be a young single man from the West Indies, while by the 1960s Indian and Pakistani men gained greater visibility in tandem with their expanding numbers.[20] Women and children took longer to receive comparable levels of attention. Black and Asian men were imagined as menials rather than professionals, doing jobs that many working-class whites considered beneath them at a time of economic expansion and full employment. Significantly, a number who came to Britain and performed unskilled work upon arrival had counted as highly skilled workers or as middle-class professionals back home. Having completed higher education, some arrived in Britain to find their qualifications unrecognized and entry into comparable careers effectively closed. As one Indian man who settled in Birmingham in the late 1950s later remarked, 'I didn't know any school-teacher at that time, I didn't know anybody working in bank or office jobs, even those people who have been graduated who worked as teachers back home, they were working in the factories or foundries.'[21] Britain may have offered higher wages, but migration commonly spelled a relative social decline. Understood as labourers (and often taking the unpopular night shifts) in the car and metal factories in West Midlands areas like Birmingham or Wolverhampton, in textile mills in West Yorkshire cities like Bradford, or as factory and service-sector workers in London, 'coloured' men tended to be viewed not as individuals but as a generic category. Some distinctions were

[18] Wendy Webster, *Imagining Home: Gender, 'Race', and National Identity, 1945–64* (London, 1998); Brah, *Cartographies*.
[19] 'Life Would Be Harder For All of Us Without Coloured Labour', *The Times*, 27 January 1965.
[20] Marcus Collins, 'Pride and Prejudice: West Indian Men in Mid-Twentieth-Century Britain', *Journal of British Studies*, 40 (2001), 391–418.
[21] Avtar Singh Jouhl, in Doreen Price and Ravi Thiara (eds.), *The Land of Money?: Personal Accounts by Post-War Black Migrants to Birmingham* (Birmingham, 1992), 16.

drawn between blacks and Asians (but often not within these broad groupings), but racial discrimination and stereotyping crossed ethnic lines.

White British attitudes towards 'coloured' peoples settling among them were strongly marked by deeply-entrenched colonial ideologies and prejudices, mindsets that outlived the end of empire to survive well into the postcolonial period. These collided head-on with distinct self-understandings and preconceptions about Britain brought by colonized and formerly colonized newcomers. When Lord Kitchener wrote his 'London is the Place for Me' calypso in 1948, he became only one of many, particularly from the Caribbean, to claim Britain as his 'mother country'. Accounts by West Indian workers and students alike stressed how their colonial upbringing meant that they arrived 'very familiar with English and British culture, had been nursed on it' in schools modelled upon British institutions.[22] But Donald Hinds, who worked as a bus conductor, recounted 'the sudden realization that all the years of coaching could offer little to his being at home in Britain'; time in his 'mother country' spelled 'the shattering of the great illusion' of allegiance and belonging.[23] Elliott Bastien, a student from Trinidad, reflected that middle-class West Indians 'feel that they know the English. They expect a certain reciprocity which in the majority of cases is non-existent. This is their first realization that they are different. Soon they are complimented on the standard of their English. Very good for a foreigner!'[24]

Even though they were formally British citizens, native speakers of English, Christian, and possessed other cultural similarities, West Indians were thus largely denied belonging on account of racial difference. The lack of reciprocity Bastien highlighted also extended to the forms of knowledge common among migrants and those amongst whom they settled. West Indians' prior exposure to British culture at home was met with Britons' ignorance about the West Indies – and, for that matter, other parts of what had been their empire until very recently. Hinds recalled one Englishman's comment that 'We knew that you were there. It was not until we saw you in the streets that we started thinking that you were real . . . It always surprised me that you seemed to know so much about us.'[25] An Indian student noted that, despite exceptions, the incomprehension he encountered in Britain about what had long ranked as the 'jewel in the British Empire' continually stunned him. Hearing his country reduced to a 'land of snakes and crocodiles and rope-dancers' became a repeated occurrence.[26]

---

[22] Mervyn Morris, 'Feeling, Affection, Respect', in Henri Tajfel and John L. Dawson (eds.), *Disappointed Guests: Essays by African, Asian, and West Indian Students* (London, 1965), 13.

[23] Donald Hinds, *Journey to an Illusion: The West Indian in Britain* (London, 1966), 170, 173–4.

[24] Elliott Bastien, 'The Weary Road to Whiteness and the Hasty Retreat into Nationalism', in Tajfel and Dawson (eds.), *Disappointed Guests*, 48.

[25] Hinds, *Journey*, 173.

[26] Syed Ali Baquer, 'The File of Regrets', in Tajfel and Dawson (eds.), *Disappointed Guests*, 112.

A controversial contribution to the historiography of British culture and imperialism, Bernard Porter's *The Absent-Minded Imperialists* argues that the vast majority of the British population at home knew little and cared even less about the overseas empire prior to decolonization, as noted in Chapter 1.[27] On the surface, episodes like those related above might appear to support Porter's contentions with respect to the early post-war decades. So too would observations that few Britons ever distinguished between, or among, West Indians and Africans. 'Trinidad, Barbados, Dominica. Where is that? What part of Africa?', Bastien summarized.[28] Yet these prevalent views suggest forms of ignorance redolent with assumed knowledge – a knowledge, incomplete and inaccurate, that rested upon a history of differential power relations between Britain, the colonies, and their respective racialized populations.

A recurrent feature of the preconceptions many white Britons had about the colonies and former colonies linked blackness with inferiority and primitiveness (and, conversely, whiteness with superiority). Colonialism and its historical associations permeated white British attitudes across a wide social spectrum, with West Indians and South Asians experiencing racial and cultural stereotyping from educated and uneducated Britons alike. After coming from Jamaica to study at Oxford in the late 1950s, Mervyn Morris repeatedly had to tell people who complemented him on his English that it was his native language as much as theirs. Without ill intent, friends unconsciously used 'phrases harkening back to slavery, such as "working like a Black" and "nigger in the woodpile"', rarely pausing to recognize the meanings inherent in stock expressions.[29] Countless narratives described encounters with Britons who believed people in the Caribbean and elsewhere lived in trees or thatched huts, wearing neither clothes nor shoes.[30] A passage in Sam Selvon's 1956 novel *The Lonely Londoners* suggested that English people eagerly held onto preconceived ideas about black people overseas. As one West Indian character reflected, 'you can't put on any English accent for them or play ladeda or tell them you studying medicine in Oxford or try to be polite and civilise [sic] they don't want that sort of thing at all they want you to live up to the films and stories they hear about black people living primitive in the jungles'.[31] Social anthropologist Sheila Patterson attributed such attitudes to diverse forms of popular culture, including children's rhymes and toys ('Ten Little Nigger Boys'

---

[27] Bernard Porter, *The Absent-Minded Imperialists: Empire, Society, and Culture in Britain* (Oxford, 2004); Bernard Porter, 'What Did They Know of Empire', *History Today* 54:10 (2004), 42–8.

[28] Bastien, 'Weary Road', 48.   [29] Morris, 'Feeling, Affection, Respect', 7.

[30] Hinds, *Journey*, 174; Sheila Patterson, *Dark Strangers: A Study of West Indians in London* (Harmondsworth, 1965), 141, 213.

[31] Sam Selvon, *The Lonely Londoners* (London, 1995; originally published 1956), 108.

and golliwogs), 'nigger minstrels', films, and journalistic portrayals of 'Negroes' either as 'inferior but agreeable' or 'exotic, violent, and primitive'.[32]

Ideas that blacks and South Asians were markedly inferior to whites rested on the notion that Britain could be credited with whatever 'civilization' once-colonized peoples had achieved. 'We civilized you Indians', one Sri Lankan was informed by a fellow passenger on a train. 'I politely admonished that it was never too late in life to study history', he noted; 'The beneficial effects of British rule in Asia are often exaggerated.'[33] An Indian student, for his part, mused that the independence of colonial peoples spread an 'unspecified fear in an ex-Empire like Britain'. Long-standing beliefs in their role as 'civilizers' made the British 'uneasy living with immigrants of races they are unused to treating as equals'.[34] Patterson attributed the durability of such preconceptions to the 'considerable confusion and insecurity among all classes in Britain as the erosion of imperial power and national prestige continues'. Although it had become 'necessary to adopt new attitudes and to form new relationships with other nations and with former colonial dependants', many seemed unwilling to do so – a reluctance that may well explain the (wilful) ignorance and disdain behind strident assertions of migrants' primitiveness, inferiority, and distance from British culture.[35] While these views may have originated with older colonial stereotypes, they gained a new lease on life as Britain confronted the twin challenges of decolonization and the arrival of the formerly colonized. As previous chapters argued, decolonizing the colonizers once based overseas was never a simple or straightforward process, accomplished overnight; nor was decolonizing domestic culture and recasting prevalent understandings about former colonial subjects.

'Coloured immigration' for some commentators was tantamount to an 'unarmed invasion', as Lord Elton provocatively entitled a study he published in 1965. Elton was one of many observers to focus on 'invaded urban areas' that had attracted substantial black and Asian settlement, such as Birmingham, Bradford, and areas of London like Paddington, Notting Hill, Southall, and Brixton.[36] The impact on these neighbourhoods, streets, homes, and 'native' residents was described as a breaching of domestic boundaries, a theme Wendy Webster's work has stressed. 'The violation of a domestic sanctuary becomes a symbol of a nation under siege', she argues. Homes and streets, and by extension the families living in them, served as symbols of 'embattled Englishness' and a national identity configured as white, decent, orderly, and threatened.[37]

---

[32] Patterson, *Dark Strangers*, 210–11.

[33] S. Weeraperuma, 'Colour and Equality', in Tajfel and Dawson (eds.), *Disappointed Guests*, 121.

[34] Adil Jussawalla, 'Indifference', in ibid., 130.   [35] Patterson, *Dark Strangers*, 211.

[36] Lord Elton, *The Unarmed Invasion: A Survey of Afro-Asian Immigration* (London, 1965), 20.

[37] Wendy Webster, *Englishness and Empire, 1939–1965* (Oxford, 2005), 180, 165–8; see also James Proctor, *Dwelling Places: Postwar Black British Writing* (Manchester, 2003), ch. 2.

Personifying this 'embattled Englishness' were resentful whites seen as adversely affected by 'coloured' neighbours. As Stuart Hall and Paul Gilroy have outlined, until the late 1960s and early 1970s the social and cultural aspects of post-war immigration that received by far the most attention were those linked to the intimate realms of private life, particularly housing and sex.[38] (The association of ethnic minorities with crime, while not absent, was less pronounced than it later became in the 1970s and 1980s.) Britain's severe housing shortage after the Second World War – stemming from the long-term decay of the existing housing stock coupled with extensive wartime destruction through aerial bombing and increased demand upon demobilization – meant the supply of accommodation in urban areas was inadequate and rents were high. Housing became a heavily racialized issue and an arena where blacks and Asians were most likely to encounter discrimination. Working-class migrants earning relatively low wages competed with working-class whites for accommodation in neighbourhoods that had become increasingly derelict and stigmatized 'twilight areas'. In his 1954 book entitled *Colour Bar*, the famous West Indian cricketer Learie Constantine summarized how 'coloured residents' were 'unable to choose freely where they will live and find themselves virtually obliged to reside in a recognized "black area" which is often a slum area'.[39] Many British landlords and landladies refused them as tenants, while others took advantage and charged higher rents for poor-quality accommodation. Encountering pervasive racial discrimination in the housing market, not to mention at work, did much to burst the bubble of optimism about life in Britain for the newly-arrived. A few years after composing 'London is the Place for Me', Lord Kitchener's calypso 'My Landlady' immortalized the rude and condescending behaviour from those who charged extortionately for squalid rooms that marred the British experiences of so many.[40]

In the slum-like surroundings to which many blacks and Asians were largely relegated, white resentment of 'coloureds' took many forms of expression. West Indians, Africans, Indians, and Pakistanis alike were condemned for inhabiting dirty, unsanitary, and overcrowded rooms and houses and for failing to keep windows, doorsteps, and gardens clean and well-tended – all of which constituted significant liminal areas where private and public spaces coincided.[41] At the same time, specific ethnic groups became singled out as the main culprits for other forms of 'un-English' behaviour that went beyond

---

[38] Stuart Hall, 'Reconstruction Work: Images of Post-war Black Settlement', in Jo Spence and Patricia Holland (eds.), *Family Snaps: The Meanings of Domestic Photography* (London, 1991), 152–64; Paul Gilroy, *'There Ain't No Black in the Union Jack': The Cultural Politics of Race and Nation* (Chicago, 1987), 79–85.

[39] Learie Constantine, *Colour Bar* (London, 1954), 65.

[40] Lord Kitchener, 'My Landlady', *London is the Place for Me*.

[41] Webster, *Englishness and Empire*, 162, 166–8, 180.

those deemed unsightly. Within a discourse of sensory assault on the white population, West Indians attracted continual complaints for offending local ears, while South Asians cooked spicy foods reprehensible to many noses. That Indians and Pakistanis 'stank of curry' whose smells travelled through doors and windows to plague their neighbours and West Indians shouted in the street, played loud music, and threw rowdy parties that lasted through the night and attracted undesirables became staple accusations.[42] As Peter Bailey has explored, sound – to which smell and other sensory stimuli can be added – is 'an expressive and communicative resource that registers collective and individual identities, including those of nation, race and ethnicity'. Immigrants' noises and odours had 'the power to appropriate, reconfigure or transgress boundaries' in ways that illuminated both their own insistent presence and native responses to it.[43]

West Indians, moreover, were deemed the worst offenders of white British sexual morality. Contemporary writers stressed that nuclear family life and marriage was often not the norm in the West Indies, particularly amongst the working classes, with casual sex, unstable unions, and illegitimate children being common.[44] When contemplating a migrant group numerically dominated by young men, many white Britons considered West Indians (along with African men) as oversexed and coveting relationships with white women. This was another example of beliefs with deep roots in colonial mentalities, this time linked to the unsubstantiated sexual 'Black Peril' that supposedly threatened white women with rape in the empire.[45]

Within domestic British society, interracial sex and private intimacy epitomized widespread white fears about the place 'coloureds' occupied within a nation that proved worryingly porous.[46] In the 1940s and 1950s, sex across

[42] Elizabeth Buettner, '"Going for an Indian": South Asian Restaurants and the Limits of Multiculturalism in Britain', *Journal of Modern History*, 80:4 (2008), 875–6; Clifford S. Hill, *How Colour Prejudiced is Britain?* (London, 1965), 77–8; R.B. Davison, *Commonwealth Immigrants* (London, 1964), 23, 25; Rashmi Desai, *Indian Immigrants in Britain* (London, 1963), 11, 20.

[43] Peter Bailey, 'Breaking the Sound Barrier', in *Popular Culture and Performance in the Victorian City* (Cambridge, 1998), 210–11; more broadly, see also '*AHR* Forum: The Senses in History', *American Historical Review*, 116:2 (2011), 307–400.

[44] Patterson, *Dark Strangers*, 201–2, 285; Peter Griffiths, *A Question of Colour?* (London, 1966), 90.

[45] Dane Kennedy, *Islands of White: Settler Society and Culture in Kenya and Southern Rhodesia, 1890–1939* (Durham, 1987), ch. 7; Jock McCulloch, *Black Peril, White Virtue: Sexual Crime in Southern Rhodesia, 1902–1935* (Bloomington, 2000); Jenny Sharpe, *Allegories of Empire: The Figure of Woman in the Colonial Text* (Minneapolis, 1993); Ann Laura Stoler, *Carnal Knowledge and Imperial Power: Race and the Intimate in Colonial Rule* (Berkeley, 2002), 58–60.

[46] Elizabeth Buettner, '"Would You Let Your Daughter Marry a Negro?": Race and Sex in 1950s Britain', in Philippa Levine and Susan R. Grayzel (eds.), *Gender, Labour, War and Empire: Essays on Modern Britain* (London, 2009), 219–37; Webster, *Imagining Home*, 48–52; Webster, *Englishness and Empire*, 152, 157–9, 167–8; Schwarz, 'Black Metropolis, White England',

racial lines was greeted with a level of white hostility out of all proportion to the numbers of men and women actually involved in relationships that ranged from casual encounters to cohabitation to marriage. Black men typically met with racism at work and elsewhere in public life, but interracial sexuality, private life, and mixed-race children showed more than anything else that blacks had come 'too close to home'.[47] In implying that black assimilation and integration within metropolitan Britain was possible, the men and women involved were frequently vilified. As one researcher writing in 1952 phrased it, 'Everywhere the British ... resented the sight of a black man with a white woman, reacting rivalrously, sometimes violently as though to an outrage, to the thought that an alien man was being admitted to the closed society, through a woman violating her social trust.'[48] In this as in many other contemporary assessments, black British subjects counted as aliens, or foreigners, in public perception if not in legal fact, with the citizenship and cultural attributes they shared with white Britons deemed much less significant than their difference in colour.

Sex and family life involving black men and white women suggested, on the one hand, a degree of British tolerance and acceptance of black settlers. On the other hand, however, white women entering into such intimacies were repeatedly condemned as deviants and moral outcasts from mainstream British society, being labelled as prostitutes, nymphomaniacs, or merely 'loose'. Britons hostile to immigration and black integration often channelled their aggressions through rejections of interracial sex and 'miscegenation' as a means of policing the imaginative boundaries of Britishness. During riots that occurred in Nottingham and the Notting Hill area of London in 1958, press reports considered opposition to the presence of black men with white women in pubs and on the streets as a central cause of the violence instigated by white working-class youths.[49]

Public discussion of the 1958 disturbances marked just one of many instances when a range of worrying social elements came together as a source of moral panic in respectable opinion. Promiscuous black men, 'low' white women, and white 'hooligan' youth subcultures, in this case the Teddy Boys, converged on the streets of Nottingham, in the 'twilight', derelict areas of Notting Hill, and in the wider public imagination.[50] As Dick Hebdige argues,

---

198–200; Chris Waters, '"Dark Strangers" in Our Midst: Discourses of Race and Nation in Britain, 1947–1963', *Journal of British Studies*, 36 (1997), 228–9; Collins, 'Pride and Prejudice', 405–10; Hall, 'Reconstruction Work'.

[47] Ruth Glass (assisted by Harold Pollins), *Newcomers: The West Indians in London* (London, 1960), 84; Patterson, *Dark Strangers*, 246–50.

[48] Ruth Landes, 'A Preliminary Statement of a Survey of Negro-White Relationships in Britain', *Man*, 52:184–185 (1952), 133.

[49] 'Why Racial Clashes Occurred', *The Times*, 27 August 1958; 'London Racial Outburst Due to Many Factors', *The Times*, 3 September 1958; Edward Pilkington, *Beyond the Mother Country: West Indians and the Notting Hill White Riots* (London, 1988).

[50] Frank Mort, *Capital Affairs: London and the Making of the Permissive Society* (New Haven, 2010), chs. 3 and 7; 'The Hooligan Age', *The Times*, 3 September 1958.

'the positions "youth" and "Negro" are often aligned in the dominant mythology', with both groupings 'viewed with the same ambivalence: happy-go-lucky and lazy, hedonistic and dangerous'. In the case of the Teddy Boys – a subculture excluded from respectable white working-class society – identification with blacks became 'repressed or inverted into an antagonism'.[51]

Other marginalized British groups, however, actively sought out social contacts with blacks. These included white homosexual men seeking sex with black men as well as 'bohemians' and social elites in search of exoticism.[52] According to Sheila Patterson, the 'small white minority' who became regulars at 'coloured clubs' and house parties included 'unattached white men' as well as a growing number of teenagers, the latter mainly attracted by jazz music and an atmosphere they found 'easy-going and uninhibited'.[53] Yet like the white women criticized for sexual transgressions, they too tended to be seen as moral deviants, or more worryingly still as indications of wider British social change for the worse.

While white neighbours may have resented the noise and vivacity emanating from 'coloured' arenas associated with drink, drugs, dancing, and illicit sex, others found them appealing precisely because they offered an alternative to a mainstream deemed stifling and traditional. Hebdige suggests that 'there existed a whole network of subterranean channels which had for years linked the fringes of the indigenous population to the equivalent West Indian subcultures. Originally opened up to the illicit traffic of "weed" and jazz, these internal exchanges provided the basis for much broader cultural exchanges'.[54] Interestingly, the musical genre associated with West Indians that appeared most attractive to young white Britons in the 1950s and early 1960s was African-American jazz rather than Trinidadian calypsos or other musical forms associated with the Caribbean, although other accounts do suggest that calypso bands were a favourite among university students.[55] Convergences between white youth cultures and black and Asian British cultures became

---

[51] Dick Hebdige, *Subculture: The Meaning of Style* (London, 1987; first published 1979), 44; see also Tony Jefferson, 'Cultural Responses of the Teds: The Defence of Space and Status', in Stuart Hall and Tony Jefferson (eds.), *Resistance Through Rituals: Youth Subcultures in Post-war Britain* (London, 1976), 81–6.

[52] Waters, '"Dark Strangers"', 229–30; Mort, *Capital Affairs*, ch. 7.

[53] Patterson, *Dark Strangers*, 247, 307.

[54] Hebdige, *Subculture*, 39–40, 44–51, 73. The white teenage protagonist of Colin MacInnes' novel *Absolute Beginners* (London, 1959), who lived in the 'Napoli' neighbourhood of London (a reference to Notting Hill), combined a passion for jazz with curiosity about his West Indian neighbours. MacInnes' other novels such as *City of Spades* (London, 1957) represented black men as homoerotic subjects. On MacInnes' work, see Tony Gould, *Inside Outsider: The Life and Times of Colin MacInnes* (London, 1993); John McLeod, *Postcolonial London: Rewriting the Metropolis* (London, 2004), ch. 1.

[55] Kenneth Ramchand, 'The Colour Problem at the University: A West Indian's Changing Attitudes', in Tajfel and Dawson (eds.), *Disappointed Guests*, 35.

much more visible and diverse in later decades, a theme that will be explored in the next chapter. But during the 1950s and early 1960s, white Britons linked with blacks in the realms of social and private life were widely condemned as emblematic of permissiveness and the decline of British culture – a culture imagined as decaying from within through white immorality working in tandem with black intrusions, not to mention by the threats posed by forms of American popular culture like jazz (and later rock 'n' roll).[56]

The political arena was not immune from concerns about the effects of unrestricted 'coloured' migration from the colonies and Commonwealth on Britain. The 1958 riots, for example, generated calls to 'Keep Britain White' and for an end to the prevailing open-door policy, but these bore no fruit until the passing of the 1962 Commonwealth Immigration Act placed limits on the numbers permitted to enter the country each year. Demands for further restrictions became more vocal by the mid-1960s and racism grew increasingly apparent within party politics. Such expressions were particularly evident in areas like the West Midlands that had experienced large influxes of 'coloured' settlement.

A political turning point came with the 1964 general election when Patrick Gordon Walker, the Labour Member of Parliament for the Smethwick borough outside Birmingham, lost his seat to the Conservative candidate Peter Griffiths.[57] During the course of a local campaign that achieved national notoriety, Griffiths' supporters turned to the racist slogan 'If you want a nigger neighbour, vote Labour.' Griffiths himself declined to take personal credit for this form of campaigning but never condemned those chanting such phrases, saying they represented a common attitude in Smethwick and deserved to be taken seriously.[58] Gordon Walker faced local ire for having opposed the 1962 Act; Griffiths, meanwhile, wanted a complete ban on further immigration. As the campaign turned nastier, Gordon Walker was reviled not only for his political stance vis-à-vis immigration but also saw himself, and his family, become subjected to racial slander. In keeping with the themes examined earlier, local rumours revolved around housing and sex: 'Gordon Walker had sold his house in Smethwick to the blacks. Gordon Walker went out to the West Indies to recruit blacks for Smethwick industry. Gordon Walker's wife was black. So was Gordon Walker. ... All Gordon Walker's daughters married black men', ran the allegations.[59] Though lacking in foundation, such insults

[56] Elton, *Unarmed Invasion*, 85; Mort, *Capital Affairs*.
[57] Elizabeth Buettner, '"This is Staffordshire not Alabama": Racial Geographies of Commonwealth Immigration in Early 1960s Britain', *Journal of Imperial and Commonwealth History*, 42:4 (2014), 710–40.
[58] Griffiths, *A Question of Colour?*, 171.
[59] Paul Foot, *Immigration and Race in British Politics* (Harmondsworth, 1965), 49; Robert Pearce, 'Introduction', in Robert Pearce (ed.), *Patrick Gordon Walker: Political Diaries 1932–1971* (London, 1991), 40–5.

nonetheless suggested how political concerns drew sustenance from cultural and social understandings about the ramifications of black settlement for local communities and the families within them – namely, that they entailed a violation of racial boundaries in domestic and neighbourhood life, and by extension the nation.

In this account of the 1964 Smethwick campaign, West Indians figured as the main cause of concern. Yet the mid-1960s witnessed a shift in discussions of immigration that reflected the sharp increase in migration from the Indian subcontinent. Whereas public discussion had centred on Caribbeans in the 1950s, in the 1960s Indians and Pakistanis often became the focus of attention, often for quite distinct reasons. In 1958, James Wickenden's analysis of *Colour in Britain* distinguished West Indians on the grounds that 'they have no separate language or dress of their own and wish to be integrated into the English pattern; they are the results of an historical upheaval' – that is, slavery – 'their ancestors having been transported many generations ago against their will and their whole social background having been destroyed ... misunderstandings of a more violent kind may arise because the West Indian thinks of himself as British in dress, speech, and custom'. Other groups, including the 'Sikhs, Pakistanis, Hindus, and West Africans', posed fewer concerns, Wickenden felt, because they 'do not wish to enter or to become integrated in the British system and probably mean to return to their own country'.[60]

Once South Asians arrived in larger numbers and it became increasingly apparent that their stay in Britain might not be as temporary as some had thought (or indeed hoped), their supposed failure to assimilate and their propensity to 'self-segregate' became re-imagined as a problem rather than a virtue.[61] While West Indians' desire to integrate had once been rejected and frowned upon, the tables turned once observers contrasted them with Asians. Lord Elton's *Unarmed Invasion* asserted that 'the West Indians at least wish for integration. Unlike the Asians ... they speak our language, they share many of our traditions and most of them are Christians ... But few Asians even desire integration. They have their own languages, their own religions ... and their own cultures, and not unnaturally they display not the slightest desire to adopt ours.'[62] In a book published two years after his victory over Patrick Gordon Walker in Smethwick, Peter Griffiths similarly wondered whether Britain's one million coloured immigrants, or 'new citizens', could be 'assimilated', asking 'Can they become Britons? Do they wish to do so?'[63] Like many others, Griffiths did not see 'new citizens' as equivalent to 'Britons', whatever their legal status.

---

[60] James Wickenden, *Colour in Britain* (London, 1958), 19.
[61] Patterson, *Dark Strangers*, 10; Judith Henderson, 'Race Relations in Britain', in Griffith *et al., Coloured Immigrants*, 49.
[62] Elton, *Unarmed Invasion*, 70.   [63] Griffiths, *A Question of Colour?*, 85.

Although the mud-slinging campaign that saw him elected to parliament foregrounded an antipathy to 'nigger neighbours', Griffiths' 1966 book provided a somewhat different assessment of West Indians as 'English-speaking Christians'. 'The West Indian culture is not entirely British but if the willingness to conform is present, the change should not be very lengthy or painful,' he remarked. 'West Indians will probably be assimilated culturally and separated only by the barrier of colour. Indians and Pakistanis will remain more isolated by religious and cultural barriers.' For South Asians, in short, such characteristics were 'likely to make assimilation for them a very slow process indeed'.[64] Griffiths' emphasis in *A Question of Colour?* – a title whose wording and qualifying punctuation were of equal significance – was a sign of much more to come. As the next chapter takes further, starting in the 1960s issues such as assimilation, integration, and whether minority groups in Britain were a subject of concern on the basis of their colour or their distinct cultures (with religious difference counting as a central aspect of cultural specificity) grew ever more apparent within British public discourse.

The 1960s also saw women and children enter into contemporary discussions about 'immigration' far more regularly. While in the 1940s and 1950s male migrants were the main focus of concern, commentary later shifted to their dependants once growing numbers of wives and children joined men who had already put down roots. Opinions about female arrivals and family reunification were divided. As *The Times* put it in 1965, '[m]ore dark women and children are coming to Britain. . . . this will mean more stable immigrant communities and a reduction in VD' – a reference to the common assertion that sexually transmitted diseases were particularly prevalent amongst immigrants, particularly blacks, on account of their supposed 'oversexed' nature and promiscuity with white women.[65] Some writers claimed that white men welcomed the arrival of more West Indian women because they provided black men with black rather than white female companionship.[66] Yet the growing presence of West Indian women and children generated concerns of their own as many British commentators stereotyped and pathologized black family life, relentlessly drawing attention to purportedly unstable relationships between black men and women, a high rate of illegitimacy, and single-parent families whose children were likely to become social 'problems'.[67] As for South Asian children, *The Times'* journalist

---

[64] Ibid., 86–7.   [65] Elton, *Unarmed Invasion*, 12; Griffiths, *A Question of Colour?*, 146.

[66] Patterson, *Dark Strangers*, 255; Sydney Collins, *Coloured Minorities in Britain: Studies in British Race Relations based on African, West Indian, and Asiatic Immigrants* (London, 1957), 253.

[67] Goulbourne and Chamberlain (eds.), *Caribbean Families*; Errol Lawrence, 'Just Plain Common Sense: The "Roots" of Racism', and 'In the Abundance of Water the Fool is Thirsty: Sociology and Black Pathology', in Centre for Contemporary Cultural Studies (CCCS), *The Empire Strikes Back: Race and Racism in 70s Britain* (London 1982), 47–94 and 95–142; Hazel Carby, 'White Woman Listen! Black Feminism and the Boundaries of Sisterhood', in CCCS

continued, 'increased numbers of children from Asia who do not speak English cause teaching problems in schools. The more settled families are in Britain the less likely they are to return home.'[68] As Chapter 8 discusses in more depth, alongside family reunification the emergence of a second, British-born generation (or alternatively a British-raised one) was, as much as anything else, a sign that Commonwealth citizens were in Britain to stay.

Once the 1962 Act had reduced the numbers permitted to arrive from the Commonwealth each year, Britons opposed to immigration campaigned for ever more stringent restrictions. Conservative Member of Parliament Enoch Powell was, and remains, among the best-known advocates of halting further primary Commonwealth migration. Furthermore, Powell, like others, targeted unrestricted family reunification as a dangerous loophole that threatened to increase Britain's coloured population exponentially despite the numerical curbs already in place. Like Griffiths, he underscored the problems posed by high birth rates among immigrant families and the pressure this placed on social services and schools.[69] In his infamous 'Rivers of Blood' speech delivered in Birmingham in 1968, Powell claimed that '[i]t can be no part of any policy that existing families should be kept divided', but they should 'be reunited in their countries of origin' rather than in Britain – one of his many calls for encouraging repatriation alongside further restrictions on settlement. Allowing the 'annual inflow of some 50,000 dependents, who are for the most part the material of the future growth of the immigrant-descended population', Powell argued, 'is like watching a nation busily engaged in heaping up its own funeral pyre'.[70] National identity, yet again, was pronounced as endangered by immigration, a threat that the second generation only enhanced.

While Powell's views were widely condemned even within his own party, further immigration restrictions were implemented in 1968 and again in 1971. Not coincidentally, the 1971 Immigration Act saw dependants' automatic right of entry curtailed. Immigration legislation in both 1968 and 1971 reconfigured the parameters of British citizenship. Afterwards, Commonwealth citizens only retained the right to unrestricted entry if they could claim British birth or British ancestry – a link based on 'patriality' which, in the words of Ann Dummett, thereby became 'a quasi-nationality'.[71] Race was not named as a criterion, but

---

(ed.), *Empire Strikes Back*, 212–35; Heidi Safia Mirza, *Young, Female and Black* (London, 1992); Webster, *Imagining Home*, ch. 3.

[68] 'Real Solution is Dispersal from Decaying City Areas', *The Times*, 29 January 1965.

[69] Griffiths, *A Question of Colour?*, 92, 128–48.

[70] J. Enoch Powell, speech in Birmingham, 20 April 1968, reprinted in John Wood (ed.), *J. Enoch Powell, Freedom and Reality* (London, 1969), 215–16. Repeated references to women, children, and family reunification in Powell's speeches also appear on 214–37.

[71] Ann Dummett, 'Britain', in Rainer Bauböck *et al.* (eds.), *Acquisition and Loss of Nationality: Politics and Trends in 15 European States, Vol. 2: Country Analyses* (Amsterdam, 2006), 568; see also 561–7.

few West Indians, South Asians, and other 'New Commonwealth' citizens could claim British ancestors (and provide watertight documentation of British forebears if so); most hailing from 'Old Commonwealth' nations like Australia, New Zealand, and Canada that had once been British settler colonies, however, could. Although implicit rather than explicit, the right to British citizenship and identity became ever more closely aligned with whiteness – not simply in many sectors of public opinion, but now newly enshrined by law.

* * *

Postcolonial arrivals in the Netherlands from the East Indies and West Indies

Citizenship and European ancestry (or lack thereof) were equally central in shaping the Netherlands' history of post-war migration from its colonies and former colonies.[72] Migration from the former Dutch East Indies, which achieved independence as Indonesia in 1949, differed markedly from that from the West Indies, a region whose Dutch possessions included Suriname as well as the Netherlands Antilles. While the flow of people from the West Indies proved more protracted in nature and indeed continues until the present day, migration from the Indonesian archipelago occurred in a fairly short space of time and involved two distinct groups. The first encompassed the 300,000 'repatriates' (of whom approximately 180,000 were Indisch, or of mixed Indonesian and European descent) examined in the previous chapter, who arrived as Dutch citizens between the late 1940s and the early 1960s. In terms of their experiences and the ways the Dutch government and wider metropolitan population viewed them, Indisch Dutch shared little other than geographical origins (and in some instances a degree of physical resemblance) with the Moluccans, the second group, who possessed neither Dutch ancestry

---

[72] On wider Dutch immigration trends since the early modern period that consider former colonial peoples alongside a range of other groups, see Jan Lucassen and Rinus Penninx, *Newcomers: Immigrants and Their Descendants in the Netherlands, 1550–1995* (Amsterdam, 1997); Herman Obdeijn and Marlou Schrover, *Komen en gaan: Immigratie en emigratie in Nederland vanaf 1550* (Amsterdam, 2008), with ch. 6 focusing on migrants from the colonies; Leo Lucassen and Jan Lucassen, *Winnaars en verliezers: Een nuchtere balans van vijfhonderd jaar immigratie* (Amsterdam, 2011). General introductions in English to the groups fore-grounded here include Hans van Amersfoort and Mies van Niekerk, 'Immigration as a Colonial Inheritance: Post-Colonial Immigrants in the Netherlands, 1945–2002', *Journal of Ethnic and Migration Studies*, 32:3 (2006), 323–46; Ulbe Bosma (ed.), *Post-colonial Immigrants and Identity Formations in the Netherlands* (Amsterdam, 2012), especially the chapter by Guno Jones, 'Dutch Politicians, the Dutch Nation and the Dynamics of Post-colonial Citizenship', 27–47; Han Entzinger, 'East and West Indian Migration to the Netherlands', in Robin Cohen (ed.), *The Cambridge Survey of World Migration* (Cambridge, 1995), 342–46; Hans van Amersfoort, *Immigration and the Formation of Minority Groups: The Dutch Experience, 1945–1975*, translated by Robert Lyng (Cambridge, 1982), 101–83.

nor citizenship. Many Moluccans nonetheless had long considered themselves *Belanda Hitam*, or 'Black Dutchman', an identity rooted in loyal service in the colonial military.[73]

Decolonization meant disbanding the Royal Dutch Indies Army (KNIL) which, beneath its predominantly Dutch officer class, recruited soldiers from the colonized population. Many of the KNIL's 62,000 native troops came from the Moluccan islands, mainly from the Protestant population on the island of Ambon. Having fought on behalf of the Dutch against the Japanese during the Second World War and then against the Indonesian nationalists, the KNIL's Moluccan soldiers, often referred to as the Ambonese, faced difficult choices in 1949: they could either accept demobilization or alternatively join the Indonesian republican army they had just fought so bitterly. Several thousand KNIL soldiers who adamantly refused to join their former enemies demanded to be demobilized in Ambon rather than elsewhere in Indonesia, where a secessionist Republic of the South Moluccas (*Republik Maluku Selatan*, or RMS) had been declared in 1950. Unsurprisingly, Sukarno's newly independent Indonesian government rejected the prospect of former KNIL soldiers swelling the ranks of RMS rebels either in Ambon or on other islands once Ambon was quickly reconquered. The Dutch government sought to demobilize its remaining Moluccan troops in Java, but its own courts forbade leaving unwilling soldiers behind in 'enemy territory'. Faced with this stalemate, in 1951 the Dutch brought the remaining 3,578 soldiers and members of their families, about 12,500 persons in total, back to the Netherlands on what they imagined to be a temporary basis.[74] Rather than offering the Moluccans the opportunity to join the Royal Dutch Army and thereby continue military life – the only occupation and lifestyle they had known – KNIL soldiers brought to the Netherlands were simply discharged upon arrival.

Not only did the Dutch state shy away from the option of integrating its ex-colonial Moluccan soldiers into the metropolitan army; equally, it did not envision that they and their dependants would ever become a settled segment of Dutch society. Their sojourn in the Netherlands having been styled as temporary until some arrangement for their return to Southeast Asia could be agreed upon, the Moluccans were housed in social isolation, in what were, no

---

[73] Dieter Bartels, 'Can the Train Ever Be Stopped Again?: Developments in the Moluccan Community in the Netherlands Before and After the Hijackings', *Indonesia*, 41 (1986), 25.

[74] J. Veenman and L.G. Jansma, *Molukkers in Nederland: Een probleeminventariserend onderzoek* (Deventer, 1981); Dieter Bartels, *Moluccans in Exile: A Struggle for Ethnic Survival* (Leiden, 1989); Hans van Amersfoort, 'The Waxing and Waning of a Diaspora: Moluccans in the Netherlands, 1950–2002', *Journal of Ethnic and Migration Studies*, 30:1 (2004), 151–74; Henk Smeets and Justus Veenman, 'More and More at Home: Three Generations of Moluccans in the Netherlands', in Hans Vermeulen and Rinus Penninx (eds.), *Immigrant Integration: The Dutch Case* (Amsterdam, 2000), 36–63; Henk Smeets and Fridus Steijlen, *In Nederland gebleven: De geschiedenis van Molukkers 1951–2006* (Amsterdam, 2006).

less, former German concentration camps located in remote areas. The distinction between the Dutch response to the Indisch Dutch repatriates and the Moluccans could not have been greater. With varying degrees of success, the state attempted to disperse the former throughout the Netherlands to discourage the formation of a 'ghetto', to bring them into the labour market, and to encourage them to adapt Dutch cultural practices – in other words, to fully integrate. By contrast, the Moluccans were kept in a state of relative geographical isolation and initially out of work. Nor were they encouraged to adapt to Dutch culture. While children from the camps were sent to school and taught Dutch, no effort was made to provide language instruction for the adults, many of whom arrived speaking only Malay. One housewife interviewed in the camps in the early 1950s 'complained that she had no contact with Dutch people at all. "I know", she said, "it is the language. Why don't they teach us Dutch? We have a radio, but I don't understand a word."'[75]

What originally had been envisioned as short-term arrangements for the Moluccans living in the camps, however, dragged on for years. Starting in the late 1950s, the Dutch embarked on building new social housing in special residential districts for them, but not in a manner intended to promote their social integration. During the 1960s, Moluccan neighbourhoods on the outskirts of small and middle-sized towns replaced life in the camps but remained ethnically homogenous areas. Moluccans gradually entered the workforce, but with few qualifications most performed only unskilled, poorly-paid jobs. For many years, the majority held onto the ideal of returning to an independent RMS and did not wish to acknowledge the possibility that their stay in the Netherlands would be permanent. Few sought to acquire Dutch citizenship, and most still remained stateless several decades after their arrival. At the outset, the Moluccans' fixation upon a return to their islands of origin, free from Indonesian control, found support within some Dutch circles, particularly amongst former colonials who shared their hatred for the Sukarno government and sided with the political aims of a community whose loyalty to the Netherlands had long bolstered the colonial order.[76] Over time, however, initial Dutch support for the RMS ideal waned; as the Dutch East Indies receded further into the background, the likelihood that the government would actively intervene to try to realize a free RMS in the face of Indonesian

[75] Tamme Wittermans, *Social Organization Among Ambonese Refugees in Holland* (Amsterdam, 1991), 22. This book stems from Wittermans' 1955 PhD thesis that drew upon fieldwork done immediately following the Moluccans' arrival. On women's lives, see also 'De Ambonese Huisvrouw', *Ambonezen in Nederland: Rapport van de Commissie ingesteld bij besluit van de Minister van Maatschappelijk Werk.* DD. 24 September 1957, Nr. U2598 ('s-Gravenhage, 1959), 25–9.

[76] Van Amersfoort, 'Waxing and Waning', 157, 172.

opposition (a political and diplomatic impossibility even in the early 1950s) became increasingly remote and far-fetched.

In holding on to their desire for a return to the Moluccan islands under a free RMS and remaining convinced that the Netherlands should assist in achieving this, the Moluccans' devotion to the Dutch diminished among both the older generation and their children raised in the camps and in neighbourhoods where the RMS ideal was nurtured. Feelings of resentment, bitterness, and betrayal grew stronger. Convinced that their parents had been treated shabbily by the Netherlands upon decolonization – first dismissed from military service, then given insufficient support for their political aspirations – a contingent among the second generation took matters into their own hands through a series of violent actions perpetrated during the 1970s. Hostage-takings, train hijackings, and other terrorist activities orchestrated by Moluccan youth worked to reactivate a common Moluccan identity which had fractured over time, yet they simultaneously alienated most Dutch (and many Moluccans as well) who were appalled by these incidents.[77] Having succeeded in raising public awareness of their community's aims and grievances, the youth involved in the violence nonetheless underscored the futility of the RMS and dream of return to the Moluccas. Moreover, the Dutch increasingly stereotyped them as a dangerous, troubled, and unintegrated underclass suffering from high unemployment and poor prospects, a 'problem' group requiring more effective state policy rather than sidelining and neglect. Moluccan violence in the 1970s finally prompted the government to acknowledge their presence as permanent and develop new policies aiming to integrate the community rather than perpetuate its social isolation.[78]

The 1970s marked a turning point in the Netherlands' history of colonial and postcolonial migration in other crucial respects as well, with arrivals from the Dutch Caribbean colony of Suriname (formerly known as Dutch Guiana) peaking on account of mass departures during the years immediately before and after its independence in 1975. Alongside migration from the Netherlands Antilles – Dutch Caribbean territories that included the islands of Curaçao, Aruba, Bonaire, St Martin, St Eustatius, and Saba – which took until the 1980s and 1990s to gather pace, the Surinamese counted as one of the main migrant groups to settle after the Second World War. West Indians had travelled to and from the Netherlands long before the war, as work by Gert Oostindie and Emy Maduro outlines, but many more made the journey starting in the 1950s.[79] As

---

[77] Bartels, 'Can the Train Ever Be Stopped Again?'; Smeets and Veenman, 'More and More at Home'.
[78] The Netherlands, *De Problematiek van de Molukse Minderheid in Nederland: Tweede Kamer der Staten-Generaal, Zitting 1977–1978, 14915, nrs. 1–2*; see for example 'Het RMS-ideaal', 27, and 'De problematiek van de tweede generatie', 28.
[79] Gert Oostindie and Emy Maduro, *In Het Land van de Overheerser II: Antillianen en Surinamers in Nederland, 1634/1667–1954* (Dordrecht, 1986); see also Allison Blakely, *Blacks in the Dutch World: The Evolution of Racial Imagery in a Modern Society* (Bloomington, 1993).

Chapter 2 described, in 1954 the Charter of the Kingdom of the Netherlands created a single nationality encompassing persons in the Netherlands, Suriname, and the Antilles. Possessing formal Dutch citizenship, both Surinamese and Antilleans had the right to travel to and reside in the Netherlands without restrictions.

Until the 1960s, migration from the Caribbean predominantly involved social elites and the middle classes who came for study or professional advancement.[80] Surinamese setting out during this era were mainly Afro-Surinamese 'Creoles' from educated, urban backgrounds, with most hailing from the capital city of Paramaribo. However, in the 1960s (and even more strikingly in the 1970s) migration patterns to the Netherlands diversified along class and ethnic lines as others came to share the view long held by better-off Creoles of the Netherlands as facilitating upward socio-economic mobility. Working-class Surinamese arrived in growing numbers and now included Indo-Surinamese 'Hindustanis' as well as Surinamese of Javanese descent. Creoles, Hindustanis, and Javanese (alongside smaller numbers of other backgrounds) reflected Suriname's ethnic diversity as an agricultural economy once dependent upon slaves from Africa and later, after the Netherlands abolished slavery in 1863, upon indentured labourers brought from India and the Dutch East Indies to work on the plantations.[81]

Their background shaped by collective histories of forced and indentured migration to the Caribbean, Dutch Surinamese writers like Edgar Cairo and Astrid Roemer used their fictional work to draw connections between a remembered history of colonial racial oppression and the discrimination their countrymen and women later encountered upon moving to the Netherlands. As Roemer's protagonist reflected in her 1983 novel *Nergens ergens* [*Nowhere Somewhere*], she had a 'love-hate relationship with Suriname'. While loving the country of her birth, she simultaneously loathed it 'because history shows

---

[80] See for example Denis Henriquez's fictional portrayal of an Aruban student in 1960s Holland, *Delft Blues* (Amsterdam, 1995), and Ellen Ombre's story 'Maalstroom', in *Maalstroom: Verhalen* (Amsterdam, 1992), 126–50. For excerpts of the latter in English translation, see Ellen Ombre, 'Maelstrom', translated by Myra Heerspink Scholz, *Callaloo*, 21:3 (1998), special issue: 'Caribbean Literature from Suriname, the Netherlands Antilles, Aruba, and the Netherlands', 587–98.

[81] Alongside works by Van Amersfoort and Van Niekerk cited earlier, see Gert J. Oostindie, 'Caribbean Migration to the Netherlands: A Journey to Disappointment?', in Malcolm Cross and Han Entzinger (eds.), *Lost Illusions: Caribbean Minorities in Britain and the Netherlands* (London, 1988), 54–72; Gert Oostindie and Inge Klinkers, *Decolonising the Caribbean: Dutch Policies in a Comparative Perspective* (Amsterdam, 2003), 177–200; Mies van Niekerk, *Premigration Legacies and Immigrant Social Mobility: The Afro-Surinamese and Indo-Surinamese in the Netherlands* (Lanham, MD, 2002; originally published Amsterdam, 2000); Mies van Niekerk, 'Afro-Caribbeans and Indo-Caribbeans in the Netherlands: Premigration Legacies and Social Mobility', *International Migration Review*, 38:1 (2004), 158–83; Mies van Niekerk, 'Paradoxes in Paradise: Integration and Social Mobility of the Surinamese in the Netherlands', in Vermeulen and Penninx (eds.), *Immigrant Integration*, 64–92.

how I ended up here. My ancestors were dragged here by force and emigrated under false pretences.' As for her attitude towards the Netherlands, she continued, 'Holland's material wealth was gained partly at the expense of my native land. After five generations of legitimate oppression I have the right to choose to which country I belong. I have chosen Holland, even though Holland has not chosen me.'[82]

Roemer's reference to this 'right to choose' is suggestive of the individualist nature of Surinamese migration. In contrast to Britain, where the state and specific employers actively recruited workers from the nation's Caribbean territories to staff particular industries and social services when confronting a labour shortage, the Netherlands rarely looked to Suriname or the Antilles. Instead, the Dutch turned to Mediterranean countries – including Italy, Spain, Portugal, and Greece, but particularly Turkey and Morocco – when seeking unskilled workers for its industries and other sectors, preferring foreign 'guest workers' they could arbitrarily dismiss far more readily than Caribbean migrants who possessed Dutch citizenship rights.[83] Rather than being targeted for recruitment, West Indians from Dutch territories actively opted to migrate in the face of economic underdevelopment, a lack of employment opportunities, and poor educational and welfare provisions at home.[84] But calling West Indians in the Netherlands 'voluntary' immigrants demands strong qualification, as Philomena Essed stresses: 'One can hardly speak of "free will" when people from much exploited colonies flee to the idealized "mother country."'[85]

As in British West Indian colonies, in Suriname and the Antilles schools instructed pupils in the Dutch language and instilled a strong awareness of their ties with the 'mother country' and its culture. Yet once in the Netherlands, even middle-class arrivals like Astrid Roemer were kept at arm's length from mainstream Dutch society and reminded that while the provisions of the 1954

---

[82] Edgar Cairo's work, including his novel *Dat vuur der grote drama's* [*That Fire of Great Dramas*] (Haarlem, 1982), and Astrid Roemer's novel *Nergens ergens* [*Nowhere Somewhere*] (Amsterdam, 1983), are discussed in Wim Rutgers, 'Dutch Caribbean Literature', translated by Scott Rollins, *Callaloo*, 21:3 (1998), 551–2. On these themes, see also Michiel van Kempen, 'De binnenkamer en de open vensters: Ontwikkelingen in de Surinaamse literatuur 1975–1988', *De Gids*, 153:1 (1990), 17–28; Astrid Roemer, 'Writing Back in the Diaspora: Surinamese Ethnic Novels', in Ineke Phaf (ed.), *Presencia criolla en el Caribe y América Latina/Creole Presence in the Caribbean and Latin America* (Frankfurt am Main and Madrid, 1996), 37–43.

[83] Many labour migrants from Spain, Italy, and elsewhere in southern Europe went home when these nations became more economically prosperous and offered better opportunities. Ongoing underdevelopment in Morocco and Turkey, by contrast, encouraged men from these communities to remain in the Netherlands and bring family members to join them. The end of the Franco era in Spain along with the fall of Portugal's dictatorship and the end of the colonial wars in the mid-1970s also encouraged many Spanish and Portuguese guest workers to return. See Lucassen and Penninx, *Newcomers*, 54–9, 46.

[84] Oostindie, 'Caribbean Migration', 62–4.

[85] Philomena Essed, *Understanding Everyday Racism: An Interdisciplinary Theory* (Newbury Park, 1991), 190.

Charter may have allowed them to choose Holland, the reverse typically did not apply. Widely treated as 'foreigners with a Dutch passport', their African and Asian ancestry and colonial origins rendered them second-class citizens in the eyes of many.[86] Native Dutch scepticism about their right to belong grew even more pronounced as Caribbean migration increased exponentially in the 1970s and became more working-class in character. Possessing limited formal education at best, poorer West Indians often lacked the exposure to Dutch culture that those higher on the colonial social ladder had gained in colonial schools. Working-class migrants also tended to be less conversant in Dutch, although it was the official language, than in Sranantongo (Sranan for short), Sarnami, or Papiamento, languages spoken by Afro-Surinamese Creoles, Indo-Surinamese Hindustanis, and Antilleans respectively.

Suriname's decolonization in 1975 owed its timing in large part to the Dutch desire to curb migration that had reached mass proportions at a time of economic downturn. But just as settlement in Britain from India and Pakistan increased in the early 1960s in an effort to 'beat the ban' that immigration restriction legislation in 1962 and 1968 promised to implement, the exodus from Suriname increased in the mid- to late 1970s once it became clear that the right to enter and settle would end in 1980.[87] With the Netherlands offering an escape from scanty educational and social welfare offerings, economic stagnation and underdevelopment, and the political uncertainties surrounding independence at home, well over one third of Suriname's population of less than 400,000 left in little more than a decade. 50,000 people made the journey in 1974 and 1975 alone and a further 30,000 arrived in 1979 and 1980, thereby maintaining their right to Dutch citizenship through settling before the five-year transitional agreement expired.[88]

Unlike the Moluccans whose military service background rendered them socially homogenous, the Surinamese opting for the Netherlands were ethnically and socially diverse and included adult men and women, young people, and children in equal measure. As was true elsewhere in Europe, however, not all attracted equal attention. Among the visual depictions of Suriname's independence in 1975 that appeared in the Dutch press, cartoons by Eppo Doeve in

[86] Van Amersfoort, *Immigration and the Formation of Minority Groups*, 168.

[87] As Suriname's independence was being negotiated, the Dutch unsuccessfully attempted to take Dutch nationality away from the Surinamese already living in the Netherlands, a move that would have turned them from citizens into aliens. See Lucassen and Penninx, *Newcomers*, 86. As for those residing in Suriname upon independence, '[m]ost white Dutch nationals ... retained their Dutch nationality (or were allowed to opt for it), whereas the non-white Dutch nationals lost this nationality' and became Afro- or Indo-Surinamese. See Ricky van Oers, Betty de Hart, and Kees Groenendijk, 'The Netherlands', in Bauböck *et al.* (eds.), *Acquisition and Loss of Nationality, Vol. 2*, 401–2.

[88] Oostindie and Klinkers, *Decolonising the Caribbean*, 177–200; Van Niekerk, 'Paradoxes', 66–7.

Figure 7.1 Eppo Doeve, 'Op weg naar de onafhankelijkheid'/'Towards
Independence', October 1975.
Credit: Collectie Persmuseum, Amsterdam. Surinamese undertaking hasty *en
masse* departures for the Netherlands upon Suriname's independence.

politically conservative newspapers highlighted the racial difference and poverty of those departing *en masse* and ridiculed them as panicked and chaotic.[89] One portrayed dark-skinned Surinamese scrambling towards KLM and Sabena jets headed from the Paramaribo airport for Amsterdam. Wearing clothing meant to identify them as Creoles or Hindustanis and clutching all manner of luggage, men and women assisted children and the elderly as they raced for the airplanes, with some seemingly so eager to leave that they clung to the wings of an aircraft that had already taken off. Not only were the prospects of a Suriname independent from the Netherlands dismissed as hopeless; the Dutch on the receiving end, Doeve implied, faced a flood of desperate and impoverished minorities, ethnically and culturally different, seeking a safety net in the Netherlands' welfare state and better employment and social prospects.

While many Surinamese did indeed view the Netherlands as a land of opportunity, upon arrival they faced racial discrimination and disappointed hopes that undercut the Dutch mythology of being a tolerant society proud of its history of welcoming newcomers. Many Dutch resented Surinamese settling in their neighbourhoods and attending schools that correspondingly became denigrated as 'black neighbourhoods' and 'black schools' of low social status, ideally to be avoided via 'white flight'. As Rinus Penninx, Jeannette Schoorl, and Carlo van Praag summarize, research done in the early 1980s in one district of Amsterdam found that 'most native residents [felt] the neighbourhood had been invaded by immigrants, which had led to [its] deteriorization and "stigmatization"'.[90] In a manner resembling earlier policies towards the Indisch, Dutch authorities attempted to disperse the Surinamese and Antillean population by allocating them 5 per cent of newly-built public housing in many parts of the country, a programme which met with white resentment for favouring 'immigrants'. Most Surinamese, however, settled in larger cities, particularly Amsterdam, The Hague, and Rotterdam, where they and their descendants now comprise 8–10 per cent of the population.[91] Although some locals complained that they were given unfair access to housing, many Surinamese in fact moved into dilapidated accommodation in districts that native Dutch contemplated only as a last resort.

Mies van Niekerk's research provides detailed assessments of distinct Afro-Surinamese and Indo-Surinamese experiences both before and after migration to the Netherlands, including their preferences for different places of

---

[89] Eppo Doeve, 'Op weg naar de onafhankelijkheid', October 1975, in Alexander Pola, *De Wereld van Eppo Doeve: Politieke Prenten 1948–1980* (Amsterdam and Brussels, 1984), 70. Eppo Doeve (the nickname of Josef Ferdinand Doeve) drew cartoons for the conservative paper *Elseviers Weekblad* and later for *Elseviers Magazine*.

[90] Rinus Penninx, Jeannette Schoorl, and Carlo van Praag, *The Impact of International Migration on Receiving Countries: The Case of the Netherlands* (Amsterdam, 1993), 186; on housing, see also 143–4, 156, 164–5; Essed, *Understanding Everyday Racism*, 22–3.

[91] Van Niekerk, *Premigration Legacies*, 11, 19.

settlement. Many Hindustanis opted for The Hague, particularly its Schilderswijk area, over other Dutch cities, joining the repatriates from Indonesia in gravitating towards a city that those who had migrated before them recommended for its sedate respectability. The Hague's status as the main centre of Asian culture in the Netherlands – initially Indisch and later Indian culture above all – was thereby maintained, enhanced, and diversified with the addition of 'twice migrants' from the Caribbean diaspora. Creoles for their part predominated among the Surinamese in Amsterdam, where they grew to form a considerable population in working-class neighbourhoods such as Bijlmermeer with new high-rise housing estates. Given the concentration of Afro-Surinamese in this district, KLM flights departing from Paramaribo's airport for Amsterdam derisively became known as the 'Bijlmermeer Express'.[92]

Such was their visibility in this deprived area of Amsterdam that, as Van Niekerk writes, for much of the Dutch public Bijlmermeer came to epitomize 'everything that had gone wrong in the city with the Surinamese immigrants'.[93] In the 1970s and 1980s, common Dutch perceptions of urban neighbourhoods where many Surinamese lived encompassed social and economic disadvantage, low levels of education and skills, high unemployment, welfare dependency, crime, and racialized forms of cultural difference.[94] Not all Surinamese attracted comparable levels of public and media attention, with the better-off and educated generating little adverse commentary. Those consistently singled out for special concern during this period were young, unemployed Afro-Surinamese men.[95] Much in evidence on the streets of Bijlmermeer and other neighbourhoods, Afro-Surinamese males were stereotyped as delinquent petty criminals who smoked *wiri* (marijuana) and were active in an informal economy revolving around *hosselen*, or 'hustling', which extended from theft and illegally hawking goods on the street to drug dealing and pimping.[96] A 1973

---

[92] Ibid., 57–60, 182–3. On Bijlmermeer, see also Kees Schuyt and Ed Taverne, *Dutch Culture in a European Perspective, Vol. 4: 1950: Prosperity and Welfare* (Basingstoke, 2004), 185–8; Leo de Klerk and Hans van Amersfoort, 'Surinamese Settlement in Amsterdam, 1973–1983', in Cross and Entzinger (eds.), *Lost Illusions*, 147–63.

[93] Van Niekerk, *Premigration Legacies*, 189.

[94] Annemarie Bodaar, 'Multicultural Urban Space and the Cosmopolitan "Other": The Contested Revitalization of Amsterdam's Bijlmermeer', in Jon Binnie *et al.* (eds.), *Cosmopolitan Urbanism* (London, 2006), 171–86.

[95] Guno Jones, 'Biology, Culture, "Postcolonial Citizenship" and the Dutch Nation, 1945–2007', *Thamyris/Intersecting*, 27 (2014), 328–30.

[96] Livio Sansone, 'Alternatieven voor regulier werk: het hosselen', in *Schitteren in de Schaduw: Overlevingsstrategieën, subcultuur en etniciteit van Creoolse jongeren uit de lagere klasse in Amsterdam 1981–1990* (Amsterdam, 1992), 72–147; Van Niekerk, *Premigration Legacies*, 31, 90–1, 117, 231; Essed, *Understanding Everyday Racism*, 221; W.E. Biervliet, 'The Hustler Culture of Young Unemployed Surinamers', in Humphrey E. Lamur and John D. Speckmann (eds.), *Adaptation of Migrants from the Caribbean in the European and American Metropolis* (Amsterdam and Leiden, 1975), 191–201.

account of prostitution in the Netherlands featured '*Caribische types*' as a notable subsector of Amsterdam's pimps, taking refuge in colonial racial stereotypes to explain Creole attitudes towards white prostitutes: 'Perversion and aggressiveness against the Dutch woman comes in response to colonial hatred', the author asserted, because '"you people have done so much to my ancestors."' Surinamese pimps, he continued, were 'frustrated' because 'they come from bad families and have bad traditions that derive from a slave colony'.[97]

Although men received a disproportionate share of negative publicity, gender-based Dutch perceptions of its black population also extended to women. Afro-Surinamese women were also criminalized, finding themselves likely candidates to be falsely accused of shoplifting and welfare fraud. Women Philomena Essed interviewed in the mid-1980s repeatedly encountered insinuations that they worked as prostitutes or, if not, simply contributed to the Netherlands' alleged overpopulation by having too many children. Black single mothers and matri-focal family traditions received considerable adverse attention as both signalling and enhancing 'social problems'.[98] Blame for blacks' purportedly aberrant sexuality and unstable, 'immoral' family life, moreover, was laid at the door of Afro-Surinamese men criticized for shirking domesticity (and commonly marriage) and failing to provide for their children. Countering pervasive sexual stereotypes and providing historical context for West Indians' family culture became important to Astrid Roemer's and Edgar Cairo's task of 'writing back'. Roemer sought to address images of the 'admirable strong black ma' and the 'irresponsible sexist black pa', in the process portraying women's investment in motherhood and powerful domestic roles in a positive rather than a negative light. As for black men, Cairo encapsulated the common preconception as '[t]he Negro doesn't think about tomorrow. When he's got money, he spends it. He goes around fucking, making children. Daddy was a rolling stone is his way of life. And that's all of the Negro.' On the contrary, he concluded: 'Well that isn't all at all.'[99]

Gender-specific Dutch ideas about the Surinamese coexisted alongside stereotypes that applied to men as well as women. As Essed argues, many common views contained colonial antecedents not far below the surface. Longstanding 'racial stereotypes of Blacks as inherently uncivilized, ugly, barbarian, dirty, aggressive and stupid ... are partly replaced by cultural beliefs portraying Blacks as aggressive, lazy, loud and as people who refuse to adapt to

---

[97] J.W. Groothuyse, *Het menselijk tekort van de pooier* (Amsterdam, 1973), 144, 149. See also 93, 111–14, 142–4, 151.

[98] Essed, *Understanding Everyday Racism*, 20, 25, 86, 167–8, 252; Van Niekerk, *Premigration Legacies*, 33, 104–12.

[99] Roemer, 'Writing Back', 40; Charles H. Rowell, 'An Interview with Edgar Cairo', *Callaloo*, 21:3 (1998), 694.

Dutch culture while abusing the benefits of the Dutch welfare system'. Dutch images of blacks as 'happy-go-lucky', music-loving, 'swinging Negroes' were equally common, creating the belief that the Surinamese 'only care about parties and good food and are less concerned with matters of the mind'. Attitudes that worked to distance the Surinamese from rationality and 'civilization' – portrayed as traditionally Dutch attributes – could then be used to justify their inferior position in the Netherlands and explain away persistent forms of social, economic, and educational disadvantage and inequality.[100]

Recurrent white presumptions that positioned the Surinamese (and particularly the Afro-Surinamese) together with drugs, prostitution, single parenthood, 'problem families', and sexual immorality in the 1970s and 1980s are suggestive of wider concerns about seismic changes that Dutch society and culture had only recently undergone – changes that entailed rethinking precisely what 'traditional' Dutch attributes indeed should be. During the years immediately preceding and directly coinciding with the mass arrival of working-class Surinamese, the Netherlands experienced tremendous social upheaval. In the 1960s and 1970s, the institutionalized division of society into Protestant, Catholic, socialist, and liberal 'pillars', a theme treated in Chapter 8, was largely discarded, and a *gedoogcultuur* ('culture of tolerance') ushered in. This heralded the spread of new attitudes towards sexual morality, greater gender equality and new roles for women, and a liberal state approach to soft drugs like marijuana and hashish as well as prostitution. Today, the global image of the Netherlands, and particularly Amsterdam, revolves as much around liberal policies concerning the drugs readily available at 'coffee shops' and the sex for sale in red light districts as it does around tulips, canals, bicycles, Vermeer, and Van Gogh.[101] So deeply ensconced has this reputation become that it is easy to forget how new and contentious this response to sex and recreational drugs was in the 1970s, when culturally conservative social sectors worried endlessly and openly about moral deterioration.[102] With West Indian migration accelerating at precisely the same time, the Surinamese epitomized wider Dutch anxieties about sexuality and the family, drug use, and moral decline. Issues that divided metropolitan society in a manner resembling British concerns about permissiveness, blacks, and white youth culture seen earlier combined and became racialized.

---

[100] Essed, *Understanding Everyday Racism*, 20, 201.

[101] Jan Nijman, 'Cultural Globalization and the Identity of Place: The Reconstruction of Amsterdam', *Cultural Geographies*, 6:2 (1999), 146–64; Léon Deben, Willem Heine Meijer, and Dick van der Vaart (eds.), *Understanding Amsterdam: Essays on Economic Vitality, City Life, and Urban Form*, 2nd rev. edn (Amsterdam, 2000); Schuyt and Taverne, *Dutch Culture*, 372, 380, 415.

[102] Cannabis was decriminalized in 1976 (just one year after Suriname's independence) when a new law drew a distinction between soft and hard drugs.

In time, the preoccupations of the 1970s and 1980s shifted to make room for new foci of social concern. In the decades after the 'exodus' surrounding Suriname's independence, the Surinamese attracted less adverse attention than before and different ethnic minority groups became the favoured candidates for public concern and widespread hostility.[103] While primary migration from Suriname dwindled after the decolonization transition period ended in 1980, that from the Netherlands Antilles sharply accelerated starting in the 1980s and 1990s in response to the decline of oil refineries and loss of employment on the islands. The influx of poor, unskilled Antilleans, many of whom spoke little Dutch and had limited job prospects in the Netherlands, resulted in stereotypes revolving around young male criminality, unemployment, and burdens placed on the welfare state that had previously been applied to the Afro-Surinamese being transferred to more recent arrivals from Curaçao and Aruba.[104] Antillean migration and the problems associated with it caused Dutch sceptical of the political status quo to question whether migration from the islands should be allowed to continue unimpeded or whether it had to be curbed. To date, the Antilles and Aruba remain part of the Kingdom of the Netherlands as constituted by the 1954 Charter and their populations retain full Dutch citizenship and settlement rights. Since 1998, however, new arrivals from the Antillean parts of the Kingdom are required to complete a one-year 'integration' course – a sign that not all who are legally Dutch are deemed sufficiently Dutch in cultural terms.[105]

Within the Netherlands' population that approaches 17 million today are approximately 40,000 first-, second-, and third-generation Moluccans, 332,000 Surinamese (43 per cent of whom are second generation), and 130,000 Antilleans (with 38 per cent in the second generation).[106] All groups continue to confront racial discrimination and cultural biases, although today Afro-Surinamese Creoles are widely considered more culturally integrated within Dutch society than either Antilleans or Indo-Surinamese. Largely on account of their religious, cultural, and linguistic differences, Indo-Surinamese Hindustanis appear less likely to intermarry and interact socially with native Dutch than Creoles.[107] Yet all of the colonial and postcolonial migrant groups

---

[103] Jones, 'Dutch Politicians', 43–5.

[104] Hans van Hulst, 'A Continuing Construction of Crisis: Antilleans, Especially Curaçaoans, in the Netherlands', in Vermeulen and Penninx (eds.), *Immigrant Integration*, 93–122; Michael Sharpe, 'Globalization and Migration: Post-Colonial Dutch Antillean and Aruban Immigrant Political Incorporation in the Netherlands', *Dialectical Anthropology*, 29:3–4 (2005), 291–314; Van Amersfoort and Van Niekerk, 'Immigration as a Colonial Inheritance', 337–40.

[105] Jones, 'Biology, Culture', 331–2; Sharpe, 'Globalization and Migration', 304.

[106] Mies van Niekerk, 'Second-Generation Caribbeans in the Netherlands: Different Migration Histories, Diverging Trajectories', *Journal of Ethnic and Migration Studies*, 33:7 (2007), 1068; Van Amersfoort and Van Niekerk, 'Immigration as a Colonial Inheritance', 333, 338. See also data provided in Obdeijn and Schrover, *Komen en gaan*, ch. 6.

[107] Van Niekerk, *Premigration Legacies*, 127, 208–14.

discussed above have fared far better than the foreign 'guest workers' and their descendants from Turkey and Morocco (who numbered over 320,000 and 275,000 in the early 2000s).[108] With respect to their socio-economic, employment, and educational status and future prospects alongside other measures of social inclusion, those with historic colonial connections and the citizenship rights stemming from these occupy an intermediary position between the native Dutch and the Turks and Moroccans.[109] Despite the disadvantages that many from Surinamese and Antillean backgrounds continue to suffer (particularly if working class), many Dutch view them as 'more like us' than the guest workers and their children (who, despite this now outdated label implying temporary residence, are a permanent part of the Netherlands' population).[110] As Chapter 8 considers further, over time religion often became a more salient marker of difference than physical appearance or other cultural attributes, with Muslims of Moroccan or Turkish origin now generating far more public concern than other religious minorities like Hindus from Suriname. Like West Indians and South Asians in Britain, those who came to the Netherlands from its past or present overseas territories confronted metropolitan public responses that changed considerably throughout the post-war period rather than remain static.

* * *

France, immigration, and *les trente glorieuses* in context

Like the Netherlands and Britain, France's history of migration from its colonies and overseas dependencies predated the era of decolonization and evolved continually over time. France's status as a nation of immigration developed in the nineteenth century, a theme explored most influentially, perhaps, in Gérard Noiriel's *Le creuset français* (*The French Melting Pot*).[111]

---

[108] Justus Veenman, 'The Socioeconomic and Cultural Integration of Immigrants in the Netherlands', *Studi Emigrazione/Migration Studies*, 40:152 (2003), 805, 818.

[109] On related issues (and what he terms the 'postcolonial bonus' stemming from cultural and historical ties as well as citizenship), see Gert Oostindie, *Postcolonial Netherlands: Sixty-five Years of Forgetting, Commemorating, Silencing* (Amsterdam, 2011), 15–16, 43–7.

[110] Louk Hagendoorn and Joseph Hraba, 'Foreign, Different, Deviant, Seclusive and Working Class: Anchors to an Ethnic Hierarchy in the Netherlands', *Ethnic and Racial Studies*, 12:4 (1989), 441–68; Van Niekerk, 'Second-Generation Caribbeans', 1075; Penninx, Schoorl, and Van Praag, *Impact of International Migration*, 204, 210–14. For introductions to Turks and Moroccans in the Netherlands, see contributions to Vermeulen and Penninx (eds.), *Immigrant Integration*; Obdeijn and Schrover, *Komen en gaan*, ch. 7.

[111] Gérard Noiriel, *The French Melting Pot: Immigration, Citizenship, and National Identity*, translated by Geoffroy de Laforcade (Minneapolis, 1996; first published in French in 1988). Among many important works in French exploring the twentieth-century history of French immigration, see Patrick Weil, *La France et ses étrangers: L'aventure d'une politique de l'immigration 1938–1991* (Paris, 1991); Philippe Dewitte (ed.), *Immigration et intégration:*

284 Migrations and multiculturalisms in postcolonial Europe

With a low birth rate that failed to keep pace with its need for manual workers, France had long attracted foreign labour and, to a lesser degree, more affluent classes. Since the 1930s, the percentage of foreigners within France's overall population has remained fairly constant, varying from between 4 and 7 per cent (and exceeding 6 per cent between the 1960s and 1990s), but their geographical origins changed markedly. Historically most immigrants hailed from within Europe, particularly from neighbouring countries such as Belgium, Italy, and Spain but also from Poland and Eastern Europe (from which France's pre-war Jewish population largely originated). European immigrants indeed remained substantial after 1945, as the growing Portuguese population during the 1960s and 1970s examined later illustrates. But from the early- to mid-twentieth century onwards, colonial subjects from North Africa, the West Indies (Antilles), sub-Saharan Africa, and Southeast Asia gradually rose from form- ing a small fraction of the population born outside the metropole to rank among the most significant in numerical, social, and political terms.[112]

The First World War heralded a significant shift in inward imperial migra- tion patterns. France could no longer rely on foreign workers to the extent previously possible at the same time as French men were taken away from agricultural and industrial work to become soldiers in the trenches. As Chapter 3 noted, the nation's manpower needs during 1914–1918 extended from the home front to the war front itself, and France looked to its colonies and overseas dependencies to fill them. With Antilleans, Indochinese, West Africans and North Africans counting as French subjects as opposed to foreigners, they could either man the fields, mines, and factories or be conscripted into the army. The *tirailleurs sénégalais* fighting for France on the Western front, although the best known, were only one of many colonial groups to come and go from metropolitan France during the war.[113] Then as later, North Africa's geographical proximity to France relative to other parts of the empire accounted for its importance as a source of workers and soldiers, and over the course of the war approximately 300,000 Algerians travelled across the Mediterranean either for work or military

---

l'état des savoirs (Paris, 1999); Benjamin Stora and Émile Temime (eds.), *Immigrances: L'immigration en France au XXe siècle* (Paris, 2007); Ahmed Boubeker and Abdellali Hajjat (eds.), *Histoire politique des immigrations (post)coloniales: France, 1920–2008* (Paris, 2008). Prominent within English-language scholarship are Maxim Silverman, *Deconstructing the Nation: Immigration, Racism, and Citizenship in Modern France* (London, 1992); Alec G. Hargreaves, *Multi-ethnic France: Immigration, Politics, Culture and Society*, 2nd edn. (New York, 2007).

[112] For more detailed data on the numbers of immigrants of different national origins over time, see especially Hargreaves, *Multi-ethnic France*, ch. 1; Janine Ponty, *L'immigration dans les textes: France, 1789–2002* (Paris, 2003), chs. 7 and 8.

[113] See Chapter 3 for further discussion of the *tirailleurs sénégalais* and the presence of the colonized in wartime and interwar France, for instance in connection with the 1931 *Exposition Coloniale*.

service.[114] Migratory and labour patterns that became accentuated during the war continued thereafter, fluctuating in the ensuing decades in line with France's domestic economic conditions and colonial circumstances. The Second World War again saw many colonial troops join in the French war effort.[115]

What accounted for late colonial migrations to metropolitan France before the end of empire? Political rights enabling travel to and work and settlement in France were paramount. To take several examples, Algerians gained the freedom to emigrate to the metropole in 1914 and were later granted full citizenship rights in France in 1947, while residents of Martinique, Guadeloupe, and French Guiana in the Caribbean and the island of Réunion in the Indian Ocean became equal French citizens (regardless of their colour) when these areas became French *départements d'outre-mer* and *territoires d'outre-mer* (Overseas Departments and Territories, or DOM-TOM) in 1946, a status they hold up to the present.[116] Africans also benefitted from imperial citizenship granted the same year that enabled free circulation within the French Union.[117] Like the DOM-TOM, until its independence in 1962 Algeria also officially ranked not as a colony but rather as three *départements*, making their inhabitants technically internal migrants and not immigrants – as indeed those from the DOM-TOM remain today.

Taking advantage of their rights to migrate, colonized elites or middle-ranking social groups tended to come for study or professional opportunities unavailable at home, and many sought to deepen their exposure to France's cultural, artistic, and intellectual life that colonial institutions had relentlessly promoted as superior. The Martinican Frantz Fanon remains the best-known example, having first seen France through military service with the Free French forces during the Second World War and later returning to study medicine and psychiatry in Lyon, but countless others shared his experiences of educational migration to Paris and other metropolitan cities.[118] Like Fanon, many became

[114] Neil MacMaster, *Colonial Migrants and Racism: Algerians in France, 1900–62* (Basingstoke, 1997), 16. On Algerian migration to France throughout the twentieth century, see Benjamin Stora, *Ils venaient d'Algérie: L'immigration algérienne en France, 1912–1992* (Paris, 1992); Alain Gillette and Abdelmalek Sayad, *L'Immigration algérienne en France*, 2nd ed (Paris, 1984); Abdelmalek Sayad, *The Suffering of the Immigrant*, translated by David Macey (Cambridge, 2004); Leo Lucassen, *The Immigrant Threat: The Integration of Old and New Migrants in Western Europe since 1850* (Urbana and Chicago, 2005), ch. 7.

[115] Martin Thomas, *The French Empire at War, 1940–45* (Manchester, 1998), esp. ch. 2.

[116] Todd Shepard, *The Invention of Decolonization: The Algerian War and the Remaking of France* (Ithaca, 2006), 39–43; David Beriss, *Black Skins, French Voices: Caribbean Ethnicity and Activism in Urban France* (Boulder, 2004), 7.

[117] Frederick Cooper, *Citizenship between Empire and Nation: Remaking France and French Africa, 1945–1960* (Princeton, 2014), chs. 2 and 3.

[118] On Fanon's experiences in France, see especially Frantz Fanon, *Black Skin, White Masks*, translated by Charles Lam Markmann (New York, 1967; originally published in French in 1952); David Macey, *Frantz Fanon: A Life* (London, 2000).

increasingly politicized by their encounters in 1940s and 1950s France, developing new 'black' identities via their contacts with other colonized peoples and African-American intellectuals which took expression in journals such as *Présence Africaine* and at international congresses that did much to galvanize anti-colonial nationalism.[119] For colonized elites, stays in France often began on the basis of cultural identification but were transformed by the experiences of racism and exposure to new cultural and political possibilities.

Even for many working-class migrants, a sense of cultural familiarity with France might encourage decisions to travel there in search of employment. This was particularly likely for Antilleans from the islands of Guadeloupe and Martinique for whom colonial schooling and other institutions inculcated a knowledge of French language and culture, yet it also applied to North Africans regardless of their linguistic aptitudes. A Moroccan man who had lived in France since 1966 reflected several years later that he and his countrymen seeking work overseas opted for France rather than another Western European country because – although he himself did not know one word of French, according to his bemused interviewer! – 'one speaks the language . . . one is used to things. France once belonged to Morocco and Morocco to France. . . . I personally came to France just as I would have gone to Casablanca or Algeria or Egypt. I consider France . . . a little like home.'[120]

Prior familiarity or a sense of cultural affiliation aside, however, most coming to France were the poor for whom migration first and foremost meant jobs, economic opportunity, and in many cases sheer survival. As one Algerian man who first arrived in France in 1954 put it in the early 1970s, 'for us, France is the country of work'.[121] Full employment and a labour shortage within France's developed economy during *les trente glorieuses*, the 'thirty glorious years' of growth and prosperity spanning the end of the Second World War and the onset of economic crisis in the mid-1970s, coincided with severe underdevelopment in overseas colonies and territories that formal political ruptures of decolonization occurring along the way did nothing to change. Indeed, upheavals caused by colonial wars preceding decolonization along with uncertainty and instability at the time of independence contributed to the continuity characterizing migration patterns across the colonial and immediate postcolonial era. Decolonization in and of itself, in short, did not alter pre-existing

[119] Philippe Dewitte, 'L'immigration: l'émergence en métropole d'une élite africaine (1946–1961)', in Pascal Blanchard, Sandrine Lemaire, and Nicolas Bancel (eds.), *Culture coloniale en France: De la Révolution à nos jours* (Paris, 2008), 451–59; V.Y. Mudimbe, *The Surreptitious Speech: Présence Africaine and the Politics of Otherness, 1947–1987* (Chicago, 1992).

[120] Juliette Minces, *Les travailleurs étrangers en France: enquête* (Paris, 1973), 177.

[121] Ibid.

tendencies. As will be seen later in this chapter, economic and political changes both within France and within ex-colonies occurring years later led to much more decisive shifts.

Workers coming to France from colonies and dependent territories by and large came from communities already severely uprooted and destabilized by colonial economic, political, and military incursions. On the islands of Martinique and Guadeloupe, the decline of agricultural economies dominated by a sugar monoculture (and once dependent upon African slave labour) caused unemployment and social unrest to skyrocket, resulting in an exodus from the plantations into cities followed by departures from the Caribbean to France that accelerated markedly after 1960.[122] Groups from Senegal, Mali, and Mauritius formed the majority of those coming from French West Africa in the 1950s and 1960s, with their overseas journeys set in motion by upheavals within the Senegal River valley caused by colonialism. Poverty plus population growth had long encouraged seasonal migrations within West Africa that ultimately paved the way for longer-distance journeys to Europe, with some men initially finding employment in ports and on ships destined for France.[123] Once connected with the metropole, they might remain working on ships circulating between France and Africa, work as dockers in port cities like Marseille, or else branch out into other forms of manual labour upon arrival.

By one estimate, France's 'black' populations from the DOM-TOM and sub-Saharan Africa approached 170,000 by the mid-1960s. 74,000 came from Martinique and Guadeloupe and 22,000 from Guiana and Réunion, while the main groups within a diverse African population included 11,000 students, 12,000 former students and their children, and 45,000 workers.[124] In the late 1990s, the Antillean community alone totalled 212,000 excluding children born after migration, by which point as many as a quarter of those born in Martinique and Guadeloupe had uprooted themselves to mainland France. Demographically, France had become the Antilles' proverbial 'third island'.[125]

The most marked increase in France's sub-Saharan African populations occurred only in the last quarter of the twentieth century, with wars and political upheaval along with persistent poverty in many parts of Central and West Africa acting as the main catalysts. While approximately 82,000 Africans from south of the Maghreb lived in France in 1975, their numbers had nearly

---

[122] Claude-Valentin Marie, 'Les Antillais en France: une nouvelle donne', *Hommes et Migrations*, 1237 (2002), 26; Alain Anselin, *L'Émigration antillaise en France: la troisième île* (Paris, 1990).

[123] Robert Delerm, 'La population noire en France', *Population*, 19:3 (1964), 515–28; Hélène Bergues, 'L'immigration de travailleurs africains noirs en France et particulièrement dans la région parisienne', *Population*, 28:1 (1973), 59–79; Minces, *Les travailleurs étrangers*, 56–7.

[124] Delerm, 'La population noire', 524.   [125] Marie, 'Les Antillais', 27.

doubled to 158,000 by 1982, later rising to 240,000 in 1990 and then to 282,000 by 1999. Most came from former French colonies, but those from the former Belgian Congo also became well represented.[126] African migration to France thus largely occurred over twenty years after the wave of decolonizations in 1960, a time lag that also characterized most arrivals from the former French Indochina. Some Vietnamese (and Cambodians and Laotians to a lesser extent) were 'repatriated' to France during the war against the Viet Minh and upon France's retreat from Vietnam in 1954, but most only came as refugees or 'boat people' following the communists' victory and America's departure in 1975. From c. 6,400 residing in France in 1954 (0.4 per cent of the foreign population), the Vietnamese only totalled slightly more than 22,300 by 1975 yet exceeded 72,000 by 1990 – a figure that included both Vietnamese nationals and those who had acquired French nationality.[127]

North African (or Maghrebi) migrants to France proved by far the most numerically significant of all colonial and postcolonial populations. Already present well before the Second World War, Algerian arrivals escalated thereafter, with Moroccans (and to a lesser degree Tunisians) initially coming in smaller numbers that gradually grew over time. French Algeria's indigenous Berber and Arab populations suffered intense upheaval through settler colonialism. Military invasion, land expropriation, and punitive systems of taxation combined to destroy the traditional economy and create a dispossessed and destitute peasantry that needed to migrate to survive. Internal migration to settler farms and coastal cities failed to provide sufficient work, and over time population growth coupled with the onset of the Algerian War in 1954 led ever greater numbers to cross the Mediterranean in search of subsistence. Although the European settlers and their lobby in the metropole initially tried to obstruct labour migration to France because they feared both losing their reserve of cheap workers and the politicization and radicalization of those who made the journey, in time they too recognized that work in France served as an essential safety valve for an overpopulated region without the means to sustain itself at home.[128]

Writing in 1957, French ethnologist Germaine Tillion described much of Algerian society as thoroughly 'pauperised' and living from 'hand to mouth', with staggering numbers reliant on overseas work to feed not only themselves but also their families and villages. 'French industry thus employs today

---

[126] Hargreaves, *Multi-ethnic France*, 70. Estimates of France's African population vary markedly; see Ponty, *L'immigration dans les textes*, 364; Dominic Thomas, *Black France: Colonialism, Immigration, and Transnationalism* (Bloomington, 2007), 26; Catherine Quiminal, 'Les Africains, divers et dynamiques', in Dewitte (ed.), *Immigration et intégration*, 113.

[127] Ida Simon-Barouh, 'Les Viêtnamiens, des "rapatriés" aux *boat people*', in Dewitte (ed.), *Immigration et intégration*, 134–5; Nicola Cooper, *France in Indochina: Colonial Encounters* (Oxford, 2001), 193–5; Hargreaves, *Multi-ethnic France*, 72.

[128] MacMaster, *Colonial Migrants*; Gillette and Sayad, *L'Immigration algérienne*.

400,000 Algerian workers and directly supports – in Algeria itself – about two million people', she estimated, at a time when Algeria's non-European population did not exceed 9 million.[129] As was also the case with West Africans, Algerian migration to France was then predominantly male as well as rotational, with men typically spending several years in France prior to returning home and younger relatives or others from their kinship group or village then following in their footsteps. Interviewed by the leading sociologist Abdelmalek Sayad in the early 1970s, 21-year-old 'Mohand A.' described how such conditions had affected individuals and entire communities for at least two generations. His father had first travelled to France over forty years before, as had countless others ever since to the extent that 'we have more people in France than in the village'. Almost the only men left in the village at any given time had already been to France and periodically returned home, only to leave again:

... there's a whole army of them, the army of men – and I am one of them – who never stop coming and going between here and France; going and coming, that's all they do. . . . Even in conversations, what do all the men in the village talk about? France! The veterans of France keep going on about their memories. Those 'on leave' talk about France, in the middle of the village; they believe they are still in France; the young men who are waiting to leave dream of France. France is all you hear them talk about . . . Our village is a village that has been "eaten" by France; no one escapes it.[130]

War in Algeria between 1954 and 1962 did nothing to curb migration to France; rather the opposite.[131] Not only did forced population resettlements in Algeria push ever greater numbers out of their ancestral villages who needed to look further afield in search of their livehihood, but the departure of conscripted French soldiers to fight the FLN insurgency left even more jobs open in the metropole that Algerians did much to fill. Countless French families, Tillion noted, 'have had to resign themselves to seeing their sons leave for Algeria, where some of them have been killed. Killed by whom? . . . By an Algerian, obviously. And who has taken the missing son's place at the factory or the workshop? An Algerian, too.'[132]

Nor did 1962 reduce the Algerian presence in France. New metropolitan arrivals at independence included not just repatriated European settlers (the *pieds-noirs* discussed in the previous chapter) but also up to 90,000 *harkis*, soldiers who had served with the French as auxiliaries who arrived together with their families. Rightly fearing retribution, torture, and death at the hands of

---

[129] Germaine Tillion, *Algeria: The Realities*, translated by Ronald Matthews (New York, 1958, originally published in French in 1957), 16, 72. As outlined below, other estimates of the total number of Algerians in late 1950s France were lower than Tillion's, yet her overall argument remains valid.
[130] Sayad, *Suffering of the Immigrant*, 12–15.
[131] Stora, *Ils venaient d'Algérie*; MacMaster, *Colonial Migrants*, ch. 11.
[132] Tillion, *Algeria*, 93–4.

their victorious opponents if they remained in independent Algeria, the *harkis'* removal to France was to some degree analogous to the Moluccans' resettlement in the Netherlands upon Indonesia's independence.[133] As for Algerians not affiliated with the French military, Neil MacMaster summarized, '[t]he newly independent Algerian government was unable to halt, as it intended, the emigration which was a mark of colonial exploitation as it had inherited a catastrophic economic situation … a combination of wartime destruction, French departure and economic sabotage, and the accumulated underdevelopment of industry and agriculture. Emigration continued to be a necessary safety-valve and source of foreign exchange earnings for the infant Republic.'[134] The c. 211,000 Algerians in France in 1954 thus rose to c. 350,000 by 1962, later escalating to nearly 474,000 by 1968, reaching nearly 711,000 by 1975, and exceeding 805,000 in 1982 – ultimately making them France's largest 'immigrant' group.[135] Decolonization did not reduce the urgent need for overseas workers' remittances among families, villages, and the postcolonial Algerian state, just as Algerian workers remained essential to the French economy at the height of the *trente glorieuses*. Like Africans from other former French colonies, they retained the right to free circulation after independence.[136]

North Africans, West Africans, and arrivals from the DOM-TOM largely filled low-paid, insalubrious, insecure, and monotonous jobs that the native French population increasingly shunned at a time of full employment. Booming industrial sectors like car manufacture employed large 'foreign' workforces, as did mining, metal and chemical factories, and the construction and public works sector.[137] Unskilled work like road sweeping also became associated with 'immigrants', while physically exhausting and accident-prone jobs loading and unloading ships in French ports made the docks where many North and West African men earned their livelihoods 'deserve their nickname of man killer', as Senegalese writer Ousmane Sembène put it in his 1956 novel *Le Docker Noir* (*Black Docker*).[138] Those originating in the DOM-TOM also

---

[133] Mohand Hamoumou, *Et ils sont devenus harkis* (Paris, 1993), ch. 12; Jean-Jacques Jordi and Mohand Hamoumou, *Les harkis, une mémoire enfouie* (Paris, 1999); Tom Charbit, *Les Harkis* (Paris, 2006); Shepard, *Invention of Decolonization*, 230–42; Fatima Besnaci-Lancou and Gilles Manceron (eds.), *Les harkis dans la colonisation et ses suites* (Ivry-sur-Seine, 2008); Vincent Crapanzano, *The Harkis: The Wound That Never Heals* (Chicago, 2011).

[134] MacMaster, *Colonial Migrants*, 189.   [135] Ponty, *L'Immigration dans les textes*, 363–4.

[136] Cooper, *Citizenship*, 415, 423–9.

[137] Minces, *Les travailleurs étrangers*, 36, 117, 210–28; Hargreaves, *Multi-Ethnic France*, 41–50; Laure Pitti, 'Carrières d'OS depuis 1945: Les Algériens à Renault-Billancourt', in Jacqueline Costa-Lascoux, Geneviève Dreyfus-Armand, and Émile Temime (eds.), *Renault sur Seine: Hommes et lieux de mémoire de l'industrie automobile* (Paris, 2007), 97–111.

[138] Sembène Ousmane, *Black Docker*, translated by Ros Schwartz (London, 1987; originally published in French in 1956), 95. As David Murphy notes in his important study *Sembène: Imagining Alternatives in Film and Fiction* (Oxford, 2000), 1, 'Ousmane Sembène' is

took on lower-status public sector jobs as their French nationality qualified them for state employment, and they commonly worked in public hospitals, in customs and excise, and in the post office. Some came to France of their own accord but many were directly recruited by the state, which formalized procedures in the early 1960s with the establishment of BUMIDOM (*Bureau pour le développement des migrations intéressant les départements d'outre-mer*, or Bureau for Migration from the Overseas Departments).[139] Although many Antilleans and those from Réunion welcomed these jobs as preferable to the limited opportunities at home, France benefited immeasurably from the availability of workers for posts they could not otherwise easily fill. In this sense, as Juliette Minces has suggested, BUMIDOM served as the principal channel enabling a '*nouvelle traite des nègres*' – a 'new slave trade'.[140]

New arrivals from France's colonies, formerly-held territories, and the DOM-TOM correspondingly settled where they found work, with Paris and its surrounding region (Île-de-France), Lyon, and the Mediterranean region of Provence-Alpes-Côte d'Azur (particularly the city of Marseille) having the highest concentrations. Overwhelmingly urban in nature, *harkis* long proved the exception to the rule as the government settled them in camps in rural areas isolated from France's larger towns and cities. Within the cities and their outskirts where the majority of North Africans, Antilleans, and West Africans moved, particular run-down working-class neighbourhoods and districts became deeply associated with their growing overseas communities, two examples being Paris' Goutte d'Or district near the Gare du Nord and the area of Marseille Sembène referred to as 'Little Harlem', or a 'little Africa in the south of France'.[141]

sometimes referred to as 'Sembène Ousmane' or simply 'Sembène'. On *Black Docker*, see Thomas, *Black France*, ch. 3; Yaël Simpson Fletcher, 'Catholics, Communists, and Colonial Subjects: Working-Class Militancy and Racial Difference in Postwar Marseille', in Sue Peabody and Tyler Stovall (eds.), *The Color of Liberty: Histories of Race in France* (Durham, 2003), 338–50.

[139] Stephanie A. Condon and Philip E. Ogden, 'Emigration from the French Caribbean: The Origins of an Organized Migration', *International Journal of Urban and Regional Research*, 15:4 (1991), 505–23; Marie, 'Les Antillais', 27–8.

[140] Minces, *Les travailleurs étrangers*, 85.

[141] Sembène Ousmane, *Black Docker*, 41; Vasoodeven Vuddamalay, Paul White, and Deborah Sporton, 'The Evolution of the Goutte d'Or as an Ethnic Minority District of Paris', *New Community*, 17:2 (1991), 245–58. On post-war Marseille, a Mediterranean port city whose geography, economy, ethnically heterogeneous immigrant communities, and culture long secured its status as the gateway to (and from) the French empire, see especially Jean-Jacques Jordi, Abdelmalek Sayad, and Émile Temime, *Histoire des migrations à Marseille, vol. 4: Le choc de la décolonisation (1945–1990)* (Aix-en-Provence, 1991); Pascal Blanchard and Gilles Boëtsch (eds.), *Marseille Porte Sud 1905–2005* (Paris, 2005); Fletcher, 'Catholics, Communists, and Colonial Subjects'; Brigitte Bertoncello and Sylvie Bredeloup, *Colporteurs africains à Marseille: Un siècle d'aventures* (Paris, 2004).

At a time when France suffered a severe housing shortage – not for nothing were many immigrant workers employed in construction – newcomers from overseas typically lived in crowded, unhealthy, and overpriced accommodation, a situation bearing some resemblance to British conditions outlined earlier. Single male workers commonly lived in lodging houses (*hôtels*) run by landlords known as 'sleep merchants' (*marchands de sommeil*), renting space in rooms where those on the night and day shifts in factories slept in rotation. Others resided in workers' hostels (*foyers*) where their activities were closely regulated. Throughout the 1950s and beyond, tens of thousands lived in *bidonvilles*, the shantytown slums that multiplied around the outskirts of Paris, Marseille, and Lyon. Algerians and Moroccans were not the only immigrants to live in *bidonvilles* – the Portuguese were also well represented in many such as Champigny in Paris – but shantytowns became best known as Maghrebi settlements despite being multi-ethnic.[142] Indeed, the very term *bidonville* was imported from North Africa where the French colonizers used it to refer to comparable settlements around Algiers or Casablanca.[143] Conditions in France's *bidonvilles* were grim: their inhabitants lived in shacks without electricity, sewers, or running water, with thousands of people depending on a single communal water pipe for all their cooking and washing needs. Lacking paved roads, overcrowded *bidonvilles* became mud baths when it rained or snowed and their residents did constant battle with rats, parasites, and the threat of fire and sickness.

Immigrant men, and increasingly their wives and children, lived largely in isolation from mainstream French society, relegated by their poverty and ethnicity to specific districts often located at a considerable distance from city centres; as such, *bidonvilles* became racialized spaces literally on the metropolitan margins. France's indigenous working classes, while historically also living and working in the suburbs, did not compete with newcomers for scarce housing in the 1950s and 1960s to the extent typical in other European

[142] Marie-Christine Volovitch-Tavares, *Portugais à Champigny, le temps des baraques* (Paris, 1995).

[143] Marie-Claude Blanc-Chaléard, 'Les immigrés et le logement en France depuis le XIXe siècle: une histoire paradoxale', in Stora and Temime (eds.), *Immigrances*, 77. On housing, see also R. D. Grillo, *Ideologies and Institutions in Urban France: The Representation of Immigrants* (Cambridge, 1985), chs. 4 and 5; Peter Jones, 'Race, Discourse and Power in Institutional Housing: The Case of Immigrant Worker Hostels in Lyons', in Maxim Silverman (ed.), *Race, Discourse and Power in France* (Aldershot, 1991), 55–70; Paul A. Silverstein, *Algeria in France: Transpolitics, Race, and Nation* (Bloomington, 2004), ch. 3; Ahmed El Gharbaoui, 'Les travailleurs maghébins immigrés dans la banlieue nord-ouest de Paris', *Revue de Géographie du Maroc*, 19 (1971), 3–56; Mehdi Lallaoui, *Du bidonville aux HLM* (Paris, 1993); Abdelmalek Sayad (with the collaboration of Éliane Dupuy), *Un Nanterre algérien, terre de bidonvilles* (Paris, 1995); Mireille Rosello, 'North African Women and the Ideology of Modernization: From Bidonvilles to Cités de Transit and HLM', in Alec G. Hargreaves and Mark McKinney (eds.), *Post-colonial Cultures in France* (London, 1997), 240–54.

Figure 7.2 'Bidonville de la Folie à Nanterre en 1964.'
Photograph by Jean Pottier of the Algerian *bidonville* (shantytown) in
Nanterre, outside central Paris, as it looked in the late 1950s and early 1960s.

countries; this came later as authorities gradually marked shantytowns for
demolition and their residents moved into social housing, as will be considered
below.[144] French workers then mixed with immigrants largely at the workplace
and, to a lesser degree, in public life. In these arenas racism was rife, and those
bearing the brunt often valued their ability to insulate themselves from it by
keeping largely to their own circles in *bidonvilles* or other neighbourhoods with
a high concentration of fellow countrymen. After their destruction, *bidonvilles*
became remembered not simply as sites of poverty and misery in the midst of
the nation's prosperity during the *trente glorieuses*, but also with nostalgia for
the spirit of community and solidarity they engendered.[145] Keeping amongst
themselves whenever possible provided some with a safe haven from French
hostility, as the account provided by an Algerian man interviewed by Sayad
illustrates: 'shut your eyes, see nothing; block your ears, hear nothing. There is

---

[144] Tyler Stovall, 'From Red Belt to Black Belt: Race, Class, and Urban Marginality in Twentieth-
Century Paris', in Peabody and Stovall (eds.), *Color of Liberty*, 351–69.
[145] Brahim Benaïcha, *Vivre au paradis: d'une oasis à un bidonville* (Paris, 1999). On family life
and growing up in a *bidonville* outside Lyon, see Azouz Begag's autobiographical novel
Shantytown Kid, translated by Naïma Wolf and Alec G. Hargreaves (Lincoln and London,
2007; originally published in French in 1986).

a remedy for that sort of racism: you stay at home, within our own limits, stay on your guard . . . why mix with them [the French]? . . . As little as possible is best . . . Stay amongst us, and you'll see: racism and racists don't exist! . . . Your poverty, your hunger, your worries: that's your racism.' Dealings with the French only brought disappointment and discrimination in this view, and while inescapable in the workplace could be avoided in leisure:

[T]here's always a frontier, you're not the same as them . . . He [the emigrant] begins to take an interest in girls: he goes to a dance, and that is where he discovers racism: you discover that there is always a barrier. The worst racism is the racism of the dance hall. . . . Even at work, you can't be anything but a labourer; they're not used to that. . . . They've never seen a Kabyle foreman, an Algerian or an Arab boss . . . our place is in the immigrant jobs, as they put it, all the filthy jobs where you lose your health and perhaps even your life.[146]

The 1967 novel entitled *Élise ou la vraie vie* (*Elise or the Real Life*) provides valuable insight into issues central to the history of French working-class and migrant (particularly Algerian) life in late 1950s France, especially workplace racism, sexual stereotypes, and the Algerian War's inescapability in Paris. Its author Claire Etcherelli drew heavily on her own experiences as a young woman from Bordeaux who moved to Paris and worked on the assembly line at the Citroën car plant a decade earlier, and much of the book is set in late 1957 and early 1958. Protagonist Élise follows her brother Lucien into factory work, and the latter's political idealism for worker solidarity amongst the down-trodden became crushed by relentless physically debilitating labour. 'If I hadn't been working with blacks, cheek by jowl, I'd have already forgotten them', he told a friend. 'But there they are, and for all that I feel exploited and diminished, next to them, I am a privileged person. They are a fuel with no value, an inexhaustible reserve. There can't be more than three or four of us in the factory who see that they are men.'[147] Shop floor racism became directed at workers from Hungary, sub-Saharan Africa, and Algeria alike, but Algerians suffered the most abuse, condemned as inherently lazy, incompetent, and devious, and collectively called 'Mohammed':[148]

The French didn't like Algerians, or any foreigners, for that matter. They accused them of taking away their jobs and then not knowing how to do them. The shared efforts, the shared sweat, the shared demands were, as Lucien said, "So much crap," so many slogans. Most of them brought their own frustrations and distrusts to the factory. It was impossible to be for the rat hunts outside and the fraternity of the workers inside the cage.[149]

---

[146] Sayad, *Suffering of the Immigrant*, 48–9.
[147] Claire Etcherelli, *Elise or the Real Life*, translated by June P. Wilson and Walter Benn Michaels (London, 1970, originally published in French in 1967), 140.
[148] Ibid., 152.   [149] Ibid., 169; see also 143, 170.

'Rat hunts outside' referred directly to the official crackdown within metropolitan France on the FLN network operating amongst Algerian workers during the war – a theme introduced in Chapter 3 and analyzed in depth by Jim House and Neil MacMaster as well as Benjamin Stora, Monique Hervo, and others. With Algerians in French cities providing crucial funding for the FLN's anticolonial campaign across the Mediterranean, French police engaged in a brutal campaign of repression. The Battle of Algiers became the Battle of Paris as police relentlessly stopped and searched Algerian men in metro stations and on the street, raiding their lodging houses and *bidonvilles* (most famously Paris' Nanterre) and holding many in custody. Most were released but only after being interrogated and often beaten and tortured; others were sent back to Algeria or simply disappeared.[150] *Élise ou la vraie vie* explores these themes via Élise's romance with her Algerian co-worker Arezki, an FLN operative who faced constant police harassment and public suspicion wherever he went. His relationship with Élise was doomed to failure, for '[i]t was not a good thing, at the start of this year 1958, to be an Algerian in Paris. He was living on borrowed time.'[151] Within months, he vanished permanently from Élise's life following yet another arrest; while his fate was never clear, she reasonably assumed that he had been killed.

The wartime context underpinned every aspect of Arezki's life in Paris, continually shaping responses to him and Élise as a mixed couple before ultimately rendering their future together impossible. The following scene at a café illustrates the common understanding of Algerian men as simultaneously a political threat, violent, and sexually predatory with French women: '"where are the police? Look at that guy sitting right next to you in a nice place where you've made a date with a nice girl ... and there's an Arab with a French girl! ... We're fighting a war with those guys ... Clean up Paris. Maybe this one has a gun in his pocket. They all have."'[152] Similarly, Élise suffered public sneers and slights from female co-workers at the factory who called her 'Aïcha'. To be labelled as one who 'goes out with Algerians' or with 'Negroes' was the ultimate insult, 'always followed by the plural' to emphasize low morals and promiscuity. Élise may have been deeply offended (albeit undeterred) by these slurs, but they came as no surprise to Arezki. 'To the French, we are sexual brutes', he shrugged.[153]

---

[150] Jim House and Neil MacMaster, *Paris 1961: Algerians, State Terror, and Memory* (Oxford, 2006); MacMaster, *Colonial Migrants*, ch. 11; Stora, *Ils venaient d'Algérie*; Alexis Spire, *Étrangers à la carte: L'administration de l'immigration en France (1945–1975)* (Paris, 2005). Particularly revealing are Monique Hervo's accounts based upon her time living and working in a Nanterre *bidonville* as a social worker during the Algerian War; see her *Chroniques du bidonville: Nanterre en Guerre d'Algérie, 1959–1962* (Paris, 2001).
[151] Etcherelli, *Elise*, 232.   [152] Ibid., 181.   [153] Ibid., 179, 248; see also 154, 160, 225.

As Arezki and his non-fictional counterparts knew well, 'the racism of the dance hall' directed at colonial men interacting with white women was nothing new. Algerian men may have borne the brunt of such stereotypes and hostilities which the 1954–1962 war of independence enhanced, but such conceptions had long applied to colonized racial 'others' more widely. As this was a predominantly male population during the 1950s and 1960s, gendered forms of discrimination and bias were rife among the native French, just as was the case with many British and Dutch. 'Arabs', 'Africans', and other 'blacks' were widely seen as sexually deviant, covetous of white women, and prone to violence and criminality.[154] Readily linked to sexual licentiousness and sexually-transmitted diseases alike, the pathologization of late-colonial and postcolonial peoples extended to the belief that they brought 'tropical' illnesses into France and suffered frequent ill health due to their purported constitutional incompatibility with the French climate.[155] With bodies and mores apt to be condemned as bestial and barbaric, in their supposed 'savagery' they served as the convenient antithesis to France's 'civilization'. Writing in 1973, Juliette Minces opined that

persuaded of their country's role as 'civilizer' and 'generous', the French only accept foreign cultures with an air of paternalism at best. Their attractions are largely limited to their exoticism as leisure pursuits (Portuguese fado, Spanish flamenco, Maghrebi couscous, etc.). When it comes to non-European civilizations, the rejection is even more categorical. Not living 'like us', 'those people' can only be uncivilized, 'savage' at worst (Maghrebis, Africans), since we alone are the carriers of civilization.

In short, 'colonial propaganda remains present' past the end of empire itself, the imperial 'civilizing mission' having become transferred to metropolitan soil.[156]

French cultural understandings of formerly colonized peoples proved highly influential in changing the nation's immigration policies between the late 1960s and the mid-1970s. The impact of the end of the protracted economic boom after 1973 cannot be underestimated, not least because of the close link between the numbers of new arrivals and the availability of work. The common-sense equation between 'immigrant' and 'worker' up until the 1970s rapidly shifted to a scenario of high ethnic minority unemployment. But as Maxim Silverman has argued, '[i]mmigration controls in contemporary France

---

[154] Todd Shepard, '"Something Notably Erotic": Politics, "Arab Men," and Sexual Revolution in Post-decolonization France, 1962–1974', *Journal of Modern History*, 84:1 (2012), 80–115.

[155] Among countless sources discussing these attitudes, see Alain Girard, 'Attitudes des Français à l'égard de l'immigration étrangère', *Population*, 26:5 (1971), 835; Bergues, 'L'immigration de travailleurs africains noirs', 70, 72, 75; Sembène Ousmane, *Black Docker*, 10–11, 25, 102; Minces, *Les travailleurs étrangers*, 409, 416–18; MacMaster, *Colonial Migrants*, 138–9, 191, 260.

[156] Minces, *Les travailleurs étrangers*, 407. On French 'civilization' versus blacks' 'barbarity', see also Sembène Ousmane, *Black Docker*, 10–11, 34, 103.

were not at first the result of the economic crisis of the 1970s; instead, they were influenced largely by concerns about assimilation, ethnic balance, and social cohesion'.[157] Anxieties about 'social problems' became increasingly prominent in official discourse well before the need for additional manual labour ground to a halt, and these underpinned the incremental moves towards state intervention. Starting in 1968, the French government introduced quotas on the number of Algerians permitted entry within a given year (initially placed at 1,000 per month but later raised to 35,000 annually), and in 1972 the Marcellin-Fontanet circulars stipulated that those eligible for regularization needed to possess both an employment contract and adequate housing. 1974 spelled the end of an era as the state curtailed primary labour migration from outside the European Economic Community. This terminated free movement into France for peoples of ex-French African territories who, having once been citizens, 'had *become* immigrants', as Frederick Cooper stresses, acting as a reminder that 'the definition of the "immigrant" in France . . . is not a given, but a product of history'.[158] Non-European immigration into France certainly did not cease in 1974; as noted earlier, some groups only saw their most marked increase in later decades. After the early 1970s, however, many new arrivals faced obstacles as *clandestins* or *sans papiers* – illegals 'without papers' whose status in France became increasingly precarious.

Even more significantly, 1974's legislation contributed immeasurably to the shift, already under way, away from male-dominated cyclical migration and towards more permanently settled populations characterized by an upsurge in family reunification within France.[159] Women, children, and families rendered ethnic minority groups increasingly visible to the French public outside male-dominated workplaces, and in many ways they came to epitomize many of the 'social problems' with which immigrants became popularly associated during and after the late 1960s. These revolved predominantly around housing, ethnically diverse neighbourhoods, and, as the next chapter discusses, schools, youth culture, and the perceived condition of women of other cultural backgrounds branded as less 'civilized'.

From the late 1960s until well into the next decade, many men who initially lived in lodging houses, workers' hostels, or *bidonvilles* were not only joined by their families but also moved into newly-built housing. Shantytowns were gradually demolished and their residents relocated first into temporary prefabricated housing (*cités de transit*) and ultimately into state-subsidized social housing known as HLM (*habitations à loyer modéré*). Taking the form of large

---

[157] Silverman, *Deconstructing the Nation*, 77.   [158] Cooper, *Citizenship*, 442, 445.
[159] Silverman, *Deconstructing the Nation*, 46–53; Weil, *La France et ses étrangers*, 69–87. Migration from the Antilles, however, traditionally involved many women travelling to the metropole not simply to join male relatives but often on their own in search of work. See Marie, 'Les Antillais', 27–8.

tower blocks, the HLM, like the shantytowns they replaced, were mainly concentrated on the suburban margins of large cities (the *banlieues*). Initially intended for France's native working-class population along with many *pieds-noirs* who had nowhere to go following their *en masse* arrival in 1962, over time they housed an increasing proportion of families from North Africa, sub-Saharan Africa, and the DOM-TOM.[160] Multi-ethnic HLM and *banlieues* became critical contact zones where immigrants quite literally came closer to home both for poorer white families living beside them and for political and media commentators observing them from the outside.

Social proximity in private life often fomented resentment of peoples with customs that separated 'us' from 'them', resentments that anti-immigration politicians seeking white working-class votes increasingly seized upon over the coming decades. While Chapter 8 delves further into the rise of the xenophobic extreme right *Front National* during and after the 1980s, it is important to stress that mainstream politicians also sought to capitalize upon popular resentment of 'others' portrayed simultaneously as a private nuisance and public burden. As the centre-right mayor of Paris Jacques Chirac infamously stated in 1991, the French worker living in an area like Goutte d'Or or in an HLM 'looks across the landing to see ... a family with a father, three or four wives, twenty or so children, who gets 50,000 francs worth of welfare benefits without working, and if you add to that the noise and the smell, the French worker goes crazy'.[161] Unemployed, welfare dependent, polygamous, and overly fecund, stereotyped families breached the domestic barriers of French homes and the French nation alike, just as immigrants in Britain attracted criticism for their loud music and cooking odours.

Public commentators frequently invoked the concept of the *seuil de tolérance* – 'threshold of tolerance' – to describe the percentage of foreigners that specific localities needed to reach to provoke hostility amongst the native population.[162] While normally applied to housing complexes or neighbourhoods, the threshold worked as a domestic metaphor and boundary marker that readily extended to encompass the nation as a whole invaded by 'too many immigrants'. As the *Front National*'s leader Jean-Marie Le Pen told an

[160] Silverstein, *Algeria in France*, 92–8; Ed Naylor, '"Un âne dans l'ascenseur": Late Colonial Welfare Services and Social Housing in Marseille after Decolonization', *French History*, 27:3 (2013), 422–47; Blanc-Chaléard, 'Les immigrés et le logement'; Jordi, Sayad, and Temime, *Histoire des Migrations à Marseille, vol. 4*, 128–40; Rosello, 'North African Women'; Stovall, 'From Red Belt to Black Belt'; Grillo, *Ideologies and Institutions*, 113–40; Lallaoui, *Du bidonville aux HLM*.
[161] 'Chirac dénonce l'inquiétude des Français', *Le Figaro*, 21 June 1991, 1, 7.
[162] Véronique de Rudder, '"Seuil de tolérance" et cohabitation pluriethnique', in Pierre-André Taguieff (ed.), *Face au racism 2: Analyses, hypothèses, perspectives* (Paris, 1991), 154–66; Neil MacMaster, 'The "Seuil de tolérance": The Uses of a "Scientific" Racist Concept', in Silverman (ed.), *Race, Discourse and Power*, 14–28.

interviewer in 1993, 'flourishing' nations were 'a bit like an apartment ... one doesn't just let anyone in'.[163] Metaphorical depictions of the nation as a house became common in political discourse not only within but beyond the extreme right, as did the analogy between immigrant and guest. Mireille Rosello astutely notes that this 'ideological logic ... can welcome or reject: political leaders can either urge the French to be more hospitable and to greet the Guest, that is, the immigrants, with open arms, or construct images of the bad Guest who overstays his or her welcome, pockets the silver, or ransacks the fridge'. More often than not they opted for the latter course, with immigrants/guests represented as equivalent to 'undesirable parasites'.[164]

Significantly, an official report dating from 1969 argued that the *seuil de tolérance* was higher for foreigners from other parts of Europe than it was for non-Europeans (20 per cent versus 15 per cent).[165] This raises three interrelated questions. First, which individuals and groups were more likely to become, or remain, popularly labelled as 'immigrants' or 'foreigners' within France? Second, what difference did French citizenship make in such 'common-sense' responses? And third, how have European foreigners compared in the popular imagination with various racialized populations from France's former empire and the DOM-TOM that remain *départements* of France today?

French public discourse long blurred the lines, often inaccurately, between those construed as 'immigrants' and 'foreigners'. 'Immigrant' was the term repeatedly applied to Antilleans and others from the DOM-TOM who entered the metropole as French nationals, as indeed had Algerians until independence in 1962. Many other colonial and postcolonial migrants eventually acquired French citizenship if they did not formally possess it upon arrival, yet remained seen as 'foreign'. Moreover, most children of 'immigrants' (real or imagined) born within the metropole officially counted as French upon reaching adult-hood but still found themselves labelled as 'foreign' by everyday people, politicians, and the media – even if, as was often the case, they had never lived outside France.[166] Holding French passports did not stop those from Martinique or Guadeloupe from becoming lumped together with sub-Saharan Africans as 'black' and 'foreign', a move that simultaneously negated their Frenchness and ignored their immense diversity on account of racialized forms of difference and colonial origins.[167] Still, while the homogenization of France's 'black' population was both ethnically and historically misleading, these groups often shared similar experiences of racism coupled with socio-

---

[163] Jonathan Marcus, *The National Front and French Politics: The Resistible Rise of Jean-Marie Le Pen* (Basingstoke, 1995), 8.
[164] Mireille Rosello, *Postcolonial Hospitality: The Immigrant as Guest* (Stanford, 2001), 33–4.
[165] De Rudder, '"Seuil de tolérance"', 154.
[166] Silverman, *Deconstructing the Nation*, 3, 37, 41.
[167] Minces, *Les travailleurs étrangers*, 411; Sembène, *Black Docker*, 57.

economic deprivation. Writing of Antilleans, Claude-Valentin Marie appraised their circumstances thus: 'Far from being distanced from these "foreigners" [the Africans] ... Antilleans occupied the same HLM and lived in the same *banlieues* where they were perceived as belonging to a single, devalued social universe, that of immigration.'[168]

In one crucial respect, however, not all 'blacks' were 'the same' in the eyes of the indigenous French: some – such as the Antilleans – were Catholic, while others – such as many Senegalese, Malians, etc. – were Muslim. As such, the latter shared with North Africans the stigma of association with Islam, a form of 'otherness' already greeted with hostility in the 1950s and 1960s but attracting even greater animosity thereafter (particularly during and after the 1980s) in response to international affairs. Islam and Muslims became synonymous with intolerant and inflexible religious fundamentalism (and often international terrorism), the oppression of women, customs deemed either barbaric or simply backward, and the inability or unwillingness to 'assimilate' or 'integrate' within a secular, republican France, themes Chapter 8 considers more extensively.[169] The Islamic faith and its adherents attracted relentless political and media opprobrium, whether expressed explicitly or implicitly. Jacques Chirac did not name the 'problem' family in the HLM as a Muslim family, but alluding to the man's multiple wives achieved this without the need for further elaboration. Alongside being associated with offensive smells and noises, Muslims violated domestic decorum in countless other respects that ranged from deviations from the nuclear family 'norm' via polygamy – practiced only by a minority – to their purported (mis-)use of bathtubs or balconies to slaughter sheep and goats at Ramadan.[170] Religious difference became the primary form of cultural difference around which racism increasingly revolved.

Such was the public emphasis upon North Africans (and Algerians first and foremost) that terms like 'immigrant', 'Algerian', and 'Arab' readily became interchangeable. 'Immigrants? You mean Arabs!' read the headline of a representative article in *Le Nouvel Observateur* in 1984. The reasons why many French so consistently singled out this group – that was not really a 'group' at all but rather a convenient composite – included colonial wars (and particularly the Algerian War of 1954–1962) and the 'terrifying' global rise of Islam after

---

[168] Claude-Valentin Marie, 'L'Europe: de l'empire aux colonies intérieures', in Taguieff (ed.), *Face au racism* 2, 299.

[169] Michèle Lamont, 'Working Men's Imagined Communities: The Boundaries of Race, Immigration, and Poverty in France and the United States', in Ulf Hedetoft and Mette Hjort (eds.), *The Postnational Self: Belonging and Identity* (Minneapolis, 2002), 182–6; Michel Wieviorka, 'Race, Culture, and Society: The French Experience of Muslims', in Nezar Alsayyad and Manuel Castells (eds.), *Muslim Europe or Euro-Islam: Politics, Culture, and Citizenship in the Age of Globalization* (Lanham, MD, 2002), 134.

[170] Alec G. Hargreaves (ed.), *Immigration in Post-war France: A Documentary Anthology* (London, 1987), 134.

the mid-1970s. 'I feel that my culture, customs, and way of life are menaced by the veritable invasion from the Maghreb and Islamic Africa into France,' was one typical response.[171] Significantly, French people with this outlook often denied that they were xenophobic, claiming they were not against foreigners *per se*. 'Blacks' not linked with Islam, for instance, might be seen pejoratively as 'big children' and associated with low-status forms of work yet appear less threatening because they were imagined as carefree, fun-loving, and loosely affiliated with African-American musical culture – stereotypes similar to those widely applied to the Afro-Surinamese in the Netherlands.

Even more suggestive were responses to new arrivals from Vietnam and elsewhere in Southeast Asia in the mid-late 1970s. As Nicola Cooper advances, the twenty-year interval between France's withdrawal from Indochina after a protracted war against the Viet Minh that ended in the humiliating defeat at Dien Bien Phu in 1954 helped ensure that the 'boat people' were not immediately associated with anti-colonial nationalism and violence. Instead, colonial myths that positioned the 'average' Vietnamese as docile, complicit, and apolitical – a grateful colonized majority – in opposition to the communist anti-colonial minority were ripe for reinvigoration once decolonization in Indochina was more safely distant, not to mention overlaid by more bitter memories of the Algerian War that directly succeeded it. Politicians and the media viewed the Vietnamese entering France in the 1970s as global 'refugees' fleeing from an oppressive communist regime, not as unwelcome erstwhile opponents of French rule.[172] What is more, their cultural differences were not construed as threatening; in place of the spectre of Islam, the Vietnamese were Buddhist or Catholic.[173] Described as polite, conformist, undemanding, hard working, appreciative, and eager to assimilate, Vietnamese 'refugees' became readily portrayed as the antithesis of the underemployed Muslim/Arab/ Maghrebi 'immigrants' either unwilling or unable to integrate within French society and culture.

Of all 'foreign' new arrivals, however, Europeans were by far the least contentious and ranked highest in the hierarchy of those seen as 'desirable immigrants'.[174] Albeit lacking the French nationality possessed by many formerly colonized and those from the DOM-TOM and often having no ability to speak French, those from nearby countries in Western, Southern, and Eastern Europe were viewed as readily assimilable both because of what they were (fellow Europeans and Christian – therefore more 'like us') and

[171] Anne Fohr *et al.*, 'Immigrés? Vous voulez dire Arabes!', *Le Nouvel Observateur*, 30 November 1984, reprinted in Hargreaves (ed.), *Immigration in Post-war France*, 53.

[172] Cooper, *France in Indochina*, ch. 10; Fohr *et al.*, 'Immigrés?', 54.

[173] Simon-Barouh, 'Les Viêtnamiens', 138–9.

[174] Girard, 'Attitudes des Français', 836–41; Minces, *Les travailleurs étrangers*, 408; Fohr *et al.*, 'Immigrés?', 53.

what they were not (racialized 'others' and often Muslim). Of the many European nationalities settling in France after 1945, the Portuguese experience provides one of the best illustrations of how European foreigners were envisioned differently than colonial and postcolonial ethnic minority groups. With their numbers skyrocketing in the early 1960s and exceeding 800,000 by the late 1970s, the Portuguese long ranked as either the largest or second-largest migrant group in France, vying with the Algerians for first and second place. Unlike the Algerians, many had entered France illegally, but the *clandestin* taint did not encumber them over the long term. France gradually regularized their status, for they were seen not simply as essential labourers but equally as readily assimilable. Within a nation whose weak birth rate was a deeply entrenched source of anxiety, North African family reunification and the birth rate of Muslim families was politically contentious and pathologized by the media (exemplified by the 'twenty or so children' Chirac referred to earlier), while the high rate of Portuguese familial migration was officially encouraged.[175]

By the 1980s, France's substantial Portuguese population largely escaped the increasingly vociferous public debates about the 'problems' associated with immigration. The Portuguese became virtually invisible, as Albano Cordeiro has argued, owing 'this absence, which is called integration' to their juxtaposition with North Africans.[176] Nonetheless, it is important to stress that their favourable position was not only relative but also improved over time. Upon arrival, they too were victims of debilitating stereotypes in the 1960s and 1970s. If 'every Algerian was Mohamed, every Portuguese was Antonio', Juliette Minces observed of French workplace attitudes.[177] As the next pages illustrate, the Portuguese travelling to France shared significant features with other migrants from France's overseas territories and former colonies. Not only did they come on account of poverty at home, live in *bidonvilles* upon arrival, and experience class and ethnic discrimination as part of a low-paid exploited workforce. Theirs was also a decolonization migration, albeit of a different kind: that from a Portuguese empire in terminal decline whose repercussions encompassed the Portuguese metropole, its overseas territories, France, and other nations alike.

* * *

---

[175] Albano Cordeiro, 'Les Portugais, une population "invisible"?', in Dewitte (ed.), *Immigration et intégration*, 106–111; see also 'Portugais de France', special issue, *Hommes et Migrations*, 1210 (1997).

[176] Albano Cordeiro, 'Le paradoxe de l'immigration portugaise', *Hommes et Migrations*, 1123 (1989), 25–6.

[177] Minces, *Les travailleurs étrangers*, 204.

Portugal: A nation of emigration and postcolonial immigration

For centuries, departure has been a persistent and integral aspect of Portugal's social history and national identity.[178] From the early modern 'Age of Discoveries' when Vasco da Gama and other maritime explorers set out to chart unknown overseas territories to the hundreds of thousands of Portuguese who settled in the colonies that emerged in their wake, leaving Portugal for Brazil, Africa, and other regions was long a common destiny for the inhabitants of one of Europe's poorer countries. In the twentieth century, Portuguese migrants headed for the nation's so-called 'overseas provinces' in Africa until colonial wars and independence closed off these destinations. As broached earlier, more-over, even more working-class Portuguese went to find work in France, Germany, and other European destinations as well as North America after the Second World War. Emigration to highly developed countries proved particularly attractive during the 1960s and early 1970s, when the economic boom in nations like France and the Netherlands acted as a 'pull' factor while colonial wars, dictator-ship, and underdevelopment at home provided the 'push'.[179] Most Portuguese left in search of work, but political opposition to the dictatorship led others into exile in Britain, France, or elsewhere abroad.[180]

Rural areas of northern Portugal accounted for a substantial share of those heading to France, which attracted the largest number of emigrants as the closest country beyond Spain (which, like Portugal itself, remained under dictatorship and economically underdeveloped). Impoverished peasants from the countryside often left illegally – possessing only the 'rabbit's passport', as the saying went – making the dangerous journey through Spain and over the mountains partly hidden on trucks and partly on foot with the help of organized smugglers. Although the Portuguese state depended on the economic benefits of emigration (not least the remittances workers sent home from abroad that not only fed their families but also helped offset the national deficit enhanced by the cost of fighting colonial wars) and entered into bilateral agreements with France, the Netherlands, and Germany, it insisted upon strict quotas on the numbers legally allowed to leave each year.[181] Both wealthy landowners and the dictatorship had a strong vested interest in limiting emigration because they

---

[178] Helena Carvalhão Buescu, 'Time Displaced: Post-colonial Experience in António Lobo Antunes', *European Review*, 13:2 (2005), 261–9.

[179] On Portuguese migration to the Netherlands, see Lucassen and Penninx, *Newcomers*, 54–9, 46.

[180] Two dissidents who relocated to London were António de Figueiredo, activist, journalist, and author of respected books including *Portugal: Fifty Years of Dictatorship* (Harmondsworth, 1975), and the artist Bartolmeu Cid do Santos. See their respective obituaries in *Guardian*, 12 December 2006, 32; *Guardian*, 8 August 2008, 37.

[181] Maria Ioannis B. Baganha, 'Portuguese Emigration After World War II', in António Costa Pinto (ed.), *Modern Portugal* (Palo Alto, 1998), 191–2; Caroline B. Brettell, 'The Emigrant, the Nation, and the State in Nineteenth- and Twentieth-Century Portugal: An Anthropological Approach', *Portuguese Studies Review*, 2:2 (1993), 54–6.

sought to maintain their supply of cheap agricultural labour as well as young men due for involuntary military service in Africa.

Anti-colonial wars that began in the early 1960s were a decisive cause of male departures.[182] Some Portuguese dodged the draft because they were ideologically anti-war and supported African nationalism ('I believe that Angola belongs to the Africans', as one young worker who arrived in Paris in 1964 later said); others simply wanted to spare themselves what seemed an interminable four to six years in the army in the name of preserving the 'overseas provinces'.[183] Nonetheless, while war lay behind many men's decisions to leave, Portuguese women were also strongly represented among this swelling diaspora on account of both family reunification as well as their own search for work. While women commonly found jobs as domestic help or in retail, men were most heavily concentrated in the construction sector. In France, women constituted approximately 30 per cent of the total resident Portuguese population as early as 1962 and over 46 per cent by 1975, making the so-called *salto* into foreign countries – the 'great leap' that became shorthand for this mass wave of emigration when well over one-tenth of Portugal's total population left – one ultimately shared almost equally across gender lines.[184]

Empire's decline and fall proved a critical turning point when arrivals in Portugal started to compete with departures in numerical terms. Not only did Portuguese settlers (*retornados*) return *en masse* from Africa; Lusophone (Portuguese-speaking) Africans also gradually acquired greater visibility within Portugal. After decolonization, the overwhelming majority of Portugal's new arrivals were from ex-colonized populations, particularly from the Cape Verde Islands but also Angola, Guinea Bissau, Mozambique, São Tomé and Príncipe, and Goa, not to mention Brazil, independent since 1822, with which a two-way traffic continues today.[185] In short, it took the protracted end of empire and the 1974 revolution to turn Portugal into a nation of immigration as well as emigration.

Just as was the case in other European imperial powers, colonized peoples (for instance, African slaves bought back from Brazil) had been present within

---

[182] Ponty, *L'immigration dans les textes*, 325–9.
[183] Minces, *Les travailleurs étrangers*, 14; see also 13–25, 44, 64, 70–1, 119.
[184] Ponty, *L'immigration dans les textes*, 311; Cordeiro, 'Les Portugais', 107–8.
[185] Maria do Céu Esteves (ed.), *Portugal, País de Imigração* (Lisbon, 1991); Bela Feldman-Bianco, 'Brazilians in Portugal, Portuguese in Brazil: Constructions of Sameness and Difference', *Identities*, 8:4 (2001), 607–50; Rui Pena Pires, *Migrações e Integração* (Oeiras, Portugal, 2003), ch. 3; Sheila Khan, 'Identidades sem chão: Imigrantes Afro-Moçambicanos: Narrativas de Vida e de Identidade, e Percepções de um Portugal Pós-colonial', *Luso-Brazilian Review*, 43:2 (2006), 1–26. Immigrants to Portugal from Goa, Timor, and Macau were, and remain, far fewer in number. On Goa, see Caroline Brettell, 'Portugal's First Post-Colonials: Citizenship, Identity, and the Repatriation of Goans', *Portuguese Studies Review*, 14:2 (2006/7), 143–70.

Portugal for centuries, albeit in relatively small numbers. Alongside African sailors whose work involved cyclical migrations between the metropole and its 'overseas provinces', by the 1940s and 1950s growing numbers of black and *mestiço* students from Cape Verde, Angola, Mozambique, and other Portuguese-controlled territories also travelled to Lisbon for higher education. Like their counterparts in other European countries, some found opportunities to hone new forms of cultural and ultimately political consciousness as Africans after coming together in Portugal. Experiences and alliances fostered in Lisbon, both among themselves and through encounters with Portuguese opponents of the dictatorship, proved decisive to the political education of a number who subsequently played key roles in anti-colonial nationalist struggles, Amílcar Cabral and Agostinho Neto being just two of the most influential.[186]

Arrivals became more regular and substantial in the 1960s, when Portugal paradoxically experienced a labour shortage at home as a result of mass emigration and the onset of colonial wars requiring men to serve in Africa. Cape Verde Islanders were recruited for unskilled jobs, particularly construction work in and around Lisbon, setting in motion a chain migration pattern that accelerated in subsequent decades.[187] As a result of substitution migration, Cape Verdeans and Africans from other former Portuguese colonies arrived to do similar low-status jobs that so many Portuguese refused at home but travelled to northwest Europe to perform for the higher wages offered abroad.[188] In countries like France, Portuguese workers may have encountered less racism than non-European newcomers, but as noted earlier they nonetheless occupied menial positions in the labour market and experienced discrimination both because they were economically disadvantaged and ethnically distinct.[189] Portugal has thus become both a sending and receiving country, reflecting what scholars including Boaventura de Sousa Santos have called its 'semi-peripheral' global position.[190] Albeit once an empowered 'centre' with respect to its former colonies and later an attractive destination for economic migrants from Lusophone Africa, Portugal still remained an underdeveloped 'periphery' vis-à-vis wealthier European

---

[186] Patrick Chabal, *Amílcar Cabral: Revolutionary Leadership and People's War* (London, 1983), ch. 2; Norrie MacQueen, *The Decolonization of Portuguese Africa: Metropolitan Revolution and the Dissolution of Empire* (London, 1997), 18.

[187] Luís Batalha, *The Cape Verdean Diaspora in Portugal: Colonial Subjects in a Postcolonial World* (Lanham, MD, 2004); Kesha Fikes, *Managing African Portugal: The Citizen-Migrant Distinction* (Durham, 2009).

[188] David Corkill, 'Economic Migrants and the Labour Market in Spain and Portugal', *Ethnic and Racial Studies*, 24:5 (2001), 836; David Corkill and Martin Eaton, 'Multicultural Insertions in a Small Economy: Portugal's Immigrant Communities', *South European Society and Politics*, 3:3 (1998), 151–2, 156.

[189] Bernd Reiter, 'Portugal: National Pride and Imperial Neurosis', *Race & Class*, 47:1 (2005), 81.

[190] Ana Paula Beja Horta, *Contested Citizenship: Immigration Politics and Grassroots Migrants' Organizations in Post-colonial Portugal* (New York, 2004), 33, 37, 47–8.

neighbours to which the Portuguese have looked for better opportunities – a status akin to that of colonized to colonizer.[191]

In the early phases of African settlement in Portugal prior to imperial collapse, those who came from Portuguese colonies arrived as Portuguese citizens thanks to the 1961 law that granted citizenship to the entire population of the nation's 'overseas provinces'. Including Africans and *mestiços* as Portuguese, for example, explains why Eusébio da Silva Ferreira, ranked as one of the twentieth century's greatest football stars and celebrated globally on a first-name basis, played for Portugal's national team throughout his career. The son of a white Angolan father and black mother born in Mozambique in 1942, Eusébio's sporting talents took him to Portugal where the 1960s saw him fêted as the *pantera negra* – 'black panther'.

The end of empire prompted a more restrictive nationality law in 1975, when citizenship was largely limited to persons of Portuguese ancestry. Exceptions were made for Goans, persons of Indian origin who had settled in Portuguese territories in Africa, and some Africans, including those who had fought in the Portuguese army during the anti-colonial wars. Overall, however, most from the former African territories lost Portuguese nationality.[192] This was the first step in a protracted renegotiation of who was legally 'Portuguese' that was to continue during and after the 1980s, a theme addressed in the next chapter. During the 1970s, however, contracting the conception of Portuguese citizenship reflected the attempt to place limits on who might legally go to Portugal during the chaotic, and violent, process of decolonization. Alongside the largely white *retornado* population which exceeded half a million were *mestiços* and Africans, including a number of political refugees. Over time, some *mestiços* (often the wealthier groups) effectively merged with (and certainly identified themselves with) the white Portuguese majority; others, particularly the poorer majority, became indistinguishable from black immigrants.[193]

One of the main effects of the new republic's 1975 nationality legislation was that persons who could previously legally arrive and settle in Portugal became illegal foreigners. This condition has structured the lives and limited the opportunities of the many Lusophone Africans who, despite these restrictions,

---

[191] Boaventura de Sousa Santos, *Pela Mão de Alice: O Social e Político na Pós-modernidade* (Porto, 1994), 58, 136; Boaventura de Sousa Santos, 'Between Prospero and Caliban: Colonialism, Postcolonialism, and Inter-identity', *Luso-Brazilian Review*, 39:2 (2002), 9–43.

[192] Ricard Morén-Alegret, *Integration and Resistance: The Relation of Social Organizations, Global Capital, Governments, and International Immigration in Spain and Portugal* (Aldershot, 2002), 96–7; Rui Manuel Moura Ramos, 'Migratory Movements and Nationality Law in Portugal', in Randall Hansen and Patrick Weil (eds.), *Towards a European Nationality: Citizenship, Immigration and Nationality Law in the European Union* (Basingstoke, 2001), 217; Brettell, 'Portugal's First Post-Colonials', 144.

[193] Batalha, *Cape Verdean Diaspora*, 87–130.

continued to come to Portugal, and indeed arrived in considerably higher numbers during the 1980s and 1990s than before. Yet the Portuguese state, although not formally allowing most of its ex-colonized populations to enter legally, proved inconsistent in both its enforcement of migration policies and its periodic efforts to regularize long-term illegal residents starting in the 1990s. For the most part, the government largely turned a blind eye to illegal settlement and employment because Africans played crucial roles in the development of the country in the wake of dictatorship and decolonization.[194] As a result, although fewer of its ex-colonized peoples reside in Portugal than is the case in Britain, France, and the Netherlands, the number of documented foreign residents, largely from Portuguese-speaking ex-colonies, now exceeds 400,000 in a total population of over 10 million.[195]

African men's importance in the construction sector, already noticeable with the Cape Verdean arrivals in the 1960s, grew exponentially in the 1980s as public works and private building projects along with the development of the tourist industry in the Algarve got underway. Portugal's entry into the European Economic Community in 1986 brought an infusion of development funds for state projects, and with ongoing Portuguese emigration the need for workers was all the more pressing. Building contractors as well as manufacturers favoured illegal immigrants because they worked for the lowest wages and received no social welfare benefits. The state silently acquiesced to this informal economy hiding in plain sight by largely failing to crack down on the sector and the Africans it exploited.[196]

Low wages and insecure, impermanent jobs – which most still considered better than their prospects in politically and economically unstable homelands – accounted for the poor living conditions African men and the family members who gradually followed them endured. A severe housing shortage brought most to shantytown slums on the outskirts of cities with the most dynamic economic sectors, namely Lisbon, Setúbal, Faro, Porto, and Aveiro – shantytowns not unlike the *bidonvilles* around Paris where Portuguese emigrants had lived themselves.[197] In environments characterized by overcrowding, poverty, dilapidation, and poor sanitation, Africans lived lives of spatial and social

---

[194] Martin Eaton, 'Foreign Residents and Illegal Immigrants in Portugal', *International Journal of Intercultural Research*, 22:1 (1998), 49–66.

[195] Maria Beatriz Rocha-Trindade, 'Portugal: Ongoing Changes in Immigration and Government Policies', *Studi Emigrazione/Migration Studies*, 39:148 (2002), 795–810; José Manuel Sobral, 'Imigração e Concepções da Identidade Nacional em Portugal', in André Barata, António Santos Pereira, and José Ricardo Carvalheiro (eds.), *Representações da Portugalidade* (Alfragide, Portugal, 2011), 149–50.

[196] Cristóbal Mendoza, *Labour Immigration in Southern Europe: African Employment in Iberian Labour Markets* (Aldershot, 2003), 121–35.

[197] Maria Lucinda Fonseca, 'Immigration and Spatial Change: The Lisbon Experience', *Studi Emigrazione/Migration Studies*, 39:145 (2002), 49–76.

marginalization.[198] Many Portuguese residing near areas where Africans settled rarely came into direct contact with them, avoiding the shantytowns which the media consistently depicted as racialized spaces of criminality, violence, and social disorder.

With many African men continuing to work on construction sites that few members of the public visited until building projects were completed, middle- and upper-class white Portuguese were more likely to encounter African women, who became commonly employed as housemaids and cleaners.[199] In the early 1990s, a councillor for housing in Lisbon observed that such people 'represent an ironic situation – because they are helping to build this city, but they don't have houses to live in'.[200] Similarly, African women's labour enhanced the domestic lives of the white families employing them as maids when they and their families had no prospect of enjoying habitations deemed 'respectable' themselves. One immigrant political leader extended the rhetoric of exclusionary domesticity to encompass the relationship of immigrants to the nation, commenting in the late 1990s that Portugal had 'opened the door to the Africans but it does not let them in the living-room. It still receives them in the hall'.[201] Martin Eaton has persuasively summarized how Africans were decisive in Portugal's transition from dictatorship to democracy by fighting the colonial wars that ultimately toppled the metropolitan government; moreover, for decades their labour had been essential to the physical development of the nation's infrastructure. Yet the majority continued to lack basic rights and decent living and working conditions, instead being relegated to the status of 'illegal' and 'foreign' and rarely considered to qualify as 'Portuguese' by the wider public, even when they possessed citizenship.[202]

If Africans' contributions to postcolonial Portugal remain under-acknowledged and their right to belong within the nation is often ignored or treated dismissively, the same cannot be said about mainstream attitudes towards Portugal's overseas history that explains the very presence of Lusophone Africans in cities like Lisbon. Imperial myths that prevailed during the dictatorship did not invariably die with it in 1974; instead, they endured to structure Portugal's postcolonial identity at a time when the nation simultaneously struggled to assert its European cultural credentials after being admitted into the European Economic Community in 1986.[203]

---

[198] Horta, *Contested Citizenship*.

[199] Batalha, *Cape Verdean Diaspora*, 144–50, 203–6; Kesha Fikes, 'Domesticity in Black and White: Assessing Badia Cape Verdean Challenges to Portuguese Ideals of Black Womanhood', *Transforming Anthropology*, 7:2 (1998), 5–19; Fikes, *Managing African Portugal*, 26–30, 90, ch. 4.

[200] Eaton, 'Foreign Residents', 63.   [201] Horta, *Contested Citizenship*, 68.

[202] Eaton, 'Foreign Residents', 53.   [203] Fikes, *Managing African Portugal*.

Figure 7.3 Vasco da Gama Bridge (from Sacavém to Montijo). Portuguese
postage stamp designed by Carlos Leitão, date of issue: 29 March 1998.
Fundação Portuguesa das Comunicações/PFA, Image no. 2481.
Image reproduction authorized by CTT Correios de Portugal, Sociedade
Aberta.

1998 proved to be a critical moment when imperial legacies selectively
became both foregrounded and ignored in Portugal. The late 1990s witnessed
a series of events that showcased versions of the nation's historic identity within
the context of present-day aspirations. Prominent among these were the completion of the Vasco da Gama Bridge across the Tagus River to commemorate
the 500th anniversary of da Gama's voyage from Europe to India, along with
Expo '98 that took place in Lisbon and attracted 11 million visitors. Expo '98
similarly placed particular importance on the 'Age of Discoveries' led by
Portuguese navigators and explorers in the late fifteenth and early sixteenth
centuries as foundational to the modern history not only of Portugal, South
America, Asia, and Africa but also to Europe as a whole, a theme explored
further in Chapter 9.[204] Thus invoked, Portugal's global history was, unsurprisingly, portrayed in resoundingly positive terms. Expo '98 provided a highly

---

[204] Marcus Power and James D. Sidaway, 'Deconstructing Twinned Towers: Lisbon's Expo '98
and the Occluded Geographies of Discovery', *Social & Cultural Geography*, 6:6 (2005),
865–83.

public platform for reasserting new versions of older ideas linked with luso-tropicalism, which, as Chapter 5 introduced, stressed Portugal's unique status as a colonizing nation in its purported lack of racism. The lusotropical ideology once used to defend the *Estado Novo's* ongoing transcontinental presence in debates with its international opponents between the 1950s and early 1970s continued to resonate decades after the so-called 'overseas provinces' had been lost – in this instance, in the depiction of Portugal as an idealized civilizing force whose overseas mission was characterized by harmony, hybridity, and racial egalitarianism.[205]

Postcolonial variants of lusotropicalism in evidence in 1998 were just as misleading as those propagated earlier to mask the realities of racial inequality, exploitation, and anti-colonial unrest that had plagued an empire in irrevocable decline. Nonetheless, they retained their appeal within Portugal as the nation strove to assert itself as more than simply a small, poor, and peripheral nation within the European Union (whose funding had paid for the Vasco da Gama Bridge and Expo '98 alike). The supposed lack of racism that informed lusotropical fantasies, moreover, was much in evidence elsewhere within Portuguese public discourse in connection with widespread understandings about the nation's relationship with its population from former African territories. The belief that racism does not exist within a tolerant, postcolonial Portugal (or at least is far less widespread and virulent than elsewhere in Europe) has been a difficult one to undermine, even in the face of the blatant social exclusion and limited opportunities that ethnic minority immigrants encounter on a daily basis.[206]

Portugal's slow (and still grudging and incomplete) recognition of racist realities and the need for multicultural policies will be treated in the next chapter.[207] As 1998 revealed, however, rendering Portugal's growing community of postcolonial peoples invisible has been a vital corollary to denials of racism's prevalence. Not only did the central roles played by low-paid African workers in building the bridge and the Expo '98 site find no official acknowledgement, but few immigrants could afford the cost of admission to visit the grounds once the Expo opened.[208] Thus, the physical infrastructure buttressing

[205] R. Timothy Sieber, 'Composing Lusophonia: Multiculturalism and National Identity in Lisbon's 1998 Music Scene', *Diaspora*, 11:2 (2002), 164–7; James D. Sidaway and Marcus Power, '"The Tears of Portugal": Empire, Identity, "Race", and Destiny in Portuguese Geopolitical Narratives', *Environment and Planning D: Society and Space*, 23:4 (2005), 527–54.

[206] Jorge Vala, Diniz Lopes, and Marcus Lima, 'Black Immigrants in Portugal: Luso-Tropicalism and Prejudice', *Journal of Social Issues*, 64:2 (2008), 287–302; Fikes, *Managing African Portugal*, ch. 1, 99, 104.

[207] Horta, *Contested Citizenship*, 16, 45–6, 100, 111; Eaton, 'Foreign Residents', 58.

[208] Morén-Alegret, *Integration and Resistance*, 219; Corkill and Eaton, 'Multicultural Insertions', 156; Sieber, 'Composing Lusophonia', 171.

these celebrations of a Portuguese identity reconfigured for postcolonial, European-focused times quite literally emerged through the poorly-paid work of ex-colonized ethnic minorities, yet once completed its structures were deployed to reassert imperial mythologies linked to durable Portuguese assertions of anti-racism. Of these human and material traces of empire, the former were pushed behind the scenes while the latter, literally the fruits of Africans' labour, were assertively incorporated into public consciousness and national self-representation.

* * *

Africans in postcolonial Belgium

Belgium had much in common with neighbouring countries as a nation attracting considerable immigration following the Second World War. Until the 1970s, an expanding economy provided work not only for Belgian nationals but also for large numbers of foreign workers in the mining and metal industries. Thereafter, economic downturn coupled with state and public concerns about the extent to which migrant workers might remain in Belgium permanently and fail to become socially or culturally integrated caused widespread debate. By the late 1980s and 1990s, extreme-right political parties had made their mark on regional and national politics on the back of anti-immigration platforms, a theme to which the next chapter will return.[209]

Similarities aside, the degree to which Belgium's history of post-war immigration is an explicitly *postcolonial* one differs markedly from that of the other nations explored earlier. In contrast to the large numbers of new arrivals in Britain, the Netherlands, France, and Portugal coming from colonies and former colonies, in Belgium the most sizable groups by far hailed from Southern Europe. Italians predominated, particularly in the 1950s, joined by large numbers from Spain and elsewhere. As in the Netherlands, however, non-Europeans, largely from Morocco and Turkey, became more numerous from the 1960s onwards. The 1991 census indicated that Belgium's total population of roughly 10 million was approximately 9–10 per cent foreign. Estimates that factored recent acquisitions of Belgian nationality into their findings revealed

---

[209] Anne Morelli (ed.), *Histoire des étrangers et de l'immigration en Belgique de la préhistoire à nos jours* (Brussels, 2004); Karen Phalet and Marc Swyngedouw, 'Measuring Immigrant Integration: The Case of Belgium', *Studi Emigrazione/Migration Studies*, XL:152 (2003), 773–804; Freddy Merckx and Liz Fekete, 'Belgium: The Racist Cocktail', *Race & Class*, 32:3 (1991), 67–78; John Fitzmaurice, 'The Extreme Right in Belgium: Recent Developments', *Parliamentary Affairs*, 45:3 (1992), 300–08; Nouria Ouali and Andrea Rea, 'Young Migrants in the Belgian Labour Market: Integration, Discrimination, Exclusion', in John Wrench, Andrea Rea, and Nouria Ouali (eds.), *Migrants, Ethnic Minorities and the Labour Market: Integration and Exclusion in Europe* (London, 1999), 21–34.

the population of Italian, Moroccan, Turkish, and other Southern European origins respectively as 297,000, 153,000, 88,000, and 98,000. By contrast, residents from Belgium's ex-colony of the Congo (called Zaïre between 1971 and 1997 and subsequently the Democratic Republic of Congo) approximated only 21,000 by the year 2000 – under 2 per cent of the entire foreign population.[210] Estimated numbers vary tremendously, however: while official data recorded roughly 27,000 Congolese in 2006, other sources placed the unofficial figure at 80,000, indicating a recent surge attributable to the growing violence, civil war, human rights abuses, poverty, and lack of educational and employment prospects in Central Africa that caused an increase in refugees, asylum seekers, and economic migrants alike.[211]

Why did Belgium prove distinct in having so few of its former colonial subjects among its immigrant population? Part of the answer stems from colonial policies prior to 1960 when the Congo achieved independence. Compared with colonial subjects going to Britain, France, and the Netherlands, only a handful of Congolese made journeys to Belgium for work or study. Some came to participate as part of the spectacle of colonial exhibitions, others were brought back as the domestic employees or dependants of returned colonizers, others arrived as sailors, and some as students.[212] Yet their numbers remained minuscule, with Belgian authorities actively discouraging Congolese sojourns (whether permanent or temporary) from becoming more widespread or protracted. The relatively weak population density in the Congo, they argued, meant that Belgium should avoid recruiting Congolese manual workers when extra labour was needed at home because doing so would deprive Belgian companies in Central Africa of their local workforce. Political and cultural motivations also underpinned this outlook. Belgian policymakers balked at the idea of providing more than a token number of Congolese students with the opportunities that studying and attaining professional qualifications in Belgium would bestow, seeking to uphold white superiority in the Congo by

---

[210] Phalet and Swyngedouw, 'Measuring Immigrant Integration', 775–6; Anne Cornet, 'Les Congolais en Belgique aux XIXe et XXe siècles', in Morelli (ed.), *Histoire des étrangers*, 377–8; Nouria Ouali, 'Analyse des données démographiques et des demandes d'asile', in Pierre Desmarez *et al.* (eds.), *Minorités ethniques en Belgique: migration et marché du travail* (Gent, 2004), 10–11; Ron Lesthaeghe, 'Transnational Islamic Communities in a Multilingual Secular Society', in Ron Lesthaeghe (ed.), *Communities and Generations: Turkish and Moroccan Populations in Belgium* (Brussels, 2000), 4.

[211] Eva Swyngedouw and Erik Swyngedouw, 'The Congolese Diaspora in Brussels and Hybrid Identity Formation: Multi-Scalarity and Diasporic Citizenship', *Urban Research & Practice*, 2:1 (2009), 71.

[212] Zana Aziza Etambala, *In het land van de Banoko: De geschiedenis van de Kongolese/Zaïrese aanwezigheid in België van 1885 tot heden* (Leuven, 1993); Bambi Ceuppens, 'Een Congolese Kolonie in Brussel', in Vincent Viaene, David Van Reybrouck, and Bambi Ceuppens (eds.), *Congo in België: Koloniale cultuur in de metropool* (Leuven, 2009), 231–50; Guy Vanthemsche, *La Belgique et le Congo: L'impact de la colonie sur la métropole*, new and rev. edn (Brussels, 2010), 94–6, 319–20.

severely limiting Africans' ability to benefit socially, culturally, and politically from a prolonged stay. Just as importantly, alongside preserving the racial and social hierarchy that favoured Europeans in Africa, Belgian authorities sought to maintain racial homogeneity at home and avoid racial mixing, or *métissage*, in the metropole.[213] Belgian subjects they may have been, but Belgian citizens with the right to settle in the metropole the Congolese were not.[214]

Such priorities outlasted colonial rule and still remained in place into the 1960s, although the years immediately following formal decolonization did find somewhat more Congolese coming to Belgium as students, professionals employed by African companies and the Congo state, and political refugees in unstable times. Nonetheless, Congolese migration to Belgium only gradually accelerated beyond these traditionally low levels in the 1980s and 1990s. By the 1990s, remaining in the Congo spelled poverty and lack of hope for the future in an atmosphere of social dissolution, political dictatorship, war, and endemic violence. The spiralling economic and political disintegration and chronic insecurity in the Democratic Republic of Congo caused a surge in Belgium's Congolese population after 2000. Europe offered better prospects for Congolese migrants and their relatives back home, for whom remittances brought improved material standards of living as well as paid for others to embark upon their own journeys to an imagined El Dorado. Many men arrived as students and, whether or not they continued to pursue their studies, often tried hard to maintain student status in order to prolong their stay in Belgium. Alongside these long-term 'professional students' were those who acquired Belgian nationality and the legal right to remain by other means, possibly by marrying a Belgian citizen.[215] Women gradually became better represented within this largely male population.

Some who initially came as students, tourists, or workers subsequently declared themselves refugees. Although the well-publicized human rights violations of the Mobutu regime made the Belgian government somewhat sympathetic to requests for political asylum (particularly after relations between the two countries sharply deteriorated in the 1990s), Congolese were much more likely to find their applications turned down than not. The categories of student, illegal migrant worker, and asylum seeker remained porous, with individuals commonly moving from one to the other over time.[216] With

---

[213] Mayoyo Bitumba Tipo-Tipo, *Migration Sud/Nord: Levier ou Obstacle? Les Zaïrois en Belgique* (Brussels, 1995), 89–90; Bonaventure Kagné, 'Africains de Belgique, de l'indigène à l'immigré', *Hommes et Migrations*, 1228 (2000), 64; Cornet, 'Les Congolais', 379–86.

[214] Patrick Hullebroeck and François Sant'Angelo, 'La politique générale d'immigration et la legislation sur les étrangers', in Morelli (ed.), *Histoire des étrangers*, 134.

[215] Mumpasi B. Lututala, 'L'élargissement de l'espace de vie des africains: comment le "pays des oncles" européens devient aussi celui des neveux africains', *Revue Tiers Monde*, 38:150 (1997), 341.

[216] Tipo-Tipo, *Migration Sud/Nord*, 53, 89–98.

some acquiring a legal right to residence or becoming Belgian citizens and others having a precarious status with no formal permission to remain, the Congolese community thus grew both numerically and in visibility.[217]

Belgium had indisputably played a leading role in sowing the seeds of political and economic instability in its former colony that led many Congolese to seek a better life in Europe, whether in Belgium, France, or elsewhere. Indeed, France (and particularly Paris) attracted a significantly larger Congolese population, with 52 per cent of the Congolese in the European Union living there in contrast to the 29 per cent residing in Belgium by the late 1990s. With Congolese heading for Europe likely to be familiar with and possibly fluent in the French language, France could seem as obvious a choice as Belgium on linguistic and other cultural grounds.[218] As the European hub of a multinational Francophone African diaspora, Paris beckoned those arriving directly from Congo as well as those who had initially migrated to Belgium and subsequently moved on, partly because they believed better opportunities awaited them across the French border.[219]

While dreams of European prosperity were typically compromised by the everyday realities of racism and low-paid jobs in the informal economy for Africans who may or may not have enjoyed the legal right to work or reside, most nevertheless sought to remain in Belgium or France and actively avoided returning to the Congo. Like postcolonial ethnic minorities in other countries discussed earlier, they fell victim to poor working conditions in combination with racial stereotypes formed during the colonial era that long outlived it. White Belgians commonly dismissed those of Central African origin as unassimilable, their culture fully distinct from and incompatible with that of Belgium.[220] Finding themselves publicly called 'Chocolate' counted among the ways they became singled out as 'other' to a greater extent than most other immigrant communities, particularly those of European origin.[221]

Many correspondingly cultivated a sense of community among themselves, sometimes by settling in the Ixelles area of Brussels that popularly became known as Matonge. Named after a district of Kinshasa, Congo's capital city, Matonge was home to Congo's diplomatic mission as well as African cultural centres, businesses, and entertainment venues. With its substantial multinational immigrant population, the neighbourhood became widely associated with the Congolese and, by extension, other African communities in the city.

---

[217] Lise Thiry, *Conversations avec des clandestins* (Mons, Belgium, 2002).
[218] Lututala, 'L'élargissement de l'espace de vie', 337–8, 342.
[219] Janet MacGaffey and Rémy Bazenguissa-Ganga, *Congo-Paris: Transnational Traders on the Margins of the Law* (Oxford and Bloomington, 2000), 55, 144. As the authors note, 18, they could just as easily have chosen Brussels rather than Paris as the focus of their study on second-economy trade that involves Central Africans from contiguous former French and former Belgian colonies in equal measure.
[220] Kagné, 'Africains de Belgique', 62–3.   [221] Cornet, 'Les Congolais', 394–5.

Many Congolese living in other parts of Brussels and further afield were drawn to Matonge by its African groceries and clothing shops, hairdressers, restaurants, and bars, making the neighbourhood central to the community's identity, consumption patterns, and leisure.[222] Congolese women played important roles in running many of the shops and *nganda*, the unlicensed bars patronized almost exclusively by African men, with trade (often contraband) and consumer activities being central to Africans' economic, social, and cultural life within the diaspora.[223] *Nganda*-based sociability exemplifies the extent to which Belgium's and France's Congolese remain to a considerable extent a closed community, interacting far more with one another than with outsiders and mentally oriented towards an eventual return to Africa once they have 'made it' in Europe.[224]

Given their typically precarious financial circumstances, many Congolese earned their living from unlicensed trading and illegal business activities, including drug dealing, and Matonge's portrayal in the Belgian media routinely revolved around racialized criminality.[225] Although African wrongdoing may well be exaggerated by Belgians insistent upon painting a negative picture of this immigrant population, researchers affirm illegal activities to be common practice among at least a minority who have acquired a disproportionate public visibility. Frequently denied access to decent jobs with good wages, some Congolese turned to crime to make ends meet as well as to afford luxury goods like designer clothing and other status objects in high demand among themselves and those they left behind in the Congo.[226] Some Congolese came to view activities such as shoplifting, theft, riding the metro without a ticket, and squatting in apartments rather than paying rent as politically justifiable on account of the 'colonial debt' they insisted Belgium owed to Africans it once ruled and ruthlessly exploited for the Congo's labour, rubber, and mineral wealth.[227]

[222] Swyngedouw and Swyngedouw, 'Congolese Diaspora in Brussels', 85–6; Mashini Dhi Mbita Mulenghe, 'L'intégration socio-économique de la population originaire d'Afrique noire dans la Région de Bruxelles-Capitale', *Revue Belge de Géographie*, 63 (1998), 56.

[223] MacGaffey and Bazenguissa-Ganga, *Congo-Paris*, 47–69, 73, 142–52.

[224] Désiré Kazadi Wa Kabwe and Aurelia Segatti, 'Paradoxical Expressions of a Return to the Homeland: Music and Literature among the Congolese (Zairean) Diaspora', in Khalid Koser (ed.), *New African Diasporas* (London, 2003), 124–39.

[225] Benoît Verhaegen, 'Exposé introductif', in Gauthier de Villers (ed.), *Belgique/Zaïre: Une histoire en quête d'avenir, Cahiers Africains* no. 9–10-11 (Brussels and Paris, 1994), 18; Césarine Bolya Sinatu *et al.*, 'Coopération, immigration: Les "bons", les "brutes" et les "truands": Le cas de figure Belgique-Zaïre', in ibid., 333–6.

[226] Ch. Didier Gondola, 'Dream and Drama: The Search for Elegance among Congolese Youth', *African Studies Review*, 42:1 (1999), 23–48. On African fashion and consumption in Europe, see also MacGaffey and Bazenguissa-Ganga, *Congo-Paris*; Thomas, *Black France*, ch. 6.

[227] Michela Wrong, *In the Footsteps of Mr Kurtz: Living on the Brink of Disaster in the Congo* (London, 2000), 51–4.

316 Migrations and multiculturalisms in postcolonial Europe

References to Belgium's colonial debt became a recurrent feature of Congolese fiction published in the 1990s, informing novels set in both Africa and Belgium. Originating at the time of decolonization among nationalists, the colonial debt philosophy resurfaced starting in the late 1980s in the context of the Mobutu regime's demands for compensation for a history of depredation, as Chapter 4 noted. As Désiré Kazadi Wa Kabwe and Aurelia Segatti summarize, 'regularly used by Mobutu as an instrument against pressures from the West or as a means of popular seduction in domestic politics ... the idea of Belgium and Western countries in general being in debt to the Congo did not remain confined to the political sphere'.[228] Congolese at home who were denied the privileges accorded to Mobutism's postcolonial beneficiaries adopted an outlook that shaped Zaïrian international relations to their own purposes, using it to justify material and moral survival strategies that revolved around getting goods or money by whatever means necessary, including fraud, theft, and looting. Those who emigrated to Europe could also find within the colonial debt a rationale that not only excused but indeed legitimated and encouraged such behaviour.[229] Frustrations sown by socio-economic exclusion, in sum, rendered the idea of the colonial debt appealing to many Congolese both at home and away.

Maguy Kabamba's 1995 novel *La dette coloniale* provides one of the most penetrating interrogations of this outlook. Centring on the experiences of a group of disenchanted Congolese youths in Brussels, it features a scene in which one character who lived on the proceeds from smuggling and auto theft excused his actions thus:

For eighty years they colonized us and Léopold II didn't think twice about turning the Congo into his private property. ... Did the Belgians ever think of us while they were plundering our wealth? Did they consider the poverty they created in our homeland? Before they came and brought us what they call 'civilization', our ancestors' granaries were never empty. ... Call me a thief, a bandit ... but we don't have a suitable means of making the Belgians pay for their pillaging of the Congo during the colonial period that also continues today. Also, we can't work in this fucking country. What else can we do?[230]

This rationale extended beyond the literary arena and into everyday life. One account from the early 1990s described a robbery at a jewellery shop in which an African was accused of the theft but later released due to insufficient evidence. Denying the charges, he nonetheless said that if he *had* been involved, he would have asked the Belgian owner whether he knew anything about gold and diamond mines in Belgium. Upon the owner's negative reply, he

[228] Désiré Kazadi Wa Kabwe and Aurelia Segatti, 'The Philosophy of the "Colonial Debt" in Contemporary Congolese (Zairean) Literature: Example or Counter-example for Congolese Youth?', *French Studies in Southern Africa*, 31 (2002), 124.

[229] Désiré Kazadi Wa Kabwe, 'Réparation, récupération et dette coloniale dans les romans congolais récents', *Cahiers d'Études africaines*, XLIV:1–2, 173–174 (2004), 141–50.

[230] Maguy Kabamba, *La dette coloniale* (Montreal, 1995), 113–14.

would then have retorted, 'this is our gold and our diamonds that you stole. I've come to recover them.'[231] Far from forgotten, the colonial past continues to shape Congolese outlooks and responses as they create new lives within a Europe dreamed of as El Dorado from afar but all too frequently yielding disappointment up close.

* * *

Conclusion: colonial debts within an integrating Europe?

During and after decolonization, then, ethnic minorities from Western Europe's (ex-) colonies and overseas territories had a keen sense of how colonial history directly shaped their migrations to and experiences within what had long been the heart of empires. By the same token, ideas about empire also shaped the ways many Europeans responded to them. Empire could be imagined as a history of Europeans' exploitation of colonized peoples for which the latter might rightfully claim a colonial debt was owned them – a debt that gave them rights to settle, earn livelihoods, and ultimately belong in a postcolonial Europe. While some Europeans also saw imperial ties as justifying citizenship rights and settlement, many opportunistically viewed late colonial and post-colonial migrants as a source of cheap labour. Others, however, considered them as simply a new manifestation of the 'white man's burden' and as further demonstration of Europe's selfless good intentions and good works vis-à-vis erstwhile colonies. References to the 'civilizing mission' or to the purportedly non-racist forms of tolerance inherent within lusotropicalist and other forms of discourse outlived decolonization, as did ideas that empire had been largely at colonizers' expense for the benefit of those over whom they ruled.

In consequence, while some might argue that ex-colonizers owed a debt to the ex-colonized, others protested the opposite. Peter Griffiths, introduced earlier in connection with his successful 1964 campaign to became a Conservative Member of Parliament in England's West Midlands on the back of an anti-immigration agenda and slogans including 'If you want a nigger neighbour, vote Labour', completely refuted any notion that Britain owned a colonial debt to former subjects that extended to metropolitan settlement as a form of repayment. Writing in 1966, his verdict combined a celebration of Britain's imperial achievements with an adamant refusal to accept ongoing British responsibility for former colonies that might extend to immigration:

We owe no debt to our ex-colonies. The great cities, the schools, hospitals, roads, bridges and airports are the legacy of colonialism. The industries, the bustling commerce and prosperous agriculture, these pay off any debt we might be said to owe. . . . The debt owed

---

[231] Tipo-Tipo, *Migration Sud/Nord*, 114; Gondola, 'Dream and Drama', 35–6.

is one of gratitude to the men and women from this country who brought prosperity to replace poverty, education in place of ignorance, health instead of disease, the Word of God to sweep away superstition and fear. How dare they discount the selfless efforts of missionaries and teachers, engineers and doctors, soldiers and administrators who gave them a heritage and an opportunity. Independence was demanded. Now they have it. We owe them no debt. We too demand independence.[232]

Griffiths' platform thus might be considered a distinct form of anti-colonial nationalism, one in which petulant ex-colonizers sought freedom from 'invasions' that marked one of imperialism's defining legacies.

Not all newcomers encountered as much hostility as South Asians, West Indians, Maghrebis, or Africans from south of the Sahara did within Britain, the Netherlands, France, Portugal, and Belgium; nor, as was discussed earlier, were these postcolonial populations viewed as an undifferentiated 'problem'. Just as Griffiths saw West Indians as better candidates for assimilation than Indians or Pakistanis because he attributed their differences primarily to colour rather than culture, he clearly deemed Eastern and Southern European immigrants who had settled in the late 1940s as European Volunteer Workers to be infinitely more promising on both grounds. 'As European Christians the Poles have found little difficulty in settling into the British community', he insisted; as for Ukrainians and those from the Baltic states, 'the second generation is completely British' and 'absorption is only a matter of time', while Britain's Hungarian and Italian populations appeared likely to travel the same path towards unproblematic integration.[233] As was seen in different national contexts earlier, other Europeans, although not free from discrimination as foreigners who were culturally distinct, lacked citizenship rights, and were typically economically disadvantaged, were repeatedly viewed more favourably than racialized colonial and postcolonial populations after 1945.[234]

Time and again, whiteness has rendered other Europeans both less contentious and less discussed than those originating in Asia, Africa, or the Caribbean. Portugal, for example, has long attracted considerable numbers of British and other Western European resident foreigners who attract little if any political, media, or scholarly attention.[235] Most, like the many middle-class retirees in the Algarve, are comparatively well off, with class acting together with race to render them relatively invisible in discussions of immigration. Wealthy Brazilians in Portugal share a similarly privileged position. But in recent years Europeans have swelled the ranks of Portugal's working classes as well, and since the 1990s Eastern Europeans have become increasingly dominant amongst

---

[232] Griffiths, *A Question of Colour?*, 199.   [233] Ibid., 29–30.
[234] Hill, *How Colour Prejudiced is Britain?*, 71; Selvon, *Lonely Londoners*, 40; Waters, '"Dark Strangers"'; Webster, *Englishness and Empire*, 153–6.
[235] Esteves (ed.), *Portugal*, 30.

the country's foreign population.[236] Valued as cheap labour within sectors like construction and domestic service and often working illegally within the informal economy like Lusophone Africans, they nonetheless have attracted comparatively little opprobrium and are widely favoured over their African counterparts. As Luís Batalha has written of Cape Verdean women's attitudes, '[b]efore, they thought the Portuguese were racist because they left the worst jobs for black people; now they think the Portuguese are racist because they prefer white European women to black women' for menial jobs.[237]

Migration to Europe from former colonies thus demands to be analyzed not only in relationship to distinct host societies but also as the counterpoint to the contemporary history of intra-European migration. If the decline and fall of overseas empires formed one crucial element of Western European history after 1945, so too did the gradual moves towards a more unified Europe that occurred alongside decolonization and accelerated in its wake – developments that Peo Hansen persuasively suggests should be more rigorously studied as interconnected phenomena rather than in isolation.[238] Starting with the Treaty of Rome in 1957, freedom of movement – of capital, goods, services, and also people – became increasingly fundamental to the ideology and aspirations of Europe's common market that ultimately became the European Union. As Andrew Geddes notes, 'free movement for nationals of member states has become a defining feature of the European Union and integral to ideas and practices relating to such things as "EU citizenship"' that was created under the Maastricht Treaty that came into effect in 1993.[239]

While movements within Europe certainly pre-dated Maastricht, they took on new meanings and eventually extended to encompass ever more nations with the EU's enlargement in the new millennium. Ten new member states, most of them former Soviet Bloc countries in Eastern Europe, entered the EU in 2004; Bulgaria and Romania then joined in 2007, and Croatia followed in 2013. Taking advantage of their ability to live and work within wealthier Western European countries, vast numbers of Eastern Europeans moved west in search of better opportunities. Like newcomers from former colonies or 'guest workers' in Germany, the Netherlands, and other countries, they played economically invaluable roles by taking low-skilled jobs, often dirty, monotonous, or dangerous, that citizens of the receiving nations shunned; others came with manual skills in short supply or with professional qualifications in high demand

---

[236] Batalha, *Cape Verdean Diaspora*, 206–11; Horta, *Contested Citizenship*, 44; Rocha-Trindade, 'Portugal: Ongoing Changes', 799.
[237] Batalha, *Cape Verdean Diaspora*, 206.
[238] Peo Hansen, 'European Integration, European Identity, and the Colonial Connection', *European Journal of Social Theory*, 5:4 (2002), 483–98.
[239] Andrew Geddes, *Immigration and European Integration: Beyond Fortress Europe?*, 2nd edn (Manchester, 2008), 48; see also Webster, 'Empire Comes Home', 129, 156–7.

by Britain's National Health Service or other public and private sectors. But like postcolonial arrivals examined earlier, however, Eastern Europeans provoked xenophobic populist responses, one of the most memorable being France's debate around the figure of the 'Polish plumber' at the time of its referendum on the European Constitution in 2005. The Polish plumber acted as a symbol of France's fears about the EU – fears that ended in 55 per cent of the French voting 'no' and rejecting the Constitution. Seized upon by those on the extreme right who played up the prospect of an unmanageable 'flood' of immigrants as well as by Eurosceptics on the left who highlighted the threat to French workers posed by migrants willing to work for low wages, the Polish plumber rapidly achieved the status of one of France's 'New Mythologies' featured in a 2007 volume published to coincide with the fiftieth anniversary of Roland Barthes' celebrated text *Mythologies*:

Armed with his moustache and spanner, the Polish plumber was erected as a symbol of globalization and a liberal Europe by the Constitution's opponents, killing off the jobs and social gains of French citizens from within the intimate spaces of their bathrooms and heating ducts.[240]

Thus portrayed as an intruder who penetrated into the most private parts of domestic life, France's demonized Polish plumber joined the ranks of other post-war immigrants described as breaching barriers theoretically meant to protect homes – and by extension nations – from foreign invasions, whether through smells, noise, or other incursions deemed culturally objectionable or an occupational threat. Like the West Indian or North African men with whom some European women willingly entered relationships in earlier decades, the Polish plumber was arguably a highly sexualized symbol as well, the masculine and moustachioed immigrant handyman chosen (indeed, invited in) over the native worker to keep the feminized French domestic realm and heating ducts in good repair.[241] Emblematic of the fear and animosity directed towards immigrants, the Polish plumber serves as an important reminder of how different groups can become singled out under specific historical conditions. The significant 'others' of one time and place may, or may not, retain their prominence under other circumstances. Common citizenship rights or, in this instance, perceptions of cultural and ethnic proximity as fellow Europeans have not protected Eastern Europeans from xenophobia, discrimination, and structural disadvantage, just as was seen on countless occasions with late

---

[240] Nicolas Baverez, 'Le plombier polonais', in Jérôme Garcin (ed.), *Nouvelles Mythologies* (Paris, 2007), 26–7; see also Raphaël Franck, 'Why Did a Majority of French Voters Reject the European Constitution?', *European Journal of Political Economy*, 21:4 (2005), 1071–6.

[241] Tellingly, Polish women workers, although well represented amongst recent EU migration trends, were not singled out as the figures around which French dissent coalesced.

colonial and postcolonial migrants in France and the other nations featured earlier.

Does the dramatic rise of East-West migration in recent years suggest that postcolonial migrants and their descendants have been displaced as the main foci of 'anti-immigrant' nationalist sentiment in Western Europe today? Although Eastern European migrants clearly encounter resentment, Adrian Favell suggests that 'from the point of view of populist politicians, they are much more desirable than other, more visible, actual and potential immigrant populations':

It might be speculated that, in the long run, West European publics are likely to be more comfortable with the scenario of getting used to Balkan and Slavic accents, rather than seeing black and brown faces in the same jobs, or (especially) hearing them speak the language of Allah. There is indeed a racial and ethnic logic inherent in the EU enlargement process: borders to the East will be opened as they are increasingly rammed shut to those from the South.[242]

Whiteness and Europeanness, both of which are conceptual categories that encompass enormous ethnic, linguistic, religious, and national diversity, acquire much of their salience and appeal when juxtaposed either implicitly or explicitly with those imagined as falling outside their confines.[243] As Favell emphasizes, those whom Western European nations most stridently seek to exclude or deny the potential to belong still overwhelmingly remain racialized, visibly different 'black' and 'brown' people who are often (albeit not invariably) Muslim. European Union integration and the integration of border-hopping Europeans, while by no means smooth or uncontested processes at the national level (as UKIP's prominence in Britain since 2013 attests), are often imagined as infinitely more straightforward and palatable prospects for the future than the inclusion of those whose presence derives from colonial legacies.

While often condemned as unable or unwilling to integrate, however, postcolonial migrants have nonetheless already remade Europe over the course of several generations. Britain, the Netherlands, France, Portugal, and Belgium have become multicultural societies thanks in large part to those who trace their origins to former empires and are now there to stay. Chapter 8 now considers some of the new identities, individual, group, and national alike, that emerged over time following histories of migration to former imperial metropoles – hybrid identities irrevocably indebted to the colonial past, but not exclusively determined by it.

---

[242] Adrian Favell, 'The New Face of East-West Migration in Europe', *Journal of Ethnic and Migration Studies*, 34:5 (2008), 712.

[243] Linda McDowell, 'On the Significance of Being White: European Migrant Workers in the British Economy in the 1940s and 2000s', in Claire Dwyer and Caroline Bressey (eds.), *New Geographies of Race and Racism* (Aldershot, 2008), 51–64.

8 Reconfiguring nations

Identities, belonging, and multiculturalism in the wake of postcolonial migration

Introduction

'Will we still be French in thirty years' time?' asked Jean Raspail in *Le Figaro Magazine* in 1985. By 2015, 'France would no longer be a nation' but rather 'nothing more than a geographical space', and his anxiety over the allegedly imperilled 'fate of our civilization' centred on the differential birth rate of two composite 'communities' into which he divided the nation's population. The first consisted of persons of French nationality together with those who had come to France from other European countries; the second of 'non-European foreigners' hailing primarily from south of the Mediterranean, 90 per cent being of the 'Islamic culture or religion'. While the fecundity of the first was weak, that of the second was estimated as three times higher and showed no signs of abating. So many non-Europeans could never be assimilated, he stressed, not least because the groups in question possessed values that made them unlikely to want – or even be able – to integrate.

Raspail continually returned to Islam along with the identity and size of the next generation of 'non-Europeans' as constituting pivotal national threats. Moreover, after family reunification in France became increasingly common in the wake of what initially had been a predominantly male labour migration, Muslim women became as significant as their children within French public discussions of the threat 'immigrants' supposedly posed to the nation. Raspail's article was accompanied by a series of graphs and charts detailing population projections and a photograph depicting Marianne, the female allegorical symbol of the republic, wearing an Islamic headscarf. This visual image was intended to support his assertion that 'darkness was falling on the old Christian country'; Islam, in other words, was descending to enshroud France's deep-rooted and cherished traditions. He predicted that by 2015 each school would have one 'Maghrebi or African' child for every two *'Français de souche'*, children of 'French stock'. While the notion of the old classroom expression 'our ancestors the Gauls' being 'imposed upon little Algerians or little Africans' might seem risible, it could be no laughing matter: 'The Gauls could be swept away and with them all that remains of our traditional cultural values'.[1] In this understanding, children of North African or sub-Saharan African immigrants not only were not, and could never be, French themselves. Even more worryingly, their very presence and difference threatened to subsume the nation's historic culture under their weight – a 'culture' he implied was homogenous, unchanging, and closed, at least to non-Europeans. Raspail proposed forced repatriation as the only viable solution to this peril.

By 1985, both Jean Raspail and his chosen subject matter had been familiar features of France's ideological landscape for well over a decade. Espousing ideas of the French *Nouvelle Droite* (New Right) that coalesced in the late 1960s and proliferated throughout the 1970s, he was one of many commentators to draw upon a long history of anxieties about France's birth rate and population decline to promote a defensive brand of ethnic nationalism. Outlets like *Le Figaro Magazine*, the weekend supplement of a conservative daily newspaper launched in 1978 that was owned and edited by prominent *Nouvelle Droite* figures, allowed these views to incrementally make their mark on public and political culture. At its core, commentators like Raspail argued, France constituted an organic community whose cultural integrity derived from ancient Greco-Roman roots.[2] This version of national identity (often but not invariably containing strong Catholic underpinnings) was one firmly fixed north of the Mediterranean – a radical and profoundly forgetful departure from the conception of the nation so recently widespread among defenders of French Algeria, who had proclaimed much of North Africa to be an integral part of France as well. Having retreated into its European hexagon so unwillingly, France was now deemed internally jeopardized by the very peoples over whom it had failed to maintain sovereignty overseas through 'reverse colonization'.[3]

---

[1] Jean Raspail, 'Serons-nous encore Français dans 30 ans?', *Le Figaro Magazine*, 26 October 1985, 123–32 (quotes taken from 123, 125, 126, 129, 132). Images of Marianne in a headscarf appeared on the cover of this issue and on p. 123; to view the cover, see www.nouve lordremondial.cc/2014/09/19/figaro-magazine-en-1985-serons-nous-encore-francais-dans-30-a ns/, accessed 28 July 2015.

[2] J.G. Shields, *The Extreme Right in France from Pétain to Le Pen* (London, 2007), 144–59; Charles Tshimanga, 'Let the Music Play: The African Diaspora, Popular Culture, and National Identity in Contemporary France', in Charles Tshimanga, Didier Gondola, and Peter J. Bloom (eds.), *Frenchness and the African Diaspora: Identity and Uprising in Contemporary France* (Bloomington, 2009), 261–3.

[3] Christopher Flood and Hugo Frey, 'Questions of Decolonization and Post-Colonialism in the Ideology of the French Extreme Right', in James D. Le Sueur (ed.), *The Decolonization Reader* (London, 2003), 404. Raspail discussed similar threats of Third World 'invasion' in his apocalyptic novel *Le camp des Saints*, first published in 1973 and soon translated into English as *The Camp of the Saints*. Ever controversial, over time it developed a following among white supremacist groups in the United States and elsewhere. See Jean-Marc Moura, 'Littérature et idéologie de la migration: "Le camp des Saints" de Jean Raspail', *Revue Européenne des Migrations Internationales*, 4:3 (1988), 115–24; Matthew Connelly and Paul Kennedy, 'Must

What Raspail's rendition wilfully overlooked was that in the mid-1980s many if not most second-generation descendants of postcolonial migrants upon whom he fixated were already French citizens, either through being born in France or by automatically becoming French after reaching the age of majority.[4] Nor was he alone on the European right. As Ahmed Boubeker observes, '[t]he foreigner is no longer one who comes from elsewhere, but rather one that is permanently reproduced within the social body ... Like a social or ethnic partition of the hexagon, there is a radical rupture between recognized citizens and second-class ones.'[5]

Did non-European ancestry render formerly colonized peoples and their descendants perennially unable and/or unwilling to belong in France and other European nations where growing numbers had been born and raised by the late twentieth and early twenty-first centuries? Were they condemned to a status as 'either/or' within essentialist constructions of cultural and national identity – as either Algerian or French, Pakistani or British, Surinamese or Dutch, among many others – regardless of their citizenship, and whether they sought to integrate or not? In grappling with these questions, this chapter assesses national responses to cultural and ethnic pluralism alongside the hybrid cultures and new ethnic identities that emerged, and continually evolved, among postcolonial diasporas across the generations and more broadly within the societies where they settled. In so doing, it positions local spaces such as the schools, multi-ethnic neighbourhoods, and cities where cosmopolitan cultures were most commonly produced, consumed, experienced, or observed as central to the history of remaking European nations after empire.

By the late twentieth century France, Britain, the Netherlands, Belgium, and Portugal were already home to ethnically-diverse citizenries, but the extent to which they accorded legitimacy and official recognition to minority cultures varied considerably and fluctuated markedly over time. Albeit multicultural in reality, they often fell far short of espousing multicultural*ism* as part of their national imaginary. Multiculturalism emerged starting in the 1970s as 'a broad set of mutually reinforcing approaches or methodologies concerning the incorporation and participation of immigrants and ethnic minorities and their modes

---

it Be the Rest Against the West?', *The Atlantic Monthly*, December 1994, www.theatlantic.com/past/politics/immigrat/kennf.htm; Lionel Shriver, 'Population in Literature', *Population and Development Review*, 29:2 (2003), 153–62.

[4] Alec G. Hargreaves, *Multi-Ethnic France: Immigration, Politics, Culture and Society*, 2nd edn. (New York, 2007), 29–30.

[5] Ahmed Boubeker, 'Le "creuset français", ou la légende noire de l'intégration', in Pascal Blanchard, Nicolas Bancel, and Sandrine Lemaire (eds.), *La fracture coloniale: La société française au prisme de l'héritage colonial* (Paris, 2005), 188–9.

of cultural/religious difference', as Steven Vertovec and Susanne Wessendorf have written.[6] At times, its champions have celebrated selected cultural attributes and practices as positive and enriching both for minorities themselves and for wider national populations alike. More often than not, however, multiculturalism has been construed either as a 'problem' in and of itself, or at best as a worthy attempt at tackling a problem – namely, that of purported minority non-integration and a lack of social cohesion.[7]

Not only have backlashes against multiculturalism proved recurrent: multiculturalism remained contentious even in societies where it had secured a relatively strong foothold and where a tolerance of difference was proudly extolled as a national trait. What is more, multiculturalism readily coexisted with widespread racism, particularly with what scholars have termed 'new' or 'neo-racism'. Based primarily on assumptions about rigid cultural distinctiveness, new racism nonetheless retained countless traces of the 'old' racism predicated upon supposed genetic inferiority: the demarcations between peoples continued to be treated as insistently permanent and absolute. Neo-racism's 'dominant theme', Étienne Balibar notes, 'is not biological heredity but the insurmountability of cultural differences, a racism which, at first sight, does not postulate the superiority of certain groups or peoples in relation to others but "only" the harmfulness of abolishing frontiers, the incompatibility of life-styles and traditions'.[8] Raspail's arguments exemplified this tendency by collapsing France's 'traditional cultural values' together with the French nation and indigenous people ('the Gauls'/'*Français de souche*') alike – all of which, he insisted, risked being 'swept away' by the relentless onslaught of 'Maghrebi or African' peoples seemingly destined to remain exclusively conjoined with 'Islamic culture or religion'. As Paul Gilroy emphasizes, new racist ideology commonly entails 'the confluence of "race", nationality and culture in the contemporary politics of racial exclusion', with the 'characteristic outcome [being] a situation in which blackness appears as a kind of disqualification from membership in the national community'.[9]

While his own studies delve most deeply into examples taken from British and other Anglophone arenas linked together by the Atlantic, Gilroy offers

---

[6] Steven Vertovec and Susanne Wessendorf, 'Introduction: Assessing the Backlash Against Multiculturalism in Europe', in Steven Vertovec and Susanne Wessendorf (eds.), *The Multiculturalism Backlash: European Discourses, Policies and Practices* (London, 2010), 4.

[7] Elizabeth Buettner, '"Going for an Indian": South Asian Restaurants and the Limits of Multiculturalism in Britain', *Journal of Modern History*, 80:4 (2008), 866.

[8] Étienne Balibar, 'Is There a "Neo-Racism"?', in Étienne Balibar and Immanuel Wallerstein, *Race, Nation, Class: Ambiguous Identities* (London, 1991), 21; see also Martin Barker, *The New Racism: Conservatives and the Ideology of the Tribe* (London, 1981).

[9] Paul Gilroy, 'Nationalism, History and Ethnic Absolutism', in *Small Acts: Thoughts on the Politics of Black Cultures* (London, 1993), 64; see also Paul Gilroy, *The Black Atlantic: Modernity and Double Consciousness* (Cambridge, MA, 1993), 2–11.

invaluable insight into broader postcolonial Western European contexts, and certainly to understanding French verdicts like Raspail's. But if his most influential analyses focused on blackness as a cause of national exclusion, over time Islam and Muslims became ever more dominant within public anxieties revolving around the presumption of ethnic minority cultural incompatibility across most of the countries examined here, with the exception of Portugal.[10] Within nations whose majority populations were at least nominally Catholic or Protestant and which had become increasingly secular since the 1960s (with Christian cultural underpinnings nonetheless remaining influential), Islam and Muslims became the chief 'others' against whom many Europeans defined their core national identities. Iran's revolution of 1979, the Ayatollah Khomeini's *fatwa* against Salman Rushdie in 1989, the first Gulf War and the Algerian civil war during the early 1990s, recurrent Palestinian and Israeli conflicts, and the 11 September 2001 terrorist attacks in the United States followed by wars in Iraq and Afghanistan counted among the definitive episodes that increased Western fears of politicized Islam. Heated debates revolving around Muslims living within Europe have often resulted in other ethnic minorities (including other religious minorities) becoming sidelined if not altogether obscured within academic scholarship as well as public discussion, regardless of their numerical and cultural importance and despite suffering other forms of racial and ethnic discrimination and socio-economic disadvantage.

Rather than exclusively singling out Muslims, those understood to be 'black', or any other single collectivity, this chapter stresses how social understandings of specific minorities in the late twentieth and early twenty-first centuries often rely upon implicit or explicit comparisons with other ethnic groups, minority and majority alike. It also acknowledges the heterogeneity within ethnic groups internally divided along socio-economic, gender, generational, and other lines. Moreover, in contrast with the static understandings of culture, ethnicity, and nationality prevalent within new racist ideologies, what Stuart Hall has termed 'new ethnicities' have regularly surfaced not only among postcolonial migrants, their children, and their grandchildren but also among majority populations. 'New ethnicities' as forms of identity that permanently generate new, historically-specific alliances and cultures, often across ethnic lines, underscore the extent to which no apparently discrete 'groups' can be treated as fixed or examined in isolation.[11] The following sections compare

---

[10] His subsequent studies go somewhat further in addressing discourses and controversies surrounding Islam in contemporary Britain. See Paul Gilroy, *After Empire: Melancholia or Convivial Culture?* (London, 2004).

[11] Stuart Hall, 'New Ethnicities', in David Morley and Kuan-Hsing Chen (eds.), *Stuart Hall: Critical Dialogues in Cultural Studies* (London, 1996), 442–51; Stuart Hall, 'What Is This "Black" in Black Popular Culture?', in Morley and Chen (eds.), *Stuart Hall*, 471–5. For a wider

conflicting understandings of cultural and national identity, belonging, change, and diversity across indigenous and diasporic populations alike, positioning these against the backdrop of local and transnational influences that have shaped them.

* * *

Butter in the melting pot? Multiculturalism in the postcolonial French republic

When Raspail's *Le Figaro Magazine* article referred to France's 'two communities' – one a population of '*Français de souche*' or 'French stock' seemingly open to other Europeans, the other 'non-European foreign' and overwhelmingly Muslim – it confronted a central facet of national identity head-on by suggesting that it was already fundamentally compromised. This binary opposition failed to address the vast differences within each artificial grouping and ignored the countless other forms of affiliation (ethnic and otherwise) available to those forcibly placed under each heading. Yet his account was a typical expression of fears about the effects of difference within, and upon, the French nation generated between the 1980s and the present day. Within this climate of anxiety, religion dominated ruminations on the state of the nation and the state of culture within a purportedly secular French republic that was 'one and indivisible' in theory, if not in practice.

The 1980s marked a watershed in French discussions of national identity that narrowed the limited scope for state-level recognition and encouragement of ethnic and cultural minority identities that had opened up at the beginning of the decade. In 1981, the newly-elected Socialist government under François Mitterrand promoted *le droit à la différence*, or 'the right to be different', which signalled an acceptance of greater French regional autonomy and cultural distinctiveness alongside an expanded public presence of diverse ethnic identities.[12] Yet official nods that favoured multiculturalism proved short-lived, squeezed out by the resurgence of republicanism as a national ideology and the rise of the extreme right *Front National* under Jean-Marie Le Pen.

Elements of the republican legacy inspiring late twentieth-century French public intellectuals and officials included some that dated back to the era of the

thematic treatment, see Elizabeth Buettner, 'Ethnicity', in Ulinka Rublack (ed.), *A Concise Companion to History* (Oxford, 2011), 247–67.

[12] Judith Vichniac, 'French Socialists and the Droit à la Différence: A Changing Dynamic', *French Politics and Society*, 9:1 (1991), 40–56; David Blatt, 'Immigrant Politics in a Republican Nation', in Alec G. Hargreaves and Mark McKinney (eds.), *Post-Colonial Cultures in France* (London, 1997), 40–55; Hargreaves, *Multi-Ethnic France*, 182–4; Adrian Favell, *Philosophies of Integration: Immigration and the Idea of Citizenship in France and Britain* (Basingstoke, 1998), 51.

Enlightenment and the French Revolution alongside others that evolved during the Third Republic (1870–1940). Liberty, equality, and fraternity; the rights of man; the freedom of the individual; purportedly 'universal' and 'civilized' cultural and political values taking precedence over those denigrated as particularistic, retrograde, 'lower', and 'barbaric': these were joined by the late nineteenth- and early twentieth-century project to iron out ongoing signs of regional cultural specificity and turn 'peasants into Frenchmen', as Eugen Weber memorably termed it.[13] Compulsory education and male military service were two of the main mechanisms meant to produce a generic French citizen owing allegiance to the centralizing state that had become assertively secular in its battle for ascendancy over Roman Catholicism for French loyalties. The separation of church and state climaxed with legislation passed in 1905, and laïcité (secularism) joined liberty, equality, and fraternity as central tenets of French republican ideology. While it was acceptable for French citizens to be Catholic (or adhere to another faith such as Judaism or, later, Islam), religion was meant to be a private matter rather than a part of public life. So too were other competing forms of identity deriving from subnational group affiliations, whether they be ethnic, regional, cultural, linguistic, or otherwise 'particular'. The primary bond was to be that tying the individual to the nation; intermediary group attachments coming between them compromised and diluted the nation's identity and integrity.[14]

Transforming peasants and Catholics into Frenchmen first and foremost meant integration within a conception of a unified, singular nation. Equally fundamental to the republican ideology of citizenship and nationality was its openness to newcomers, a crucial dimension given the high rate of immigration into France during the nineteenth and twentieth centuries. Citizenship in France was meant to be 'elective' as opposed to 'organic', Adrian Favell succinctly summarizes, with 'an individual's identity ... not definitively determined by their racial or cultural origins'.[15] Frenchness should be available to those willing to adhere to its ostensibly unitary culture and traditions and integrate within the polity. Foreigners amenable to integration and full immersion within le creuset français, or French melting pot, were thus not barred from doing so, nor were their descendants.[16]

---

[13] Eugen Weber, Peasants into Frenchmen: The Modernization of Rural France (Stanford, 1976).

[14] Excellent summaries in English include Jeremy Jennings, 'Citizenship, Republicanism, and Multiculturalism in Contemporary France', British Journal of Political Science, 30:4 (2000), 575–98; Cécile Laborde, 'The Culture(s) of the Republic: Nationalism and Multiculturalism in French Republican Thought', Political Theory, 29:5 (2001), 716–35.

[15] Favell, Philosophies of Integration, 69.

[16] See Chapter 7, alongside Gérard Noiriel, The French Melting Pot: Immigration, Citizenship, and National Identity, translated by Geoffroy de Laforcade (Minneapolis, 1996; first published in French in 1988).

Citizenship rights, in sum, were based not solely upon *jus sanguinis* (bloodline); *jus soli* (birthplace or place of residence) also opened many doors. But France's willingness for immigrants to become citizens – and, as the previous chapter outlined, many labelled 'immigrants' who came from (ex-)colonies and overseas territories were legally citizens upon arrival – was in fact highly conditional, demanding that the persons in question set aside other ethnic group identities deemed to be in competition with Frenchness. Of France's entrenched opposition to recognizing minority groups and cultures or their claims to specific rights, Jeremy Jennings notes the main reasons why multiculturalism has been so widely rejected within France: 'It sanctions unequal rights. It countenances communities closed in upon themselves. It places culture before politics, groups before individuals.'[17] 'Un-French' in the extreme, multiculturalism was 'Anglo-Saxon', an even more damning verdict in its association with American (and to a lesser extent British) approaches to minorities believed to foster ethnic hostilities, segregation, and ghettoization.[18] Republicanism, on the other hand, 'became a vehicle for inclusion *and* exclusion' in its insistence upon universalism over particularism, its hostility to cultural pluralism, and its requirement for integration.[19] While in France the prospect of belonging existed in theory, it was often withheld in practice to those blamed for failing to subscribe to republican ideologies.

The possibility of exclusion loomed large not only for postcolonial migrants, particularly Muslims, but also for their children born on French soil and for whom *jus soli* might normally apply. Scholars such as Jean-Loup Amselle persuasively argue that the postcolonial reluctance to countenance multiculturalism within France owes an immeasurable debt to the colonial legacy, in particular to the nation's extended history of promoting its rule overseas as a 'civilizing mission' (which, during the Third Republic, coincided with efforts to 'civilize' rural peasants at home – a programme arguably akin to internal colonization).[20] Responses to non-European ethnic minorities in France in recent decades have antecedents in the valorization of French culture over the cultures of allegedly 'inferior races' in the empire, as does the encouragement

---

[17] Jennings, 'Citizenship, Republicanism, and Multiculturalism', 589.

[18] Ibid., 587; Favell, *Philosophies of Integration*, 61–2. For an assessment of the strong anti-American current long evident in France, see Jean-François Revel, *Anti-Americanism* (San Francisco, 2003).

[19] Jennings, 'Citizenship, Republicanism, and Multiculturalism', 597.

[20] Jean-Loup Amselle, *Affirmative Exclusion: Cultural Pluralism and the Rule of Custom in France*, translated by Jane Marie Todd (Ithaca, 2003); Alice L. Conklin, *A Mission to Civilize: The Republican Idea of Empire in France and West Africa, 1895–1930* (Stanford, 1997); Hafid Gafaiti's and Driss Maghraoui's contributions to Tyler Stovall and Georges Van Den Abbeele (eds.), *French Civilization and Its Discontents: Nationalism, Colonialism, Race* (Lanham, MD, 2003). Weber evaluates the possibility that rural French society during the Third Republic experienced forms of intervention comparable to colonized populations in *Peasants into Frenchmen*, ch. 29.

of assimilation as the road to political rights and naturalization for what in reality never amounted to more than a small portion of the colonized population. 'Assimilation', Alec Hargreaves aptly stresses, remains 'tainted by its colonial connotations', living on in the aftermath of empire in accusations that many immigrants and their children have failed to integrate within French society.[21]

Debates about immigration, integration, and French national identity perceived as under threat have revolved overwhelmingly around Algerians and their descendants, paying relatively little attention to other groups – that is, unless they were Muslim and thus were presumed to share some of the same problematic qualities, as were many other Maghrebis and sub-Saharan Africans. Algerians' paramount position is closely tied to their nation's centrality to France's overseas history for well over a century, not least the history of its decolonization. As outlined in Chapter 3, the end of French Algeria in 1962 after a war that had dragged on since 1954 was France's most protracted, violent, and publicly divisive decolonization by far. The loss of Algeria divided France in a literal sense, redrawing the nation's borders on account of Algeria's status not as a colony but as three French *départements*. Just as Algerian independence had altered France by contracting its territory, so too did many in France fear that Algerians who had crossed the Mediterranean and become permanent residents might further 'reduce' the nation, this time through importing cultural difference accused of being intractable as well as incommensurate with France's 'universal' culture in its obdurate ethnic (and religious) particularism.

Memories of, and support for, the *Algérie française* cause did not disappear in France after 1962. Repatriated settlers (*pieds-noirs*) and military personnel who had fought long and hard to keep Algeria French later provided a disproportionately high level of recruits for new-right and extreme-right organizations and political parties, most famously the *Front National*.[22] Its controversial leader Jean-Marie Le Pen's biography in the mid-late 1950s involved periods of military service first in Indochina and later in Algeria as a paratrooper during the Battle of Algiers. After achieving political notoriety he found himself periodically dogged by allegations of involvement in the torture of FLN suspects.[23] Founded in 1972, the *Front National* languished in the

[21] Hargreaves, *Multi-Ethnic France*, 151.

[22] Emmanuelle Comtat, *Les pieds-noirs et la politique: Quarante ans après le retour* (Paris, 2009), ch. 5; John Veugelers, 'Ex-Colonials, Voluntary Associations, and Electoral Support for the Contemporary Far Right', *Comparative European Politics*, 3 (2005), 408–31; Jonathan Marcus, *The National Front and French Politics: The Resistible Rise of Jean-Marie Le Pen* (Basingstoke, 1995), 57–8; Edward G. Declair, *Politics on the Fringe: The People, Policies, and Organization of the French National Front* (Durham, 1999), 22–5, 213; Flood and Frey, 'Questions of Decolonization', 408.

[23] Shields, *Extreme Right*, 66, 108–9.

political wilderness for over a decade before achieving its electoral break-through in 1983 on the back of its racist, anti-immigration platforms.[24] While support has waxed and waned since then, on average the party regularly receives the votes of between 10 and 15 per cent of the French electorate. Indicatively, its strongest showings consistently have been in greater Paris, the region surrounding Lyon, northeast France, and along the Mediterranean coast, all areas with high concentrations of non-European immigrants, high levels of unemployment, and often significant *pied-noir* settlement (as is the case in the Mediterranean region).

Although the *Front National* was known for slogans like 'Two million unemployed is two million immigrants too many', the extreme right's antipathy found its strongest expression in discussions revolving around culture, family, and nation.[25] Overtly eugenic in tone, the *Front National*'s anti-abortion and pro-natalist agenda saw in the family the source of France's strength and equally its weakness. It espoused demographic ideas and fears nearly identical to those Jean Raspail contributed to *Le Figaro Magazine*. A low birth rate among native French families meant that 'The nation is disappearing. Nature abhors a vacuum and this vacuum will be filled', Le Pen stated:

The influx of traditionally prolific immigrant families in the name of family reunification is a precursor of the demographic submersion of France and the substitution of a population originating in the Third World for the French population, which is doomed to become a minority in its own country ... Make no mistake: *it is the very existence of the French people which is at stake*.[26]

The *Front National*'s conception of the French nation and French culture was thus distinctly at odds with republican ideology. Frenchness was envisioned as deriving from ancestry, blood, and heritage; rather than being theoretically open to all comers who ascribed to republican values, France needed protection from those Le Pen termed illegitimate 'stowaways' who should be forcibly repatriated.[27] Moreover, in contrast to the emphasis upon secularism within republican

---

[24] Françoise Gaspard, *A Small City in France: A Socialist Mayor Confronts Neofascism*, translated by Arthur Goldhammer (Cambridge, MA, 1995). On the *Front National*'s evolution and policies, see Valérie Igounet, *Le Front National de 1972 à nos jours: Le parti, les hommes, les idées* (Paris, 2014); Nonna Mayer and Pascal Perrineau (eds.), *Le Front National à découvert* (Paris, 1989); Marcus, *National Front*; Peter Fysh and James Wolfreys, *The Politics of Racism in France* (Basingstoke, 2003); Declair, *Politics on the Fringe*; Shields, *Extreme Right*, chs. 7–11; David Art, *Inside the Radical Right: The Development of Anti-Immigrant Parties in Western Europe* (New York, 2011), 120–35.

[25] Marcus, *National Front*, 53.

[26] Front National, *La vraie opposition: Le Front National* (Paris, Autumn 1984), 15, 12, cited in Pierre-André Taguieff, 'The Doctrine of the National Front in France (1972–1989): A "Revolutionary Programme"? Ideological Aspects of a National-Populist Mobilization', *New Political Science*, 8:1&2 (1989), 45.

[27] Taguieff, 'Doctrine of the National Front', 43.

discourse, Le Pen's party has included many supporters who might be described as 'Catholic fundamentalists' – persons who might well share Raspail's feeling that 'darkness was falling on the old Christian country'. Evidence of anti-Semitism is also not difficult to find within its rhetoric.[28]

Significant though the differences may be, however, views espoused by the *Front National* overlap with mainstream republican philosophy in revealing ways, for example in the intense hostility to Muslims in France and the adamant refusal to accommodate multiculturalism. French cultural homogeneity is assumed in the case of the former (for whom ethnic minorities of different cultures fall permanently outside the nation) and demanded by the latter (whose champions argue that immigrants must integrate and take up France's purportedly universal culture). While republicanism insists upon integration yet repeatedly accuses postcolonial immigrants and their children of failing to achieve it, the *Front National* suggests that cultural differences can never be overcome. As Pierre-André Taguieff concludes, 'the fear and the vehement denunciation of the mixing of people and/or of races, if not of cultures, defines the hard core of Le Pen's racism. The postulate of the inassimability of certain categories of "foreigners", thereby set up as being absolute, fixed in substantial collective identities, sums up the basic conviction.'[29] Although many within the political mainstream have found it easy to accuse the *Front National* of a racism that remains deeply imbued with biological essentialism, the party is nonetheless heavily reliant upon a 'neo-racist' static conception of cultural difference. Racism predicated upon culture was not confined to the extreme right, but rather spread far more widely throughout the political and social spectrum.

The *Front National*'s ascent after 1983 does much to explain a number of critical shifts in France's stance towards immigrants, ethnic minorities, Muslims, and cultural pluralism, along with the resurgence of republican ideologies concerning integration, citizenship, and secularism.[30] From the mid-1980s until the present, the Socialists and especially the centre-right parties have responded defensively to the growth in popular support for the *Front National*. Fearing even further desertion by voters discontented with mainstream party policies, left and right alike altered their positions in response to extreme-right platforms, resulting in what some commentators have termed a *lepénisation* of French politics.[31] In efforts to appear tougher on immigration, between the mid-1980s and the early 1990s successive governments made

[28] Declair, *Politics on the Fringe*, 19, 213; Shields, *Extreme Right*, 221–4.
[29] Taguieff, 'Doctrine of the National Front', 61.
[30] Favell, *Philosophies of Integration*, 48, 52; Hargreaves, *Multi-Ethnic France*, ch. 5.
[31] Pierre Tévanian and Sylvie Tissot, *Mots à maux: Dictionnaire de la lepénisation des esprits* (Paris, 1998).

family reunification more difficult and enacted new regulations concerning illegal immigrants and conditions of residency. Socialist nods in the direction of *le droit à la différence* came to an end, in part because of resilient scepticism concerning sub-national group identities and in part because the *Front National* appropriated the idea for themselves. All nations, they agreed, had the right to maintain and protect their own ethnic culture and identity (assumed as singular, fixed, and mirroring the nation's geographical limits) – the French just as much as those supposedly destined to remain North African wherever they happened to live.[32] *Le droit à la différence* was a laudable objective, in other words, if it was achieved by repatriating 'foreigners' to enjoy their much-vaunted difference in their countries of origin while preserving France for the 'true' French – a subconscious delayed reaction, perhaps, to the *pieds-noirs'* mass repatriation when the dream of *Algérie française* died and the territorial confines of France receded.

Having lost more ground to the *Front National* than the left on the basis of public hostility to immigration-related issues, centre-right parties worked even harder to reclaim the initiative. Extended discussions about reforming the nationality code began in the mid-1980s and ultimately bore fruit in the 1993 Pasqua laws revising the conditions of citizenship for the children of immigrants. French nationality was no longer automatically granted to those born in France to foreign parents when they reached the age of majority: a range of special conditions now applied, foremost among which was the requirement that they formally request citizenship rather than receive it passively.[33] The new laws reinforced the official stress upon the elective nature of French citizenship, and in this respect drew upon a long-standing plank of republican ideology. Yet the extent to which the 1993 legislation constituted a fundamental shift away from *jus soli* in the direction of *jus sanguinis* cannot be underestimated. Young men and women born in France who were not of recent foreign descent were not required to affirm their loyalties actively, whereas second-generation youth were – even if they had never resided in any other country but France. 1993 marked a critical moment when France veered 'toward an ethnic conception of the nation', Amselle suggests.[34] Even though the Pasqua laws were partly overturned after a government under the Socialists returned to power in 1997, the message they sent about the differential conditions of Frenchness for descendants of postcolonial migrants continued to resonate loud and clear. The onus was placed upon them to demonstrate their affiliation to a nation whose mainstream remained highly reluctant to accept

---

[32] Flood and Frey, 'Questions of Decolonization', 401, 405; Herman Lebovics, *Bringing the Empire Back Home: France in the Global Age* (Durham, 2004), 132, 135.

[33] Favell, *Philosophies of Integration*, 66–9; Patrick Weil and Alexis Spire, 'France', in Rainer Bauböck *et al.* (eds.), *Acquisition and Loss of Nationality: Politics and Trends in 15 European States, Vol. 2: Country Analyses* (Amsterdam, 2006), 198–202.

[34] Amselle, *Affirmative Exclusion*, 114, 119, 154.

them, often on the basis of their alleged 'non-integration' that stemmed from 'communitarian' cultural and religious particularism.

Since the mid-1980s, the reigning republican consensus put on the defensive by the extreme right has rallied around a strongly integrationist agenda heavily focused on Muslim youth. Government officials and the media relentlessly provided the public with reports of the domestic presence of international Islamist fundamentalism, identified as gaining a strong foothold among young men of North African descent living on high-rise housing estates in the deprived *banlieues* ringing French cities. Cast as petty criminals, delinquents, and vandals, adolescent males and men in their twenties were made to personify the *banlieues de l'islam*, sites incubating anti-social behaviour, drug use, non-integration, and potential religion-inspired terrorism alike.[35] Fears of an Islamic 'fifth column' present in France reached new heights in 1995 when bombings in Paris and Lyon were attributed to enemies both from without (the Algerian Armed Islamic Group) and within (the *banlieues*).[36]

* * *

Gendered fears and stereotypes surrounding Maghrebi-descended youth also applied to adolescent girls, around whom revolved one of the most significant and drawn-out controversies about the place of Islam in France: the question of whether headscarves should be permitted or prohibited in public schools. Just as the previous chapter examined how the image of the beleaguered or crowded house or apartment readily served as a metaphor for the nation experiencing immigration, so too did schools and the *banlieues* become pivotal sites for analyzing the place of 'immigrants' within the republic – particularly once the category of 'immigrants' included permanently-settled families with children rather than a mainly male workforce often imagined as temporary. In Jean-Marie Le Pen's book *Les Français d'abord* (*French First*), all three became spaces that readily testified to the extent to which France was being 'invaded' or 'colonized'. 'When we look at these apartments conquered one after the next, these concrete walls, these concrete cities which spring up all around our cities, these changing populations, these schools which have literally been colonized, we well know that the danger is great', he intoned.[37]

[35] Gilles Kepel, *Les banlieues de l'islam: Naissance d'une religion en France* (Paris, 1987).
[36] Thomas Deltombe and Mathieu Rigouste, 'L'ennemi intérieur: la construction médiatique de la figure de l'"Arabe"', in Blanchard, Bancel, and Lemaire (eds.), *La fracture coloniale*, 199; Thomas Deltombe, *L'islam imaginaire: La construction médiatique de l'islamophobie en France, 1975–2005* (Paris, 2005), 57; Ahmed Boubeker, 'La "petite histoire" d'une génération d'expérience: Du mouvement beur aux banlieues de l'islam', in Ahmed Boubeker and Abdellali Hajjat (eds.), *Histoire politique des immigrations (post)coloniales: France, 1920–2008* (Paris, 2008), 185; Paul A. Silverstein, *Algeria in France: Transpolitics, Race, and Nation* (Bloomington, 2004), ch. 4.
[37] Jean-Marie Le Pen, *Les Français d'abord* (Paris, 1984), 101.

Nor was the *Front National* alone in seeing schools as situated on the front line in the encounter between France and its immigrant/Muslim population. Champions of the republican ethos did so as well, with key 'battles' occurring in 1989, 1994, and 2003–2004 around female pupils' rights to wear head coverings variously called *foulards* (headscarves), *voiles* (veils), the *chador*, or the *hijab*.[38] An item of clothing that had long been worn, largely unremarked, by some (but far from all) Muslim schoolgirls in France suddenly became elevated to the status of recurrent furore in national politics and the media.

That 'Islamic headscarves' should move to the heart of such an emblematic struggle in late twentieth- and early twenty-first-century France can be attributed to a combination of domestic and imperial antecedents that informed how France confronted current events. As noted earlier, since the Third Republic state schools have played a central role in the larger project of creating French citizens by instilling in the coming generation a national civic identity at the expense of other loyalties, including religious affiliations, seen to be in competition with it. Roman Catholicism's long-standing dominance in France's schools was dealt a decisive blow with the separation of church and state in 1905; thereafter, state schools were reimagined as bastions of *laïcité*. A republican secular tradition was thus readily available to be drawn upon in connection with educational policy, and 1989 became a key moment when domestic developments and international affairs came together to pit republican *laïcité* against a religious opponent – no longer Roman Catholicism but now Islam. Coinciding with months of intense republican celebrations organized to commemorate the bicentennial of the French Revolution, 1989 saw years of steadily rising negative publicity surrounding 'fundamentalist' Islam and Muslims' supposed incompatibility with France's integrationist demands come to a head in the immediate wake of international public outcry in the West over the Ayatollah Khomeini's *fatwa* against Salman Rushdie.

Tensions exploded that autumn when the principal of a school in Creil, near Paris, expelled three schoolgirls who refused to remove their headscarves when requested to do so. Thus began fifteen years of periodic and inconclusive '*foulards* affairs' that finally culminated in a law banning 'ostentatious' religious insignia at state schools in 2004. Renewed attention to Islamic militancy in the aftermath of the 11 September 2001 attacks in the United States and the

---

[38] Of many French examinations of the struggles over headscarves, see especially Saïd Bouamama, *L'affaire du foulard islamique: La production d'un racisme respectable* (Roubaix, 2004); Charlotte Nordmann (ed.), *Le foulard islamique en questions* (Paris, 2004); Pierre Tévanian, *La voile médiatique: Retour sur la construction de l''affaire du foulard islamique'* (Paris, 2005). The best studies in English include Joan Wallach Scott, *The Politics of the Veil* (Princeton, 2007); John R. Bowen, *Why the French Don't Like Headscarves: Islam, the State, and Public Space* (Princeton, 2007); Cécile Laborde, *Critical Republicanism: The Hijab Controversy and Political Philosophy* (Oxford, 2008).

Front National's strong showing in the 2002 elections help explain its timing. Significantly, the 2004 law tolerated selected religious symbols it classified as 'discreet' or 'inconspicuous', such as small Christian crosses or Jewish Stars of David, but it failed to identify a convincingly comparable token item permissible for Muslims. Between 1989 and 2004, the status of Judaism in France never counted as the central issue driving debates surrounding religious signs and public schools. Instead, an often vociferous animosity towards Islam worked in combination with the refusal to address the 'diffuse hegemony of Catholic culture' in everyday French life.[39]

The republican status quo that might more aptly be termed 'Catho-*laïcité*' or '*laïcité sacrée*' (sacred secularism) extends to religiously-inflected portrayals of state schools as having a '"sacred" mission' and providing '"sanctuaries" where children can become enlightened'.[40] Muslim girls figured as those most in need of this civic refuge, a view with roots in colonial-era gender and racial ideologies that laid the groundwork for postcolonial French stereotypes of Islam as uniquely oppressive to women. Nineteenth-century assumptions about 'Arab' societies as being immoral and backward took sexual expression in oft-repeated narratives focused on harems, polygamy, and veiling carried over into the twentieth. Until the end of French rule, efforts to modernize indigenous society were justified by the need to defend Muslim women from misogynistic patriarchy, literally by bringing them out from behind the veil – by force if necessary. During the 1954–1962 war, the so-called 'battle of the veil' in 1958 involved French soldiers tearing away the head coverings of Algerian women whose recalcitrant stance towards this form of alleged 'liberation' provided further testament to their repression by an inferior culture.[41]

So symbolic was the veil for the French, Joan Scott suggests, that after decolonization it survived as a potent reminder of Algeria's stubborn backwardness and France's humiliation alike: 'It was the piece of cloth that represented the antithesis of the *tricolore* [French flag], and the failure of the

---

[39] Laborde, *Critical Republicanism*, 69; see also Bowen, *Why the French Don't Like Headscarves*, 20; Scott, *Politics of the Veil*, 101.

[40] Laborde, *Critical Republicanism*, 69; Pierre Tévanian, 'A Conservative Revolution within Secularism: The Ideological Premises and Social Effects of the March 15, 2004, "Anti-Headscarf" Law', translated by Naomi Baldinger, in Tshimanga, Gondola, and Bloom (eds.), *Frenchness and the African Diaspora*, 189.

[41] Julia Clancy-Smith, 'Islam, Gender, and Identities in the Making of French Algeria, 1830–1962', in Julia Clancy-Smith and Frances Gouda (eds.), *Domesticating the Empire: Race, Gender, and Family Life in French and Dutch Colonialism* (Charlottesville, 1998), 154–74; Todd Shepard, *The Invention of Decolonization: The Algerian War and the Remaking of France* (Ithaca, 2006), 186–92; Scott, *Politics of the Veil*, 62–7; Neil MacMaster, *Burning the Veil: The Algerian War and the 'Emancipation' of Muslim Women, 1954–62* (Manchester, 2009); Frantz Fanon, *A Dying Colonialism*, translated by François Maspero (Harmondsworth, 1970; originally published in French in 1959), 32–3.

civilizing mission.'[42] In the ongoing fixation upon the Muslim female body and clothing, the colonial past still reverberates in postcolonial France.[43] If the 'battle of the veil' ultimately had been conceded across the Mediterranean in 1962, that against the *foulard* or *hijab* might still be won in France – if, that is, French schools could become settings where girls might be 'rescued' from the strictures of the traditional, male-dominated Muslim family.[44] The imperative to emancipate them helped reinforce sexual equality as a French republican 'primordial value', literally situated at the centre of *liberté, egalité, fraternité*, and *laïcité*.[45] Diverging from this stance confirmed the status of 'other': foreign, culturally backward, and unintegrated.

The obdurate French focus on Islamic headscarves is only the most widely-discussed instance of the way the condition of Muslim girls and women – imagined by turns as victims and/or as offering strongest proof of cultural resilience that spelled non-integration – is seen as emblematic of the 'problems of immigration' and, relatedly, the 'problems of *les jeunes issus de l'immigration*', or 'youth of immigrant origin'. Alongside controversies surrounding *foulards* (and more recently burkas and other garments), other gender issues associated with Muslims of either North African or West African origin have attracted intense public scrutiny and condemnation, including polygamy, forced marriages, and female excision (also commonly referred to as genital mutilation or clitoridectomy).[46] While protecting women from abuse and human rights violations remains essential, sensationalized media coverage out of all proportion to the numbers of families involved became politically exploited by Islamophobic opponents of immigration and multiculturalism.[47]

---

[42] Scott, *Politics of the Veil*, 66.   [43] Laborde, *Critical Republicanism*, 132–3.

[44] Jane Freedman and Carrie Tarr, 'Introduction', in Jane Freedman and Carrie Tarr (eds.), *Women, Immigration, and Identities in France* (Oxford, 2000), 2–3; see also Camille Lacoste-Dujardin, 'Maghrebi Families in France', in Freedman and Tarr (eds.), *Women, Immigration, and Identities in France*, 57–68.

[45] Scott, *Politics of the Veil*, 173; Bowen, *Why the French Don't Like Headscarves*, 6. This rendition of gender equality as located at the heart of Frenchness, of course, relies upon ignoring the tortuous path women travelled to achieve political (and other) rights in France, where their right to vote only dates from 1944.

[46] In 2010, the French government significantly stepped up its policing of women's clothing associated with Islam, going beyond the 2004 legislation concerning headscarves in state schools by forbidding women (of all ages) from wearing burkas or otherwise covering their faces in public.

[47] Catherine Raissiguier, 'Gender, Race, and Exclusion: A New Look at the French Republican Tradition', *International Feminist Journal of Politics*, 1:3 (1999), 435–57; Catherine Raissiguier, 'Women from the Maghreb and Sub-Saharan Africa in France: Fighting for Health and Basic Human Rights', in Obioma Nnaemeka and Joy Ngozi Ezeilo (eds.), *Engendering Human Rights: Cultural and Socioeconomic Realities in Africa* (New York, 2005), 111–28; Tévanian and Tissot, *Mots à maux*, 162–4; Trica Danielle Keaton, *Muslim Girls and the Other France: Race, Identity Politics, and Social Exclusion* (Bloomington, 2006), ch. 5. For an example of populist media coverage linking polygamy and burkas, see Rose-Laure

Habitual depictions of Islam as a fixed, undifferentiated phenomenon and Muslims as forming a homogeneous 'community' in France come at the expense of an informed understanding of the highly diverse character of the religion and its adherents. When positive reference is made to 'moderate', 'good' Muslims, it often serves as a simplistic means of redirecting attention back towards those dismissed as 'radical' and thus 'bad'.[48] French analyses of Islam rarely do justice to the many ways of being a Muslim that range from a low level of sporadic religious engagement and relative agnosticism to more fundamentalist stances that dominate the public spotlight – nor do they usually attempt to comprehend the precise meanings of practices associated with Islam to those who value them. One poll conducted shortly before the 2004 ban on headscarves in schools, for example, found that only 14 per cent of Muslim women wore the *hijab* while 51 per cent considered themselves regularly observant.[49] Over more than a decade of debate, young women's personal reasons for wearing headscarves were seldom listened to or taken seriously.

Interviews reveal a far more complex set of stories. Some girls and women donned head coverings on account of familial expectations and pressures, but others willingly did so to assert their own identity, seeing them as a sign of dignity, sexual respectability, spiritual dedication, or connection to their cultures of origin.[50] Crucially, many protested that they were not in fact 'oppressed' by their parents but had freely chosen their attire as an expression of their *liberté*, drawing upon a republican idiom in asserting their status as individual agents and not helpless victims. In short, they considered themselves French *and* North African-descended *and* Muslim, rejecting the either/or identities offered to them by the state. Theirs was a hybrid identity of which they were proud, one they insisted was compatible with belonging in France – but belonging on their own terms. Integration in France was possible while retaining cultural and religious distinctiveness, they claimed, and should not require abandoning their 'particularity' as a precondition for national inclusion.

* * *

Controversies surrounding Islamic headscarves first erupted at the end of a decade when, in the wake of increased family reunification, a sizable second generation raised and educated in France came of age and asserted new forms of cultural affiliation. North African-descended youth in their teens and early

Bendavid and Flore Olive, 'Burqa: Les mariées étaient en noir', *Paris Match*, 3181 (6–12 May 2010), 62–7.

[48] Jocelyne Cesari, *Musulmans et républicains: Les jeunes, l'islam et la France* (Paris, 1998); Deltombe and Rigouste, 'L'ennemi intérieur', 199–200.

[49] Scott, *Politics of the Veil*, 3.

[50] Françoise Gaspard and Farhad Khosrokhavar, *Le foulard et la République* (Paris, 1995); Ismahane Chouder, Malika Latrèche, and Pierre Tévanian, *Les filles voilées parlent* (Paris, 2008).

twenties known as *beurs* became the most recognizable segment of a group that received wide public attention starting in the early 1980s. Maghrebi youth reversed the syllables of *Arabe*, a ubiquitous form of insult, to make a new word, *beur*, indicating not simply a protest against racism but also the assertion of an identity different from that of their parents and from other ethnic groups in France alike.[51] *Beurs* achieved a high level of visibility through a combination of anti-racist activism and cultural expression, not to mention through their involvement in riots that have periodically recurred since the early 1980s. Second-generation Maghrebis, sometimes working alongside other ethnic minority youth, became involved in organizations such as SOS-Racisme and were core participants in the 1983 March for Equality and Against Racism (often referred to as the *Marche des Beurs*). The so-called '*beur* movement' also encompassed the emergence of *beur* radio, filmmaking, and fiction, with two of the best-known novels being Mehdi Charef's *Le thé au harem d'Archi Ahmed* (later translated as *Tea in the Harem*) and Azouz Begag's *Le Gone du Chaâba* (*Shantytown Kid*).[52]

Beur cultural creativity that blossomed in the 1980s, although not ignoring religion, largely foregrounded generational distinctiveness and experiences of racism, violence, poverty, lack of opportunity, and social exclusion. These often derived from growing up in shantytowns and later in the *banlieues*, the deprived outskirts of large French cities. Alongside youth from other postcolonial ethnic minority backgrounds, *beurs* turned to forms of expression ranging from music to writing to rioting to make themselves heard. They contested dominant representations that reduced a complex range of social, economic, and cultural issues to demonized ideas about Islam, responding with critiques of France's treatment of low-income *banlieue* residents and a new set of cultural formations alike. These reflect the common ground they shared with others of their generation across ethnic lines. In talking back to those who insisted on a centralized, monolithic model of French national identity to which they allegedly failed to adhere, *banlieue* youth offered alternative forms of

---

[51] Sylvie Durmelat, 'Petite histoire du mot beur: ou comment prendre la parole quand on vous la prête', *French Cultural Studies*, 9 (1998), 191–207.

[52] Mehdi Charef, *Tea in the Harem*, translated by Ed Emery (London, 1989; first published in French in 1983); Azouz Begag, *Shantytown Kid*, translated by Naïma Wolf and Alec G. Hargreaves (Lincoln, NE and London, 2007; first published in French in 1986). On *beur* identity, activism, filmmaking, and fiction, see Adil Jazouli, *L'action collective des jeunes maghrébins de France* (Paris, 1986); Alec G. Hargreaves, *Voices from the North African Immigrant Community in France: Immigration and Identity in Beur Fiction* (New York, 1991); Michel Laronde, *Autour du roman beur: immigration et identité* (Paris, 1993); Saïd Bouamama, *Dix ans de marche des beurs: Chronique d'un mouvement avorté* (Paris, 1994); Richard L. Derderian, *North Africans in Contemporary France: Becoming Visible* (New York, 2004); Silverstein, *Algeria in France*, chs. 4 and 5; Carrie Tarr, *Reframing Difference: Beur and Banlieue Filmmaking in France* (Manchester, 2005); Nacira Guénif-Souilamas, *Des 'beurettes' aux descendantes d'immigrants nord-africains* (Paris, 2000).

affiliation at once locally specific *within* France and global/transnational *beyond* France. In the process, they claimed new ways of belonging *to* France that testified to their integration, rather than the reverse. Rejecting binary forms of belonging that restricted one to being *either* French *or* North African/Muslim/black, they, like so many Muslim girls who wanted to wear headscarves to school, protested not only that multiple identities were possible but that multiculturalism was positive.

Multiculturalism has long been a fact of life in France's *banlieues*, which have never been analogous to African-American 'ghettoes' pervaded by ethnic segregation. As Loïc Wacquant insists, the very notion that French suburbs are akin to areas of Chicago or Harlem is 'a sociological absurdity' given their multi-ethnic populations that included many working-class whites (of French and other European backgrounds) alongside those of Maghrebi, sub-Saharan African, or Antillean origin.[53] Socio-economic marginality, however, combined with spatial marginality to produce resiliently racialized portrayals of *banlieue* residents whatever their background.[54] Recurrent youth-focused moral panics surrounding *banlieues* as sites combining poverty, crime, and cultural alienation largely ignore whites in the rush to attribute most problems to cultural and ethnic difference and the non-assimilation of *les jeunes issus de l'immigration* – for example in repeated allusions to the *banlieues de l'islam*. Alternative portrayals illustrate how diverse neighbourhoods have produced youth cultures and friendship networks united by age, circumstances, and locality but not ethnicity. The highly acclaimed 1995 film *La haine* (*Hatred*) provides only one of many illustrations, fictional and factual alike, of a '*black blanc beur*' (black white *beur*) group of male friends living on the same housing estate whose diverse parental origins proved less relevant than the common social exclusion, unemployment, police harassment, and leisure interests that brought them together.[55]

Popular music exemplifies *banlieue* hybridity. In the 1980s, Algerian *raï* was a central aspect of Franco-Maghrebi identity among both parents and children, enabling the former to look back to their homeland and giving the latter a means of bridging their ancestral culture and the French arenas where they had grown up. Over time, however, those coming of age shifted their musical preferences from *raï* to a multiplicity of international styles that extended far beyond those rooted in either their parents' (and later

---

[53] Loïc Wacquant, *Urban Outcasts: A Comparative Sociology of Advanced Marginality* (Cambridge, 2008), 160.

[54] Tyler Stovall, 'From Red Belt to Black Belt: Race, Class, and Urban Marginality in Twentieth-Century Paris', in Sue Peabody and Tyler Stovall (eds.), *The Color of Liberty: Histories of Race in France* (Durham, 2003), 358–9.

[55] Ginette Vincendeau, *La Haine* (London, 2005); Tarr, *Reframing Difference*, ch. 3; Mireille Rosello, *Declining the Stereotype: Ethnicity and Representation in French Cultures* (Hanover and London, 1998), 2–10 and ch. 3.

grandparents') countries of origin or France. Favoured cultural affiliations of French-born minority youth – Maghrebi-descended or otherwise – and their white friends and neighbours gravitated more and more towards a combination of African-American and Afro-Caribbean popular musics, rap and hip hop first and foremost but also fusions incorporating Jamaican reggae, ragamuffin, ragga, funk, and *zouk* from Guadeloupe and Martinique, among others.[56] Transnational through and through, *banlieue* youth cultures of the 1990s and 2000s drew upon aspects of what Paul Gilroy has called a 'black Atlantic' arena of cultural transmissions alongside ongoing borrowings from across the Mediterranean. Such is the influence of African diasporic communities and cultures, often but not exclusively Anglophone, that it has become common for French-born youth whose parents came from former French colonies to call themselves by the English term 'black', finding this self-chosen label more empowering than *noir* or *Africain* – words some associate with derogatory colonial-era imagery and an older generation of immigrants rather than themselves.[57]

Via diverse global music styles, musicians and their audiences from the *banlieues* stake their claim to belonging within France but on their own terms. French rappers and other bands, like their wider generational cohorts, tend overwhelmingly to foreground their strong affiliations with multi-ethnic localities within the nation at the same time as they search far beyond France for their inspirations and cultural politics. Feeling at home in and identifying with specific *quartiers* or *banlieues* of cities like Marseille, Lyon, and Paris where they grew up is as common among second-generation youth as it is among those of their age and class of French ancestry, an issue continually ignored by those who exclusively fixate upon whether those of Maghrebi descent either do or do not 'want to integrate' in France.[58] In their view, they

---

[56] Joan Gross, David McMurray, and Ted Swedenburg, 'Arab Noise and Ramadan Nights: Rai, Rap, and Franco-Maghrebi Identities', in Jonathan Xavier Inda and Renato Rosaldo (eds.), *The Anthropology of Globalization: A Reader* (Malden, MA and Oxford, 2002), 198–232; George Lipsitz, *Dangerous Crossroads: Popular Music, Postmodernism and the Poetics of Place* (London, 1994), ch. 6; David L. Looseley, *Popular Music in Contemporary France: Authenticity, Politics, Debate* (Oxford, 2003), ch. 3; Chris Warne's and Steve Cannon's contributions to Hargreaves and McKinney (eds.), *Post-Colonial Cultures in France*; Rupa Huq, *Beyond Subculture: Pop, Youth and Identity in a Postcolonial World* (London, 2006), chs. 4 and 6.

[57] Gilroy, *Black Atlantic*; Tshimanga, 'Let the Music Play', 248–76, 284; Dominic Thomas, *Black France: Colonialism, Immigration, and Transnationalism* (Bloomington, 2007), 11–12; Alain-Philippe Durand (ed.), *Black, Blanc, Beur: Rap Music and Hip-Hop Culture in the Francophone World* (Lanham, MD, 2002). On this wider theme, see Trica Danielle Keaton, T. Denean Sharpley-Whiting, and Tyler Stovall (eds.), *Black France/France Noire: The History and Politics of Blackness* (Durham, 2012), especially the points made by Rémy Bazenguissa-Ganga, 'Paint it "Black": How Africans and Afro-Caribbeans Became "Black" in France', 157, 160.

[58] Jocelyne Cesari, Alain Moreau, and Alexandra Schleyer-Lindenmann, *'Plus marseillais que moi, tu meurs!': Migrations, identités et territoires à Marseille* (Paris, 2001), 175; Silverstein,

already have – but within an actual France that is culturally plural and hybrid, not within an imaginary France that is culturally homogeneous.

Famously illustrating musical hybridity and its possibilities was Zebda, a group formed in 1980s Toulouse. Three of its members were *beurs* while the remaining four were white with French, Italian, Spanish, and other European immigrant backgrounds. Zebda's music encompassed elements of *la chanson française* (French song), rock, dub, rap, hip hop samples, reggae, and North African instruments and acoustics to produce what one commentator called '*un melting-pot de sons*' – 'a melting pot of sounds'.[59] *Métissage* (mixing) was integral to its artistic ethos, politics, and indeed its very name. 'Zebda', the Arabic word for butter, played upon the similarities between the French equivalent (*beurre*) and *beur*, words pronounced exactly the same. The band refused to recognize *beurs* as anything other than French or their identity as incompatible with Frenchness – a stance linked to the group's insistence not only that the second generation was already well integrated (melting into a wider whole) but that plurality and difference deserved respect.[60]

In its lyrics – mainly French, but with occasional Arabic words – and band members' public statements, Zebda simultaneously subscribed to republican values while problematizing them and exposing their limitations. 'I'm integrated, where's the solution?'; 'I'm French, I've got the documents to prove it, I'm well integrated'; 'I'm secular and republican': comparable statements recur in Zebda's songs and summarize the band's demands for inclusion.[61] Zebda critiqued republican hypocrisy and racism, most famously in the 1995 song '*Le Bruit et l'odeur*', or 'Noise and Smell', where it took on Jacques Chirac's notorious 1991 diatribe condemning 'immigrant' families (as discussed in Chapter 7). Samples from Chirac's speech alternated with lines insisting that cities like Toulouse owed their development and identity to immigrants from within and outside Europe, whose labours and contributions gave them the right to stand up and be counted:

> Who paved this street?
> Who built this city?

Algeria in France, 120, 162, 197–8; Ahmed Boubeker, 'Nouvelles générations et conscience politique', in Nicolas Bancel, Léla Bencharif, and Pascal Blanchard (eds.), *Lyon, Capitale des Outre-Mers: Immigration des Suds et culture coloniale en Rhône-Alpes et Auvergne* (Paris, 2007), 182–205; Stephanie Decouvelaere, '"Ça vient de la rue": French Rap's Perspective on French Society', *Wasafiri*, 23:4 (2008), 36–42.

[59] Danielle Marx-Scouras, *La France de Zebda 1981–2004: Faire de la musique un acte politique* (Paris, 2005), 123.

[60] Ibid., 25, 100; Barbara Lebrun, *Protest Music in France: Production, Identity and Audiences* (Farnham and Burlington, VT, 2009), 76–7.

[61] These lyrics from 'Quinze Ans' (1999), 'France 2' (1995), and 'Le Bruit et l'odeur' (1995) are analyzed in Marx-Scouras, *La France de Zebda*, 32, 138, 156–7; Lebrun, *Protest Music*, 78–80, 84.

And who lives in it?
To those who complain about the noise
To those who condemn the smell
Let me introduce myself
My name is Larbi, Mamadou, Juan, along with
Guido, Henri, Chico, Ali.[62]

Zebda's resistance to Chirac, the *Front National*, and others has been echoed by many hip hop and rap groups whose response has often proved far more strident and adversarial by comparison. Rappers Suprême NTM, a group that achieved fame in the early–mid 1990s, chose both a name (NTM was the abbreviation for *Nique ta mère*, translated as 'Fuck your mother') and wrote songs (like *'Nique la police'*) calculated to provoke a public reaction.[63] *Banlieue* youth more broadly responded to the cycle of state racism, police brutality, and biased media portrayals of their communities as non-integrated and 'communitarian' with slogans like *'Va t'faire intégrer!'* – 'Go integrate yourself!', an obvious adaptation of *'Va te faire foutre'*, or 'Go fuck yourself'.[64] If society and the state continually rejected their claims that they already belonged, the reasoning went, then why bother trying?

Anger at racial and social discrimination, public contempt, brutal methods of policing, and the depressed, impoverished, and seemingly hopeless conditions of their neighbourhoods periodically erupted into violence and rioting. This occurred most spectacularly in the autumn of 2005, when unrest that began in the suburb of Clichy-sous-Bois outside Paris spread to 300 cities and towns. Nicolas Sarkozy, then France's minister of the interior and later president, dismissed participants as *racaille* (scum, or rabble), a response that succeeded only in fuelling a pervasive sense of rage and disillusionment. Like other officials and prominent public commentators, Sarkozy appeared wilfully deaf to the underlying social, economic, and political problems – not least disproportionately high unemployment – that led to resentment and violence amongst whites as well as ethnic minority groups, preferring instead to round up what had become the usual suspects when seeking root causes. 'There are more problems for the child of a black African or North African immigrant than for the son of a Swede, Dane, or Hungarian', he proclaimed, 'because of culture, because of polygamy, because their social origins create more difficulties' – a choice of examples perhaps unsurprising coming from a politician who himself

---

[62] Marx-Scouras, *La France de Zebda*, 113 (see also 101); Lebrun, *Protest Music*, 77, 80.

[63] On Suprême NTM and other rap groups, see especially Tshimanga, 'Let the Music Play'; Decouvelaere, '"Ça vient de la rue"'; Gross, McMurray, and Swedenburg, 'Arab Noise', 215–18.

[64] Florence Bernault, 'Colonial Syndrome: French Modern and the Deceptions of History', in Tshimanga, Gondola, and Bloom (eds.), *Frenchness and the African Diaspora*, 144; Marx-Scouras, *La France de Zebda*, 145.

was of Hungarian descent.[65] 'Hooliganism' derived from African family culture, a secretary of the *Académie française* insisted. In an echo of Chirac's proclamations fourteen years before, she continued, 'there are three or four wives and 25 children living in one apartment. They are so packed that they are no longer even apartments but rather God knows what! No wonder these children run around in the streets'.[66]

France faced dangers emanating from multiple foreign cultures, this reasoning ran, that from the 'primitive' African family and that associated with the violence and rap music from the African-American 'ghetto'. These came together in the figure of the maladjusted *banlieue* youth, usually one presumed to be Muslim.[67] Philosopher Robert Redeker's verdict in *Le Figaro* stressed that the 2005 riots demonstrated the disastrous consequences of tolerating difference and cultural pluralism. 'Why be astonished at non-integration when these youth feel themselves justified in what they are, authorized to reject the rules of citizenship because everything is legitimated? ... It isn't poverty, that is to say the social situation, that engenders deviant and insane violence, but rather nihilism', Redeker argued. 'The over-estimation of cultures, of all cultures, and the fetishization of difference' created only 'the impossibility, for populations descended from foreign cultures, of amalgamating within France's national and republican culture'. In short, if 'a verse by Racine is worth no more than a dish of couscous, how can one be shocked when the libraries are burned?'[68]

* * *

Suggestions that rioting in the *banlieues* was symptomatic of a wholesale rejection of French traditions, namely republicanism, have not found unanimous support, however. As Didier Lapeyronnie and others note, 'rioting belongs to the normal repertoire of political action', counting as an integral part of 'France's broader revolutionary tradition of sedition, mutiny, riots, and disturbances'.[69] Just as some Muslim women proclaimed their right to wear

---

[65] 'M. Larcher fait le lien entre polygamie et violences urbaines', *Le Monde*, 16 November 2005.

[66] Hélène Carrère d'Encausse, quoted in Lorraine Millot, 'Beaucoup de ces Africains sont polygames ...', *Libération*, 15 November 2005.

[67] Graham Murray, 'France: The Riots and the Republic', *Race & Class*, 47:4 (2006), 34, 43; Didier Gondola, 'Transient Citizens: The Othering and Indigenization of Blacks and Beurs within the French Republic', in Tshimanga, Gondola, and Bloom (eds.), *Frenchness and the African Diaspora*, 147, 163; Laurent Dubois, *Soccer Empire: The World Cup and the Future of France* (Berkeley, 2010), 234.

[68] Robert Redeker, 'Le nihilisme culturel imprègne les émeutes banlieusards', *Le Figaro*, 28 November 2005.

[69] Didier Lapeyronnie, 'Primitive Rebellion in the French Banlieues: On the Fall 2005 Riots', translated by Jane Marie Todd, in Tshimanga, Gondola, and Bloom (eds.), *Frenchness and the African Diaspora*, 25 (the second quotation is taken from this volume's 'Introduction: Examining Frenchness and the African Diaspora', 10); Lebrun, *Protest Music*, 84.

head coverings as an expression of their *liberté*, other voices have explored forms of radical dissent that fit well within French popular political traditions. Faïza Guène's *Kiffe kiffe demain*, a novel first published in 2004, explores how Maghrebi-descended youth have multiple cultural inventories from outside as well as inside France upon which to draw.

Translated into English as *Just Like Tomorrow*, Guène's novel centres on the lives of 15-year-old Doria and her illiterate mother Yasmina on a run-down housing estate outside central Paris. Abandoned by Doria's father, they rely upon Yasmina's low salary as a cleaner alongside state welfare and help from friends and neighbours, most of whom are also North Africans or their French-born children. Doria's scholastic failures resemble those of her male counterparts, many of whom had dropped out of school on a downward spiral involving drug dealing and car theft followed by prison and negligible job opportunities.

Doria, Yasmina, and their neighbours occupy a spatially, economically, and culturally marginal position in the eyes of wider society and mainstream culture. Chastised by one of her French teachers for 'sullying our beautiful literature' on account of a mispronunciation, Doria was told that '[i]t's because of PEOPLE-LIKE-YOU that our Frrrench herrrritttage is in a coma!'[70] By contrast, Guène highlights the ways her characters actively include themselves within national traditions. Doria's conversations with her friend Hamoudi repeatedly invoke Rimbaud, while their close friend Aunt Zohra's linguistic malapropisms are jokingly likened by her sons both to the French literary canon and rap culture: 'They say she does re-mixes of Molière's great French language. They've tagged her "DJ Zozo."'[71] 'High', 'popular', and 'immigrant' cultures are not portrayed as exclusive but rather as coexisting and interacting, refreshing evidence that France was dynamic instead of ossified.

Taking charge of their lives rather than passively accepting adverse circumstances becomes the pivotal theme in a novel whose main characters are ethnic minority women and girls conventionally pitied as oppressed and resigned to their fate. Yasmina's immigrant women co-workers go on strike and successfully bargain for higher wages, and she enrols in literacy and job training classes and becomes more confident and independent. Contemplating the improvement in her mother's situation at the end of the novel, Doria wonders what more might be achieved and concludes that *banlieue* residents needed to become politicized. Recalling 'that joker Napoleon saying: "Every conquered nation needs a revolution"', she envisions herself heading an uprising on their

---

[70] Faïza Guène, *Just Like Tomorrow*, translated by Sarah Adams (London, 2006), 142. For an assessment, see Brinda J. Mehta, 'Negotiating Arab-Muslim Identity, Contested Citizenship, and Gender Ideologies in the Parisian Housing Projects: Faïza Guène's *Kiffe kiffe demain*', *Research in African Literatures*, 41:2 (2010), 173–202.

[71] Guène, *Just Like Tomorrow*, 28; see also 19–20.

estate – one, however, that would 'be a smart revolution with nobody getting hurt, and we'll all rise up to make ourselves heard. Life isn't just about rap and football. We'll be like the poet Rimbaud, fired up by "the sobbing of the Oppressed, the clamour of the Cursed."'[72]

Guène thus looked to French historical inspirations when contemplating the 'smart revolution' the marginalized desperately need, whatever their ethnic background. '[W]hat we need answering today are social questions', she emphasized in an interview. 'They think it's a war between the whites and the blacks and the Arabs. They think it's a war between the secularists and the Muslims. But it's above all a war between the rich and the poor.' Her rejection of violence suggests one reason for the novel's tremendous success in France, where it has sold hundreds of thousands of copies and become required reading at French schools. Having herself grown up on a Paris housing estate as the daughter of Algerian parents, Guène wrote *Kiffe kiffe demain* when she was only twenty, becoming an ideal candidate for elevation to celebrity status as the 'voice of the suburbs' by a public hungry for a story with an upbeat ending after the 2005 riots.[73] *Kiffe kiffe demain* counts as an example of the acclaim accorded to selected achievements and cultural contributions by members of postcolonial minority groups that are few and far between in France. Despite widespread concerns over the effects of cultural and ethnic pluralism in France, 'celebratory multiculturalism' occasionally manifests itself – but in what forms, and with what implications?

* * *

In France as in other countries, food and music along with a handful of novels and films provide ready examples of mainstream white society's selective appropriation and enjoyment of postcolonial cultural diversity. *Raï* music became familiar and attracted a crossover community of listeners beyond those of North African descent; dishes like couscous did the same.[74] New gastronomic additions and musical innovations became widely accepted forms of cultural plurality – sometimes ephemeral, sometimes long-lasting and every-day – among enthusiastic consumers eager to experience the 'pleasures of multiculturalism' as a form of leisure and fun.[75] In reality, however,

---

[72] Ibid., 178–9 (see also 87–8).

[73] Jim Wolfreys, "'I Think They've Identified the Wrong War'", *Socialist Review*, May 2006; Jason Burke, 'Voice of the Suburbs', *Observer* (London), 23 April 2006.

[74] Driss Maghraoui, 'French Identity, Islam, and North Africans: Colonial Legacies, Postcolonial Realities', in Stovall and Van Den Abbeele (eds.), *French Civilization*, 213.

[75] Nacira Guénif-Souilamas, 'Zidane: Portrait of the Artist as Political Avatar', translated by Naomi Baldinger, in Tshimanga, Gondola, and Bloom (eds.), *Frenchness and the African Diaspora*, 221; Silverstein, *Algeria in France*, 168; Gross, McMurray, and Swedenburg, 'Arab Noise', 213, 217.

mainstream acceptance remained limited, conditional, and politicized. Couscous, for example, might be elevated to the status of a 'national dish' yet still signal unwelcome practices amongst those of Maghrebi origin who traditionally counted it as a dietary staple.[76] Among the questions authorities asked a lawyer from Morocco seeking French naturalization in 2002 was how often she ate couscous, with her answer taken as a sign of her (low) level of integration.[77] Its consumption beyond the North African community readily figured as harmless enjoyment, whether everyday or exotic, but 'excessive' consumption within it retained worrying connotations.

Other culinary practices and musical forms popular amongst immigrants and their descendants never remotely managed to gain widespread acceptance, retaining their stigma as un-French, 'foreign', and uncivilized – further examples, in other words, of offensive 'noise and smell'. Meat prepared according to Islamic ritual practices generates considerable controversy, with Muslim butchers and their customers often accused of animal cruelty as a result. Brigitte Bardot, French film icon of the 1950s and 1960s and later infamous for far-right political sympathies and animal rights activism, has repeatedly railed against immigration and the 'Islamization' of France as epitomized by halal slaughter. Illegal animal sacrifices to mark Eid demonstrated the 'savagery and cruelty of Muslim traditions' that 'dishonoured the land of France', she proclaimed. Animals bled to death in 'apartment courtyards, stairwells, bathtubs, car trunks, wheelbarrows, gutters, etc.' were seemingly ubiquitous, with 'rubbish chutes in tower blocks clogged by the skins and entrails of sheep'. In short, 'France, a civilized country that had abandoned and forgotten such practices in the Middle Ages', should refuse to accept these 'barbaric' and 'most primitive traditions'.[78] Just as France had suffered from German invasion and oppression during the First and Second World Wars, Bardot wrote, the hexagon faced a succession of new foreign onslaughts ranging from the euro that had vanquished 'our national "franc"' to Muslims who 'not only do not submit to our laws and customs, but over the course of time try to impose theirs upon us'.[79] '*Française de souche*, I am' began her 'Open Letter to My Lost France' published in *Le Figaro* in 1997. 'Along with General de Gaulle and the Eiffel Tower, I am probably the most famous French person in the world', she admonished readers. Once chosen to model for a well-known sculptor's bust of Marianne, she announced her

---

[76] Denis Saillard, 'La cuisine', in Jean-Pierre Rioux (ed.), *Dictionnaire de la France coloniale* (Paris, 2007), 764.

[77] Bowen, *Why the French Don't Like Headscarves*, 196.

[78] Brigitte Bardot, *Le Carré du Pluton: Mémoires* (Paris, 1999), 683, 679.

[79] Brigitte Bardot, *Un cri dans le silence: Révolte et nostalgie* (Paris, 2003), 133; *Le Carré du Pluton*, 683, 693–4.

intention to remain 'representative of the image of France' by speaking out against submitting to 'a surplus foreign population, notably Muslim'.[80]

Although Bardot was not alone in her beliefs, it is important to stress that her views about Islam and France have not gone uncontested. She has been convicted and repeatedly fined for inciting racial and religious hatred, the 'Open Letter' sparking one of her many trips to court. French opinion about multiculturalism remains divided, and even social sectors normally sceptical (or indeed outright hostile) to pluralism have found opportunities to celebrate some of its effects. Sports have offered a number of occasions when black and *beur* athletes have found fame and adulation for their talents and been feted as national heroes. The French football team's victory over Brazil in the 1998 World Cup provided the best-known example. With the majority of the team comprised of ethnic minority French citizens like Zinedine Zidane (whose parents came from Algeria) and Lilian Thuram (born in Guadeloupe and raised in a *banlieue* outside Paris), those celebrating the nation's victory found ample opportunity to extol the benefits of a multicultural France. Jean-Marie Le Pen's opponents viewed the victory of a team that he had once dismissed as consisting of 'foreigners' and 'fake French' as a symbolic defeat of the *Front National*'s racism. France had gained a second *tricolore*: alongside the *bleu-blanc-rouge*, the blue, white, and red national flag, waved that of the *black-blanc-beur*.[81]

Genuine though the national ovations to the 1998 team were, the World Cup counted as a momentary episode rather than a permanent validation of *la France métissée* (mixed France). Significantly, the meanings of 1998's victory for France's minority youth were highly qualified even at the moment when the public's idolization of the team was at its peak. The *black-blanc-beur* team's feat was evidence of what subscribing to France's republican culture could achieve, some commentators argued. In their veneration of football heroes who had grown up in the *banlieues*, suburban youth might be more likely to see the value of patriotism. As Laurent Dubois states, 'the victory was co-opted and used for particular, and limited, political ends', rapidly becoming 'channeled into a traditional interpretation of "integration" in France, in which immigrants were expected to fit into rather than add to and expand the culture'.[82] If *black-blanc-beur* had arguably found a place in postcolonial France, it remained hedged with limitations.

* * *

---

[80] 'Lettre ouverte à ma France perdue', reprinted in Bardot, *Le Carré du Pluton*, 693–4.
[81] Dubois, *Soccer Empire*, 97–8, 104–5, 157, 163; Guénif-Souilamas, 'Zidane'; Silverstein, *Algeria in France*, 125, 128–9, 198; Lebovics, *Bringing the Empire Back Home*, 9, 136–42.
[82] Dubois, *Soccer Empire*, 168 (see also 125–6, 164).

Union Jack, Union Black: new ethnicities and approaches to integration in Britain

As the transitory recasting of France's *tricolore* into the *black-blanc-beur* suggests, flags offer iconic possibilities both for reasserting conventional forms of national identity and for imagining alternatives to exclusionary national 'norms'. Flags have gained even more potent meanings in late twentieth- and early twenty-first-century Britain among those who defensively perceive their nation to be challenged from within by ethnic minorities, and equally by those who demand its reconfiguration to reflect the realities of a multicultural society. Britain's Union Jack as well as the Cross of St George (England's national flag representing its patron saint and featuring a red cross over a white background) became closely associated with what Paul Gilroy terms 'ethnic absolutism': a 'politics of "race" … fired by conceptions of national belonging and homogeneity which not only blur the distinction between "race" and nation, but rely on that very ambiguity for their effect'. Britishness and Englishness were readily seen as equivalent to whiteness and its corresponding 'cultural ties which mark the boundaries of "race"', resulting in the 'exclusion of blacks from the definitions of nationality which matter most'.[83] Through its very title *'There Ain't No Black in the Union Jack'*, Gilroy's seminal study underscored the flag's emblematic status as a visual tool for racist, neo-fascist parties of the extreme right such as the National Front following its establishment in 1967 and, later, the British National Party as they promoted visions of a nation and culture freed from the pernicious influence of non-white immigrants and their descendants.[84]

Such appropriations of the Union Jack became vehemently contested by scholars, anti-racist organizations, and an increasingly assertive group of British ethnic minority activists, writers, and artists.[85] The Black Art movement came of age in the 1980s with a militant stance against the exclusion of minorities from the British art establishment. Its critical reinterpretations of race and the black experience both in Britain and abroad drew on a range of global inspirations in style and subject matter alike.[86] By the 1990s and 2000s,

---

[83] Paul Gilroy, *'There Ain't No Black in the Union Jack': The Cultural Politics of Race and Nation* (Chicago, 1987), 45, 52.

[84] Ibid., 120–4; see also Susanne Reichl, 'Flying the Flag: The Intricate Semiotics of National Identity', *European Journal of English Studies*, 8:2 (2004), 205–17; Michael Billig, *Banal Nationalism* (London, 1995), 41. For concise overviews of the National Front and British National Party, see John Solomos, *Race and Racism in Britain*, 3rd edn. (Basingstoke, 2003), ch. 8; Alan Sykes, *The Radical Right in Britain: Social Imperialism to the BNP* (Basingstoke, 2005), chs. 5 and 6; Matthew J. Goodwin, *New British Fascism: Rise of the British National Party* (Abingdon, 2011).

[85] Institute of International Visual Arts, *Black People and the British Flag* (London, 1993).

[86] Rasheed Araeen (ed.), *The Other Story: Afro-Asian Artists in Post-war Britain* (London, 1989); David A. Bailey, Ian Baucom, and Sonya Boyce (eds.), *Shades of Black: Assembling Black Arts*

selected minority artists had achieved both national and international recognition, and few could match Chris Ofili's success and critical acclaim.

Born in Manchester in 1968 to Nigerian parents, Ofili won the prestigious Turner Prize in 1998 for paintings that drew upon a thoroughly transnational set of artistic influences. A study trip to Zimbabwe in the early 1990s inspired him to adopt the dotted patterns found in San cave painting and first suggested the use of elephant dung as an artistic material, both of which came to count among the signature features of his work, as did recurrent references to African-American popular culture such as hip hop. After 2000, Ofili's extended stays in Trinidad also informed work in which the interconnected African diaspora in the Caribbean, the United States, and Britain was inextricably linked to a Pan-African sensibility.[87]

Being chosen to represent Britain at the 2003 Venice Biennale cemented Ofili's status as both a leading British artist and one whose output refused compartmentalization within the confines of one national culture. His exhibit involved redecorating the British Pavilion with red, black, and green paint, carpeting, and paintings that featured black lovers in a jungle-like romantic setting.[88] Outside the Pavilion hung Ofili's 'Union Black': a flag where red, black, and green replaced the standard red, white, and blue of the Union Jack. A clear rebuttal to the racist slogans prevalent in earlier decades, Ofili not only put black into the Union Jack; he did so via colours associated with a Pan-African ethos and black nationalism ever since the Jamaican Marcus Garvey made use of this schema for the flag of his Universal Negro Improvement Association in the 1910s and 1920s. For Garvey and the many he later inspired, red connoted the spilled blood of black people, green represented nature, and black referred to skin colour.[89] 'I thought, seeing as though I'm British and have African ancestry, I would like to try to make a British flag that was for African-British people', Ofili stressed, one that simultaneously counteracted racist and nationalist symbols of Britishness.[90]

As the designated British representative on the premier stage of contemporary international art, Ofili's 'Union Black' was enthusiastically endorsed as an acceptable vision of Britishness suited to a diverse, multicultural society, one in

in 1980s Britain (Durham, 2005); Stuart Hall, 'Black Diaspora Artists in Britain: Three "Moments" in Post-war History', History Workshop Journal, 61 (2006), 1–24.

[87] Judith Nesbitt, 'Beginnings', in Judith Nesbitt (ed.), Chris Ofili (London, 2010), 8–21.

[88] Marla C. Berns, 'Africa at the Venice Biennale', African Arts, 36:3 (2003), 8. Ofili's exhibit was undertaken in collaboration with the architect David Adjaye.

[89] On the political significance of red, green, and black (as well as gold) in the history of black nationalist movements, see Ernest Cashmore, Rastaman: The Rastafarian Movement in England (London, 1979), 156–61; Crispin Sartwell, 'Red, Gold, Black and Green: Black Nationalist Aesthetics', Contemporary Aesthetics, Special Volume 2 (2009).

[90] Chris Ofili and Thelma Golden, 'A Conversation', in Chris Ofili, Within Reach: British Pavilion 50th Venice Biennale, 15 June to 2 Nov. 2003, 23.

tune with the official approval accorded to ethnic and cultural difference during the early years of Tony Blair's New Labour government.[91] Yet successful black artists like Ofili, and by extension validated forms of black cultural expression, remain tokenistic exceptions to the rule of ongoing marginalization. By and large, as Rasheed Araeen asserts, they are kept outside the mainstream and 'their significance is controlled and contained within the larger spectacle of multiculturalism'.[92] Approaches to and attitudes towards multiculturalism in early twenty-first-century Britain were divided and often cautious at best, just as they had been for decades. Having 'first declared itself multicultural in the mid 1960s', John Solomos observes, Britain 'still faces the dilemma of what kind of multicultural society it should become'; moreover, it has failed to reach any consensus concerning the extent to which multiculturalism should be acknowledged or promoted at all.[93]

* * *

To what extent have Britain's ethnic minorities been expected to conform to an imagined, uniform, 'British way of life', and to what extent have cultural differences configured along ethnic lines been encouraged? In a 1966 speech, Labour Home Secretary Roy Jenkins signalled a shift in official outlooks away from promoting assimilation, which he likened to a 'flattening process' or 'a "melting-pot", which will turn everybody out in a common mould', and towards integration as the preferred goal. Integration should not mean 'the loss, by immigrants, of their own national characteristics and culture' but rather 'equal opportunity, accompanied by cultural diversity, in an atmosphere of mutual tolerance'.[94]

Jenkins' conception of integration as the most appropriate British approach to its minorities thus differed markedly from the stance common in France. In dismissing the notion of the 'melting pot', he explicitly portrayed Britain as a nation with a long history of internal diversity. Rather than conceiving itself as 'one and indivisible' in its cultural uniformity (ideally, if not in reality) as France did, Britain made space not just for the English but also for 'the rest of us', including the Welsh '(like myself)', Scots, Irish, Jews, 'the mid-European', and 'still more recent arrivals'.[95] Indeed, this was a main reason why Britain

---

[91] Mainstream British press coverage was largely positive; see Fiachra Gibbons, 'Artist's Bold Display of Black Power Takes Venice By Storm', *Guardian* (London), 13 June 2003; Richard Brooks, 'Artist Turns the Union Jack Black', *Sunday Times*, 15 June 2003.

[92] Rasheed Araeen, 'The Success and Failure of Black Art', *Third Text*, 18:2 (2004), 151.

[93] Solomos, *Race and Racism*, 211.

[94] Roy Jenkins, 'Racial Equality in Britain', in Anthony Lester (ed.), *Essays and Speeches by Roy Jenkins* (London, 1967), 267. On the shift from assimilation to integration in the 1960s, see Floya Anthias and Nira Yuval-Davis, *Racialized Boundaries* (London, 1992), 158–60; Avtar Brah, *Cartographies of Diaspora: Contesting Identities* (London, 1996), 23, 25, 229–30.

[95] Jenkins, 'Racial Equality', 267; Favell, *Philosophies of Integration*, 94–7, 104.

could claim itself to be a 'tolerant' nation – a notion to which Jenkins repeatedly returned throughout his text, and that will receive further attention in the following sections.

After praising the contributions immigrant workers made to the nation's economy, Jenkins reminded his listeners that 'we are beginning to move from the era of the first generation immigrant to the second generation immigrant . . . Many [children] were born in this country, many more wholly educated here. They are not so much Asians or West Indians as coloured Britons, dressing and speaking much as we do, and looking for the same opportunities as the rest of us.' As such, it was imperative that every effort be made to combat racial discrimination and promote equality.[96] Just as Chris Ofili was later to describe himself as British with African ancestry, Jenkins also considered the children of New Commonwealth immigrants to be British, the difference being in his use of 'coloured' as opposed to Asian, West Indian, or African (although it is telling that he, like others, persisted in referring to 'coloured Britons' as 'second generation immigrants'). But not everyone agreed, perhaps most famously Conservative politician Enoch Powell. Several months after his notorious 1968 'Rivers of Blood' speech discussed in the last chapter, Powell insisted that '[t]he West Indian or Asian does not by being born in England, become an Englishman. In law he becomes a United Kingdom citizen by birth; in fact he is a West Indian or an Asian still'.[97] Even when legal Britishness was not disputed, this reasoning went, those descended from immigrants failed to count as 'English', an identity linked to cultural attributes they seemingly could never hope to possess on account of their race – presuming, that is, that they even wanted to do so.

Powell's public interventions had manifold repercussions, including a boost to extreme-right groups like the National Front. Furthermore, although mainstream Conservatism sidelined Powell, both he and the National Front made a deep impression on Tory approaches to race-related issues. The National Front gained greater visibility in the 1970s, and while it remained a fringe party in terms of electoral success its platforms were taken up by Margaret Thatcher after she assumed leadership of the Conservative Party and lent legitimacy to its position on questions of race, immigration, and nationality.[98] In a 1978 television interview she described how many people feared Britain 'might be

[96] Jenkins, 'Racial Equality', 271.
[97] Enoch Powell, speech given in Eastbourne, 16 November 1968, reprinted in John Wood (ed.), *J. Enoch Powell, Freedom and Reality* (London, 1969), 237; on Powell and immigration in the late 1960s, see especially Camilla Schofield, *Enoch Powell and the Making of Postcolonial Britain* (Cambridge, 2013), ch. 4. Powell's comments on the second generation clearly resemble the opinions later expressed by Raspail discussed earlier; like Raspail, moreover, he too focused on the high immigrant birth rate, 232–3.
[98] Favell, *Philosophies of Integration*, 106–8; Solomos, *Race and Racism*, 177–82; Sykes, *Radical Right*, 109–16; Goodwin, *New British Fascism*, 28–34.

rather swamped by people with a different culture'; as such, it was urgent that immigration be halted in order to preserve 'fundamental British characteristics' and ensure good race relations. Epitomizing 'new racism', her elision between racial and cultural difference positioned both as antithetical to what Britishness 'fundamentally' entailed. Stating that many voters resented both the Conservatives and Labour for failing to tackle popular concerns about race, she warned that this was 'driving some people to the National Front. They do not agree with the objectives of the National Front, but they say that at least they are talking about some of the problems'.[99] After the Conservatives returned to power in 1979, their appropriation of many National Front (as well as Powellite) ideas caused the extreme right to enter a period of decline in the 1980s.[100] Nonetheless, the ideological momentum gathered in the 1970s remained critical long afterwards, aided and abetted by ongoing economic crisis, state racism, and divided public responses to the legitimacy of ethnic minority difference spanning the decades.

From the 1960s to the 1980s, minority children, adolescents, and young adults featured as a main subject of concern, increasingly bearing the brunt of institutional and popular racism and ultimately emerging as leaders in the fight against it. Education became a key arena in which multiculturalism both as everyday reality and as policies designed to manage ethnic diversity was played out in schools and neighbourhoods with a high rate of West Indian and South Asian settlement. While children of Commonwealth immigrants were meant to be schooled in the 'British way of life', their integration also required combatting racism and inequality, which policymakers believed could be achieved by confronting white ignorance about ethnic minority cultures through multicultural teaching. Intended to be mutually enriching, efforts to provide exposure to other cultures by according them space within school curricula simultaneously provoked intense criticism from those championing cultural diversity and created a backlash among those fiercely opposed to it. Ray Honeyford, the headmaster of a Bradford middle school whose main intake was immigrants' children, made a series of critical journalistic interventions in the early 1980s that positioned him firmly within the latter camp.[101]

[99] Michael Hatfield, 'People Fear Swamping by Immigrants, Mrs Thatcher Says', *The Times*, 31 January 1978.
[100] Anna Marie Smith, *New Right Discourse on Race and Sexuality: Britain, 1968–1990* (Cambridge, 1994), ch. 4; Goodwin, *New British Fascism*, ch. 2.
[101] Mark Halstead, *Education, Justice and Cultural Diversity: An Examination of the Honeyford Affair, 1984–85* (London, 1988), ch. 4; Philip Lewis, *Islamic Britain: Religion, Politics and Identity among British Muslims* (London, 1994), 147–53; Seán McLoughlin, 'Writing a BrAsian City: "Race", Culture and Religion in Accounts of Postcolonial Bradford', in N. Ali, V.S. Kalra, and S. Sayyid (eds.), *A Postcolonial People: South Asians in Britain* (London, 2006), 126–30; Dervla Murphy, *Tales from Two Cities: Travels of Another Sort* (London, 1987), ch. 6.

In provocatively titled articles such as 'Multi-ethnic Intolerance' and 'Multiracial Myths?' Honeyford rejected the notion that schools had any duty 'to foster and maintain distinctive, foreign cultures in opposition to the majority culture'.[102] His attitude towards the South Asian and West Indian parents and family culture of the pupils at his school was openly condescending and hostile. West Indians' 'creole, pidgin' English counted as part of the 'linguistic confusion' reigning in classrooms that was compounded by Asian children whose parents often knew little or no English. Asian parents included 'half-educated and volatile' Sikhs along with Pakistanis from a 'backward' country, among whom 'the hysterical political temperament of the Indian sub-continent became evident'.[103] He mocked the notion that anything positive could emerge from a curriculum that gave space to these cultures:

'Cultural enrichment' is the approved term for the West Indian's right to create an ear-splitting cacophony for most of the night to the detriment of his neighbour's sanity, or for the Notting Hill Festival whose success or failure is judged by the level of street crime which accompanies it. At the schools' level the term refers to such things as the Muslim parent's insistence on banning his daughter from drama, dance and sport i.e. imposing a purdah mentality in schools committed to the principle of sexual equality . . .[104]

Honeyford's opinions bore close resemblance both to well-established British reservations about minorities that revolved around offensive sounds, purported lawlessness, and other adverse effects on domestic and neighbourhood life (as discussed in Chapter 7) as well as to French hostility towards cultural diversity. Although the French frequently have labelled multiculturalism as an 'Anglo-Saxon' phenomenon and sought to dissociate their own national approach to minorities from British and American models, Honeyford's position shared common ground with French opponents of diversity in public contexts. Significantly, many of his criticisms focused on religious difference, particularly patriarchal Muslim attitudes towards girls' education and sexual equality (deemed characteristic of 'religious fanaticism').[105] Islamic culture was also condemned via his reference to demands for halal meat to be served in schools then gathering pace in cities like Bradford in the first half of the 1980s. With halal methods of slaughter widely seen as a form of 'barbaric horror' by their opponents on the grounds of

[102] R. Honeyford, 'Multi-Ethnic Intolerance', *The Salisbury Review* (Summer 1983), 13; Raymond Honeyford, 'When East Is West', *Times Educational Supplement*, 2 September 1983, 19; Raymond Honeyford, 'Multiracial Myths?', *Times Educational Supplement*, 19 November 1982, 20.
[103] Ray Honeyford, 'Education and Race – An Alternative View', *The Salisbury Review*, Winter 1984, 30–2.
[104] Ibid., 30.
[105] Honeyford, 'When East Is West', 19; Honeyford, 'Multi-Ethnic Intolerance', 13.

animal protection in a manner similar to Brigitte Bardot's campaigns in France, Honeyford was not alone in asking how educators could reconcile 'the English regard for animal welfare' with Muslim 'indifference to animal care'.[106]

As Honeyford's writings suggest, concern about religious (and particularly Muslim) forms of cultural difference was on the rise in 1980s Britain as well as in France. Yet his opposition to the alleged 'multiracialist assault' on education did not revolve exclusively around Muslims and Islam. He was equally concerned about the implications of poetry by writers like the Jamaican-born Linton Kwesi Johnson being taught alongside works by Shakespeare and Wordsworth, thereby highlighting similar fears about the place of the cultural canon as were expressed in France.[107]

With his trademark dub poetry written and performed in the Jamaican vernacular that fused the language and rhythms of reggae music together with a call for black resistance to racism in Britain, Linton Kwesi Johnson's message and medium alike stood for much that Honeyford opposed.[108] Reggae was noise pollution incarnate, in his view; similarly, Johnson's poem to which he disparagingly referred ('Forces of Victory', first published in a collection entitled *Inglan is a Bitch*) celebrated the protracted defence of the Notting Hill Carnival by first- and second-generation British West Indians in the face of official attempts to prohibit or restrict it in the late 1970s – the very festival that Honeyford, and others, took as a byword for disorder and criminality, as is explored further below. Johnson committed the sin of political as well as linguistic subversion in his attack on Britain posed by the words 'an wi fite an wi fite / an defeat di state'.[109] No wonder Honeyford considered his work to epitomize much that was wrong with multiculturalism and its champions: characterized by 'anti-British prejudice', multiculturalists encompassed 'well-meaning liberals ... suffering from a rapidly dating post-Imperial guilt ... and a hard-core of left-wing political extremists', among whom featured '[a]n influential group of black intellectuals of aggressive disposition, who know little of the British traditions of understatement, civilised discourse and respect for reason'.[110] Multiculturalists, moreover, fostered 'a critical view of British imperialism', 'harmful colour

---

[106] Honeyford, 'When East Is West', 19. On halal slaughter as a 'barbaric horror', see Dave Harrison, 'Whose Rights in Bradford?', *Guardian*, 5 March 1984; Wendy Berliner, 'Bigotry Boils Up Over Asian Meat', *Guardian*, 26 March 1984. On demands for and opposition to halal food, see Roger Charlton and Ronald Kaye, 'The Politics of Religious Slaughter: An Ethno-Religious Case Study', *New Community*, 12:3 (1985), 490–503; Humayun Ansari, *'The Infidel Within': Muslims in Britain since 1800* (London, 2004), 202–3, 354–5; Lewis, *Islamic Britain*, ch. 6.
[107] Honeyford, 'Multi-Ethnic Intolerance', 13; Honeyford, 'Education and Race', 30.
[108] John McLeod, *Postcolonial London: Rewriting the Metropolis* (London, 2004), 126–38.
[109] Honeyford, 'When East Is West', 19; Linton Kwesi Johnson, 'Forces of Victory', in *Inglan is a Bitch* (London, 1980), 22–3.
[110] Honeyford, 'Multi-Ethnic Intolerance', 13; Honeyford, 'Education and Race', 32.

consciousness', and 'anti-white solidarity' amongst the various groups – West Indian and Asian alike – who came together and claimed themselves to be 'black'.[111]

For Honeyford, critiquing imperial history, being 'anti-British', and being 'anti-white' became seemingly one and the same. His views suggest not only the extent to which the imperial past survived as a key facet of Britishness needing to be defended from recrimination and 'assault', but also how British national identity readily converged with white cultural homogeneity. Minorities were fanatical, 'volatile', of 'hysterical political temperament', 'aggressive', and 'anti-white' (and thus racist); British culture, by contrast, was 'understated', 'civilised', and 'reasonable'. British 'good-natured toler-ance' stood in opposition to the 'extremism' of 'multi-ethnic intolerance', and was dependent on it to endow Britishness with meaning.[112] The 'mutual tolerance' Roy Jenkins had envisioned was thereby rendered impossible, not by white racism but by a composite multi-ethnic 'other'.

By the 1980s, multiculturalism had come under attack not only from the right but from the left. Anti-racists insisted that the aspects of ethnic minority cultures that were accorded space in the classroom and public culture amounted to little more than the so-called '3 Ss': 'saris, samosas, and steel bands' stereotypes akin to mere cultural tourism.[113] As a state response to discrimination in the 1970s and 1980s, multiculturalism was, in the words of Stephen May, 'a well-meaning but ultimately vacuous approval of cultural difference' rather than an effective strategy to combat racism and inequality.[114] Hazel Carby argued that:

the articulation by black movements of the need for an awareness of black history and culture, formed in struggles against imperialism and colonialism, and essential in the struggle against contemporary forms of racism, was turned by the state into a superficial gesture in an attempt to control the rising level of politicized black consciousness. The multicultural curriculum was from its inception part of state strategies of social control.

Multiculturalism was 'irrelevant to the black struggle in Britain'; the '3 Ss', as Barry Troyna and Jenny Williams noted, 'was advanced as the operational mode through which the 3 Rs (resistance, rejection and rebellion) would be contained and defused'.[115]

[111]   Honeyford, 'Multiracial Myths?', 20–1; Honeyford, 'Education and Race', 30.
[112]   Honeyford, 'Multi-Ethnic Intolerance', 12; Honeyford, 'Education and Race', 32.
[113]   Barry Troyna and Jenny Williams, *Racism, Education, and the State* (London, 1986), 24; James Donald and Ali Rattansi, 'Introduction', in James Donald and Ali Rattansi (eds.), *'Race', Culture and Difference* (London, 1991), 2; Ali Rattansi, 'Changing the Subject? Racism, Culture and Education', in Donald and Rattansi (eds.), *'Race', Culture and Difference*, 11–48.
[114]   Stephen May, 'Multiculturalism', in David Theo Goldberg (ed.), *A Companion to Racial and Ethnic Studies* (Malden, MA, 2002), 129.
[115]   Hazel V. Carby, 'Schooling in Babylon', in Centre for Contemporary Cultural Studies, *The Empire Strikes Back: Race and Racism in 1970s Britain* (London, 1982), 194–5; Troyna and Williams, *Racism, Education and the State*, 24.

* * *

What precisely was the 'black struggle' to which Carby referred, and how and when did it emerge? The 'colour consciousness' those like Honeyford derided as 'harmful' and 'aggressive' came of age between the mid-1960s and late 1970s, when the '3 Rs' aptly encapsulated the attitude of growing numbers of Afro-Caribbeans, South Asians, and other 'blacks' in Britain. Mobilization escalated in response to racism and discrimination encountered in schooling, housing, employment (and increasingly unemployment, which skyrocketed in the 1970s and 1980s and had a disproportionately high impact on minorities), and on the street. Parents agitated against teachers' tendency to consign their children to 'ESN' ('Educationally Sub-Normal') classes and schools, for example, and the campaign demanding Honeyford's dismissal caused Bradford's local authorities to push him into early retirement. But it was not long before minority youth either born or largely raised in Britain took centre stage in the fight against racism. In their rising militancy, they asserted new forms of political and cultural consciousness that reflected new ethnic identities distinct from those of their parents' generation, identities that grew out of a combination of British experiences and an appreciation for global struggles against oppression.

Black Power and Rastafarianism provided two important inspirations for Afro-Caribbean- and West African-descended youth (particularly males) starting in the late 1960s. If Enoch Powell's political pronouncements gave a fillip to neo-fascist organizations like the National Front and subsequently influenced Thatcherite, New Right approaches to racial issues, right-wing racist politics (coupled with racist policing) in turn galvanized black militancy. Attempting both to make sense of and combat the discrimination they faced in Britain's inner cities, youth looked to international movements including civil rights and especially Black Power in the United States, Pan-Africanism inspired by historical figures like Marcus Garvey, and struggles against imperialism in Britain's former colonies and further afield.[116] Linton Kwesi Johnson (born in Jamaica in 1952 and settled in Britain since the early 1960s) joined the Black Panthers and looked to reggae when evolving his dub poetry, effectively combining African-American and Jamaican cultural forms in ways that spoke

---

[116] Evan Smith, 'Conflicting Narratives of Black Youth Rebellion in Modern Britain', *Ethnicity and Race in a Changing World: A Review Journal*, 1:3 (2010), 16–31; A. Sivanandan, 'From Resistance to Rebellion', in *A Different Hunger: Writings on Black Resistance* (London, 1982), 15–20; Gilroy, *'There Ain't No Black'*, 173–8; Paul Gilroy, 'Steppin' out of Babylon – Race, Class and Autonomy', in Centre for Contemporary Cultural Studies, *The Empire Strikes Back*, 290–5; Anne-Marie Angelo, 'The Black Panthers in London, 1967–1972: A Diasporic Struggle Navigates the Black Atlantic', *Radical History Review*, 103 (2009), 17–35; R.E.R. Bunce and Paul Field, 'Obi Egbuna, C.L.R. James and the Birth of Black Power in Britain: Black Radicalism in Britain 1967–1972', *Twentieth Century British History*, 22:3 (2011), 391–414.

to his generation's experiences of everyday British life.[117] Reggae's cultural and political messages underpinned Rastafarianism's growing impact in 1970s Britain. With its combination of Biblical references and the elevation of Ethiopian emperor Haile Selassie to the status of living god, Rastafarianism was a religious as well as a political movement that took up Garvey's Pan-Africanist messages from the 1910s and 1920s that imagined Africa and Ethiopia (often interchangeably) as blacks' true home from which slavery had forced them. Its goal of repatriation to Africa enabled redemption and release from the suffering imposed by 'Babylon' (a reference to the white- or Western-controlled world, colonialism, or the British establishment) and also provided its adherents with a set of orientations that exceeded both where they or their parents were from and where they were at in any direct territorial sense. As one young man interviewed in late 1970s London responded when asked what his nationality was, 'I'm from Ethiopia, but I was born in the West Indies'.[118]

Looking 'back to Africa' meant not simply making concrete plans to resettle there (a road ultimately taken by few), but entailed reasserting the positive value of African, and African diasporic, cultures in the face of white hostility going back centuries that remained ever-present in Britain. Within a society that overwhelmingly seemed to reject their culture and question their right to be there, some Rastas responded in kind: 'blacks ... were never and can never be part of this country where we do not belong', another stated.[119] Their attitudes placed them at odds not only with their parents, whom they dismissed as misguided or overly complacent in their efforts either to belong in Britain or peacefully withdraw from its mainstream (as many first-generation West Indians did in religious terms, for example, in turning to their own Pentecostal churches when British Christian congregations failed to make them feel welcome), but also in opposition to the British authorities.[120] They resisted Babylon's coercive apparatuses through beliefs made manifest visibly (through dreadlocks and distinctive clothing and woollen hats in red, green, and gold) as well as audibly (via reggae and its sound systems). Smoking *ganja* was imbued with religious significance, but its illegality made it one of many ways

---

[117] 'Interview with Linton Kwesi Johnson by Mervyn Morris (1982/86)', reprinted in E.A. Markham (ed.), *Hinterland: Caribbean Poetry from the West Indies and Britain* (Newcastle upon Tyne, 1989), 250–61.

[118] Cashmore, *Rastaman*, 1; more broadly, see Dick Hebdige, 'Reggae, Rastas and Rudies', in Stuart Hall and Tony Jefferson (eds.), *Resistance Through Rituals: Youth Subcultures in Postwar Britain* (London, 1976), 135–54; Dick Hebdige, *Subculture: The Meaning of Style* (London, 1979), chs. 3 and 4; Gilroy, *'There Ain't No Black'*, 187–209.

[119] Cashmore, *Rastaman*, 137.

[120] Barbara Bush, 'The Dark Side of the City: Racialized Barriers, Culture and Citizenship in Britain c. 1950–1990s', in Werner Zips (ed.), *Rastafari: A Universal Philosophy in the Third Millennium* (Kingston, 2006), 169–201; Cashmore, *Rastaman*, 39–41, 73, 120, 192–3.

that Rastas came into conflict with Britain's forces of law and order. The equation of drug use and criminality with reggae and Rastafarianism became common sense in the eyes of the police, who epitomized all that Babylon stood for and all that Rastas rejected.

Rastafarianism's significance in political terms greatly exceeded its religious dimensions. Far more than simply advocating a literal return to Africa, Rastafarianism and the music inseparable from it advocated resistance in the here and now. As reggae's most famous spokesman Bob Marley sang, 'Get up, stand up ... Stand up for your rights'; 'Get up, stand up, don't give up the fight.'[121] Rebellion among blacks in Britain took many forms, encompassing cultural assertiveness, political resistance, and insurgency on the streets, sometimes all at once. By the late 1970s, London's Notting Hill Carnival provided an important stage upon which these became enacted.

The street festival taking place each August in Notting Hill emerged in 1965, initially as a modest event that brought white and black locals and their cultures together. Trinidadian-style carnival culture featuring calypso, steel bands, and masquerading predominated by the early 1970s, but soon other Caribbean-origin peoples and influences, especially Jamaican, grew more prominent while direct white involvement markedly diminished. Attracting 100,000 people by 1974, the Race Today Collective (whose affiliates included many of the event's core supporters and organizers) could confidently claim that the Notting Hill Carnival represented 'the measure of the stage of development of the West Indian community in Britain'.[122] By the mid- to late 1970s, members of the second generation had made an indelible stamp on the event in which reggae and Rastafarian-associated cultures cohabited with steel bands, calypso, and other musical forms. These factors proved decisive in rendering the Carnival 'an expression of, and an instrument for, the development of a new homogeneous West Indian culture that transcended affiliations to islands of origin, to confront the economic and political realities of contemporary Britain'.[123]

After a surge in violent public confrontations between black youth and the police in 1976 which were repeated in later years, whites on the right of the political spectrum increasingly associated the Carnival with excessive noise levels together with law and order offences like mugging (widely depicted as a 'black crime' in 'common sense' racism).[124] Carnival organizers entered into a long battle with local government, the police, and white residents who sought

---

[121] 'Get Up, Stand Up', written by Bob Marley and Peter Tosh, from The Wailers, *Burnin'* (Island Records, 1973).

[122] 'Carnival in a Strange Land', *Race Today*, October 1974, 270.

[123] Abner Cohen, *Masquerade Politics: Explorations in the Structure of Urban Cultural Movements* (Oxford, 1993), 40.

[124] Stuart Hall *et al.*, *Policing the Crisis: Mugging, the State, and Law and Order* (London, 1978); Gilroy, *'There Ain't No Black'*, ch. 3.

to have it banned or severely restricted well into the 1980s. But its becoming universally recognized as a 'West Indian' public event did not preclude members of other ethnic groups from attending or showing appreciation. The number of casual white onlookers at the Notting Hill Carnival fluctuated over time, ultimately rising considerably in tandem with the neighbourhood's gentrification since the late 1980s. Well before then, however, some white youth came because they too enjoyed reggae or sympathized with blacks in their conflicts with the police, if not always both. Reggae won an enthusiastic reception among selected white youth subcultures as early as the 1960s, leaving its musical and political mark on the late 1970s punk scene due to the 'oppositional resonance of black cultural forms'.[125] With its profusion of monarchist pageantry and Union Jacks, Queen Elizabeth II's 1976 Silver Jubilee provoked a backlash against nationalist symbols by bands like the Sex Pistols (especially with their song 'God Save the Queen'). 'Punks and Niggers are almost the same thing' proclaimed the Sex Pistols' John Lydon, similarly positioned against dominant forms of conservative patriotic Britishness predicated on exclusion.[126]

Cross-cultural borrowings and alliances in opposition to racist culture and politics reached new levels in the late 1970s and early 1980s. Musical fusions like the two-tone movement saw bands combine reggae with punk, while reggae and punk musicians and fans came together at a series of Rock Against Racism concerts beginning in 1976. An organization affiliated with the Anti-Nazi League, Rock Against Racism brought white leftists together with ethnic minorities to counter the rise of groups like the National Front among youth.[127] Nonetheless, minority youth of diverse ethnic backgrounds often viewed whites who claimed common cause with them as unable to fully relate to their plight or share their priorities. White members of socialist, communist, and anti-racist groups along with the Labour Party could well be suspect allies insistent on the primacy of collective class struggles rather than the particularities of the black experience. Encouraging though they were, rallying cries like 'Black and White – Unite and Fight' proved an inadequate means of defending and asserting minority rights in the face of popular and institutional racism in Britain.[128] 'Punks and Niggers' clearly were *not* 'the

---

[125] Simon Jones, *Black Culture, White Youth: The Reggae Tradition from JA to UK* (Basingstoke, 1988), 150.

[126] Lipsitz, *Dangerous Crossroads*, chs. 5 and 6; Hebdige, 'Reggae, Rastas and Rudies'; Hebdige, *Subculture*, 28–9, 63–7; Gilroy, *'There Ain't No Black'*, 122–6, 170–1.

[127] Gilroy, *'There Ain't No Black'*, ch. 4; Virinder S. Kalra, John Hutnyk, and Sanjay Sharma, 'Re-Sounding (Anti)Racism, or Concordant Politics?: Revolutionary Antecedents', in Sanjay Sharma, John Hutnyk, and Ashwani Sharma (eds.), *Dis-Orienting Rhythms: The Politics of the New Asian Dance Music* (London, 1996), 127–55; Ian Goodyer, *Crisis Music: The Cultural Politics of Rock Against Racism* (Manchester, 2009); Hebdige, *Subculture*, 58–9, 64.

[128] Sivanandan, 'From Resistance to Rebellion', 41; Brah, *Cartographies*, 83; Tariq Mehmood, *Hand on the Sun* (Harmondsworth, 1983), 63–4, 91–4, 120.

same thing', and many youth from diverse African- and Asian-descended backgrounds looked to solidarity with other minorities as 'blacks' as a more effective means of combatting racism in politics, policing, and other realms of everyday life.

'Black' became an important collective identity under which many of West Indian, South Asian, and other origins (especially those born or brought up in Britain) mobilized in the late 1970s and 1980s. Just as the Notting Hill Carnival signalled and helped create a West Indian identity that spanned many Caribbean islands of origin, so too did 'black' emerge as a political colour under which different ethnic minorities in Britain could come together and 'make sense of their common exclusion from Britain and Britishness', as Paul Gilroy put it.[129] This exclusion took new legal form when the British Nationality Act was passed in 1981, which marked a decisive retreat from the *jus soli* tradition dating back 700 years whereby children born in Britain counted as British nationals regardless of whether their parents were legally resident at the time. From then on, only children with a parent who was either a British citizen or possessed formal settlement status would automatically be accorded citizenship – a shift that made descent an even stronger criterion for citizenship than had been the case following previous nationality and immigration legislation implemented since the 1960s.[130]

During a period punctuated by recurrent episodes of protest and urban unrest, it was common for minority youth of one background to lend moral and often practical support to others opposing state racism and the far right. Confrontations in Bradford, Southall, and Brixton in 1976, 1979, and 1981 illuminate this dynamic. During the same year as clashes between West Indian–descended youth and the police occurred during the Notting Hill Carnival in 1976, their counterparts from South Asian backgrounds engaged in other high-profile demonstrations in response to the steady rise of state and popular racism. Working-class Asian families had long been burdened by growing unemployment alongside official crackdowns that spread once the 1971 Immigration Act facilitated the arrest and deportation of suspected illegal immigrants. The police not only appeared indifferent to the racist harassment they suffered; they also stood accused of enabling the activities of groups like the National Front and thereby enhancing their political legitimacy.

---

[129] Gilroy, *'There Ain't No Black'*, 236; Hall, 'What Is This "Black"', 471–5; Anandi Ramamurthy, 'The Politics of Britain's Asian Youth Movements', *Race & Class*, 48:2 (2006), 44–7; Brah, *Cartographies*, 96–102; Gerd Baumann, *Contesting Culture: Discourses of Identity in Multi-Ethnic London* (Cambridge, 1996), 161–72; Smith, 'Conflicting Narratives'.

[130] Ann Dummett, 'United Kingdom', in Bauböck *et al.* (eds.), *Acquisition and Loss of Nationality, Vol. 2*, 551, 568–70; Marc Morjé Howard, *The Politics of Citizenship in Europe* (New York, 2009), 159–60.

Tensions spilled over during the 'Battle of Bradford' fought on Saturday 24 April 1976.[131] West Yorkshire's chief constable allowed over 1,000 supporters of the National Front to march through the largely Asian neighbourhood of Manningham to mark St George's Day (23 April).[132] This event featured prominently in *Hand on the Sun*, an autobiographical novel by Tariq Mehmood published in 1983 that chronicled the lives of Pakistan-born teen-agers raised in the city. Seeing the National Front descend upon their neigh-bourhood under police escort and calling for repatriation made those like Jalib, the novel's protagonist, realize that the police would never protect them. Instead, they had to defend themselves, not simply make polite requests for peace and reconciliation as older community leaders were accused of doing to no avail. The police, the National Front, and 'the symbol of the enemy, the Union Jack, waving above the sea of deep blue' merged to become one, but the second generation (of South Asian and West Indian origin alike) retaliated, throwing stones and bricks at the police and chasing the Front from the area.[133]

Murders and assaults that the police were reluctant to recognize as racially motivated created further waves of youth militancy and calls for self-organiza-tion and self-protection. Bangladeshis in the Brick Lane area of London's East End, where the National Front had a substantial following among working-class whites, suffered repeated attacks in the late 1970s and organized protests against police complicity with the far right.[134] In Southall, the fatal stabbing of a Sikh teenager by a white gang in 1976 led to days of demonstrations featuring massive sit-ins surrounding the police station.[135] The Southall Youth Movement emerged soon afterwards and sparked similar Asian Youth Movements in other cities like Bradford.[136] Many Asians were eager to work

---

[131] Mehmood, *Hand on the Sun*, 140; Mehmood's novel is also discussed in McLoughlin, 'Writing a BrAsian City', 120–4.

[132] 'Race Brawls: 55 Held', *Observer*, 25 April 1976; Michael Nally, 'National Front Gains Worry Bradford', *Observer*, 9 May 1976; 'Defend Manningham', *Race Today*, 8:5 (1976), 100; Roger Ballard, 'Up Against the Front', *New Society*, 36:709 (6 May 1976), 285–6.

[133] Mehmood, *Hand on the Sun*, 119; see also 112–25, 140.

[134] 'Law and Order Hoo! Hoo!', *Race Today*, 10:4 (1978), 76–7; Dilip Hiro, *Black British White British: A History of Race Relations in Britain* (London, 1991), 168–77.

[135] Campaign Against Racism and Fascism (CARF), *Southall: Birth of a Black Community* (London, 1981), 51; see also Diana Geddes, 'Asians Clash with Police in Protest over Killing', *The Times*, 7 June 1976; Lindsay Mackie, 'A Long Day in Southall', *Guardian*, 7 June 1976; 'Southall: New Passions, New Forces', *Race Today*, 8:6 (1976), 131–2. More generally, see Sandhya Shukla, *India Abroad: Diasporic Cultures of Postwar America and England* (Princeton, 2003), ch. 2.

[136] Dilip Hiro and Ian Mather, 'We Won't be Sheep, Say Young Asians', *Observer*, 13 June 1976; Philip Jordan and Lindsay Mackie, 'Growing Militancy in the Pit of Disillusion', *Guardian*, 1 July 1980. More broadly, see 'Charting the Asian Self-Defence Movement', *Race Today*, 10:6 (1978), 128–31; Ramamurthy, 'Politics', 42–3; Sivanandan, 'From Resistance to Rebellion', 39–40; Hiro, *Black British White British*, 168–77.

together with West Indians to fight racial oppression and protect themselves when the police would not.

Subsequent incidents cemented this growing militancy, none more so than the clashes recurring in Southall on 23 April 1979.[137] St George's Day again proved a highly combustible moment when the local council flew the Union Jack over the town hall to mark the occasion while simultaneously granting the National Front permission to hold a political meeting on the premises.[138] Southall's ethnic minority communities and their anti-racist white allies staged a peaceful protest, only to be met by over 2,500 police officers in riot gear who beat and arrested hundreds of demonstrators. Blair Peach, a white member of the Anti-Nazi League, was killed, his death never properly subjected to internal police investigation.[139]

As the Campaign Against Racism and Fascism put it, responses to the provocation and brutality in Southall on St George's Day 1979 'showed that a black community had indeed been born'.[140] The Southall Youth Movement and other local Asian Youth Movements established several years before were joined by new organizations, some of which addressed gender issues that the male-dominated AYMs typically sidelined. Women's groups such as the Organisation of Women of African and Asian Descent and Southall Black Sisters emerged in 1978 and 1979. They aimed to confront minority women's oppression not only by British authorities by also from within their own ethnic communities, working to fight problems encompassing immigration law, domestic violence, and forced marriage, amongst other campaigns. For Southall Black Sisters, a 'black' identity 'allowed for united action against the state' that fragmentation into discrete Afro- or Asian-descended subgroups would have rendered more difficult.[141]

Dialogue and cultural borrowings across ethnic lines recurred throughout the late 1970s and early 1980s. Transnational black symbolism was prominent within the Asian Youth Movements, which took the Black Power clenched fist as a logo befitting its militant stance.[142] Among the journals published by the AYMs was Bradford's *Kala Tara*, Urdu for 'Black Star' – a reference to the Black Star Line, the shipping company founded in 1919 by Marcus Garvey's Universal Negro

---

[137] Shivdeep Singh Grewal, 'Capital of the 1970s?: Southall and the Conjuncture of 23 April 1979', *Socialist History Journal*, 23 (2003), 1–34.

[138] National Council for Civil Liberties, *Southall 23 April 1979: The Report of the Unofficial Committee of Enquiry* (Nottingham, 1980), 7, 22.

[139] Southall Rights, *A Report on the Events of 23rd April 1979* (Southall, 1980); Baumann, *Contesting Culture*, 58–9; Sivanandan, 'From Resistance to Rebellion', 44.

[140] CARF, *Southall*, 64.

[141] Rahila Gupta, 'Some Recurring Themes: Southall Black Sisters, 1979–2003 – and Still Going Strong', in Rahila Gupta (ed.), *From Homebreakers to Jailbreakers: Southall Black Sisters* (London, 2003), 15.

[142] Ramamurthy, 'Politics', 45. See also an extended treatment in Anandi Ramamurthy, *Black Star: Britain's Asian Youth Movements* (London, 2013).

· KALA TARA

PAPER OF ASIAN YOUTH MOVEMENT BRADFORD.   No. 1.   20p.

Figure 8.1 *Kala Tara: Paper of the Asian Youth Movement, Bradford*, no. 1 (1979), 1. Tandana – the Glowworm, Archives, SC2.
Credit: www.tandana.org. Inaugural cover image featuring the Asian Youth Movement's logo, the Black Power fist, and the slogan 'Here to Stay, Here to Fight'.

Improvement Association.[143] In contrast to the back-to-Africa ideology that informed Garvey's movement and later Rastafarianism, however, the AYMs rebuffed far-right calls for their repatriation to their parents' lands of origin (where they had often never lived themselves, and to which they therefore could not be 'repatriated' in the first place). Instead, they insisted they were 'Here to stay, here to fight'.

Fighting indeed continued, and in 1981 'riots' involving youth of many ethnic backgrounds (including whites) occurred in many British cities and towns. Brixton became the best-known episode sparked by mainly Afro-Caribbean youth in protest against police harassment and the capricious use of their ability to 'stop and search' those suspected of criminal activity.[144] As Linton Kwesi Johnson argued in poems like 'Di Great Insohreckshan' and 'Mekin Histri', uprisings in Brixton, Toxteth, Moss Side, Southall, and elsewhere revealed the fight against 'Babylon' to be thoroughly multi-ethnic in nature, drawing on the pent-up frustrations and activism of blacks, whites, and Asians alike.[145]

Alongside acts of solidarity with black Britons of African descent, Asian youth simultaneously developed their own cultural forms that extended back to their parents' cultural imports as well as outwards to encompass other influences made possible by coming of age in Britain. By the early to mid-1980s, British Asians produced modernized forms of *bhangra*, a form of Punjabi folk music, by incorporating aspects of Western pop that expanded its audience to encompass a new generation. One Southall-based musician remembered how once 'Asians were lost, they weren't accepted by whites, so they drifted into the black culture, dressing like blacks, talking like them, and listening to reggae. But now *Bhangra* has given them "their" music and made them feel that they do have an identity. No matter if they are Gujaratis, Punjabis or whatever, – *Bhangra* is Asian music for Asians.'[146] *Bhangra*'s following in Britain was not limited to one particular national, religious, class, or caste background, illustrating how an extremely diverse range of South Asian peoples and cultures had the potential selectively to coalesce as 'Asians' in diaspora.

---

[143] *Kala Tara* alongside much other AYM visual and printed material has been digitized as part of the invaluable Tandana-Glowworm archive (www.tandana.org) coordinated by Anandi Ramamurthy.

[144] Solomos, *Race and Racism*, ch. 7 (see especially 160–4); Kobena Mercer, *Welcome to the Jungle: New Positions in Black Cultural Studies* (New York, 1994), 5–16.

[145] Linton Kwesi Johnson, 'Mekin Histri' and 'Di Great Insohreckshan', in *Selected Poems* (London, 2006), 60–1, 64–6.

[146] Veeno Bewan, 'Upcoming: Cobra', *Ghazal and Beat*, 4 (March 1988), 8, cited in Baumann, *Contesting Culture*, 156. On *bhangra*, see Sabita Banerji and Gerd Baumann, 'Bhangra 1984–8: Fusion and Professionalization in a Genre of South Asian Dance Music', in Paul Oliver (ed.), *Black Music in Britain: Essays on the Afro-Asian Contribution to Popular Music* (Buckingham, 1990), 137–52; Tony Ballantyne, *Between Colonialism and Diaspora: Sikh Cultural Formations in an Imperial World* (Durham, 2006), ch. 4; and especially Sharma, Hutnyk, and Sharma (eds.), *Dis-Orienting Rhythms*.

Yet 'Asian music for Asians' did not evolve in new-found isolation from other 'black' cultures. A plethora of post-*bhangra* styles emerged in the late 1980s and 1990s, where performers fused *bhangra* and indeed other Indian, Pakistani, and Bangladeshi musical inspirations with reggae, rap, hip hop, techno, and a host of other sounds, many being African-American or Jamaican and often arriving by way of everyday engagement with multi-ethnic Britain. Often loosely categorized under the heading of 'Asian underground' dance music, performers included Apache Indian (Steve Kapur) from Birmingham, who combined *bhangra* with reggae and reggae-derived ragga (and whose 1993 cover art of the album *No Reservations* incorporated Rastafarian colours alongside images of India's flag); Asian Dub Foundation, which drew upon rap, jungle, and punk in addition to dub; the classically-trained musician Talvin Singh, who organized London club nights and con-tributed 'tabla-tronics' (electronic tabla) to compilation CDs like 1997's *Anokha: Soundz of the Asian Underground*; Fun^Da^Mental, who fused rap with Islamic devotional and Indian film music; and Black Star Liner, a group whose white and Asian musicians combined Asian and Middle Eastern instruments and sounds with those of rock guitar, reggae, and dub in albums like 1999's *Bengali Bantam Youth Experience!*. Anti-racist political messages were commonly integral to their creative output, as were anti-colonial themes (as Chapter 9 considers further). Direct references to transnational movements, both implicit and explicit, pervaded musical styles, instrumentalization, and lyrics alike. Fun^Da^Mental's plea for Afro-Asian unity in opposition to racism combined with a staunch allegiance to Islam, and their tracks included samples of voices like Gandhi, Black Panther leaders, Malcolm X, and Louis Farrakhan of the Nation of Islam. Black Star Liner, meanwhile, took its very name from Marcus Garvey's shipping line.[147]

* * *

As British Asian youth were drawing upon and contributing to multi-ethnic black cultures, however, signs that 'blackness' as a multi-ethnic political colour was breaking down grew impossible to ignore. In his highly influential essays, Stuart Hall has described how 'the black subject' and 'the black experience' were 'not stabilised by Nature or by some other essential guarantee . . . they are constructed historically, culturally, politically'. Open to continual change and

---

[147] Sharma, Hutnyk, and Sharma (eds.), *Dis-Orienting Rhythms*; John Hutnyk, *Critique of Exotica: Music, Politics and the Culture Industry* (London, 2000); Huq, *Beyond Subculture*, ch. 4; Virinder S. Kalra, 'Vilayeti Rhythms: Beyond Bhangra's Emblematic Status to a Translation of Lyrical Texts', *Theory, Culture & Society*, 17:3 (2000), 80–102; Shukla, *India Abroad*, ch. 6; Lipsitz, *Dangerous Crossroads*, ch. 6; Les Back, *New Ethnicities and Urban Culture: Racisms and Multiculture in Young Lives* (London, 1996), 219–29; Rehan Hyder, *Brimful of Asia: Negotiating Ethnicity on the UK Music Scene* (Aldershot, 2004); Barry Didcock, 'Black Star Rising', *Sunday Herald* (Glasgow), 29 August 1999.

negotiation, 'black' identities were plural as opposed to monolithic, and by the late 1980s 'the end of the essential black subject' was indisputable.[148] Differences among blacks were manifest not simply in class, gender, and sexual diversity but also through increasingly fragmented ethnic and cultural forms of orientation.[149] Blackness was a 'false essentialism', Tariq Modood argued in 1994, and one that was particularly problematic for (and indeed never had been universally accepted among) British Asians. 'Political blackness', in emphasizing the need to unify and combat colour-based racism,

systematically obscures the cultural antipathy to Asians (and, no doubt, others), how Asian cultures and religions have been racialised, and the elements of discrimination that Asians (and others) suffer. If colour (or colour and class) were the sole basis of racism in British society it would be impossible to explain the finding of all the white attitude surveys over more than a decade that self-assigned racial prejudice against Asians is higher, sometimes much higher, than against black people.[150]

Operating in tandem with the rise of a 'new racism' predicated upon cultural difference rather than physical distinctions (of which skin colour was typically paramount), colour-coded 'black' activism and allegiances became difficult to sustain, especially for Asians.

Asians not only largely ceased to be 'black'; 'Asian' itself, always a composite 'invented category' – another 'false essentialism' – became subjected to 'the powerful centrifugal pull of Hindu, Sikh, and Muslim identities'.[151] While the Asian Youth Movements of the late 1970s and early 1980s crossed denominational lines and focused on secular issues, the coming years saw seismic shifts both in the ways Asians saw themselves and in wider social perceptions which increasingly foregrounded religion. World events played a significant role in reshaping diasporic identities as well as British attitudes towards its South Asian–descended population, among them being the rise of right-wing Hindu communal politics with its anti-Muslim agenda in India.[152] Islam and Muslims, however, came to dominate public awareness in Britain in a way that Hinduism and Hindus or Sikhism and Sikhs never did. More than anything else, events – global, national, and local – after the 1988 publication of Salman Rushdie's novel *The Satanic Verses* turned Britain's attention towards its Muslim population, which then totalled approximately 1 million (the majority

---

[148] Hall, 'New Ethnicities', 446, 444; Hall, 'What Is This "Black"', 474.
[149] Gilroy, *Black Atlantic*, 86.
[150] Tariq Modood, 'Political Blackness and British Asians', *Sociology*, 28:4 (1994), 865.
[151] Philip Lewis, 'Arenas of Ethnic Negotiation: Cooperation and Conflict in Bradford', in Tariq Modood and Pnina Werbner (eds.), *The Politics of Multiculturalism in the New Europe: Racism, Identity and Community* (London, 1997), 142, 129.
[152] Shukla, *India Abroad*, chs. 4 and 6; Dhooleka S. Raj, *Where Are You From?: Middle-Class Migrants in the Modern World* (Berkeley, 2003); Ramamurthy, 'Politics', 39, 57–8; Stacey Burlet and Helen Reid, 'Cooperation and Conflict: The South Asian Diaspora after Ayodhya', *New Community*, 21:4 (1995), 587–97.

being of Pakistani or Bangladeshi origin). A relentless fixation on Muslim minorities ensued, periodically escalating and remaining a dominant political and cultural issue up to the present day.

As was also the case internationally, countless Muslims in Britain found passages within *The Satanic Verses* deeply offensive and a blasphemous insult to the Prophet, the Qur'ān, and Islam, and unsuccessfully sought to have the novel banned. Muslims in Bradford became prominent leaders of mass demonstrations, most spectacularly when the Bradford Council for Mosques organized a public book-burning early in 1989 that received intense media coverage. What became known as the 'Rushdie Affair' took a new turn when the Ayatollah Khomeini issued a *fatwa*, or religious edict, from Iran on 14 February 1989 calling for Rushdie's death, and by extension that of others involved with the book's publication and distribution. Rushdie himself, long resident in Britain, went into hiding under police protection. Both the novel itself and the resoundingly hostile response to their concerns within much of Britain (seen, for example, in the state's refusal to extend blasphemy laws to encompass Islam) made many Muslims despair of having their religion and values respected. Some concluded that whatever official lip service had been paid to multiculturalism was meaningless in actual fact. In mainstream opinion, meanwhile, Muslims (and especially Pakistanis) were 'portrayed as a radical assault upon British values, a threat to the state and an enemy to good race relations', as Modood encapsulated.[153]

The protracted furore surrounding some Muslims' position on *The Satanic Verses* and the Ayatollah's death sentence saw the crystallization of a public discussion of Britishness in which national identity and British values became construed as diametrically opposed to those ascribed to 'British Muslims' – typically (and incorrectly) discussed as a homogenous group and assumed to share a uniform and undifferentiated attitude towards Rushdie and Islam more generally. Whereas Britain and Britishness epitomized progressive Western liberalism, freedom of expression, the rule of law, and secularism, Islam stood for dogmatic extremism, backwardness, barbarism, and fundamentalism. Britishness, in sum, meant tolerance; Islam inevitably denoted intolerance.[154] To return to Roy Jenkins' conception of integration, the Rushdie Affair, rather like Honeyford's earlier accusations, testified that the 'atmosphere of mutual tolerance' was non-existent because it remained one-sided. Muslims' 'un-British' approach to *The Satanic Verses* and the *fatwa* provided resounding

---

[153] Tariq Modood, 'British Asian Muslims and the Rushdie Affair', *Political Quarterly*, 61:2 (1990), 152.

[154] Talal Asad, 'Multiculturalism and British Identity in the Wake of the Rushdie Affair', *Politics and Society*, 18:4 (1990), 455–80; Ruvani Ranasinha, 'The Fatwa and Its Aftermath', in Abdulrazak Gurnah (ed.), *The Cambridge Companion to Salman Rushdie* (Cambridge, 2007), 45–58; Lewis, *Islamic Britain*, 153–64.

proof that they had failed to integrate and indeed actively isolated themselves from mainstream society and rejected its dominant (secular) values.

The Rushdie Affair had manifold and long-lasting repercussions, particularly the demonization of Britain's Muslim population as embodying forms of cultural difference deemed incompatible with the nation. Racism increasingly took the form of Islamophobia – a shift from a colour-based to a cultural- and predominantly faith-based animosity – and Muslims became differentiated from others of South Asian backgrounds.[155] As Dilip Hiro observed, '[w]ithin a year of the publication of *The Satanic Verses*, the term "British Muslims" had entered the day-to-day lexicon. Yet nobody used the corresponding phrase "British Sikhs" or "British Hindus". The non-Muslim immigrants and their descendants continued to be described merely as "Asians" or "British Asians" – that is, without any identification of their religious affiliation'.[156] Indeed, many Hindus and Sikhs acquiesced to this erosion of a unitary 'Asian' identity, seeming only too happy to distance themselves from public association with a group that increasingly monopolized the status of a racialized cultural and religious 'problem'. Nor did other blacks seem eager to support Muslim campaigns against *The Satanic Verses* and its author.[157] Whereas the late 1970s and early 1980s had witnessed significant acts of solidarity among ethnic minorities of different African and Asian backgrounds and Ray Honeyford had condemned West Indians, Sikhs, and Muslims in equal measure, less than a decade later Muslims had become the primary scapegoat. Repeatedly accused of having the lowest level of integration of all Britain's minorities, Muslims were declared guilty of 'self-segregation', not the victims of racism and discrimination.

Events since 1989 reveal the marked extent to which Britain continues to live in the Rushdie Affair's shadow. Fixation upon purported non-integration and cultural identities construed on an either/or basis continued, resurfacing the following year when Norman Tebbit, once chairman of the Conservative Party, notoriously proclaimed that second-generation youth failed to pass the 'cricket test of loyalty'. When England competed against Pakistan, India, or the West Indies in international matches, 'Which side do they cheer for?': 'If all the time somebody is looking back over their shoulder to the country from which their family came instead of to the country where they live and are making their home, you scratch your head if you are an integrationist and ask, "Are they

---

[155] Ralph Grillo, 'British and Others: From "Race" to "Faith"', in Vertovec and Wessendorf (eds.), *Multiculturalism Backlash*, 50–71; Ceri Peach, 'Britain's Muslim Population: An Overview', in Tahir Abbas (ed.), *Muslim Britain: Communities under Pressure* (London, 2005), 18.

[156] Hiro, *Black British White British*, 193.

[157] Modood, 'Political Blackness', 869; Ramamurthy, 'Politics', 58; Lewis, 'Arenas', 130, 134; Lewis, *Islamic Britain*, 1. Growing socio-economic disparities also explain why many increasingly affluent Hindus and Sikhs distinguished themselves from Muslims, who suffer far higher levels of poverty on average.

really integrated or are they just living here?"'[158] Hybrid identities and multi-cultural orientations resisting containment within a single and exclusive national category – British or 'other' – had no place within Tebbit's brand of 'integrationist' thinking, and were suggestive of the extent to which multi-culturalism had become discredited on the Conservative public policy agenda. Branded a 'failure', multiculturalism was declared 'dead', killed off by Muslim responses to Rushdie.[159]

* * *

Yet the 1990s also witnessed the acceleration of parallel, mutually-reinforcing processes, already under way, in which rhetoric focused on integration (and especially the presumed lack thereof among Muslims) coexisted with increas-ingly widespread forms of celebratory multiculturalism within the spheres of leisure and consumption.[160] These simultaneous and symbiotic tendencies continue into the present. Over time, for example, the Notting Hill Carnival's meanings became politically contained until it could be enjoyed as an unpro-blematic occasion when 'the streets of West London come alive with the sounds and smells of Europe's biggest street festival'. Once an epicentre of resistant and potentially subversive positive assertions of blackness, the Carnival today is feted as 'vibrant', 'colourful', and 'Caribbean', attracting millions and legitimized as a tourist-friendly contender for the honour of 'London's most exciting annual event'.[161]

Carnival's changing reputation was partly attributable to Notting Hill's social gentrification, but other neighbourhoods and cities long well known for their combination of socio-economic deprivation and racial tensions also became arenas where local authorities looked to multiculturalism, especially when it took the form of food and restaurants, as a desperately-needed source of regeneration. Bradford along with the Brick Lane area of east London (both flashpoints of recurrent British Asian confrontations with the National Front, other white racists, and the police during and after the 1970s) counted among Britain's self-proclaimed 'Curry Capitals' by the late 1990s. Whereas the 'smell of curry' once ranked high among the reasons why many whites claimed to find South Asian immigrants culturally offensive in the 1960s, in later decades 'Indian' restaurants or curry houses attracted a growing white clientele until they became widely marketed as a revered part of local heritage. In the

---

[158] Richard Ford and Jonathan Braude, '"Cricket Test" is Defended by Tebbit', *The Times*, 21 April 1990; Helen Johnstone, 'Tebbit Test of Loyalty Dismissed as Absurd', *The Times*, 21 April 1990.

[159] Ranasinha, 'Fatwa', 48; Lewis, *Islamic Britain*, 4; Asad, 'Multiculturalism', 474.

[160] Barnor Hesse, 'Introduction: Un/Settled Multiculturalisms', in Barnor Hesse (ed.), *Un/Settled Multiculturalisms: Diasporas, Entanglements, 'Transruptions'* (London, 2000), 10, 21–2.

[161] www.thenottinghillcarnival.com, accessed 8 March 2011.

case of Bradford, 'going for an Indian' acquired the status of a 'Yorkshire institution' and Asian-run restaurants qualified as one of the city's 'traditional industries' – one of the few, in fact, after textile manufacture's collapse – with residents and visitors alike encouraged to partake of 'traditional Indian cuisine in the heart of Brontë country'. Praised as 'the positive side of ... multiculturalism' in Bradford, curry's champions on the national stage were no less enthusiastic. As Labour Foreign Secretary Robin Cook announced in April 2001, chicken tikka masala, a restaurant mainstay, was 'a true British national dish ... a perfect illustration of the way Britain absorbs and adapts external influences', epitomizing 'multiculturalism as a positive force for our economy and society'.[162]

Cook's assertions typified New Labour's affirmative approach to ethnic cultural diversity after the party returned to power under Tony Blair in 1997, and they testify to two interconnected tendencies. First, they suggest the extent to which new ways of 'being British' that could accommodate forms of diversity associated with postcolonial minorities had spread, taking root among significant swathes of society. Paul Gilroy, among other scholars, analyzes how by the early twenty-first century Britain had developed a deeply-entrenched cosmopolitan 'convivial culture' characterized by 'a routine, everyday exposure to difference' and 'spontaneous and ordinary hybridity'. '[T]he convivial metropolitan cultures of the country's youth', he continued, remain

a bulwark against the machinations of racial politics. This enduring quality of resistance among the young ... is much more than an effect of multicultural consumerism and communicates something of the irrevocably changed conditions in which factors of identity and solidarity that derive from class, gender, sexuality and region have made a strong sense of racial difference unthinkable to the point of absurdity.[163]

'Creeping multiculturalism' of this nature remains patchy, however, because 'racialized exclusion, racially-compounded disadvantage, household poverty, unemployment and educational under-achievement persist'.[164] Racially-motivated assaults and police racism continued, as the 1993 murder of Stephen Lawrence by white youths in south London and the controversies following the exposure of institutional racism pervading the police investigation starkly revealed. 'It is perfectly possible for young officers', Stuart Hall commented, 'to love reggae, eat Vindaloo curry every Saturday night, have a few black friends, and still think that "good policing" requires them to act on the assumption that a young black man carrying a holdall at a bus-stop after dark almost

---

[162] Buettner, '"Going for an Indian"', 887–8, 865.
[163] Gilroy, *After Empire*, 109, 132, 166, 131–2; see also Back, *New Ethnicities*.
[164] Stuart Hall, 'From Scarman to Stephen Lawrence', *History Workshop Journal*, 48 (1999), 188, 191.

certainly just committed a robbery and should be "sussed" – stopped and searched'.[165]

Hailing some forms of multicultural diversity went hand in hand with denouncing other aspects – often grouped under the heading of Islamic fundamentalism, extremism, and terrorism since the late 1980s – seen to pose more of a threat to British values and the nation's 'way of life'. In his analysis of the debates sparked by the Rushdie Affair about what 'being British' should mean, Talal Asad astutely pointed out as early as 1990 that it remained unclear

whether 'diversity' is an intrinsic feature of the British way of life or something allowed only when divergences do not contradict an essential – and therefore unchangeable – Britishness. When immigrants bring new practices, beliefs and discourses with them to Britain, do they extend the scope of British life, *or are they (conditionally) tolerated* by the authentic British who are also the cultural majority?[166]

Some 'hybrid cultural forms' have been 'comfortably accommodated by urban consumer capitalism and by the liberal celebration of . . . "the rich and diverse heritage which has added to Britain's wealth of culture and tradition"', Asad argues, while others, particularly those involving faith and political allegiance, appear 'to threaten the assumptions on which British secular identity is constructed'.[167]

Asad's questions remain pressing and stubbornly unresolved in the early twenty-first century. Soon after Robin Cook's speech extolling the Britishness of chicken tikka masala, New Labour's commitment to 'multiculturalism as a positive force for our economy and society' found itself repeatedly put to the test in a series of crises, domestic and international, that punctuated the rest of 2001 and continued thereafter. Spring and summer 2001 saw violent clashes in Bradford, Oldham, and Burnley involving young Asians and the police, instigated by a combination of white gang provocation, long-term deprivation and unemployment, competition for scarce jobs and social assistance, and inflammatory racism and Islamophobia fomented by the British National Party whose fortunes were on the rise.[168] The 'northern riots' were the most serious Britain had seen since the 1980s, and countless political and media commentators placed the blame on Muslims who were accused of self-segregation and stubbornly refusing to integrate at the expense of highlighting socio-economic causes and racist politics.[169] Post mortems quickly became harnessed to Britain's response to the terrorist attacks in the United States on 11

---

[165] Ibid., 195. See also Stuart Hall, 'Conclusion: The Multi-Cultural Question', in Hesse (ed.), *Un/Settled Multiculturalisms*, 209–41.

[166] Asad, 'Multiculturalism', 459 (emphasis added).   [167] Ibid., 474.

[168] Goodwin, *New British Fascism*, chs. 3 and 4.

[169] Ash Amin, 'Ethnicity and the Multicultural City: Living with Diversity', *Environment and Planning A*, 34 (2002), 959–80; Arun Kundnani, 'From Oldham to Bradford: The Violence of the Violated', *Race & Class*, 43:2 (2001), 105–10; Buettner, '"Going for an Indian"', 891–4.

September and the ensuing wars in Afghanistan and Iraq that further fuelled anti-Muslim discourse. The 7 July 2005 suicide bombings on the London transport network perpetrated by British-born Muslims brought up in Yorkshire (three of Pakistani and one of Jamaican origins) raised the tenor of Islamophobia to an even higher pitch. Time and again, multiculturalism was declared 'dead' by numerous self-appointed coroners from across the political spectrum, just as had been the case during the Rushdie Affair. New Labour's response involved a retreat away from earlier celebrations of diversity and hybridity, cautious and qualified though they had been, that veered sharply towards 1960s-style assimilationism.[170]

New Labour's conciliatory stance towards racist, xenophobic, and Islamophobic politics and outlooks nonetheless left space for acceptable forms of cultural diversity – arguably, as Hall put it, for 'a kind of difference that doesn't make a difference of any kind'.[171] Britain's love of chicken tikka masala and other dishes made familiar and everyday through curry houses, for instance, survived the latest so-called 'death' of multiculturalism, even though the vast majority of Britain's 'Indian' restaurants have always been owned and operated by Bangladeshi or Pakistani Muslims. Intercultural cuisine could become thoroughly integrated within mainstream British life, even while its creators and purveyors stood accused of non-integration and self-segregation as never before.[172] Like the Notting Hill Carnival, curry now ranks among the '3 S' – style examples of cultural and artistic forms and occasions whose meanings, to reiterate Araeen's verdict on Britain's black artists, became 'controlled and contained within the larger spectacle of multiculturalism'.

Recent positive public responses to particular types of 'black' culture, predominantly those linked to transnational African diasporic cultures, can be better understood when seen in the light of the decades-long ascent and consolidation of anxieties about Muslims and Islam. Chris Ofili's transfusion of the Pan-African colour palette into the Union Jack did not discredit him as Britain's official representative at the first Venice Biennale to take place after the cataclysms of 2001. Although Ofili intended his 'Union Black' to serve as a critical comment on the ways the Union Jack had grown so closely associated with racist forms of nationalism, his very adaptation of it could be construed as a form of dialogue *with, and within,* British national identity, rather than as a

---

[170] Les Back *et al.*, 'New Labour's White Heart: Politics, Multiculturalism and the Return of Assimilation', *Political Quarterly*, 73:4 (2002), 445–54; Abbas (ed.), *Muslim Britain*; Gilroy, *After Empire*, 1.

[171] Hall, 'What Is This "Black"', 467.

[172] Buettner, '"Going for an Indian"', 891–2. After all, even Enoch Powell reportedly enjoyed dining at Indian restaurants in and around his West Midlands constituency in the late 1960s – the same years when he made his most virulent pronouncements opposing immigration. See Mike Phillips and Trevor Phillips, *Windrush: The Irresistible Rise of Multi-Racial Britain* (London, 1999), 248–9.

stance in irrevocable opposition to it – as was the case with common-sense ideas about British Muslims and Islam. After 2001, blacks' relative acceptability was readily apparent in many British social and political sectors, including the far right. As BNP leader Nick Griffin admitted in 2002, 'We can put up with the blacks. The question of Islam is another matter . . . As things now stand, we are going to end up with an Islamic republic some time in the future.'[173] 'Putting up with the blacks': a very limited form of 'tolerance', to be sure, and certainly a far cry from a warm welcome or full accommodation – not least in a party that continued to exclude non-whites from membership.[174] Nonetheless, it enabled the BNP to contrast its own position to that of its portrayal of Islam. Alongside its relative silence on the issue of blackness, the acronym within the title of the party's 2002 pamphlet *The Truth about ISLAM: Intolerance, Slaughter, Looting, Arson and Molestation of Women* spoke volumes.[175]

Far-right organizations like the BNP continue to rally around the Union Jack as a symbol of exclusionary nationalism, but since the late 1990s the flag of Britain increasingly shared the stage with that of England, the Cross of St George, in some instances to the extent of being pushed off it.[176] Now flown by English football fans during international matches and World Cups and emblazoned across the faces of the English Defence League (a group formed in 2009 with Muslims being its stated enemy), the England flag's current prominence as a cultural and political symbol of English nationalism comes at a time when the Union itself has diminishing powers in other respects as well. In the face of devolution according greater autonomy to Scotland, Wales, and Northern Ireland, the growing demands for independence among many Scots, and the deepening inroads carved by the European Union into Britain's sovereignty, the Union faces multiple challenges from both within and without that extend well beyond threats perceived to emanate from multiculturalism at home and an Islam that crosses national borders.[177]

---

[173] Andrew Anthony, 'Flying the Flag', *Observer*, 1 September 2002.

[174] Art, *Inside the Radical Right*, 101–2.

[175] British National Party, *The Truth about ISLAM: Intolerance, Slaughter, Looting, Arson and Molestation of Women* (2002 leaflet), discussed in Chris Allen, 'From Race to Religion: The New Face of Discrimination', in Abbas (ed.), *Muslim Britain*, 56.

[176] Krishan Kumar, *The Making of English National Identity* (Cambridge, 2003), 252, 262–3; Gilroy, *After Empire*, 117; Jim Pines, 'Rituals and Representations of Black "Britishness"', in David Morley and Kevin Robins (eds.), *British Cultural Studies: Geography, Nationality, and Identity* (Oxford, 2001), 57–66.

[177] Kumar, *Making*, ch. 8. On the English Defence League, see Matthew Taylor, 'EDL Is Fuelling Islamist Extremism, Say Police', *Guardian*, 20 November 2010. As a resurgent signifier of embattled English nationalism, it is at once suggestive and deeply ironic that the Cross harkens back to the crusades, another era of self-definition against an Islamic 'other', and that in St George England chose a patron saint who not only was foreign, but born in the Middle East. See Paul Bagguley and Yasmin Hussain, 'Flying the Flag for England? Citizenship, Religion and Cultural Identity among British Pakistani Muslims', in Abbas (ed.), *Muslim Britain*, 213–15; Reichl, 'Flying the Flag', 210–13.

In the summer of 2012, moreover, the Union Jack again revealed its infinitely malleable potential by becoming integral to a celebration of Britain's ethnic diversity during the London Olympics. Standouts among the many feted British medallists included women's heptathlon champion Jessica Ennis, whose father came from Jamaica and mother came from England, and the winner of the men's 5,000- and 10,000-meter track events, Mo Farah, born in Somalia and raised in Britain since childhood (and a practicing Muslim). Pictures of Ennis and Farah after their victories enswathed in the Union Jack instantly counted among the most memorable images of the games that generated a widespread sense of pride in the host nation's achievements. Many commentators eagerly proclaimed the London Olympics 'a multicultural success'.[178] Jackie Kay, a poet of Nigerian and Scottish origins, went so far as to say that

Mo Farah may have changed my opinion of the Union flag: when it was draped around his shoulders I was shocked by how attractive it looked. I noticed the stunning design as if for the first time. It's not the flag's fault, the way it has frightened me for years. Well, it seems the tide of the river of blood may be turning. Farah's got the flag back. That Hurrah Farah photograph will become one of the iconic images of Britishness.[179]

Whether or not Kay's hopeful prediction will come to pass remains to be seen. Sceptics would point towards earlier episodes of black athletes' Olympic successes in which the Union Jack figured prominently to highlight how ephemeral similar euphoric moments have proved in the past.[180] In a poll conducted by the *Guardian* newspaper at the end of the games, 53 per cent of those surveyed felt that '[m]ore often than not immigrants … do not bring anything positive, and the likes of the Olympic-winning athletes are an exception'.[181] To date, no matter how many times minorities – whether 'immigrants' or British-born – have taken 'the flag back' and made it their own, they have not yet been allowed to keep hold of it unconditionally.

* * *

Postcolonial cultures in a multicultural Netherlands

Dutch responses to ethnic minorities and cultures underwent considerable change in the era spanning the arrival of Indisch Dutch repatriates and Moluccans between the late 1940s and early 1960s and the mass settlement of West Indians and Mediterranean labour migrants that grew in the 1960s and

[178] Lizzy Davies, 'Notting Hill Carnivalgoers Hope to Put the Seal on London's Summer-Long Party', *Observer*, 26 August 2012.
[179] 'London 2012: It Changed Us, and How the World Sees Us', *Observer*, 9 September 2012.
[180] Pines, 'Rituals and Representations', 57–8, invokes the example of Linford Christie in the 1990s.
[181] Tom Clark and Owen Gibson, 'London 2012's Team GB Success Sparks Feelgood Factor', *Guardian*, 10 August 2012.

1970s. As discussed in Chapters 6 and 7, Indisch Dutch faced intense official pressure to assimilate within Dutch society, but the fiction that other groups counted as temporary as opposed to permanent residents proved difficult to uproot. It took dramatic events such as the violence perpetrated by second-generation Moluccans, the surge in migration from Suriname surrounding its independence, and the sharp rise in Turkish and Moroccan family reunification to render traditional arguments that these groups would one day return home patently untenable by the late 1970s. With its goal of promoting 'integration but not without preserving cultural identity', the 1983 Minorities Memorandum became the most significant of a series of initiatives signalling a new official approach to the place of postcolonial and other minorities within Dutch society. This paved the way for a new Nationality Act in 1984 that facilitated the process of acquiring Dutch citizenship among both the first and second generation alike, allowing those born in the Netherlands the right to opt for nationality via *jus soli*.[182]

Like in Britain, the 1980s came to represent the 'heyday of multiculturalism' in the Netherlands when the aim of cultural assimilation was rejected.[183] Minority cultures gained a foothold in Dutch school curricula, and communities had access to a range of institutional channels through which to organize and promote their interests with state support. As long as integration was not jeopardized (respect for cultural difference went hand in hand with the promotion of Dutch language instruction, for example), the multicultural approach could be deployed to enhance the nation's pride in its historic reputation for tolerating and making space for diversity and combating racial and religious discrimination.

The multicultural 'consensus' prevailing in the 1980s (at least among political elites) began revealing fractures in the 1990s, but the backlash against it gathered growing momentum in the new millennium.[184] With the United States' terrorist attacks of 11 September 2001 providing a backdrop to the

---

[182] Ricky van Oers, Betty de Hart, and Kees Groenendijk, 'The Netherlands', in Bauböck *et al.* (eds.), *Acquisition and Loss of Nationality, Vol. 2*, 410, 425–9; Howard, *Politics of Citizenship*, 83–7.

[183] Hans Vermeulen, 'Immigration, Integration and the Politics of Culture', *Netherlands Journal of Social Sciences*, 35 (1999), 15–18; Jan Lucassen and Rinus Penninx, *Newcomers: Immigrants and Their Descendants in the Netherlands, 1550–1995* (Amsterdam, 1994), 3, 15–16, 154, 158; Hans Vermeulen and Rinus Penninx, 'Introduction', in Hans Vermeulen and Rinus Penninx (eds.), *Immigrant Integration: The Dutch Case* (Amsterdam, 2000), 1–4, 22, 25.

[184] For excellent summaries, see Peter Geschiere, *The Perils of Belonging: Autochthony, Citizenship, and Exclusion in Africa and Europe* (Chicago, 2009), ch. 5; Baukje Prins and Sawitri Saharso, 'From Toleration to Repression: The Dutch Backlash Against Multiculturalism', in Vertovec and Wessendorf (eds.), *Multiculturalism Backlash*, 72–91; Han Entzinger, 'The Rise and Fall of Multiculturalism: The Case of the Netherlands', in Christian Joppke and Ewa Morawska (eds.), *Toward Assimilation and Citizenship: Immigrations in Liberal Nation-States* (New York, 2003), 59–86.

national furore provoked by the murders of right-wing Dutch politician Pim Fortuyn in 2002 and the filmmaker Theo van Gogh in 2004 – both of whom were renowned for their vituperative critiques of multiculturalism and particularly Islam – detractors from the multicultural status quo relentlessly focused their attention on the Netherlands' Muslim communities to the almost total exclusion of other minorities.[185] In consequence, *allochtonen* (persons of non-Dutch nationality and/or born outside the Netherlands, as well as their children until the third generation, as distinct from *autochtonen*, or native Dutch) like the Indisch Dutch, Moluccans, Surinamese, and Antilleans whose ties to the Netherlands are rooted in colonialism have not been the target of recent multicultural debates, for relatively few are Muslim.[186] Labour migrants and their families of Moroccan and Turkish origin, by contrast, found their religion and culture under attack and a cause of widespread suspicion and hostility.[187]

While the debates raging around cultural pluralism, integration, and Islam occurring within France and Britain are closely linked with their respective postcolonial North African- and South Asian-descended populations, this is far less the case in the Netherlands, let alone in Belgium or Portugal as will be explored later in this chapter. In the Netherlands as elsewhere, postcolonial diasporas and cultures along with nativist responses to them have taken shape within a wider framework of national, and indeed transnational, developments. Postcolonial minorities gained new places within a post-war Dutch society simultaneously experiencing widespread secularization, domestic social transformations, and an expanding range of international cultural influences.

Foremost among these shifts was the decline of pillarization (*verzuiling*) that had structured and compartmentalized almost every aspect of individual and social life among the Dutch along religious and ideological lines since the late nineteenth century. The four main pillars – Roman Catholic, Protestant, liberal, and socialist – were accorded state recognition whereby pluralism (and

---

[185] See especially Ian Buruma, *Murder in Amsterdam: The Death of Theo van Gogh and the Limits of Tolerance* (London, 2006); Leo Lucassen and Jan Lucassen, 'The Strange Death of Dutch Tolerance: The Timing and Nature of the Pessimist Turn in the Dutch Migration Debate', *Journal of Modern History*, 87:1 (2015), 72–101; Paul M. Sniderman and Louk Hagendoorn, *When Ways of Life Collide: Multiculturalism and Its Discontents in the Netherlands* (Princeton, 2007); Paul Scheffer, *Immigrant Nations* (Cambridge, 2011); Ron Eyerman, *The Assassination of Theo van Gogh: From Social Drama to Cultural Trauma* (Durham, 2008), especially ch. 4; Jan Lucassen and Arie de Ruijter (eds.), *Nederland Multicultureel en Pluriform?: Een aantal conceptuele studies* (Amsterdam, 2002); Bauke Prins, *Voorbij de onschuld: Het debat over integratie in Nederland*, 2nd edn. (Amsterdam, 2004); Thomas Beaufils and Patrick Duval (eds.), *Les identités néerlandaises: De l'intégration à la désintégration?* (Villeneuve d'Ascq, France, 2006).

[186] Gert Oostindie, *Postcolonial Netherlands: Sixty-five Years of Forgetting, Commemorating, Silencing* (Amsterdam, 2011), 15–16, 43–7.

[187] Marcel Coenders, Marcel Lubbers, Peer Scheepers, and Maykel Verkuyten, 'More Than Two Decades of Changing Ethnic Attitudes in the Netherlands', *Journal of Social Issues*, 64:2 (2008), 269–85.

religious pluralism first and foremost) became institutionalized; each pillar had its own separate schools, political, voluntary, and leisure associations, newspapers and broadcasting media, and health and welfare provisions. Still holding sway as late as the 1950s, pillarization collapsed in the face of the decline in church attendance, youth revolts, social mobility, and the consolidation of the welfare state during the 1960s.[188] Ethnic minority newcomers also played a role, making 'distinctions between elements of Dutch stock seem less significant, differences that with the spread of pillarization had become more and more obtrusive', one scholar suggested.[189] In encountering new forms of diversity, native Dutch society struck many commentators as increasingly homogenous compared with the era when pillarization was at its height; the differences between Catholics and Protestants, not to mention those between working-class socialists and bourgeois liberals, came to seem far less acute.

Nonetheless, a system that had been an inescapable part of life until so recently still held sway both in popular memory and through its enduring official salience. Within what had become a highly secularized society, pillarization's legacies included the opportunities the state continued to offer groups to organize along religious lines.[190] It also shaped multicultural policies and fed into an essentializing view of cultures as bounded, internally coherent and homogeneous, and mutually distinct. Ironically, in a country that had only just undergone radical religious and cultural change in a short space of time, both 'Dutch' culture and identity and 'immigrant' culture and identity were widely imagined as frozen and discrete entities – arguably analogous to two separate post-pillarization pillars, particularly when the 'immigrant' culture in question became conflated with a 'Muslim' one.[191]

The history of the Netherlands' postcolonial diasporic populations demonstrates how *allochtonen* and *autochtonen* alike were fluid, not frozen categories and identities, each undergoing cultural transformations through multicultural possibilities working in tandem with other shifts. Far from presenting straightforward examples of successful or failed assimilation or integration, changes took distinct form among different social sectors over time and across the

---

[188] Arend Lijphart, *The Politics of Accommodation: Pluralism and Democracy in the Netherlands*, 2nd rev. edn. (Berkeley, 1975); essays published in *Netherlands Journal of Social Sciences*, 35 (1999); Kees Schuyt and Ed Taverne, *Dutch Culture in a European Perspective, Vol. 4: 1950: Prosperity and Welfare* (Basingstoke, 2004), 325–43; James C. Kennedy and Jan P. Zwemer, 'Religion in the Modern Netherlands and the Problems of Pluralism', *BMGN-Low Countries Historical Review*, 125:2–3 (2010), 237–67.

[189] William Petersen, *Ethnicity Counts* (New Brunswick and London, 1997), 199; see also Vermeulen, 'Immigration, Integration, and the Politics of Culture', 12–13.

[190] Rinus Penninx, Jeannette Schoorl, and Carlo van Praag, *The Impact of International Migration on Receiving Countries: The Case of the Netherlands* (Amsterdam, 1993), 210–14.

[191] Marlou Schrover, 'Pillarization, Multiculturalism and Cultural Freezing: Dutch Migration History and the Enforcement of Essentialist Ideas', *BMGN-Low Countries Historical Review*, 125:2–3 (2010), 329–54.

generations, with youth culture and urban life offering particularly fertile grounds for the development of hybrid and cosmopolitan configurations. Albeit becoming more visible by the late twentieth century, signs that Indisch repatriates, the Surinamese, and other groups would make prominent (if uneven) contributions to the Dutch cultural landscape were already apparent in the 1950s and indeed earlier, particularly in the realm of food, music, and leisure. Global cultural forms taking hold within the Netherlands proved inseparable from postcolonial populations who acted as conduits in the process of cultural transfer.

* * *

Culinary practices, as Chapter 6 argued, ranked high among the cultural mores of the Indisch Dutch targeted for reform between the late 1940s and early 1960s. Steering Indies repatriates away from their traditional spicy, rice-based dishes towards Dutch meals featuring meat and potatoes became emblematic of the drive towards assimilation. Yet repatriates withstood the pressure to completely change their diet, which became a key marker of postcolonial group identity after migration. Some found their economic niche by setting up *toko's*, or small groceries that sold Indonesian vegetables, rice, and spices to other repatriates and to Moluccan customers. In time, Indies cuisine also took hold among growing segments of native Dutch society. Not only did exotic ingredients enter a growing number of Dutch homes via *toko's* and later supermarkets; restaurants specializing in Indonesian food soon followed, run either by repatriates or by Chinese entrepreneurs who recognized a growing market. Students seeking an inexpensive, informal meal and ex-soldiers who had spent time in the Indies in the 1940s and grew to appreciate its culinary offerings were gradually joined by others eager to partake of a diversifying range of international dining options in the 1970s. By the 1980s and continuing to the present day, restaurants and cookbooks featuring *nasi goreng* (fried rice), *bami* (noodles), *sambal* (red hot pepper paste), and *sate* (meat served on skewers with peanut sauce) were popular not just in The Hague with its substantial repatriate population but nationwide. Like curry in Britain, the Indies-style *rijsttafel* (rice table) made the transition from culinary pariah to common crossover staple within the space of a generation.[192] By 2006, a UNESCO

---

[192] Anneke H. van Otterloo, 'Foreign Immigrants and the Dutch at Table, 1945–1985: Bridging or Widening the Gap?', *Netherlands Journal of Sociology/Sociologia Neerlandica*, 23:2 (1987), 126–43; Anneke H. van Otterloo, 'Chinese and Indonesian Restaurants and the Taste for Exotic Food in the Netherlands: A Global-Local Trend', in Katarzyna Cwiertka with Boudewijn Walraven (eds.), *Asian Food: The Global and the Local* (Richmond, Surrey, 2002), 153–66; Annemarie Cottaar, 'Een oosterse stad in het westen: Etnisch-culinaire pioniers in Den Haag', *Tijdschrift voor Sociale Geschiedenis*, 26:4 (2000), 261–80.

report counted Indisch food culture as part of the 'canon' of Dutch heritage and nothing less than 'a fine example of the national patrimony'.[193]

Dutch East Indies repatriates also contributed to the nation's cultural life in ways less commonly recognized today. Once the *rijsttafel* entered mainstream Dutch diets it never left; by contrast, Indisch youth who played decisive roles in introducing American rock 'n' roll to the Netherlands in the 1950s have been remembered and celebrated only sporadically. Rock 'n' roll's surge in international popularity coincided with the repatriates' departure from independent Indonesia, but at the outset few native Dutch youth possessed the musical abilities to form their own bands. Guitars were not part of the traditional Dutch repertoire at home, but they had been central to musical culture in the Indies. Young repatriates arrived in the Netherlands with previous exposure to stringed instruments as well as to American music – rock 'n' roll as well as country and Hawaiian genres – they had listened to back home. Indisch Dutch youth formed bands that played live performances enthusiastically attended by Dutch teenagers as well as their peers who shared an Indies background. Most of their songs were covers of American hits but reinterpreted with an original sound to become 'Indorock', a genre where the music of Elvis Presley, Jerry Lee Lewis, and selected Hawaiian or Indonesian *krontjong* sounds converged.[194]

Indorock's broader appeal did not survive long past its heyday in the late 1950s and early 1960s, when it dominated the live Dutch rock scene. Indobands' overall audience plummeted once native Dutch youth gained the musical expertise to form their own groups attractive to mainstream teenage rock 'n' roll fans. However, while white Dutch youth abandoned Indorock for 'Nederbeat' and other American- and British-influenced pop genres in the early 1960s, Indobands still found eager listeners and dancers at Indisch parties and regular gatherings like the Pasar Malam Besar that became an annual festival in The Hague starting in 1959. Superseded by other performers and sounds at the national level though it was, Indorock's ephemeral moment during a critical decade in the emergence of European rock 'n' roll testifies to the pioneering roles decolonization migrants played in importing American popular culture – briefly suffused with Indies influences – to the Netherlands. Just as importantly, ongoing enthusiasm for the forms of Indies culture that Indobands made available to repatriates in the Netherlands once their wider appeal diminished contradicts the once-prevalent depiction of the Indisch Dutch as completely assimilated. Festivals like the Pasar Malam Besar featuring Indisch food, music, and literature also served as a social reunion for repatriates, illustrating

---

[193] Lizzy van Leeuwen, *Ons Indisch erfgoed: Zestig jaar strijd om cultuur en identiteit* (Amsterdam, 2008), 329, 344–5.

[194] Lutgard Mutsaers, 'Indorock: An Early Eurorock Style', *Popular Music*, 9:3 (1990), 307–20; Mel van Elteren, *Imagining America: Dutch Youth and Its Sense of Place* (Tilburg, 1994), 103–18, Van Leeuwen, *Ons Indisch erfgoed*, 78–93.

an ongoing connection to their culture of origin in ways that enabled colonial memories to take shape and circulate within the group and ultimately become shared with others.[195]

Cultural survival, revival, spread, and evolution were also apparent among the Surinamese, taking different forms among those of Hindustani and Afro-Creole origin. Netherlands-based diasporas became a driving force behind the proliferation of Surinamese vernacular literatures written in the Sranantongo (Sranan) language used amongst Creoles, the Sarnami prevalent amongst Surinamese of Indian descent, and also in Dutch.[196] Migration and alienation stimulated a new awareness of heritage and roots that manifested itself differently over time and across the first and second generations. Afro-Surinamese writer Astrid Roemer has described how for those who made the journey, 'Suriname has become a language, transformed into stories, stories, stories. Newspaper articles. Letters from home. Phone calls. Occasional visits. Many Surinamese living in Holland have said to me: You give Suriname back to us. But I thought: I'm not giving Suriname back to them. All I'm doing . . . [is adding] new chapters to the story that Suriname has become to us.'[197] Gradually, Surinamese 'stories' ceased to revolve exclusively around recapturing the Suriname they had left but became something new. For Roemer as for others of African descent, this commonly extended to an awareness of being 'black' as opposed to, or alongside, Creole – a black identity deriving as much from Suriname as from creative engagement with African-descended cultures in the United States, the Caribbean, and the Afro-Caribbean diaspora elsewhere in Europe that migration to the Netherlands had facilitated.

Afro-Surinamese migrants provided native Dutch with access to African-American culture long before their numbers rose so sharply during and after the 1960s. In the interwar years, American-style jazz became popular in Amsterdam and other Dutch cities via Surinamese performers like Theodoor Kantoor, who assumed the Americanized stage name of Teddy Cotton and played at venues with names like the Cotton Club and Negro Palace.[198] An infinitely larger, socially diverse, and permanent population in the wake of the

---

[195] Claudia Huisman, 'De l'exil a l'intégration des Indos aux Pays-Bas: quel avenir pour leur identité?', in Beaufils and Duval (eds.), *Les identitiés néerlandaises*, 255–73; Van Leeuwen, *Ons Indisch erfgoed*.

[196] See especially assessments by Michiel van Kempen, including 'Vernacular Literature in Suriname', *Callaloo* 21:3 (1998), 630–44; 'De binnenkamer en de open vensters: Ontwikkelingen in de Surinaamse literatuur 1975–1988', *De Gids*, 153:1 (1990), 17–28; 'À l'extérieur du stade. La littérature immigrée surinamienne aux Pays-Bas', in Beaufils and Duval (eds.), *Les identités néerlandaises*, 275–96.

[197] Joost Niemöller, 'A Gaping Wound: An Interview with Astrid H. Roemer', *Callaloo*, 21:3 (1998), 507; see also Charles H. Rowell, 'An Interview with Astrid H. Roemer', *Callaloo*, 21:3 (1998), 509.

[198] Gert Oostindie and Emy Maduro, *In het Land van de Overheerser II: Antillianen en Surinamers in Nederland, 1634/1667–1954* (Dordrecht, 1986), 50–4.

Surinamese decolonization exodus of the 1970s soon produced a generation of young people who, whether because they were born in or had settled in the Netherlands at an early age, did not simply look back to Suriname for their cultural and geographic affiliations. By the 1980s and 1990s, Afro-Surinamese (along with Antillean) youth had become inseparably intertwined with a transnational black culture most noticeably apparent in the realms of fashion, style, and particularly music generated in diaspora – produced within, and between, the many nations within a linguistically diverse 'black Atlantic' arena.[199] Reggae, rasta, rap, and hip hop successively made their mark in the Netherlands in large part via the Afro-Surinamese contribution to these genres. Creole, or black, youth took up American musical influences alongside those emanating from the Caribbean, especially Jamaica, that reached the Netherlands partly refracted through the West Indian youth culture then flowering in neighbouring Britain. On Dutch soil, they adapted these syncretic black musical forms so that they stretched back to Suriname while simultaneously tapping into everyday life experiences in ethnically-mixed urban neighbourhoods like Amsterdam's Bijlmermeer. In consequence, Dutch rap and hip hop encompassed American influences but could also incorporate Sranan lyrics, Surinamese kawina, and Antillean salsa. In the Netherlands, moreover, hip hop and rap artists and audiences extended beyond black, Afro-Surinamese, and Antillean youth to include their white working-class peers who had grown up alongside them in Bijlmermeer or in equally diverse areas of Amsterdam, Rotterdam, and other Dutch cities with significant minority populations. In the process, they crossed and blurred the social and cultural lines between *allochtonen* and *autochtonen*.[200]

New ethnicities and transnational cultures also emerged within other ethnic groups. Global influences shaping Indisch Dutch youth culture in the

---

[199] Gilroy, *Black Atlantic*.

[200] Livio Sansone, 'The Making of Black Culture: The New Subculture of Lower-Class Young Black Males of Surinamese Origin in Amsterdam', *Critique of Anthropology*, 14:2 (1994), 173–98; Livio Sansone, *Schitteren in de Schaduw: Overlevingsstrategieën, subcultuur en etniciteit van Creoolse jongeren uit de lagere klasse in Amsterdam 1981–1990* (Amsterdam, 1992), 148–92; Van Elteren, *Imagining America*, 184–202; Mir Wermuth, 'Weri Man! Een Studie naar de Hiphop-Cultuur in Nederland', in *Kunst en Beleid in Nederland 6* (Amsterdam, 1993), 63–112; Ulf Hannerz, 'Cities as Windows on the World', in Léon Deben, Willem Heine Meijer, and Dick van der Vaart (eds.), *Understanding Amsterdam: Essays on Economic Vitality, City Life, and Urban Form*, 2nd rev. edn. (Amsterdam, 2000), 179–96; Mies van Niekerk, *Premigration Legacies and Immigrant Social Mobility: The Afro-Surinamese and Indo-Surinamese in the Netherlands* (Lanham, MD, 2002; originally published Amsterdam, 2000), 58, 217; Mies van Niekerk, 'Second-Generation Caribbeans in the Netherlands: Different Migration Histories, Diverging Trajectories', *Journal of Ethnic and Migration Studies*, 33:7 (2007), 1076; Christine Delhaye, Sawitri Saharso, and Victor van de Ven, 'Immigrant Youths' Contribution to Urban Culture in Amsterdam', in Nancy Foner *et al.* (eds.), *New York and Amsterdam: Immigration and the New Urban Landscape* (New York, 2014), 287–309.

Netherlands in the 1950s and early 1960s and Surinamese and Antillean youth culture since the 1980s were also apparent, if very different in form, among second-generation Moluccans who became radicalized in the 1970s. Some developed a highly visible politics of protest against their community's treatment after migration, the Dutch state's failure to help further their parents' aim of returning to an independent Republic of the South Moluccas (RMS) freed from Indonesian rule, and first-generation elders they perceived as overly quiescent. The train hijackings, hostage takings, and other terrorist acts they orchestrated (discussed in Chapter 7) drew inspiration from international movements including Black Power and the Black Panthers in the United States, the Palestinian cause, and youth protest. Their radicalism died down after the mid- to late 1970s, yet a commitment to perpetuating a Moluccan identity remained prominent amongst the third generation. Some continued to espouse nationalist RMS ideologies, some identified with broader-based transnational Third World movements, and some revisited their historic roots through a range of cultural activities; regardless of their stance, most continued to assert a distinct identity vis-à-vis other Dutch ethnic groups.[201]

In the case of the Indo-Surinamese (or Hindustani) population, living in the Netherlands led to a re-engagement with a wider Indian diaspora as well as with India itself. Migration to Suriname in the late nineteenth and early twentieth centuries attenuated ties with India amongst earlier generations, but 'twice migrants' found that relocation to the Netherlands enabled them to reconnect with their South Asian roots and heritage if they chose. Their relative proximity to Britain's large and dynamic South Asian communities allowed them to readily tap into the media forms – especially Bollywood film and music, alongside British Asian television programmes – that linked Britain and the subcontinent. Even more than their parents, second-generation Indo-Surinamese have avidly drawn upon a burgeoning array of Indian consumer and media products ranging from cinemas and film rentals to music, dance, and theatre performances to clothing shops and fashion shows available across a diversifying and expanding diaspora. So prominent did these manifestations of Indian culture become in The Hague, where half the Indo-Surinamese had settled, that the city has been referred to as 'Dollywood' – a meeting of Den Haag and Bollywood.[202]

---

[201] See especially Dieter Bartels, 'Can the Train Ever Be Stopped Again?: Developments in the Moluccan Community in the Netherlands before and after the Hijackings', *Indonesia*, 41 (1986), 23–45; Henk Smeets and Justus Veenman, 'More and More at Home: Three Generations of Moluccans in the Netherlands', in Vermeulen and Penninx (eds.), *Immigrant Integration*, 40, 55, 60.

[202] Van Niekerk, *Premigration Legacies*, 214–17; Van Niekerk, 'Second-Generation Caribbeans', 1076. On 'Dollywood' and related themes, see Sanderien Verstappen and Mario Rutten, 'Bollywood and the Indian Diaspora: Reception of Indian Cinema among Hindustani Youth in the Netherlands', in Gijsbert Oonk (ed.), *Global Indian Diasporas: Exploring Trajectories*

* * *

The reorientation towards South Asia suggests, on the one hand, the desire for cultural preservation amongst many Indo-Surinamese. On the other hand, Mies van Niekerk notes that among both Afro- and Indo-Surinamese 'these ethnic and transnational identifications are expressions of their cultural roots that only make sense in the Dutch context. The current celebration of ethnic diversity and multiculturalism offers a receptive ground for adhering to the cultural aspects and symbolic meanings of transnationalism'.[203] As will be argued in the following sections, it is necessary to qualify the assertion that multiculturalism is celebrated in any straightforward and all-encompassing sense in the Netherlands. Nonetheless, Dutch attitudes and policies that derive from pillar-ization traditions provided ethnic groups with the means of maintaining or rediscovering specific forms of group identity – particularly if these derive from or encompass non-Christian religious differences. Decades after depillar-ization took place within native Dutch society, its residual structures still work to make space for Hindus and Muslims to establish their own broadcasting and other media channels in addition to state-supported primary schools with the goal of transmitting their religions, languages, and cultures to children of the next generation. Groups most likely to organize separately in these arenas include Turkish and Moroccan Muslims as well as both Hindu and Muslim Indo-Surinamese; Afro-Surinamese, despite the importance of *winti* religious practices within their culture, are far less likely to do so.[204]

Scholars exploring the extent to which different ethnic groups have inte-grated in the Dutch context argue that religious difference, and specifically Muslim and Hindu religious difference, lies behind a relative lack of cultural and social integration and ongoing separatism – or at least the perception thereof – among these groups. Religion, far more than colour, has become

---

of Migration and Theory (Amsterdam, 2007), 211–33, especially 216–17. Dollywood in its Dutch/Surinamese/Indian context should not, of course, be confused with the theme park of the same name founded by American country-western singer Dolly Parton in Tennessee.

[203]   Mies van Niekerk, 'Premigration Legacies and Transnational Identities: Afro-Surinamese and Indo-Surinamese in the Netherlands', in Holger Henke and Karl-Heinz Magister (eds.), *Constructing Vernacular Culture in the Trans-Caribbean* (Lanham, MD, 2008), 14.

[204]   Van Niekerk, *Premigration Legacies*, 212–13, 217; Lucassen and Penninx, *Newcomers*, 26, 97–8, 158–9, 162; Vermeulen and Penninx, 'Introduction', 27–8; Jan Rath, Rinus Penninx, Kees Groenendijk, and Astrid Meyer, 'The Politics of Recognizing Religious Diversity in Europe: Social Reactions to the Institutionalization of Islam in the Netherlands, Belgium, and Great Britain', *Netherlands Journal of Social Sciences*, 35 (1999), 57–8, 64. As Thijl Sunier argues in 'Muslim Migrants, Muslim Citizens, Islam and Dutch Society', *Netherlands Journal of Social Sciences*, 35 (1999), 69–82, although Surinamese Muslims were a small minority (c. 30,000 at the end of the 1990s) within the Netherlands' total Muslim population, '[a]s people from a former Dutch colony who did not have any problem with the Dutch language and were much more familiar with Dutch circumstances, they had advantages over Turkish and Moroccan Muslims. Surinamese Muslims have long played a prominent role in the institutionalisation of Islam in the Netherlands', 73.

the most culturally significant form of difference in the Netherlands, as in many other postcolonial European contexts. To date, Indo-Surinamese (whether Hindu or Muslim) as well as Moroccans and Turks have fewer cultural inter-actions, social contacts, friendships, and marriages with native Dutch than do Afro-Surinamese, Moluccans, and Indisch Dutch repatriates.[205] Social distance between native Dutch and Afro-Surinamese has declined since mass migration in the 1970s, when many whites saw Creoles' difference as a cultural threat. Although racial discrimination and stereotypes of the Afro-Surinamese remain common, their alleged sexual immorality, involvement with drugs, and orien-tation towards leisure and 'having a good time' are now perceived differently. As Peter van der Veer, Ian Buruma, and others have argued, the 'Dutch way of life' has changed markedly in recent decades, making some ethnic minority groups now appear more in step with a newly-reconfigured national culture while others have become its antithesis. Indisch Dutch repatriates and Afro-Surinamese count amongst the former, while Muslims from Morocco and Turkey predominate amongst the latter.

What Muslims represent to many Dutch, it is suggested, is the unwelcome return of constricting religious traditions into a society that had so recently freed itself from equivalent Christian shackles.[206] Depillarization and secular-ization since the 1960s became, Van der Veer summarizes, celebrated 'as a liberation, especially from obstacles to enjoyment'. A 'Calvinist ethos of frugality and moral strictness' that 'portrayed enjoyment as something poten-tially sinful' – previously seen, for example, in critical responses to the Indies repatriates' supposedly excessive and improvident approach to hospitality and the much-vaunted love of music and partying amongst Afro-Surinamese – was overcome by a new emphasis on consumerism and sexual liberty.[207] Both at home and abroad, the Dutch cultural reputation came to revolve around toler-ance, gender equality, sexual freedom, homosexual rights, and a liberal approach to drug-taking. In short, aspects of the *gedoogcultuur* (the 'culture of tolerance' introduced in Chapter 7) that many found so worrying in the 1960s and 1970s later became central to a changed national identity.

---

[205] Vermeulen, 'Immigration, Integration, and the Politics of Culture'; Mies van Niekerk, 'Afro-Caribbeans and Indo-Caribbeans in the Netherlands: Premigration Legacies and Social Mobility', *International Migration Review*, 38:1 (2004), 176; Van Niekerk, 'Second-Generation Caribbeans', 1073–4, 1077; Van Niekerk, *Premigration Legacies*, 127, 208–10; Justus Veenman, 'The Socioeconomic and Cultural Integration of Immigrants in the Netherlands', *Studi Emigrazione/Migration Studies*, 40:152 (2003), 818; Philomena Essed and Sandra Trienekens, '"Who Wants To Feel White?": Race, Dutch Culture and Contested Identities', *Ethnic and Racial Studies*, 31:1 (2008), 60–3.

[206] Buruma, *Murder in Amsterdam*, 33–4, 54–7, 69, 241, 245.

[207] Peter van der Veer, 'Pim Fortuyn, Theo van Gogh, and the Politics of Tolerance in the Netherlands', *Public Culture*, 18:1 (2006), 111–24, especially 118.

Within this context, postcolonial newcomers' highly stereotyped sexual mores, 'fun-loving' tendencies, and centrality within the internationalization and hybridization of Dutch cuisine and youth culture could be construed as 'modern' and positive in a way that Muslim cultures rarely were.[208] For Dutch who valued women's and gay liberation – so recently won – Muslim attitudes towards gender issues epitomized the extent to which they were non-integrated, culturally alien, anti-modern, and intolerant. In the words of Pim Fortuyn, the openly gay politician murdered in 2002, 'I have no desire to have to go through the emancipation of women and homosexuals all over again' in the face of Islamic 'backwardness'.[209] Describing the collapse of the multicultural consensus by the early twenty-first century, Ian Buruma stresses that for the Dutch who 'felt like world pioneers in a new age of sexual and religious liberation ... The Muslims are the spoilsports, unwelcome crashers at the party,' espousing values deemed 'irreconcilable with a secular, liberal state'.[210]

Unlike Islam, Hinduism as practiced amongst the Indo-Surinamese population is not similarly disparaged as a social intrusion feared to be violent and illiberal. As was also the case in Britain, the international Western discourse condemning Muslims as intolerant and threatening had no comparable equivalent for Hindu diasporas. Despite their desire to preserve their cultural roots, the Indo-Surinamese do not constitute a widespread source of anxiety among the native Dutch. Rather, events like the Hindustanis' annual Milan Festival, held since 1984, have joined other public cultural showcases like the Indisch repatriates' long-established Pasar Malam Besar (now called the Tong Tong Fair), the Antillean (now Solero) Summer Carnival (dating from 1984), and the Afro-Surinamese Kwakoe Summer Festival (held in Bijlmermeer since 1975). All attract an increasingly multi-ethnic group of visitors eager to enjoy the food, music, dancing, and other cultural performances held to be characteristic of these respective communities. Like ethnic restaurants and gastronomy, such events epitomize the highly selective ways multiculturalism might become valued as never before as a source of cosmopolitan pleasure and leisure – and often safely containable as such – not to mention as a means of mobilizing

---

[208] On 'modern' attitudes about women and gender roles among different ethnic groups, for example, see Wilfred Uunk, 'The Cultural Integration of Immigrants in the Netherlands: A Description and Explanation of Modern Attitudes of Turks, Moroccans, Surinamese, Antilleans, and the Indigenous Population', in Louk Hagendoorn, Justus Veenman, and Wilma Vollebergh (eds.), *Integrating Immigrants in the Netherlands: Cultural versus Socio-Economic Integration* (Aldershot, 2003), 225.

[209] Pim Fortuyn, cited in Buruma, *Murder in Amsterdam*, 56–7; see also Art, *Inside the Radical Right*, 179–87; Prins and Saharso, 'From Toleration to Repression'.

[210] Buruma, *Murder in Amsterdam*, 126–7, 245.

ethnic identities.[211] Multiculturalism as it pertains to Muslim minorities, however, typically connotes the opposite, remaining a source of fear rather than fun.

Early twenty-first century hostility towards multiculturalism that centres on Muslims, however, cannot be treated in isolation from the history and cultural evolution of the country's non-Muslim postcolonial populations. In 2009, the far-right Dutch politician Geert Wilders, infamous for statements proclaiming that Muslim immigration was turning Europe into 'Eurabia' and warning that the Netherlands faced a 'Muslim tsunami' and 'Moroccan colonizers', became the focus of further media controversy, this time over revelations about his own genealogy.[212] Archival research revealed that Wilders, while born in the Netherlands, was descended from Indisch Dutch Jews on his mother's side – a hitherto unknown dimension of his public biography. An Amsterdam weekly magazine published an article by the anthropologist Lizzy van Leeuwen that sparked tremendous media attention, with journalists adding that as the descendant of a mixed-race 'Indo' Wilders undoubtedly had Muslim ancestry himself given Indonesia's status as the world's largest Islamic country.[213] Muslim antecedents, however distant and partial amongst a group whose members were largely Protestant or Roman Catholic upon arrival, became singled out in 2009 when they were all but ignored at the time of mass repatriation over half a century earlier – a fact that speaks volumes about the changed place of Islam in Dutch (and other European) discussions of migration and ethnic diversity across the intervening decades. What is more, Van Leeuwen argues, Wilders was not alone among first- and second-generation Indisch Dutch in vociferously espousing anti-immigrant and anti-Muslim politics. Since the late 1970s, a significant number of Indisch repatriates have

---

[211] Patricia Gosling and Fitzroy Nation, *Ethnic Amsterdam: A Complete Guide to the City's Faces, Places and Cultures* (Amsterdam, 2001), 8; Annemarie Bodaar, 'Multicultural Urban Space and the Cosmopolitan "Other": The Contested Revitalization of Amsterdam's Bijlmermeer', in Jon Binnie *et al.* (eds.), *Cosmopolitan Urbanism* (London, 2006), 171–86; Marga Alferink, 'Post-Colonial Migrant Festivals in the Netherlands', in Ulbe Bosma (ed.), *Post-Colonial Immigrants and Identity Formations in the Netherlands* (Amsterdam, 2012), 99–116. Ethnic festivals (along with postcolonial migrants' organizations more generally) as a source of evolving identity politics were explored under the joint research programme 'Bringing History Home: Postcolonial Identity Politics in the Netherlands' (www.kitlv.nl/bringinghistoryhome.html). Important studies to emerge under its auspices include Van Leeuwen's *Ons Indisch erfgoed*; Ulbe Bosma, *Terug uit de koloniën: Zestig jaar postkoloniale migranten en hun organisaties* (Amsterdam, 2009); Oostindie, *Postcolonial Netherlands*.
[212] On Wilders' party, see Niek Pas, *The State of the Right: The Netherlands* (Paris, March 2011), www.fondapol.org; Art, *Inside the Radical Right*, 185–7.
[213] Lizzy van Leeuwen, 'Wreker van zijn Indische grootouders: De politieke roots van Geert Wilders', *De Groene Amsterdammer*, 36, 2 September 2009. Many journalists took up Van Leeuwen's story and added their own interpretations, including 'Geert Wilders' Indonesian Roots Define His Politics, Says Anthropologist', *NRC Handelsblad*, 4 September 2009; Perro de Jong, 'Geert Wilders Is One of Us, Say Indies Immigrants', *Radio Netherlands Worldwide*, 4 September 2009, www.rnw.nl/english/article/geert-wilders-one-us-say-indies-immigrants, accessed 22 September 2009.

become active within right-wing anti-immigration politics and in opposing multicultural state policies. Having arrived in the Netherlands with a strong hatred towards the Indonesian nationalists who toppled Dutch colonial rule, many became extremely patriotic. Equally important, having initially encountered racial discrimination and then resented being compared with Turkish and Moroccan labour migrants, they later were commended as the best-integrated of all post-war newcomers.[214] For repatriates asserting their identity as integrated and Dutch while retaining and celebrating their colonial heritage, Muslims in the Netherlands became the primary 'others' against whom they redefined themselves.

* * *

Belgium's African population and new ethnicities in a divided nation

With its post-war history of high immigration from within and outside Western Europe, Belgium too has experienced the growth of religious minorities, particularly Muslims from Morocco and Turkey. Central Africans from Belgium's ex-colonies, who form but a fraction of the overall immigrant population, do not feature strongly within public discourse about religious minorities that foreground anxieties about Islam.[215] Native Belgian perceptions of foreigners and their descendants, while differing according to the group in question, have taken shape within a wider context of national reconfiguration, particularly since the 1960s. Like the Netherlands, Belgium also experienced depillarization and widespread secularization, but this has occurred alongside the sharp rise in divisions along regional, ethnic, cultural, and linguistic lines within the nation-state itself – divisions which have, to a considerable extent, replaced traditional political and ideological loyalties. With a total population approximating 11 million, Belgium consists of three regions (Flanders, Wallonia, and the capital city of Brussels), three 'communities' (Flemish, Walloon, and the German-speaking minority), and four linguistic regions (the Dutch-, French-, and German-speaking areas, as well as a bilingual Dutch-speaking and Francophone Brussels). An officially-recognized linguistic frontier within the nation became implemented in 1963, a development followed by a succession of constitutional reforms dating from 1970, 1980, and 1988. This

---

[214] Van Leeuwen, 'Wreker van zijn Indische grootouders'; Van Leeuwen, *Ons Indisch erfgoed*, 149–50.

[215] Anxieties about Islam in Belgium share many similarities with those prevalent in other Western European countries; see for example Jan Blommaert, 'Integration Policies and the Politics of Integration in Belgium', in Marco Martiniello (ed.), *Multicultural Policies and the State: A Comparison of Two European Societies* (Utrecht, 1998), 75–88.

culminated in 1993 with a new constitution and a federalized, decentralized political structure that granted a high degree of regional autonomy. These changes both reflected and worked to enhance sub-national identities along ethno-linguistic lines – 'new ethnicities', in other words, amongst the native population. Regional aspirations and pluralism pose a serious threat to the Belgian nation-state and have encouraged ongoing claims to greater autonomy and secessionism amongst a significant and stridently vocal minority, particularly among nationalist-minded Flemings.[216]

Within a fractured and plural Belgian nation, foreigners, immigrants, and their descendants severely compromise the prominent Flemish/Walloon binary, simultaneously problematizing it and helping to explain its dynamics. Internal fragmentation and federalization occurred side by side with the growth of immigration, with the result being that 10 per cent of the nation's population now have foreign passports and fully 25 per cent are of immigrant roots, with some having immigrant ancestry dating back only a generation or two. Anne Morelli and Jean-Philippe Schreiber stress that such people largely do not take on either Flemish or Walloon identities that are based upon backward-looking ethnolinguistic and regional origins: 'While it is quite possible to "feel Belgian", it is rather difficult to "feel Flemish" or to "feel Walloon" especially if one realizes that the mere luck of the draw upon arrival accounted for the fact that one's father got a job in a Walloon mine whereas one's uncle ended up in a Flemish one.' In failing to identify as Walloon or Flemish, the foreign-born and foreign-descended might thus count among the 'last Belgians'.[217] To an exponentially greater degree than in France, Britain, the Netherlands, or Portugal, foreigners in Belgium became situated within what was already a multicultural society, divided from within. As Eugeen Roosens aptly notes, 'immigrants or alien residents are entering an ethnically prestructured field: what has been happening and is going on among the Flemings and the Francophones is influencing how newcomers are perceived'.[218]

In postcolonial Belgium, rhetorical recourse to a language of colonization frequently punctuated hostile exchanges between Dutch-speaking Flemings and French-speaking Walloons. Bambi Ceuppens' analysis persuasively charts

---

[216] For background, see Kas Deprez and Louis Vos (eds.), *Nationalism in Belgium: Shifting Identities, 1780–1995* (Basingstoke, 1998), especially the editors' 'Introduction', 1–19; Georges Van Den Abbeele, 'The Children of Belgium', in Tyler Stovall and Georges Van Den Abbeele (eds.), *French Civilization and Its Discontents: Nationalism, Colonialism, Race* (Lanham, MD, 2003), 323–42; Catherine Labio, 'The Federalization of Memory', *Yale French Studies*, 102, special issue: 'Belgian Memories' (2002), 1–8; John Fitzmaurice, *The Politics of Belgium: A Unique Federalism* (London, 1996).

[217] Anne Morelli and Jean-Philippe Schreiber, 'Are Immigrants the Last Belgians?', in Deprez and Vos (eds.), *Nationalism in Belgium*, 249, 252, 255.

[218] Eugeen Roosens, 'Multicultural Society: The Case of Flemish Brussels', in Martiniello (ed.), *Multicultural Policies and the State*, 60.

ways in which Francophones feared colonization by Flemings, who comprise 60 per cent of Belgium's population. Flemings, for their part, drew even more readily upon this terminology and outlook, proclaiming themselves to be dominated by Francophone 'imperialists' in terms of language and their purported contempt for Flemish culture and the Dutch language. The antipathy many nationalist Flemings, particularly the extreme-right anti-immigration party VB (formerly known as the *Vlaams Blok* and later as *Vlaams Belang*, or Flemish Interest) expressed towards foreigners, Ceuppens states, operated within this predominant native binary. The VB 'define[d] and redefine[d] different categories of people as "foreigners", from disenfranchised Muslim immigrants and asylum-seekers to Francophone Belgians. Indeed ... behind the ever-changing array of various allochthons lurks the Francophone co-citizen as the enduring and ultimate "Other" who stands accused of trying to impose a Gallicized culture'.[219] As one of its leaders Filip Dewinter asked, 'How can a party resist the Francification of Brussels without resisting its Moroccanization?'[220]

The VB's Flemish nationalism has long been inseparable from its stance towards foreigners. Established in the late 1970s, the party only experienced its electoral breakthrough a decade later at the same time as France's *Front National*, its staunch ally in the European Parliament. Significantly, it broadened its popular appeal *not* via its assertively Flemish platform but through its campaign to repatriate North African and Turkish migrant workers. So strong was its racist anti-immigration dimension that the VB worked closely with Le Pen's party, despite its opposition to French influence within Belgium.[221] Immigrants, and those of immigrant descent, have been commonly accused of being Francophone-inclined, since many originated from countries like Italy where other romance languages were spoken, from former French overseas territories like Morocco, or from the former Belgian Congo, where French was (and remains) a far more common second language among the population than Dutch.[222]

[219] Bambi Ceuppens, 'Allochthons, Colonizers, and Scroungers: Exclusionary Populism in Belgium', *African Studies Review*, 49:2 (2006), 163; see also 151, 157, 168. As Bart Maddens, Jaak Billiet, and Roeland Beerten outline how those having a strong Flemish (as opposed to Belgian) identification tended to view foreigners more negatively than did Walloons with a strong Walloon identity. See 'National Identity and the Attitude Towards Foreigners in Multi-National States: The Case of Belgium', *Journal of Ethnic and Migration Studies*, 26:1 (2000), 45–60.
[220] Art, *Inside the Radical Right*, 146.
[221] Jos Bouveroux, 'Nationalism in Present-Day Flanders', in Deprez and Vos (eds.), *Nationalism in Belgium*, 210–11, 214; John Fitzmaurice, 'The Extreme Right in Belgium: Recent Developments', *Parliamentary Affairs*, 45:3 (1992), 300–8.
[222] Georges Van Den Abbeele, 'No Joking Matter: The "Other" Belgium', *Social Identities*, 7:4 (2001), 515; Morelli and Schreiber, 'Are Immigrants the Last Belgians?', 253.

Flemish anxieties revolving around Francophone 'imperialism' are most acute with respect to the cultural and demographic composition of the capital. Officially a bilingual region, Brussels constitutes a highly fraught terrain. Geographically encompassed by Flanders and historically a Flemish city, Brussels with its population of about 1 million is predominantly French-speaking; indeed, Francophones (both Belgian and foreign) outnumber Dutch speakers by a ratio of five to one. Flemish concerns about Francophone 'colonization' of the capital concern French-speaking native Belgians and foreigners alike, with the latter being a multinational group that collectively comprises as much as 30 per cent of its inhabitants. Brussels' status as not only the national capital but also the capital of the European Union means that its foreign population includes (in roughly equal numbers) both working-class migrants from non-industrialized countries alongside numerous professional 'Eurocrats' and employees of multinational corporations or NATO who count as expatriates as opposed to immigrants.[223]

Few foreigners, whether poor or rich, seem inclined to learn Dutch, and affluent expatriates include high numbers of native French speakers as well as countless others for whom French is their second language.[224] The city's cosmopolitan, international orientation has also made English, coupled with Anglo-American culture, an increasingly powerful presence. In consequence, as Ceuppens argues, Anglophone influences and the European Union, in tandem with non-European immigrants, are all candidates for Flemish concern and often outright animosity. 'Unlike many Francophones who have long identified with an international culture ... many Flemings consider themselves victims ... of all sorts of haughty imperialists', she asserts, 'threatened by various types of "foreigners": Anglophones, asylum-seekers, Eastern European "thieves", Eurocrats, Francophones, Muslims, illegal immigrants, non-European labor immigrants, "niggers", refugees, Walloons, and so on'.[225] Within this multicultural framework, the position of Central Africans formerly under Belgian colonial rule emerged within the context of multiple divisions, including those within the indigenous population on the one hand and those between subsections of native Belgian society and a range of recently-arrived groups on the other.

* * *

---

[223] Adrian Favell and Marco Martiniello, 'Multi-National, Multi-Cultural and Multi-Levelled Brussels: National and Ethnic Politics in the "Capital of Europe"', Online Working Paper Series for 'Transnational Communities' (1999), edited by Steven Vertovec and Ali Rogers, 2–5, 11, www.transcomm.ox.ac.uk/working%20papers/favell.pdf, accessed 17 November 2010; Deprez and Vos, 'Introduction', in Deprez and Vos (eds.), *Nationalism in Belgium*, 17.

[224] Roosens, 'Multicultural Society', 46–7.

[225] Ceuppens, 'Allochthons, Colonizers, and Scroungers', 164, 167.

Exemplifying the internationalization and social transformation of Brussels is
Matonge, the Ixelles area introduced in the last chapter that became well known
for its Congolese population, businesses, and cultural life. Despite having its
name derived from an area of Kinshasa, however, Matonge's ethnic diversity
greatly exceeds Central African dimensions. With 55 per cent of the district's
population being Belgian and 45 per cent of other nationalities, its foreign
population encompasses French, Italians, Spanish, Portuguese, Moroccans,
and many other groups, symbolizing more than any other area Brussels' status
as the EU capital and point of attraction for non-EU minorities combined.
While only 2 per cent of Matonge's residents came from the Democratic
Republic of Congo per se, 8 per cent in total originated from other parts of
Africa to give the neighbourhood a pronounced sub-Saharan character.[226]
Matonge's importance to Belgium's Congolese and other African populations
greatly exceeded the numbers actually resident there: the large number of
African food and clothing shops, hairdressers, bars, restaurants, and spaces
for live music and other cultural events encouraged many living elsewhere in
and outside Brussels to visit regularly and interact with one another – not only
with those from their nation of origin, but also with those of other African
backgrounds.[227]

Matonge's reputation amongst better-off Belgians and other Europeans
combined fear with fascination. As an area with considerable poverty, poor
housing, litter, drug dealing, and other social problems, it was known for a high
crime rate and ethnic tensions that culminated in riots in 2001. In equal
measure, however, since the 1990s it has experienced signs of gentrification,
attracting growing numbers of students, intellectuals, artists, and yuppies
among its residents as well as visitors who gravitated towards what became
trendy bistros, bars, cafés, and the occasional 'alternative' designer boutique.
Bohemians, EU professionals, and others found in Matonge pleasurable opportunities to consume ethnic exoticism in the form of shopping, food, drink,
African music featured at many bars and restaurants, and people-watching. By
2005, Brussels' tourism authority began to officially promote the neighbourhood as a place worthy of a visit – a move closely connected with a wider
regeneration programme that followed the 2001 riots.[228] Comparable to
London's Brick Lane, Matonge became celebrated in promotional material as
a 'vibrant ethnic and cultural melting pot', 'exotic', and 'eclectic', with a

[226] Eva Swyngedouw and Erik Swyngedouw, 'The Congolese Diaspora in Brussels and Hybrid
Identity Formation: Multi-Scalarity and Diasporic Citizenship', *Urban Research & Practice*,
2:1 (2009), 69, 72, 85–6; Anya Diekmann and Geraldine Maulet, 'A Contested Ethnic Tourism
Asset: The Case of Matonge in Brussels', *Tourism Culture and Communication*, 9:1–2 (2009),
96–7.
[227] Sarah Demart, 'Histoire orale à Matonge (Bruxelles): un miroir postcoloniale', *Revue
Européenne des Migrations Internationales*, 29:1 (2013), 133–55.
[228] Diekmann and Maulet, 'A Contested Ethnic Tourism Asset', 95, 99, 101.

'colourful crowd of fashionable locals, students, and eurocrats' there for the viewing.[229]

Concerted efforts to celebrate diversity extended to an annual cultural festival called *Matonge en Couleurs* ('Colourful Matonge') starting in 2001. Featuring African-oriented public concerts, literary events and book stalls, and plentiful eating and drinking every June, it was no coincidence that its origins followed closely on the heels of the riots (in which one young African was killed by police) earlier that year. Meant to constitute a 'multicultural celebration of solidarity, dialogue, and intercultural reconciliation', it invited people of all backgrounds to come and enjoy themselves together.[230] Amongst its stated goals was the enhancement of social cohesion – an intention that implies the frequent lack thereof in reality.

Despite efforts to promote Matonge's 'ethnic' characteristics, their rate of success has been mixed. As Anya Diekmann and Geraldine Maulet have summarized of civic tourism initiatives centred around Matonge, 'the combination of the African ambiance and the urban degradation makes for a somewhat negative image and summons the visitors to systematically associate the two characteristics'; as a result, stereotypes of African groups may well be reinforced among the wider population.[231] Colourful though it may be, Matonge remains widely associated with crime and black youth gangs and thus often kept at arm's length.

Significantly, despite the hope for greater dialogue and solidarity expressed in connection with *Matonge en Couleurs*, most people choosing to visit come to mingle with those sharing their cultural background, not to interact with 'the other'.[232] The area thus serves distinct functions for non-African and African residents and visitors, with both mainly coming to socialize amongst themselves. Scholarship often characterizes the Congolese diaspora as a closed community, with many of its members withdrawing and keeping largely to themselves.[233] It has, nonetheless, diversified considerably over time and now encompasses a first as well as a second generation.

Given that Belgium's Congolese population only grew more numerous during and after the 1980s, attention was often focused on first-generation immigrants as opposed to the emerging second generation of children and young people either born or mainly raised in Europe. Among the first generation, the notion that residence in Belgium was but a temporary interlude prior to

---

[229] John Brunton, 'Island Inside the City', in 'Brussels: Another Side of Town', *Guardian*, 10 May 2008, 3, published in association with the Belgian Tourist Office.

[230] See http://users.skynet.be/fb175085/matongecolours/index.html, accessed 2 November 2009.

[231] Diekmann and Maulet, 'A Contested Ethnic Tourism Asset', 99, 105.

[232] Ibid., 100; Roosens, 'Multicultural Society', 44, 48–9.

[233] Désiré Kazadi Wa Kabwe and Aurelia Segatti, 'Paradoxical Expressions of a Return to the Homeland: Music and Literature among the Congolese (Zairean) Diaspora', in Khalid Koser (ed.), *New African Diasporas* (London, 2003), 124.

returning home was deeply entrenched, an assumption strongly reinforced by Congolese literature and music. Just as many works of Surinamese literature came to be written and published in the Netherlands, so too was much Congolese music produced and recorded in Europe, particularly Paris, and then circulated throughout the Congo, other African countries, and among Africans living in Europe.[234] Since the 1980s, leading overseas-based musicians like Papa Wemba served as go-betweens, circulating stories of the diaspora to those back home through their lyrics and perpetuating many myths of migration among emigrés themselves. Utopian notions of a triumphant return to the Congo following the fulfilment of material ambitions in Belgium or other countries served to glorify time overseas and became the subject matter of many songs, not to mention a number of literary works. In reality, however, disappointment and failure characterized the European lives of many Congolese who repeatedly postponed going back, both because they had not achieved their goals and also on account of ongoing political insecurity, war, and violence in Central Africa. With dreams often unfulfilled, many nevertheless continued to gravitate towards symbols of status primarily directed towards those at home and fellow expatriates, most famously the European designer clothing and branded accessories that underpinned the *sapeur* cultural movement revolving around elegance, fashion, and style.[235] However endlessly deferred their return often proved to be, the assumption of its inevitability remained central to their mental orientation. Literary and musical representations of a Congolese community permanently settled in Belgium, France, or elsewhere remained few and far between.

Compatriots' concerns that some Congolese were in danger of losing their cultural heritage abroad were in themselves testament to the reality that many failed to go home, instead putting down roots, marrying (both among themselves and across ethnic and national lines), and having children in Belgium. Anxieties about the diaspora's deculturation were particularly pronounced with respect to women and girls. Some African women became important players in building associations that aimed to preserve their culture, but many – often younger – exchanged women's fashions such as the *pagne* for Western dress and adopted new eating habits, preferring *frites* (fries, or chips) to African foods. Congolese men commonly criticized women and girls as having become too emancipated and 'revolutionary' in Europe, losing respect for their

---

[234] Mayoyo Bitumba Tipo-Tipo, *Migration Sud/Nord: Levier ou Obstacle? Les Zaïrois en Belgique* (Brussels, 1995), 58–64.

[235] Kabwe and Segatti, 'Paradoxical Expressions', 124–39. On the *sapeurs* and *la Sape* (closely associated with Papa Wemba's influence) see also Ch. Didier Gondola, 'Dream and Drama: The Search for Elegance among Congolese Youth', *African Studies Review*, 42:1 (1999), 23–48; Janet MacGaffey and Rémy Bazenguissa-Ganga, *Congo-Paris: Transnational Traders on the Margins of the Law* (Oxford and Bloomington, 2000); Thomas, *Black France*, ch. 6.

husbands' and fathers' authority.[236] With many African immigrant families badly off due to high unemployment and underemployment, women's work frequently provided crucial economic support, further destabilizing conventional gender roles and the status of men as the main breadwinners and domestic authority figures.[237]

With the emergence of a quantifiable second generation being so recent, it is difficult to gauge the extent to which Central African–descended youth will identify with their parents' cultural origins, with local Belgian cultures, or create altogether new identities. Evidence to date suggests that they will do a combination of all three, as has commonly been the case among second-generation postcolonial communities in France, Britain, and the Netherlands examined earlier. Adopting, and helping to develop, a transnational 'black' or Pan-African identity is common among Belgium's second-generation African population whose members take inspiration from a confluence of Congolese, other African, Afro-Caribbean, African-American, and black British and European cultures rendered ever more widely available via a globalized media.[238] Residing in neighbourhoods (Matonge being only one of many) with large immigrant populations originating from a wide variety of sub-Saharan African countries, the Maghreb, and elsewhere facilitates the emergence of new ethnic and cultural identities not restricted to those associated with the Congo and/or Belgium. Geographical proximity and a shared French language also means that African music produced in Paris finds a ready outlet across the border in Belgium. The *Matonge en Couleurs* festival indicatively featured local rap, hip hop, and reggae as well as music from Benin, Cameroon, Burundi, Cape Verde, and the Democratic Republic of Congo, performed by Africans and diasporic Africans alike.[239]

Belgian uproar about the dangers posed by African youth gangs operating in Brussels (and Matonge especially) highlights the diverse forms of threatening 'otherness' their presence and behaviour represent. One racist diatribe by Bruno Gheerbrant published in 2005 focused on a gang linked to drug dealing, rapes, stabbings, abductions, and muggings known as *Black Démolition*, stressing the group's African-American orientation through its nomenclature; its members were mainly Congolese but also included West Africans, Rwandans,

---

[236] Anne Cornet, 'Les Congolais en Belgique aux XIXe et XXe siècles', in Anne Morelli (ed.), *Histoire des étrangers et de l'immigration en Belgique de la préhistoire à nos jours* (Brussels, 2004), 391–2.

[237] Anne Morelli, 'Les Zaïrois de Belgique sont-ils des immigrés?', in Gauthier de Villers (ed.), *Belgique/Zaïre: Une histoire en quête d'avenir, Cahiers Africains* no. 9–10–11 (Brussels and Paris, 1994), 153.

[238] Swyngedouw and Swyngedouw, 'Congolese Diaspora', 79–82.

[239] The 2009 programme for *Matonge en Couleurs* featured Brussels-based rap and dance groups including Poison Hypnotik, 5 Block Style, and Anonyme Colorz. See http://users.skynet.be/fb175085/images/matcoul2009programme.jpg, accessed 2 November 2009.

and Burundians. Said to include many young men who had arrived in Belgium as children during the 1990s as refugees from civil wars and the Rwandan genocide, *Black Démolition* and other gangs stood accused of importing violence from Africa and combining it with leanings towards the culture of inner-city America. Such was the increased prevalence of crime, Gheerbrant wrote, that Bruxelles (Brussels) had become 'Bronxelles' – akin, in other words, to the South Bronx in New York City. Such violence was intrinsic to African life, he opined; 'in Africa itself one finds even worse . . . black gangs in Belgium, with their violence and sadism, are a kind of social constant independent of geography or social or historical circumstances. It could have been predicted with complete confidence that they would appear once the African population reached a certain number.'[240]

While Geertbrant refused to consider the historical specificity informing both the circumstances of postcolonial Africa (and Belgium's important role in creating the underlying conditions for them) and the presence of Africans in postcolonial Belgium, he nonetheless flagged the legacy of colonialism as responsible for the danger that Africans posed on Belgian soil. Belgian politicians, like their counterparts in France and other countries, were made to shoulder the blame for failing to keep such people out:

Our rulers came of age when there were still African empires, and when Europeans still claimed their goal was to civilize the savage. Politicians today seem to think they can go the previous generation one better: if civilization could not be brought to Africa, they can bring Africans to Europe and make them good little Belgians and Frenchmen. What we now see before our eyes – in the streets . . . in the crime figures – is proof that Africans do not become Belgians or Frenchmen . . . The Africans of *Black Démolition* are responsible for their crimes, but they are not responsible for having committed them in Belgium.[241]

In this populist formulation, a range of external dangers confronted Belgium in the guise of its African population: insufficient control over immigration by a complacent national political elite, the misguided survival of the colonial civilizing mission, and Africans' innate 'savagery' and inability to assimilate. Equally worrying, Belgium's African-descended youth appeared more likely to lean towards African-American hip hop and rap than to orient themselves towards national or sub-national cultures, whether Belgian, Flemish, or Walloon. Instead, they threatened to transform Brussels into 'Bronxelles', thus enhancing the tendency of the nation's capital to be reshaped along increasingly cosmopolitan and globalized lines. In tapping into African diasporic cultures emanating from neighbouring France as well as from the United

---

[240] Bruno Gheerbrant, 'Black Démolition', June 2005, translated and published in *American Renaissance*, 2006, www.amren.com/mtnews/archives/2006/04/black_dmolition.php, accessed 2 November 2009. The New Century Foundation behind this publication has been identified as a white supremacist organization by the U.S. Anti-Defamation League.

[241] Ibid.

States alongside Africa itself, Belgium's second-generation Africans thus bring together three sources of imported cultural otherness some Belgians resent as signs of cultural colonization, symbolizing a potent convergence of African, American/Anglophone, and French/Francophone outside influences. The new ethnicities they work to develop rest uneasily alongside those of their auto-chthonous counterparts, particularly but not exclusively among assertively nationalist Flemings.

* * *

Portugal and its diasporas: hybrid cultures and the limits of lusotropicalism in the aftermath of migration

After the 1974 Carnation Revolution terminated the *Estado Novo* dictatorship and brought democracy together with rapid decolonization in Africa, Portugal simultaneously retreated inward and looked north, achieving its goal of inte-gration within the European Economic Community (now the European Union) by 1986. However seismic the change in its political order and however abrupt its downsizing from imperial metropole to small rectangle on the southwest fringe of Europe, Portugal nonetheless underwent the transition with a clear and confident sense of its national identity and culture. Unlike Belgium, postcolonial Portugal did not confront centrifugal forces pulling it ever further apart from within along ethnic, linguistic, or regional lines to the extent of placing national integrity at risk. As a state whose European frontiers origi-nated in late medieval times and which had lacked numerically significant ethnic, cultural, or religious minorities since the eighteenth century, defining what 'Portugal' was without an empire and who 'the Portuguese' were might well have appeared a straightforward process.[242] Yet the reality proved much more complex: in the late 1970s and 1980s, understandings of the parameters of Portuguese nationality and the Portuguese community were in a state of flux. Continuities with the past coexisted with new forms of inclusion and exclusion.

Decolonization was largely responsible for inaugurating changed concep-tions of the nation and those deemed legitimate members of it, but the coming decades revealed a postcolonial Portugal whose identity remains inseparable from its centuries-long history of global engagement and migration. Core symbolic manifestations of contemporary Portuguese national culture owe their form and meaning to both historic and ongoing patterns of outward migration *from* as much as inward migration *to* Portugal. Indeed, the former

---

[242] Nuno G. Monteiro and António Costa Pinto, 'Cultural Myths and Portuguese National Identity', in António Costa Pinto (ed.), *Contemporary Portugal: Politics, Society and Culture* (New York and Boulder, 2003), 47–9.

Figure 8.2 Poster advertising Portugal Day, Kennington Park, London, 12 June 2011. By prominently featuring the armillary sphere that appears on the national flag, this image associates both contemporary Portugal and the Portuguese diaspora with symbols that invoke the maritime and imperial heritage of the 'Age of Discoveries'.

are far more openly acknowledged than the latter. The national flag, for instance, features Portugal's coat of arms coupled with an armillary sphere, a navigation instrument dating from the era of the maritime 'Discoveries' that saw pioneering Portuguese navigators embark on caravels to Asia and America via Africa. Similarly, every year the tenth of June brings the celebration of one of the nation's most important holidays, Portugal Day – short for *Dia de Portugal, de Camões e das Comunidades Portuguesas*, or Day of Portugal, Camões, and the Portuguese Communities. While 10 June was chosen for being the day Luís Vaz de Camões died in 1580, his reputation has never been more alive than in the twentieth- and early twenty-first century. As Portugal's most venerated author of the poem *Os Lusíadas* (*The Lusiads*), which revisited Vasco da Gama's journey to India at the close of the fifteenth century, Camões remains as habitually glorified after 1974 as he was under the preceding *Estado Novo* dictatorship. Significantly, Camões was not just a poet but a sailor himself who travelled East in da Gama's wake, thus making him emblematic of the millions of Portuguese to leave home for distant lands from the early modern era until the present – the very 'Portuguese Communities' living outside Portugal who are explicitly included within annual commemorations of what the nation means and whom it metaphorically includes.[243]

The *Dia de Portugal, de Camões e das Comunidades Portuguesas* and the national flag both demonstrate the extent to which Portugal retains – and foregrounds – an overtly expansive conception of its history, culture, and population surviving well beyond its dramatic retreat from Africa in the mid-1970s and more extended period of withdrawal from smaller territories in Asia. Personifying this are Portuguese emigrants past and present and the communities they collectively form in diaspora. Although widespread emigration has long been an economic necessity rooted in chronic rural poverty, underdevelopment, and a lack of opportunity at home, negative 'push' factors created by adversity nonetheless elevated those who travelled abroad into exemplary representatives of the nation. Writing of the years following the transition to democracy in 1974, Caroline Brettell describes contemporary emigrants 'as symbolic transformations of [the navigators] for they have carried on the tradition of the Portuguese explorers – a tradition of reaching out beyond the shores of a small country situated at the margins of Europe'. Stoically facing hardship, parting from loved ones, sending money home to better the lot of those left behind, and transmitting Portuguese culture

---

[243] 10 June is also widely celebrated across the Portuguese diaspora; see Daniel Melo, 'Fátima, Folclore e Futebol?: Portugalidade e Associativismo na Diáspora', in André Barata, António Santos Pereira, and José Ricardo Carvalheiro (eds.), *Representações da Portugalidade* (Alfragide, 2011), 180–3; Daniel Melo and Eduardo Caetano da Silva, 'Associativismo, emigração e nação: o caso português', in Daniel Melo and Eduardo Caetano da Silva (eds.), *Construção da Nação e Associativismo na Emigração Portuguesa* (Lisbon, 2009), 52–3.

throughout the world counted among the qualities rendering the emigrant a heroic figure and the migration process 'Portugal's national rite of passage'.[244]

Inseparable from these patterns of behaviour and their valued place within Portuguese society and culture are the emotional sentiments closely attached to them, encapsulated in the concept of *saudade* – a term connoting melancholy, suffering, loss, and longing. Since the early twentieth century, *saudade* became increasingly central to ideas about the Portuguese national character – what João Leal has called the country's 'ethnic psychology' or 'collective soul'. It is as closely associated with the experience of dislocation and uprooting that migration entails for those who leave as it is with the feelings of sadness and loss they share with those left behind. *Saudade* (twinned with *fado* folk songs, its ubiquitous mode of expression) consolidated its status as the primary sensibility ascribed to 'Portugueseness' in the 1960s and 1970s, when over a million left to work abroad in Western Europe and North America. *Saudade* together with *fado* ('fate') music received official validation under the *Estado Novo* as a means of perpetuating a sense of group belonging and a collective identity that united Portuguese separated by time and distance. The emotional investment in *saudade* ideally paid financial dividends as well. Through fostering dreams of eventual return after making good, 'Portuguese political authorities were interested in making sure that the emigrants would actively transform their savings into remittances deposited in Portuguese banks, allowing the economy of the country to directly benefit ... In fact, the Portuguese economy from the 1960s to the present has depended upon [them]'.[245]

Just as the dictatorship's perpetual celebration of the 'Discoveries' and its associated maritime and literary heroes survived its overthrow, so too did *saudade, fado*, and the Portuguese diaspora remain essential aspects of Portuguese culture after the consolidation of democracy. If the sentiments and sounds of *saudade* initially appeared politically tainted after having been fervently espoused by a discredited *ancien régime*, they soon regained their paramount position in the late 1970s and 1980s.[246] By contrast, the cultural, economic, and political importance of the emigrant had never been in question. Not only did remittances remain critical for the economies of the nation and countless individual families alike. Just as importantly, insisting that the *Comunidades Portuguesas* made up of emigrants and their descendants abroad still belonged within the nation facilitated the emergence of a postcolonial

[244] Caroline B. Brettell, 'The Emigrant, the Nation, and the State in Nineteenth- and Twentieth-Century Portugal: An Anthropological Approach', *Portuguese Studies Review*, 2:2 (1993), 57, 59.

[245] João Leal, 'The Making of *Saudade*: National Identity and Ethnic Psychology in Portugal', in Ton Dekker, John Helsloot, and Carla Wijers (eds.), *Roots and Rituals: The Construction of Ethnic Identities* (Amsterdam, 2000), 270–1, 278. On *fado*'s cultural centrality, see Lila Ellen Gray, 'Memories of Empire, Mythologies of the Soul: *Fado* Performance and the Shaping of *Saudade*', *Ethnomusicology*, 51:1 (2007), 106–30.

[246] Leal, 'Making of *Saudade*', 278–9; Gray, 'Memories of Empire', 121.

Figure 8.3a–c 'Homenagem ao emigrante'/'Homage to the Emigrant': 1979
Portuguese postage stamp series designed by Lima de Freitas. Date of issue:
21 February 1979; Fundação Portuguesa das Comunicações/PFA, Image nos.
1415, and 1417.
Credit: Image reproductions authorized by CTT Correios de Portugal,
Sociedade Aberta.

'imagined community' capable of supplanting an ideology that the *Estado
Novo* regime had steadfastly proclaimed until its final days. Up until the 1974
revolution Portugal had construed itself as a geographically discontinuous,
'pluricontinental' nation extending well beyond its modest, southwest
European confines via the colonies it misleadingly termed 'overseas

402 Migrations and multiculturalisms in postcolonial Europe

provinces', as Chapter 5 discussed. With the shift to democracy and decolonization Portugal maintained its identity as a nation proud of transcending its borders – the difference being that it did so through its transnational diaspora rather than incorporating territories and peoples in Africa and Asia.

New nationality legislation initiated in 1975 and reinforced in 1981 consolidated this transition. It occurred in response to concerns about escalating migration from the former colonies together with Portugal's concerted overtures towards greater European integration. As previous chapters examined, before decolonization Portuguese citizenship had extended to include anyone born in Angola, Mozambique, Guinea, the Cape Verde Islands, and other 'overseas provinces' regardless of race – a key plank of the *Estado Novo*'s claim that Portugal was as much a multiracial as it was a pluricontinental nation. Laws passed in 1975 and 1981 retreated from the principle of *jus soli* (citizenship derived from place of birth) to one based upon *jus sanguinis* (citizenship via Portuguese ancestry). Ethnicity and descent became the main criteria, and the results were threefold. *Retornados* who hastily fled from ex-settler communities in Angola and Mozambique in the mid-1970s could be reintegrated within the nation on account of being either fully or partly of Portuguese ancestry, even if born in Africa and having one African parent; acquiring or regaining Portuguese nationality was made easier for those born abroad who were descended from Portuguese emigrants; and millions of Africans formerly eligible for citizenship on account of being born in territories once defined as part of Portugal retroactively became foreigners (or, if already resident in Portugal, immigrants), with restricted rights to migrate and settle after decolonization.[247] Nationality laws were further revised in 1994, but the emphasis upon *jus sanguinis* was retained. Until a new law came into effect in 2006 that veered back towards older *jus soli* traditions, Portuguese citizenship became harder to obtain for children of immigrants – including those born in Portugal.[248]

In sum, by the 1980s what Ana Paula Beja Horta describes as 'a conception of the nation as an imagined community of descent that transcended territorial boundaries' prevailed that prioritized the reincorporation of the 'Portuguese of the Diaspora', both those who had returned home and those still based abroad.[249] In looking forward to full integration within the European

---

[247] Ana Paula Beja Horta, *Contested Citizenship: Immigration Politics and Grassroots Migrants' Organization in Post-Colonial Portugal* (New York, 2004), 51, 55; Ricard Morén-Alegret, *Integration and Resistance: The Relation of Social Organisations, Global Capital, Governments and Immigration in Spain and Portugal* (Aldershot, 2002), 96–7.

[248] Maria Ioannis Baganha and Constança Urbano de Sousa, 'Portugal', in Bauböck *et al.* (eds.), *Acquisition and Loss of Nationality, Vol. 2*, 435–76 (especially 470–2); Howard, *Politics of Citizenship*, 87–90; José Manuel Sobral, 'Imigração e Concepções da Identidade Nacional em Portugal', in Barata, Pereira, and Carvalheiro (eds.), *Representações da Portugalidade*, 164.

[249] Horta, *Contested Citizenship*, 51; see also Brettell, 'The Emigrant, the Nation, and the State', 61.

Economic Community, Portugal asserted a European cultural and ethnic identity, thereby 'impos[ing] a future by alienating the past'[250] – that of an empire that had styled itself a 'multiracial nation'. Embracing the *Portuguese diaspora* thus went hand in hand with delegitimizing *ethnic minority diasporas within Portugal* whose grounds for belonging seemed more in tune with colonial than postcolonial times.

Once European integration was an established fact in the 1990s, however, Portugal stepped up attempts to forge stronger international relations beyond Europe with Portuguese-speaking nations. Efforts came to fruition in 1996 with the establishment of the *Comunidade dos Países de Língua Portuguesa* (CPLP), the Community of Portuguese Language Countries. Reconnecting with former colonies ranging from long-independent Brazil to recently-decolonized Cape Verde, Guinea-Bissau, São Tomé and Príncipe, Angola, and Mozambique (with East Timor joining in 2002) was done with a view to closer diplomatic, economic, and cultural ties and greater multilateral cooperation. The CPLP's rationale stemmed from the shared historical and cultural heritage that manifested itself in a common language and had allegedly generated a lasting 'community of affection', but these claims left it open to accusations of neo-colonial intentions and an amnesia about the brutal realities of colonialism. To its detractors and sceptics inside and outside Portugal, the Community represented a throwback to the hypocritical ideals of an egalitarian, non-racist lusotropicalism that had flourished under the *Estado Novo* from the 1950s to 1974, now revived under the guise of Lusophone commonality (*lusofonia*).

The coming years saw the CPLP widely condemned as a largely superficial and ineffectual project, one hampered not least by retrograde colonial-era ideological shackles and ambiguities. Nevertheless, it testified to the continued importance of former colonies to Portugal's identity within postcolonial Europe. Initiatives like the CPLP were both a counterpoint to Portugal's Europeanization and a form of compensation. As a poor nation only recently made a member, Portugal had never been a leading player within the EU upon which it depended enormously for loans and financing for desperately-needed development projects. Its relative weight diminished further still in the 2000s with the EU's enlargement into Eastern Europe. In some eyes, the CPLP served 'the dual purpose of guaranteeing some singularity to a country that feels increasingly diluted in Europe and "invaded" by Spain, whilst attempting to cement old self-assur[ed] notions, like "the unique ability to interplay with other cultures", or the "non-racist character" of the Portuguese people'.[251]

---

[250] Horta, *Contested Citizenship*, 21; see also 268–9.

[251] Luís António Santos, 'Portugal and the CPLP: Heightened Expectations, Unfounded Disillusions', in Stewart Lloyd-Jones and António Costa Pinto (eds.), *The Last Empire: Thirty Years of Portuguese Decolonization* (Bristol, 2003), 75. For critical views of the CPLP and the deployment of *lusofonia* discourses, see Michel Cahen, 'Des caravelles pour

* * *

Portugal's national self-image in the 1990s and 2000s thus has been uneasily split between its assertively European geographical, ethnic, and cultural dimensions and its resurgent idealized identification with a multi-ethnic Lusophone community and culture spread across continents. This dichotomy accounts for many of the tensions and contradictions pervading Portugal's approach towards its resident postcolonial immigrant and immigrant-descended ethnic minority populations. Contemporary versions of lusotropical myths of mid-twentieth-century vintage survive in the routine assertion that Portugal is categorically a non-racist – and in fact anti-racist – society that overwhelmingly accepts diversity and hybridity.[252]

So strong was this belief that the state acted belatedly in developing and implementing multicultural policies and forming a coherent response to racist incidents that, by definition, ran counter to the dominant narrative of racial and cultural accommodation. Legislation to establish a Multicultural Education Programmes Coordination Bureau, for instance, was introduced as late as 1991. The preface to the 1991 act reveals how deeply embedded notions of tolerance as a national trait rooted in centuries-old colonial traditions remained:

Portuguese culture, distinguished for its universalism and its awareness thereof and for its long links with other cultures which, over the centuries, have made it welcome diversity, comprehend differences and great particularity with open arms, is an open and varied culture enriched by the diffusion of a people which has sought overseas a further dimension to its identity. Today, Portugal is proud to be the chance product of a mysterious alchemy which found in the sea, that great unknown, its ideal medium and its path to adventure.[253]

Political pronouncements that grudgingly admitted the reality of racism found it difficult to abandon the cherished mythology of tolerance as the norm. '*Even in our society*', the 1991 document continued, 'displays of intolerance are

le futur?: Discours politique et idéologie dans l'"institutionnalisation" de la Communauté des pays de langue portuguaise', *Lusotopie*, 1997, 391–433; Alfredo Margarido, *A Lusofonia e os Lusófonos: Novos Mitos Portugueses* (Lisbon, 2000); R. Timothy Sieber, 'Composing Lusophonia: Multiculturalism and National Identity in Lisbon's 1998 Musical Scene', *Diaspora*, 11:2 (2002), 164–7, 181–2.

[252] Miguel Vale de Almeida, *An Earth-Coloured Sea: 'Race', Culture, and the Politics of Identity in the Postcolonial Portuguese-Speaking World* (New York, 2004), 45–6; Marta Araújo, 'The Colour That Dares Not Speak Its Name: Schooling and "The Myth of Portuguese Anti-Racism"', paper presented at the International Conference on 'Equality and Social Inclusion in the 21st Century: Developing Alternatives', Belfast, 1–3 February 2006; Jorge Vala, Diniz Lopes, and Marcus Lima, 'Black Immigrants in Portugal: Luso-Tropicalism and Prejudice', *Journal of Social Issues*, 64:2 (2008), 287–302.

[253] Ministério da Educação, 'Despacho normativo 6391, DR no. 60, 13 de Março 1991' (Criação do Secretariado Coordenador dos Programas de Educação Multicultural), cited and translated by Carlos Manuel and Neves Cardoso, 'The Colonialist View of the African-Origin "Other" in Portuguese Society and Its Education System', *Race, Ethnicity and Education*, 1:2 (1998), 198.

emerging, as are cases of physical and psychological violence directed at ethnic minorities, the result of the proliferation of simplistic doctrines and extremist groups which must be strenuously combated'.[254]

Complacency about the position of minorities and a reluctance to admit that racism and discrimination not only existed but demanded a robust response extended in part from the reconfiguration of the nation's political landscape after 1974. Once freed from an authoritarian dictatorship, most Portuguese resoundingly rejected new forms of extremist, neo-fascist politics. In late 1970s and 1980s Portugal, no electorally significant right-wing or far-right party emerged dedicated to fomenting public xenophobia and racism that was in any way analogous to France's *Front National* or to broadly comparable movements in the other countries considered earlier. Considerable consensus about immigrants and minorities reigned across the political spectrum, and indeed within public opinion more broadly.[255] This not only bolstered common-sense understandings about Portuguese tolerance as the laudable norm, but provoked fraught discussions at moments of crisis when racism became impossible to ignore.

Widely-held Portuguese convictions about race were subjected to new challenges in the 1990s. Over the course of the decade, Portugal gradually implemented anti-discrimination and multicultural educational and cultural policies, though often with little enthusiasm on account of the conviction that such measures were largely unnecessary.[256] Militant racism and acts of physical violence against ethnic minorities remained relatively rare but concerns that the situation was worsening grew stronger, particularly after a racial attack occurring in the centre of Lisbon in 1995 – significantly, on 10 June, the Day of Portugal, Camões, and the Portuguese Communities. Alcindo Monteiro, a man of Cape Verdean origin who had long held Portuguese nationality, died after being stabbed by a skinhead gang, leading to violent acts of retaliation on the streets followed by intense criticism of the police for their delayed response.

The 10 June tragedy had tremendous repercussions, prompting a mass antiracist march alongside protracted national soul-searching about Portugal's much-vaunted convention of tolerance. Political leaders uniformly condemned

---

[254] Ibid., 198–9; emphasis added.

[255] António Costa Pinto, 'The Radical Right in Contemporary Portugal', in Luciano Cheles, Ronnie Ferguson, and Micalina Vaughan (eds.), *The Far Right in Western and Eastern Europe*, 2nd edn. (London, 1995), 108–28; António Costa Pinto, 'Dealing with the Legacy of Authoritarianism: Political Purges and Radical Right Movements in Portugal's Transition to Democracy, 1974-1980s', in Stein Ugelvik Larsen (ed.), *Modern Europe after Fascism, 1943–1980s*, Vol. II (Boulder, 1998), 1679–718; David Corkill and Martin Eaton, 'Multicultural Insertions in a Small Economy: Portugal's Immigrant Communities', *South European Society and Politics*, 3:3 (1998), 160; Morén-Alegret, *Integration and Resistance*, 103.

[256] Luís Batalha, *The Cape Verdean Diaspora in Portugal: Colonial Subjects in a Postcolonial World* (Lanham, MD, 2004), 196–8; Kesha Fikes, *Managing African Portugal: The Citizen-Migrant Distinction* (Durham, 2009), 39, 49–53; Horta, *Contested Citizenship*, 56–8, 270.

Monteiro's death and organized a state-financed funeral that was widely attended by leading public dignitaries, including President Mário Soares. Like others, however, Soares denounced Monteiro's killers by stressing that their actions deviated from Portugal's tradition of 'respect' for other races. While some Portuguese argued that 10 June 1995 should serve as a sorely-needed wakeup call to the bankruptcy of hypocritical lusotropical ideals, most preferred the more comforting familiar interpretations. Resoundingly deplored though it was, Monteiro's fate was more commonly viewed through the prism of the alleged 'norm', that of racial harmony and acceptance, to which it stood as a contemptible exception.[257] Skinhead racism, moreover, was effectively dismissed as 'non-Portuguese', an example of '*males importados*' ('imported evils') allegedly more characteristic of other European nations' racist tendencies that had found their way across the border than a home-grown phenomenon.[258]

Rhetorically banishing racism to Portugal's disreputable social margins by acknowledging only its most overt and incontestable forms enabled mainstream attitudes and behaviour to emerge largely unscathed and resiliently intact. Numerous studies have revealed that while most white Portuguese publicly insist they are not racist, everyday prejudices along with subtle (and not-so-subtle) racial ideas abound. Lusotropical convictions indeed remain alive and well in the early twenty-first century but still run parallel with covert forms of racial prejudice and derogatory opinions, sometimes expressed openly, about minorities and particularly 'blacks'.[259]

A closer look at the schooling experiences of ethnic minority children and adolescents highlights the limited impact of multicultural education policies and the extent to which the supposed lack of racism in Portugal fails to correspond with daily realities for many young people of African descent. Research at schools in Lisbon and Porto undertaken by Marta Araújo since 2003 suggests that state education policies stressing the need to respect cultural diversity often do little to curb discrimination based on pupils' appearance and understandings of 'racial' characteristics common among both white teachers and students. 'Black' children are regularly the target for racist name-calling and other forms of bullying. Comments such as 'Black people smile like monkeys' came as no surprise to pupils who, in some instances, had become

[257] F.L. Machado, 'Des étrangers moins étrangers que d'autres?: La régulation politico-institutionnelle de l'immigration au Portugal', in Évelyne Ritaine (ed.), *L'Europe du Sud face à l'immigration: Politique de l'Étranger* (Paris, 2005), 119–22; Corkill and Eaton, 'Multicultural Insertions', 160.
[258] Isabel Ferin Cunha, 'Nós e os otros artigos de opinião da imprensa portuguesa', *Lusotopie* (1997), 455.
[259] Maria I. Baganha, José Carlos Marques, and Graça Fonseca, *Is An Ethclass Emerging in Europe?: The Portuguese Case* (Lisbon, 2000), 55–7; Vala, Lopes, and Lima, 'Black Immigrants'.

so accustomed to such forms of abuse that one girl reported, 'They call me nigger and that's all'. In many cases teachers appear to do little to challenge such episodes, preferring to push them under the carpet by recasting them entirely. One teacher who recounted her discussion with a girl who had been hit and called *Preta* by a white classmate responded by equating this historically pejorative racial term with *Negra*, which in Portuguese refers to a dark or black colour. 'You can't interpret them calling you Black (*Preta*) as an insult, because the colour of your skin is dark (*Negra*) and you have to recognise that with pride.'[260] Anti-racist myths are thereby upheld despite voluminous evidence to the contrary.

Insistence that racism was non-Portuguese, however, did not preclude an overt focus on cultural difference, whether for the purposes of celebration or condemnation. When schools finally introduced multicultural education policies in the 1990s, Portugal (like other European countries in whose footsteps it followed) approached cultural diversity in ways more likely to reinforce than fight ethnic stereotypes. 'Benevolent multiculturalism' in the classroom often relied upon pre-existing understandings linking African-descended peoples to 'traditional' forms of imported music and dance, while doing little to address discrimination, socio-economic inequality, and racism.[261] The examples of diversity granted a qualified public endorsement (yet still widely, if often covertly, imagined as inferior) at school were commonly those brought from pupils' parents' lands of origin. By contrast, new forms of cultural specificity that evolved in Portugal within the second generation itself were more often than not condemned as suspect – a sign that they had 'failed' to integrate.

Portuguese representations of immigrant-descended youth often saw them as devoid of any virtues their parents may have possessed, such as a capacity for hard work. Instead, so-called '*jovens de origem africana*' ('youths of African origin') remained widely identified in the media and wider public opinion as a social problem – lazy and idle, scholastic underachievers, unemployed, poor, prone to delinquency and urban criminality, and linked with drugs.[262] Although anxieties about Islam, and Islamic 'extremism', among the second generation are nowhere near as widespread in Portugal as in other countries examined earlier, in other respects public concerns revolve around similar forms of alleged misbehaviour and cultural marginality.[263] Just as violent racism was imaginatively cordoned off from the 'tolerant' Portuguese majority, so too were

[260] Araújo, 'Colour', 3, 7–8, 14, 17.
[261] Batalha, *Cape Verdean Diaspora*, 218; Araújo, 'Colour', 7–8.
[262] Machado, 'Des étrangers moins étrangers que d'autres?', 133; Batalha, *Cape Verdean Diaspora*, 151, 189, 212; Horta, *Contested Citizenship*, 109.
[263] Portugal's contemporary and historical encounters with Islam and Muslims differ markedly from those of the other nations considered here. Still predominantly Roman Catholic today and with the ideological link between Portugueseness and Catholicism augmented under the *Estado Novo*, Portugal also experienced over seven centuries of Muslim occupation between

youth descended from African immigrants repeatedly depicted as 'foreign' (like their parents) and non-Portuguese in political discussions and the media – regardless of birthplace (often in Portugal), length of residence in Portugal (if not since birth, then usually since early childhood), or actual nationality (often Portuguese). 'The boundary based on "race" is still quite active and is pushing black Cape Verdean youth into the category of *preto* or *africano*, terms which are used by the mainstream as synonyms', Luís Batalha notes – a situation equally applicable to those whose families came from Angola or elsewhere in former Portuguese Africa and who were understood as falling outside the Portuguese 'community' after decolonization.[264]

* * *

Public marginalization of 'black' youth extends not simply from racialization that renders them 'other'. In Portugal as elsewhere, conceptions of ethnicity also derive from understandings about class and urban space. Extensive socio-economic deprivation among postcolonial minorities accounts for their over-representation in poor neighbourhoods on the urban periphery where those who formerly lived in shantytowns were rehoused throughout the 1990s. Within housing estates habitually stigmatized in public discourse, ethnically-diverse communities that have developed hybrid transnational cultures arose that are analogous to those in France's *banlieues* and multi-ethnic neighbourhoods in other postcolonial European nations. Commonly portrayed in the media as if everyone living there was exclusively, homogeneously, and ever-problematically 'black' or 'African', in reality their residents claim origins in many African countries; moreover, they are also home to substantial white working-class populations.[265]

United by socio-economic exclusion, limited prospects, spatial segregation, and the experience of racial discrimination in Portugal, African-descended youth born or brought up in Portugal converged across ethnic lines far more habitually than their parents, whose primary identification was more likely to be Cape Verdean, Mozambican, Angolan, or another country of origin. Youth commonly came together as 'black', effectively appropriating wider tendencies

---

the eighth and fourteenth centuries. As AbdoolKarim Vakil notes, a powerful 'narrative of national history as *Reconquista* [Reconquest]' meant that 'the making of Portugal' entailed 'the erasure of Islam'. Its Muslim population remains relatively small, estimated at under 40,000 (less than 0.5 per cent of its total population) in the early twenty-first century. Perhaps in consequence, in the wake of 11 September 2001 Portugal did not experience a rise of Islamophobia comparable to other European nations. See AbdoolKarim Vakil, 'Muslims in Portugal: History, Historiography, Citizenship', *Euroclio Bulletin*, 18 (2003), 16 (downloaded from www.euroclio.edu on 24 February 2012); Nina Clara Tiesler, 'Novidades no terreno: muçulmanos na Europa e o caso português', *Análise Social*, 39:173 (2005), 827–49.

[264] Batalha, *Cape Verdean Diaspora*, 196.

[265] Maria Lucinda Fonseca, 'Immigration and Spatial Change: The Lisbon Experience', *Studi Emigrazione/Migration Studies*, 39:145 (2002), 62–7; Horta, *Contested Citizenship*, 147–8.

to flatten differences among them and turning them to their own positive purposes, in the process creating new forms of identity in diaspora. New ethnicities took shape that are situational and locally-based, revolving around identities and a sense of belonging rooted in their neighbourhoods that encompass white and black youth alike.[266] They find expression through multi-ethnic peer groups and friendship networks, taking cultural form through shared tastes in fashion, style, and particularly music.

Syncretic youth cultures strongly shaped by an African-descended second generation of diverse backgrounds but also readily making space for local white peers demonstrate how age, shared class disadvantages, and daily proximity work to create distinct geographical affiliations and expressive cultures. Rap and hip hop's ubiquity and contextual specificity exemplify how neighbourhood-level interactions draw upon national and global cultures, combine them anew, and adapt them to local purposes. Like multi-ethnic youth cultures in other nations examined earlier, contemporary Portuguese variants involve mingling African-American musical genres and cultural messages with other cross-ethnic, postcolonial cultures specific to a European setting that are distinct, but not entirely divorced from, participants' own heritage. A cosmopolitan, transnational, 'black' identity that accommodated white urban social counterparts was the result, manifesting itself in a generationally-specific musical, linguistic, and stylistic idiom.[267] Cultural borrowings across ethnic lines were as standard in rap lyrics and rhythms as they were in everyday sociability. English-language (particularly African-American) words and slang mingled with Portuguese, Angolan, Cape Verdean, and other vocabulary to create a form of creole that could only have emerged in Lisbon's socially marginal and racialized *bairros* (districts). Rappers from the Lisbon metropolitan area correspondingly integrated musical genres from Cape Verde and elsewhere into their own productions.[268]

Rap offered disadvantaged urban youth a means to protest against racism, social rejection, and the stigma of living in 'bad neighbourhoods' and to assert

[266] António Concorda Contador, 'Consciência de geração e etnicidade: de segunda geração aos novos luso-africanos', *Sociologia, Problemas e Práticas*, 26 (1998), 57–83; Fikes, *Managing African Portugal*, 47–8, 87, 144, 151; Dora Possidónio, 'The Descendants of Angolans and Luso-Angolans in the Lisbon Metropolitan Area: Aspects of Their Integration', *Finisterra*, 39:77 (2004), 50–4.

[267] Teresa Fradique, *Fixar o Movimento: Representações da Música RAP em Portugal* (Lisbon, 2003), 64, 103, 114–16, 133; Batalha, *Cape Verdean Diaspora*, 214–18; Timothy Sieber, 'Popular Music and Cultural Identity in the Cape Verdean Post-Colonial Diaspora', *Etnográfica*, 9:1 (2005), 132, 137. *Rapública* (Sony Music, 1994) was a definitive compilation of tracks by leading Portuguese-based musicians reflecting the rap scene that had emerged by the mid 1990s.

[268] Neusa Maria Mendes de Gusmão, *Os Filhos de África em Portugal: Antropologia, Multiculturalidade e Educação* (Lisbon, 2004), 154, 196–7 (alongside chs. 3 and 4 more generally).

pride in both their families' ethnic heritage and in their own lives and cultural choices. As Otávio Raposo's research highlights, rap became a vehicle for expressing a critical distance from dominant constructions of Portuguese national identity and 'community' that worked to exclude those devalued as *pretos*.[269] Theirs was not the same 'imagined community' of the Portuguese nation as that celebrated on 10 June within Portugal and amongst its far-flung emigrant offspring who helped make up the composite *Comunidades Portuguesas* extending from descent. Nor was it akin to the CPLP, the Community of Portuguese Language Countries, whose sense of 'community' (such that it was) stemmed from shared Lusophone traditions rooted in colonialism. Rather, theirs was a multicultural, multi-ethnic 'affective community' that was simultaneously subnational (revolving around neighbourhood alliances and loyalties) and supranational (looking outwards towards African, African-American, Afro-Caribbean, and other diasporic African cultural formations) but which remained contingent upon Portuguese life experiences.[270] To quote Chullage, a Lisbon-based rapper who achieved prominence in the early 2000s, this cultural space was not that of Portugal but rather 'Pretugal' – one reflecting yet also challenging pervasive societal rejection (in which *pretos* were tacitly equated with *africanos* and not envisioned as legitimately part of Portugal) via dynamic self-affirmation.[271]

Much more than simply a resistant and oppositional form of affiliation, 'Pretugal' serves as an invitation to rethink dominant notions of what Portugal and Portuguese culture are – and who the Portuguese are – so that lusotropicalism might finally be laid to rest and ancestry-based conceptions of nationality surpassed. 'Pretugal' signals a hybrid Portuguese reality shaped by a convergence of global and local cultures and identities, *an actually existing cultural hybridity* quite distinct from idealized versions that fuelled self-congratulatory lusotropicalist assertions that a carefree tolerance of mixing, difference, and multiculturalism was a common Portuguese trait. Critiques of durable lusotropicalist ideas by Timothy Sieber and Miguel Vale de Almeida argue that Portuguese celebrations of hybridity overwhelmingly have treated it as something that Portugal exported, not something defining what Portugal inherently was. 'The Portuguese nation … has seldom been described as miscegenated and *mestiça* itself', Almeida notes. 'In the discourses of national identity, emphasis has been placed on what the Portuguese have given to others –

---

[269] Otávio Raposo, "'Heart There and Body Here in Pretugal": In Between Mestizagem and the Affirmation of Blackness', *BUALA: African Contemporary Literature*, 21 October 2010, downloaded from www.buala.org on 5 January 2012.

[270] Ibid.; on 'affective communities', see especially Leela Gandhi, *Affective Communities: Anticolonial Thought, Fin-de-siècle Radicalism, and the Politics of Friendship* (Durham, 2006).

[271] Raposo, "'Heart There'"; Chullage, 'Pretugal', *Rapensar: Passado Presente Futuro* (2004).

a gift of "blood" and culture – not on what they have received from others.' Once 'the others are among us' – 'others' from regions historically marked by the impact of Portuguese colonial culture – they were not seen primarily in terms of their similarity but rather in terms of their difference. Within Portugal, 'others' retained a 'cultural authenticity [that] places them outside nationality, although they are allowed to enjoy multiculturalism'.[272] This tendency, Sieber suggests, resembled 'older lusotropicalist ideas that celebrated miscegenation and hybridity in the colonies, while preserving essentialist and racialized conceptions of Portuguese "at home," as pure, superior, and homogeneous'.[273]

'Pretugal' allows a different story to be told, one of deeply-embedded inward flows of peoples and cultures alongside outward migrations. This alternative narrative foregrounds heterogeneity as integral within Portugal and Portuguese culture, and not simply in recent decades as a late colonial or postcolonial novelty. It was present long before African-descended youth and their white friends and neighbours in Portuguese cities remade rap and hip hop in response to their own daily lives and added new cultural layers to musical inspirations from the United States and elsewhere. It also pre-dated the arrival of African migrants from Portugal's erstwhile 'overseas provinces' who bought Cape Verdean musical styles like *morna* with them when they made the journey in the mid-late twentieth century. Diversity and cultural fusions through imported influences were nothing new: they lay at the very heart of Portugal's invented national traditions, and never more strongly than in *fado* songs.

Since the 1990s, new scholarship has succeeded in rewriting *fado*'s history and challenging cherished myths about its roots and 'Portugueseness'. Common wisdom long venerated *fado* as music that dated from the time of the 'Discoveries', owing its origins and melancholy to early modern Portuguese sailors longing for home and its survival to its ability to express the emotions of Portugal's homesick emigrants throughout the twentieth century. *Fado* thus became as emblematic of traditions emphasizing Portugal's maritime pioneers and the millions of emigrants who followed them as it was of pride in the circulation of Portuguese culture across continents, where it inspired allegedly derivative musical genres, like *morna*, in the Cape Verde Islands. Musicologists now position *fado* as far more modern, emerging as part of Portuguese popular culture only between the 1820s and 1850s. Moreover, they insist *fado* to be a synthetic music with origins in Afro-Brazilian culture that was subsequently imported to Portugal – a product of triangular cultural convergences in which the Portuguese-dominated slave trade from Angola to Brazil was central – rather than exported as a native Portuguese style across Lusophone arenas.[274]

---

[272] Almeida, *Earth-Colored Sea*, 66, 80.   [273] Sieber, 'Composing Lusophonia', 180.

[274] Kimberly DaCosta Holton, 'Fado Historiography: Old Myths and New Frontiers', *Portuguese Cultural Studies*, 0 (Winter 2006), 1–17; Gray, 'Memories of Empire'; José Ramos Tinhorão, *Fado: Dança do Brasil, Cantar de Lisboa: O Fim de um Mito* (Lisbon, 1994).

Reconceiving an aspect of Portuguese identity as symbolically central as *fado* as a hybrid, cross-cultural import, not an indigenous and 'pure' national artefact, reveals how much it has in common with cultural forms seen as 'other', like *morna*.[275] Both genres represent dynamic fusions marked by multiple histories of migration to as much as from Portugal, not to mention other journeys and relocations to Brazil, North America, and other European countries. Not simply emblematic of the emotions of Portuguese emigrants and those parted from them, *fado* can be seen in terms of its sonic and textual resemblance to Cape Verdean *morna* songs, which revolve around strikingly similar themes – departures to and returns from overseas, undertaken out of economic necessity; the sea itself; longing and sadness; hope and despair – in short, *saudade*. Bound together through the shared traditions of migration that inspired them, *fado* and *morna* confound the distinction between 'Portuguese' and 'Cape Verdean other'. Instead, their analogous qualities help bridge an artificial divide by revealing convergences and a two-way traffic between Portugal's diasporas at home and away.

* * *

Conclusion: national dynamism and defensiveness

In the decades since the end of overseas empires, Western European cultures have never been as globalized and hybrid, with the leading importers of diversity being ethnic minority groups descended from colonized populations once 'empires struck back' in former metropoles. Ever fluid rather than perennially frozen, cultures have recurrently crossed state and ethnic lines and remade individual and group identities as well as places. Although historians can easily identify precedents in earlier eras, anthropologists have argued that the increased frequency and speed of global mobility and communications in the late twentieth century had a uniquely corrosive effect upon supposedly 'natural' associations linking distinct localities with particular 'native' ethnic groups and cultures. Led by Arjun Appadurai, James Clifford, Akhil Gupta, and James Ferguson, scholars describe this phenomenon as 'deterritorialization', a process involving uprootings and the cross-border traffic of people together with ideas, beliefs, practices, capital, and commodities. 'Reterritorialization' has been its constant companion: once transferred to other locations, the peripatetic and migratory transformed not only themselves but also their new surroundings and the peoples amongst whom they settled.[276]

---

[275] Sieber, 'Popular Music', 141–3.

[276] Arjun Appadurai, *Modernity at Large: Cultural Dimensions of Globalization* (Minneapolis, 1996), see especially 37–40, 48–9; James Clifford, *The Predicament of Culture* (Cambridge, MA, 1988), 338; James Clifford, 'Traveling Cultures', in *Routes: Travel and Translation in the*

Within European nations where ethnicities, cultures, and spaces have been continually remade by a combination of supra- and subnational forces, profound tensions divide those at the vanguard who are spearheading this dynamic process – or simply responding positively to it – from those seeking to protect 'authentic' national cultures (no matter how imaginary) from change (no matter how inevitable).[277] In this context, as Gupta and Ferguson have noted, it is ironic if unsurprising 'that as actual places and localities become ever more blurred and indeterminate, *ideas* of culturally and ethnically distinct places become perhaps even more salient'.[278] Appadurai suggests that authenticity, which 'measures the degree to which something is more or less what it *ought* to be', is a criterion likely to 'emerge just after its subject matter has been significantly transformed'.[279] So it has proven in the countries explored here, where anxious and energetic efforts to define and defend allegedly genuine Frenchness, Britishness, Dutchness, and other composite qualities supposedly characteristic of their 'native' majorities (in contrast to the minority cultures provoking concern) have proven as recurrent and as they have inconclusive and lacking in consensus, even in nations far less internally divided than Belgium.[280] National myths such as tolerance of diversity or secularism have been periodically resurrected in efforts to characterize and extol national and often transnational Western European values, despite the ways in which they regularly fail to depict the reality of life in postcolonial Europe for many individuals and groups. Since the 1980s, this has been most glaringly apparent in Europe's encounters with Islam, both in its transnational forms and in its local and everyday manifestations as Europe grapples with its own Muslim minorities.

Almost exactly three decades after Jean Raspail asked 'will we still be French in thirty years' time?' in 1985, Paris experienced several days of terrorist violence perpetrated by young French Muslim men in January 2015. Having grown up in the disadvantaged *banlieues* and become radicalized via global events and jihadist movements, notably Al-Qaeda and Islamic State, two attacked the editorial offices of the satirical magazine *Charlie Hebdo*, killing

---

Late Twentieth Century (Cambridge, MA, 1997), 17–46; Akhil Gupta and James Ferguson, 'Beyond "Culture": Space, Identity, and the Politics of Difference', in Inda and Rosaldo (eds.), *Anthropology of Globalization*, 65–80. For an excellent overview, see Jonathan Xavier Inda and Renato Rosaldo, 'Introduction: A World in Motion', in Inda and Rosaldo (eds.), *Anthropology of Globalization*, 1–34.

[277] Inda and Rosaldo, 'Introduction', 21; Appadurai, *Modernity at Large*, 9, 161; Hall, 'What Is This "Black"', 468.

[278] Gupta and Ferguson, 'Beyond "Culture"', 69.

[279] Arjun Appadurai, 'On Culinary Authenticity', *Anthropology Today*, 2:4 (1986), 25.

[280] Geschiere, *Perils*, 154; 'Full Text of Gordon Brown's Speech', *Guardian*, 27 February 2007; 'Cameron: Stop Being Bashful about Britishness', www.bbc.co.uk/news/uk-27853591, 15 June 2014, acessed 19 January 2015; Pierre Nora, 'Lettre ouverte à Frédéric Mitterrand sur la Maison de l'histoire de France', *Le Monde*, 11 November 2010.

many of its staff together with several policemen (including one who was Muslim). They selected their target on account of *Charlie Hebdo*'s provocative portrayal of the Prophet Muhammad in cartoons that many Muslims deemed deeply offensive. In a separate incident, another killer singled out Jews and took hostages at a kosher supermarket, resulting in several more deaths. As France and its neighbours mourned the victims and condemned terrorist acts, some struggled to make sense of the tragedy and tried to separate the inexcusable criminal actions of several individuals from the Muslim majority who resoundingly condemned them. Others retreated into what had long since become familiar territory by envisioning Islam as a monolith that posed an inherent danger to French and broader Western lives and traditions, namely secularism and freedom of expression, including the freedom to insult and cause deliberate offense. France's deeply-entrenched unwillingness to countenance public expressions of cultural distinctiveness and religious identity had long rendered it difficult to develop a sensitive approach to difference, and the January tragedies made it highly unlikely that the road ahead would be any smoother. While many in France argued that integration was the solution, the *Front National* (now led by Jean-Marie Le Pen's daughter Marine) stepped up its longstanding exclusionary agenda.

In the face of the realities of hybridity, perpetual change, and difference, defences of purported national 'authenticity' and 'traditions' continue unabated. New Jeremiahs eagerly present themselves, ever ready to join the lengthening parade of figures like Raspail in bemoaning threats to France and to 'being French'.[281] Fears and pessimism about the status and security of national cultures in the wake of empire, postcolonial migration, and a host of other factors have in fact become as traditional and authentic to France and its postcolonial European counterparts alike as the aspects of their identities deemed so fragile. With the demands that living with diversity makes on all parties concerned having by no means been reconciled, the next chapter turns to the other unfinished history within today's multicultural societies: the fraught process of remembering and forgetting empires in Europe after decolonization, a process in which former colonizers and the formerly colonized have both played important roles.

---

[281] Michel Houellebecq counts as one of a number of prominent voices.

Part III

Memories, legacies, and further directions

9   Remembering and forgetting empires

Introduction

In its exhibit entitled *Mwana Kitoko – Beautiful White Man*, the Belgian Pavilion at the 2001 Venice Biennale staged ten new paintings by Luc Tuymans, one of Europe's leading contemporary artists. At the British Pavilion two years before, Chris Ofili's *Union Black* (discussed in the previous chapter) had engaged with British national symbols and a transnational black culture reflecting the multicultural aftermath of empire; Tuymans' contribution to the next Biennale in turn probed his own country's deeply problematic colonial and decolonization history itself. His *Mwana Kitoko* series challenged many long-standing Belgian understandings and fantasies about the Congo, starting with those that had taken centre stage when King Baudouin toured the colony in 1955 (see Chapter 4). Tuymans excavated André Cauvin's state-approved *Bwana Kitoko* documentary project produced in commemoration of the king's visit, contesting its assumptions at the most fundamental level by renaming it. In replacing 'Bwana Kitoko' ('noble lord') with 'Mwana Kitoko' ('beautiful boy'), Tuymans reinstated a Congolese way of describing Baudouin in 1955 that the colonial authorities, finding it overly irreverent, had modified at the time. Adding 'white man' underscored the role of race in the king's emergent persona as a twenty-five-year-old who had recently ascended the throne in divisive circumstances after Belgium emerged from the trauma of Nazi wartime occupation.

Throughout his series, Tuymans subjected still-dominant Belgian narratives and memories of the Congo to critical scrutiny, not least by confronting the less-than-'beautiful' part that the 'white man' (including King Baudouin himself) played in Central African history.[1] Three paintings recast Cauvin's film footage from the 1955 tour, respectively depicting Baudouin's majestic descent

---

[1] Detailed analyses of Tuymans' trajectory as an artist and his *Mwana Kitoko* paintings include Robert Storr, Philippe Pirotte, and Jan Hoet, *Luc Tuymans: Mwana Kitoko (Beautiful White Man)* (Gent, 2001), particularly Philippe Pirotte's chapter, 'Mwana Kitoko (Beautiful White Man)', 81–115; Madeleine Grynsztejn and Helen Molesworth (eds.), *Luc Tuymans* (New York, 2009), especially 156–71; Ulrich Loock *et al.*, *Luc Tuymans* (London, 2003). Tuymans discussed his subject matter and approach to it in Luc Tuymans, *Doué pour la peinture: Conversations avec Jean-Paul Jungo* (Geneva, 2006), 21–3, 66–8.

Figure 9.1 Luc Tuymans, *Mwana Kitoko* (2000), depicting King Baudouin's descent from his aircraft at the start of his tour of the Belgian Congo in 1955. Credit: Studio Luc Tuymans, Antwerp, Belgium.

from his aircraft, his trip into Léopoldville by motorcade (portrayed by featuring African spectators watching the procession from the upper-floor window of a building), and the leopard skin laid down for him when he reached his destination (an image showing African hands dutifully straightening the skin together with the king's feet after walking across it). Tuymans set out to represent the rituals and pageantry of power while emphasizing its shadowy and unsettling nature – a power replete with clearly recognizable ceremonial trappings and scripted performances but in which the individuals involved lack clear facial features, or even faces. Baudouin's sunglasses and blurred physiognomy render him an impersonal, shielded figure whose aloof authority is conveyed by a stiff white military uniform and sword, while the out-of-focus depiction of the requisite African onlookers viewing his procession makes their actual response to the royal arrival impossible to decipher.

Four paintings then move forward to decisive figures and events surrounding the Congo's independence in 1960 and 1961: a portrait of Patrice Lumumba, as vital, expressive, and instantly recognizable as the African nationalist icon he was (and remains) as the Belgian King is obscure, impassive, and anonymized, followed by three that look obliquely at Lumumba's murder orchestrated soon after independence. One features ominous black cars that carried him by night to a remote location, where he and two of his political allies were shot against a tree; another shows Moïse Tshombe and his Katangan affiliates, as shadowy and shady as King Baudouin, plotting and conspiring against Lumumba; and the third, *Chalk*, being an image of hands encased in black gloves, each holding out a small white object. *Chalk* obliquely alluded to a story circulated decades after Lumumba's assassination by one of the Belgian police officers present at the murder, who claimed to have taken away two of Lumumba's teeth as trophies when the rest of his corpse was dissolved in a bath of acid.[2]

Tuymans' series concluded with *The Mission*, an austere building with a large cross standing before it showing one of the institutional mainstays of Belgium's heavily Catholic colonial agenda, followed by two paintings that returned back to present-day postcolonial Belgium. *Sculpture* featured an antique statue of an African man, portrayed as primitive, that Tuymans spotted in a restaurant in his home town of Antwerp.[3] Last of all came *Diorama*, a faint image of a stuffed rhinoceros still on view behind glass at the Royal Museum

---

[2] Gauthier de Villers, 'Histoire, justice et politique: À propos de la commission d'enquête sur l'assassinat de Patrice Lumumba, instituée par la Chambre belge des représentants', *Cahiers d'Études africaines*, XLIV:1–2 (2004), 197; Ludo De Witte, *The Assassination of Lumumba*, translated by Ann Wright and Renée Fenby (London, 2001), 141–2.

[3] Tuymans subsequently reflected in an interview how this Flemish port city that had long connected Belgium and colonial Africa as the point of ships' arrival and departure (and still owed its fortunes to international trade and flows of foreign capital) had paradoxically become a stronghold of the xenophobic far-right Flemish nationalist party, the *Vlaams Blok*. Tuymans, *Doué pour la peinture*, 23, 67–8.

Figure 9.2 Luc Tuymans, *Lumumba* (2000).
Credit: Studio Luc Tuymans, Antwerp, Belgium.

Figure 9.3 Luc Tuymans, *Sculpture* (2000).
Credit: Studio Luc Tuymans, Antwerp, Belgium.

for Central Africa in the Brussels suburb of Tervuren. At an institution first established in 1898 as the Musée du Congo and inhabiting its current grandiose premises since 1910, at the dawn of the twenty-first century visitors could still re-enter a world of colonial-era representations showcasing heroic Belgian 'pioneers' in the Congo, artefacts extolling the nation's 'civilizing mission', and depictions of Africans as savage and primitive, such as those that once directly inspired Hergé's drawings in *Tintin au Congo*.[4] *Sculpture* and *Diorama* pointed towards historic Belgian acts of slaughter, pillage, and appropriation along with the everyday survival of racist colonial relics (and the mentalities making it acceptable to keep them on open display) in contemporary Belgian public spaces, long after the leading African nationalist to contest Belgium's colonial legacy and neo-colonial ambitions in the Congo had been deposed and physically 'disappeared'. But unlike the faceless King Baudouin, Tuymans' *Lumumba* and the African statue both make direct eye contact with their viewers, insisting on their humanity and that they be newly reckoned with in postcolonial times. Not merely reducible to an exoticized, denigrated decorative object or murdered and obliterated as a political inconvenience, they demand respect, recognition, and reassessment alike.

Through his subject matter, Tuymans situated African people, artefacts, and colonial events as central to Belgium's present as well as its past. Through his style of painting, he explored the embodiment and workings of dominance and power – and the power and limits of representation – in all its cloudy indeterminacy, ghostliness, and things unseen or deliberately covered up. Violence and the insinuation of gruesome horror pervade the series despite never being explicitly conveyed, becoming all the more disquieting for being imagined or implied. Throughout the *Mwana Kitoko* paintings, Tuymans suggested both that there were other stories needing to be told than the ones proudly trumpeted by the colonial authorities and their publicists, the royal entourage determined to deny brutal truths and the king's own knowledge and approval of them, and the postcolonial institutions and actors still peddling uncritical and nostalgic versions of Belgium's history in the Congo. Yet his work simultaneously underscored that the past, in all its haziness, can never be fully recaptured and that history and memory are inevitably incomplete, inconclusive, and often faulty or repressed, destined to remain as unsettled as they were unsettling. Together with focusing on the concrete historical traces that remained, Tuymans alluded to further evidence that might still surface about colonialism and decolonization, not least that which might yield a clearer account of

---

[4] Guido Gryseels, Gabrielle Landry, and Koeki Claessens, 'Integrating the Past: Transformation and Renovation of the Royal Museum for Central Africa, Tervuren, Belgium', *European Review*, 13:3 (2005), 637–8; Jean Muteba Rahier, 'The Ghost of Leopold II: The Belgian Royal Museum of Central Africa and Its Dusty Colonialist Exhibition', *Research in African Literatures*, 34:1 (2003), 58–84.

Lumumba's assassination. Like Lumumba's teeth that were alleged to have survived the acid bath designed to eradicate his body without trace (but which were never actually handed over), the deadly effects of Belgium's time in the Congo still remained the subject of rumour, incomplete knowledge, patchy evidence, accusations, and denials of responsibility for atrocities, remaining unfinished business forty years later. While the full story might never come out, revisiting colonialism and decolonization in ways surpassing Belgian self-congratulation and a shirking of high-level responsibility for wrongdoings nonetheless remained an imperative postcolonial task.

Tuymans' return to Belgium's colonial history and legacy at the turn of the millennium counts among the innumerable instances of the ongoing presence of the imperial past in Europe decades after decolonization. Whether in Belgium, France, Britain, the Netherlands, or Portugal, this history remains alive today and is subject to different modes of remembering, misremembering, recasting, or amnesia at the national, subnational, group, and individual level. It exists in the countless books with imperial settings and subject matter dating from colonial times that remain part of national culture, texts as diverse as Camões' sixteenth-century epic *The Lusiads*, Rudyard Kipling's prodigious Victorian and Edwardian literary output, *Tintin au Congo* and the Babar stories dating from the 1930s, and Albert Camus' mid-twentieth-century writings about Algeria. These now share the stage with a growing corpus of new postcolonial stories of empire, some well-known, others far less so. Empire retains its indelible mark on an evolving and globalized literary canon in Europe, seen in the works of authors as diverse as Salman Rushdie, Ousmane Sembène, Marguerite Duras, António Lobo Antunes, and innumerable others who have decisively reshaped the literary landscape. Just as importantly, alongside new contributions to imperial history directed at both scholars and a general readership, private stories of empire continually circulate orally and in writing as personal or familial colonial experiences become shared between individuals and across social networks to reach wider audiences.

Books, conversations, radio and television documentaries, and feature films coexist with manifold material remains of empire that survive in homes and attics, consumer goods, and public spaces. Family photograph albums, keep-sakes, and writings; the latest incarnation of the *tirailleur sénégalais* still featured on the packaging of the Banania breakfast drink in France; the street names, statues, and memorials dedicated to imperial-era figures and events still scattered throughout European cities and towns, large and small; colonial-inspired décor in commercial establishments, like the statue Tuymans found in the Antwerp restaurant; art exhibits, arts festivals, or anniversaries of defining events; museums and archives old and new devoted wholly or in part to colonial history – the examples are endless. All remain part of private and public life, enabling different renditions of a past which are partly shared and partly specific to particular people and communities living within these nations today.[5] Yet ready access to the imperial past has never meant a consensual interpretation of its meanings or led to a generalized willingness to probe either its history or present-day implications. The fact that memories of empire also resurface through court cases, accusations of racism or historic human rights abuses, media furores, official inquiries, and contentious political pronouncements suggests their potential to reflect and stir vociferous contemporary debates.

Memories of any historical phenomenon are destined to be partial and incomplete, and those of empire in late twentieth- and early twenty-first century Europe are no exception. Without aspiring to the impossible task of being comprehensive or encyclopaedic, this chapter considers selected examples, often returning to themes raised in Parts I and II, to illuminate central tendencies and broach the following issues. Who works hardest to keep memories of empire alive and make particular histories and narratives of colonial engagement public? Although anyone can (and does) revisit empire – whether fondly or critically, consistently or occasionally, thoughtfully or unreflectively – many of those most committed to doing so have been individuals, social groups, and institutions claiming a direct connection to the imperial past and who seek recognition for their specific versions of it. Europeans who once lived overseas themselves together with ethnic minorities and their descendants from former colonies who now form part of European citizenries have been leading players in memory cultures, as have a range of highly active social networks representing them. So too were veterans of decolonization-era wars and counterinsurgencies. Their involvement does much to account both for the persistence and deep-rootedness of some stories about the imperial past and the eruption of new narratives and controversies at particular moments since decolonization. No matter how prominent certain memories, together with some deafening silences, might prove, they are never inevitably static or uniformly held.

---

[5] Among many important studies (more of which are cited throughout this chapter), see Robert Aldrich, *Vestiges of the Colonial Empire in France: Monuments, Museums and Colonial Memories* (Basingstoke, 2005); Susan Legêne, *Spiegelreflex: Culturele sporen van de koloniale ervaring* (Amsterdam, 2010); Dominic Thomas (ed.), *Museums in Postcolonial Europe* (London, 2010); Pascal Blanchard, Sandrine Lemaire, and Nicolas Bancel (eds.), *Culture coloniale en France: De la Révolution française à nos jours* (Paris, 2008); Herman Lebovics, *Bringing the Empire Back Home: France in the Global Age* (Durham, 2004); Andrew Thompson, *The Empire Strikes Back?: The Impact of Imperialism on Britain from the Mid-Nineteenth Century* (Harlow, 2005); Andrew Thompson (ed.), *Britain's Experience of Empire in the Twentieth Century (Oxford History of the British Empire Companion Series)* (Oxford, 2012); Stuart Ward (ed.), *British Culture and the End of Empire* (Manchester, 2001); Rachael Gilmour and Bill Schwarz (eds.), *End of Empire and the English Novel Since 1945* (Manchester, 2011). Dietmar Rothermund (ed.), *Memories of Post-imperial Nations: The Aftermath of Decolonization, 1945–2013* (Cambridge, 2015) appeared too late to be drawn upon for this chapter.

Rather, they are prone to change over time in tune with new historical contexts in which they circulate and in accordance with the shifting social demographics of multi-ethnic European nations decisively reshaped through migration, generational change, and dynamic political and cultural landscapes.

Varying markedly both within postcolonial nations and across social groups, memories of empire generate vastly different levels of interest and degrees of willingness to revisit this past, whether to extol, condemn, or critically weigh its historical and contemporary significance. Which aspects of imperial history have circulated most readily in postcolonial Europe, and which remain neglected, silenced, and marginalized by comparison – often because they have become submerged underneath or entangled with other memories, some imperial, others not? Specific historical constellations have worked to trigger a return to empire with especial intensity long after decolonization. In Belgium, this happened approximately forty years after the Congo's violent transition to a neo-colonial and incomplete form of independence.

* * *

Triggers of entangled imperial memories and forgettings

It was no accident that Luc Tuymans tackled Belgium's problematic colonial legacy precisely when he did in his *Mwana Kitoko* series painted and exhibited in 2000 and 2001. After decolonization, silence and ignorance about the colonial past held sway among most Belgian social sectors that had not been directly engaged with it. The Congo ceased to be part of school curricula, and ruling Christian Democrats (the party that had been in government in 1960 and remained pre-eminent for decades afterwards) made no effort to reassess the nation's recent history as an African colonizer, least of all self-critically. As Chapters 4 and 8 introduced, Belgium's postcolonial decades witnessed the draining out of what Antoine Tshitungu Kongolo has called the 'common pool of historical and symbolic references' in a nation increasingly divided between French-speaking Wallonia and Dutch-speaking Flanders. Federalization worked towards the evaporation of a collective national memory, including that concerning colonialism – Belgium's 'last national project', as Sarah De Mul puts it.[6] In the immediate aftermath of Congolese independence, those in search of colonial critics found them in Africa, not Belgium itself, where attitudes, such that they were expressed at all, tended towards the complacent

---

[6] Antoine Tshitungu Kongolo, 'Colonial Memories in Belgian and Congolese Literature', *Yale French Studies*, 102 (2002), 85; Sarah De Mul, 'The Holocaust as a Paradigm for the Congo Atrocities: Adam Hochschild's *King Leopold's Ghost*', in Elleke Boehmer and Sarah De Mul (eds.), *The Postcolonial Low Countries: Literature, Colonialism, and Multiculturalism* (Lanham, MD, 2012), 173.

if not outright celebratory.[7] For decades, books by professional historians had a limited reception outside academia, and general impressions of colonialism were far more likely to have been informed by a visit to the time-warped museum filled with pro-colonial propaganda at Tervuren.

This seemingly stable and relatively placid, marginal, and uncontentious place of colonial history in Belgian public culture was thrown into a tailspin when a series of public controversies erupted in the late 1990s. Belgium's Congolese past became catapulted into the spotlight in a manner unprecedented since independence in the media storm initially sparked by the publication of two studies (and followed up by several documentaries) that achieved a level of mainstream attention that few history books manage.[8] Adam Hochschild's *King Leopold's Ghost* appeared in English in 1998 and in French and Dutch translation in 1999, revisiting the horrors inflicted on Africans in the quest for wealth from rubber and other raw materials under the *fin-de-siècle* Congo Free State presided over by King Léopold II from afar. Although the stories he told had been explored by many scholars before him, Hochschild's bestseller provided a general readership with minute descriptions of European brutalities ranging from forced labour, mass killings, habitual beatings, and hands severed as punishment as the Congolese were coerced into delivering high quotas of natural rubber, building roads, and servicing other projects. Hochschild's graphic treatment extended to the attention-grabbing contention that the native population had declined from 20 million to 10 million – 'a death toll of Holocaust dimensions'.[9] 1999 also saw the publication of Ludo De Witte's *The Assassination of Lumumba*, a deeply-researched study that contradicted received Belgian wisdom about Congolese decolonization. De Witte produced compelling evidence that went against the favoured Belgian argument that the 1961 murder of the Congo's democratically-elected prime minister counted as a sordid 'Bantu affair' committed by African political enemies. Instead, he emphasized Belgian actions, knowledge, and encouragement of Lumumba's

---

[7] Jan Vandersmissen, 'Cent ans d'instrumentalisation de Léopold II, symbole controversé de la présence belge en Afrique centrale', in Sébastien Jahan and Alain Ruscio (eds.), *Histoire de la colonisation: Réhabilitations, falsifications et instrumentalisations* (Paris, 2007), 229.

[8] Excellent accounts of these episodes and their implications include Geert Castryck, 'Whose History is History? Singularities and Dualities of the Public Debate on Belgian Colonialism', in Sven Mörsdorf (ed.), *Being a Historian: Opportunities and Responsibilities Past and Present* (CLIOHRES.net, 2010), 1–18; Georgi Verbeeck, 'Coming to Terms with the (Post-)Colonial Past in Belgium: The Inquiry into the Assassination of Patrice Lumumba', in Harriet Jones, Kjell Östberg, and Nico Randeraad (eds.), *Contemporary History on Trial: Europe Since 1989 and the Role of the Expert Historian* (Manchester, 2007), 46–61; Martin Ewans, 'Belgium and the Colonial Experience', *Journal of Contemporary European Studies*, 11:2 (2003), 167–180; De Mul, 'Holocaust as a Paradigm'. Further fuelling these controversies were highly-publicized films condemning Belgium's colonial past, Peter Bate's documentary *White King, Red Rubber, Black Death* (2004) and Raoul Peck's *Lumumba* (2000).

[9] Adam Hochschild, *King Leopold's Ghost: A Story of Greed, Terror, and Heroism in Colonial Africa* (New York, 1998), 4, 233.

'definitive elimination' that extended to the highest levels of the nation's political establishment, up to and including its monarchy.[10]

Such was the furore sparked by De Witte's claims that the Belgian parliament set up a commission of inquiry into the circumstances of Lumumba's death in 2000, the conclusions of which were released late in 2001. The commission upheld De Witte's verdicts that Belgians both participated in Lumumba's murder on the ground and aided and encouraged it at every step, extending from officials, military, and police in Africa to government ministers in Brussels. It also confirmed that King Baudouin had full knowledge that Lumumba's life was in danger and never attempted to intervene. The report concluded that Belgium bore a clear 'moral responsibility' for Lumumba's death, and Foreign Minister Louis Michel issued an official state apology to Lumumba's family and to the Congolese people – an apology revealingly not accompanied by one from the palace, presided over for nearly twenty years by King Albert II after his elder brother's death in 1993.

Regardless of this spate of revelations that culminated in a state proclamation, there remained a great deal that Belgium's authorities did not wish to delve into too deeply at the turn of the millennium. Many were left unsatisfied by the outcomes, including Lumumba's son François, who pointed out that admitting and regretting Belgium's 'moral responsibility' was not the same thing as accepting 'responsibility' pure and simple.[11] Despite their explicit purpose being to reveal, the commission's findings were meant to close the issue, turn the page, and usher in a new era of Belgian–African relations. Both the commission and wider responses to the issues aired concerning the Congo Free State and decolonization eras were signs of changing times in Belgium's international and domestic politics across the 1990s. Alongside the end of the Mobutu regime in the Democratic Republic of Congo and the gradual international reckoning with the tragedy of the 1994 Rwandan genocide (which saw Belgium's prime minister formally apologize for Belgium's own role in the catastrophe in April 2001), Belgium also witnessed a changing of its own political guard at home. Together with King Baudouin's death, the election of a moderate coalition government of liberals, socialists, and greens in 1999 placed conservative Christian Democrats in opposition for the first time in forty years, thereby facilitating new national overtures towards contemporary Central Africa and the colonial past alike that the previous status quo worked to inhibit.[12]

---

[10] De Witte, *Assassination of Lumumba.*   [11] De Villers, 'Histoire, justice et politique', 212–15.
[12] Alongside Castryck, 'Whose History is History?' and Verbeeck, 'Coming to Terms with the (Post-) Colonial Past', see especially Valérie Rosoux, 'La mémoire de la colonisation: Fer de lance ou talon d'Achille de la politique étrangère belge?', in Serge Jaumain and Éric Remacle (eds.), *Mémoire de guerre et construction de la paix: Mentalités et choix politiques, Belgique—Europe—Canada* (Brussels, 2006), 157–79.

Equally important in shaping the tenor of controversies surrounding colonial history are the federal schisms within Belgian politics that have widened drastically since the 1990s. Belgian interest in colonial legacies often has less to do with the Congo's past than with Belgium's own future as a nation.[13] Postcolonial returns to empire became incorporated within debates about the fate of the Belgian nation-state and representative of the forces working for or against it. Until decolonization, monarchy and colony had provided closely connected symbols and myths that helped unify Belgium across its Walloon and Flemish regional and linguistic divides; without the colony, royalty was one of the few national symbols that remained. Historical accounts that implicated King Léopold II in mass murder of 'Holocaust' proportions and extreme human rights abuses, or contended that King Baudouin had condoned and encouraged Lumumba's assassination, did not simply tarnish the historical record and taint Belgian colonialism's nineteenth-century beginnings and early-1960s ending. They provided useful ammunition to those eager to attack the monarchy as an institution and through it the increasingly fragile Belgian state itself in the present day. Damning reassessments of and apologist responses to Belgium's colonial record, in sum, form part of Belgo-Belgian arguments splitting Francophones and Flemings: the former are far more likely to defend a unitary Belgian nationalist discourse, the monarchy, and colonial heritage, while the latter are more likely to critique all three. For separatist Flemings, especially the far-right *Vlaams Belang*, colonialism counts as a Francophone inheritance from which they seek to dissociate Flanders, regardless of the actual extent of Flemish involvement in colonial enterprises.[14]

In light of these bi-national tendencies at work, it may be no coincidence that none of the critics mentioned earlier are Francophone Belgians. Adam Hochschild is American, while Ludo De Witte and Luc Tuymans both come from Flanders – even if, it must be stressed, neither subscribes to Flemish nationalist politics (Tuymans, indeed, has used his art to deflate central Flemish myths and symbols). Nor is it irrelevant that *De Stoete(n) Ostendenoare*, a shadowy anarchist leftist group that claimed responsibility for vandalizing public monuments featuring Léopold II and Baudouin, operates in the Flemish city of Oostende. That dousing statues of Léopold and Baudouin with red paint or powder to represent blood spilled in the Congo, or sawing off the hand of one of the African figures positioned at the base of Léopold's pedestal on the 1931 *'Dank van de Congolezen'* ('With thanks from the

---

[13] Bambi Ceuppens, 'U bent mij vergeten, I presume?', 30 January 2007 posting on Mondiaal Nieuws, www.mo.be/artikel/u-bent-mij-vergeten-i-presume, accessed 6 June 2014.

[14] Véronique Bragard and Stéphanie Planche, 'Museum Practices and the Belgian Colonial Past: Questioning the Memories of an Ambivalent Metropole', in Thomas (ed.), *Museums in Postcolonial Europe*, 60; Vandersmissen, 'Cent ans d'instrumentalisation de Léopold II', 237–8; De Villers, 'Histoire, justice et politique', 198.

Congolese') monument towering over Oostende's seafront in 2004, counts as colonial critique is obvious. The group issued explicit statements of its intention to remind contemporaries of the 'severed hands' scandals during the Congo Free State and counter the monument's original purpose of insisting on Congolese gratitude to Léopold for rescuing them from the Arab slave trade, and of Baudouin's complicity in Lumumba's assassination by targeting his statue in retaliation on the anniversary of Lumumba's death in 2005.[15] Far less transparent are the possible connections between *De Stoete(n) Ostendenoare*'s stance on Belgian colonial crimes and the wider separatist spirit dividing Belgium from within.

* * *

As the Belgian case indicates, European imperialism and decolonization have been interpreted through the prisms of other contemporary and historical events spanning from the local to the global, prisms that work to distort or obscure as much as they reveal. National and subnational frameworks for remembering coexisted with international ones, whether extra-European or intra-European. Together with the United States' colossal impact on post-war Europe itself, American-led military interventions ranging from Vietnam in the 1960s to Afghanistan and Iraq in the 'war on terror' after 2000 have shaped perceptions of the end of European empires from the decolonization era to the present day. Overseas empires and their collapse, moreover, also competed for attention or collided with Europe-focused histories and memories, particularly recollections of the Second World War, fascism, and dictatorship, often becoming submerged beneath them. Portugal offers a distinct example, having been technically neutral in the 1939–1945 conflict and with the dictatorship most shaping its twentieth-century history being its home-grown Salazarist *Estado Novo*, a case the last section of this chapter considers. Elsewhere, whether in Britain or in the colonizing nations subjected to wartime occupation, the dictatorship casting the longest shadow was the Third Reich.

The polemicists discussed earlier who aimed to expose historical misdeeds committed by Belgium's monarchy and topple deeply-entrenched nationalist myths about a colonial record worthy of pride found powerful weapons in claims that it was akin to a Holocaust or genocide. Not only was the Rwandan genocide fresh in the minds of scholars and the wider public looking back on colonialism after the mid-1990s: more important still was the longstanding dominance of the Second World War and Holocaust perpetrated by the Nazis

---

[15] Michael Meeuwis, 'Het activisme van de verminking/L'activisme de la mutilation', *Forum: Nieuwsbrief van de Belgische Vereniging van Afrikanisten*, 25 (July 2005), 3–12, http://cas1 .elis.ugent.be/avrug/erfgoed/pdf/vermink.pdf; Vandersmissen, 'Cent ans d'instrumentalisation de Léopold II', 230; 'De Stoeten Ostendenoare slaat weer toe', 21 August 2013, www.nieuws blad.be/article/detail.aspx?articleid=BLEFO_20130821_006, both accessed 6 June 2014.

and their collaborators as the paradigmatic benchmark in the history of mass atrocities. Just as German occupation and wartime collaboration coloured Belgium's approach to the Congo in the 1950s as well as French and Dutch attitudes towards struggles to remain in Southeast Asia and Algeria between 1945 and 1962, as Part I explored, memories of Europe's war and Jewish Holocaust (and their perpetrators and victims) have since interacted with and shaped subsequent postcolonial returns to the imperial past.

Acting as what Michael Rothberg describes as a 'template of cruelty', the Holocaust became a dominant means of making sense of numerous other historic episodes and human tragedies occurring before, during, and after the early 1940s, from the transatlantic slave trade and slavery during the colonial era to the violence of decolonization that scarred empires' end. Provoking countless comparisons and contrasts that serve a variety of agendas, one of the results of its 'universalization' has been 'the unmooring of the Holocaust from its historical specificity and its circulation instead as an abstract code for Evil'.[16] To be sure, deployments of Holocaust analogies can be highly problematic, running a severe risk of historical inaccuracies, misrepresentation, and sensationalism.[17] Nonetheless, as was seen in late 1990s Belgium, prior grappling with *the* Holocaust, together with European wartime experiences more broadly, also had the potential to generate new forms (albeit patchy ones) of scholarly and public awareness of imperial and decolonization-era occupations, wars, and violence later. France and the Netherlands illustrate how these opened up possibilities for historical narratives that surpass the conventionally Eurocentric to gain ground.

When its eight-year undeclared war in Algeria ended with decolonization in 1962, French authorities attempted to put the conflict that had divided the metropole behind. Between 1962 and 1982, France enacted a succession of amnesties and pardons for its soldiers, police, and politicians for crimes committed during the Algerian 'events' that stymied the threat of new prosecutions and gradually rehabilitated those already accused or convicted. Even leading OAS figures on the run and in exile could ultimately resurface without fear of standing trial, and others were released from jail. Pardons extended as high as the men jailed for attempting to assassinate de Gaulle and the generals who led the failed 1961 putsch attempt, even the head of the OAS himself. General Raoul Salan knew he had the crisis of May 1968 to thank for his

---

[16] Michael Rothberg, *Multidirectional Memory: Remembering the Holocaust in the Age of Decolonization* (Stanford, 2009), 264, 229. See also De Mul, 'Holocaust as a Paradigm'; Andreas Huyssen, 'Present Pasts: Media, Politics, Amnesia', *Public Culture*, 12:1 (2000), 21–38; Andreas Huyssen, 'Diaspora and Nation: Migration into Other Pasts', *New German Critique*, 88 (2003), 147–64.

[17] Stephen Howe, 'Colonising and Exterminating? Memories of Imperial Violence in Britain and France', *Histoire@Politique: Politique, culture, société*, 11 (2010), 1.

freedom from a sentence of life imprisonment after only six years, when de Gaulle agreed to new terms in exchange for a guarantee of the army's loyalty in the face of civil unrest that put the republic at risk. As concessions to those on the losing side of decolonization, amnesties and pardons were intended to calm rough seas and repair the cracks in the foundations of a reconfigured postcolonial republic. Preventing Algerian War deeds from being brought to justice or fully researched in archives rendered inaccessible acted as powerful tools to silence the past. War victims were deprived of legal redress and new public exposés were hindered, inhibiting France from developing a collective memory of the imbroglio.[18]

Official measures to encourage amnesia about the sordid end of *Algérie française* succeeded for at least twenty years. Benjamin Stora characterizes the two decades after 1962 as a time of orchestrated *oubli* (forgetting) at the public level as France looked forward to a new future and revisited only selective facets of its recent past. Both the resilient omnipresence of Second World War memory and the events of May 1968 helped smother the Algerian debacle sandwiched between them. Yet *Algérie française* was by no means forgotten: it remained the focus of an uninterrupted flow of publications, its memory continuing to circulate intensely among those whose lives had been directly shaped by it as uprooted *pieds-noirs*, soldiers, officers, and political figures staunchly committed to its cause. Defeated *Algérie française* partisans for whom the war and decolonization remained an ever-present source of fury and resentment dominated this genre, but theirs was overwhelmingly a private or group engagement that remained '*intériorisé* ', or internalized. As the next section takes further, their narratives comprised 'mosaics of individual consciousness refusing to melt into an impossible collective memory' or oblivion, as Stora phrased it.[19] What ultimately enabled more thorough reappraisals of the Algerian War was the public reassessment of the very topics that had long taken precedence over it: the Vichy period of Nazi occupation, collaboration, and resistance.

Starting in the early 1970s, France began a painful, drawn-out process of seeing popular myths about the Vichy era challenged and discredited. Until then, Vichy crimes had been laid at the door of Germans and a small minority of elite French collaborators, enabling the French majority to be heroically associated with the resistance. Documentaries and new historical work gradually demanded

[18] Stéphane Gacon, *L'Amnistie: De la Commune à la guerre d'Algérie* (Paris, 2002), 255–319, especially 288–93; Benjamin Stora, *La gangrène et l'oubli: La mémoire de la guerre d'Algérie* (Paris, 1991), 214–20, 281–3; Olivier Dard, *Voyage au coeur de l'OAS* (Paris, 2005); 351–70; Rémi Kauffer, *OAS: Histoire de la guerre franco-française* (Paris, 2002), 403, 412; François Malye and Benjamin Stora, *François Mitterrand et la guerre d'Algérie* (Paris, 2010), 289; Raphaëlle Branche, 'The State, the Historians and the Algerian War in French Memory, 1991–2004', in Jones, Östberg, and Randeraad (eds.), *Contemporary History on Trial*, 159.

[19] Stora, *La gangrène*, ch. 17; quote taken from 242.

that the French roots of Vichy policies, home-grown anti-Semitism, and wide-spread collaboration and acquiescence be reckoned with, even if many people remained loathe to accept French responsibility for the actions and ideologies of a thoroughly disgraced regime.[20] Tackling the history and memory of Vichy was still ongoing in the 1990s, when President Chirac made official statements of repentance for specific French acts perpetrated against the Jews during the period.[21] Remaking the memory of Vichy culminated in 1997 and 1998, when Maurice Papon was tried and ultimately sentenced to ten years' imprisonment for 'complicity in crimes against humanity' for his role as a civil servant in multiple round-ups and deportations of Jews from Bordeaux. The subject of massive media coverage, Papon's trial marked France's transition from the 'Vichy syndrome' to the 'Algeria syndrome' as his subsequent colonial career and position as prefect of the Paris police during the Algerian War became aired in the proceedings.[22] Expert witnesses provided the public with detailed descriptions of Papon's ordering and overseeing of police repression of Algerians in Paris, the most notorious incident being the deaths of hundreds of peaceful protestors against a curfew during the night of 17 October 1961.

Papon was not in court on account of Algerian deaths, however, but rather for facilitating Jewish extermination between 1942 and 1944. Indeed, as Richard Golsan notes, 'a trial for crimes against humanity dealing with Papon's role on 17 October 1961 in Paris would have been legally impossible because by definition crimes against humanity according to French law can, in effect, *only have been committed during World War II and only under the aegis of a government practicing "a politics of ideological hegemony" – for all intents and purposes, Nazi Germany'*. This, together with the amnesties protecting Algerian War actions from prosecution, rendered 17 October 'ultimately inconsequential in legal terms' in the late 1990s. Yet while 'the historical period that mattered' was still Vichy, Papon's trial marked 'the definitive entry of the October massacre into public memory', Michael Rothberg summarizes, becoming a catalyst for the intensification of debates about torture and murders committed on both sides of the Mediterranean in 1954–1962.[23]

Between 1998 and 2002, torture during the Algerian War became subject to more French public debate than at any time since the conflict itself. Algerians who had suffered torture recounted their experiences, and prominent elderly

---

[20] Henry Rousso, *The Vichy Syndrome: History and Memory in France since 1944*, translated by Arthur Goldhammer (Cambridge, MA, 1991).

[21] Benjamin Stora, entretiens avec Thierry Leclère, *La guerre des mémoires: La France face à son passé colonial* (Paris, 2007), 75.

[22] Neil MacMaster, 'The Torture Controversy (1998–2002): Towards a "New History" of the Algerian War?', *Modern and Contemporary France*, 10:4 (2002), 450.

[23] Richard J. Golsan, 'Introduction: Maurice Papon and Crimes Against Humanity in France', in Richard J. Golsan (ed.), *The Papon Affair: Memory and Justice on Trial* (New York, 2000), 5; Rothberg, *Multidirectional Memory*, 286.

French military figures reflected upon what had been an endemic and institutionalized practice. In newspaper articles, General Jacques Massu acknowledged and regretted torture as both unnecessary and ineffectual in the effort to break the FLN, while General Paul Aussaresses, by contrast, unapologetically considered torture an indispensable weapon in his brutally detailed memoir. Aussaresses was taken to court by human rights campaigners who wanted the wider issue to be reopened, and although the public prosecutor decided against trying him for 'crimes against humanity' the court fined him and his publishers for 'apologising for crimes of war' in 2002. Financially negligible though the punishment was, the verdict nonetheless marked the first occasion that a court had acknowledged that the French had committed *'crimes de guerre'* in Algeria.[24] Just as significantly, by 2002 the Algerian War officially qualified as having been a 'war' at long last (rather than as 'operations for the maintenance of order in North Africa', 'events', or other exculpatory euphemisms). This change happened as late as 1999 when a new law was passed by the National Assembly in response to demands from veterans hitherto excluded from receiving war benefits. Signs of a broader willingness to revisit atrocities came with the fortieth anniversary of the 17 October massacre in 2001, which was marked by ceremonies, demonstrations, and the mayor of Paris dedicating a commemorative plaque on the Pont Saint-Michel, near where many Algerians had drowned in the Seine. The following year saw a new national memorial to French soldiers killed in North Africa between 1952 and 1962 inaugurated on the Quai Branly in Paris.

If France finally seemed able to re-confront its Algerian past after forty years, the 'accelerations of memory' occurring around the turn of the millennium nevertheless remained far from complete.[25] State admission that the Algerian War really had been a war was not the same as accepting full state responsibility for atrocities like 17 October, and those campaigning on behalf of its victims felt the Pont Saint-Michel plaque to constitute the 'start of recognition', not the end.[26] Indeed, the next years brought further returns to French Algeria and the war as diverse constituencies sought to have their stories about its meanings heard and accorded space in public discourse. As the next section considers, France embarked on a new round of 'memory wars' fought between minorities of Maghrebi heritage, *pieds-noirs*, and other colonial critics and apologists.[27] Some sought further forms of official recognition

---

[24] MacMaster, 'Torture Controversy', 454; Branche, 'The State, the Historians and the Algerian War', 165–6.

[25] Benjamin Stora, '1999–2003, guerre d'Algérie, les accélérations de la mémoire', in Mohammed Harbi and Benjamin Stora (eds.), *La guerre d'Algérie* (Paris, 2004), 725–44.

[26] Jim House and Neil MacMaster, *Paris 1961: Algerians, State Terror, and Memory* (Oxford, 2006), 315, 319.

[27] Stora, *La guerre des mémoires*.

and apology, while others staged a backlash against the concept of repentance and mounted new defences of the colonial past in new political contexts.

Since 2001, moreover, returns to the Algerian War have taken place against a new backdrop, one in which the 'war on terror' and international debates about torture after 11 September regularly take precedence over the Second World War as the main lens through which the 1954–1962 conflict has recently been viewed. Torture, as Michael Rothberg writes, was 'a practice that triggered memory of Nazism at one moment' – namely, during France's struggle against decolonization – and 'could later serve as a trigger in France for memory of the Algerian War itself'.[28] Having finally come out from behind the Second World War in French memory, the lost fight to retain *Algérie française* not only remains intertwined with other events. As the last section of this chapter explores, it continues to loom over the memory of the rest of the French empire, which often disappears underneath its weight.

* * *

It proved just as difficult for the Netherlands' military struggle against Indonesian nationalists between 1945 and 1949 to surface from beneath the Second World War in Dutch collective memory as it had for the Algerian War in France. 1945 was overwhelmingly recalled as the year of Dutch liberation at the end of a war, not the start of brutal Dutch efforts to forcibly prevent Indonesians from liberating themselves. As will be explored further later, postcolonial repatriates from the former East Indies acted as crucial agents in extending Dutch memories of the Second World War beyond a Eurocentric focus in which the Third Reich, Nazi Germany's occupation of the Netherlands, and the Allied liberation reigned supreme. Shining a determined spotlight on their specific ordeals led to the inclusion of the Pacific War and Japanese occupation of Dutch-held territory within the national war experience decades after the East Indies ceased to be Dutch. Yet as Elspeth Locher-Scholten rightly emphasizes, '[f]or the general public, Pacific war memories were easier to accept than those of the unpopular war of decolonization, which had first been forgotten and then called into question'.[29] Commemorating those who had been victims of the Japanese was one thing; pointing the finger at Dutch perpetrators of ruthless violence in what ultimately proved a futile struggle against Indonesian nationalism proved another matter entirely.

Public silence over 1945–1949 was only broken after the 1968 massacre committed by American troops in the Vietnamese village of My Lai made international headlines. A Dutch television documentary aired at the beginning

[28] Rothberg, *Multidirectional Memory*, 17.
[29] Elspeth Locher-Scholten, 'From Urn to Monument: Dutch Memories of World War II in the Pacific, 1945–1995', in Andrea L. Smith (ed.), *Europe's Invisible Migrants* (Amsterdam, 2003), 128.

of 1969 opened a Pandora's box shut for twenty years, featuring veterans, now middle-aged, reflecting critically on their own actions in Southeast Asia a generation before.[30] The broadcast sparked what became known as the 'Hueting affair' on account of its interview with the psychologist Joop Hueting, who had served as a nineteen-year-old conscript in the Dutch army during the so-called 'police actions' of 1947 and 1948. Viewers heard him confess that 'I took part in war crimes. I saw men commit them … villages would be riddled while no one at the time saw the military exigency. During interrogations suspects would be tortured in the most hideous ways even though there was no evidence this was necessary. Retaliations were organised, again with no clear military urgency'.[31] Many Dutch veterans reacted angrily to Hueting's admissions, while others welcomed the chance to publicly describe witnessing or taking part in similar transgressions and express their regrets.

What made the Hueting episode so controversial was not simply the nature of the counterterrorism acts he described (and the fact that he did so to the large audience watching television) but the manner in which he described them: as 'war crimes', a term instantly associated in the public imagination with Nazi atrocities.[32] Although the coalition government ruling in 1969 had no wish to revisit military activities that were part of a failed effort to hold on to Indonesia, such was the media storm that political leaders felt there was no alternative to holding an official inquiry. Its published result was the *Excessennota*, known as such because its authors, with state approval, settled on the euphemistic term 'excesses' rather than 'war crimes' to play down the extent of Dutch soldiers' misdeeds. The report provided plentiful information about numerous instances of military misconduct, to be sure, but these were circumscribed and neutralized by portraying them as wrongdoings committed by individuals who had deviated from acceptable standards of behaviour – standards that had been upheld by the majority – not as systematically inherent within the entire Dutch counterinsurgency campaign.[33] The government's strategy to contain the fallout succeeded and the controversy subsided, yielding little more in its

---

[30] Frank van Vree, '"Our Tortured Bride": The Japanese Occupation of the Dutch East Indies in Dutch Films and Documentaries', in Remco Raben (ed.), *Representing the Japanese Occupation of Indonesia: Personal Testimonies and Public Images in Indonesia, Japan, and the Netherlands* (Amsterdam, 1999), 209–10; Peter Romijn, 'Learning on "the job": Dutch War Volunteers Entering the Indonesian War of Independence, 1945–46', *Journal of Genocide Research*, 14:3 (2012), 317–18.

[31] Stef Scagliola, 'The Silences and Myths of a "Dirty War": Coming to Terms with the Dutch-Indonesian Decolonisation War (1945–1949)', *European Review of History—Revue européenne d'Histoire*, 14:2 (2007), 248–9.

[32] 'The Psychology Professor and the Nation's Bad Dreams: An Interview with J.E. Hueting', *Itinerario*, 20:2 (1996), 17.

[33] *Nota: Betreffende het archievonderzoek naar gegevens omtrent excessen in Indonesië begaan door nederlandse militairen in de periode 1945–1950: Aan de Heer Voorzitter van de Tweede Kamer der Staten-Generaal, Zitting 1968–1969-10 008 3 (2)* ('s-Gravenhage, 1969).

immediate aftermath than a few respected academic publications that critically probed the matter further (but which never attracted a sizable mainstream audience).[34] What had momentarily become a burning issue was doused with cold water, petering out into a tepid outcome in which neither the Dutch military nor the politicians of 1945–1949 had to face a full investigation into their behaviour and policies in Indonesia.[35]

Following the 'Hueting affair' and *Excessennota*, Dutch public discussions of Indonesian decolonization subsided for close to another two decades before the next controversy erupted between 1987 and 1988. This time, it was triggered by the leading Dutch historian of the Second World War, Lou de Jong, director of the state-sponsored Netherlands Institute for War Documentation. De Jong was a household name thanks to his television and radio programmes and twenty-seven-volume series of books meant to provide a comprehensive treatment of the Dutch war experience that adorned thousands of bookshelves across the country. Although most concerned the metropole, it was his later volumes focusing on the former East Indies that appeared in the 1980s that proved among the most polemical. In 1984, De Jong incurred the wrath of Dutch ex-colonials convinced that his rendition of Dutch rule prior to the Japanese occupation was biased by anti-colonial views and accorded too much space to Indonesian nationalism and the colonial authorities' repression of it; their legal efforts to have offending portions re-written by a more 'objective' historian floundered in the courtroom. Trouble returned three years later when drafts of his account of '*de worsteling met de Republiek Indonesië*' ('the struggle with the Republic of Indonesia') after Japan's surrender were leaked to the press prior to publication. These provoked a furious response among vocal veterans and their conservative supporters, their criticisms honing in on one offending paragraph: that in which De Jong referred to Dutch troops' 'war crimes' as opposed to 'excesses', thus deviating from the consensual formulation that had become habitual since 1969. His detractors went so far as to initiate a criminal libel case, which, although dismissed, caused him to bow down to intense pressure and revert back to labelling military misconduct as 'excessive use of violence' or 'counter-terror' by the time the volume appeared in print in 1988. That same year, the 'Nationaal Indië-monument' dedicated to soldiers who served in the Indies between 1945

---

[34] See especially J.A.A. van Doorn and W.J. Hendrix, *Ontsporing van geweld: Over het Nederlands/Indisch/Indonesisch conflict* (Rotterdam, 1970) and the authors' related publications discussed in Chapter 2.

[35] As had also been the case in France after the Algerian War, moreover, a general amnesty agreed on by the Netherlands and Indonesia in 1949 inhibited the prospect of individuals facing legal prosecution for their actions, even if the will had existed to initiate cases—which it categorically did not in 1969. See Scagliola, 'Silences and Myths', 243.

and 1962 was unveiled in Roermond, the scene of annual remembrance ceremonies ever since.[36]

De Jong's foray into (and prompt retreat out of) 'war crimes' territory
revealed the intense and coordinated determination of veterans' groups to
defend their reputation against accusations of extreme and unwarranted violence, while the Roermond monument's inauguration showed a considerable
degree of official sympathy for their position. Many ex-soldiers had intense
misgivings about their experiences in the lost battle to hold on to the Indies ever
since the late 1940s, arguing that they had simply been following orders, and
these showed no signs of abating as they advanced into old age. Some felt
guilty, traumatized, or conflicted about their own actions or those they witnessed firsthand; others were self-righteous, defensive, and bitter about what
they perceived as betrayal and abandonment by politicians and the lack of
understanding, respect, and appreciation for their services and sacrifices from
either the public or the state that preferred to forget decolonization.[37]

Divisions among Dutch soldiers' and veterans' attitudes during their military
service and in later recollections of it could also be found among their counterparts who fought decolonization wars on behalf of France, Portugal, or Britain.
Some ex-soldiers had been fully committed to and passionate about their mission
to fight alleged 'terrorists' and 'extremists' at the time and remained so long
afterwards. Others, especially many conscripts as opposed to professional soldiers and officers, had never wanted to be sent to fight end-of-empire wars, or
wars that the political establishment refused to label as such, in the first place.
That French conscripts were sent to fight an increasingly unpopular war on
behalf of the *Algérie française* cause that most did not feel personally invested
in meant that many harboured resentments at the time and long afterwards.[38]

---

[36] See Peter Romijn, 'Myth and Understanding: Recent Controversy about Dutch Historiography
on the Netherlands-Indonesia Conflict', in Robert S. Kirsner (ed.), *The Low Countries and
Beyond* (Lanham, MD, 1993), 219–29; Madelon de Keizer (ed.), *'Een dure verplichting en een
kostelijk voorrecht': Dr. L. de Jong en zijn geschiedwerk* ('s-Gravenhage, 1995); Boudewijn
Smits, *Lou de Jong 1914–2005: Historicus met een missie* (Amsterdam, 2014), ch. 27. For
coverage of the 'excesses' as well as the Hueting episode, see L. de Jong, *Het Koninkrijk der
Nederlanden in de Tweede Wereldoorlog, Deel 12: Epiloog*, vol. 2 (Leiden, 1988), 1011–60.
Reactions to the various volumes appeared in J.Th.M. Bank *et al.* (eds.), *Het Koninkrijk der
Nederlanden in de Tweede Wereldoorlog, Deel 14: Reacties*, vol. 2 ('s-Gravenhage, 1991); on
the decolonization of the Indies, see 900–28, especially the section concerning 'De Paragraaf
"oorlogsmisdrijven', 900–18. On the Nationaal Indië-monument 1945–1962, see www.nim-
roermond.nl/herdenking.htm.

[37] Tessel Pollmann, 'The Unreal War: The Indonesian Revolution Through the Eyes of Dutch
Novelists and Reporters', *Indonesia*, 69 (2000), 105–6.

[38] On French conscripts, see Benjamin Stora, *Le livre, mémoire de l'histoire: Réflexions sur le livre
et la guerre d'Algérie* (Paris, 2005), 23–45; Benjamin Stora, *Appelés en guerre d'Algérie* (Paris,
1997); Philip Dine, *Images of the Algerian War: French Fiction and Film, 1954–1992* (Oxford,
1994), ch. 5. Much work remains to be done about British soldiers sent to fight colonial
insurgencies in Kenya, Malaya, Cyprus, and elsewhere through no choice of their own as part

Similarly, men drafted into the Portuguese army to defend the 'overseas provinces' in Africa against guerrilla opponents between 1961 and 1974 often had strong reservations from the start. Fighting in Guinea, Angola, and Mozambique left over 9,000 Portuguese dead and tens of thousands of others with physical disabilities or mental traumas that haunted them long after their returns home following the Carnation Revolution and the decolonizations that rapidly ensued. Colonial war narratives became prominent themes not only in the autobiographical writings of ex-combatants but most famously in the fiction of a number of Portugal's most highly-acclaimed novelists, including Lídia Jorge's renditions of women's wartime experiences and the highly complex novels of António Lobo Antunes, a psychiatrist whose military service took him to Angola.[39]

Ex-soldiers' writings revisit comrades' deaths and the injuries, psychological wounds, and anguish afflicting the survivors. For them, understandably, decolonization wars proved impossible to forget, their emotions diversely expressed as shame, criticism of the wars waged, anger that they had been forced to participate, denial of atrocities perpetrated in the name of what became a lost cause, sanitized recollections of doing their duty, and self-victimization.[40] Like many of their own stories, occasional documentaries, films, and newspaper retrospectives on colonial war experiences often favoured portrayals that emphasized soldiers' integrity, bravery, camaraderie, resilience, and endurance in adverse circumstances – in short, their heroism.[41] Understanding Portuguese soldiers, alongside families mourning soldiers' deaths, as war victims was common in a post-revolutionary, postcolonial society. However, veterans' position was in fact a highly uncertain one, as Margarida Calafate Ribeiro puts it, 'caught between being the victim', a mere cog in a monstrous machine, 'and being the image of the former power that everyone wanted to forget'.[42] Soldiers testify to the impossibility of arriving at

---

of their National Service obligation. For an excellent beginning, see Richard Vinen, *National Service: Conscription in Britain, 1945–1963* (London, 2014).

[39] Margarida Calafate Ribeiro, *Uma História de Regressos: Império Guerra Colonial e Pós-colonialismo* (Porto, 2004), especially 259–95 on Lobo Antunes and 363–421 on Jorge; Norberto do Vale Cardoso, *A Mão-de-Judas: Representações da Guerra Colonial em António Lobo Antunes* (Alfragide, 2011); 'Facts and Fictions of António Lobo Antunes', special issue, *Portuguese Literary and Cultural Studies*, 19/20 (2011).

[40] Paulo de Medeiros, 'Hauntings: Memory, Fiction and the Portuguese Colonial Wars', in T.G. Ashplant, Graham Dawson, and Michael Roper (eds.), *The Politics of War and Commemoration* (London, 2000), 201–21. See also Rui de Azavedo Teixeira (ed.), *A Guerra Colonial: Realidade e Ficção* (Lisbon, 2001).

[41] Marcus Power, 'Geo-politics and the Representation of Portugal's African Colonial Wars: Examining the Limits of the "Vietnam Syndrone"', *Political Geography*, 20 (2001), 461–91; Carolin Overhoff Ferreira, 'Decolonizing the Mind? The Representation of the African Colonial Wars in Portuguese Cinema', *Studies in European Cinema*, 2:3 (2005), 227–39.

[42] Margarida Calafate Ribeiro, 'Empire, Colonial Wars and Post-colonialism in the Portuguese Contemporary Imagination', *Portuguese Studies*, 18 (2002), 186; on soldiers' self-victimization, see also Manuel Loff, 'Coming to Terms with the Dictatorial Past in Portugal after 1974:

anything approaching a uniform social understanding of struggles to maintain empire after decolonization. Not only were those directly involved unable to reach any agreement about their experiences, but the chasms separating their memories from those common within metropoles where many did not wish to remember these episodes at all often proved unbreachable.

The Dutch fight against Indonesian nationalists remained even more contentious and unresolved as the fiftieth anniversary of the start of the conflict drew near.[43] Despite the public prominence of individuals and pressure groups intent on defending their reputation, in 1995 elderly veterans were still divided among themselves about the morality of their actions; so too were prominent Dutch politicians about how to approach the colonial past. Some sought a meaningful public debate on the nation's decolonization policy, or argued that 17 August 1945 be recognized as the real anniversary of Indonesia's independence rather than 27 December 1949 – in other words, that the Dutch finally acknowledge the date celebrated by Indonesians ever since independence was declared immediately after Japan's surrender – or called for an official apology to be issued for Dutch actions between 1945 and 1949. Yet none materialized: when Queen Beatrix visited Indonesia just days after the fiftieth anniversary of 17 August 1945, she admitted that 'Holland was at first not prepared to accept the Indonesian endeavor towards complete and immediate independence. Because of this, the separation between our countries has become a long process, that has cost much pain and bitter struggle'. 'Deep regret' was conveyed, but no formal state apology.[44]

Although a third of Dutch respondents to an opinion poll in 1995 believed an apology was right and 49 per cent believed Dutch soldiers had committed grave misdeeds in the late 1940s, this was not yet sufficient to tip the balance in favour of a new approach to the end of empire or yield official gestures to formerly colonized peoples on the receiving end of counterterrorism brutality.[45] Many Dutch remained ambivalent or defensive about the nation's and its soldiers' actions in the late 1940s, not least the veterans themselves. Since then, generational change and the passing of the vast majority of those personally involved has opened up possibilities for a new approach and making amends, but even

---

Silence, Remembrance and Ambiguity', in Stefan Troebst and Susan Baumgartl (eds.), *Postdiktatorische Geschichtskulturen im Süden und Osten Europas: Bestandsaufnahme und Perspektiven* (Göttingen, 2010), 109, 119.

[43] Leonard Doyle, 'Colonial Atrocities Explode Myth of Dutch Tolerance', *Independent* (London), 29 May 1994; Jon Henley, 'Dutch Haunted by Dirty War', *Guardian* (London), 31 January 1995; Gillian Sharpe, 'End of War Brings Future Without Empire', *Christian Science Monitor* (Boston), 17 August 1995.

[44] Vincent J.H. Houben, 'A Torn Soul: The Dutch Public Discussion of the Colonial Past in 1995', *Indonesia*, 63 (1997), 47–66, especially 61; Maarten Kuitenbrouwer, 'The Never-Ending Debt of Honour: The Dutch in the Post-Colonial World', *Itinerario*, 20:2 (1996), 34–5.

[45] Kuitenbrouwer, 'Never-Ending Debt', 35.

today this remains incomplete. By the time of the sixtieth anniversary of the Indonesian independence declaration in 2005, the Dutch government finally recognized 17 August 1945 as the date of *de facto* independence, but its foreign minister still refused to issue an apology.[46] In 2011, the Dutch state was found liable in court for the December 1947 massacre of 430 villagers at Rawagede, formally apologized to the surviving widows, and agreed to pay them compensation. This was later repeated in 2013 after another trial found in favour of Indonesian widows whose husbands were killed in South Sulawesi by Captain Raymond Westerling's troops between December 1946 and February 1947.[47] Despite public admissions of responsibility and credible words of contrition, however, these remain limited to isolated instances. To date, the Netherlands has yet to deliver a full apology for years of widespread decolonization violence, let alone engage in an in-depth national reckoning with its policies in its former empire.[48]

* * *

In Britain, popular attitudes about the Second World War fundamentally moulded deeply-held beliefs about Britain's distinctiveness from Western Europe, doing much to explain the relative absence of public memories about end-of-empire conflicts and decolonization after 1945. Assumptions of uniqueness and superiority vis-à-vis continental neighbours both as an imperial power and as an ultimate victor in war were widely shared, as Chapter 1 explored. Never subjected to German invasion and occupation, Britain's war against the Axis powers as the United States' primary (albeit subordinate) ally remains firmly embedded as its 'finest hour' in national mythology until the present day. The righteous and triumphant struggle against fascism resulted in what Paul Gilroy calls the 'totemic power of the great anti-Nazi war' coupled with 'the mysterious evacuation of Britain's postcolonial conflicts from national consciousness' – a removal he rightly suggests to be 'a significant cultural and historic event in its own right'.[49] In mainstream British memories of the Second World War, moreover, its imperial dimensions and Pacific arenas became increasingly sidelined over time, yielding a largely Eurocentric conflict in which the Anglo-American alliance, the German enemy, European war theatres, and an emphasis on white British experiences on the home front and war

---

[46] 'Dutch Withhold Apology in Indonesia', *New York Times*, 17 August 2005.

[47] Anne Barrowclough, 'Dutch Apologise for Java Massacre 64 Years Ago', *The Times* (London), 9 December 2011; Lidy Nicolasen, 'Weduwen Sulawesi krijgen twee ton schadevergoeding', *De Volkskrant* (Amsterdam), 8 August 2013.

[48] These landmark human rights cases were publicly debated at the 'Apologies and the Dutch East Indies' meeting sponsored by the Netherlands Institute for War Documentation in Amsterdam on 7 May 2014; see the video report at www.niod.nl/en/roads-justice/apologies-and-dutch-east-indies.

[49] Paul Gilroy, *After Empire: Melancholia or Convivial Culture?* (London, 2004), 96–7.

fronts alike left relatively little space for acknowledging colonial peoples' contributions to what had been a resoundingly imperial war.[50] Excluding postcolonial minorities from a heroic national war story and consigning post-war anti-colonial struggles to general oblivion, Gilroy concludes, has reinforced the cultural exclusion of minorities from British national identity long after their settlement.[51]

Thus contracted to European and transatlantic proportions while simultaneously envisioning Britain as safely *outside* Europe, the Second World War's dominance ensured that subsequent military engagements, many of which involved fighting colonial insurgencies, could neither compete with 1939–1945 nor destabilize the confident sense that Britain stood apart and above other European nations in the way it approached its empire and decolonization. Plentiful scholarship on the war's global and imperial ramifications and on British decolonization struggles reveals a fuller picture, but examples of academic studies or books written for non-expert audiences that have succeeded in overturning prevailing conceptions remain exceptional. Three accounts that attracted considerable attention both within and beyond specialist academic circles since 2000 have, by turns, defended and maligned Britain's historic imperial reputation in ways that illuminate wider tendencies: Niall Ferguson's *Empire: How Britain Made the Modern World* (2003), Caroline Elkins' *Britain's Gulag: The Brutal End of Empire in Kenya* (2005), and David Anderson's *Histories of the Hanged: The Dirty War in Kenya and the End of Empire* (2005).[52]

Written to accompany a popular television series broadcast in 2003, Ferguson's *Empire* became a bestseller whose influence rapidly exceeded other conveniently available narratives of Britain's imperial past by a considerable margin. With the national curriculum devoting little attention to the subject

---

[50] Alongside Gilroy's discussions in *After Empire* (especially ch. 3) and *Between Camps: Nations, Cultures, and the Allure of Race* (London, 2000), see in particular Sonya O. Rose, *Which People's War?: National Identity and Citizenship in Britain 1939–1945* (Oxford, 2003); Wendy Webster, *Englishness and Empire 1939–1965* (Oxford, 2005). Although thousands of British soldiers and civilians had also suffered Japanese internment in Southeast Asia, they were fewer in number than their Dutch counterparts and made much less of an impact in dislodging European-focused war memories in the post-war era in Britain than had been the case in the Netherlands. See Felicia Yap, 'Voices and Silences of Memory: Civilian Internees of the Japanese in British Asia during the Second World War', *Journal of British Studies*, 50:4 (2011), 917–40.

[51] Gilroy, *Between Camps*, 5.

[52] My discussion of Ferguson's, Elkins', and Anderson's books partly draws upon my earlier analysis in Elizabeth Buettner, '"Setting the Record Straight"?: Imperial History in Postcolonial British Public Culture', in Ulrike Lindner, Maren Möhring, Mark Stein, and Silke Stroh (eds.), *Hybrid Cultures—Nervous States: Britain and Germany in a (Post)Colonial World* (Amsterdam, 2010), 89–104. For a perceptive critique of Ferguson's *Empire* television series, see Jon Wilson, 'Niall Ferguson's Imperial Passion', *History Workshop Journal*, 56 (2003), 175–83.

in secondary schools, British university students enrolling in imperial history courses after 2003 regularly claimed that their initial interest had been sparked by Ferguson's multimedia contributions.[53] What themes and arguments drove what proved such a compelling account that captured the attention of a wide reading and viewing public?

In contrast to Gilroy and other critics, Ferguson began by proposing that the case against the British empire was well-known, using this assumption as his rationale for giving little space to imperial detractors (reminding his readers that in any case 'the Radical critique of imperialism was an over-simplification').[54] 'There is no need here to recapitulate in any detail the arguments against imperialism', he claimed (or, by implication, to take them seriously); it was widely considered 'one of history's Bad Things' and ranked as 'unfashionable'.[55] True, '[s]lavery and the slave trade cannot be and are not disclaimed, any more than ... the expropriation of the Matabele or the Amritsar massacre'.[56] By and large, however, such regrettable aspects receive short shrift. 'Blemishes' are briefly invoked to clear the decks for Ferguson's una-bashed emphasis on the positive side of Britain's imperial 'balance sheet'.[57] '[T]he legacy of Empire is not just "racism, racial discrimination, xenophobia and related intolerance" – which in any case existed long before colonialism', he stressed; 'the fact remains that no organization in history has done more to promote the free movement of goods, capital and labour than the British Empire in the nineteenth and early twentieth centuries. And no organization has done more to impose Western norms of law, order and governance around the world', implemented by 'remarkably non-venal institutions'. The British directly involved in this history, including members of his own family, were not its only beneficiaries: both colonizers and colonized were better with the empire than they would have been without it.[58]

Throughout his book and television series, Ferguson featured plentiful anecdotes about British rogues, heroes, and do-gooders. The first populated the eighteenth-century empire (described as 'at best, amoral') with its fair share of opportunists and get-rich-quick schemers out for themselves.[59] The nineteenth century, however, succeeded in ridding empire of its British villains, consigning them to the dustbin of history as imperialism reformed itself and became predominantly characterized by altruism. Most bad imperialists were cordoned off at a safe chronological distance from the present, leaving the later stages of empire free for the valorization of good intentions and selfless good

---

[53] Periodic conversations about Ferguson's impact on students with colleagues at other British universities suggest my own experiences in teaching undergraduates and postgraduates at the University of York until 2013 to be broadly representative.
[54] Niall Ferguson, *Empire: How Britain Made the Modern World* (London, 2003), 284.
[55] Ibid., xvii, 188, 366.   [56] Ibid., xxvi.   [57] Ibid., 366.   [58] Ibid., xxii; see also xxvi–xxvii.
[59] Ibid., 113.

works. Nationalism and anti-colonial insurgents receive little space and decolonization even less (the latter meriting less than ten pages out of more than 400) – the lack of attention to the end of empire perhaps justified on account of its having supposedly been 'self-liquidating'.[60] Empire's rise and glorious heyday thus constitute the bulk of Ferguson's text, while its decline and fall are perfunctorily described, with scant attention to events that might mar Britain's commendable record.

Throughout his account overwhelmingly geared towards accentuating the positives, Ferguson makes occasional momentary detours into other empires to show Britain's to the best advantage or to put possible failings into perspective. Indeed, when subsequently defending himself against the accusation that he was an 'apologist for the British empire', he emphasized that 'the opposite of empire is not always no empire. So if it hadn't been the British, it might have been somebody worse. In any case, empires have been with us as a means of power and control for centuries and centuries, so you might as well cast a moral judgment on rain as on the British empire'.[61] When it came to arguments about the drain of wealth from colony to metropole, the Dutch were far worse in the East Indies than the British were in India; France also behaved badly ('In Algeria, New Caledonia and Indochina too, there was a policy of systematic expropriation of native land which made a mockery of Gallic rhetoric about universal citizenship'.).[62] Germany's colonial practices in early twentieth-century Africa also came in for criticism, while Belgian profiteering and abuses in the Congo under Léopold II were singled out for particular condemnation.[63] But of all the comparisons it was those between competing empires during the Second World War that best allowed Britain's to shine: those of Japan under Emperor Hirohito, Italy under Mussolini, and first and foremost the Third Reich under Hitler.[64] The war, Ferguson concluded, became not only Britain's 'finest hour' but also the empire's:

When faced with the choice between appeasing or fighting the worst empires in all history, the British Empire had done the right thing. ... In 1940, under Churchill's inspired, indomitable, incomparable leadership, the Empire had stood alone against the truly evil imperialism of Hitler. Even if it did not last for the thousand years that Churchill hopefully suggested it might, this was indeed the British Empire's 'finest hour'.

Yet what made it so fine, so authentically noble, was that the Empire's victory could only ever have been Pyrrhic. In the end, the British sacrificed her Empire to stop the Germans, Japanese, and Italians from keeping theirs. Did not that sacrifice alone expunge all the Empire's other sins?[65]

---

[60] Ibid., xxiv.   [61] John Crace, 'Unforgiven, unrepentant', *Guardian*, 30 May 2006.
[62] Ferguson, *Empire*, 216, 296.   [63] Ibid., 218.
[64] Ibid., 152, 218, 295–7, 335, 338–43, 363–6.   [65] Ibid., 362–3.

If the road from 'finest hour' to final hours was to prove a short one, it could be recalled with pride as one worth travelling, especially if the journey could be justified as the price of the fight against fascism and not remembered as one peopled with anti-colonial detractors who fought for decolonization from within the empire's confines. With Britain's former empire exonerated from accusations of wrongdoing, Ferguson concluded his account by claiming that imperialism still had a positive and necessary role to play in today's world, and that the only power able to undertake it was the United States. More than anything, the terrorist attacks of 11 September 2001 proved it was America's duty to step up and fulfil its responsibilities in regions of the world lacking good government. Al-Qaeda's most decisive onslaught and the United States' and Britain's subsequent invasions and occupations of Afghanistan and Iraq cast long shadows over Ferguson's work, both in *Empire* as well as his immediate follow-up project, *Colossus: The Rise and Fall of the American Empire*.[66] The same events following 11 September inspired Gilroy's account that was informed by political stances and verdicts on empire that were fundamentally opposed to Ferguson's. '[C]ountless tales of colonial brutality' continue to be ignored, he suggests, 'because a sanitized history of the imperial project is required by those who wish to bring it back to life'.[67] Regardless of their political leanings, in the early twenty-first century many find it impossible to dissociate judgements about British imperialism from judgements about contemporary American and British foreign policy and efforts to combat Islamist violence, including recourse to detention camps at Guantanamo Bay, Abu Ghraib, and elsewhere.

Critical perspectives like Gilroy's have abounded in academic studies as well as work targeted at a wider audience for decades, but few have received public attention that came close to rivalling that accorded to affirmative accounts like Ferguson's.[68] Caroline Elkins' and David Anderson's books on 1950s Kenya published in 2005 attracted considerable notice, but the response to their work from outside scholarly circles suggests how difficult it remains for narratives that challenge the imperial record to gain a foothold in public consciousness.[69] In deeply-researched studies about British methods of cracking down on the

---

[66] Ibid., 373–81; Niall Ferguson, *Colossus: The Rise and Fall of the American Empire* (London, 2004).

[67] Gilroy, *After Empire*, 52.

[68] John Newsinger, *The Blood Never Dried: A People's History of the British Empire* (London, 2006); Richard Gott, *Britain's Empire: Resistance, Repression and Revolt* (London, 2011); Pankaj Mishra, *From the Ruins of Empire: The Revolt Against the West and the Remaking of Asia* (London, 2012).

[69] Caroline Elkins, *Britain's Gulag: The Brutal End of Empire in Kenya* (London, 2005); David Anderson, *Histories of the Hanged: The Dirty War in Kenya and the End of Empire* (New York, 2005). Elkins' book also appeared as *Imperial Reckoning: The Untold Story of Britain's Gulag in Kenya* (New York, 2005).

Mau Mau insurgency and the brutal treatment of suspects, Elkins and Anderson marshalled copious evidence against received versions of the last years of empire as a peaceful time of orderly, dignified, and planned retreat predicated upon a benevolent, welfare-oriented civilizing mission. Elkins' arguments about Kikuyu internment camps proved the most polemical. Some reviewers in the British press took issue with the high African death rates she proposed, while others chaffed at the book's title, *Britain's Gulag*, and its analogies between British behaviour in their colony and repression enacted by the Nazis or in the Soviet Union under Stalin.

Whereas Niall Ferguson had invoked the Nazis to show the British empire in a positive light, Elkins used the comparison to achieve the opposite, namely, to undercut virtuous British self-understandings deriving from the war by illustrating their own role in end-of-empire atrocities soon after. The caption on her book's back cover left prospective readers in no doubt either of its tactical reliance on received Eurocentric common historical wisdom, or of its intention to put it into new perspective by painstakingly detailing the 'combined effects of exhaustion, disease, starvation and systematic brutality' that led to the deaths of 'possibly a hundred thousand or more' Mau Mau detainees between 1952 and 1960:

Britain fought in the Second World War to save the world from fascism. But just a few years after the defeat of Hitler came the Mau Mau uprising in Kenya – a mass armed rebellion by the Kikuyu people, demanding the return of their land and freedom. The draconian response of Britain's colonial government was to detain nearly the entire Kikuyu population of one-and-a-half-million – to hold them in camps or confine them in villages ringed with barbed wire – and to portray them as sub-human savages.[70]

Of the reviews published in the British press, most concurred that Elkins' and Anderson's accounts offered much in terms of a corrective version of events in 1950s Kenya, but many appearing in conservative-leaning papers qualified their endorsement in highly significant ways. Writing in the *Daily Telegraph*, one reviewer noted how the 'terrible doings' described are 'painful to those of us who love Kenya and admire what some distinguished white settlers have achieved there' – settlers who often 'worked very hard for small return'.[71] Another, while stating that 'there can be no excuse for what happened' in Kenya, emphasized that 'both authors are righteously indignant at Britain's conduct of the war, yet do not say what alternatives existed. They make no attempt to put themselves in the authorities' shoes, faced with nightly massacres in which oath-taking and witchcraft played an unpredictable part'.

[70] Elkins, *Britain's Gulag*, 147, 153, 179–81, 335; quotes take from the back cover. Scholars have also critiqued the book's use of Nazi and Soviet comparisons; see Howe, 'Colonising and Exterminating?'.

[71] Max Hastings, 'The dark side of Empire', *Daily Telegraph*, 10 January 2005.

Elkins' and Anderson's versions were dismissed as 'one-sided': 'neither author was in Kenya during Mau Mau. They present an image of the British that will be unrecognisable to the many thousands of doctors, vets, nurses, teachers, farmers, engineers, district and administrative officers who gave their lives to that country without ever torturing, raping, or murdering anyone'.[72]

Other commentators conceded that some Britons involved in counterinsurgency may have acted inappropriately but insisted that these formed but a small minority, just as Dutch defenders of military operations in late 1940s Indonesia pleaded that violence was a question of individual incidents and not deployed systematically. In large part, however, the British government and colonial administration were absolved from much of the responsibility, which was shifted onto white settlers or the 'loyal Kikuyu' who were also instrumental collaborators in repressing Mau Mau.[73] Niall Ferguson, for his part, argued that events like Mau Mau and its repression were not the British imperial norm.[74] The master narrative of a benevolent, well-intentioned, and decent British empire could thereby be largely upheld and the damage to its legacy limited and ringfenced.

Controversies about Britain's conduct during the Mau Mau revolt did not subside in the wake of Anderson's and Elkins' books. Since 2005, the evidence they uncovered made them both expert witnesses in a lengthy court case initiated in 2009 by a London law firm on behalf of five elderly Mau Mau veterans, who had suffered appalling injuries from beatings, sexual assaults, castration, and other forms of torture while incarcerated as suspected 'terrorists'. The British government tried hard to stymie the case, arguing that too much time had elapsed and too few reliable witnesses could be found; Britain even went so far as to insist that responsibility lay instead with Kenya's own authorities, despite the fact that Kenya was years away from independence at the time.[75] It was only when the High Court ruled that the claimants had a viable legal case in 2013 that the government responded with an out-of-court financial settlement and rhetorical gesture. Over 5,000 surviving Kenyans abused as Mau Mau detainees were promised £19.9 million in compensation and granted a partial official recognition of misdeeds. As Foreign Secretary William Hague stated in the House of Commons:

we understand the pain and grievance felt by those who were involved in the events of the emergency in Kenya. The British government recognises that Kenyans were subject to torture and other forms of ill-treatment at the hands of the colonial administration.

[72] Nicholas Best, 'They died cursing the British', *Sunday Telegraph*, 16 January 2005.
[73] On 'loyal Kikuyu', see Robert Oakeshott, 'Mau Mau and all that', *Spectator*, 5 March 2005.
[74] Niall Ferguson, 'Home truths about famine, war and genocide', *Independent*, 30 April 2007.
[75] 'Mau Mau uprising: Bloody history of Kenya conflict', www.bbc.com/news/uk-12997138, accessed 7 April 2011.

The British government sincerely regrets that these abuses took place and that they marred Kenya's progress towards independence.[76]

Revealingly, however, Britain stopped short of accepting legal liability for what its colonial administration had done, and countless other Kenyan claims remained unresolved. Clearly, it was hoped that settling out of court would defuse the issue and put an end to further damaging disclosures. The 2013 ruling and ensuing announcement were unprecedented nonetheless: never before had the government admitted to committing acts of torture in the empire or come as close to apologizing for imperial atrocities. As Elkins put it, 'Britons can no longer hide behind the rhetoric of unequivocal imperial success. Instead, British liberalism in the empire – with its alleged spread of civilisation, progress, liberty and rule of law justifying any coercive actions – has been irreversibly exposed'.[77] Anderson, for his part, hoped that 'maybe we in Britain have also now begun to come to terms with our imperial past. It is a step in the right direction'.[78] But opinions remained strongly divided: judging from comments posted on the Internet, while many people applauded the decision as fully justified and long overdue, many others ardently resented the idea that Britain should pay compensation or express remorse, even for the most egregious forms of misrule let alone for empire more generally.[79] Hostility was to be anticipated given how the prospect of the trial had been covered in the conservative press. Reminding his readers of the murders of the Ruck settler family and their African 'houseboy' in 1953 (see Chapter 1), a journalist for the *Daily Mail* stated:

Let's be clear. Atrocities committed by the British against Kenyans are to be condemned. This was not a pretty war by any means and most definitely not Britain's finest hour ... But in the finger-pointing ... it is well to remember the Rucks and their innocent six-year-old son slashed to death in his bed. There is another side to the coin of British brutality – that of the horrors inflicted by the Mau Mau.[80]

In the early twenty-first century, Britain, like Belgium, the Netherlands, and France, has thus seen selected episodes from the imperial past subjected to

---

[76] 'Mau Mau torture victims to receive compensation – Hague', www.bbc.com/news/uk-227900 37, accessed 6 June 2013.

[77] Caroline Elkins, 'Britain has said sorry to the Mau Mau. The rest of the empire is still waiting', *Guardian*, 7 June 2013.

[78] Professor David Anderson, 'Justice for Kenya's Colonial Torture Victims', www2.warwick.ac .uk/knowledge/culture/maumau/, accessed 20 August 2014. See also articles by Stephen Howe, David M. Anderson, Huw Bennett, and Caroline Elkins included in the 'Mau Mau Judgement' section of the *Journal of Imperial and Commonwealth History*, 39:5 (2011).

[79] See online comments posted in response to Elkins' piece in *The Guardian* (www.theguardian .com/commentisfree/2013/jun/06/britain-maumau-empire-waiting) and the BBC reports quoted earlier.

[80] Tony Rennell, 'Justifiably the British are accused of brutality in 1950s Kenya. But why aren't the Mau Mau butchers also in the dock?', *Daily Mail* (London), 12 April 2011.

intense bouts of critical reappraisal. Indictments coexist in tension with positive imperial associations that remain widely held, the latter proving extremely difficult to dislodge even once new light has been shone on particular cases. Apologists are quick to label these as unrepresentative exceptions (despite ample historical evidence to the contrary) within an imperial legacy worthy of pride, righteousness, and satisfaction that must be defended from detractors. Not only did postcolonial Britain continue to draw upon narratives of empire as a success story that had been circulated before and during the era of decolonization; the intervening decades had produced new portrayals of colonialism as an acceptable source of nostalgia. Empire became a popular theme in British heritage films, television productions, literature, non-fiction, fashion, and interior decoration, with white adventures during the Raj in India or amidst settler society in Kenya finding their place in the cultural mainstream.[81] Reaching its apex in the 1980s, the imperial revival was already evident in the previous decade with radio programmes like *Plain Tales from the Raj* and *Plain Tales from the Dark Continent*. As Britain cast a fond and reverential look back upon a disappeared colonial world replete with adventure, glamour, romance, and achievement, it accorded starring roles to those who could offer something that later generations of historians born after decolonization never could: firsthand experience. Aging ex-colonizers' stories were promoted as the 'real' history of empire, told by and about Britons who had lived it and thus could 'set the record straight'. In the process, they reinforced a celebratory narrative that remains popular and that critics have yet to overturn.

* * *

Repatriates and ethnic minorities as leading defenders, critics, and initiators of public discussion

Across postcolonial Europe, repatriated former colonials have repeatedly counted among the most vocal and determined contributors to discussions about the colonial past. Britons who later shared their memories of past times in bygone colonial arenas, Indisch Dutch reconstructing life in the East Indies after their resettlement in the postcolonial Netherlands, Portugal's *retornados* from Africa, France's large and politicized *pied-noir* population of ex-*Algérie*

---

[81] Salman Rushdie, 'Outside the Whale' (1984), in *Imaginary Homelands: Essays and Criticism 1981–1991* (London, 1991), 87–101; John McBratney, 'The Raj Is All The Rage: Paul Scott's *The Raj Quartet* and Colonial Nostalgia', *North Dakota Quarterly*, 55:3 (1987), 204–9; Elizabeth Buettner, *Empire Families: Britons and Late Imperial India* (Oxford, 2004), 267–70; Patricia M.E. Lorcin, *Historicizing Colonial Nostalgia: European Women's Narratives of Algeria and Kenya 1900–Present* (Basingstoke, 2011), Part III; Will Jackson, 'White Man's Country: Kenya Colony and the Making of a Myth', *Journal of Eastern African Studies*, 5:2 (2011), 344–68.

française settlers, Belgians who once lived and worked in the Congo, and others offered renditions of colonialism in which personal experiences and wider European imperial projects became inseparable. Private, family, and community ties with empire, often over the course of generations, encouraged returns to colonial times that blended with fond recollections of formative phases of the life cycle. Happy memories of childhood, youth, early adulthood and married life, and rewarding careers in an atmosphere characterized by tropical conviviality, a valued sense of community and belonging, and affectionate relationships (including friendly relationships with the colonized) prevailed. For many, the stark contrast between colonial times and the disruptive transitions and crises that followed sharpened nostalgic sentiments. Whether returns to past times were undertaken alone in private thoughts, in writing down memories to be shared with others, or in conversations, they were deeply anchored in postcolonial social contexts that worked to reactivate memories at specific moments.

Britain's former colonials illustrate how the decades after the sun had set on the empire but when surviving participants hovered in its twilight encouraged dual processes of memory making and its gradual dissemination to wider social groups. Initially, Britons who had lived and worked in imperial India, Africa, or other overseas arenas reminisced privately or in the company of fellow ex-colonizers. Participating in organizations devoted to Asian and African heritage, attending reunions of retired overseas service personnel, and reading and contributing to these associations' newsletters, magazines, and ultimately Internet discussion groups provided valued opportunities for face-to-face or long-distance engagement with people of similar backgrounds.[82] These outlets facilitated the consolidation and transmission of individual memories and the building of a widely shared story of the past. Retirement gave many people greater opportunities to engage and also brought home the reality that their time to reconnect with their imperial past was running out. Writing memoirs, donating their papers and mementoes to libraries and archives, and taking part in oral history and documentary projects offered the chance to pass

---

[82] I have examined one London-based organization, the British Association for Cemeteries in South Asia founded in 1976, in Elizabeth Buettner, 'Cemeteries, Public Memory and Raj Nostalgia in Postcolonial Britain and India', *History & Memory*, 18:1 (2006), 5–42, and considered related issues at greater length in Elizabeth Buettner, '"We Don't Grow Coffee and Bananas in Clapham Junction You Know!": Imperial Britons Back Home', in Robert Bickers (ed.), *Settlers and Expatriates: Britons Over the Seas (Oxford History of the British Empire Companion Series)* (Oxford, 2010), 302–28. On 'Rhodesian' identity perpetuated across time and space after Zimbabwe's independence in 1980, see Tony King, 'Rhodesians in Hyperspace: The Maintenance of a National and Cultural Identity', in Karim H. Karim (ed.), *The Media of Diaspora* (London, 2003), 177–88; Donal Lowry, 'Rhodesia 1890–1980: "The Lost Dominion"', in Bickers (ed.), *Settlers and Expatriates*, 147–8.

along their experiences and opinions that many were eager to take before it was 'too late'.

Between the mid-1970s and the 1980s, British firsthand accounts of life in the colonies gradually moved beyond close-knit circles of family, friends, and old acquaintances and into public culture.[83] Some people simply wanted to make their papers or interviews available for posterity by transferring them to archives or responded to invitations to clear out their attics or have their memories recorded, while others embarked on purposeful projects to correct what they resented as inaccurate or biased conceptions of empire. Rehabilitating colonialism and understandings about Britons who had been most intimately connected with it were paramount aims. 'Old India hands' and 'old Africa hands' penned autobiographies, histories, and fictional renditions of colonial times, often with the intention of combatting stereotypes that colonials lived easy lives of privilege as the beneficiaries of exploitative and racially unequal societies. In reality, many Britons had gone to the empire on account of the opportunities it offered for incomes, status, and leisure that exceeded those they could enjoy back home. But in recollections recorded with the aim of reinforcing a positive legacy of personal, familial, and national imperial endea-vours, they emphasized hard work, sacrifices, lasting achievements, and good relations with colonial subjects. M.M. Kaye, one of the best known of countless chroniclers of late British India who published a series of widely-read novels and autobiographies, spoke for many when recalling her own early-twentieth century childhood as the daughter of an Indian Civil Servant in 1990. The family's Indian domestic servants were 'firm friends and allies', while the Indians who worked for her father 'loved and revered him and would be forever grateful for the encouragement he had given them':

men of my race who spent their lives in Indian service were not overpaid and pampered 'Burra-Sahibs' lording it over 'the natives', but were really people like [my father] who worked themselves to the bone to serve, to the best of their ability, a country and a people whom they had come to love so much.

Kaye hoped that 'a time may come when the world will look back on the era of the Pax Britannica as a golden age, and not, as the present tendency seems to be, a dark, disgraceful period of brutal colonial repression'.[84] Portrayals like these that exonerated empire and Britons active in it by using personal experiences as a weapon against critics reinforced the foundations of a resoundingly

[83] Buettner, *Empire Families*, 252–70.
[84] M.M. Kaye, *The Sun in the Morning: My Early Years in India and England* (New York, 1990), 91, 383, 303, 419. Mary Margaret Kaye (1908–2004) wrote three autobiographies, murder mysteries that often had imperial settings, and a number of historical novels, the best known of which was *The Far Pavilions* (1978) that was made into a television miniseries in 1984 and into a musical that debuted in London's West End in 2005.

celebratory imperial eulogy that outlived Kaye and her generation, remaining alive in public consciousness thanks to its circulation via multiple media.

As the British example suggests, at least several decades could elapse between decolonization and returns home and concerted efforts to tell their stories publicly and play a part in shaping wider understandings of the colonial past. Portugal's *retornados*, for instance, have taken much longer than British ex-colonials to share personal memories of Portuguese Africa with a broader general public exceeding their own circles, a time lag corresponding to Portugal's belated decolonization history in the mid-1970s. Having little visibility as a distinct group after their return, close to forty years later their stories gradually became available in leading bookshops. Titles like *África Eterna: Testemunhos de um tempo que não se esquece* (*Eternal Africa: Testimonies of an Unforgettable Time*) were advertised as '*uma história de amor por África*' ('a love story for Africa'), and many centred on fondly-recalled overseas lives followed by a time of '*perda, incerteza e coragem*' ('loss, uncertainty, and courage'). One book about the 1975 airlift that brought several hundred thousand to Portugal from Angola stressed the hardships of those who fled with little or nothing, returning as 'refugees' who had 'escaped with their lives'.[85] Along with compilations of personal stories are works of fiction such as the acclaimed 2011 novel *O Retorno* (*The Return*), Dulce Maria Cardoso's story of a family's traumatic resettlement in a society that viewed them with hostility, told from the standpoint of an adolescent and closely patterned on her own family's experiences.[86]

Retornados' input into discourses of late colonialism and decolonization that circulate beyond themselves still appears to be gathering momentum. However, their main themes – deep-seated grievances about decolonization and their often abrupt departures described as 'exoduses' in which they 'lost everything', and bitter misgivings about finding themselves unwelcome in metropolitan society – already bear close resemblance to the subjects long prominent in the stories of earlier waves of repatriates to other countries, including the Indisch Dutch and French *pieds-noirs*. In their self-victimization, their narratives also overlap with those by and about Portuguese veterans noted earlier. Whether they will prove as central to the remaking of national histories and memories of colonialism as their counterparts elsewhere remains to be seen.

---

[85] Catarina Carvalho *et al.* (eds.), *África Eterna: Testemunhos de um tempo que não se esquece* (Alfragide, 2012); Rita Garcia, *S.O.S. Angola: Os Dias da Ponte Aérea* (Alfragide, 2011); quotes are taken from the front and back covers of Garcia's book. See also Sarah Adamopoulos, *Voltar: Memória do Colonialismo e da Descolonização* (Lisbon, 2012).

[86] Dulce Maria Cardoso, *O Retorno* (Lisbon, 2011) was also published in French translation in 2014. Born in 1964, Cardoso moved to Angola with her family as a baby and returned to Portugal in 1975.

East Indies repatriates arriving in the Netherlands faced intense social pressure to assimilate into metropolitan society and leave their colonial past behind as befitting a post-decolonization era, as Chapter 6 explored. Never encouraged to perpetuate a separate identity that dated back to colonial times, initially their Indies memories were overwhelmingly private ones, exchanged informally among family, friends, and close acquaintances whose experiences were similar. Yet by the late 1950s a re-forged Indisch group identity was already discernible. Indies-oriented publications, clubs, associations, and reunions multiplied and a new Indisch community spirit was created in the Netherlands – one in which the colonial class and racial divisions pervading it were increasingly effaced but in which elites, often but never exclusively white, became the driving force. The *Tong-Tong* magazine, Indies-themed literature, illustrated books and memoirs, and periodic events such as the Pasar Malam Besar ('great evening bazaar' in colonial colloquial parlance) taking place in The Hague (where many Indisch had resettled) emerged as forums and vehicles that worked to consolidate, perpetuate, and reinvent an Indisch imagined community intent on looking backward. Within it, the Dutch East Indies that were no more were fondly and sentimentally recalled as an idyllic time – *tempo doeloe*, Malay for 'the good old days' – that ended abruptly and tragically in 1942 with the arrival of the Japanese.[87]

After 1942 nothing was the same again: Europeans were interned *en masse* in civilian and prisoner-of-war camps from which many never returned alive, Eurasians suffered severe deprivation outside the camps, and those who survived until Japan's surrender on 15 August 1945 faced the wave of Indonesian nationalist violence that came in its wake. Decolonization and their ultimate departure further enhanced feelings of victimhood that were already strong as a result of wartime sufferings. Migrants to the Netherlands found their Indies

---

[87] Among the excellent studies now available on the topics drawn upon here, see Wim Willems, 'No Sheltering Sky: Migrant Identities of Dutch Nationals from Indonesia', in Smith (ed.), *Europe's Invisible Migrants*, 33–59; Wim Willems, *Tjalie Robinson: Biografie van een Indo-schrijver* (Amsterdam, 2008); Lizzy van Leeuwen, *Ons Indisch erfgoed: Zestig jaar strijd om cultuur en identiteit* (Amsterdam, 2008); Andrew Goss, 'From *Tong-Tong* to Tempo Doeloe: Eurasian Memory Work and the Bracketing of Dutch Colonial History, 1957–1961', *Indonesia*, 70 (2000), 9–36; Sarah De Mul, 'Nostalgia for Empire: "Tempo Doeloe" in Contemporary Dutch Literature', *Memory Studies*, 3:4 (2010), 423–8; Paul Bijl, 'Dutch Colonial Nostalgia Across Decolonisation', *Journal of Dutch Literature*, 4:1 (2013), 128–49; and many contributions by Pamela Pattynama, including *Bitterzoet Indië: Herinnering en nostalgie in literatuur, foto's en films* (Amsterdam, 2014); '(Un)happy Endings: Nostalgia in Postimperial and Postmemory Dutch Films', in Boehmer and De Mul (eds.), *Postcolonial Low Countries*, 97–122. For broader overviews that highlight Indisch themes at many junctures, see Gert Oostindie, *Postcolonial Netherlands: Sixty-five Years of Forgetting, Commemorating, Silencing* (Amsterdam, 2011); Ulbe Bosma, *Terug uit de koloniën: Zestig jaar postkoloniale migranten en hun organisaties* (Amsterdam, 2009); Ulbe Bosma and Marga Alferink, 'Multiculturalism and Settlement: The Case of Dutch Postcolonial Migrant Organisations', *Journal of International Migration and Integration*, 13:3 (2012), 265–83.

experiences, culture, and identity ignored, misunderstood, and unrecognized, and those of mixed descent were commonly subjected to Dutch racism. Occasions to revisit their Indies origins by reading and writing about them and meeting with one another paved the way for what would coalesce into an increasingly confident, active, and outwardly-directed Indisch lobby by the 1970s. Cultural assertiveness was accompanied by demands for national recognition as well as official compensation for their losses and privations. Along with disseminating popular books revolving around rosy portrayals and sepia-tinted photographs of a pre-war *tempo doeloe* that attracted a larger audience, the Indisch gradually succeeded in winning a recognized place in Dutch national commemorative culture via incessant returns to the Second World War years that made an indelible mark.[88]

If the furore provoked by the controversies that erupted in 1969 about Dutch 'war crimes' committed between 1945 and 1949 soon fizzled out, fading from public discussion via a feeble retreat into an insistence that they were merely unfortunate 'excesses', repatriates' relentless focus on the Second World War proved a far more effective means of raising consciousness of colonial history in the postcolonial Netherlands soon after debates about 'excesses' subsided. Pervasive forms of Second World War commemoration that initially focused almost exclusively on European events proved amenable to a broadening-out to encompass its Pacific arena in which the Indies-based Dutch could be unproblematically remembered as war victims – an infinitely more palatable form of remembering empire than grappling with much thornier questions of decolonization atrocities perpetrated by Dutch veterans. Dutch who had never been to the East Indies might well have found photographs and stories about *tempo doeloe* appealing in their portrayals of a romanticized and exotic distant world, but invoking the war experienced in the former colony as well as the metropole made Indisch sufferings comprehensible despite their distinctiveness.

Throughout the 1970s and 1980s, Indisch repatriate initiatives lay behind the inauguration of vast numbers of war memorials and annual remembrance ceremonies on 15 August. This culminated in the unveiling of the national Indisch Monument in The Hague in 1988, where ceremonies turned into annual

---

[88] On *tempo doeloe* photographs, see E. Breton de Nijs (a pseudonym used by Rob Nieuwenhuys), *Tempo Doeloe: fotografische documenten uit het oude Indië, 1870–1914* (Amsterdam, 1961); Rob Nieuwenhuys, *Komen en blijven: Tempo Doeloe, een verzonken wereld: fotografische documenten uit het oude Indië, 1870–1920* (Amsterdam, 1982; 2nd edn, 1998); Dorine Bronkhorst and Esther Wils, *Tropenecht: Indische en Europese kleding in Nederlands-Indië* (The Hague: Stichting Tong Tong, 1996); Pattynama, *Bitterzoet Indië*, ch. 7. On the Second World War, see especially Raben (ed.), *Representing the Japanese Occupation*, particularly Raben's introduction and chapters by Elsbeth Locher-Scholten and Frank van Vree; Locher-Scholten, 'From Urn to Monument'; Esther Captain, *Achter het kawat was Nederland: Indische oorlogservaringen en –herinneringen 1942–1995* (Kampen, 2002); Hans Meijer, *Indische rekening: Indië, Nederland en de backpay-kwestie, 1945–2005* (Amsterdam, 2005), along with many works cited earlier.

Figure 9.4 Indisch Monument, The Hague, inaugurated 1988.
Photograph by author, 2013.

events.[89] What had once been overwhelmingly Indisch group rituals to mourn the dead and reflect on their own ordeals as survivors ultimately became national occasions. Although annual commemorations of the Netherlands' liberation from Nazi occupation every 4 and 5 May still take precedence, 15 August has joined them as a state ritual with attendant media coverage and is now officially recognized as the day the war ended. Through war memorialization, Indisch Dutch thus succeeded both in asserting their separate identity and gaining visible recognition for their experiences while also embedding them in Dutch national culture – one which, as the last chapter noted, has also made space for Indisch-style food and the Pasar Malam Besar, now called the Tong Tong Festival, an event that celebrated its fiftieth anniversary in 2008 and attracts well over 100,000 visitors every June.[90]

---

[89] www.indieherdenking.nl. An indication of the dominance of Second World War memorials among monuments concerned with the colonial past can be found in Gert Oostindie, Henk Schulte Nordholt, and Fridus Steijlen (with photographs by Eveline Kooijman), *Postkoloniale Monumenten in Nederland/Post-colonial Monuments in the Netherlands* (Leiden, 2011).

[90] www.tongtongfair.nl; www.stichtingtongtong.nl.

Understandings of *Algérie française* common among repatriated *pieds-noirs*, army officers, and others who ardently espoused its cause proved harder to transmit to others in France after decolonization. Like the Indisch Dutch, they too were indelibly associated with the memory of war, but with the lost and divisive Algerian War that most in the metropole were happy to forget as opposed to the Second World War that dominated collective memory in France and the Netherlands alike. This was central to the *pieds-noirs'* uncertain position in postcolonial France. As Philip Dine puts it, '[w]ithout the *pieds-noirs* there would have been no Algerian war: it was they who constituted "French Algeria", and it was their entrenchment which made the 1954–62 conflict both so inevitable and so intractable'.[91] Feeling unwelcome and rejected, socially marginalized, and sold out by decolonization after resettling north of the Mediterranean, many *pieds-noirs* turned inwards and found practical and emotional support in the hundreds of new associations that sprang up to defend their interests. These groups fought for state indemnification for losses of property and livelihoods in North Africa, and after their campaigns scored successes their *Maisons des rapatriés* (repatriates' centres) and sponsored events continued to provide social spaces and occasions for *pieds-noirs* to stay connected and retrospectively recreate *Algérie française* in the imagination.[92]

For decades, repatriate associations and activities were largely inwardly-focused. While the metropolitan mainstream had willed itself to move on from the Algerian War, many *pieds-noirs* were still fighting it, even amongst each other. Decolonization failed to dampen their passionate commitment to the struggle against the FLN or the hatred for those perceived to have betrayed *Algérie française* and its ideals. De Gaulle unsurprisingly remained loathed long after his death, but even leading *pied-noir* activists could find themselves on the receiving end of diehard acts committed by the OAS. That its staunchest partisans never considered themselves *ex*-OAS even after decades had elapsed was revealed with brutal clarity in 1993, when Jacques Roseau, co-founder and leading spokesman of the best-known repatriate association and a former OAS militant himself, was gunned down in the town of Montpellier. Condemning him as a 'pro-Arab traitor' for shaking hands with a member of the FLN in a television debate, the three men convicted of Roseau's murder all openly admitted to OAS credentials, one proudly proclaiming that he would remain OAS until he died.[93]

---

[91] Dine, *Images*, 146.   [92] See Chapter 6.
[93] Kauffer, *OAS*, 11–16; Benjamin Stora, *Le transfert d'une mémoire: De l''Algérie française' au racisme anti-arabe* (Paris, 1999), 64–65; Vincent Quivy, *Les soldats perdus: Des anciens de l'OAS racontent* (Paris, 2003), 16. Roseau had also committed the sin of supporting neo-gaullist politicians rather than the *Front National*.

This shocking incident suggests why *pied-noir* perceptions of the past were so strongly at odds with those of most people in France after empire. With the exception of the *Front National* and other far-right groups that retained a strong ideological commitment (and often personal ties) to the lost *Algérie française* cause, few were so attached to this past or so resentful of decolonization (indeed, the vast majority of *pieds-noirs* themselves would never have gone as far as Roseau's killers). Theirs was an oppositional memory, a counterpoint to the national tide of willed amnesia. '*Nostalgérie*' for the years up until 1954 was the *pied-noir* equivalent of the pre-1942 *tempo doeloe* of Indisch Dutch recollection. *Algérie française* became a paradise lost after the 1962 exodus, an idyllic time and beautiful place in which relationships between Europeans and Arabs were considered analogous to those within a contented family. In *pied-noir* refashionings of the past, the FLN was dismissed as an unrepresentative minority amidst a peaceful and compliant population.[94]

Pied-noir memory work after resettlement focused on an invented golden age before the rise of ethnic hostilities as well as on defending settlers' reputation against alleged metropolitan misconceptions. In 1955 Albert Camus, the best-known literary figure to emerge from the community, had complained of press coverage that made Algeria appear 'peopled by a million *colons* with riding crops and cigars, mounted on Cadillacs'. *Pieds-noirs* were still contesting *gros colon* (colonists who were big, in the sense of being rich and symbolically fat) imagery decades later, emphasizing instead that most settlers were humble people of modest means and often quite poor, much like Camus himself before his rise to fame.[95] Ordinary, everyday people living worthy but unspectacular lives, they nonetheless played a part in what had been France's distinguished 132-year Algerian presence that provided education, hospitals, ports, and an invaluable modern infrastructure in what they continued to insist had been part of France, not a colony. As an eighty-year-old man living in Marseille put it in 1999, 'the *pieds-noirs* were neither more nor less than the people of a French province who found themselves expelled from their province'.[96] France simply needed to recognize what *pieds-noirs* considered self-evident 'truths': that France's presence had been of great benefit, and that

---

[94] Joëlle Hureau, *La mémoire des pieds-noirs* (Paris, 2001); Dominique Farques, *Mémoire de Pieds-Noirs* (Paris, 2008); Andrea L. Smith, *Colonial Memory and Postcolonial Europe: Maltese Settlers in Algeria and France* (Bloomington, 2006), ch. 7; Dine, *Images*, ch. 6; Antoine Prost, 'The Algerian War in French Collective Memory', in Jay Winter and Emmanuel Sivan (eds.), *War and Remembrance in the Twentieth Century* (Cambridge, 1999), 168; Stora, *La gangrène*, 240; Anne Roche, 'Pieds-noirs: le "retour"', *Modern & Contemporary France*, NS 2:2 (1994), 151–64; William B. Cohen, 'Pied-Noir Memory, History, and the Algerian War', in Smith (ed.), *Europe's Invisible Migrants*, 129–45.
[95] Clarisse Buono, *Pieds-noirs de père en fils: Voix et regards* (Paris, 2004), 83 (for Camus quote), 142; Smith, *Colonial Memory*, 179.
[96] Buono, *Pieds-noirs de père en fils*, 73–4.

the real victims of *Algérie française* were most certainly not 'those people over there' but rather the *pieds-noirs* who became exiled when it ended.

Pied-noir efforts to engender metropolitan recognition of their version of French Algeria were most strikingly apparent in southeastern France where many had resettled after 1962. In Marseille, Marignane, Fréjus, Toulon, and other towns and cities, they and their political allies in the *Front National* and other parties have initiated countless memorials to their heroes of the fight against decolonization, like the crossroads in Toulon named after General Salan or the many *stèles* (memorial columns) honouring OAS 'martyrs' who died valiantly attempting to save *Algérie française* from its betrayers. Their municipal impact generated considerable controversy as human rights campaigners and others strongly denounced the rehabilitation of OAS terrorists and murderers and sought to have the *stèles* removed.[97] Long underway but restricted in their wider influence, local initiatives gathered pace throughout the 1990s and 2000s until they gradually converged with, and helped reorient, changing national memories of colonialism, specifically of France's history in Algeria.

France's return to its colonial past in the 1990s may have ended with the spate of Algerian War torture accounts in the media, but signs that revisionist tendencies were simultaneously underway were equally apparent. In 1994, Albert Camus' unfinished novel *Le premier homme* (*The First Man*) was released with great fanfare thirty-four years after his death in a car crash, the public eagerly devouring the autobiographical account of an impoverished upbringing and the European settler community by one of France's most highly acclaimed literary figures. Together with a new biography, Camus' posthumous book did much to rehabilitate his reputation that his settler sympathies and inability to condemn *Algérie française* outright had compromised among intellectuals by the time of his death amidst what had descended into a venomous Franco–French split over the Algerian War. His compassionate and laudatory treatment of Algeria's Europeans reinforced apologist *pied-noir* myths vindicating the *petits blancs* (small whites), lending them new cultural legitimacy and widespread publicity given his immense cultural stature.[98]

Colonial justifications bearing considerable similarity to *pied-noir* self-defences also became increasingly apparent within mid-1990s conservative political discourse after Jacques Chirac became France's president. Chirac, who had served as a lieutenant in Algeria in the 1950s, made a number of public

---

[97] Dard, *Voyage*, 395–403; contributions by Jean-Philippe Ould-Aouida, François Nadiras, and Vincent Geisser in Jahan and Ruscio (eds.), *Histoire de la colonisation*, Part III; Romain Bertrand, *Mémoires d'empire: La controverse autour du 'fait colonial'* (Broissieux, 2006), 17, 27, 48, 55; Stora, *Le transfert*, 67–8.

[98] Albert Camus, *The First Man*, translated by David Hapgood (London, 1995; first published 1994); Nancy Wood, *Vectors of Memory: Legacies of Trauma in Postwar Europe* (Oxford, 1999), ch. 6; Philip Dine, '(Still) *A la recherche de l'Algérie perdue*: French Fiction and Film, 1992–2001', *Historical Reflections/Réflexions Historiques*, 28:2 (2002), 263–8.

statements in which he spoke of 'the civilizing work of France' in the colonial era, praising its 'pioneers' and 'builders' thus:

Pacification, development of the territories, the spread of education, the establishment of modern medical practices, and the creation of administrative and legal institutions are all marks of that indisputable work to which the French presence contributed, not only in northern Africa but also on every continent. ... over thirty years after the return to the metropole of [the French of Algeria] it is right to recall the importance and richness of the work accomplished there and of which [France] is proud.

Thus, as Nicolas Bancel observes, 'advances in what was politically "sayable" within the "republican Right" came about through a return, little noticed at the time, to the favorite themes of colonial propaganda, which until then had been confined to a few circles on the far right'.[99] What began as a trickle gradually turned into a flood, with defenders of France's colonial era and especially its history in Algeria becoming increasingly assertive as French behaviour during the Algerian War came under fire during and after 1998.

Renewed controversies about decolonization-era torture occurred alongside other excavations of France's earlier history of participation in the African slave trade and colonial slavery that led to the Taubira law of 2001. Described further later, this declared slavery to have been a 'crime against humanity' – a milestone that broadened out the definition beyond its embeddedness in the Second World War. Commemorations and high-level state condemnations of slavery and the deluge of Algerian torture narratives contributed to a backlash against repentance that culminated in the 23 February 2005 law, article 4 of which rendered it instantly notorious. This stipulated that French school curricula and required textbooks had to give space to the 'positive role of the French presence overseas, notably in North Africa' – a regulation with implications for scholarly research as well as classroom teaching. The law represented the fruits of a concerted campaign to take French reassessments of the colonial era beyond its darkest moments of slavery and torture to promote an allegedly 'neutral', and indeed often glowing, reinterpretation focused on celebration rather than shame-faced contrition.[100]

Although Chirac had article 4 retracted in 2006 after a coordinated campaign against it by scholars and other critics, its road to implementation spoke volumes about the extent to which pro-colonial and particularly pro-*Algérie française* voices had succeeded in moving their perspectives from the margins

[99] Bertrand, *Mémoires d'empire*, 29–30; Nicolas Bancel, translated by Jane Marie Todd, 'The Law of February 23, 2005: The Uses Made of the Revival of France's "Colonial Grandeur"', in Charles Tshimanga, Didier Gondola, and Peter J. Bloom (eds.), *Frenchness and the African Diaspora: Identity and Uprising in Contemporary France* (Bloomington, 2009), 171.

[100] On the 23 February 2005 law, see especially Stora, *La guerre des mémoires*, 18–23; Bertrand, *Mémoires d'empire*; Bancel, 'The Law of February 23, 2005'; Claude Liauzu and Gilles Manceron (eds.), *La colonisation, la loi et l'histoire* (Paris, 2006).

to the centre of national historical discourse and memory. 'Individuals can form groups with the aim of transforming their collective memories into social action only when these memories are compatible with social norms and values accepted by the larger community', Antoine Prost argues, noting that *pied-noir* memory had long proved too discordant to perform this task.[101] The 2005 law illustrates how much the scene had changed, albeit neither completely nor consensually. On the one hand, it was repatriate initiatives to promote their historical narratives together with conservative politicians who coveted the votes of *pieds-noirs* and their sympathizers and assented to their affirmative, self-interested version of history that placed the law onto the agenda and secured its passage. To come into being, the law required political and cultural preconditions that rendered colonial rehabilitation possible in the first place.[102] But in their ultimately successful fight to have article 4 removed, however, its opponents ensured that France's colonial history became hotly debated in the mainstream media at a level that greatly exceeded discussions usually restricted to narrow academic circles.[103] Like the torture controversies preceding it, the uproar surrounding article 4 exemplified how contentious and unresolved the colonial past (and the history of French Algeria and the position of the *pieds-noirs* first and foremost) still remains in twenty-first-century France.

Belgium's former colonials (*anciens coloniaux*) demonstrate similar motives and patterns of private and organizational activity specific to their times. *Anciens* had long partaken in a vibrant associational life through numerous groups that held periodic reunions and published newsletters and magazines featuring nostalgic reminiscences, book reviews, and members' articles about Central Africa's history, ethnography, and natural environment.[104] These forums allowed members to keep up with and exchange news about old acquaintances as well as engage with topics deemed worthy of contemporary interest. Until the 1990s, *anciens* primarily spoke to each other about colonial times, either because they assumed outsiders lacked interest or because they suspected hostile responses to the colonial record. Memories were discussed or written down largely for family together with an inner circle who shared similar experiences and opinions. Thirty years after the Congo's independence, however, the scene started to change. The more *anciens* entered into retirement and

---

[101] Prost, 'Algerian War', 176.   [102] Bertrand, *Mémoires d'empire*, 66–8, 203.

[103] Claude Liauzu, 'Une loi contre l'histoire', *Le Monde diplomatique* (Paris), April 2005, 28; Sandrine Lemaire, 'Une loi qui vient de loin', *Le Monde diplomatique*, January 2006, 28; Jon Henley, 'French angry at law to teach glory of colonialism', *Guardian*, 15 April 2005.

[104] Rosario Giordano, *Belges et Italiens du Congo-Kinshasa: Récits de vie avant et après l'Indépendance* (Paris, 2008), 28; Florence Gillet, 'Congo rêvé? Congo détruit ... Les anciens coloniaux belges aux prises avec une société en repentir. Enquête sur la face émergée d'une mémoire', *Cahiers d'Histoire du Temps Présent*, 19 (2008), 86–90, which estimates that out of the approximately 30,000 *anciens* alive when research was undertaken in 2005, 56 per cent belonged to at least one, if not several, of the 39 different organizations representing them.

saw members of their cohort pass away, the more they recognized that time was running out if they hoped to make an impact on wider perceptions of Belgium's colonial era before it became 'too late'.[105]

Alongside penning written accounts, *anciens* participated in other memorial projects such as the Musée Africain de Namur, first established in the early twentieth century and located in the Francophone capital city of Wallonia. Most working on its behalf were members of the local *Cercle Royal Namurois des Anciens d'Afrique* (CRNAA), which, as its name indicates, was highly royalist and befitting an institution whose collections centred on honouring the Congo Free State, King Léopold II, and the heroic European 'pioneers' who 'pacified' the Congo and 'liberated' Africans from the slave trade. As Karel Arnaut argues, commitment to the museum became a means of struggling against their own 'disappearance and marginalisation'.[106]

Defending Belgian colonialism (be it times well before their own, or the years leading up to decolonization they had experienced personally) grew all the more urgent in response to the wave of historical accusations and deluge of bad publicity sparked by Hochschild's and De Witte's books followed by highly critical television documentaries focused on the Léopold II era and Lumumba murder. Fighting back by refuting charges of chronic Belgian violence, racism, and self-interest vis-à-vis the Congolese brought forth repeated proclamations of pride in colonial achievements, idealizations of colonial life for the colonized, and portrayals of Belgians as victims rather than beneficiaries of empire. *Anciens* founded *l'Association Mémoire du Congo* in 2002 as a direct response to hostile reports in order to gather and disseminate their own versions of the colonial past, while the long-established *Union Royale Belge pour les Pays d'Outre-Mer* (UROME, or Royal Belgian Overseas Union) issued a book entitled *La colonisation belge: Un grand aventure*.[107] An umbrella group encompassing twenty-eight smaller local or profession-specific colonial associations whose total membership approached 10,000, UROME (whose royalist leanings were as identifiable through its name as they were with the CRNAA) stepped up its extensive, multilingual website as a means of spelling out its aims. 'To restore the image of the Belgian colonial period, including the one preceding it, the Congo Free State', UROME 'will seek historical, scientific, objective, honest and impartial truth' and 'combat all libel and disinformation against the Belgian colonial era, if necessary by means

[105] Marie-Bénédicte Dembour, *Recalling the Belgian Congo: Conversations and Introspections* (New York, 2000), 68, 78. For a representative account characteristic of its time, see Gérard Jacques, *Lualaba: Histoires de l'Afrique profonde* (Brussels, 1995), especially 5, 35, 56, 96.
[106] Karel Arnaut, 'Belgian Memories, African Objects: Colonial Re-collection at the Musée Africain de Namur', *Ateliers*, 23 (2001), 29–49; alternative downloadable version available via www.africana.ugent.be/file/7 (where the quote appears on p. 7).
[107] Giordano, *Belges et Italiens*, 87; Gillet, 'Congo rêvé?', 93; www.memoiresducongo.org.

of legal procedures'.[108] To this end, its website listed Belgium's colonial achievements in meticulous detail, precisely quantifying the numbers of schools established, and the numbers of Congolese educated in them; the numbers enjoying medical care and how much the indigenous population grew; how many kilometres of roads, railway lines, and waterways were built; how many hydroelectric power plants were established and how many kilowatts of energy these produced. Together with this vast economic infrastructure that also extended to mining, agriculture, and trade, Belgium, those visiting the site learn, achieved the unification of many disparate groups of Congolese and voluntarily bestowed independence on them in 1960, bequeathing a democratic constitution, elected parliament, and universal suffrage – and all within just three generations, or the space of one lifetime.[109]

The aim of (re-)establishing 'the truth' – to which they themselves claimed a unique means of access – about Belgium's time in Central Africa still preoccupied the *anciens* over a decade after the debates about the Congo Free State atrocities and Lumumba's death had crested in the wider political and media arena. On the occasion of the fiftieth anniversary of the Congo's independence in 2010, both UROME and the CRNAA took the opportunity (again) to explain how Belgium should be proud of its colonial achievements that benefitted the Congolese and not suffer sensationalized accusations that violence in Central Africa had underpinned colonial rule. In letters to the media in the summer of 2010, their representatives labelled the controversy over severed hands at the time of Léopold II to be an outright 'lie', attributing such practices to Arab slave traders and '*africains islamisés*' *before* the Belgians ever arrived on the scene and installed a sound colonial administration. Rather than referring to the notorious use of the *chicotte* (whip), one statement went so far as to demand an end to Belgium's '*auto flagellation*' over colonialism when there was nothing to blame itself for.

Violence, in short, was not suffered by Africans but rather by Belgians – whether symbolically self-inflicted as a form of misconceived postcolonial guilt, or inflicted by Africans who participated in the 'anti-white racism which existed, and which still exists at the heart of Matonge' in Brussels. Whites who had come under physical attack during the *Force publique* mutiny of July 1960 were resurrected to prove this point, with raped women and girls taking centre stage as archetypal martyrs once again (see Chapter 6).[110] After a

---

[108] www.urome.be/en/aims.htm, accessed 23 April 2014.   [109] www.urome.be/fr2/introd.htm.
[110] Cercle Royal Namurois des Anciens d'Afrique asbl, Bulletin trimestriel, no. 3–2010, pp. 5, 6–7, 9–10, 31–2 (www.urome.be/fr2/membres/CRNAA_Bulletin_3–10.pdf). As had been the case in 1960, moreover, sexual violence suffered by African women under colonialism never entered the discussion. For a perceptive analysis of this wider issue, see Nancy Rose Hunt, 'An Acoustic Register, Tenacious Images, and Congolese Scenes of Rape and Repetition', *Cultural Anthropology*, 23:2 (2008), 220–52.

long period in which sexual violence suffered by whites at decolonization had receded from public discussion, tales of their violation by African soldiers in 1960 became reactivated by colonialism's defenders in the heated controversies raging around the turn of the millennium, just like the Ruck family murders in 1953 Kenya that later resurfaced in the *Daily Mail* in 2011 Britain. Recoiling from Belgium's official apology for Lumumba's death delivered as a follow-up to the commission of inquiry, the son of Count Harold d'Aspremont Lynden, the Minister of African Affairs in the early 1960s who De Witte (and the commission) had deemed complicit in the assassination, argued publicly that no apology should ever have been made: after all, Lumumba had presided over the rape and murder of Belgians, and no one had ever apologized to them. Many *anciens* completely agreed with him.[111]

Writing of postcolonial France, Achille Mbembe has stressed that the 'discourse against repentance' seeks nothing less than 'the rehabilitation of the colonial *oeuvre*. It asserts that the true victims of colonization were not the *indigènes*, but the *colons*. The former owe gratitude to the latter.'[112] This applies as much to Belgian discussions as to the French and British cases discussed earlier. Far from accepting the charge of perpetrator, some Belgians withdrew into the familiar habit of asserting a national status of innocent victim of aggression at the hands of others, be they Germans in two world wars, Congolese who refused to consider themselves thankful for colonial rule in 1960 and were 'anti-white', or historians daring to contradict reassuring national myths.[113] Belgium's *anciens coloniaux* provide an intriguing example of how, as Karel Arnaut phrases it, 'what looks like a middle-class, not-too-bad-off group of people with rather mainstream, if slightly

---

[111] Paul Vaute, 'Le fils du ministre Harold d'Aspremont Lynden écoeuré par les excuses du gouvernement et le projet d'une fondation: Louis Michel fait d'un génocidaire un héros', *La Libre Belgique*, 11 November 2001, discussed in Rahier, 'Ghost of Leopold II', 80; see also Gillet, 'Congo rêvé?', 96–7, 122–3, 131–2. Count Harold d'Aspremont Lynden's son Arnoud later featured prominently in a documentary in which he and Jacques Brassinne, an *ancien* who had written studies of decolonization and Lumumba's death that De Witte later attacked, strive to refute accusations of Belgian responsibility. Directed by Sven Augustijnen, *Spectres* (2011), however, not only showcases their efforts to dodge blame and insist that 'No one has anything to hide!'; it leaves both men, and their arguments, open to audience scrutiny of their motivations and personal interest in telling the stories they do. Alongside the film itself, see T.J. Demos and Hilde van Gelder (eds.), *In and Out of Brussels: Figuring Postcolonial Africa and Europe in the Films of Herman Asselberghs, Sven Augustijnen, Renzo Martens, and Els Opsomer* (Leuven, 2012), Part II, together with the essay by T.J. Demos, *Sven Augustijnen's Spectropoetics* (Brussels, 2011).

[112] Achille Mbembe, *Sortir de la grande nuit: Essai sur l'Afrique décolonisée* (Paris, 2010), 166; see also Bertrand, *Mémoires d'empire*, 184; Daniel Lefeuvre, *Pour en finir avec la repentance coloniale* (Paris, 2006). Paul Gilroy notes the British tendency to focus on white victims rather than white beneficiaries of empire in *After Empire*, 103, 115.

[113] Bragard and Planche, 'Museum Practices', 59–60. Significantly, the historian Jean Stengers took issue with Hochschild's book by claiming Léopold II as Hochschild's victim; see Vandersmissen, 'Cent ans d'instrumentalisation de Léopold II', 237.

conservative, ideas about politics and society, construct themselves as a sub-ordinate, marginalised minority'.

Examined comparatively across postcolonial Europe, not all former colo-nials are as materially well off as Arnaut suggests Belgians are, but time and again they have portrayed their position as defenders of imperial legacies as akin to a 'subaltern' group fighting a rear-guard action against a dominant mainstream which veers towards the critical or the forgetful.[114] Yet in one undeniable respect they are indeed a group whose direct influence is destined to decline, if only by dint of generational change. Some larger groups such as *pieds-noirs* and Indisch Dutch may well transfer selected aspects of a group identity rooted in a colonial past into the second, third, and subsequent gen-erations, but this appears a less likely prospect in other cases.[115] As *anciens coloniaux* gradually recede as an active group through aging and death, they leave behind them a large body of writings, memorabilia, and recorded inter-pretations available to be drawn on after their passing by anyone eager to hear their versions of history, whether to reproduce and share them or deploy them critically. Meanwhile, in the late twentieth and early twenty-first centuries imperial stories propagated by a largely white group of ex-colonizers have faced growing competition for attention and influence from those circulated by younger, postcolonial generations.[116] This forms part of a multi-ethnic chal-lenge to rethink national and imperial myths, one in which Europe's minorities with a far greater claim to qualify as 'subordinate' and 'marginalised' play increasingly important roles.

* * *

While ethnic majorities (and especially individuals and groups with close personal ties to colonialism) have dominated the process of revisiting colonial questions in Western Europe, diasporic minorities descended from colonized peoples nonetheless made significant contributions to ongoing debates. Their critical interventions come in response to positive interpretations circulated by those keen to defend and exonerate the colo-nial past, contributing to the emergence of a counter-narrative to celebra-tory and selective stories. Writers of (or descended from) South Asian, African, and West Indian backgrounds have completely revolutionized Britain's literary and scholarly canon, for instance, rendering it thoroughly

---

[114] Arnaut, 'Belgian Memories, African Objects', 17.
[115] Buono, *Pieds-noirs de père en fils*; Marlene de Vries, *'Indisch is een gevoel': De tweede en derde generatie Indische Nederlanders* (Amsterdam, 2009); Van Leeuwen, *Ons Indisch erf-goed*, 138–50; www.indisch3.nl.
[116] Laurent Licata and Olivier Klein, 'Holocaust or Benevolent Paternalism?: Intergenerational Comparisons on Collective Memories and Emotions about Belgium's Colonial Past', *International Journal of Conflict and Violence*, 4:1 (2010), 55.

postcolonial. Salman Rushdie's internationally-acclaimed fiction provides only the most obvious evidence of the debt contemporary literature, sociology, and cultural analysis in Britain owes to scholars and novelists like Stuart Hall, Paul Gilroy, Hanif Kureishi, Zadie Smith, and a host of other ethnic minority intellectuals. Their influence on literature and academic conversations comes alongside efforts by lesser-known figures to contest deeply-embedded received notions about Europe's surviving colonial heritage. Bienvenu Mbutu Mondondo, a Congolese national long resident in Brussels, provides a powerful example, putting one of Belgium's most beloved national icons on trial: Tintin.

Between 2007 and 2012, Mondondo did battle with Hergé's *Tintin au Congo* in the courtroom, initiating what was to stretch into a series of calls for a ban on the book's publication, sale, and distribution. His initial inspiration came upon learning that Britain's Commission for Racial Equality had asked retailers to stop selling the comic on account of its 'imagery and words of hideous racial prejudice, where the "savage natives" look like monkeys and talk like imbeciles'; such a book was best consigned to 'a museum, with a big sign saying "old fashioned, racist claptrap"'.[117] Mondondo accused *Tintin au Congo* of violating Belgium's 1981 anti-racism legislation in that it circulated and reinforced colonial-era prejudices with pernicious contemporary consequences. Having arrived in Belgium as a student in 1989, he described everyday experiences of racism and insisted that Belgian perceptions of him and other Congolese extended in no small part from Tintin's durable cultural resonance. Like the public debates raging several years earlier in which *fin-de-siècle* atrocities were contentiously framed as akin to a Holocaust in the Congo, Mondondo invoked laws against Nazi Holocaust denial in support of his position. As he told an interviewer, Belgium should institute comparable legislation against anyone minimizing the horrific impact of colonialism between 1885 and 1960 that killed twenty million people.[118]

Mondondo's lengthy campaign attracted cross-border support from France's *Conseil Représentatif des Associations Noires* (CRAN, or Representative Council of Black Associations) but faced seemingly insurmountable odds against a favourable verdict. In 2012, Belgian courts rejected the plea that Hergé's story was tantamount to racial harassment, constituted a consciously

---

[117] Commission for Racial Equality, 'CRE Statement on the children's book "Tintin in the Congo"', press release, 12 July 2007, cited in Jogchum Vrielink, 'Effort to Ban Tintin Comic Book Fails in Belgium', www.theguardian.com/law/2012/may/14/effort-ban-tintin-congo-fails, accessed 26 November 2013; see also Daniel Couvreur, 'Tintin face à son passé africain', *Le Soir* (Brussels), 30 September 2011; Daniel Couvreur, 'Interdire Tintin au Congo serait "inconstitutionel"', *Le Soir*, 28 October 2011.

[118] Didier Pasamonik, interview with Bienvenu Mbutu Mondondo, 'Cette bande dessinée est raciste', 31 August 2007, www.actuabd.com/Bienvenu-Mbutu-Mondondo-Cette-bande-dessinee-est-raciste, accessed 26 November 2013.

malicious violation of personal dignity, or acted as an incitement to racial hatred. Hergé's publishers and (posthumously) Hergé himself were thereby exonerated; as a headline in *La Libre Belgique* announced, 'Tintin can stay in the Congo'.[119] Mondondo and CRAN duly announced their intention to appeal, claiming that what was at issue was not past racist intentions but rather current racist effects.[120]

As-yet unsuccessful efforts to ban *Tintin au Congo* mark another instance of unfinished colonial business in present-day Belgium structured by contemporary historical debates, political questions, and cultural preconceptions about the Congolese diaspora. In daring to take on two figures with the stature of Hergé and his much-loved creation, Mondondo found himself pitted against what the public prosecutor defended as 'a work of undeniable artistic quality' that counted as 'a recognized masterpiece of our national literary inheritance'.[121] In the course of the five-year legal saga, moreover, Mondondo was subjected to hostile media attention, aggressive verbal attacks, and accusations that he was nothing more than a self-promoting opportunist opposed to free speech. His social identity and political leanings were publicized as equally dubious and used to discredit the sincerity of his motives. Still declaring himself a student at the age of thirty-nine, he closely fit widely-held stereotypes of the Congolese in Belgium whose claims to be at university but whose attendance was irregular at best were ridiculed as a flimsy pretext to claim indefinite residence, as Chapter 7 explored.[122] What is more, as *Le Soir*'s well-known Africa correspondent Colette Braeckman informed its Francophone readers in 2007, Mondondo had a prior history of political activism that rendered his campaign against *Tintin au Congo* suspect. His involvement in protests against recent state efforts to improve Belgium's relations with the Democratic Republic of Congo under Laurent Kabila situated him together with Congolese asylum seekers who feared being sent back if international relations assumed better footing. To further their own ends, they resorted to exploiting Walloon–Flemish political rifts. Mondondo counted among those who encouraged Belgians of Congolese origin to boycott Francophone politicians and build links with Flemish nationalists, Braeckman asserted, 'who view colonialism as the doings of the Francophone bourgeoisie of the time' but conveniently ignored the long-standing dominance of Flemish missionaries in evangelical work in the Congo.[123] Not only was Mondondo flying in the face of an alleged national

---

[119] 'Tintin peut rester au Congo', *La Libre Belgique* (Brussels), 13 February 2012.
[120] 'Tintin au Congo: les plaignants feront appel', *Le Soir*, 13 February 2012; '"Tintin au Congo à nouveau sur la sellette?', *La Libre Belgique*, 5 October 2012.
[121] Daniel Couvreur, 'Le procureur du Roi ne veut pas interdire "Tintin au Congo"', *Le Soir*, 29 October 2011.
[122] Pasamonik, interview with Bienvenu Mbutu Mondondo.
[123] Colette Braeckman, '"Tintin au Congo": une occasion de faire du bruit', *Le Soir*, 26 September 2007.

literary masterpiece; he was also tied together with Flemish separatists intent on the destruction of Belgium itself.

Postcolonial minorities in France, meanwhile, have turned to the imperial past to claim their place in national history and right to belong in France after empire, as well as to contest exclusionary racism by exposing its colonial roots. Starting in the 1990s, West African immigrants who lacked French residence rights as *sans-papiers* (those without papers) returned to the First and Second World Wars to make a case for their right to remain. They reinvoked the *tirailleur sénégalais* figure who retained positive associations in French popular memory and remained an everyday presence in millions of French kitchens through the Banania logo to assert that 'they and their ancestors were not, after all, "strangers" to France', as Gregory Mann's research reveals.[124] Even if few *sans-papiers* were the literal descendants of *tirailleurs sénégalais* who had come to France's aid on the western front in 1914–1918 and again in the forces of liberation from Nazi occupation, the sacrifices of earlier generations, they felt, more than justified Africans' inclusion in France's history and present-day population alike.

The campaign to recast dominant national memories of the Second World War to give space to the North and West African soldiers who helped liberate the French hexagon from the Germans also lay behind Rachid Bouchareb's 2006 film *Indigènes*. Bouchareb's effort to recover unjustly forgotten war heroes and win them a recognized place in the epochal events that lay at the centre of national historical consciousness proved a tremendous critical and commercial success. Along with selling three million tickets at the French box office, *Indigènes* secured an Oscar nomination and an international release under the English-language title *Days of Glory*. The film struck a chord in no small part because it sought to integrate loyal colonial troops into a shared republican memory as part of France's common glory, not place them in opposition to it. *Indigènes*, as Benjamin Stora points out, paid no attention to what happened between France and its colonies after 1945, making it seem 'as if, in the end, these territories had remained French'.[125] Stora correctly predicted that Bouchareb's next film, *Hors la loi* (*Outside the Law*, released in 2010), would fail to receive a similarly warm welcome in France, focusing as it did on the crises of Algerian decolonization that still remained divisive half a century later. The film's story revolved around one Algerian family's saga between losing their land in the 1920s, experiencing French reprisals following the Sétif uprising of 8 May 1945, and their ultimate move to the *bidonvilles* of Paris, where two of the three brothers became prominent European-based FLN

---

[124] Gregory Mann, 'Immigrants and Arguments in France and Africa', *Comparative Studies in Society and History*, 45:2 (2003), 379.

[125] Stora, *La guerre des mémoires*, 55. See also Mireille Rosello's discussion of *Indigènes* in *The Reparative in Narratives: Works of Mourning in Progress* (Liverpool, 2009), 109–13.

leaders. *Hors la loi* divided French opinion between *Front National* and conservative detractors who condemned it as 'anti-French' and those who applauded it as a significant step in the right direction of increasing public recognition of France's violent road to decolonization.[126]

With *Indigènes* and *Hors la loi*, Bouchareb, born in Paris to parents of Algerian origin, affirmed his place within a constellation of second-generation minority efforts to shed new light on the oppressive dimensions of France's colonial and decolonization history that so many others preferred to ignore. Since the 1980s, descendants of Algerian migrants have worked to reclaim events such as the 17 October 1961 killings and create new public memories after more than two decades of public forgetting. Victims of police violence and especially their children eager to know the truth about episodes their parents often preferred not to discuss produced a 'history from below' that gradually raised awareness of the tragedy in a manner far exceeding the impact of work by professional historians.[127] Leïla Sebbar's acclaimed 1999 novel *La Seine était rouge (Paris, octobre 1961)* (translated as *The Seine Was Red*) featured adolescents determined to learn about their parents' painful experiences at last and communicate them to others. Their memory work extended to visiting famous Paris historic landmarks such as La Santé prison to inscribe new Algerian histories next to conventional metropole-centred reference points that had long defined them as sites of French Revolution or Second World War memory alone. To the prison's 'Liberty Equality Fraternity' emblem and its plaque reading 'On November 11 1940 in this prison were held high school and university students who, at the call of General de Gaulle, were the first to rise up against the occupation', they added '1954–1962 in this prison were guillotined Algerian resisters who rose up against the French occupation'. Using the same red paint to represent the blood spilled, their graffiti outside the Concorde metro station informed passers-by that 'on this spot Algerians were savagely beaten by Prefect Papon's police on October 17 1961'.[128]

Activism in both fictional and real forms paved the way for greater scholarly attention as well as the official plaque laid on the Pont Saint-Michel in 2001 to commemorate the 17 October deaths. Second- and third-generation returns to the past, moreover, were not restricted to the Algerian War. Minorities contested colonial nostalgia and racist imagery still visible in everyday French culture, whether it be in colonial-style restaurant motifs or Banania's ongoing

---

[126] Mark Brown, 'Film protests reopen Algerian war wounds', *Guardian*, 22 May 2010.
[127] Rothberg, *Multidirectional Memory*, 227–8, 233–4, 270; Stora, *La guerre des mémoires*, 12, 40; House and MacMaster, *Paris 1961*, ch. 12.
[128] Leïla Sebbar, *The Seine Was Red: Paris, October 1961*, translated by Mildred Mortimer (Bloomington, 2008), 14–15, 67. See also Rothberg's discussion in *Multidirectional Memory*, 296–308.

allusion to the *tirailleur sénégalais* in its advertising.[129] In 2005, a year in which riots in the *banlieues* involving youth of Maghrebi, African, and Antillean backgrounds dominated the headlines, minorities both took part in protests against article 4 of the 23 February law and launched their own group initiatives. Together with the *Conseil Représentatif des Associations Noires* (the group that later assisted Mondondo in his fight against *Tintin au Congo* in Belgium), the far more militant *Indigènes de la République* collective politicized contemporary disadvantages by connecting them directly to France's colonial past.

By asserting their right to belong in France as legitimate 'natives *of* the republic' and protesting their continued discrimination by historicizing it in terms of its origins in France's oppression of the 'natives' in the colonies, their chosen *Indigènes* appellation perfectly captured a politics that crossed ethnic lines. The movement's initial *appel* ('call to action') spoke of socio-economic exclusion and institutional racism as a form of 'indigenizing' that placed postcolonial migrants and their descendants on the margins of French society, epitomized by the *banlieues*, 'labeled as zones of disorder that the Republic sets out to conquer all over again'. Postcolonial minorities endured police brutality, while 'the old colonial tactics to control Islam are recycled', the citizenship of those born in France was systematically attacked, and the African *tirailleurs* used as 'canon fodder during the two World Wars' were still denied due recognition as war veterans. Past and present sufferings converged in a France that 'was still a Colonial State' in which citizens from the overseas departments and territories were 'relegated to the status of immigrants'. What was needed, the *Indigènes* insisted, was the '[d]ecolonizing of the Republic' in which 'Equality is a myth'. 'The state and society must critically examine their colonial past and present', its authors stressed, to counteract 'the legacy of a "universal chauvinism" aiming to "civilize" the savages and their children'.

'WE, descendants of slaves and African deportees, daughters and sons of the colonized and the immigrants, militants involved in the battle against oppression and discrimination produced by the postcolonial Republic, call those engaged in these struggles to come together in the Conference for Anti-Colonialism', the *Indigènes* argued, and gain inspiration from anti-colonial resistance as well as the French who once resisted Nazism. Returning to the common connection between the surfeit of Second World War memories and amnesia surrounding France's fight against decolonization, they planned their first demonstration for 8 May 2005, the sixtieth anniversary of the day when

---

[129] www.bodegon-colonial.fr, and discussed by Stéphane Coloneaux, 'Mon grand-père "Y'a bon Banania", *L'Humanité*, 7 October 2002, www.humanite.fr/node/272551; www.mrap.fr/contre-le-racisme-sous-toutes-ses-formes/discriminations/aby2019a-bon-bananiabb-un-arret-histori que. All accessed 15 September 2014. See also Sylvie Durmelat, 'Introduction: Colonial Culinary Encounters and Imperial Leftovers', *French Cultural Studies*, 26:2 (2015), 116–18.

'the paradox of the Republic was revealed'. 8 May 2005 needed to go beyond remembering France's liberation from the Nazis to extend to the commemoration of France's simultaneous massacre of thousands of Algerians in Sétif. Looking back into a history that exceeded the hexagon thus became a means of perpetuating an anti-colonial activism appropriate to new times and the postcolonial condition of France.[130]

Although the previous efforts to galvanize an alternative set of imperial memories discussed earlier show the *Indigènes'* activities to be part of a broader acceleration of group recollections made public, their refusal to limit their attention to specific colonial events or colonized groups rendered theirs a highly significant development. Earlier returns to the imperial past had focused overwhelmingly on *either* France's long history of repressing Algerians in the metropole as well as in North Africa *or* its history of participation in the slave trade and slavery, to name two important examples, but rarely united the two into a wider protest against the colonial past and its present-day legacy. In France as well as in the Netherlands, initiatives that gradually succeeded in putting the history of slavery onto the public agenda came about first and foremost through pressure from their Afro-Caribbean populations. France's Taubira law of 2001 that made slavery a 'crime against humanity' alongside commemorations of significant anniversaries of abolition would never have come about without concerted battles for recognition waged by Antillean peoples, not least Christiane Taubira herself, a Guianese deputy in France's National Assembly. Equally, the slow recognition gradually accorded to the historic victims of slavery by the Dutch state, such as the National Monument to the Dutch History of Slavery unveiled by Queen Beatrix in Amsterdam's Oosterpark in 2002, stemmed directly from commemorative activism by members of the Netherlands' Afro-Surinamese- and Antillean-descended communities.[131] But as was also the case with returns to the history of slavery and abolition in Britain, these were overwhelmingly the concern of peoples of African descent along with white activists, not other minority groups. Ascendant memories of slavery in Europe serve as an important reminder of how returns to the colonial past often remain group-specific, even when they succeed in gaining a stronger foothold within a wider collective historical consciousness. This was even more true of South Asian critiques of empire in Britain.

---

[130] Quotes are taken from 'A Call to Action: "We Are the Natives of the Republic!", January 18, 2005', translated by Florence Bernault, in Tshimanga, Gondola, and Bloom (eds.), *Frenchness and the African Diaspora*, 277–81. See Florence Bernault's excellent analysis of the *Indigènes* movement in 'Colonial Syndrome: French Modern and the Deceptions of History' in the same volume, 120–45, together with Stora, *La guerre des mémoires*, 68, 72, 93, 97, and Bertrand, *Mémoires d'empire*, 110, 118.

[131] Stora, *La guerre des mémoires*, 72–3, 103–5; Oostindie, *Postcolonial Netherlands*, 148–57.

South Asian anti-colonialism in Britain was apparent before, during, and long after India and Pakistan won independence. The Indian Workers' Association formed in the Midlands in the 1930s not only championed the freedom struggle then being waged on the Indian subcontinent but continued to remain involved in anti-colonial activism long after 1947. In the late 1960s, Asians in Britain joined forces with other minorities in a Black People's Alliance protesting apartheid in South Africa, white settler domination in Rhodesia, and American involvement in Vietnam.[132] By the 1980s, Britain's Asian communities had decades of political struggle behind them that spanned continents, but members of the second generation found themselves unable to learn about this heritage in British schools. With most of their teachers appearing to know little and care even less about the history and cultures of the subcontinent, they gained access to an anti-colonial heritage outside the classroom through older members of their own communities who passed along stories of earlier fights against colonial oppression.

In their own struggles against British racism and exclusion, Asian Youth Movements in Bradford, Birmingham, Southall, and elsewhere drew inspiration from Indian sufferings under colonialism as they asserted their right to belong and combat continuing forms of British oppression. Like arguments about the 'colonial debt' Belgium owed its Congolese migrants discussed in Chapter 7, Asian youth in Tariq Mehmood's autobiographical novel set in Bradford claimed that 'It is the wealth of our people that they have stolen from us over the centuries. It's not a favour to let us come here. It is our right!' No one should be labelled an 'illegal immigrant', they felt, for 'black people had a right to come to this country by virtue of their history, the colonization of their lands and the enslavements of their peoples by Britain, and to live here free of restraints and harassment'.[133] In their search for heroes who took a stand against injustice, they reached back in time to the Rani of Jhansi, who valiantly fought the British during the 1857 uprising, and other martyrs to the cause of freedom. Rather than opt for famous nationalists known for non-violence like Gandhi or Nehru, they preferred Udham Singh, the diasporic Punjabi whose nationalism took more radical forms and culminated in avenging the Amritsar massacre of 1919 in a lecture hall in 1940 London.[134]

When Udham Singh appeared at a meeting at Caxton Hall toting a revolver with which he shot and killed Sir Michael O'Dwyer, the retired Lieutenant Governor of Punjab whose hard-line policy led to the deaths of hundreds of

---

[132] 'Battle of the Strand in South Africa and Rhodesia Protest', *The Times*, 13 January 1969; '6,000 in Grosvenor Square Fail Against "Calm Wall"', *The Times*, 28 October 1968.

[133] Tariq Mehmood, *Hand on the Sun* (Harmondsworth, 1983), 115, 128; see also 27, 86–8, 97–8, 123.

[134] Anandi Ramamurthy, *Black Star: Britain's Asian Youth Movements* (London, 2013), 69–71; see also 3–5, 12.

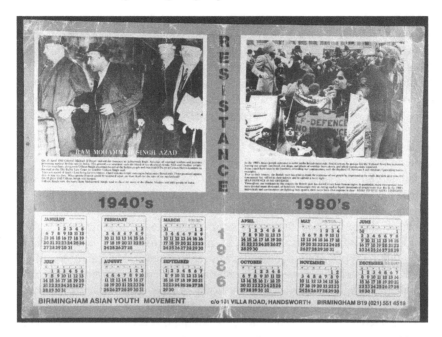

Figure 9.5 1986 calendar issued by the Birmingham Asian Youth Movement, featuring photographs of Udham Singh in 1940 next to Asians proclaiming the right to self-defence in 1980s Britain. Tandana – the Glowworm, Archives, MH98.
Credit: www.tandana.org.

peaceful protestors at Jallianwala Bagh twenty-one years earlier, his actions were publicly dismissed by the British police and India Office as those of a mere 'fanatic . . . resorting to terrorist methods', as a report of his trial in *The Times* put it.[135] Within months, Singh had been sentenced to death by hanging and buried at London's Pentonville Prison, the authorities hoping that in pathologizing the assassination its political radicalism would be contained and forgotten. But his memory remained alive, particularly in Punjab but also among Punjabis (often but not exclusively Sikhs) and other South Asians who had migrated to Britain. Indian campaigns ultimately secured the return of his remains to Punjab in 1974, where Prime Minister Indira Gandhi commended him for having 'sacrificed his life for the independence of the country'.[136] Accorded the status of *Shaheed* (martyr), Udham Singh has been recognized as one of the most influential Sikhs

[135] 'The Trial of Udham Singh', *The Times*, 6 June 1940.
[136] 'Executed Sikh's Remains Go Home', *The Times*, 20 July 1974.

of the twentieth century, honoured as a patriot in India by statues, periodic commemorations, a museum in Amritsar, street names, and a number of films praising his revolutionary life and heroic death. In Britain, he featured in Asian Youth Movement material, became the subject of television documentaries and theatre productions, was invoked in 1990s songs by Asian Dub Foundation and the Apna Group, and lent his name to several South Asian community centres and welfare organizations in London and Birmingham. Last but not least, activists in Birmingham worked together with scholars in Punjab to secure the release and publication of closed British archival material to shed further light on hitherto hidden aspects of his life, politics, and death.[137]

Udham Singh's road to execution has thus been taken up by many admirers determined to shape his legacy not as merely a cold-blooded murderer but as having committed a legitimate political act to avenge British crimes at Amritsar. Regardless of the profusion of film, music, writings, and public buildings dedicated to him, however, he, his motives for O'Dwyer's assassination, and the types of anti-colonialism it represented in 1940 and long afterwards remain almost completely unfamiliar among non-Asians in Britain. Despite bicontinental efforts on many fronts to recover his legacy and correct perceived misconceptions, Udham Singh is still an unknown figure within most of the society in which he committed the killing that secured his reputation in his homeland and among its overseas diasporas. His legacy (and lack thereof) provides an instructive example of how particular colonial histories can circulate intensely within specific groups but completely fail to spread beyond them and take root among others, in this instance the overwhelming majority of people in postcolonial Britain.

Paradoxically, peoples of South Asian backgrounds appear to have been much more effective in enhancing popular memories of the Raj in Britain that veer towards the nostalgic than in disseminating stories of colonial oppression and resistance. For decades, postcolonial literary stars like Salman Rushdie and intellectuals such as Maria Misra, Priyamvada Gopal, and Pankaj Mishra have indeed made important arguments against tendencies to whitewash the empire's reputation in their books, essays, and journalism.[138] Far better

---

[137] Louis E. Fenech, 'Contested Nationalisms: Negotiated Terrains: The Way Sikhs Remember Udham Singh "Shahid"' (1899–1940)', *Modern Asian Studies*, 36:4 (2002), 827–8; Florian Stadtler, '"For every O'Dwyer … there is a Shaheed Udham Singh": The Caxton Hall Assassination of Michael O'Dwyer', in Rehana Ahmed and Sumita Mukherjee (eds.), *South Asian Resistances in Britain, 1858–1947* (London, 2012), 19–32; Mehmood, *Hand on the Sun*, 88; Virinder S. Kalra, '*Vilayeti* Rhythms: Beyond Bhangra's Emblematic Status to a Translation of Lyrical Texts', *Theory, Culture & Society*, 17:3 (2000), 89–93; Peter Lennon, 'Shadow of a Gunman', *Guardian*, 6 January 1996; Navtej Singh and Avtar Singh Jouhl (eds.), *Emergence of the Image: Redact Documents of Udham Singh* (New Delhi, 2002).

[138] Rushdie, 'Outside the Whale'; Misra's, Gopal's, and Mishra's commentaries appeared frequently in the *Guardian*.

known among the general public, however, are 'Indian' restaurants that prominently deploy Raj associations to attract customers. With a substantial number of British Asian restauranteurs opting for restaurant names and interior decoration that harken back to colonial times by offering their predominantly white clientele a meal at the 'Viceroy', 'Memsahib', 'Bengal Lancer', 'Jewel in the Crown', or 'Last Days of the Raj', invoking the Raj without critique in a culturally recognizable way seemed far better for business.[139]

Across postcolonial Europe, in sum, memories of empire are closely tied to the history of inward migrations. Repatriates and formerly colonized ethnic minorities – and the ways these groups have been perceived among metropolitan societies – propelled defensive and affirmative returns to the imperial past from those who benefitted from colonial structures as well as harsh condemnation by those who recall empire as a site of their own, or their ancestors', oppression. Without significant numbers of one or both groups, European perceptions of national imperial history would be far different today. As Gert Oostindie puts it of the Netherlands, 'the rediscovery of colonial history and its legacies ... was forced by migrants who derived their identities primarily from that past', a pattern equally discernible in the other countries explored here.[140] Nonetheless, the transferral of ideas about empire from those most intimately linked to it to other social sectors remains a partial process. Some group memories remain what Benjamin Stora has called 'cloistered', largely confined to those with specific imperial experiences and family histories; others have spread outwards to reconfigure wider collective conceptions of empire.[141]

Despite countless examples of the memory work performed by minorities who circulate their own narratives of colonial history, however, public awareness of them remains low overall when compared with the impact better-off white ex-colonizers and Indisch repatriates have had on moulding postcolonial European memory cultures. Stora's assessment of France in 2007 that 'group carriers of a pro-colonial memory have more allies in French society than anti-colonialists' aptly characterizes other European nations after decolonization as well.[142] Can ethnic minorities who, much more often than not, have critical stories of the colonial past to tell hope to make as strong a mark on national conceptions of empire that repatriates have achieved? So far, although the selective emergence of minority narratives has created dissonance, they have yet to overturn or fully displace either positive memories or a preference not to remember empires at all among the mainstream. Postcolonial minorities remain

[139] Elizabeth Buettner, '"Going for an Indian": South Asian Restaurants and the Limits of Multiculturalism in Britain', *Journal of Modern History*, 80:4 (2008), 895; Elizabeth Buettner, 'Chicken Tikka Masala, Flock Wallpaper, and "Real" Home Cooking: Assessing Britain's "Indian" Restaurant Traditions', *Food & History*, 7:2 (2009), 205, 212.
[140] Oostindie, *Postcolonial Netherlands*, 239; see also 208.
[141] Stora, *La guerre des mémoires*, 15.   [142] Ibid., 24.

engaged in an ongoing struggle to have their own imperial pasts and post-migration lives recognized within multicultural European societies – societies that often remain reluctantly multicultural at best and grant them only partial or grudging inclusion.[143]

* * *

Cacophony and silence: selective memories of colonialism and decolonization

While a large body of academic work now positions overseas histories as part of European histories, the process of integrating empire into Europe's past and present remains far from complete. New scholarship about empires has boomed within history and many other academic disciplines since the 1990s, but its findings and arguments have not frequently spread beyond specialist circles to become common knowledge.[144] What we find in public life are partial reappearances and recoveries, often sporadic and ephemeral, as opposed to full recognition or reckonings with empires' consequences, with Eurocentric understandings of nations and peoples in isolation from empire still taking precedence. White European voices still predominate in memory-making, regardless of efforts by minorities to tell different stories or occasional contributions made to debates by the citizens of independent postcolonial nations in Asia, Africa, and the Caribbean.[145]

Europe's material legacies of empire, moreover, often suggest a will to forget this past after decolonization. In towns and cities across France, countless memorials, street names, and statues still exist today that date from the age of empire itself, whereas few were commissioned during the era of 'Greater France's' decline or after its fall. As Robert Aldrich concludes, 'no one wanted monuments to a dying empire'; decolonization, whether notoriously violent and domestically divisive or not, was a letdown not conducive to the commemorative enthusiasm seen during the empire's heyday.[146] Some French

---

[143] Initiatives such as Black History Month (dating from the 1980s) and the Black Cultural Archives in Brixton provide two British examples of efforts to place minority histories and cultures on the map. See www.blackhistorymonth.org.uk; Hannah Ellis-Petersen, 'Black Cultural Archives Unveils New Centre in Brixton', *Guardian*, 29 July 2014.

[144] Bertrand, *Mémoires d'empire*, 132; Stora, *La guerre des mémoires*, 28–9. France's intense debate about the 23 February 2005 law stands out as exceptional.

[145] Giordano, *Belges et Italiens*, 161, 170; Ann Laura Stoler and Karen Strassler, 'Castings for the Colonial: Memory Work in "New Order" Java', *Comparative Studies in Society and History*, 42:1 (2000), 4–48; Paul Bijl, 'Colonial Memory and Forgetting in the Netherlands and Indonesia', *Journal of Genocide Research*, 14:3–4 (2012), 441–61. The elderly Mau Mau plaintiffs who travelled to London to tell their stories in court discussed earlier mark a rare instance when African voices were belatedly heard in Britain.

[146] Aldrich, *Vestiges*, 15.

'vestiges of empire' were reinvented for new times, as happened with museum collections of non-Western artefacts newly showcased at the Musée du Quai Branly in Paris in 2006, or put to different uses, like the Palais du Porte Dorée built for the 1931 *Exposition Coloniale*. Once housing the Musée des Colonies, the Palais was renovated as the new national immigration museum (la Cité Nationale de l'Histoire de l'Immigration) and reopened in 2007.[147] In France as in other former colonizing nations, most imperial-era monuments remain in place with little sign of concerted objection from the public encountering them. Rather than becoming sites of post-imperial celebration or the focus of campaigns for their removal, most attract more interest from the birds perching upon them than from locals or tourists. London's Trafalgar Square provides a case in point.

Towered over by the column topped by a statue of naval hero Lord Horatio Nelson, who died at sea during the Battle of Trafalgar in 1805, two out of the four monumental plinths within one of London's most highly-visited attractions feature statues of mid-nineteenth-century empire builders and defenders. Sir Charles Napier's career in the empire culminated with his conquest of Sindh (now part of Pakistan) in the early 1840s, while Sir Henry Havelock achieved fame for recapturing Lucknow during the Indian revolt in 1857. Long after their history in the limelight peaked, today few passers-by seem even remotely aware of who these erstwhile figures were, let alone voice objection to their ongoing public presence. In 2000, London's mayor Ken Livingstone proposed removing them to a less prominent location and suggested that neither was still meaningful for present-day Londoners. He personally knew nothing about them, and speculated 'that not one person in 10,000 going through Trafalgar Square knows any details about the lives of those two generals', arguing that they be replaced with more familiar figures. Although his suggestion provoked predicable outrage from conservatives and the military who resented the attempt to 'erase a fundamental part of our nation's heritage from the heart of our capital city', the idea never advanced beyond the stage of fleeting media commentary before evaporating into thin air.[148] Havelock and Napier still have

---

[147] Among a growing number of studies of these examples, see many of the contributions to Thomas (ed.), *Museums in Postcolonial Europe*, especially Robert Aldrich, 'Colonial Museums in Postcolonial Europe', 12–31; Caroline Ford, 'Museums After Empire in France and Overseas France', *Journal of Modern History*, 82:3 (2010), 625–61; Maureen Murphy, *Un Palais pour une cité: du Musée des Colonies à la Cité Nationale de l'Histoire de l'Immigration* (Paris, 2007).

[148] Paul Kelso, 'Mayor attacks generals in battle of Trafalgar Square', *Guardian*, 20 October 2000; Philip Johnston, 'Old statues given marching orders … by the Left', *Telegraph*, 20 October 2000. Relevant discussions include Deborah Cherry, 'Statues in the Square: Hauntings at the Heart of Empire', *Art History*, 29:4 (2006), 660–97; Bill Schwarz, '"Strolling Spectators" and "Practical Londoners": Remembering the Imperial Past', in Jo Littler and Roshi Naidoo (eds.), *The Politics of Heritage: The Legacies of 'Race'* (London, 2005), 192–209.

yet to move an inch, remaining ignored and seemingly unproblematic for most people, hiding in plain sight.[149]

Far more captivating than statuary of imperial vintage to the millions from Britain and around the world who visit Trafalgar Square each year are the temporary structures that adorn the fourth plinth, rather that the figure of King George IV ensconced upon the third. Between 2010 and 2012, British-Nigerian sculptor Yinka Shonibare's 'Nelson's Ship in a Bottle' featured a rendition of the H.M.S. *Victory* with its sails made of colourful batik fabrics of multiple Dutch, Indonesian, and African origins.[150] Like the succession of ethnic festivals held annually in the square including celebrations marking Vaisakhi (the Sikh New Year), Diwali, Eid, St Patrick's Day, and the Chinese New Year, Shonibare's popular commission illustrated how London spaces could be multicultural in terms of their artefacts, visitors, and resident population, yet simultaneously filled with relics of empire seemingly consigned to oblivion. Ringed by the National Gallery, Canada House, and the South African High Commission and located just a stone's throw from what was formerly Rhodesia House (now occupied by the Zimbabwean Embassy), London's symbolic hub has long been a site of political protest. That demonstrators against the 1956 Suez invasion, apartheid South Africa, Rhodesia under UDI, Zimbabwe under Mugabe, and wars waged in Afghanistan and Iraq since 2001 have invaded this space that was designed to celebrate British imperial grandeur through monuments to empire builders attests to the many contradictory ways in which imperial pasts, unevenly recalled, coexist with postcolonial priorities.

Public apathy about Napier and Havelock suggests the irregular ways in which empires have been revisited after decolonization, even by critics eager to highlight their most damning features. In Britain, the history of transatlantic slavery long inseparable from its history of empire, together with the brutality meted out to Mau Mau suspects in 1950s Kenya, have generated particularly negative publicity. Of the two, slavery predominated: in Britain as well as the Netherlands, Belgium, and France, postcolonial returns to the history of slavery and the slave trade from the 1990s onwards performed important functions, one of which was to contrast what most contemporaries agree to have been a uniquely atrocious practice with other colonial histories deemed to reflect favourably on Europe. Britain's national and local re-engagements with slavery climaxed

---

[149] As Jay Winter has written of European First World War memorials, Trafalgar Square similarly qualifies among the sites that have 'no fixed meanings, immutable over time'. Their initial significance changed, until '[o]ther meanings derived from other needs or events [were] attached to them, or no meaning at all'. Jay Winter, *Sites of Memory, Sites of Mourning: The Great War in European Cultural History* (Cambridge, 1995), 98.

[150] www.london.gov.uk/priorities/arts-culture/fourth-plinth/commissions/yinka-shonibare -mbe, accessed 30 September 2014; see also points made by Alan Rice, 'Tracing Slavery and Abolition's Routes and Viewing Inside the Invisible: The Monumental Landscape and the African Atlantic', *Atlantic Studies*, 8:2 (2011), 258–9.

Figure 9.6 Yinka Shonibare, 'Nelson's Ship in a Bottle', exhibited on the
fourth plinth in Trafalgar Square, London, 2010–2012, now located at the
National Maritime Museum, Greenwich.
Photograph by Bernhard Rieger, 2014.

around the bicentenary of its abolition of the slave trade in 1807. Prime Minister
Tony Blair expressed 'regret' (without, however, offering a full apology) for
slavery in 2006, and in 2007 Britain's museums and media were inundated with
slavery-themed exhibitions, television programming, and radio broadcasts.[151]
Laudable though these were, many commemorative activities preferred to stress
not Britain's history as a slave-trading nation and slave-holding empire but rather
its pioneering humanitarian role as the 'great emancipator' – even though slavery
itself lasted nearly another thirty years after the trade ended. Emphasizing
Britain's anti-slavery credentials – 'a matter of national honour' – lent the
spate of memorializations a self-congratulatory air that competed with repentant
looks back to better understand a shameful past.[152]

---

[151] Laurajane Smith, Geoffrey Cubitt, Ross Wilson, and Kalliopi Fouseki (eds.), *Representing
Enslavement in Museums: Ambiguous Engagements* (New York, 2011); James Walvin, 'The
Slave Trade, Abolition and Public Memory', *Transactions of the Royal Historical Society*, sixth
series, 19 (2009), 139–49.

[152] Douglas Hamilton, Kate Hodgson, and Joel Quirk, 'Introduction', in Hamilton, Hodgson, and
Quirk (eds.), *Slavery, Memory, and Identity: National Representations and Global Legacies*
(London, 2012), 5, 9–11; Ross Wilson, 'Remembering to Forget? The BBC Abolition Season
and Media Memory of Britain's Transatlantic Slave Trade', *Historical Journal of Film, Radio*

After abolitionism became more widespread, it became an important means of favourable self-comparison between nations that advertised themselves as opposing slavery and societies where the practice persisted. King Léopold II's insistence that Belgians were instrumental in combatting the Arab slave trade in the Congo was used to justify Belgium's presence ever since the era of the Congo Free State, a defence still invoked today by parties determined to refute accusations of rapacious profiteering and inhuman brutality in the territory. For Belgian apologists for either the Free State, the post-1908 colonial era, or both, the horrors suffered by Africans were decidedly *pre*-colonial, miseries from which Belgium had liberated them. The postcolonial Netherlands, for its part, could not deny its own imperial history of slavery, not least given the fact that it abolished it only in 1863, long after Britain and France. Repentance for slavery could, however, be geographically contained to the Dutch West Indies, leaving the East Indies as a facet of Dutch history ripe for celebration. In 2002, the same year that the Dutch government proclaimed its 'deep remorse' for participation in the slave trade and slavery in the Caribbean and inaugurated its national slavery monument in Amsterdam, the nation simultaneously embarked on a series of state-funded festivities marking the Dutch East India Company's (VOC's) four-hundredth anniversary that were overwhelmingly triumphal in nature. If the West India Company's gruesome slave-trading history was one of national contrition, the VOC still represented a source of pride – a monumental history of national achievement as the world's first 'multinational trading company' that rendered the Netherlands' 'Golden Age' a time of seafaring pre-eminence. Revealingly, as Gert Oostindie observes, those coordinating the 2002 events chose 'to place most emphasis on the early period of the VOC (1602–1620) and its maritime and commercial aspects, rather than its function as a violent protocolonial state ... the predecessor to the nineteenth- and twentieth-century colonial state of the Dutch East Indies'.[153] In the process, the VOC's own intensive involvement in slavery was conveniently sidelined, allowing its history to shine while its West Indian counterpart was condemned.

Most Europeans, even those keenest to extol their nation's colonial records, agree that transatlantic slavery was reprehensible and thus a suitable topic for overdue repentance. Safely distant in time, slavery enables gestures of recognition to be extended to minority groups whose ancestors suffered under it. By the same token, however, postcolonial memories of slavery in Europe also attest to how segments of the colonial past can readily become cordoned off as apt

---

and Television, 28:3 (2008), 391–403. Charles Forsdick notes French tendencies to highlight abolition at the expense of slavery itself. See 'The Panthéon's Empty Plinth: Commemorating Slavery in Contemporary France', *Atlantic Studies*, 9:3 (2012), 279–97.

[153] Oostindie, *Postcolonial Netherlands*, 134; see also 131–4, 146, 148, together with Gert Oostindie, 'Squaring the Circle: Commemorating the VOC After 400 Years', *Bijdragen tot de Taal-, Land- en Volkenkunde*, 159, Part I (2003), 135–61, especially 148–53.

subjects for regret or denunciation, only to leave other imperial histories and legacies comparatively unscathed. Focussed attention on European culpability for transatlantic slavery along with selected decolonization episodes like Britain's merciless crackdown on the Mau Mau, the Netherlands' counter-terrorism operations in post-1945 Indonesia, Belgium's involvement in Lumumba's assassination, and France's engagement in torture in the Algerian War makes these examples stand out as low points of empire for many people, and justifiably so. Yet casting these in the darkest possible form nonetheless helps other colonial times and places to appear all the brighter in contrast. Contentious histories become the extremes split off from what is then held up as the imperial norm, with appealing colonial myths and fantasies allowed to remain largely intact. For all the light shed on Britain's actions in 1950s Kenya after the court case began in 2009, massacres and routine uses of torture in other parts of its post-war empire from Cyprus to Malaya were left under-scrutinized, their faraway victims without justice, and the British public still under-informed about them.[154]

Similarly, in Belgium the colonial Congo between 1908 and the late 1950s could still be distinguished from the Free State era under Léopold II as well as decolonization, the two junctures upon which recent public recriminations had focused. Sandwiched in between, the era could be claimed as a time of achievement, 'a success story, dramatically interrupted by an all too sudden independence', as Georgi Verbeeck phrases it.[155] In the Netherlands, fond returns to *tempo doeloe* in the East Indies before the Japanese occupation and debates, often ephemeral, about the nationalist insurgency and Dutch counter-insurgency that soon followed it were not mutually exclusive but occurred side by side. 'As the atrocities, "excesses", or "war crimes" were being researched and exposed, a widespread nostalgia for life in the colonies began to flourish in the Netherlands; stores displayed books with glossy pictures of white people in tropical dress lounging beneath the beautiful palm trees', Tessel Pollmann notes. 'Any book focusing on the post-war history of Indonesia found and finds no buyers.'[156] Whatever might once have been wrong with Dutch governance could be brushed aside as predating the 'ethical policy' that emerged in the late nineteenth century, with ongoing colonial exploitation and the denial of indigenous political rights that encouraged Indonesian nationalism ignored in favour of romanticized depictions of European and Indisch lifestyles.

---

[154] Ian Cobain, 'Mau Mau veterans ruling: where other torture claims could come from', *Guardian*, 5 October 2012; Richard Norton-Taylor, 'UK urged to accept responsibility for 1948 Batang Kali massacre in Malaya', *Guardian*, 18 June 2013; David Anderson, 'It's not just Kenya. Squaring up to the seamier side of empire is long overdue', *Guardian*, 25 July 2011.
[155] Verbeeck, 'Coming to Terms', 49; see also Licata and Klein, 'Holocaust or Benevolent Paternalism?', 55.
[156] Pollmann, 'Unreal War', 106.

In France, controversies about torture in 1954–1962 Algeria at the end of the 1990s and the concomitant public nods towards condemning slavery made many defenders of empire all the more insistent that there was not one French colonial era, but several. A brutal initial period of conquest, unfortunate though it was, paved the way for a second period when the 'positive role' that lay at the centre of article 4 of the 23 February 2005 law came into its own. Early colonial violence was followed by the benefits of peace, economic development, medical advances, and other achievements of which France could justifiably still be proud. The French were not all slavers and torturers, this argument ran, but the carriers of modernity and civilization. What Romain Bertrand describes as '*la légende rose*' (rose-tinted myth) acted as a rejoinder to re-airings of the darkest moments of empire, those of initial invasion and occupation, slavery, and decolonization-era torture.[157] This left much of French imperial history, like that of French Indochina, protected from critical scrutiny – or, indeed, from much public scrutiny at all.

* * *

France's collective memories of colonial Indochina and the war that ended it are similarly ridden with omissions and silences. Like colonialism and decolonization in French sub-Saharan Africa, French Indochina has received little of the public attention slowly accorded to Algeria, in part due to the comparably few European repatriates and ethnic minority migrants from Southeast Asia who might otherwise have encouraged backward glances.[158] Paradoxically, the United States' war in Vietnam that divided world opinion and sparked Dutch memories of Indonesia's decolonization and the brief debate about 1940s 'war crimes' at the end of the 1960s failed to resurrect France's unsuccessful struggle to keep hold of the very region of American engagement. In France, its own lost war in Indochina waged from 1946 to 1954 remained buried beneath the Second World War that preceded it as well as the Algerian War and the American struggle in Vietnam that followed.

French Indochina gained new space in French collective memory in the 1980s and early 1990s through returns to the past that kept colonial times before the Japanese occupation and the war of decolonization cordoned off into a separate sphere. Marguerite Duras' Prix Goncourt-winning 1984 novel *L'Amant* (*The Lover*), which drew closely on her own sexual relationship

---

[157] Bertrand, *Mémoires d'empire*, 97–105.

[158] Controversies that flared up around President Sarkozy's pronouncements on a visit to Dakar in 2007 remained largely confined to specialists in France and mark an exception that proves the rule. Sarkozy caused outrage and insult when he spoke of Africans as not having fully 'entered into history' or embraced progress, with many Africans resenting it as a racist colonial throwback. See Adame Ba Konaré (ed.), *Petit précis de remise à niveau sur l'histoire africaine à l'usage du président Sarkozy* (Paris, 2008); Jean-Pierre Chrétien (ed.), *L'Afrique de Sarkozy: Un déni d'histoire* (Paris, 2008).

with a wealthy Chinese man as a French adolescent growing up in and around Saigon at the end of the 1920s, was released as a film in 1992, as was Régis Wargnier's *Indochine*, set mainly in the 1930s and starring Catherine Deneuve as the rich and glamourous owner of a rubber plantation. Amidst lush tropical landscapes and picturesque French colonial architecture, interracial romances and the seductive appeal of the 'other' gave their many readers and viewers an Indochina characterized by natural beauty, eroticism, and touristic appeal at precisely the time when Vietnam was opening up as a tourism destination. In France, 'Indochine' had come to mean something very different from 'Vietnam': the latter carried connotations of America's unpopular war rein-voked in films like *Platoon* and *Rambo*, while an imagined 'Indochine' of the interwar years could remain distinct as an attractive setting for French adventures, sexual encounters, and rose-tinted postcolonial nostalgia.[159]

Although colonial iniquities, Vietnamese anti-colonialism, and the spread of communism were not absent from Wargnier's film, politics and oppression took a back seat in these lavish, expensively-produced, and highly popular French returns to its erstwhile empire in Southeast Asia at its height. 'The bloody history of French colonial rule is entirely missing from this romantic fantasy', Panivong Norindr aptly concludes of the genre, one preoccupied with a mythical, golden-age '*Indochine avant l'ouragan*' ('Indochina before the hurricane').[160] France's lost struggle against the Viet Minh had little place in this sentimental and revisionist return to the past. France's futile battle received separate treatment in a third film that reached cinemas the same year as *L'Amant* and *Indochine*, Pierre Schoendoerffer's *Dien Bien Phu*. Like the official rhetoric that accompanied the inauguration of France's Indochina war memorial, cemetery, and museum in the town of Fréjus a year later in 1993, Schoendoerffer (himself a veteran) portrayed French forces and their loyal Indochinese peasant-soldier allies as heroic defenders of a lost ideal, fighting an epic struggle side by side that remained noble and glorious even in defeat.[161]

---

[159] Alain Ruscio and Serge Tignères, *Dien Bien Phu, Mythes et réalités: Cinquante ans de passions françaises (1954–2004)* (Paris, 2005), 363–80; Nicola Cooper, *France in Indochina: Colonial Encounters* (Oxford, 2001), ch. 11; Nikki Cooper, 'Dien Bien Phu—Fifty Years On', *Modern & Contemporary France*, 12:4 (2004), 445–57; Panivong Norindr, *Phantasmatic Indochina: French Colonial Ideology in Architecture, Film, and Literature* (Durham, 1996), ch. 6; Pierre Brocheux, 'The Death and Resurrection of Indo-China in French Memory', *European Review*, 8:1 (2000), 59; Eric T. Jennings, 'From *Indochine* to *Indochic*: The Lang Bian/Dalat Palace Hotel and French Colonial Leisure, Power and Culture', *Modern Asian Studies*, 37:1 (2003), 193–4.

[160] Norindr, *Phantasmatic Indochina*, 132, 137.

[161] Ruscio and Tignères, *Dien Bien Phu*, 381–8; Pierre Journoud and Hugues Tertrais (eds.), *1954–2004: La bataille de Dien Bien Phu entre histoire et mémoire* (Paris, 2004), especially points made in chapters by Anne Logeay, 'Qui se souvient de Dien Bien Phu?: Quelques remarques sur l'érosion de la mémoire', 189–91, and Pierre Journoud, 'Dien Bien Phu: Du témoignage à l'histoire', 207–19.

Neither Schoendoerffer's tribute nor the Fréjus site honouring those who died fighting for France attempted either a critical reassessment of colonialism or an understanding of the strength and appeal of communist opposition to it. 'Commemoration takes precedence over comprehension' at Fréjus, Robert Aldrich argues; in highlighting heroic sacrifice and victimhood, the site 'ignores the darker side of colonialism' together with the reasons why the war was ever fought.[162]

Postcolonial French returns to the Indochina war proved as fleeting as they were uninspiring for most but the dwindling minority who experienced it as professional soldiers. Fréjus' memorial attracts a limited number of visitors, and even important anniversaries have failed to generate widespread attention. Tellingly, the fiftieth anniversary of Dien Bien Phu in May 2004 was submerged by commemorations of the sixtieth anniversary of the Allied D-Day landings in Normandy that marked the beginning of France's liberation from Nazi occupation – yet another instance when the distant colonial war became overshadowed by the hexagon-centred Second World War memory looming over it. Faced with what Nikki Cooper calls a seemingly insurmountable 'wall of indifference', the limited understanding of the 1946–1954 conflict centres on its Cold War dimensions at the expense of the colonial. As part of the fight to defend the 'free world' from communism, the war was waged for a 'just cause'; that it was also a war to reconquer a colony and a war of national independence has been largely forgotten.[163]

* * *

To date, many aspects of colonial history thus have never become subjected to thorough reappraisal or lasting scrutiny. Moreover, even intense debates could be followed by a retreat back into more palatable memories and comfortable forms of forgetting after the controversy subsided. As the example of Belgium's Royal Museum for Central Africa at Tervuren suggests, signs of a decisive move towards a more critical approach to the colonial past did not necessarily produce a 180-degree shift from older conventional approaches to it. Long resistant to change under directors who continued to honour both Léopold II's ambitions and the colonial period that followed it through the 1990s, the museum appointed a new head, Guido Gryseels, in 2001 at the height of the national tumult about Belgian crimes at the turn of the previous century and in 1960–1961. Gryseels aimed to rebrand what had become an infamously stagnant, antiquated institution still showcasing colonial-style propaganda via modernizing its exhibitions, reaching out to Africans both in

---

[162] Aldrich, *Vestiges*, 133 (and 123–33 more generally).
[163] Cooper, 'Dien Bien Phu', 445, 451.

Africa and among Belgium's African diasporas, and incorporating more up-to-date perspectives.[164]

Reform was firmly on the agenda, but the museum promptly began planning for an exhibit staged in 2005 that its detractors complained was a blatantly defensive response to Adam Hochschild's assertion that the Congo had suffered a 'forgotten Holocaust' under Léopold. Its organizers disputed the contention that the Congo's population declined by 50 per cent and rejected the notion that the deaths which did occur could properly be labelled a genocide: not only were there too few Europeans based in the region to have carried out such a large-scale destruction of human life, but diseases and other factors also accounted for African mortality. Evidence of European-inflicted physical brutality and killing were indisputable, but the extent of the violence was both played down and attributed to the bad conduct of a limited number of perpetrators. Like the defensive Dutch assertions about 1940s Indonesia or British qualifications about Mau Mau seen earlier, Tervuren's 2005 exhibit contended that atrocities were not a routine feature underpinning the entire workings of the Congo Free State but constituted unacceptable individual excesses – excesses which, moreover, were stamped out once the Congo officially became Belgium's colony in 1908.[165] In attempting to steer perceptions towards a more moderate and, at times, revisionist stance, the 2005 exhibition thus marked a significant step back from the radical critiques that had originally inspired it. Plans for the Tervuren museum's overhaul continued thereafter; closed to the public for renovation in 2013 with a projected reopening scheduled for 2017, it is clear that it will not retreat to its *status quo ante* as the diehard champion of the alleged achievements of the Congo Free State and the 1908–1960 colonial era that followed it.[166] Nevertheless, judging from 2005, the extent to which it will fundamentally challenge its own ideological origins that are materially inscribed into the building and its grounds remains to be seen.

After the furore sparked by Hochschild's and De Witte's assertions died down, Belgium's colonial memory became one 'torn between nostalgia and shame' and 'international accusations and national self-defence', as Véronique

---

[164] Rahier, 'Ghost of Leopold II', 74; Gryseels, Landry, and Claessens, 'Integrating the Past'. Encouraging signs that Congolese views of the past would be accorded more attention came with the museum's 2010 exhibition 'Indépendance! Congolese Tell Their Stories of 50 Years of Independence'. See Véronique Bragard, '"Indépendance!": The Belgo-Congolese Dispute in the Tervuren Museum', *Human Architecture: Journal of the Sociology of Self-Knowledge*, 9:4 (2011), 93–104.

[165] Jan-Bart Gewald, 'Review Essay: More than Red Rubber and Figures Alone: A Critical Appraisal of the Memory of the Congo Exhibition at the Royal Museum for Central Africa, Tervuren, Belgium', *International Journal of African Historical Studies*, 39:3 (2006), 474, 483–4; Bragard and Planche, 'Museum Practices', 57; Castryck, 'Whose History is History?', 4. The exhibition catalogue provides some indication of its scope. See Jean-Luc Vellut (ed.), *La Mémoire du Congo: Le temps colonial* (Gand, 2005).

[166] For updates, watch this space: www.africamuseum.be/home.

484 Memories, legacies, and further directions

Bragard and Stéphanie Planche summarize.[167] The fiftieth anniversary of the Congo's independence in 2010 saw the publication of a spate of *anciens'* nostalgic recollections of 'the most beautiful time of my life' together with a new bestselling history of the Congo by David Van Reybrouck. Van Reybrouck's highly respected book did not neglect controversial themes, but it was far less categorically damning of Belgian actions than either Hochschild's or De Witte's accounts. Vigorous critiques had ebbed somewhat and narratives restabilized that could accommodate apologist perspectives as well as somewhat more measured assessments.[168]

Ignoring or forgetting colonialism altogether, moreover, still remained a popular option, even in Flanders, where anti-colonial critiques went much further than in Wallonia. However visible and radical *De Stoete(n) Ostendenoare*'s vandalism of the '*Dank van de Congolezen*' monument in Oostende may have been, several days passed with no one officially reporting the missing hand from the African figure, leaving the perpetrators to announce their action themselves. Meanwhile, the Flemish city of Antwerp continues to enjoy one of its culinary specialties, a variety of chocolates affectionately called *Antwerpse handjes* – 'little Antwerp hands'. Few residents or visitors appear to make a conscious association between a source of municipal pride (whose origins, its devotees insist, derive from local folklore) and the scandal surrounding the 'severed hands' in *fin-de-siècle* Central Africa, regardless of how publicly and recently the episode has been revisited.[169]

* * *

Portuguese memories of empire after decolonization reveal similar selective tendencies. The 1961–1974 wars in Africa that brought down the *Estado Novo* dictatorship in Lisbon and led to rapid decolonization subsequently lost the battle for a place in public consciousness to the democratic revolution they sparked. 25 April 1974 remains predominantly remembered for its metropolitan events and consequences, not for the colonial dynamics fundamental to them. Even among many veterans, Portugal's colonial wars were apt to be compared to the United States' fight in Vietnam during the same period and

[167] Bragard and Planche, 'Museum Practices', 60–1.
[168] Idesbald Goddeeris and Sindani E. Kiangu, 'Congomania in Academia: Recent Historical Research on the Belgian Colonial Past', *BMGN-Low Countries Historical Review*, 126:4 (2011), 61–3, 71; Idesbald Goddeeris, 'Postcolonial Belgium: The Memory of the Congo', *Interventions: International Journal of Postcolonial Studies*, 17:3 (2015), 434–51. David Van Reybrouck's *Congo: een geschiedenis* (Amsterdam, 2010) has since appeared in French, German, and English translations.
[169] See www.visitflanders.us/discover/flanders/flemish-specialities/antwerpse-handjes; http://lumumba.be/blog/2005/03/congolese-handjes-finest-belgian.html; http://sites.northwestern.edu/akih/2013/02/21/chocolates-as-cultural-blind-spots-responding-to-civilization, accessed 15 June 2014. Grateful thanks to Niek Lohmann for alerting me to the *handjes*' place in Antwerp culture.

disconnected from their metropolitan contexts.[170] Additionally, with the wars in Africa 'displaced by the events of the revolution in Portugal', Paulo de Medeiros summarizes, 'Portuguese soldiers never really faced public condemnation for their actions in war, and were celebrated instead as the heroes who had rescued the nation from authoritarian rule'.[171] Whether heroicized for their bravery in Africa and initiating political change at home, or depicted as war victims who suffered death, injury, or mental trauma, as noted earlier, Portugal's veterans never were confronted with public accusations of unacceptable military violence or 'war crimes' when fighting insurgencies, unlike their counterparts elsewhere. This was despite the fact that the virtually bloodless revolution at home, symbolized by the red carnations that gave it its name, came at the cost of more than a decade of bloodshed far away that claimed countless African casualties.

Postcolonial Portugal has never probed the end-of-empire actions of its military or civilian personnel or settler population in Africa, let alone held anyone to account for massacres, torture, killings, or the use of napalm, all of which were recurrent, in the name of fighting anti-colonialism. Nor has there been any recognition that official apologies to formerly-colonized societies might be in order. Instead, as Manuel Loff puts it, the Africans who were the true 'liberators of the Portuguese in the 1970s have been forgotten or rejected by most of them and their children'.[172] So too were the sufferings of their ancestors who bore the brunt of the Portuguese slave trade, slavery, forced labour, racism, inequality, and other forms of violence over the course of centuries. Anti-colonial critique remained a minority pursuit in post-1974 Portugal, even once the fall of the political order that had defended the maintenance of the 'overseas provinces' at all costs created unprecedented opportunities to condemn the old regime's colonial misdeeds.[173] While it is not difficult to find denunciations of the wars and the abusive and racist nature of the *Estado Novo*'s overseas policy in postcolonial Portuguese literature and art – with the novelist António Lobo Antunes, film artist Filipa César, and painter Franscico Vidal (born in Portugal of Cape Verdean and Angolan parents) among those providing powerful alternative depictions of the injustices perpetrated under late colonialism – the wider collective consciousness appears largely impervious to their oppositional stance.[174] Both the cause and the

---

[170] Power, 'Geo-politics', 469–70.   [171] De Medeiros, 'Hauntings', 208.

[172] Loff, 'Coming to Terms', 121; see also 67, 109–12, 117–19.

[173] Elsa Peralta, 'Fictions of a Creole Nation: (Re)Presenting Portugal's Imperial Past', in Helen Vella Bonavita (ed.), *Negotiating Identities: Constructed Selves and Others* (Amsterdam, 2011), 212; Ferreira, 'Decolonizing the Mind?', 234–7.

[174] Francisco Bethencourt, 'Desconstrução da memória imperial: literatura, arte e historiografia', in Margarida Calafate Ribeiro and Ana Paula Ferreira (eds.), *Fantasmas e fantasias: Imperiais no Imaginário Português Contemporâneo* (Porto, 2003), 69–81; José António B. Fernandes Dias, 'Pós-colonialismo nas artes visuais, ou talvez não', in Manuela Ribeiro Sanches (ed.),

2

6

result of the general disinclination to overhaul deeply-entrenched attitudes was the survival of key elements of Salazarism's ideology: the resilient belief in Portugal's exceptionalism as an overseas power and the endurance of lusotropical myths revolving around its alleged benevolence, lack of racism, and unique acceptance of cultural difference, exchanges, and hybridity.

In Portugal after empire, then, as Chapters 7 and 8 introduced, the remnants of earlier colonial ideologies continued to thrive. Furthermore, while colonialism itself was not regretted, decolonization often was, and many clearly preferred not to think about negative aspects of the nation's history that they could not change.[175] Portuguese soldiers, for example, may have been construed as victims or heroes rather than perpetrators of racist violence, but like their African opponents they too became cloaked with widespread social amnesia. In Lisbon, the memorial in Belém inaugurated in 1994 to the Portuguese who died in the wars in Africa provides a case in point. Not only does the 'Monument to the Overseas Combatants' dedicated 'in memory of all the soldiers who died serving Portugal' use terminology that could just as readily have been deployed by *Estado Novo* stylists before 1974 and fail to include any mention of colonialism, why the wars were waged against it, or that African deaths vastly outnumbered Portuguese. For much of the time, the monument is virtually devoid of visitors, with only the soldiers standing guard in evidence. Though situated only a short walk away from the most popular historic tourist attractions of Lisbon, few visitors, whether Portuguese or foreign, venture away from the sights that drew them to the Belém district in the first place, namely, those linked to the 'Age of Discoveries' of the fifteenth and sixteenth centuries.[176]

The will to forget the lost fight against anti-colonial forces and the loss of empire itself did not mean that all chapters of Portugal's imperial history were neglected after decolonization. Far from it: if the end of empire provoked unpleasant memories and was marginalized by the Carnation Revolution which became recast as a domestic one and shorn of its overseas causes and consequences, the beginnings of empire remained as ripe for national

---

'Portugal não é um país pequeno': Contar o 'império' na pós-colonialidade (Lisbon, 2006), 333–4; www.artafrica.info/html/expovirtual/expovirtual_i.php?ide=2, accessed 5 January 2012; Filipa César, 'Das fragile Gedächtnis der Bilder', www.woz.ch/1315/filipa-cesar/das-fragile-gedaechtnis-der-bilder; http://mudam.lu/en/expositions/details/exposition/filipa-cesar, both accessed 11 June 2013.

[175] Loff, 'Coming to Terms', 96, 108–21; Ana Duarte Melo, 'The Last Empire', *Index on Censorship*, 28:1 (1999), 40; Rosa Cabecinhas and João Feijó, 'Collective Memories of Portuguese Colonial Action in Africa: Representations of the Colonial Past among Mozambicans and Portuguese Youths', *International Journal of Conflict and Violence*, 4:1 (2010), 38–41.

[176] Ellen W. Sapega, 'Remembering Empire/Forgetting the Colonies: Accretions of Memory and the Limits of Commemoration in a Lisbon Neighborhood', *History & Memory*, 20:2 (2008), 28–32; Power, 'Geo-politics', 487.

Figure 9.7 Monument to the Overseas Combatants, Belém, Lisbon; inaugurated 1994.
Photograph by author, 2012. Portugal's flag with its golden armillary sphere harkening back to the maritime 'Discoveries' flies overhead. Aside from the soldiers standing guard, this site typically attracts few visitors (compare this with the nearby Monument to the Discoveries from 1960 shown in Figure 5.2).

celebration as they were before 1974. Statues, street names, squares, and public sculpture honouring the navigators and early colonial governors or featuring maritime symbols remain ubiquitous throughout the built environment of Portuguese towns and cities, many long pre-dating 1974 but others of post-colonial, post-dictatorship vintage.[177] Within the space of a few hundred meters in Belém, tourists flock to see the early sixteenth-century Torre de Belém (Tower of Belém) perched on the shore of the Tagus River, the point of embarkation for many of the voyages of discovery, together with the Jerónimos Monastery dating from the same era. Replete with elephant statues, nautical carvings and motifs, and the ornate tombs of both Da Gama and

---

[177] Francisco Bethencourt, 'A Memória da Expansão', in Francisco Bethencourt and Kirti Chaudhuri (eds.), *História da Expansão Portuguesa, Vol. 5: Último Império e Recentramento (1930–1998)* (Navarra, 2000), 442–80; Sapega, 'Remembering Empire'.

Camões (whose supposed remains were transferred there in the late nineteenth century), the monastery's showcasing of the 'Discoveries' is complemented by the Monument to the Discoveries (*Padrão dos Descubrimientos*) situated directly across the square, overlooking the riverfront. Built under the *Estado Novo* to mark the five-hundredth anniversary of Prince Henry 'the Navigator's' birth in 1960, it incorporates statues of Magellan, Da Gama, Camões, and many other leading lights alongside Prince Henry himself (as illustrated by Figure 5.2 in Chapter 5).

All three Belém landmarks remain as crowded with sightseers today as ever, still occupying centre stage in the nation's architectural heritage and cultural understanding of its past as one characterized by global grandeur. In 1998, they were joined by prominent new additions to Lisbon's urban landscape, the Vasco da Gama Bridge built to mark the fifth centenary of his arrival in India (as seen in Figure 7.3 in Chapter 7) and the grounds and buildings constructed for Expo '98 – an event whose organizing 'Oceans' theme left considerable space for highlighting Portugal's maritime heritage that reshaped global and national history alike. Unmentioned were the responses and experiences of faraway peoples on the receiving end of the 'Discoveries', such as the Indians who marked the Da Gama quincentenary with protests as opposed to new monuments erected in his honour, or the contributions of low-waged African workers fundamental to their construction and upkeep discussed in Chapter 7.[178] Neither the racism and violence that accompanied and followed Portugal's intrepid navigators, nor the dark aspects of Da Gama's character, nor the exploitation of black immigrant workers in the creation of postcolonial monuments dedicated to his achievements were allowed to mar the celebrations or disfigure the reputation of new landmarks that survive as the legacy of these commemorative occasions.

Still ubiquitous and overwhelmingly uncontentious material features of public life and popular memory, the 'Discoveries' that crowned the nation's early modern golden age and subsequent self-understanding acted as a lens through which memories of other Portuguese historic events have been viewed.[179] In his 1988 novel *As Naus* (literally meaning *The Ships*, but uncoincidentally published in English translation as *The Return of the Caravels*), António Lobo Antunes transposed Da Gama and other maritime figures into mid-1970s Lisbon at the time of decolonization, thereby merging

[178] On Expo '98 and the Vasco da Gama Bridge, see points introduced in Chapter 7, as well as R. Timothy Sieber, 'Remembering Vasco da Gama: Contested Histories and the Cultural Politics of Contemporary Nation-Building in Lisbon, Portugal', *Identities*, 8:4 (2001), 549–81; Marcus Power and James D. Sidaway, 'Deconstructing Twinned Towers: Lisbon's Expo '98 and the Occluded Geographies of Discovery', *Social & Cultural Geography*, 6:6 (2005), 865–83; David Tomory, 'Reluctant Heritage', *Index on Censorship*, 28:1 (1999), 67–8.
[179] Cabecinhas and Feijó, 'Collective Memories'.

the two temporalities in a reworking of Camões' epic *The Lusiads*. *O Regresso das Caravelas* (*The Return of the Caravels*) also formed part of the title of João Paulo Guerra's popular history of Portuguese decolonization (a book whose cover fittingly featured the 1960 Monument in Belém looming behind packing crates delivered home upon the retreat from Africa). Other writers have used 'the return of the caravels' to describe inward population movements from the former empire, whether of *retornados* or Africans.[180]

Nor were the 'Discoveries' far away as Portugal celebrated the fortieth anniversary of its Carnation Revolution in April 2014. In press coverage and an endless round of ceremonies marking 'Forty Years of Democracy', once again the revolution's colonial dimensions took a back seat to the domestic as commentators used the occasion to reflect upon Portugal's current difficulties since the 2008 economic crisis. The depressing realities of debt, austerity, high unemployment, and Portugal's abject dependency on the hated *troika* (the International Monetary Fund, European Central Bank, and European Commission) as it attempted a recovery with no end in sight cast a pall over the festivities that coincided with what many deemed the country's most challenging period since the end of the authoritarian regime.[181] What better time, then, to offer an uplifting antidote in the form of another return to Portugal's glorious maritime past? Marking the end of a week otherwise dominated by reminiscences and verdicts about 1974 and its aftermath, the World of Discoveries, an 'interactive museum and theme park' costing €8 million, opened in Porto. As its director hoped, its replicas of galleons and caravels, guides wearing navigators' costumes, and simulated seas and tropical forests populated by model rhinos and elephants would offer visitors a chance to 'travel back in time' and regain national pride through a return to Portugal's historic zenith. For €14 for adults, €8 for children, and €11 for students and pensioners, 'the Portuguese could go back to what we once were' for a day, carrying away with them new inspiration by recalling 'the greatness of a nation'.[182] Not only did recalling the 1974 revolution or the contraction of empire inseparable from it offer no appealing competition to recalling empire's illustrious commencement; the grim realities of the early twenty-first century

---

[180] António Lobo Antunes, *The Return of the Caravels*, translated by Gregory Rabassa (New York, 2002); João Paulo Guerra, *Descolonização Portuguesa: O Regresso das Caravelas* (Alfragide, 2009); Adamopoulos, *Voltar* (whose cover image is the same as Guerra's); M. Margarida Marques, Nuno Dias, and José Mapril, 'Le "retour des caravelles" au Portugal: de l'exclusion des immigés à l'inclusion des lusophones?', in Évelyne Ritaine (ed.), *L'Europe du Sud face à l'immigration: Politique de l'Étranger* (Paris, 2005), 151.

[181] See newspaper coverage of the fortieth anniversary, including reports and editorials in *Público*, the Lisbon daily, between 24 and 26 April 2014.

[182] Sara Gerivaz, 'A partir de hoje já é possível embarcar numa viagem até aos Descobrimentos', *Público*, 25 April 2014; www.worldofdiscoveries.com. Bijl, 'Dutch Colonial Nostalgia', 144, makes a related point about the VOC-themed roller coaster ('The Flying Dutchman') at the Netherlands' most popular amusement park.

made the latest revival of Portugal's pioneering global heyday centuries before into a source of comfort and dignity once again.

* * *

Conclusion

As opportunities to take stock and reassess the past, anniversaries of turning points in the history of empire are inevitably ephemeral by nature. Often not marked much at all, even when they are these histories are prone to receding into the background after momentary returns to the limelight as fickle public interest refocuses itself elsewhere. For much of the time, critical awareness – indeed, *any* awareness at all – of colonial and decolonization history still competes against pride, nostalgia, and amnesia, while much historiography and public historical consciousness still remains centred on Europe.

Reckoning with the imperial past in Europe remains unfinished business, a series of periodic, piecemeal, and unsystematic engagements as opposed to consistently conscious and concerted efforts.[183] Recurrent failures to work through imperial pasts and their ongoing implications have provoked some critics to ask whether the European nations examined throughout this book have completely decolonized at all. 'Portugal has never really given up her colonies', Landeg White has argued:

Decolonisation is a process of recognising that the time to depart is overdue and (perhaps) that one should never have been there in the first place. Portugal's departure was more akin to mass deportation, an entirely different psychological experience. It bequeaths the illusion that history has somehow gone wrong and requires correction . . . [that this turn of events is] not part of the 'national truth'.[184]

Writing of Britain, Bill Schwarz similarly asks, 'Are we already postcolonial? Or have we yet to become so?' With 'internal mental structures of colonial power' proving so apt 'to outlive their epoch', European nations that long lay at the heart of empires still need to fully come to terms with the lessons they can teach and accept their status as *former* empires.[185] Rethinking their historical 'national truths' and present-day identities offers not simply an invaluable chance to develop more inclusive approaches to their diverse peoples and cultures that count among their most important imperial legacies; they also invite new ways of understanding what it means to be European after decolonization.

---

[183] Ann Laura Stoler, 'Colonial Aphasia: Race and Disabled Histories in France', *Public Culture*, 23:1 (2011), 121–56.
[184] Landeg White, 'Empire's Revenge', *Index on Censorship*, 28:1 (1999), 54–5.
[185] Bill Schwarz, 'Actually Existing Postcolonialism', *Radical Philosophy*, 104 (2000), 16.

Epilogue
Thoughts towards new histories of contemporary Europe

In June 2004 on the Hobbemaplein, a small square in The Hague, members of the Netherlands' Indo-Surinamese community proudly unveiled a two-part monument to their collective history of colonial and postcolonial migrations. Despite its chosen name, the National Hindustani Immigration Monument (*Nationaal Hindustaans Immigratiemonument*) was in fact much more than national. It commemorated a history of two uprootings and resettlements that stretched from indentured labourers' departure from colonial British India for what was then Dutch Guiana (Suriname) starting in 1873 to the mass Indo-Surinamese migration to the Netherlands in the decolonization era a century later. Three decades on and with a substantial proportion having clustered in and around the city, the Indo-Surinamese had become '*Hindoestaanse Hagenaars*', or 'Hindustanis of The Hague'. One bronze sculpture designed by a Surinamese artist featured boats, airplanes, sacks, and suitcases on one side and people in transit on its reverse to depict the two phases of intercontinental migration. Several meters away stood a statue of Mohandas Gandhi, an inspirational migrant himself given his own journeys from Gujarat to Victorian London as a student, to South Africa as a lawyer and activist who fought for Indian diasporic rights, and back to India where he achieved global acclaim as the foremost Indian nationalist who campaigned for independence by non-violent means.

The monument's two components thereby invoked a heritage that greatly exceeded the confines of the Netherlands and its ex-colony in South America to incorporate British South Asia and South Africa, rendering it trans-imperial as much as it was emblematic of (ex-)metropolitan-colonial population flows. Designed by a Dutch artist of Portuguese descent, moreover, the Gandhi sculpture also provided indirect testament to the intra-European movements and diasporas that complemented those coming from Europe's former colonies. On The Hague's Hobbemaplein, the local, national, continental, and intercontinental converged, with the global not reducible to one former European empire alone. And as Indo-Surinamese celebrated their successful re-rooting, socio-economic progress, and cultural adaptation in the Netherlands without having forsaken

Figure E.1 National Hindustani Immigration Monument (*Nationaal Hindustaans Immigratiemonument*), The Hague; inaugurated 2004. Photograph by author, 2013.

Figure E.2 Mohandas Gandhi statue, part of the National Hindustani
Immigration Monument (*Nationaal Hindustaans Immigratiemonument*),
The Hague; inaugurated 2004.
Photograph by author, 2013.

their roots, their guests of honour endorsed their presence and transition. Together with the city's mayor, the Dutch Minister for Integration congratulated them with the words '*U doet het goed*', or 'You're doing well' – a far cry from the relentless level of public concern then being expressed about other migrant groups who were Muslim as opposed to predominantly Hindu.[1]

The early twenty-first century Indo-Surinamese community and their monument in The Hague indicate how migration, arrivals, and broader resettlement processes that heralded wide-ranging cultural transformations qualify as the most visible and sometimes spectacular manifestations of the imperial past and the end of empire in Western Europe. As many of this book's core themes and illustrations have suggested, ships and planes readily became transformed into iconic images of arrival, gracing postage stamps, cartoons, newspaper and magazine photographs, and film footage circulated in cinemas and on television.[2] Tintin and Milou's and King Baudouin's respective descents from their ocean liner and Sabena jet in the Belgian Congo in 1930 and 1955; the airlift that orchestrated the panicked departure in July 1960 of thousands of white colonials who fled back to Belgium when violence broke out upon the Congo's independence (a history that repeated itself by boat as *pieds-noirs* crossed the Mediterranean *en masse* from Algeria to France in 1962, and again by plane when Portuguese settlers left southern Africa in the mid-1970s); the *S.S. Empire Windrush*'s arrival from Jamaica in 1948 that came to symbolize the growing West Indian presence in post-war Britain; the KLM flights that carried Surinamese of diverse ethnic backgrounds to the Netherlands in the 1970s; the planes and trains that brought Portuguese migrants home for family visits from France and other Northern European countries after they left as labour migrants while their nation was embroiled in fighting colonial wars: modes of transport and the millions of people taking advantage of them in the decades when empires ended survive as familiar images of an era when decolonizations and migrations coincided.[3]

Europe experienced new modes of continental and global interconnectedness that became signs of their times, just as the Portuguese caravels of the 'Discoveries' age, the Dutch East India Company vessels of seventeenth- and

---

[1] For press coverage, see Perdiep Ramesar, 'Hofstad krijgt immigratiemonument', *Haagsche Courant* (The Hague), 21 January 2004; 'Twee hindoe-monumenten; Hindoestanen herdenken hun volksverhuizingen', *Trouw* (Amsterdam), 25 June 2004; 'Hindoestaanse verankering', *Haagsche Courant*, 26 June 2004.

[2] Insightful analyses of postage stamps as symbolic of wider national assumptions about empire and migration include Gilles Dubus, 'Quand les timbres-poste reconnaissent ou ignorent les migrants et les réfugiés', *Revue européenne des migrations internationales*, 12:2 (1996), 87–104; Igor Cusack, 'Tiny Transmitters of Nationalist and Colonial Ideology: The Postage Stamps of Portugal and Its Empire', *Nations and Nationalism*, 11:4 (2005), 591–612.

[3] Matthew Mead, '*Empire Windrush*: The Cultural Memory of an Imaginary Arrival', *Journal of Postcolonial Writing*, 45:2 (2009), 137–49.

Figure E.3 Advertisement, Lalla Rookh restaurant, Wijttenbachstraat 290, 1093 JK Amsterdam, the Netherlands, c. 2014.

eighteenth-century vintage, and passenger steamships carrying European set-tlers and expatriates to and from their imperial destinations remained emble-matic of the birth and growth of empires in European public memory long after empires' ultimate demise.[4] Images of slave ships also survive in the public consciousness as powerful reminders of a long history of African oppression that remains integral to black diasporic identities today.[5] For their part, the Indo-Surinamese in the Netherlands still memorialize the *Lalla Rookh*, the ship that brought the first indentured workers from Calcutta to Dutch Guiana in

[4] Elizabeth Buettner, *Empire Families: Britons and Late Imperial India* (Oxford, 2004), introduc-tion; Bernhard Rieger, *Technology and the Culture of Modernity in Britain and Germany, 1890–1945* (Cambridge, 2005), ch. 6; Angela Woollacott, "'All This Is the Empire, I Told Myself': Australian Women's Voyages "Home" and the Articulation of Colonial Whiteness', *American Historical Review*, 102:4 (1997), 1003–29; Ulbe Bosma, 'Sailing through Suez from the South: The Emergence of an Indies-Dutch Migration Circuit, 1815–1940', *International Migration Review*, 41:2 (2007), 511–36.

[5] Anita Rupprecht, "'A Limited Sort of Property": History, Memory and the Slave Ship *Zong*', *Slavery and Abolition*, 29:2 (2008), 265–77.

1873, in annual ceremonies marking its date of arrival and in other portrayals of their community's culture and heritage.

Migrations outwards and inwards alike thus continually transformed European history as well as wider global dynamics from the fifteenth to the twentieth centuries as overseas empires expanded, transformed, consolidated, and collapsed. Many travellers linked particular European metropoles with their respective colonies, but this was never to the exclusion of other imperial and post-imperial geographies of circulation, as the British-Indian-Surinamese-Dutch example indicates. As Chapters 6–8 pointed out, Europe's current minority communities include Moroccans in the Netherlands and Belgium as well as in France (which once counted Morocco as a protectorate within its empire and Union), Congolese from the former Belgian colony in Paris as well as Brussels, and Portuguese in France, the Netherlands, and many other Northern European countries, including Germany and Britain. Europeans once based in former empires might also choose other metropoles as their place of residence when (and indeed if) they returned to Europe after empire, like the *pieds-noirs* who resettled in Spain rather than France or the British ex-colonials who opted for Portugal's Algarve region as their preferred retirement destination.

Criss-crossings between imperial and post-imperial spaces helped render many places in contemporary Western Europe sites of transnational and cosmopolitan 'super-diversity', as Steven Vertovec has called it, a scenario that saw Francophone Africans, Portuguese, and innumerable other groups join Indians, Pakistanis, Bangladeshis, Irish, and West Indians in London and many other parts of Britain.[6] Alongside newcomers from Asia, Africa, the Middle East, and the Caribbean migrating from the 'Global South' to Western Europe were those traveling East to West within Europe, a movement accelerating after the Berlin Wall fell in 1989 and particularly once the European Union gained many new member states in Eastern and Southeastern Europe since 2004. Empires 'striking back' may thus have accounted for much of Europe's cultural and ethnic mix, but wider global and continental population flows increasingly spelled the 'diversification of diversity' during and after the 1990s, a shift in which intra-European dynamics grew ever more central.[7] If French discussions about the European Constitution in 2005 turned to the contentious figure of the 'Polish plumber', as Chapter 7 noted, public debates about the impact of

---

[6] Steven Vertovec, 'Super-Diversity and Its Implications', *Ethnic and Racial Studies*, 30:6 (2007), 1024–54. This wider topic is influentially analyzed by, among others, Yasemin Nuhoglu Soysal, *Limits of Citizenship: Migrants and Postnational Membership in Europe* (Chicago, 1995); Étienne Balibar, *We, the People of Europe?: Reflections on Transnational Citizenship* (Princeton, 2004); Nina Glick Schiller, Tsypylma Darieva, and Sandra Gruner-Domic, 'Defining Cosmopolitan Sociability in a Transnational Age: An Introduction', *Ethnic and Racial Studies*, 34:3 (2011), 399–418.

[7] Vertovec, 'Super-Diversity', 1025.

immigration and multiculturalism in Britain currently vacillate schizophrenically between Muslims and Eastern Europeans as the most significant demonized 'others' who expose widespread levels of anxiety, hostility, and bigotry, as the recent ascent of the UK Independence Party (UKIP) attests. Since 2013, concerns about the rise of migration from Southeastern and Eastern Europe have sparked a rise in demands for the terms of Britain's European Union membership to be renegotiated among Conservatives and UKIP adherents eager for a referendum that some hope would take Britain out of the EU altogether.

Forty years earlier in 1973 as Britain acceded to the EU as it was then, the European Economic Community, J.G.A. Pocock delivered the lecture that was later published as 'British History: A Plea for New Subject'. Seeking deeper and more explicit scholarly engagements with Britain's development as a composite of Scotland, Wales, and Ireland as well as England and whose history was one of four nations in addition to an overseas empire, he claimed that '[w]ithin very recent memory, the English have been increasingly willing to declare that neither empire nor commonwealth ever meant much in their consciousness, and that they were at heart Europeans all the time' – immediately noting '[t]he obvious absurdity of the second part of the claim'.[8] Pocock's intervention proved one of the most seminal contributions that inspired scholars to explore Britain's domestic history beyond the conventional focus on England alone and equally as closely connected with its former empire and Commonwealth. With respect to the prospect of the English (or other Britons) jettisoning other identities and interests for a European orientation, however, he need not have worried: few among the general public and the Britain-focused historical profession ever came remotely close to being Europeans 'at heart', with the latter group often appearing as Europhobic in their research into Britain's past as prominent politicians on the right were about Britain's present and future. If becoming part of the EEC/European Union was heralded as a proud achievement and welcomed as an economic opportunity and a chance to reinvent themselves by many member states, to many Britons it signalled a loss of sovereignty and global stature, a sign that their nation had descended from being the elevated and exceptional heart of an oceanic empire to a disempowered component of a European herd dominated by continentals.[9]

It is precisely this tendency towards exceptionalism (one which is characteristic not only of British thinking and historiography but which recurs across the

---

[8] J.G.A. Pocock, 'British History: A Plea for a New Subject', *Journal of Modern History*, 47:4 (1975), 602.

[9] Krishan Kumar, 'Britain, England and Europe: Cultures in Counterflow', *European Journal of Social Theory*, 6:1 (2003), 5–23; Bill Schwarz, 'Britain, America, and Europe', in David Morley and Kevin Robins (eds.), *British Cultural Studies: Geography, Nationality, and Identity* (Oxford, 2001), esp. 160–6; Menno Spiering, *A Cultural History of British Euroscepticism* (Basingstoke, 2014).

other countries explored here) that this book has sought to work against. Across national borders, ideas and racisms of the late colonial and contested decolonization eras re-entered Europe once again and in new ways with the rising level of migration – of ex-colonizers returning and ex-colonized arriving – after 1945. Regardless of where one looks, imperial mentalities remained alive both during and after decolonization as many Europeans proved unwilling or unable to decolonize their minds to adjust to a new era. As Western Europe was remade at the end of empire, many imperial holdovers survived to influence approaches to ethnic and cultural diversity between the end of the Second World War and the present day. In this and other respects, the divide between the colonial and postcolonial eras often becomes blurry. Ideologies of empire still had an influence on European identity politics and polemics around race, minorities, and cultural difference long after 1945. As the chapters of *Europe after Empire* have made clear, we continue to see new (yet sadly familiar) attempts to legitimize both imperial practices of the past and proclamations of benign colonial histories and intentions that were allegedly distinct from (and usually superior to) those of other colonizers. Insistent singularities and supposed imperial uniqueness are echoed by often hollow claims about particular countries' special talents for approaching cultural diversity in postcolonial Europe.

If this book has persuaded readers that it is no longer possible to examine late colonialism, decolonization, migrations to Europe, approaches to multicultural societies, and imperial memories and legacies through a single national-imperial lens, it has achieved one of its most important aims. Failure to compare and contrast national experiences of overseas decolonization, the inward flows of peoples and cultures, and attitudes towards empires recently brought to a close inhibits our understanding of these issues as far more than specific national histories. It was not simply individual nations that had already been reconstructed by empire which were remade once again when empires ended; this process in fact described the history of most of Western Europe. The geopolitical, demographic, and cultural transformations described throughout the preceding chapters were transimperial and transnational phenomena that point towards the need to examine comparisons and common histories (despite the differences that inevitably become apparent), not isolate and contain them. Continuing to pursue the latter course risks undervaluing their historical significance, for they illuminate a continent in transition – not just its constituent countries. Put differently, taking the 'imperial turn' should encourage a 'continental turn', not close it down.

Having made tremendous progress in charting empire, its dismantling, and its inward-bound populations heralding intense cultural change as part of Britain's own history, scholars still have much to accomplish if they are to give due attention to the connected histories of Britain and Europe during and after decolonization. To varying degrees, however, the same applies to those studying the other nations explored throughout this book whose decolonization and postcolonial histories also converged with the European integration process described in Part I in ways that have been largely forgotten or ignored. Linking Europe's decolonization and integration histories offers a means of moving beyond bilateral examinations of one metropole and its ex-empire to examine how colonialism and decolonization were shared *European* experiences. The late- and postcolonial migrations that overlapped with intra-European movements briefly touched upon earlier and in Part II serve as only some of the many stories still only partly told. Others include a fuller account of the inseparability of EU member states' ties to the wider world and the integration project's origins, evolution, and modes of understanding Europe's own identity, a topic thus far broached by only a small number of promising studies.[10] Although much of their subject matter still requires further in-depth research to substantiate wider claims, they highlight the need for further work that goes beyond bounded national decolonization experiences.

Reassessments of 1950s schemes for a 'Eurafrican' project, for example, demonstrate how 'the origins of the EU cannot be separated from the perceived necessity to preserve and prolong the colonial system', as Peo Hansen and Stefan Jonsson put it.[11] Key French policymakers firmly intended to preserve hegemony over African territories as they moved forward in negotiating France's inclusion in an emergent EEC as one of its founding and most powerful member nations. '*Eurafrique*' ideas envisioned an ongoing African role for Western European nations, with national colonial projects morphing into 'a joint European colonization of Africa' – one in which Germany too could again play an active part long after losing its own African colonies when defeated in the First World War.[12] *Eurafrique* would ideally keep Western Europe in Africa and communist Eastern European influences out while simultaneously containing radical forms of anti-colonialism. In Egypt, however, the Suez Crisis of late 1956 proved that European power had distinct limits. France's humiliation after

---

[10] Giuliano Garavini, *After Empires: European Integration, Decolonization, and the Challenge from the Global South 1957–1986* (Oxford, 2012). Many of this book's core arguments are also discussed in Giuliano Garavini, 'The Colonies Strike Back: The Impact of the Third World on Western Europe, 1968–1975', *Contemporary European History*, 16:3 (2007), 299–319.

[11] Peo Hansen and Stefan Jonsson, 'Bringing Africa as a "Dowry to Europe": European Integration and the Eurafrican Project, 1920–1960', *Interventions: International Journal of Postcolonial Studies*, 13:3 (2011), 461. Other examinations of *Eurafrique* aspirations published in English include Peo Hansen and Stefan Jonsson, *Eurafrica: The Untold History of European Integration and Colonialism* (London, 2013); Frederick Cooper, *Citizenship between Empire and Nation: Remaking France and French Africa, 1945–1960* (Princeton, 2014), 202–10, 263–70; Gary Wilder, 'Eurafrique as the Future Past of "Black France": Sarkozy's Temporal Confusion and Senghor's Postwar Vision', in Trica Danielle Keaton, T. Denean Sharpley-Whiting, and Tyler Stovall (eds.), *Black France/France Noire: The History and Politics of Blackness* (Durham, 2012), 57–87 (esp. 69–70).

[12] Hansen and Jonsson, 'Bringing Africa', 443.

invading the Canal Zone and being forced to withdraw after American pressure forced its British partner to back down made policymakers decide that leadership in Western Europe was necessary if France hoped to remain prominent on the world stage towered over by the Americans and Soviets. As France signed the Treaty of Rome the following year, some observers went so far as to credit General Nasser as being 'the federator of Europe', his actions in nationalizing the Suez Canal acting as the final triggers that convinced France (if not Britain) to look within Europe as it contemplated the scope of its future capabilities.[13]

Although the *Eurafrique* fantasy petered out by the end of the 1950s, the EEC maintained neo-colonial forms of presence that ranged from economic to political to military forms of influence that outlived formal ends of empire. That said, when the EEC was inaugurated in 1957 many of its six founding member states were still so colonial that neo-colonialism remained a future prospect. Belgium still held the Congo, Rwanda, and Burundi; Italy maintained a foot-hold in parts of its former North African empire; the Netherlands was deter-mined to remain in West New Guinea; and France's Union still spread far into West and Equatorial Africa and the Pacific. Only Luxemburg could not claim the colonizing identity so integral to other EEC members' present or, in the case of West Germany, its pre-1918 past. French negotiators who wanted the entire French Union, including its African territories, to be part of the projected European community *per se* may not have carried the day, but even so the 'European' entity born with the Treaty of Rome in fact extended far beyond Europe's continental confines. Until its independence in 1962, Algeria's three *départements* were juridically part of France itself and thus part of the EEC for the first five years of its existence, while France's overseas departments and territories in Guiana, Martinique, Guadeloupe, and Réunion continue to be part of the EU today – as do the Dutch Antillean islands that were then, and still are, part of the Kingdom of the Netherlands.

Later EEC members joined carrying their own colonial and postcolonial baggage. When Spain entered in 1986, it brought its North Africa enclaves of Ceuta and Melilla along with it; Britain (like Denmark) also retained overseas territories whose inhabitants, such as the Falkland Islanders, now carry EU passports. Like Britain's Commonwealth loyalties which long competed with Europe for attention before its 1973 accession and Portugal's decolonization and democratization which paved the way for a European future, the EU as it exists today emerged from intercontinental empires in decline or in the shadow of their dismantling. Fragmentary remains of empires past endow the EU with a

---

[13]   Peo Hansen, 'European Integration, European Identity and the Colonial Connection', *European Journal of Social Theory*, 5:4 (2002), 491.

continuing global reach, its territory spanning the South Atlantic, the Caribbean, North Africa, the Indian Ocean, and the Pacific.[14]

Western Europe's global and imperial dimensions, however, are typically glossed over if not completely obliterated from institutionally dominant forms of EU self-understanding and self-portrayal. Reconstructed European identities-in-the-making emphasized selected facets of its internal history at the expense of its historic and contemporary transcontinental scope. In the EU's own preferred story of its origins, its ability to draw upon a long venerable heritage and overcome past tragedies was meant to put the recent past of two world wars and the experience of fascism, totalitarianism, and genocide behind, for Germany after Hitler and Italy after Mussolini as much as for the countries Germany had invaded, occupied, or fought against. European integration spelled democracy and freedom versus dictatorship (in Portugal, Spain, and Greece after the mid-1970s as much as for the original six EEC nations) along with economic modernization, the spread of affluence (real or aspirational), liberalism, a commitment to human and civic rights, and above all peace and solidarity after a recent history of war and division. Repudiating and transcending the traumatic Nazi past and the Holocaust proved a way of consolidating a common post-war identity, one that could act as a unifying counterweight to the communist states to its East and to American power that reached deeply into Western Europe from across the Atlantic.

In condemning the recent past plagued by destructive nationalism and war, those consolidating European myths and claims to fame reached further back in time to extol Europe's roots in classical Greek and Roman civilizations, its cultures of Christianity modernized through secularization and religious toleration, the Industrial Revolution, scientific advances, Enlightenment values, and the rights of man associated with the era of the French Revolution. But this master narrative of Europe's trajectory 'from Greece to peace' relied on forgetting much about the colonialism that had been part of its history since the fifteenth century.[15] To the extent that postcolonial Europe looked back at the colonial past that had characterized the EEC's pre-history and beginnings, it did so to sing its own praises as an exporter of the gifts of Western civilization and modern European institutions across the globe from the time of the maritime 'Discoveries' onwards. Colonial raw materials, exports, and labour that helped make Western Europe what it was were conveniently omitted, as were centuries of colonial violence. The Nazi past and the genocide suffered by Europe's racialized internal others, Jews above all, demanded transnational memorial atonement; colonized external others exploited and repressed on other

[14] Ibid.; Gurminder K. Bhambra, 'Postcolonial Europe, or Understanding Europe in Times of the Postcolonial', in Chris Rumford (ed.), *The Sage Handbook of European Studies* (London, 2009), 69–85.
[15] Peo Hansen, 'In the Name of Europe', *Race & Class*, 45:3 (2004), 49.

continents required banishment from the collective memory. Although the transnational collective memory of slavery that Europe's black minorities have succeeded in moving onto the public agenda provides a partial exception to this rule, overall the shutting out of empires' misdeeds applies as much to chronologically distant episodes of colonial conquest and oppression as to the wars and counterinsurgencies fought in the decolonization era. These included conflicts like France's Algerian War fought within the EEC's own original borders which, like other instances, severely undermined and tainted Europe's espoused ideals of democracy, liberty, and peace. As Nora Fisher Onar and Kalypso Nicolaïdis summarize, '[i]t is as if the EU, as an imagined community, has exorcized the demons of its Member States by forgetting their colonial past and successfully entrenching the myth of its own "virgin birth"'.[16] Powerful beliefs in its historical role as global benefactor were preserved, while the self-interested and destructive actions of its member states which betrayed their own core values remained publicly unrecognized.

In sum, forgetting colonialism's dark history was as appealing to the transnational community that evolved into today's EU as it was for the individual postcolonial nations that comprised it, as Chapter 9 considered. Failure to openly reckon with the many paradoxes riddling Europe today underpins the EU's ongoing and unresolved dilemmas, often unacknow-ledged, about what – and who – Europe includes and excludes among its current and future member states and citizenries. In its gradual extension from the founding six nations of 1957 to encompass Britain, Ireland, and Denmark in 1973, Greece in 1981, Portugal and Spain in 1986, Sweden, Finland, and Austria in 1995, and much of the former Eastern bloc during and after 2004 thanks to the USSR's collapse after 1989, the EU proved again and again the flexibility of its borders and frontiers. At the same time, however, it balked at requests for admission from Turkey and Morocco, claiming that these nations were manifestly un-European – despite Algeria, Morocco's next-door neigh-bour, having once comprised part of the EEC before its independence and despite the EU's inclusion of Spain's Ceuta and Melilla enclaves, both of which are sandwiched between Morocco and the Mediterranean.

Denying Morocco and Turkey's claims to possible EU belonging had to do with their location as well as their culture, widely seen in Europe as inseparable from Islam. Dismissing their pretentions to Europeanness went hand in hand with taking full advantage of the EU's small North African, Spanish-held outposts in the fight to curb illegal African migration northwards across the

---

[16] Nora Fisher Onar and Kalypso Nicolaïdis, 'The Decentring Agenda: Europe as a Post-Colonial Power', *Cooperation and Conflict*, 48:2 (2013), 292. Similar themes are also discussed in Bhambra, 'Postcolonial Europe'; Hansen, 'European Integration'; Hansen, 'In the Name of Europe'; see also contributions to Kalypso Nicolaïdis, Berny Sèbe, and Gabrielle Maas (eds.), *Echoes of Empire: Memory, Identity and Colonial Legacies* (London, 2015), Part III.

Mediterranean via full recourse to harsh and elaborate security apparatuses installed in the effort to shore up a 'fortress Europe' from non-European others, often Muslim but always ethnically distinct.[17] What is more, it corresponded closely to the widespread hesitancy among the EU's constituent nations to recognize the millions of Muslims already settled within them, most of whom are now EU citizens. Ever on its guard against those it considered illegitimate non-European 'others' outside its formal borders, the same 'logic' was broadly applied to many of the delegitimized postcolonial minority 'others' located inside its geographical perimeters.[18] As the 2015 refugee crisis further underscores, migration, whether an already accomplished fact, current issue, or future prospect, has proved a resilient question that today's EU is far from resolving, whether it be migration from South to North or from East to West.

Both European Union history and decolonization history warrant new shifts in scholarly agendas that would further globalize the former and Europeanize the latter. Undertaking empirically detailed yet conceptually informed work on their entangled histories might ultimately achieve for specialist literature on the EU's evolution what is now well underway for colonialism and decolonization, namely its inclusion within the mainstream historiography of post-1945 Europe.[19] Exploring these links will raise new questions that can only be answered by a much wider network of scholars examining both national and subnational case studies and transnational processes. New histories could then emerge that probe connections not just between ex-Western European metropoles and their ex-colonies, but across Europe itself. We still know far too little about how Western Europeans – from political decision makers to everyday people alike – responded to crises of empires in decline affecting their European neighbours, let alone about the intertwined histories of socialist Eastern Europe's 'Second World' with the former 'Third World' empires held by the Western European 'First World' during the Cold War, several of

[17] Related issues are cogently examined in Luiza Bialasiewicz *et al.*, 'Interventions in the New Political Geographies of the European "Neighborhood"', *Political Geography*, 28 (2009), 79–89; Luiza Bialasiewicz, 'Off-Shoring and Out-Sourcing the Borders of EUrope: Libya and EU Border Work in the Mediterranean', *Geopolitics*, 17 (2012), 843–66.

[18] Bo Stråth, 'A European Identity: To the Historical Limits of a Concept', *European Journal of Social Theory*, 5:4 (2002), 388; more generally, see Bo Stråth (ed.), *Europe and the Other and Europe as the Other* (Brussels, 2000); Stuart Hall, 'Europe's Other Self', *Marxism Today*, 35:8 (1991), 18–19.

[19] For perceptive discussions of EU historiography, see Wolfram Kaiser, Brigitte Leucht, and Morten Rasmussen, 'Origins of a European Polity: A New Research Agenda for European Union History', in Wolfram Kaiser, Brigitte Leucht, and Morten Rasmussen (eds.), *The History of the European Union: Origins of a Trans- and Supranational Polity, 1950–72* (London, 2009), 1–11; Wolfram Kaiser and Antonio Varsori (eds.), *European Union History: Themes and Debates* (Basingstoke, 2010); Mark Gilbert, 'A Polity Constructed: New Explorations in European Integration History', *Contemporary European History*, 19:2 (2010), 169–79.

many promising fields that are now receiving more sustained attention.[20] Decolonization as a simultaneously global and a pan-European phenomenon might then be illuminated as a set of experiences that were as much personal, cultural, and social as they were political in their manifold resonances and repercussions.

---

[20] Inspiring studies that have appeared to date include Robert Gildea, James Mark, and Niek Pas, 'European Radicals and the "Third World": Imagined Solidarities and Radical Networks, 1958–73', *Cultural and Social History*, 8:4 (2011), 449–71; Niek Pas, *Aan de weg van het nieuwe Nederland: Nederland en de Algerijnse oorlog* (Amsterdam, 2008); David C. Engerman, 'The Second World's Third World', *Kritika: Explorations in Russian and Eurasian History*, 12:1 (2011), 183–211; Quinn Slobodian, *Foreign Front: Third World Politics in Sixties West Germany* (Durham, 2012); Jennifer Ruth Hosek, *Sun, Sex, and Socialism: Cuba in the German Imaginary* (Toronto, 2012); Oscar Sanchez-Sibony, *Red Globalization: The Political Economy of the Soviet Cold War from Stalin to Krushchev* (Cambridge, 2014). Scholars whose emergent and forthcoming work looks set to shape this broader terrain include James Mark, Péter Apor, Anne E. Gorsuch, Kim Christiaens, Tobias Rupprecht, and Young-Sun Hong. See for example Péter Apor and James Mark, 'Socialism Goes Global: Decolonization and the Making of a New Culture of Internationalism in Socialist Hungary, 1956–1989', *Journal of Modern History*, 87:4 (2015); Anne E. Gorsuch, '"Cuba, My Love": The Romance of Revolutionary Cuba in the Soviet Sixties', *American Historical Review*, 120:2 (2015), 497–526. Headed by James Mark of the University of Exeter, the (UK) Arts and Humanities Research Council-funded collaborative research project on 'Socialism Goes Global: Cold War Connections Between the "Second" and "Third Worlds", 1945–1991' (2014–2018) will map productive ways forward, as will the new research project coordinated by James Mark and Andrew Thompson concerning 'The Decolonisation Revolution: The Remaking of Europe during and after the Cold War'. On the former, see http://imperialglobalexeter.com/2014/09/03/socialism-goes-global-cold-war-connections-between-the-second-and-third-worlds-1945–1991/.

Bibliography

What follows is a partial bibliography of secondary sources only. Additional secondary literature as well as the primary sources consulted for this book are cited as footnotes to relevant chapter text.

Abbas, Tahir (ed.), *Muslim Britain: Communities Under Pressure* (London, 2005).

Abbeele, Georges Van Den, 'No Joking Matter: The "Other" Belgium', *Social Identities*, 7:4 (2001), 511–24.

Aldrich, Robert, *Greater France: A History of French Overseas Expansion* (Basingstoke, 1996).

Aldrich, Robert, *Vestiges of the Colonial Empire in France: Monuments, Museums and Colonial Memories* (Basingstoke, 2005).

Aldrich, Robert, and Christopher Hilliard, 'The French and British Empires', in John Horne (ed.), *A Companion to World War I* (Oxford, 2012), 524–39.

Alexander, Martin S., Martin Evans, and J.F.V. Keiger (eds.), *The Algerian War and the French Army, 1954–62: Experiences, Images, Testimonies* (Basingstoke, 2002).

Ali, N., V.S. Kalra, and S. Sayyid (eds.), *A Postcolonial People: South Asians in Britain* (London, 2006).

Almeida, Miguel Vale de, *An Earth-Coloured Sea: 'Race', Culture, and the Politics of Identity in the Postcolonial Portuguese-Speaking World* (New York, 2004).

Amersfoort, Hans van, *Immigration and the Formation of Minority Groups: The Dutch Experience, 1945–1975*, translated by Robert Lyng (Cambridge, 1982).

Amersfoort, Hans van, 'The Waxing and Waning of a Diaspora: Moluccans in the Netherlands, 1950–2002', *Journal of Ethnic and Migration Studies*, 30:1 (2004), 151–74.

Amersfoort, Hans van, and Mies van Niekerk, 'Immigration as a Colonial Inheritance: Post-Colonial Immigrants in the Netherlands, 1945–2002', *Journal of Ethnic and Migration Studies*, 32:3 (2006), 323–46.

Amin, Ash, 'Ethnicity and the Multicultural City: Living With Diversity', *Environment and Planning A*, 34 (2002), 959–80.

Amselle, Jean-Loup, *Affirmative Exclusion: Cultural Pluralism and the Rule of Custom in France*, translated by Jane Marie Todd (Ithaca, 2003).

Andall, Jacqueline, and Derek Duncan (eds.), *Italian Colonialism: Legacy and Memory* (Bern, 2005).

Anderson, David, *Histories of the Hanged: Britain's Dirty War in Kenya and the End of Empire* (London, 2005).

Angelo, Anne-Marie, 'The Black Panthers in London, 1967–1972: A Diasporic Struggle Navigates the Black Atlantic', *Radical History Review*, 103 (2009), 17–35.

Ansari, Humayun, *'The Infidel Within': Muslims in Britain since 1800* (London, 2003).

Anthias, Floya, and Nira Yuval-Davis, *Racialized Boundaries* (London, 1992).

Appadurai, Arjun, *Modernity at Large: Cultural Dimensions of Globalization* (Minneapolis, 1996).

Appadurai, Arjun, 'On Culinary Authenticity', *Anthropology Today*, 2:4 (1986), 24–5.

Araeen, Rasheed (ed.), *The Other Story: Afro-Asian Artists in Post-War Britain* (London, 1989).

Araeen, Rasheed, 'The Success and Failure of Black Art', *Third Text*, 18:2 (2004), 135–52.

Arnaut, Karel, 'Belgian Memories, African Objects: Colonial Re-Collection at the Musée Africain de Namur', *Ateliers*, 23 (2001), 29–49; alternative downloadable version available via www.africana.ugent.be/file/7.

Art, David, *Inside the Radical Right: The Development of Anti-Immigrant Parties in Western Europe* (New York, 2011).

Asad, Talal, 'Multiculturalism and British Identity in the Wake of the Rushdie Affair', *Politics and Society*, 18:4 (1990), 455–80.

Ashton, S.R., 'British Government Perspectives on the Commonwealth, 1964–71: An Asset or a Liability?', *Journal of Imperial and Commonwealth History*, 35:1 (2007), 73–94.

Back, Les, *New Ethnicities and Urban Culture: Racisms and Multiculture in Young Lives* (London, 1996).

Back, Les *et al.*, 'New Labour's White Heart: Politics, Multiculturalism and the Return of Assimilation', *Political Quarterly*, 73:4 (2002), 445–54.

Bailey, David A., Ian Baucom, and Sonya Boyce (eds.), *Shades of Black: Assembling Black Arts in 1980s Britain* (Durham, 2005).

Bailkin, Jordanna, *The Afterlife of Empire* (Berkeley, 2012).

Balibar, Étienne, *We, the People of Europe?: Reflections on Transnational Citizenship* (Princeton, 2004).

Balibar, Étienne, and Immanuel Wallerstein, *Race, Nation, Class: Ambiguous Identities* (London, 1991).

Ballantyne, Tony, *Between Colonialism and Diaspora: Sikh Cultural Formations in an Imperial World* (Durham, 2006).

Ballard, Roger (ed.), *Desh Pardesh: The South Asian Presence in Britain* (London, 1994).

Ballinger, Pamela, 'Borders of the Nation, Borders of Citizenship: Italian Repatriation and the Redefinition of National Identity after World War II', *Comparative Studies in Society and History*, 49:3 (2007), 713–41.

Bancel, Nicolas, Léla Bencharif, and Pascal Blanchard (eds.), *Lyon, Capitale des Outre-Mers: Immigration des Suds et culture coloniale en Rhône-Alpes et Auvergne* (Paris, 2007).

Barata, André, António Santos Pereira, and José Ricardo Carvalheiro (eds.), *Representações da Portugalidade* (Alfragide, 2011).

Barker, Martin, *The New Racism: Conservatives and the Ideology of the Tribe* (London, 1981).

Bartels, Dieter, *Moluccans in Exile: A Struggle for Ethnic Survival* (Leiden, 1989).

Batalha, Luís, *The Cape Verdean Diaspora in Portugal: Colonial Subjects in a Postcolonial World* (Lanham, MD, 2004).

Bauböck, Rainer *et al.* (eds.), *Acquisition and Loss of Nationality: Politics and Trends in 15 European States, Vol. 2: Country Analyses* (Amsterdam, 2006).

Baumann, Gerd, *Contesting Culture: Discourses of Identity in Multi-Ethnic London* (Cambridge, 1996).

Bayly, C.A., 'The Origins of Swadeshi (Home Industry): Cloth and Indian Society, 1700–1930', in Arjun Appadurai (ed.), *The Social Life of Things: Commodities in Cultural Perspective* (Cambridge, 1986), 285–321.

Bayly, Christopher, and Tim Harper, *Forgotten Armies: Britain's Asian Empire and the War with Japan* (London, 2004).

Bayly, Christopher, and Tim Harper, *Forgotten Wars: The End of Britain's Asian Empire* (London, 2007).

Bean, Susan S., 'Gandhi and *Khadi*, the Fabric of Indian Independence', in Annette B. Weiner and Jane Schneider (eds.), *Cloth and Human Experience* (Washington, DC, 1989), 355–76.

Beaufils, Thomas, and Patrick Duval (eds.), *Les identités néerlandaises: De l'intégration à la désintégration?* (Villeneuve d'Ascq, France, 2006).

'Belgian Memories', special issue, *Yale French Studies*, 102 (2002).

Bender, Gerald J., *Angola Under the Portuguese: The Myth and the Reality* (Trenton, NJ, 2004; originally published London, 1978).

Ben-Ghiat, Ruth, and Mia Fuller (eds.), *Italian Colonialism* (New York, 2005).

Berenson, Edward, Vincent Declert, and Christophe Prochasson (eds.), *The French Republic: History, Values, Culture* (Ithaca, 2011).

Beriss, David, *Black Skins, French Voices: Caribbean Ethnicity and Activism in Urban France* (Boulder, 2004).

Bertrand, Romain, *Mémoires d'empire: La controverse autour du 'fait colonial'* (Broissieux, 2006).

Besnaci-Lancou, Fatima, and Gilles Manceron (eds.), *Les harkis dans la colonisation et ses suites* (Ivry-sur-Seine, 2008).

Bethencourt, Francisco, 'Desconstrução da memória imperial: literatura, arte e historiografia', in Margarida Calafate Ribeiro and Ana Paula Ferreira (eds.), *Fantasmas e fantasias: Imperiais no Imaginário Português Contemporâneo* (Porto, 2003), 69–81.

Bethencourt, Francisco, 'A Memória da Expansão', in Francisco Bethencourt and Kirti Chaudhuri (eds.), *História da Expansão Portuguesa, Vol. 5: Último Império e Recentramento (1930–1998)* (Navarra, 2000), 442–80.

Bhambra, Gurminder K., 'Postcolonial Europe, or Understanding Europe in Times of the Postcolonial', in Chris Rumford (ed.), *The Sage Handbook of European Studies* (London, 2009), 69–85.

Bialasiewicz, Luiza, 'Off-Shoring and Out-Sourcing the Borders of EUrope: Libya and EU Border Work in the Mediterranean', *Geopolitics*, 17 (2012), 843–66.

Bialasiewicz, Luiza *et al.*, 'Interventions in the New Political Geographies of the European "Neighborhood"', *Political Geography*, 28 (2009), 79–89.

Bickers, Robert (ed.), *Settlers and Expatriates: Britons over the Seas, Oxford History of the British Empire Companion Series* (Oxford, 2010).

Bijl, Paul, 'Colonial Memory and Forgetting in the Netherlands and Indonesia', *Journal of Genocide Research*, 14:3–4 (2012), 441–61.

Bijl, Paul, 'Dutch Colonial Nostalgia Across Decolonisation', *Journal of Dutch Literature*, 4:1 (2013), 128–49.

Birmingham, David, and Phyllis M. Martin (eds.), *History of Central Africa*, Vol. 2 (London, 1983).

Blake, Robert, and Wm. Roger Louis (eds.), *Churchill* (Oxford, 1993).

Blanchard, Pascal, Nicolas Bancel, and Sandrine Lemaire (eds.), *La fracture coloniale: La société française au prisme de l'héritage colonial* (Paris, 2005).

Blanchard, Pascal, Sandrine Lemaire, and Nicolas Bancel (eds.), *Culture coloniale en France: De la Révolution à nos jours* (Paris, 2008).

Bloembergen, Marieke, and Vincent Kuitenbrouwer (eds.), 'A New Dutch Imperial History', special issue, *BMGN – Low Countries Historical Review*, 128:1 (2013).

Blommaert, Jan, 'Integration Policies and the Politics of Integration in Belgium', in Marco Martiniello (ed.), *Multicultural Policies and the State: A Comparison of Two European Societies* (Utrecht, 1998), 75–88.

Blunt, Alison, *Domicile and Diaspora: Anglo-Indian Women and the Spatial Politics of Home* (Malden, MA and Oxford, 2005).

Boehmer, Elleke, and Sarah De Mul (eds.), *The Postcolonial Low Countries: Literature, Colonialism, and Multiculturalism* (Lanham, MD, 2012).

Bosma, Ulbe (ed.), *Post-Colonial Immigrants and Identity Formations in the Netherlands* (Amsterdam, 2012).

Bosma, Ulbe, *Terug uit de koloniën: Zestig jaar postkoloniale migranten en hun organisaties* (Amsterdam, 2009).

Bosma, Ulbe, and Marga Alferink, 'Multiculturalism and Settlement: The Case of Dutch Postcolonial Migrant Organisations', *Journal of International Migration and Integration*, 13:3 (2012), 265–83.

Boubeker, Ahmed, and Abdellali Hajjat (eds.), *Histoire politique des immigrations (post)coloniales: France, 1920–2008* (Paris, 2008).

Bowen, John R., *Why the French Don't Like Headscarves: Islam, the State, and Public Space* (Princeton, 2007).

Boxer, C.R., *Race Relations in the Portuguese Empire 1415–1825* (Oxford, 1963).

Bozo, Frédéric, *Two Strategies for Europe: De Gaulle, the United States, and the Atlantic Alliance* (Lanham, MD, 2001).

Bradley, Mark Philip, and Marilyn B. Young (eds.), *Making Sense of the Vietnam Wars: Local, National, and Transnational Perspectives* (Oxford, 2008).

Braeckman, Colette, *Lumumba, un crime d'État: Une lecture critique de la Commission parlementaire belge* (Brussels, 2009).

Bragard, Véronique, '"Indépendance!": The Belgo-Congolese Dispute in the Tervuren Museum', *Human Architecture: Journal of the Sociology of Self-Knowledge*, 9:4 (2011), 93–104.

Brah, Avtar, *Cartographies of Diaspora: Contesting Identities* (London, 1996).

Branch, Daniel, *Defeating Mau Mau, Creating Kenya: Counterinsurgency, Civil War, and Decolonization* (Cambridge, 2009).

Branche, Raphaëlle, 'Sexual Violence in the Algerian War', in Dagmar Herzog (ed.), *Brutality and Desire: War and Sexuality in Europe's Twentieth Century* (Basingstoke, 2009), 247–60.

Branche, Raphaëlle, 'The State, the Historians and the Algerian War in French Memory, 1991–2004', in Harriet Jones, Kjell Östberg, and Nico Randeraad (eds.), *Contemporary History on Trial: Europe Since 1989 and the Role of the Expert Historian* (Manchester, 2007), 159–73.

Branche, Raphaëlle, *La Torture et l'armée pendant la guerre d'Algérie, 1954–1962* (Paris, 2001).

Branche, Raphaëlle, and Sylvie Thénault (eds.), *La France en guerre 1954–1962: Expériences métropolitaines de la guerre d'indépendance algérienne* (Paris, 2008).

Bravo, Philip, 'The Case of Goa: History, Rhetoric and Nationalism', *Past Imperfect*, 7 (1998), 125–54.

Brettell, Caroline B., 'The Emigrant, the Nation, and the State in Nineteenth- and Twentieth-Century Portugal: An Anthropological Approach', *Portuguese Studies Review*, 2:2 (1993), 51–65.

Brettell, Caroline B., 'Portugal's First Post-Colonials: Citizenship, Identity, and the Repatriation of Goans', *Portuguese Studies Review*, 14:2 (2006/2007), 143–70.

Brocheux, Pierre, and Daniel Hémery, *Indochina: An Ambiguous Colonization, 1858–1954*, translated by Ly Lan Dill-Klein *et al.* (Berkeley, 2009).

Brown, Judith M., *Global South Asians: Introducing the Diaspora* (Cambridge, 2006).

Brown, Judith M., and Wm. Roger Louis (eds.), *The Oxford History of the British Empire, Vol. IV: The Twentieth Century* (Oxford, 1999).

Brown, Judith M., and Anthony Parel (eds.), *The Cambridge Companion to Gandhi* (Cambridge, 2011).

Brownell, Josiah, '"A Sordid Tussle on the Strand": Rhodesia House during the UDI Rebellion (1965–80)', *Journal of Imperial and Commonwealth History*, 38:3 (2010), 471–99.

Buettner, Elizabeth, 'Cemeteries, Public Memory and Raj Nostalgia in Postcolonial Britain and India', *History & Memory*, 18:1 (2006), 5–42.

Buettner, Elizabeth, 'Chicken Tikka Masala, Flock Wallpaper, and "Real" Home Cooking: Assessing Britain's "Indian" Restaurant Traditions', *Food & History*, 7:2 (2009), 203–30.

Buettner, Elizabeth, *Empire Families: Britons and Late Imperial India* (Oxford, 2004).

Buettner, Elizabeth, 'Ethnicity', in Ulinka Rublack (ed.), *A Concise Companion to History* (Oxford, 2011), 247–67.

Buettner, Elizabeth, 'Extended Families or Bodily Decomposition?: Biological Metaphors in the Age of European Decolonization', in Martin Thomas and Richard Toye (eds.), *The Rhetoric of Empire: Arguing Colonialism in the Public Sphere* (Manchester, in press).

Buettner, Elizabeth, '"Going for an Indian": South Asian Restaurants and the Limits of Multiculturalism in Britain', *Journal of Modern History*, 80:4 (2008), 865–901.

Buettner, Elizabeth, '"Setting the Record Straight"?: Imperial History in Postcolonial British Public Culture', in Ulrike Lindner, Maren Möhring, Mark Stein, and Silke Stroh (eds.), *Hybrid Cultures – Nervous States: Britain and Germany in a (Post) Colonial World* (Amsterdam, 2010), 89–104.

Buettner, Elizabeth, '"This is Staffordshire not Alabama": Racial Geographies of Commonwealth Immigration in Early 1960s Britain', *Journal of Imperial and Commonwealth History*, 42:4 (2014), 710–40.

Buettner, Elizabeth, '"We Don't Grow Coffee and Bananas in Clapham Junction You Know!": Imperial Britons Back Home', in Robert Bickers (ed.), *Settlers and Expatriates: Britons over the Seas, Oxford History of the British Empire Companion Series* (Oxford, 2010), 302–28.

Buettner, Elizabeth, '"Would You Let Your Daughter Marry a Negro?": Race and Sex in 1950s Britain', in Philippa Levine and Susan R. Grayzel (eds.), *Gender, Labour, War and Empire: Essays on Modern Britain* (London, 2009), 219–37.

Bunce, R.E.R., and Paul Field, 'Obi Egbuna, C.L.R. James and the Birth of Black Power in Britain: Black Radicalism in Britain 1967–1972', *Twentieth Century British History*, 22:3 (2011), 391–414.

Buono, Clarisse, *Pieds-noirs de père en fils: Voix et regards* (Paris, 2004).

Burbank, Jane, and Frederick Cooper, *Empires in World History: Power and the Politics of Difference* (Princeton, 2010).

Burton, Antoinette (ed.), *After the Imperial Turn: Thinking with and through the Nation* (Durham, 2003).

Buruma, Ian, *Murder in Amsterdam: The Death of Theo van Gogh and the Limits of Tolerance* (London, 2006).

Bush, Barbara, 'The Dark Side of the City: Racialized Barriers, Culture and Citizenship in Britain c. 1950–1990s', in Werner Zips (ed.), *Rastafari: A Universal Philosophy in the Third Millennium* (Kingston, 2006), 169–201.

Bush, Barbara, *Imperialism and Postcolonialism* (London, 2014).

Butler, Larry, and Sarah Stockwell (eds.), *The Wind of Change: Harold Macmillan and British Decolonization* (London, 2013).

Cabecinhas, Rosa, and João Feijó, 'Collective Memories of Portuguese Colonial Action in Africa: Representations of the Colonial Past among Mozambicans and Portuguese Youths', *International Journal of Conflict and Violence*, 4:1 (2010), 28–44.

Cahen, Michel, 'Des caravelles pour le futur?: Discours politique et idéologie dans l'"institutionnalisation" de la Communauté des pays de langue portuguaise', *Lusotopie*, 1997, 391–433.

Cannadine, David, *In Churchill's Shadow: Confronting the Past in Modern Britain* (London, 2002).

Captain, Esther *et al.* (eds.), *De Indische zomer in Den Haag: Het cultureel erfgoed van de Indische hoofdstad* (Leiden, 2005).

'Caribbean Literature from Suriname, the Netherlands Antilles, Aruba, and the Netherlands', special issue, *Callaloo*, 21:3 (1998).

Carrington, William J., and Pedro J.F. de Lima, 'The Impact of 1970s Repatriates from Africa on the Portuguese Labor Market', *Industrial and Labor Relations Review*, 49:2 (1996), 330–47.

Carruthers, Susan L., *Winning Hearts and Minds: British Governments, the Media and Colonial Counter-Insurgency 1944–1960* (London, 1995).

Cashmore, Ernest, *Rastaman: The Rastafarian Movement in England* (London, 1979).

Castelo, Cláudia, *'O modo português de estar no mundo': O luso-tropicalismo e a ideologia colonial portuguesa (1933–1961)* (Porto, 1998).

Castryck, Geert, 'Whose History is History? Singularities and Dualities of the Public Debate on Belgian Colonialism', in Sven Mörsdorf (ed.), *Being a Historian: Opportunities and Responsibilities Past and Present* (CLIOHRES.net, 2010), 1–18.

Centre for Contemporary Cultural Studies, *The Empire Strikes Back: Race and Racism in 70s Britain* (London 1982).

Ceuppens, Bambi, 'Allochthons, Colonizers, and Scroungers: Exclusionary Populism in Belgium', *African Studies Review*, 49:2 (2006), 147–86.

Ceuppens, Bambi, *Congo Made in Flanders?: Koloniale vlaamse visies op 'blank' en 'zwart' in Belgisch Congo* (Gent, 2003).

Chabal, Patrick, *Amílcar Cabral: Revolutionary Leadership and People's War* (London, 1983).

Chafer, Tony, *The End of Empire in French West Africa: France's Successful Decolonization?* (Oxford, 2002).

Chakrabarty, Dipesh, *Provincializing Europe: Postcolonial Thought and Historical Difference* (Princeton, 2000).

Chapman, James, *Licence to Thrill: A Cultural History of the James Bond Films* (New York, 2000).

Clancy-Smith, Julia, 'Islam, Gender, and Identities in the Making of French Algeria, 1830–1962', in Julia Clancy-Smith and Frances Gouda (eds.), *Domesticating the Empire: Race, Gender, and Family Life in French and Dutch Colonialism* (Charlottesville, 1998), 154–74.

Clarence-Smith, Gervase, *The Third Portuguese Empire 1825–1975: A Study in Economic Imperialism* (Manchester, 1985).

Clayton, Anthony, *The Wars of French Decolonization* (London, 1994).

Clifford, James, *The Predicament of Culture* (Cambridge, MA, 1988).

Clifford, James, 'Traveling Cultures', in *Routes: Travel and Translation in the Late Twentieth Century* (Cambridge, MA, 1997), 17–46.

Coenders, Marcel, Marcel Lubbers, Peer Scheepers, and Maykel Verkuyten, 'More Than Two Decades of Changing Ethnic Attitudes in the Netherlands', *Journal of Social Issues*, 64:2 (2008), 269–85.

Cohen, Abner, *Masquerade Politics: Explorations in the Structure of Urban Cultural Movements* (Oxford, 1993).

Cohen, William B., 'Legacy of Empire: The Algerian Connection', *Journal of Contemporary History*, 15 (1980), 97–123.

Colley, Linda, 'Britishness and Otherness: An Argument', *Journal of British Studies*, 31:4 (1992), 309–29.

Collins, Marcus, 'Pride and Prejudice: West Indian Men in Mid-Twentieth-Century Britain', *Journal of British Studies*, 40 (2001), 391–418.

'Colonial and Postcolonial Italy', special issue, *Interventions: International Journal of Postcolonial Studies*, 8:3 (2006).

Comtat, Emmanuelle, *Les pieds-noirs et la politique: Quarante ans après le retour* (Paris, 2009).

Conklin, Alice L., 'Boundaries Unbound: Teaching French History as Colonial History and Colonial History as French History', *French Historical Studies* 23:2 (2000), 215–38.

Conklin, Alice L., *A Mission to Civilize: The Republican Idea of Empire in France and West Africa, 1895–1930* (Stanford, 1997).

Conklin, Alice L., Sarah Fishman, and Robert Zaretsky, *France and Its Empire since 1870: The Republican Tradition* (New York, 2011).

Connelly, Matthew, *A Diplomatic Revolution: Algeria's Fight for Independence and the Origins of the Post-Cold War Era* (Oxford, 2002).

Connelly, Matthew, and Paul Kennedy, 'Must it Be the Rest Against the West?', *The Atlantic Monthly* (December 1994).

Conrad, Sebastian, *German Colonialism: A Short History* (Cambridge, 2012).

Contador, António Concorda, 'Consciência de geração e etnicidade: de segunda geração aos novos luso-africanos', *Sociologia, Problemas e Práticas*, 26 (1998), 57–83.

Conway, Martin, *The Sorrows of Belgium: Liberation and Political Reconstruction, 1944–1947* (Oxford, 2012).

Conway, Martin, and Kiran Klaus Patel (eds.), *Europeanization in the Twentieth Century: Historical Approaches* (London, 2010).

Conway, Martin, and Peter Romijn (eds.), *The War on Legitimacy in Politics and Culture 1936–1946* (Oxford, 2008).

Cooper, Frederick, *Africa since 1940: The Past of the Present* (Cambridge, 2002).

Cooper, Frederick, *Citizenship between Empire and Nation: Remaking France and French Africa, 1945–1960* (Princeton, 2014).

Cooper, Frederick, *Colonialism in Question: Theory, Knowledge, History* (Berkeley, 2005).

Cooper, Nicola, *France in Indochina: Colonial Encounters* (Oxford, 2001).

Cooper, Nikki, 'Dien Bien Phu – Fifty Years On', *Modern & Contemporary France*, 12:4 (2004), 445–57.

Coquery-Vidrovitch, Catherine, *Enjeux politiques de l'histoire coloniale* (Marseille, 2009).

Cordeiro, Albano, 'Le paradoxe de l'immigration portugaise', *Hommes et Migrations*, 1123 (1989), 25–32.

Corkill, David, 'Economic Migrants and the Labour Market in Spain and Portugal', *Ethnic and Racial Studies*, 24:5 (2001), 828–44.

Corkill, David, and Martin Eaton, 'Multicultural Insertions in a Small Economy: Portugal's Immigrant Communities', *South European Society and Politics*, 3:3 (1998), 149–68.

Cottaar, Annemarie, 'Een oosterse stad in het westen: Etnisch-culinaire pioniers in Den Haag', *Tijdschrift voor Sociale Geschiedenis*, 26:4 (2000), 261–80.

Cottaar, Annemarie, and Wim Willems, *Indische Nederlanders. Een onderzoek naar beeldvorming* (The Hague, 1984).

Crapanzano, Vincent, *The Harkis: The Wound That Never Heals* (Chicago, 2011).

Cross, Malcolm, and Han Entzinger (eds.), *Lost Illusions: Caribbean Minorities in Britain and the Netherlands* (London, 1988).

Cunha, Isabel Ferin, 'Nós e os otros artigos de opinião da imprensa portuguesa', *Lusotopie*, 1997, 435–67.

Cusack, Igor, 'Tiny Transmitters of Nationalist and Colonial Ideology: The Postage Stamps of Portugal and Its Empire', *Nations and Nationalism*, 11:4 (2005), 591–612.

Dard, Olivier, *Voyage au coeur de l'OAS* (Paris, 2005).

Darwin, John, *After Tamerlane: The Rise and Fall of Global Empires, 1400–2000* (New York, 2008).

Darwin, John, *Britain and Decolonisation: The Retreat from Empire in the Post-War World* (Basingstoke, 1988).

Darwin, John, 'British Decolonization since 1945: A Pattern or a Puzzle?', *Journal of Imperial and Commonwealth History*, 12:2 (1984), 187–209.

Darwin, John, *The Empire Project: The Rise and Fall of the British World-System 1830–1970* (Cambridge, 2009).

Deben, Léon, Willem Heine Meijer, and Dick van der Vaart (eds.), *Understanding Amsterdam: Essays on Economic Vitality, City Life, and Urban Form*, 2nd rev. edn. (Amsterdam, 2000).

Decouvelaere, Stephanie, '"Ça vient de la rue": French Rap's Perspective on French Society', *Wasafiri*, 23:4 (2008), 36–42.

Deighton, Anne, 'The Past in the Present: British Imperial Memories and the European Question', in Jan-Werner Müller (ed.), *Memory and Power in Post-War Europe: Studies in the Presence of the Past* (Cambridge, 2002), 100–20.

Deltombe, Thomas, *L'islam imaginaire: La construction médiatique de l'islamophobie en France, 1975–2005* (Paris, 2005).

Demart, Sarah, 'Histoire orale à Matonge (Bruxelles): un miroir postcoloniale', *Revue Européenne des Migrations Internationales*, 29:1 (2013), 133–55.

Dembour, Marie-Bénédicte, *Recalling the Belgian Congo: Conversations and Introspections* (New York, 2000).

Demos, T.J., *Sven Augustijnen's Spectropoetics* (Brussels, 2011).

Deprez, Kas, and Louis Vos (eds.), *Nationalism in Belgium: Shifting Identities, 1780–1995* (Basingstoke, 1998).

Derderian, Richard L., *North Africans in Contemporary France: Becoming Visible* (New York, 2004).

Desmarez, Pierre *et al.* (eds.), *Minorités ethniques en Belgique: migration et marché du travail* (Gent, 2004).

Dewitte, Philippe (ed.), *Immigration et intégration: l'état des savoirs* (Paris, 1999).

Diekmann, Anya, and Geraldine Maulet, 'A Contested Ethnic Tourism Asset: The Case of Matonge in Brussels', *Tourism Culture and Communication*, 9:1–2 (2009), 93–105.

Dimier, Véronique, 'For a New Start: Resettling French Colonial Administrators in the Prefectoral Corps', *Itinerario*, 28:1 (2004), 49–66.

Dine, Philip, *Images of the Algerian War: French Fiction and Film, 1954–1992* (Oxford, 1994).

Dine, Philip, '(Still) *A la recherche de l'Algérie perdue*: French Fiction and Film, 1992–2001', *Historical Reflections/Réflexions Historiques*, 28:2 (2002), 255–75.

Doel, H.W. van den, *Afscheid van Indië: De val van het Nederlandse imperium in Azië* (Amsterdam, 2000).

Donadey, Anne, '"Y'a bon Banania": Ethics and Cultural Criticism in the Colonial Context', *French Cultural Studies*, 11:31 (2000), 9–29.

Donald, James, and Ali Rattansi, *'Race', Culture and Difference* (London, 1991).

Doorn, Jacques van, *The Soldier and Social Change: Comparative Studies in the History and Sociology of the Military* (London, 1975).

Doorn, J.A.A. van, and W.J. Hendrix, *Ontsporing van geweld: Over het Nederlands/Indisch/Indonesisch conflict* (Rotterdam, 1970).

Doorn, Jacques van, and Willem J. Hendrix, *The Process of Decolonisation 1945–1975: The Military Experience in Comparative Perspective* (Rotterdam, 1987).

Dorfman, Ariel, 'Of Elephants and Ducks', in *The Empire's Old Clothes: What the Lone Ranger, Babar, and Other Innocent Heroes Do To Our Minds* (New York, 1983), 17–64.

Dubois, Laurent, *Soccer Empire: The World Cup and the Future of France* (Berkeley, 2010).

Dubus, Gilles, 'Quand les timbres-poste reconnaissent ou ignorent les migrants et les réfugiés', *Revue européenne des migrations internationales*, 12:2 (1996), 87–104.

Duiker, William J., *The Communist Road to Power in Vietnam* (Boulder, 1981).

Dunn, Kevin C., *Imagining the Congo: The International Relations of Identity* (New York, 2003).

Durmelat, Sylvie, 'Introduction: Colonial Culinary Encounters and Imperial Leftovers', *French Cultural Studies*, 26:2 (2015), 115–29.

Durmelat, Sylvie, 'Petite histoire du mot *beur*: ou comment prendre la parole quand on vous la prête', *French Cultural Studies*, 9 (1998), 191–207.

Eaton, Martin, 'Foreign Residents and Illegal Immigrants in Portugal', *International Journal of Intercultural Research*, 22:1 (1998), 49–66.

Elkins, Caroline, *Britain's Gulag: The Brutal End of Empire in Kenya* (London, 2005).

Elkins, Caroline, and Susan Pedersen (eds.), *Settler Colonialism in the Twentieth Century* (New York, 2005).

Elteren, Mel van, *Imagining America: Dutch Youth and Its Sense of Place* (Tilburg, 1994).

Essed, Philomena, *Understanding Everyday Racism: An Interdisciplinary Theory* (Newbury Park, 1991).

Essed, Philomena, and Sandra Trienekens, '"Who Wants To Feel White?": Race, Dutch Culture and Contested Identities', *Ethnic and Racial Studies*, 31:1 (2008), 52–72.

Esteves, Maria do Céu (ed.), *Portugal, País de Imigração* (Lisbon, 1991).

Etambala, Zana Aziza, *Congo '55–'65: Van koning Boudewijn tot president Mobutu* (Tielt, 1999).

Etambala, Zana Aziza, *In het land van de Banoko: De geschiedenis van de Kongolese/ Zaïrese aanwezigheid in België van 1885 tot heden* (Leuven, 1993).

Etemad, Bouda, 'Europe and Migration after Decolonization', *Journal of European Economic History*, 27:3 (1998), 457–70.

Evans, Martin, *Algeria: France's Undeclared War* (Oxford, 2012).

Evans, Martin, *The Memory of Resistance: French Opposition to the Algerian War (1954–1962)* (Oxford, 1997).

Eyerman, Ron, *The Assassination of Theo van Gogh: From Social Drama to Cultural Trauma* (Durham, 2008).

Favell, Adrian, 'The New Face of East-West Migration in Europe', *Journal of Ethnic and Migration Studies*, 34:5 (2008), 701–16.

Favell, Adrian, *Philosophies of Integration: Immigration and the Idea of Citizenship in France and Britain* (Basingstoke, 1998).

Favell, Adrian, and Marco Martiniello, 'Multi-National, Multi-Cultural and Multi-Levelled Brussels: National and Ethnic Politics in the "Capital of Europe"', in Steven Vertovec and Ali Rogers (eds.), *Online Working Paper Series for 'Transnational Communities'* (1999), 2–5, 11, www.transcomm.ox.ac.uk/working%20papers/favell.pdf.

Feldman-Bianco, Bela, 'Brazilians in Portugal, Portuguese in Brazil: Constructions of Sameness and Difference', *Identities*, 8:4 (2001), 607–50.

Feldman-Bianco, Bela, 'Colonialism as a Continuing Project: The Portuguese Experience', *Identities*, 8:4 (2001), 477–81.

Ferreira, Carolin Overhoff, 'Decolonizing the Mind? The Representation of the African Colonial Wars in Portuguese Cinema', *Studies in European Cinema*, 2:3 (2005), 227–39.

Fikes, Kesha, *Managing African Portugal: The Citizen-Migrant Distinction* (Durham, 2009).

Fisher Onar, Nora, and Kalypso Nicolaïdis, 'The Decentring Agenda: Europe as a Post-Colonial Power', *Cooperation and Conflict*, 48:2 (2013), 283–303.

Fitzmaurice, John, *The Politics of Belgium: A Unique Federalism* (London, 1996).

Flood, Christopher, and Hugo Frey, 'Questions of Decolonization and Post-Colonialism in the Ideology of the French Extreme Right', in James D. Le Sueur (ed.), *The Decolonization Reader* (London, 2003), 399–413.

Foner, Nancy *et al.* (eds.), *New York and Amsterdam: Immigration and the New Urban Landscape* (New York, 2014).

Fonseca, Maria Lucinda, 'Immigration and Spatial Change: The Lisbon Experience', *Studi Emigrazione/Migration Studies*, 39:145 (2002), 49–76.

Foray, Jennifer L., *Visions of Empire in the Nazi-Occupied Netherlands* (Cambridge, 2012).

Ford, Caroline, 'Museums after Empire in France and Overseas France', *Journal of Modern History*, 82:3 (2010), 625–61.

Forsdick, Charles, 'The Panthéon's Empty Plinth: Commemorating Slavery in Contemporary France', *Atlantic Studies*, 9:3 (2012), 279–97.

Fradique, Teresa, *Fixar o Movimento: Representações da Música RAP em Portugal* (Lisbon, 2003).

Frey, Marc, 'Dutch Elites and Decolonization', in Jost Dülffer and Marc Frey (eds.), *Elites and Decolonization in the Twentieth Century* (Basingstoke, 2011), 56–73.

Frey, Marc, 'The Indonesian Revolution and the Fall of the Dutch Empire: Actors, Factors, and Strategies', in Marc Frey, Ronald Pruessen, and Tan Tai Yong (eds.), *The Transformation of Southeast Asia: International Perspectives on Decolonization* (New York, 2003), 83–104.

Fysh, Peter, and James Wolfreys, *The Politics of Racism in France* (Basingstoke, 2003).

Garavini, Giuliano, 'The Colonies Strike Back: The Impact of the Third World on Western Europe, 1968–1975', *Contemporary European History*, 16:3 (2007), 299–319.

Gaspard, Françoise, *A Small City in France: A Socialist Mayor Confronts Neofascism*, translated by Arthur Goldhammer (Cambridge, MA, 1995).

Geddes, Andrew, *Immigration and European Integration: Beyond Fortress Europe?*, 2nd edn. (Manchester, 2008).

Geschiere, Peter, *The Perils of Belonging: Autochthony, Citizenship, and Exclusion in Africa and Europe* (Chicago, 2009).

Ghosh, Durba, 'Another Set of Imperial Turns?', *American Historical Review*, 117:3 (2012), 772–93.

Gifford, Prosser, and Wm Roger Louis (eds.), *The Transfer of Power in Africa: Decolonization, 1940–1960* (New Haven, 1982).

Gildea, Robert, James Mark, and Niek Pas, 'European Radicals and the "Third World": Imagined Solidarities and Radical Networks, 1958–73', *Cultural and Social History*, 8:4 (2011), 449–71.

Gillet, Florence, 'Congo rêvé? Congo détruit ... Les anciens coloniaux belges aux prises avec une société en repentir. Enquête sur la face émergée d'une mémoire', *Cahiers d'Histoire du Temps Présent*, 19 (2008), 79–133.

Gilroy, Paul, *After Empire: Melancholia or Convivial Culture?* (London, 2004).

Gilroy, Paul, *The Black Atlantic: Modernity and Double Consciousness* (Cambridge, MA, 1993).

Gilroy, Paul, *Small Acts: Thoughts on the Politics of Black Cultures* (London, 1993).

Gilroy, Paul, *'There Ain't No Black in the Union Jack': The Cultural Politics of Race and Nation* (Chicago, 1987).

Giordano, Rosario, *Belges et Italiens du Congo-Kinshasa: Récits de vie avant et après l'Indépendance* (Paris, 2008).

Goddeeris, Idesbald, 'Postcolonial Belgium: The Memory of the Congo', *Interventions: International Journal of Postcolonial Studies*, 17:3 (2015), 434–51.

Goddeeris, Idesbald, and Sindani E. Kiangu, 'Congomania in Academia: Recent Historical Research on the Belgian Colonial Past', *BMGN-Low Countries Historical Review*, 126:4 (2011), 54–75.

Goldsworthy, David, *Colonial Issues in British Politics, 1945–1961: From 'Colonial Development' to 'Wind of Change'* (Oxford, 1971).

Goldsworthy, David, 'Keeping Change Within Bounds: Aspects of Colonial Policy during the Churchill and Eden Governments, 1951–57', *Journal of Imperial and Commonwealth History*, 18:1 (1990), 81–108.

Golsan, Richard J. (ed.), *The Papon Affair: Memory and Justice on Trial* (New York, 2000).

Gondola, Ch. Didier, 'Dream and Drama: The Search for Elegance among Congolese Youth', *African Studies Review*, 42:1 (1999), 23–48.

Goodwin, Matthew J., *New British Fascism: Rise of the British National Party* (Abingdon, 2011).

Goss, Andrew, 'From *Tong-Tong* to Tempo Doeloe: Eurasian Memory Work and the Bracketing of Dutch Colonial History, 1957–1961', *Indonesia*, 70 (2000), 9–36.

Gouda, Frances, with Thijs Brocades Zaalberg, *American Visions of the Netherlands East Indies/Indonesia: US Foreign Policy and Indonesian Nationalism, 1920–1949* (Amsterdam, 2002).

Goulbourne, Harry, and Mary Chamberlain (eds.), *Caribbean Families in Britain and the Trans-Atlantic World* (London, 2001).

Gray, Lila Ellen, 'Memories of Empire, Mythologies of the Soul: *Fado* Performance and the Shaping of *Saudade*', *Ethnomusicology*, 51:1 (2007), 106–30.

Gregory, Derek, *The Colonial Present* (Oxford, 2004).

Grewal, Shivdeep Singh, 'Capital of the 1970s?: Southall and the Conjuncture of 23 April 1979', *Socialist History Journal*, 23 (2003), 1–34.

Grillo, R.D., *Ideologies and Institutions in Urban France: The Representation of Immigrants* (Cambridge, 1985).

Gryseels, Guido, Gabrielle Landry, and Koeki Claessens, 'Integrating the Past: Transformation and Renovation of the Royal Museum for Central Africa, Tervuren, Belgium', *European Review*, 13:3 (2005), 637–47.

Gupta, Rahila (ed.), *From Homebreakers to Jailbreakers: Southall Black Sisters* (London, 2003).

Gurnah, Abdulrazak (ed.), *The Cambridge Companion to Salman Rushdie* (Cambridge, 2007).

Gusmão, Neusa Maria Mendes de, *Os Filhos de África em Portugal: Antropologia, Multiculturalidade e Educação* (Lisbon, 2004).

Hagendoorn, Louk, and Joseph Hraba, 'Foreign, Different, Deviant, Seclusive and Working Class: Anchors to an Ethnic Hierarchy in the Netherlands', *Ethnic and Racial Studies*, 12:4 (1989), 441–68.

Hagendoorn, Louk, Justus Veenman, and Wilma Vollebergh (eds.), *Integrating Immigrants in the Netherlands: Cultural versus Socio-Economic Integration* (Aldershot, 2003).

Halen, Pierre, *'La petit Belge avait vu grand': Une littérature coloniale* (Brussels, 1993).

Halen, Pierre, and János Riesz (eds.), *Patrice Lumumba entre dieu et diable: Un héros africain dans ses images* (Paris, 1997).

Hall, Catherine (ed.), *Cultures of Empire: A Reader: Colonizers in Britain and the Empire in the Nineteenth and Twentieth Centuries* (Manchester, 2000).

Hall, Catherine, and Sonya O. Rose (eds.), *At Home with the Empire: Metropolitan Culture and the Imperial World* (Cambridge, 2006).

Hall, Stuart, 'Black Diaspora Artists in Britain: Three "Moments" in Post-War History', *History Workshop Journal*, 61 (2006), 1–24.

Hall, Stuart, 'Europe's Other Self', *Marxism Today*, 35:8 (1991), 18–19.

Hall, Stuart, 'From Scarman to Stephen Lawrence', *History Workshop Journal*, 48 (1999), 187–97.

Hall, Stuart, 'New Ethnicities', in David Morley and Kuan-Hsing Chen (eds.), *Stuart Hall: Critical Dialogues in Cultural Studies* (London, 1996), 442–51.

Hall, Stuart, 'Reconstruction Work: Images of Post-War Black Settlement', in Jo Spence and Patricia Holland (eds.), *Family Snaps: The Meanings of Domestic Photography* (London, 1991), 152–64.

Hall, Stuart, 'What Is This "Black" in Black Popular Culture?', in David Morley and Kuan-Hsing Chen (eds.), *Stuart Hall: Critical Dialogues in Cultural Studies* (London, 1996), 468–78.

Hall, Stuart et al., *Policing the Crisis: Mugging, the State, and Law and Order* (London, 1978).

Hall, Stuart, and Martin Jacques (eds.), *The Politics of Thatcherism* (London, 1983).

Hall, Stuart, and Tony Jefferson (eds.), *Resistance Through Rituals: Youth Subcultures in Post-War Britain* (London, 1976).

Halstead, Mark, *Education, Justice and Cultural Diversity: An Examination of the Honeyford Affair, 1984–85* (London, 1988).

Hamilton, Douglas, Kate Hodgson, and Joel Quirk (eds.), *Slavery, Memory, and Identity: National Representations and Global Legacies* (London, 2012).

Hansen, Peo, 'European Integration, European Identity and the Colonial Connection', *European Journal of Social Theory*, 5:4 (2002), 483–98.

Hansen, Peo, and Stefan Jonsson, *Eurafrica: The Untold History of European Integration and Colonialism* (London, 2013).

Hansen, Randall, *Citizenship and Immigration in Post-War Britain: The Institutional Origins of a Multicultural Nation* (Oxford, 2000).

Hansen, Randall, and Patrick Weil (eds.), *Towards a European Nationality: Citizenship, Immigration and Nationality Law in the European Union* (Basingstoke, 2001).

Harbi, Mohammed, and Benjamin Stora (eds.), *La guerre d'Algérie* (Paris, 2004).

Hardiman, David, *Gandhi in His Time and Ours: The Global Legacy of His Ideas* (London, 2003).

Hargreaves, Alec G., *Multi-Ethnic France: Immigration, Politics, Culture and Society*, 2nd edn. (New York, 2007).

Hargreaves, Alec G., *Voices from the North African Immigrant Community in France: Immigration and Identity in Beur Fiction* (New York, 1991).

Hargreaves, Alec G., and Mark McKinney (eds.), *Post-Colonial Cultures in France* (London, 1997).

Harper, T.N., *The End of Empire and the Making of Malaya* (Cambridge, 1999).

Hebdige, Dick, *Subculture: The Meaning of Style* (London, 1987; first published 1979).

Helsloot, John, 'De strijd om Zwarte Piet', in Isabel Hoving, Hester Dibbets, and Marlou Schrover (eds.), *Cultuur en migratie in Nederland: Veranderingen van het alledaagse 1950–2000* (The Hague, 2005), 249–71.

Helsloot, John, '*Zwarte Piet* and Cultural Aphasia in the Netherlands', *Quotidian: Journal for the Study of Everyday Life*, 3 (2012), 1–20.

Hervo, Monique, *Chroniques du bidonville: Nanterre en Guerre d'Algérie, 1959–1962* (Paris, 2001).

Hesse, Barnor (ed.), *Un/Settled Multiculturalisms: Diasporas, Entanglements, 'Transruptions'* (London, 2000).

Hiro, Dilip, *Black British White British: A History of Race Relations in Britain* (London, 1991).

Hochschild, Adam, *King Leopold's Ghost: A Story of Greed, Terror, and Heroism in Colonial Africa* (New York, 1998).

Hodge, Joseph M., 'British Colonial Expertise, Post-Colonial Careering and the Early History of International Development', *Journal of Modern European History*, 8:1 (2010), 24–46.

Hoefte, Rosemarijn, 'The Difficulty of Getting it Right: Dutch Policy in the Caribbean', *Itinerario*, 25:2 (2001), 59–72.

Hoefte, Rosemarijn, and Gert Oostindie, 'The Netherlands and the Dutch Caribbean: Dilemmas of Decolonisation', in Paul Sutton (ed.), *Europe and the Caribbean* (London, 1991), 71–98.

Holton, Kimberly DaCosta, '*Fado* Historiography: Old Myths and New Frontiers', *Portuguese Cultural Studies*, 0 (Winter 2006), 1–17.

Horne, Alistair, *A Savage War of Peace: Algeria 1954–1962* (New York, 1979).

Horta, Ana Paula Beja, *Contested Citizenship: Immigration Politics and Grassroots Migrants' Organizations in Post-Colonial Portugal* (New York, 2004).

Houben, Vincent J.H., 'A Torn Soul: The Dutch Public Discussion of the Colonial Past in 1995', *Indonesia*, 63 (1997), 47–66.

House, Jim, and Neil MacMaster, *Paris 1961: Algerians, State Terror, and Memory* (Oxford, 2006).

Howard, Marc Morjé, *The Politics of Citizenship in Europe* (New York, 2009).

Howe, Stephen, *Anticolonialism in British Politics: The Left and the End of Empire, 1918–1964* (Oxford, 1993).

Howe, Stephen, 'Colonising and Exterminating? Memories of Imperial Violence in Britain and France', *Histoire@Politique: Politique, culture, société*, 11 (2010).

Howe, Stephen, 'Internal Decolonization? British Politics since Thatcher as Post-Colonial Trauma', *Twentieth Century British History*, 14:3 (2003), 286–304.

Howe, Stephen (ed.), *The New Imperial Histories Reader* (London, 2010).

Hunt, James D., *Gandhi in London* (New Delhi, 1978).

Hunt, Nancy Rose, *A Colonial Lexicon: Of Birth Ritual, Medicalization, and Mobility in the Congo* (Durham, 1999).

Hunt, Nancy Rose, 'Tintin and the Interruptions of Congolese Comics', in Paul S. Laudau and Deborah D. Kaspin (eds.), *Images and Empires: Visuality in Colonial and Postcolonial Africa* (Berkeley, 2002), 90–123.

Huq, Rupa, *Beyond Subculture: Pop, Youth and Identity in a Postcolonial World* (London, 2006).

Hureau, Joëlle, *La mémoire des pieds-noirs* (Paris, 2001).

Hutnyk, John, *Critique of Exotica: Music, Politics and the Culture Industry* (London, 2000).

Igounet, Valérie, *Le Front National de 1972 à nos jours: Le parti, les hommes, les idées* (Paris, 2014).

Inda, Jonathan Xavier, and Renato Rosaldo (eds.), *The Anthropology of Globalization: A Reader* (Malden, MA and Oxford, 2002).

Isaacman, Allen, and Barbara Isaacman, *Mozambique from Colonialism to Revolution, 1900–1982* (Boulder, 1983).

Jackson, Ashley, 'Empire and Beyond: The Pursuit of Overseas National Interests in the Late Twentieth Century', *English Historical Review*, 122:499 (2007), 1350–66.

Jackson, Ben, and Robert Saunders (eds.), *Making Thatcher's Britain* (Cambridge, 2012).

Jahan, Sébastien, and Alain Ruscio (eds.), *Histoire de la colonisation: Réhabilitations, falsifications et instrumentalisations* (Paris, 2007).

James, Winston, 'The Black Experience in Twentieth-Century Britain', in Philip D. Morgan and Sean Hawkins (eds.), *The Black Experience and the Empire, Oxford History of the British Empire Companion Series* (Oxford, 2004), 347–86.

Jarausch, Konrad H., and Thomas Lindenberger, 'Contours of a Critical History of Contemporary Europe: A Transnational Agenda', in Konrad H. Jarausch and Thomas Lindenberger (eds.), *Conflicted Memories: Europeanizing Contemporary Histories* (New York, 2007), 1–20.

Jaumain, Serge, and Éric Remacle (eds.), *Mémoire de guerre et construction de la paix: Mentalités et choix politiques, Belgique – Europe – Canada* (Brussels, 2006).

Jennings, Eric T., 'From *Indochine* to *Indochic*: The Lang Bian/Dalat Palace Hotel and French Colonial Leisure, Power and Culture', *Modern Asian Studies*, 37:1 (2003), 159–94.

Jennings, Eric T., *Vichy in the Tropics: Pétain's National Revolution in Madagascar, Guadeloupe, and Indochina, 1940–1944* (Stanford, 2001).

Jennings, Jeremy, 'Citizenship, Republicanism, and Multiculturalism in Contemporary France', *British Journal of Political Science*, 30:4 (2000), 575–98.

Jerónimo, Miguel Bandeira, and António Costa Pinto (eds.), *The Ends of European Colonial Empires: Cases and Comparisons* (Basingstoke, 2015).

Jerónimo, Miguel Bandeira, and António Costa Pinto (eds.), 'International Dimensions of Portuguese Late Colonialism and Decolonization', special issue, *Portuguese Studies*, 29:2 (2013).

Jones, Guno, 'Biology, Culture, "Postcolonial Citizenship" and the Dutch Nation, 1945–2007', *Thamyris/Intersecting*, 27 (2014), 315–36.

Jones, Guno, 'Dutch Politicians, the Dutch Nation and the Dynamics of Post-Colonial Citizenship', in Ulbe Bosma (ed.), *Post-Colonial Immigrants and Identity Formations in the Netherlands* (Amsterdam, 2012), 27–47.

Jong, L. de, *The Collapse of a Colonial Society: The Dutch in Indonesia during the Second World War* (Leiden, 2002).

Jong, Louis de, *The Netherlands and Nazi Germany* (Cambridge, MA, 1990).

Joppke, Christian, and Ewa Morawska (eds.), *Toward Assimilation and Citizenship: Immigrations in Liberal Nation-States* (New York, 2003).

Jordi, Jean-Jacques, *De l'exode à l'exil: Rapatriés et pieds-noirs en France: L'exemple marseillais, 1954–1992* (Paris, 1993).

Jordi, Jean-Jacques, and Mohand Hamoumou, *Les harkis, une mémoire enfouie* (Paris, 1999).

Jordi, Jean-Jacques, Abdelmalek Sayad, and Émile Temime, *Histoire des migrations à Marseille, vol. 4: Le choc de la décolonisation (1945–1990)* (Aix-en-Provence, 1991).

Journoud, Pierre, and Hugues Tertrais (eds.), *1954–2004: La bataille de Dien Bien Phu entre histoire et mémoire* (Paris, 2004).

Kabwe, Désiré Kazadi Wa, 'Réparation, récupération et dette coloniale dans les romans congolais récents', *Cahiers d'Études africaines*, XLIV:1–2, 173–174 (2004), 141–50.

Kabwe, Désiré Kazadi Wa, and Aurelia Segatti, 'Paradoxical Expressions of a Return to the Homeland: Music and Literature among the Congolese (Zairean) Diaspora', in Khalid Koser (ed.), *New African Diasporas* (London, 2003), 124–39.

Kabwe, Désiré Kazadi Wa, and Aurelia Segatti, 'The Philosophy of the "Colonial Debt" in Contemporary Congolese (Zairean) Literature: Example or Counter-Example for Congolese Youth?', *French Studies in Southern Africa*, 31 (2002), 119–44.

Kagné, Bonaventure, 'Africains de Belgique, de l'indigène à l'immigré', *Hommes et Migrations*, 1228 (2000), 62–7.

Kahin, George McTurnan, *Nationalism and Revolution in Indonesia* (Ithaca, 1952).

Kahler, Miles, *Decolonization in Britain and France: The Domestic Consequences of International Relations* (Princeton, 1984).

Kaiser, Wolfram, *Using Europe, Abusing the Europeans: Britain and European Integration, 1945–63* (Basingstoke, 1996).

Kaiser, Wolfram, Brigitte Leucht, and Morten Rasmussen (eds.), *The History of the European Union: Origins of a Trans- and Supranational Polity, 1950–72* (London, 2009).

Kaiser, Wolfram, and Antonio Varsori (eds.), *European Union History: Themes and Debates* (Basingstoke, 2010).

Kalra, Virinder S., '*Vilayeti* Rhythms: Beyond Bhangra's Emblematic Status to a Translation of Lyrical Texts', *Theory, Culture & Society*, 17:3 (2000), 80–102.

Kauffer, Rémi, *OAS: Histoire de la guerre franco-française* (Paris, 2002).

Kay, Diana, and Robert Miles, *Refugees or Migrant Workers?: European Volunteer Workers in Britain, 1946–1951* (London, 1992).

Keaton, Trica Danielle, *Muslim Girls and the Other France: Race, Identity Politics, and Social Exclusion* (Bloomington, 2006).

Keaton, Trica Danielle, T. Denean Sharpley-Whiting, and Tyler Stovall (eds.), *Black France/France Noire: The History and Politics of Blackness* (Durham, 2012).

Kempen, Michiel van, 'De binnenkamer en de open vensters: Ontwikkelingen in de Surinaamse literatuur 1975–1988', *De Gids*, 153:1 (1990).

Kennedy, Dane, 'Constructing the Colonial Myth of Mau Mau', *International Journal of African Historical Studies*, 25:2 (1992), 242–60.

Kennedy, Dane, 'Decolonization and Disorder', *East Asian Journal of British History*, 3 (2013), 95–111.

Kennedy, Dane, 'Imperial History and Post-Colonial Theory', *Journal of Imperial and Commonwealth History*, 24:3 (1996), 345–63.

Kennedy, Dane, *Islands of White: Settler Society and Culture in Kenya and Southern Rhodesia, 1890–1939* (Durham, 1987).

Kennedy, James C., and Jan P. Zwemer, 'Religion in the Modern Netherlands and the Problems of Pluralism', *BMGN-Low Countries Historical Review*, 125:2–3 (2010), 237–67.

Kent, John, *America, the UN and Decolonisation: Cold War Conflict in the Congo* (London, 2010).

Kepel, Gilles, *Les banlieues de l'islam: Naissance d'une religion en France* (Paris, 1987).

Khan, Sheila, 'Identidades sem chão: Imigrantes Afro-Moçambicanos: Narrativas de Vida e de Identidade, e Percepções de um Portugal Pós-colonial', *Luso-Brazilian Review*, 43:2 (2006), 1–26.

Khan, Yasmin, *The Great Partition: The Making of India and Pakistan* (New Haven, 2007).

Khan, Yasmin, *The Raj at War: A People's History of India's Second World War* (London, 2015).

King, Russell, Tony Warnes, and Allan Williams, *Sunset Lives: British Retirement Migration to the Mediterranean* (Oxford, 2000).

King, Tony, 'Rhodesians in Hyperspace: The Maintenance of a National and Cultural Identity', in Karim H. Karim (ed.), *The Media of Diaspora* (London, 2003), 177–88.

Kirk-Greene, Anthony, *Britain's Imperial Administrators, 1858–1966* (London, 2000).

Kirk-Greene, Anthony, 'Decolonisation: The Ultimate Diaspora', *Journal of Contemporary History*, 36:1 (2001), 133–51.

Kuisel, Richard F., *Seducing the French: The Dilemma of Americanization* (Berkeley, 1993).

Kuitenbrouwer, Maarten, 'The Never-Ending Debt of Honour: The Dutch in the Post-Colonial World', *Itinerario*, 20:2 (1996), 20–42.

Kuitenbrouwer, Vincent, 'Beyond the "Trauma of Decolonization": Dutch Cultural Diplomacy during the West New Guinea Question (1950–62)', *Journal of Imperial and Commonwealth History* (in press).

Kuitenbrouwer, Vincent, '"A Newspaper War"?: Dutch Information Networks during the South African War (1899–1902)', *BMGN – Low Countries Historical Review*, 128:1 (2013), 127–50.

Kumar, Krishan, 'Britain, England and Europe: Cultures in Counterflow', *European Journal of Social Theory*, 6:1 (2003), 5–23.

Kumar, Krishan, *The Making of English National Identity* (Cambridge, 2003).

Kundnani, Arun, 'From Oldham to Bradford: The Violence of the Violated', *Race & Class*, 43:2 (2001), 105–31.

Laborde, Cécile, *Critical Republicanism: The Hijab Controversy and Political Philosophy* (Oxford, 2008).

Laborde, Cécile, 'The Culture(s) of the Republic: Nationalism and Multiculturalism in French Republican Thought', *Political Theory*, 29:5 (2001), 716–35.

Lagrou, Pieter, *The Legacy of Nazi Occupation: Patriotic Memory and National Recovery in Western Europe, 1945–1965* (Cambridge, 2000).

Langbehn, Volker, and Mohammad Salama (eds.), *German Colonialism: Race, the Holocaust, and Postwar Germany* (New York, 2011).

Lawrence, Mark Atwood, and Fredrik Logevall (eds.), *The First Vietnam War: Colonial Conflict and Cold War Crisis* (Cambridge, MA, 2007).

Lazreg, Marina, *Torture and the Twilight of Empire: From Algiers to Baghdad* (Princeton, 2008).

Le Sueur, James D., *Uncivil War: Intellectuals and Identity Politics during the Decolonization of Algeria*, 2nd edn. (Lincoln, NE, 2005).

Leal, João, 'The Making of *Saudade*: National Identity and Ethnic Psychology in Portugal', in Ton Dekker, John Helsloot, and Carla Wijers (eds.), *Roots and Rituals: The Construction of Ethnic Identities* (Amsterdam, 2000), 267–87.

Lebovics, Herman, *Bringing the Empire Back Home: France in the Global Age* (Durham, 2004).

Lebovics, Herman, *True France: The Wars over Cultural Identity, 1900–1945* (Ithaca, 1992).

Lee, J.M., 'Commonwealth Students in the United Kingdom, 1940–1960: Student Welfare and World Status', *Minerva*, 44:1 (2006), 1–24.

Leeuwen, Lizzy van, *Ons Indisch erfgoed: Zestig jaar strijd om cultuur en identiteit* (Amsterdam, 2008).

Legêne, Susan, *Spiegelreflex: Culturele sporen van de koloniale ervaring* (Amsterdam, 2010).

Legêne, Susan, and Martijn Eickhoff, 'Postwar Europe and the Colonial Past in Photographs', in Chiara De Cesari and Ann Rigney (eds.), *Transnational Memory: Circulation, Articulation, Scales* (Berlin, 2014), 287–311.

Léonard, Yves, 'Salazarisme et lusotropicalisme, histoire d'une appropriation', in *Lusotopie 1997* (Paris, 1997), 211–26.

Leonhard, Jörn, and Ulrike von Hirschhausen (eds.), *Comparing Empires: Encounters and Transfers in the Long Nineteenth Century* (Göttingen, 2011).

Lewis, Joanna, '"Daddy Wouldn't Buy Me a Mau Mau": The British Popular Press and the Demoralization of Empire', in E.S. Atieno Odhiambo and John Lonsdale (eds.), *Mau Mau and Nationhood: Arms, Authority and Narration* (Oxford, 2003), 227–50.

Lewis, Philip, *Islamic Britain: Religion, Politics and Identity among British Muslims* (London, 1994).

Liauzu, Claude, *Histoire de l'anticolonialisme en France: Du XVIe siècle à nos jours* (Paris, 2007).

Liauzu, Claude, and Gilles Manceron (eds.), *La colonisation, la loi et l'histoire* (Paris, 2006).

Licata, Laurent, and Olivier Klein, 'Holocaust or Benevolent Paternalism?: Intergenerational Comparisons on Collective Memories and Emotions about

Belgium's Colonial Past', *International Journal of Conflict and Violence*, 4:1 (2010), 45–57.

Lijphart, Arend, *The Politics of Accommodation: Pluralism and Democracy in the Netherlands*, 2nd rev. edn. (Berkeley, 1975).

Lijphart, Arend, *The Trauma of Decolonization: The Dutch and West New Guinea* (New Haven, 1966).

Lindner, Ulrike, Maren Möhring, Mark Stein, and Silke Stroh (eds.), *Hybrid Cultures – Nervous States: Britain and Germany in a (Post)Colonial World* (Amsterdam, 2010).

Lipsitz, George, *Dangerous Crossroads: Popular Music, Postmodernism and the Poetics of Place* (London, 1994).

Lloyd-Jones, Stewart, and António Costa Pinto (eds.), *The Last Empire: Thirty Years of Portuguese Decolonization* (Bristol, 2003).

Loff, Manuel, 'Coming to Terms with the Dictatorial Past in Portugal after 1974: Silence, Remembrance and Ambiguity', in Stefan Troebst and Susan Baumgartl (eds.), *Postdiktatorische Geschichtskulturen im Süden und Osten Europas: Bestandsaufnahme und Perspektiven* (Göttingen, 2010), 55–121.

Logevall, Fredrik, *Embers of War: The Fall of an Empire and the Making of America's Vietnam* (New York, 2012).

Lonsdale, John, 'Mau Maus of the Mind: Making Mau Mau and Remaking Kenya', *Journal of African History*, 31 (1990), 393–421.

Lorcin, Patricia M.E., *Historicizing Colonial Nostalgia: European Women's Narratives of Algeria and Kenya 1900–Present* (Basingstoke, 2011).

Louis, Wm. Roger, *Ends of British Imperialism: The Scramble for Empire, Suez and Decolonization: Collected Essays* (London, 2006).

Louis, Wm. Roger, *Imperialism at Bay 1941–1945: The United States and the Decolonization of the British Empire* (Oxford, 1977).

Louis, Wm. Roger, and Ronald Robinson, 'The Imperialism of Decolonization', *Journal of Imperial and Commonwealth History*, 22:3 (1994), 462–511.

Lubkemann, Stephen C., 'The Moral Economy of Portuguese Postcolonial Return', *Diaspora*, 11:2 (2002), 189–213.

Lucassen, Jan, and Arie de Ruijter (eds.), *Nederland Multicultureel en Pluriform?: Een aantal conceptuele studies* (Amsterdam, 2002).

Lucassen, Jan, and Rinus Penninx, *Newcomers: Immigrants and Their Descendants in the Netherlands, 1550–1995* (Amsterdam, 1997).

Lucassen, Leo, *The Immigrant Threat: The Integration of Old and New Migrants in Western Europe since 1850* (Urbana and Chicago, 2005).

Lucassen, Leo, and Jan Lucassen, 'The Strange Death of Dutch Tolerance: The Timing and Nature of the Pessimist Turn in the Dutch Migration Debate', *Journal of Modern History*, 87:1 (2015), 72–101.

Lucassen, Leo, and Jan Lucassen, *Winnaars en verliezers: Een nuchtere balans van vijfhonderd jaar immigratie* (Amsterdam, 2011).

Luttikhuis, Bart, and A. Dirk Moses (eds.), *Colonial Counterinsurgency and Mass Violence: The Dutch Empire in Indonesia* (London, 2014).

Lynn, Martin (ed.), *The British Empire in the 1950s: Retreat or Revival?* (Basingstoke, 2006).

Mabon, Armelle, 'La tragédie de Thiaroye, symbole du déni d'égalité', *Hommes et migrations*, 1235 (2002), 86–95.

Macey, David, *Frantz Fanon: A Life* (London, 2000).

MacGaffey, Janet, and Rémy Bazenguissa-Ganga, *Congo-Paris: Transnational Traders on the Margins of the Law* (Oxford and Bloomington, 2000).

MacKenzie, John M., 'Comfort and Conviction: A Response to Bernard Porter', *Journal of Imperial and Commonwealth History*, 36:4 (2008), 659–68.

MacKenzie, John M. (ed.), *European Empires and the People: Popular Responses to Imperialism in France, Britain, the Netherlands, Belgium, Germany and Italy* (Manchester, 2011).

MacKenzie, John M. (ed.), *Imperialism and Popular Culture* (Manchester, 1986).

MacMaster, Neil, *Burning the Veil: The Algerian War and the 'Emancipation' of Muslim Women, 1954–62* (Manchester, 2009).

MacMaster, Neil, *Colonial Migrants and Racism: Algerians in France, 1900–62* (Basingstoke, 1997).

MacMaster, Neil, 'The Torture Controversy (1998–2002): Towards a "New History" of the Algerian War?', *Modern and Contemporary France*, 10:4 (2002), 449–59.

MacQueen, Norrie, *The Decolonization of Portuguese Africa: Metropolitan Revolution and the Dissolution of Empire* (London, 1997).

MacQueen, Norrie, 'Portugal's First Domino: "Pluricontinentalism" and Colonial War in Guinea-Bissau, 1963–1974', *Contemporary European History*, 8:2 (1999), 209–30.

Maddens, Bart, Jaak Billiet, and Roeland Beerten, 'National Identity and the Attitude Towards Foreigners in Multi-National States: The Case of Belgium', *Journal of Ethnic and Migration Studies*, 26:1 (2000), 45–60.

Mamdani, Mahmood, *When Victims Become Killers: Colonialism, Nativism, and the Genocide in Rwanda* (Princeton, 2001).

Manela, Erez, *The Wilsonian Moment: Self-Determination and the International Origins of Anticolonial Nationalism* (Oxford, 2007).

Mann, Gregory, 'Immigrants and Arguments in France and Africa', *Comparative Studies in Society and History*, 45:2 (2003), 362–85.

Mann, Gregory, *Native Sons: West African Veterans and France in the Twentieth Century* (Durham, 2006).

Manuel, Carlos, and Neves Cardoso, 'The Colonialist View of the African-Origin "Other" in Portuguese Society and Its Education System', *Race, Ethnicity and Education*, 1:2 (1998), 191–206.

Margarido, Alfredo, *A Lusofonia e os Lusófonos: Novos Mitos Portugueses* (Lisbon, 2000).

Marie, Claude-Valentin, 'Les Antillais en France: une nouvelle donne', *Hommes et Migrations*, 1237 (2002), 26–39.

Marques, M. Margarida, Nuno Dias, and José Mapril, 'Le "retour des caravelles" au Portugal: de l'exclusion des immigés à l'inclusion des lusophones?', in Évelyne Ritaine (ed.), *L'Europe du Sud face à l'immigration: Politique de l'Étranger* (Paris, 2005).

Martiniello, Marco (ed.), *Multicultural Policies and the State: A Comparison of Two European Societies* (Utrecht, 1998).

'Mau Mau Judgement', section of *Journal of Imperial and Commonwealth History*, 39:5 (2011).

Maxwell, Kenneth, *The Making of Portuguese Democracy* (Cambridge, 1995).

May, Alex (ed.), *Britain, the Commonwealth and Europe: The Commonwealth and Britain's Applications to Join the European Communities* (Basingstoke, 2001).

May, Alex, 'The Commonwealth and Britain's Turn to Europe, 1945–73', *Round Table*, 102:1 (2013), 29–39.

May, Stephen, 'Multiculturalism', in David Theo Goldberg (ed.), *A Companion to Racial and Ethnic Studies* (Malden, MA, 2002), 124–44.

Mayer, Nonna, and Pascal Perrineau (eds.), *Le Front National à découvert* (Paris, 1989).

Mbembe, Achille, *Sortir de la grande nuit: Essai sur l'Afrique décolonisée* (Paris, 2010).

McDowell, Linda, 'On the Significance of Being White: European Migrant Workers in the British Economy in the 1940s and 2000s', in Claire Dwyer and Caroline Bressey (eds.), *New Geographies of Race and Racism* (Aldershot, 2008), 51–64.

McLeod, John, *Postcolonial London: Rewriting the Metropolis* (London, 2004).

McMahon, Robert J., *Colonialism and Cold War: The United States and the Struggle for Indonesian Independence, 1945–49* (Ithaca, 1981).

Mead, Matthew, '*Empire Windrush*: The Cultural Memory of an Imaginary Arrival', *Journal of Postcolonial Writing*, 45:2 (2009), 137–49.

Medeiros, Paulo de, 'Hauntings: Memory, Fiction and the Portuguese Colonial Wars', in T.G. Ashplant, Graham Dawson, and Michael Roper (eds.), *The Politics of War and Commemoration* (London, 2000), 201–21.

Medeiros, Paulo de, 'Postcolonial Memories and Lusophone Literatures', *European Review*, 13:1 (2005), 151–61.

Medina, João, 'The Old Lie: Some Portuguese Contemporary Novels on the Colonial Wars in Africa (1961–74)', *Portuguese Studies*, 15 (1999), 149–61.

Meeuwis, Michael, 'Het activisme van de verminking/L'activisme de la mutilation', *Forum: Nieuwsbrief van de Belgische Vereniging van Afrikanisten*, 25 (July 2005), http://cas1.elis.ugent.be/avrug/erfgoed/pdf/vermink.pdf.

Mehta, Brinda J., 'Negotiating Arab-Muslim Identity, Contested Citizenship, and Gender Ideologies in the Parisian Housing Projects: Faïza Guène's *Kiffe kiffe demain*', *Research in African Literatures*, 41:2 (2010), 173–202.

Melo, Daniel, and Eduardo Caetano da Silva (eds.), *Construção da Nação e Associativismo na Emigração Portuguesa* (Lisbon, 2009).

Mendoza, Cristóbal, *Labour Immigration in Southern Europe: African Employment in Iberian Labour Markets* (Aldershot, 2003).

Mendy, Peter Karibe, 'Portugal's Civilizing Mission in Colonial Guinea-Bissau: Rhetoric and Reality', *International Journal of African Historical Studies*, 36:1 (2003), 35–58.

Merckx, Freddy, and Liz Fekete, 'Belgium: The Racist Cocktail', *Race & Class*, 32:3 (1991), 67–78.

Miège, Jean-Louis, and Colette Dubois (eds.), *L'Europe retrouvée: les migrations de la décolonisation* (Paris, 1994).

Misra, Maria, *Vishnu's Crowded Temple: India since the Great Rebellion* (London, 2007).

Modood, Tariq, 'British Asian Muslims and the Rushdie Affair', *Political Quarterly*, 61:2 (1990), 143–60.

Modood, Tariq, 'Political Blackness and British Asians', *Sociology*, 28:4 (1994), 859–76.

Modood, Tariq, and Pnina Werbner (eds.), *The Politics of Multiculturalism in the New Europe: Racism, Identity and Community* (London, 1997).

Monaville, Pedro, 'La crise congolaise de juillet 1960 et le sexe de la décolonisation', *Sextant*, 25 (2008), 87–102.

Morelli, Anne (ed.), *Histoire des étrangers et de l'immigration en Belgique de la préhistoire à nos jours* (Brussels, 2004).

Morén-Alegret, Ricard, *Integration and Resistance: The Relation of Social Organizations, Global Capital, Governments, and International Immigration in Spain and Portugal* (Aldershot, 2002).

Mort, Frank, *Capital Affairs: London and the Making of the Permissive Society* (New Haven, 2010).

Mul, Sarah De, 'Nostalgia for Empire: "Tempo Doeloe" in Contemporary Dutch Literature', *Memory Studies*, 3:4 (2010), 413–28.

Mulenghe, Mashini Dhi Mbita, 'L'intégration socio-économique de la population originaire d'Afrique noire dans la Région de Bruxelles-Capitale', *Revue Belge de Géographie*, 63 (1998), 55–70.

Murphy, Philip, *Monarchy and the End of Empire: The House of Windsor, the British Government and the Postwar Commonwealth* (Oxford, 2013).

Murphy, Philip, *Party Politics and Decolonization: The Conservative Party and British Colonial Policy in Tropical Africa, 1951–1964* (Oxford, 1995).

Murray, Graham, 'France: The Riots and the Republic', *Race & Class*, 47:4 (2006), 26–45.

Mutsaers, Lutgard, 'Indorock: An Early Eurorock Style', *Popular Music*, 9:3 (1990), 307–20.

Naranch, Bradley, and Geoff Eley (eds.), *German Colonialism in a Global Age* (Durham, 2014).

Naro, Nancy Priscilla, Roger Sansi-Roca, and David H. Treece (eds.), *Cultures of the Lusophone Black Atlantic* (New York, 2007).

Naylor, Ed, '"Un âne dans l'ascenseur": Late Colonial Welfare Services and Social Housing in Marseille after Decolonization', *French History*, 27:3 (2013), 422–47.

Ndaywel è Nziem, Isidore, *Histoire générale du Congo: De l'héritage ancien à la République Démocratique* (Paris and Brussels, 1998).

Nicolaïdis, Kalypso, Berny Sèbe, and Gabrielle Maas (eds.), *Echoes of Empire: Memory, Identity and Colonial Legacies* (London, 2015).

Niekerk, Mies van, 'Afro-Caribbeans and Indo-Caribbeans in the Netherlands: Premigration Legacies and Social Mobility', *International Migration Review*, 38:1 (2004), 158–83.

Niekerk, Mies van, *Premigration Legacies and Immigrant Social Mobility: The Afro-Surinamese and Indo-Surinamese in the Netherlands* (Lanham, MD, 2002; originally published Amsterdam, 2000).

Niekerk, Mies van, 'Second-Generation Caribbeans in the Netherlands: Different Migration Histories, Diverging Trajectories', *Journal of Ethnic and Migration Studies*, 33:7 (2007), 1063–81.

Noiriel, Gérard, *The French Melting Pot: Immigration, Citizenship, and National Identity*, translated by Geoffroy de Laforcade (Minneapolis, 1996; first published in French in 1988).

Nordmann, Charlotte (ed.), *Le foulard islamique en questions* (Paris, 2004).

Norindr, Panivong, *Phantasmatic Indochina: French Colonial Ideology in Architecture, Film, and Literature* (Durham, 1996).

Nzongola-Ntalaja, Georges, *The Congo from Leopold to Kabila: A People's History* (London, 2002).

Obdeijn, Herman, and Marlou Schrover, *Komen en gaan: Immigratie en emigratie in Nederland vanaf 1550* (Amsterdam, 2008).

O'Brien, Rita Cruise, *White Society in Black Africa: The French of Senegal* (London, 1972).

O'Harrow, Stephen, 'Babar and the *Mission Civilisatrice*: Colonialism and the Biography of a Mythical Elephant', *Biography*, 22:1 (1999), 86–103.

Øien, Cecilie, 'Of Homecomings and Homesickness: The Question of White Angolans in Post-Colonial Portugal', in Eve Rosenhaft and Robbie Aitken (eds.), *Africa in Europe: Studies in Transnational Practice in the Long Twentieth Century* (Liverpool, 2013), 183–200.

Omissi, David, 'Europe through Indian Eyes: Indian Soldiers Encounter England and France, 1914–1918', *English Historical Review*, 122:496 (2007), 371–96.

Oostindie, Gert, *Postcolonial Netherlands: Sixty-Five Years of Forgetting, Commemorating, Silencing* (Amsterdam, 2011).

Oostindie, Gert, 'Squaring the Circle: Commemorating the VOC after 400 Years', *Bijdragen tot de Taal-, Land- en Volkenkunde*, 159, Part I (2003), 135–61.

Oostindie, Gert, and Inge Klinkers, *Decolonising the Caribbean: Dutch Policies in a Comparative Perspective* (Amsterdam, 2003).

Oostindie, Gert, and Emy Maduro, *In het Land van de Overheerser II: Antillianen en Surinamers in Nederland, 1634/1667–1954* (Dordrecht, 1986).

Oostindie, Gert, Henk Schulte Nordholt, and Fridus Steijlen (with photographs by Eveline Kooijman), *Postkoloniale Monumenten in Nederland/Post-Colonial Monuments in the Netherlands* (Leiden, 2011).

Otterloo, Anneke H. van, 'Chinese and Indonesian Restaurants and the Taste for Exotic Food in the Netherlands: A Global-Local Trend', in Katarzyna Cwiertka with Boudewijn Walraven (eds.), *Asian Food: The Global and the Local* (Richmond, 2002), 153–66.

Otterloo, Anneke H. van, 'Foreign Immigrants and the Dutch at Table, 1945–1985: Bridging or Widening the Gap?', *Netherlands Journal of Sociology/Sociologia Neerlandica*, 23:2 (1987), 126–43.

Owen, Nicholas, *The British Left and India: Metropolitan Anti-Imperialism, 1885–1947* (Oxford, 2007).

Owen, Nicholas, '"More Than a Transfer of Power": Independence Day Ceremonies in India, 15 August 1947', *Contemporary Record*, 6:3 (1992), 415–51.

Palumbo, Patrizia (ed.), *A Place in the Sun: Africa in Italian Colonial Culture from Post-Unification to the Present* (Berkeley, 2003).

Pas, Niek, *Aan de weg van het nieuwe Nederland: Nederland en de Algerijnse oorlog* (Amsterdam, 2008).

Pas, Niek, *The State of the Right: The Netherlands* (Paris, March 2011), www.fonda pol.org.

Pattynama, Pamela, *Bitterzoet Indië: Herinnering en nostalgie in literatuur, foto's en films* (Amsterdam, 2014).

Paul, Kathleen, *Whitewashing Britain: Race and Citizenship in the Postwar Era* (Ithaca, 1997).

Peabody, Sue, and Tyler Stovall (eds.), *The Color of Liberty: Histories of Race in France* (Durham, 2003).

Peach, Ceri, 'Postwar Migration to Europe: Reflux, Influx, Refuge', *Social Science Quarterly*, 78:2 (1997), 269–83.

Penninx, Rinus, Jeannette Schoorl, and Carlo van Praag, *The Impact of International Migration on Receiving Countries: The Case of the Netherlands* (Amsterdam, 1993).

Penvenne, Jeanne Marie, *African Workers and Colonial Racism: Mozambican Strategies and Struggles in Lourenço Marques, 1877–1962* (Portsmouth, NH, 1995).

Peralta, Elsa, 'Fictions of a Creole Nation: (Re)Presenting Portugal's Imperial Past', in Helen Vella Bonavita (ed.), *Negotiating Identities: Constructed Selves and Others* (Amsterdam, 2011), 193–217.

Phalet, Karen, and Marc Swyngedouw, 'Measuring Immigrant Integration: The Case of Belgium', *Studi Emigrazione/Migration Studies*, XL:152 (2003), 773–804.

Phillips, Mike, and Trevor Phillips, *Windrush: The Irresistible Rise of Multi-Racial Britain* (London, 1999).

Piniau, Bernard, *Congo-Zaïre 1874–1981: La perception du lointain* (Paris, 1992).

Pinto, António Costa (ed.), *Contemporary Portugal: Politics, Society and Culture* (New York and Boulder, 2003).

Pinto, António Costa, 'Dealing with the Legacy of Authoritarianism: Political Purges and Radical Right Movements in Portugal's Transition to Democracy, 1974–1980s', in Stein Ugelvik Larsen (ed.), *Modern Europe after Fascism, 1943–1980s*, Vol. II (Boulder, 1998), 1679–718.

Pinto, António Costa (ed.), *Modern Portugal* (Palo Alto, 1998).

Pinto, António Costa, *O Fim do Império Porguguês* (Lisbon, 2001).

Pinto, António Costa, 'The Radical Right in Contemporary Portugal', in Luciano Cheles, Ronnie Ferguson, and Micalina Vaughan (eds.), *The Far Right in Western and Eastern Europe*, 2nd edn. (London, 1995), 108–28.

Pinto, António Costa, and Nuno Severiano Teixeira, 'From Africa to Europe: Portugal and European Integration', in António Costa Pinto and Nuno Severiano Teixeira (eds.), *Southern Europe and the Making of the European Union, 1945–1980s* (New York, 2002), 3–40.

Pires, Rui Pena, *Migrações e Integração* (Oeiras, 2003).

Pires, R. Pena *et al.*, *Os Retornados: Um Estudo Sociográfico* (Lisbon, 1984).

Pocock, J.G.A., 'British History: A Plea for a New Subject', *Journal of Modern History*, 47:4 (1975), 601–21.

Poddar, Prem, Rajeev S. Patke, and Lars Jensen (eds.), *A Historical Companion to Postcolonial Literatures – Continental Europe and Its Empires* (Edinburgh, 2008).

Ponty, Janine, *L'immigration dans les textes: France, 1789–2002* (Paris, 2003).

Porter, Bernard, *The Absent-Minded Imperialists: Empire, Society, and Culture in Britain* (Oxford, 2004).

Porter, Bernard, 'Further Thoughts on Imperial Absent-Mindedness', *Journal of Imperial and Commonwealth History*, 36:1 (2008), 101–17.

'Portugais de France', special issue, *Hommes et Migrations*, 1210 (1997).

Potter, Simon J., and Jonathan Saha, 'Global History, Imperial History and Connected Histories of Empire', *Journal of Colonialism and Colonial History*, 16:1 (2015).

Power, Marcus, 'Geo-Politics and the Representation of Portugal's African Colonial Wars: Examining the Limits of the "Vietnam Syndrome"', *Political Geography*, 20 (2001), 461–91.

Power, Marcus, and James D. Sidaway, 'Deconstructing Twinned Towers: Lisbon's Expo '98 and the Occluded Geographies of Discovery', *Social & Cultural Geography*, 6:6 (2005), 865–83.

Proctor, James, *Dwelling Places: Postwar Black British Writing* (Manchester, 2003).

Prost, Antoine, 'The Algerian War in French Collective Memory', in Jay Winter and Emmanuel Sivan (eds.), *War and Remembrance in the Twentieth Century* (Cambridge, 1999), 161–76.

Raben, Remco, 'A New Dutch Imperial History?: Perambulations in a Prospective Field', *BMGN – Low Countries Historical Review*, 128:1 (2013), 5–30.

Raben, Remco (ed.), *Representing the Japanese Occupation of Indonesia: Personal Testimonies and Public Images in Indonesia, Japan, and the Netherlands* (Amsterdam, 1999).

'Racial France', special issue, *Public Culture*, 23:1 (2011).

Rahier, Jean Muteba, 'The Ghost of Leopold II: The Belgian Royal Museum of Central Africa and Its Dusty Colonialist Exhibition', *Research in African Literatures*, 34:1 (2003), 58–84.

Ramamurthy, Anandi, *Black Star: Britain's Asian Youth Movements* (London, 2013).

Ramamurthy, Anandi, 'The Politics of Britain's Asian Youth Movements', *Race & Class*, 48:2 (2006), 38–60.

Ranger, Terence, 'Zimbabwe and the Long Search for Independence', in David Birmingham and Phyllis Martin (eds.), *History of Central Africa: The Contemporary Years since 1960* (London, 1998), 203–29.

Raposo, Otávio, '"Heart There and Body Here in Pretugal": In Between Mestizagem and the Affirmation of Blackness', *BUALA: African Contemporary Literature* (21 October 2010), www.buala.org.

Reichl, Susanne, 'Flying the Flag: The Intricate Semiotics of National Identity', *European Journal of English Studies*, 8:2 (2004), 205–17.

Reiter, Bernd, 'Portugal: National Pride and Imperial Neurosis', *Race & Class*, 47:1 (2005), 79–91.

Reybrouck, David Van, *Congo: een geschiedenis* (Amsterdam, 2010).

Reynolds, David, *Britannia Overruled: British Policy and World Power in the Twentieth Century*, 2nd edn. (Harlow, 2000).

Ribeiro, Margarida Calafate, 'Empire, Colonial Wars and Post-Colonialism in the Portuguese Contemporary Imagination', *Portuguese Studies*, 18 (2002), 132–214.

Ribeiro, Margarida Calafate, *Uma História de Regressos: Império Guerra Colonial e Pós-colonialismo* (Porto, 2004).

Rich, Paul, *Race and Empire in British Politics* (Cambridge, 1986).

Ricklefs, M.C., *A History of Modern Indonesia Since c.1200*, 4th edn. (Basingstoke, 2008).

Rigouste, Mathieu, *L'Ennemi intérieur: La généalogie coloniale et militaire de l'ordre sécuritaire dans la France contemporaine* (Paris, 2009).

Rioux, Jean-Pierre (ed.), *Dictionnaire de la France coloniale* (Paris, 2007).

Ritaine, Évelyne (ed.), *L'Europe du Sud face à l'immigration: Politique de l'Étranger* (Paris, 2005).

Rocha-Trindade, Maria Beatriz, 'Portugal: Ongoing Changes in Immigration and Government Policies', *Studi Emigrazione/Migration Studies*, 39:148 (2002), 795–810.

Romijn, Peter, 'Learning on "the Job": Dutch War Volunteers Entering the Indonesian War of Independence, 1945–46', *Journal of Genocide Research*, 14:3 (2012), 317–36.

Romijn, Peter, 'Myth and Understanding: Recent Controversy about Dutch Historiography on the Netherlands-Indonesia Conflict', in Robert S. Kirsner (ed.), *The Low Countries and Beyond* (Lanham, MD, 1993), 219–29.

Rose, Sonya O., 'From the "New Jerusalem" to the "Decline" of the "New Elizabethan Age": National Identity and Citizenship in Britain, 1945–56', in Frank Biess and Robert G. Moeller (eds.), *Histories of the Aftermath: The Legacies of the Second World War in Europe* (New York, 2010), 231–47.

Rose, Sonya O., *Which People's War?: National Identity and Citizenship in Britain 1939–1945* (Oxford, 2003).

Rosello, Mireille, *Declining the Stereotype: Ethnicity and Representation in French Cultures* (Hanover and London, 1998).

Rosello, Mireille, *Postcolonial Hospitality: The Immigrant as Guest* (Stanford, 2001).

Rosello, Mireille, *The Reparative in Narratives: Works of Mourning in Progress* (Liverpool, 2009).

Ross, Kristin, *Fast Cars, Clean Bodies: Decolonization and the Reordering of French Culture* (Cambridge, MA, 1995).

Rothberg, Michael, *Multidirectional Memory: Remembering the Holocaust in the Age of Decolonization* (Stanford, 2009).

Rothermund, Dietmar, 'The Self-Consciousness of Post-Imperial Nations: A Cross-National Comparison', *India Quarterly: A Journal of International Affairs*, 67:1 (2011), 1–18.

Rothermund, Dietmar (ed.), *Memories of Post-imperial Nations: The Aftermath of Decolonization, 1945–2013* (Cambridge, 2015).

Ruscio, Alain, 'French Public Opinion and the War in Indochina: 1945–1954', in Michael Scriven and Peter Wagstaff (eds.), *War and Society in Twentieth-Century France* (New York, 1991), 117–29.

Ruscio, Alain (ed.), *L'Affaire Henri Martin et la lutte contre la guerre d'Indochine* (Pantin, 2005).

Ruscio, Alain, *Les communistes français et la guerre d'Indochine, 1944–1954* (Paris, 1985).

Ruscio, Alain, and Serge Tignères, *Dien Bien Phu, Mythes et réalités: Cinquante ans de passions françaises (1954–2004)* (Paris, 2005).

Rushdie, Salman, 'Outside the Whale' (1984), in *Imaginary Homelands: Essays and Criticism 1981–1991* (London, 1991), 87–101.

Said, Edward W., *Culture and Imperialism* (New York, 1993).

Sanches, Manuela Ribeiro (ed.), *'Portugal não é um país pequeno': Contar o 'império' na pós-colonialidade* (Lisbon, 2006).

Sansone, Livio, 'The Making of Black Culture: The New Subculture of Lower-Class Young Black Males of Surinamese Origin in Amsterdam', *Critique of Anthropology*, 14:2 (1994), 173–98.

Sansone, Livio, *Schitteren in de Schaduw: Overlevingsstrategieën, subcultuur en etniciteit van Creoolse jongeren uit de lagere klasse in Amsterdam 1981–1990* (Amsterdam, 1992).

Santos, Boaventura de Sousa, 'Between Prospero and Caliban: Colonialism, Postcolonialism, and Inter-Identity', *Luso-Brazilian Review*, 39:2 (2002), 9–43.

Sapega, Ellen W., 'Remembering Empire/Forgetting the Colonies: Accretions of Memory and the Limits of Commemoration in a Lisbon Neighborhood', *History & Memory*, 20:2 (2008), 18–38.

Sartwell, Crispin, 'Red, Gold, Black and Green: Black Nationalist Aesthetics', *Contemporary Aesthetics*, Special Volume 2 (2009).

Sayad, Abdelmalek, *The Suffering of the Immigrant*, translated by David Macey (Cambridge, 2004).

Scagliola, Stef, 'The Silences and Myths of a "Dirty War": Coming to Terms with the Dutch-Indonesian Decolonisation War (1945–1949)', *European Review of History – Revue européenne d'Histoire*, 14:2 (2007), 235–62.

Scheffer, Paul, *Immigrant Nations* (Cambridge, 2011).

Schiller, Nina Glick, Tsypylma Darieva, and Sandra Gruner-Domic, 'Defining Cosmopolitan Sociability in a Transnational Age: An Introduction', *Ethnic and Racial Studies*, 34:3 (2011), 399–418.

Schilling, Britta, *Postcolonial Germany: Memories of Empire in a Decolonized Nation* (Oxford, 2014).

Schofield, Camilla, *Enoch Powell and the Making of Postcolonial Britain* (Cambridge, 2013).

Schrover, Marlou, 'Pillarization, Multiculturalism and Cultural Freezing: Dutch Migration History and the Enforcement of Essentialist Ideas', *BMGN-Low Countries Historical Review*, 125:2–3 (2010), 329–54.

Schuster, John, 'The State and Post-War Immigration into the Netherlands: The Racialization and Assimilation of Indonesian Dutch', *European Journal of Intercultural Studies*, 3:1 (1992), 47–58.

Schuyt, Kees, and Ed Taverne, *Dutch Culture in a European Perspective, Vol. 4: 1950: Prosperity and Welfare* (Basingstoke, 2004).

Schwarz, Bill, 'Actually Existing Postcolonialism', *Radical Philosophy*, 104 (2000), 16–24.

Schwarz, Bill, 'Black Metropolis, White England', in Mica Nava and Alan O'Shea (eds.), *Modern Times: Reflections on a Century of English Modernity* (London, 1996), 176–207.

Schwarz, Bill, *Memories of Empire, Vol. 1: The White Man's World* (Oxford, 2011).

Schwarz, Bill (ed.), *West Indian Intellectuals in Britain* (Manchester, 2003).

Scott, Joan Wallach, *The Politics of the Veil* (Princeton, 2007).

Sèbe, Berny, 'Itinéraires intellectuels et méthodologiques en Grande-Bretagne: De *l'imperial history* aux *postcolonial studies* en passant par les *French studies*', in Le Collectif Write Back, *Postcolonial Studies: Modes d'emploi* (Lyon, 2013), 89–104.

Sharma, Sanjay, John Hutnyk, and Ashwani Sharma (eds.), *Dis-Orienting Rhythms: The Politics of the New Asian Dance Music* (London, 1996).

Sharpe, Jenny, *Allegories of Empire: The Figure of Woman in the Colonial Text* (Minneapolis, 1993).

Shepard, Todd, *The Invention of Decolonization: The Algerian War and the Remaking of France* (Ithaca, 2006).

Shepard, Todd, '"Something Notably Erotic": Politics, "Arab Men," and Sexual Revolution in Post-Decolonization France, 1962–1974', *Journal of Modern History*, 84:1 (2012), 80–115.

Shields, J.G., *The Extreme Right in France from Pétain to Le Pen* (London, 2007).

Shipway, Martin, *Decolonization and Its Impact: A Comparative Approach to the End of Colonial Empires* (Malden, MA, 2008).

Shipway, Martin, *The Road to War: France and Vietnam, 1944–1947* (Oxford, 1996).

Shukla, Sandhya, *India Abroad: Diasporic Cultures of Postwar America and England* (Princeton, 2003).

Sidaway, James D., and Marcus Power, '"The Tears of Portugal": Empire, Identity, "Race", and Destiny in Portuguese Geopolitical Narratives', *Environment and Planning D: Society and Space*, 23:4 (2005), 527–54.

Sieber, R. Timothy, 'Composing Lusophonia: Multiculturalism and National Identity in Lisbon's 1998 Music Scene', *Diaspora*, 11:2 (2002), 163–88.

Sieber, R. Timothy, 'Remembering Vasco da Gama: Contested Histories and the Cultural Politics of Contemporary Nation-Building in Lisbon, Portugal', *Identities*, 8:4 (2001), 549–81.

Sieber, Timothy, 'Popular Music and Cultural Identity in the Cape Verdean Post-Colonial Diaspora', *Etnográfica*, 9:1 (2005), 123–48.

Silverman, Maxim, *Deconstructing the Nation: Immigration, Racism, and Citizenship in Modern France* (London, 1992).

Silverman, Maxim (ed.), *Race, Discourse and Power in France* (Aldershot, 1991).

Silverstein, Paul A., *Algeria in France: Transpolitics, Race, and Nation* (Bloomington, 2004).

Sivanandan, A., *A Different Hunger: Writings on Black Resistance* (London, 1982).

Smeets, Henk, and Fridus Steijlen, *In Nederland gebleven: De geschiedenis van Molukkers 1951–2006* (Amsterdam, 2006).

Smith, Andrea L., *Colonial Memory and Postcolonial Europe: Maltese Settlers in Algeria and France* (Bloomington, 2006).

Smith, Andrea L. (ed.), *Europe's Invisible Migrants* (Amsterdam, 2003).

Smith, Anna Marie, *New Right Discourse on Race and Sexuality: Britain, 1968–1990* (Cambridge, 1994).

Smith, Evan, 'Conflicting Narratives of Black Youth Rebellion in Modern Britain', *Ethnicity and Race in a Changing World: A Review Journal*, 1:3 (2010), 16–31.

Smith, Joy L., 'The Dutch Carnivalesque: Blackface, Play and Zwarte Piet', *Thamyris/Intersecting*, 27 (2014), 219–38.

Smouts, Marie-Claude (ed.), *La situation postcoloniale* (Paris, 2007).

Sniderman, Paul M., and Louk Hagendoorn, *When Ways of Life Collide: Multiculturalism and Its Discontents in the Netherlands* (Princeton, 2007).

Soares, António Goucha, 'Portugal and the European Union: The Ups and Downs in 20 Years of Membership', *Perspectives on European Politics and Society*, 8:4 (2007), 460–75.

Solomos, John, *Race and Racism in Britain*, 3rd edn. (Basingstoke, 2003).

Sorum, Paul Clay, *Intellectuals and Decolonization in France* (Chapel Hill, 1977).

Soysal, Yasemin Nuhoglu, *Limits of Citizenship: Migrants and Postnational Membership in Europe* (Chicago, 1995).

Spiering, Menno, *A Cultural History of British Euroscepticism* (Basingstoke, 2014).

Spire, Alexis, *Étrangers à la carte: L'administration de l'immigration en France (1945–1975)* (Paris, 2005).

Spruyt, Hendrik, *Ending Empire: Contested Sovereignty and Territorial Partition* (Ithaca, 2005).

Stadtler, Florian, '"For Every O'Dwyer ... There Is a Shaheed Udham Singh": The Caxton Hall Assassination of Michael O'Dwyer', in Rehana Ahmed and Sumita Mukherjee (eds.), *South Asian Resistances in Britain, 1858–1947* (London, 2012), 19–32.

Stanard, Matthew G., *Selling the Congo: A History of European Pro-Empire Propaganda and the Making of Belgian Imperialism* (Lincoln, NE, 2011).

Stockwell, A.J., 'Leaders, Dissidents and the Disappointed: Colonial Students in Britain as Empire Ended', *Journal of Imperial and Commonwealth History*, 36:3 (2008), 487–501.

Stockwell, Sarah (ed.), *The British Empire: Themes and Perspectives* (Oxford, 2008).

Stoler, Ann Laura, *Carnal Knowledge and Imperial Power: Race and the Intimate in Colonial Rule* (Berkeley, 2002).

Stoler, Ann Laura, *Race and the Education of Desire: Foucault's History of Sexuality and the Colonial Order of Things* (Durham, 1995).

Stoler, Ann Laura, and Frederick Cooper, 'Between Metropole and Colony: Rethinking a Research Agenda', in Ann Laura Stoler and Frederick Cooper (eds.), *Tensions of Empire: Colonial Cultures in a Bourgeois World* (Berkeley, 1997), 1–56.

Stora, Benjamin, 'Algeria: The War Without a Name', *Journal of Imperial and Commonwealth History*, 21:3 (1993), 208–16.

Stora, Benjamin, *Ils venaient d'Algérie: L'immigration algérienne en France, 1912–1992* (Paris, 1992).

Stora, Benjamin, *La gangrène et l'oubli: La mémoire de la guerre d'Algérie* (Paris, 1991).

Stora, Benjamin, *Le livre, mémoire de l'histoire: Réflexions sur le livre et la guerre d'Algérie* (Paris, 2005).

Stora, Benjamin, *Le transfert d'une mémoire: De l''Algérie française' au racisme anti-arabe* (Paris, 1999).

Stora, Benjamin, and Émile Temime (eds.), *Immigrances: L'immigration en France au XXe siècle* (Paris, 2007).

Stora, Benjamin, entretiens avec Thierry Leclère, *La guerre des mémoires: La France face à son passé colonial* (Paris, 2007).

Storr, Robert, Philippe Pirotte, and Jan Hoet, *Luc Tuymans: Mwana Kitoko (Beautiful White Man)* (Gent, 2001).

Stovall, Tyler, and Georges Van Den Abbeele (eds.), *French Civilization and Its Discontents: Nationalism, Colonialism, Race* (Lanham, MD, 2003).

Stråth, Bo (ed.), *Europe and the Other and Europe as the Other* (Brussels, 2000).

Stucki, Andreas, '"Beyond Civilization": Rhetoric of Empire in the Portuguese and Spanish "Overseas Provinces"', in Martin Thomas and Richard Toye (eds.), *The Rhetoric of Empire: Arguing Colonialism in the Public Sphere* (Manchester, in press).

Stucki, Andreas, 'Imperium in iberischer Perspektive: Historiografie, Diskurse, Kultur', *Mittelweg*, 36 (2013–2014), 3–17.

Subrahmanyam, Sanjay, 'The "Kaffirs of Europe": A Comment on Portugal and the Historiography of European Expansion in Asia', *Studies in History*, 9:1, n.s. (1993), 131–46.

Swyngedouw, Eva, and Erik Swyngedouw, 'The Congolese Diaspora in Brussels and Hybrid Identity Formation: Multi-Scalarity and Diasporic Citizenship', *Urban Research & Practice*, 2:1 (2009), 68–90.

Sykes, Alan, *The Radical Right in Britain: Social Imperialism to the BNP* (Basingstoke, 2005).

Taguieff, Pierre-André, 'The Doctrine of the National Front in France (1972–1989): A "Revolutionary Programme"? Ideological Aspects of a National-Populist Mobilization', *New Political Science*, 8:1&2 (1989), 29–70.

Taguieff, Pierre-André (ed.), *Face au racism 2: Analyses, hypothèses, perspectives* (Paris, 1991).

Talbot, Ian, and Gurharpal Singh, *The Partition of India* (Cambridge, 2009).

Tarr, Carrie, *Reframing Difference: Beur and Banlieue Filmmaking in France* (Manchester, 2005).

Tévanian, Pierre, *Retour sur la construction de l''affaire du foulard islamique'* (Paris, 2005).

Thénault, Sylvie, *Histoire de la guerre d'indépendance algérienne* (Paris, 2005).

Thiong'o, Ngũgĩ wa, *Decolonising the Mind: The Politics of Language in African Literature* (Nairobi, 1986).

Thomas, Dominic, *Black France: Colonialism, Immigration, and Transnationalism* (Bloomington, 2007).

Thomas, Dominic (ed.), *Museums in Postcolonial Europe* (London, 2010).

Thomas, Martin, *Fight or Flight: Britain, France, and Their Roads from Empire* (Oxford, 2014).

Thomas, Martin, *The French Empire at War, 1940–45* (Manchester, 1998).

Thomas, Martin, *The French North African Crisis: Colonial Breakdown and Anglo-French Relations, 1945–62* (Basingstoke, 2000).

Thomas, Martin, Bob Moore, and L.J. Butler, *Crises of Empire: Decolonization and Europe's Imperial States, 1918–1975* (London, 2008).

Thomas, Martin, and Richard Toye (eds.), *The Rhetoric of Empire: Arguing Colonialism in the Public Sphere* (Manchester, in press).

Thompson, Andrew (ed.), *Britain's Experience of Empire in the Twentieth Century*, Oxford History of the British Empire Companion Series (Oxford, 2012).

Thompson, Andrew, *The Empire Strikes Back?: The Impact of Imperialism on Britain from the Mid-Nineteenth Century* (Harlow, 2005).

Tiesler, Nina Clara, 'Novidades no terreno: muçulmanos na Europa e o caso português', *Análise Social*, 39:173 (2005), 827–49.

Tipo-Tipo, Mayoyo Bitumba, *Migration Sud/Nord: Levier ou Obstacle? Les Zaïrois en Belgique* (Brussels, 1995).

Toye, Richard, *Churchill's Empire: The World That Made Him and the World He Made* (London, 2010).

Troyna, Barry and Jenny Williams, *Racism, Education, and the State* (London, 1986).

Tshimanga, Charles, Didier Gondola, and Peter J. Bloom (eds.), *Frenchness and the African Diaspora: Identity and Uprising in Contemporary France* (Indianapolis, 2009).

Tyre, Stephen, 'The Memory of French Military Defeat at Dien Bien Phu and the Defence of French Algeria', in Jenny Macleod (ed.), *Defeat and Memory: Cultural Histories of Military Defeat in the Modern Era* (Basingstoke, 2008), 214–33.

Vakil, AbdoolKarim, 'Muslims in Portugal: History, Historiography, Citizenship', *Euroclio Bulletin*, 18 (2003).

Vala, Jorge, Diniz Lopes, and Marcus Lima, 'Black Immigrants in Portugal: Luso-Tropicalism and Prejudice', *Journal of Social Issues*, 64:2 (2008), 287–302.

Vanthemsche, Guy, *Belgium and the Congo, 1885–1960*, translated by Alice Cameron and Stephen Windross, revised by Kate Connelly (Cambridge, 2012).

Varsori, Antonio, 'Is Britain Part of Europe?: The Myth of British "Difference"', in Cyril Buffet and Beatrice Heuser (eds.), *Haunted by History: Myths in International Relations* (Providence, RI, 1998), 135–56.

Veenman, Justus, 'The Socioeconomic and Cultural Integration of Immigrants in the Netherlands', *Studi Emigrazione/Migration Studies*, 40:152 (2003), 805–28.

Veer, Peter van der, 'Pim Fortuyn, Theo van Gogh, and the Politics of Tolerance in the Netherlands', *Public Culture*, 18:1 (2006), 111–24.

Verbeeck, Georgi, 'Coming to Terms with the (Post-)Colonial Past in Belgium: The Inquiry into the Assassination of Patrice Lumumba', in Harriet Jones, Kjell Östberg, and Nico Randeraad (eds.), *Contemporary History on Trial: Europe Since 1989 and the Role of the Expert Historian* (Manchester, 2007), 46–61.

Vermeulen, Hans, and Rinus Penninx (eds.), *Immigrant Integration: The Dutch Case* (Amsterdam, 2000).

Verstappen, Sanderien, and Mario Rutten, 'Bollywood and the Indian Diaspora: Reception of Indian Cinema among Hindustani Youth in the Netherlands', in Gijsbert Oonk (ed.), *Global Indian Diasporas: Exploring Trajectories of Migration and Theory* (Amsterdam, 2007), 211–33.

Vertovec, Steven, 'Super-Diversity and Its Implications', *Ethnic and Racial Studies*, 30:6 (2007), 1024–54.

Vertovec, Steven, and Susanne Wessendorf, *The Multiculturalism Backlash: European Discourses, Policies and Practices* (London, 2010).

Veugelers, John, 'Ex-Colonials, Voluntary Associations, and Electoral Support for the Contemporary Far Right', *Comparative European Politics*, 3 (2005), 408–31.

Viaene, Vincent, David Van Reybrouck, and Bambi Ceuppens (eds.), *Congo in België: Koloniale cultuur in de metropool* (Leuven, 2009).

Vichniac, Judith, 'French Socialists and the *Droit à la Différence*: A Changing Dynamic', *French Politics and Society*, 9:1 (1991), 40–56.

Villers, Gauthier de (ed.), *Belgique/Zaïre: Une histoire en quête d'avenir, Cahiers Africains no. 9–10–11* (Brussels and Paris, 1994).

Villers, Gauthier de, *De Mobutu à Mobutu: Trente ans de relations Belgique-Zaïre* (Brussels, 1995).

Vinen, Richard, *National Service: Conscription in Britain, 1945–1963* (London, 2014).

Visram, Rozina, *Asians in Britain: 400 Years of History* (London, 2002).

Wacquant, Loïc, *Urban Outcasts: A Comparative Sociology of Advanced Marginality* (Cambridge, 2008).

Wall, Irwin M., *France, the United States and the Algerian War* (Berkeley, 2001).

Ward, Stuart (ed.), *British Culture and the End of Empire* (Manchester, 2001).

Ward, Stuart, 'The European Provenance of Decolonization', *Past and Present* (in press).

Waters, Chris, '"Dark Strangers" in Our Midst: Discourses of Race and Nation in Britain, 1947–1963', *Journal of British Studies*, 36 (1997), 207–38.

Webster, Wendy, *Englishness and Empire 1939–1965* (Oxford, 2005).

Webster, Wendy, 'Home, Colonial and Foreign: Europe, Empire and the History of Migration in 20th-Century Britain', *History Compass*, 8:1 (2010), 32–50.

Webster, Wendy, *Imagining Home: Gender, 'Race', and National Identity, 1945–64* (London, 1998).

Weil, Patrick, *La France et ses étrangers: L'aventure d'une politique de l'immigration 1938–1991* (Paris, 1991).

Wermuth, Mir, 'Weri Man! Een Studie naar de Hiphop-Cultuur in Nederland', in *Kunst en Beleid in Nederland 6* (Amsterdam, 1993), 63–112.

Wesseling, H.L., 'The Giant that was a Dwarf, or the Strange History of Dutch Imperialism', *Journal of Imperial and Commonwealth History*, 16:3 (1988), 58–70.

Westad, Odd Arne, *The Global Cold War: Third World Interventions and the Making of Our Times* (Cambridge, 2007).

White, Nicholas J., 'Reconstructing Europe Through Rejuvenating Empire: The British, French, and Dutch Experiences Compared', *Past & Present*, 210, Supplement 6 (2011), 211–36.

Wieviorka, Michel, 'Race, Culture, and Society: The French Experience of Muslims', in Nezar Alsayyad and Manuel Castells (eds.), *Muslim Europe or Euro-Islam: Politics, Culture, and Citizenship in the Age of Globalization* (Lanham, MD, 2002).

Wijngaert, Mark Van Den, Lieve Beullens, and Dana Brants, *Pouvoir et monarchie: La Belgique et ses rois*, translated from the Dutch by Anne-Laure Vignaux (Brussels, 2002).

Wilder, Gary, *Freedom Time: Negritude, Decolonization, and the Future of the World* (Durham, 2015).

Wilder, Gary, *The French Imperial Nation-State: Negritude and Colonial Humanism between the Two World Wars* (Chicago, 2005).

Willems, Wim, *De Uittocht uit Indië: 1945–1995* (Amsterdam, 2001).

Willems, Wim, and Leo Lucassen (eds.), *Het onbekende vaderland: De repatriëring van Indische Nederlanders (1946–1964)* ('s-Gravenhage, 1994).

Wilson, Jon, 'Niall Ferguson's Imperial Passion', *History Workshop Journal*, 56 (2003), 175–83.

Wilson, Ross, 'Remembering to Forget? The BBC Abolition Season and Media Memory of Britain's Transatlantic Slave Trade', *Historical Journal of Film, Radio and Television*, 28:3 (2008), 391–403.

Witte, Ludo De, *The Assassination of Lumumba*, translated by Ann Wright and Renée Fenby (London, 2001).

Wood, Nancy, *Vectors of Memory: Legacies of Trauma in Postwar Europe* (Oxford, 1999).

Yap, Felicia, 'Voices and Silences of Memory: Civilian Internees of the Japanese in British Asia during the Second World War', *Journal of British Studies*, 50:4 (2011), 917–40.

Young, Crawford, *Politics in the Congo: Decolonization and Independence* (Princeton, 1965).

Young, Robert J.C., *Postcolonialism: An Historical Introduction* (Malden, MA, 2001).

Zimmerer, Jürgen (ed.), *Kein Platz an der Sonne: Erinnerungsorte der deutschen Kolonialgeschichte* (Frankfurt am Main, 2013).

Index

CPSIA information can be obtained
at www.ICGtesting.com
Printed in the USA
LVHW040726140123
737124LV00001B/22